THE QURAN

The First
Poetic Translation

By

Fazlollah Nikayin

The Ultimate Book, Inc.
Skokie, Illinois

.ıl acknowledgment is made to:

.ıic Azad University for an initial

nation to commence the project.

THE ULTIMATE BOOK, INC.

P.O.Box 4577, Skokie, Ill. 60076,

Phone (847) 6775603   Fax (847) 6772693

http://www.theultimatebook.com

Printed in the United States of America

by

R.R. Donnelley & Sons

77 W. Wacker Drive,

Chicago, IL 60616

Dedicated to

The memory of my learned father,

Al-Haaj Mohammad Reza Nikayin,

to the inspiring instructions of a pious

man who wishes not to be named,

and, certainly, to all believers in God

Almighty throughout the world.

CONTENTS

Acknowledgements   vii

Foreword   ix - xii

List of chapters (Suras)   xiii - xvi

The Quran   1 - 1084

Acknowledgements

All who encouraged me and supported this project did so, I am certain, to please God only. I must, however, express my heartfelt gratitude to some of the kindest, from among many, by mentioning their names; they are:

Dr. Abdullah Jasbi, Dr. Ataollah Mohajerani, Mohammad Reza Najian, Ahmed Mokri, Jamal Sadatian, Hameed-Reza Alamolhuda, Dr. Saeed Soltani-far, S. Mojtaba Husseini, S. Masood Husseini, Mohammad Sa'id Bahman-Pour, Nader Ebrahimi, Dr. Mohammed Reza Taherian, S. Hussein Kimiafar, Hamid Morshedzadeh Tehrani, Miss Houri Sanizadeh, Hashem Taleb, Dr. Saeed Satvat-Manesh, S. Mohammad Marandi, Paul Kriwaczek, Hojjatol-Islam Mohammad Reza Nurallahian Mohajer, Mehdi Faridzadeh, and a best friend, Quemars Saberi, the proprietor of the Persian, Satirical Weekly "Gol-Agha", who was always helpful, despite his complete lack of English knowledge, for he trusted that I was doing something in the cause of God! And three Chicago-based persons, who were instrumental in setting up the Ultimate Book: Dr Nader Khorzad, Mr. Sohrab ChamanAra and my sister Nasrin Nazemi (Nikaeen).

I must also thank Mr. Mir Hussain Khan, for producing the electronic version of the original manuscript, Mr. Bob Kotlinski for final design and editing, and my wife and my younger son, Seena, for their patience during the last ten years, and my energetic nephew, Arash, for his help in many areas.

FOREWORD

In the Name of the Merciful God

"Indeed We rendered Al-Quran
Easy for recollection..."
(54-17)

How often may people, who speak no Arabic, have come
across such comments concerning the Holy Quran:

"...that intimate symphony, the very sounds of which move
men to tears and ecstacy...the Koran cannot be translated:
that is the belief of old-fashioned sheykhs and the view of
the present translator!"[1]

" The rhetoric and rhythm of the Arabic of the Quran are
so characteristic, so powerful, so highly emotive, that any
version whatsoever is bound in the nature of things to be
but a poor copy of the glittering splendour...and the radiant beauty of the original...it is neither prose or poetry but
a unique fusion of both."[2]

"...much of the power of the original is lost in translation;
indeed most Muslims believe that the Qur'an cannot be
translated properly..."[3]

---

1. Pickthall, M., the Glorious Koran, George Allen & Unwin, London, 1957.

2. Arberry, A.J., The Quran Interpreted, Cambridge, 1962.

3. Jones A., in Foreword to the Koran, translated by J.M. Rodwell, Everyman,
J.M. Dent, London 1994.

ix

"The Koran is the earliest and by far the finest work of classical Arabic...a literary masterpiece of surpassing excellence."[4]

Such are the comments made by some learned men who had a command of the Arabic language; but there have been other famous learned men who came to know the Quran through translations:

" As tedious a piece of reading as I ever undertook, a wearisome, confused jumble, crude, incondite..."[5]

"...the endless incoherent rhapsody of fable and precept and declamation, which seldom excites a sentiment or an idea..."[6]

What these gentleman had at their disposal was George Sale's dull, prosaic translation of the Quran, indeed the very best available at the time. Pickthall, an Englishman and a convert to Islam who did read Arabic, however, not only refutes such unenlightened opinions, but goes a step further to stress:

"It is a fact that the Koran is marvellously easy for believers to commit to memory. Thousands of people in the East know the whole Book by heart. This translator who finds great difficulty in remembering well-known English quotations accurately, can remember page after page of the Koran in Arabic with perfect accuracy."[7]

---

4. N.J. Dawood, the Koran, Penguin, London 1974.

5. Thomas Carlyle (1795-1881), British Historian.

6. Edward Gibbon, the 19th Century British Historian.

7. Pickthall, M.

Well then, is there a way for people who are not well-versed in Arabic ever to have a taste of the divine original that Pickthal and many others have so highly praised?

> "I wish a translator could do justice to those marvellously terse sentences in the original",[8] says Yousuf Ali, and Prof. Irving comments"... translations which evoke no reverence or beauty in the minds of the listeners... Later on some poetic spirit may bring us the noble paraphrase that we likewise need."[9]

My new translation of the Holy Quran, in the absence of an Arabic-speaking, Muslim FitzGerald,[10] is therefore a most humble effort intended, if God will, to carry over, into the English language some of the beauty and sublimity, elegance and eloquence and the enchanting force of the original, to echo those captivating, little nuances, which in the Quran, are always lying between prose and poetry, and to let non-Muslims acquaint themselves with a Book that is to Muslims both scripture and literature at the same time.

Throughout my ten year labour of love, I have paid utmost attention not to deviate an iota from the 'meaning' by constant consultation with the most noted and authentic exegeses in Arabic and Persian, and I have not allowed any 'sectarian' interpretations whatsoever to creep into my translation: I always let the Book itself inspire me, only and finally.

---

8. Yousuf Ali, the Holy Quran, King Fahd Printing Complex, Medina, 1990; footnote 5866.

9. T.B. Irving, the Quran, Amana Books, Vermont, 1985.

10. FitzGerald, Edward (1809-83), English poet who translated some of the poems of Omar Khayyam; his brilliant translation is, however, a free paraphrase of the original, a style not permissible in the translation of holy texts.

From amongst previous translations in English, my debt to Abdullah Yousuf Ali, Abul-A'la Maududi and Mohammad Ali, is not to be measured, not for their unattractive style of translation which I never followed, but for the wealth of Koranic information and illucidations they have provided for their readers. My own footnotes, however, are most brief, and never didactic or interpretative; yet the oft-repeated footnotes may bother some of the readers. I apologize for this, but they are meant for people who may be reading parts of the Book at different times.

The verses are rendered in the *iambic,* the majesty of the English poetry, and though often in pentameters, they vary in their lengths according to the requirements of the original verse being translated. There is no fixed rhyme scheme: Rhymes of all sorts, parallel, lopsided, internal, etc. have been employed at the service of more fluency in communicating the Message, without regard to the stylistics of the original Arabic which has no application in English.

Finally if, in the translation of some 6236 verses of varying lengths, I have somewhere come near reflecting the eloquence and beauty of the original in the mirror of the English language, the credit should undoubtedly go to my life-time companions: Shakespeare, Milton, Dryden, Byron, Pope, Coleridge, FitzGerald and surely to the masterly translators of the Holy Bible, Authorized King James Version; may their beautiful souls be increasingly blessed by the Most Merciful.

Fazlollah Nikayin
Tehran, March 2000

THE QURAN

List of Chapters (*Suras*)

Nos.	Name in English	Name in Arabic	Page
1	The Opening	Al-Faatiha	1
2	The Cow	Al-Baqara	2
3	The House of Imran	Aali-Imraan	72
4	The Women	Al-Nisaa	114
5	The Heavenly Food	Al-Maa'ida	155
6	The Livestock	Al-An'aam	188
7	The Heights	Al-A'raaf	224
8	The Spoils	Al-Anfaal	266
9	Repentance	Al-Taubah	282
10	Jonah	Yoonus	312
11	Hood	Hood	333
12	Joseph	Yoosuf	356
13	The Thunder	Al-Ra'd	377
14	Abraham	Ibraaheem	388
15	The Rocky Tract	Al-Hijr	399
16	The Bees	Al-Nahl	411
17	The Night Journey	Al-Israa	434
18	The Cave	Al-Kahf	454
19	Mary	Maryam	475
20	Taa Haa	Taa Haa	490
21	The Prophets	Al-Anbiyaa	511
22	The Pilgrimage	Al-Hajj	529
23	The Believers	Al-Mo'minoon	545
24	The Light	Al-Noor	561

25	The Criterion	Al-Furqaan	577
26	The Poets	Al-Shu'araa	590
27	The Ant	Al-Naml	613
28	The Narration	Al-Qasas	629
29	The Spider	Al-Ankaboot	647
30	The Romans	Al-Room	660
31	Luqmaan	Luqmaan	672
32	The Adoration	Al-Sajda	679
33	The Confederates	Al-Ahzaab	685
34	Sheba	Sabaa	702
35	The Originator	Al-Faatir	714
36	Y.S.	Yaa Sean	724
37	Ranged in Order	Saaffaat	736
38	Saad	Saad	754
39	The Multitudes	Al-Zumar	767
40	The Believer	Al-Mo'min	783
41	The Well-Explained	Fussilat	799
42	The Counsel	Al-Shuraa	810
43	Golden Ornaments	Al-Zukhruf	822
44	The Smoke	Al-Dukhaan	836
45	Kneeling Down	Al-Jaathiya	843
46	The Sandy Plains	Al-Ahqaaf	850
47	Mohammad	Mohammad	858
48	The Victory	Al-Fatah	865
49	The Chambers	Al-Hujuraat	872
50	Qaaf	Qaaf	877
51	The Dispersers	Al-Dhariyaat	884
52	The Mountain	Al-Toor	891
53	The Pleiades	Al-Najm	897
54	The Moon	Al-Qamar	904
55	The Beneficent	Al-Rahmaan	911
56	The Occurrence	Al-Waaqia	919
57	The Iron	Al-Hadeed	928

58	The Disputing woman	Al-Mujaadila	
59	The Gathering	Al-Hashr	
60	The Examiner	Al-Mumtahina	
61	Ranks	Al-Saff	952
62	Friday	Al-Jumu'ah	955
63	The Hypocrites	Al-Munaafiqoon	958
64	Common Loss and Gain	Al-Taghaabun	961
65	Divorce	Al-Talaaq	965
66	The Prohibition	Al-Tahreem	969
67	The Kingdom	Al-Mulk	972
68	The Pen	Al-Qalam	977
69	The Sure Occurrence	Al-Haaqqa	983
70	Elevations	Al-Ma'aarij	988
71	Noah	Nooh	992
72	The Jinn	Al-Jinn	996
73	Wrapped in Mantle	Al-Muz-zam-mil	1000
74	Enwrapped	Al-Mud-dath-thir	1003
75	Resurrection	Al-Qiaama	1008
76	Man	Al-Insaan	1012
77	The Emissaries	Al-Mursalaat	1016
78	The Important News	Al-Naba'a	1020
79	Extractors	Al-Naazi'aat	1024
80	He Frowned	'Abasa	1028
81	Cessation	Al-Takweer	1031
82	Cleft Asunder	Al-Infitaar	1034
83	The Defrauders	Al-Mutaf-fefeen	1036
84	Bursting Asunder	Al-Inshiqaaq	1040
85	Constellations	Al-Burooj	1043
86	The Piercing Star	Al-Taariq	1045
87	The Most High	Al-A'laa	1047
88	The Overwhelming	Al-Ghaashia	1049
89	The Dawn	Al-Fajr	1051
90	The Town	Al-Balad	1054

91	Sol	Al-Shams	1056
92	The Night	Al-Lail	1058
93	Morning Light	Al-Dzoha	1060
94	Broadened Breast	Inshiraah	1062
95	Teen	Al-Teen	1063
96	Blood-clot	Al-Alaq	1064
97	The Glory	Al-Qadr	1066
98	The Evidence	Al-Bayyina	1067
99	The Shaking	Al-Zilzaal	1069
100	Snorting Steeds	Al-'Aadiaat	1070
101	The Smiter	Al-Qaari'a	1071
102	Worldly Gains	Al-Takaathur	1072
103	Time	Al-Asr	1073
104	The Slanderer	Al-Humaza	1074
105	Elephant	Al-Pheel	1075
106	Quraish	Quraish	1076
107	Charity	Al-Maa'oon	1077
108	Abundance	Al-Kauthar	1078
109	The Disbelievers	Al-Kaafiroon	1079
110	Help	Al-Nasr	1080
111	Fibre	Al-Masad	1081
112	Unity	Al-Ikhlaas	1082
113	The Dawn	Al-Falaq	1083
114	The Men	Al-Naas	1084

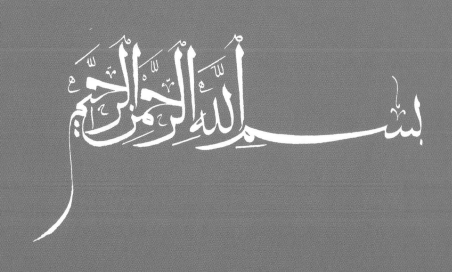

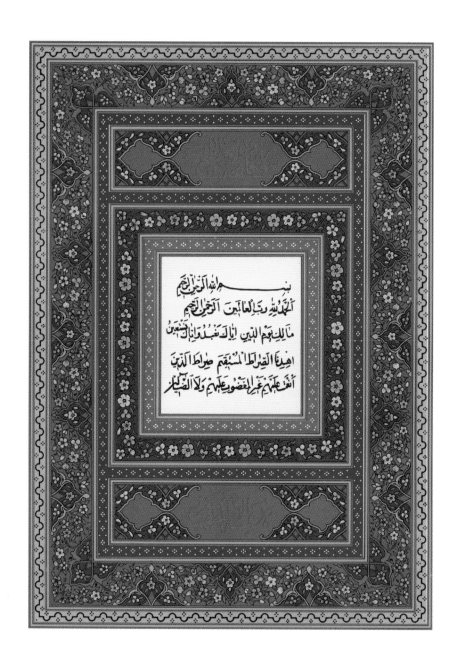

بِسْمِ اللَّهِ الرَّحْمَٰنِ الرَّحِيمِ

الْحَمْدُ لِلَّهِ رَبِّ الْعَالَمِينَ الرَّحْمَٰنِ الرَّحِيمِ

مَالِكِ يَوْمِ الدِّينِ إِيَّاكَ نَعْبُدُ وَإِيَّاكَ نَسْتَعِينُ

اهْدِنَا الصِّرَاطَ الْمُسْتَقِيمَ صِرَاطَ الَّذِينَ

أَنْعَمْتَ عَلَيْهِمْ غَيْرِ الْمَغْضُوبِ عَلَيْهِمْ وَلَا الضَّالِّينَ

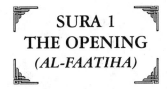

SURA 1
THE OPENING
(AL-FAATIHA)

1.   *In the Name of God, the Beneficent, the Merciful.*

2.   All praise be unto God the One,[1]
      The Lord of all Dominion,

3.   The Most Beneficent, Most Clement,

4.   The Sovereign of the Day of Judgment.

5.   You only do we worship,
      And unto You alone,
      Do we appeal for help.

6.   Direct us to the Direct Path,

7.   The path of people You have blessed,
      Who were not objects of Your Wrath,
      Nor strayers lost.

---

1. Allah

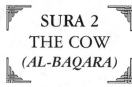

SURA 2
THE COW
(AL-BAQARA)

In the Name of God, the Beneficent, the Merciful

1.   Alif Laam Meem;[1]

2.   This is the Book, without a doubt; the Guide,
       For the godfearing e'er on guard,

3.   Who do believe in what is Hidden,
       And set up prayers and, from the bounty,
       We have unto them given,
       They give in charity,[2]

4.   Those who believe in what is being,
       Sent down to you,[3] and everything,
       Sent down before you, and have firm
       And full faith in the world to come.

5.   These are the truly-guided by their Lord,
       And it is they indeed,
       Who shall succeed.

6.   Those who have been rejecters,
       Whether you warn them or not warn,

---

1. A.L.M. such letters of the Arabic alphabet are prefixed to a number of suras
   of the Quran and commentators' opinions differ as to their significance. They,
   however, make no difference as far as the Guidance of the Quran in
   concerned.

2. The Arabic original means: "spend in the way of Allah, including charity,
   alms and the needs of the community."   3. The Holy Prophet.

It shall be all the same to them,
They won't become believers,

7.   For Allah sets a seal
Upon their hearts and ears,
And on their eyes there is a veil;
A torment grave is to be theirs!

8.   Also there are some folk who say:
" In God and the Last Day, we certainly believe",
But they in fact do not believe!

9.   They are attempting to deceive
Allah and those who do believe;
They are deceiving none but their own selves,
Only they can't perceive;

10.   Deep in their hearts is a disease,
And God increases this disease;
They shall be sternly punished
For their hypocrisies!

11.   Whenever they are warned:
"Do not make mischief in the land!"
They say: "We're only doing good!"

12.   Evil-doers are they indeed,
Though this they may not understand.

13.   And when they're told:
"Believe[1] as other people have believed",

---

1. Be true believers.

They say: "shall we believe
As the fools have believed?"
Certainly they themselves are fools,
Although they may not so perceive.

14.   And when they meet the faithful,
They claim: "We are believers too."
And, when alone with their own devils,[1]
They say: "We are indeed with you,
It's only mocking what we do!"

15.   God's mocking them by keeping them in sin,
To blindly blunder in rebellion!

16.   These are the folks who barter,
Guidance for error, so their bargain,
Is not to bring them any gain:
And they'll receive no guidance ever.

17.   Their parable is surely that of men,
Who start a fire, and when it does illumine
Around them, lo! Allah puts out their light,
Leaving them in deep darkness, seeing naught,

18.   Deaf, dumb and blind are they, so they will never
Come back unto the passage right;

19.   Or they are like some men beneath a stormy,
Dark cloud that's charged with thunder and with
lightning,
Thrusting their fingers in their ears to keep
Themselves from thunder-claps for fear of dying;

1. Their heathen chiefs or their idols.

God thus surrounds the disbelievers;

20.   The lightning almost takes away their sight,
        Where'er it flashes on them, they move forward,
        And when it darkens, they don't move; if God
        So pleased, He could have certainly deprived
        Them of their hearing and their sight, for God
        Is the Omnipotent.

21.   O Men! Worship your Lord: the One
        Who brought you into being,
        As well as those before you, thus you can
        Become upright, godfearing.

22.   He is the One who made the earth a cushion,
        For you and made the sky your canopy,
        And rain He sent down from the heavens,
        To bring forth fruits for your provisions;
        Therefore you should not set up idols
        To rival God, now that you have the ken.

23.   And if you doubt what We send down
        Unto Our servant, then produce
        One *sura*¹ like it, and do call upon
        The idols you set up, instead of God,
        If you are truthful men.

24.   But if you fail, and you are sure to fail,
        Then fear the Fire of which the fuel,
        Is human flesh and stone, prepared,

---

1. Chapter.

Only for disbelievers.

25. But give good news to those who have believed,
    And did good works, that surely they've deserved
    Gardens with running streams:
    Each time they are provided with a portion
    Of fruits therein, they utter "why, we were
    Provided with such fruits before!"
    Because the likes of them are to them given;
    Therein they will have spouses chaste and pure,
    And there they will abide for ever.

26. Certainly God does not disdain to cite,
    Any examples, from a gnat and smaller;
    The faithful know that these are certain truths
    From their own Lord, but disbelievers utter:
    "What does God mean by such a parable?
    He guides as many people
    As He leads into error!"
    Nay, by them He misleads,
    Only the evil-doers,

27. Who violate the covenant of God,
    After confirming it, and those who sever,
    What God commanded to be joined,
    And spread corruption in the land;
    These are indeed the losers.

28. How could you disbelieve in Allah,
    When you were lifeless, and He did
    Bring you to life; and later on,
    He'll cause you to be dead,
    To bring you back to life again,

And then you will to Him return.

29. He is the One who did for you create,
All that the earth contains,
And turning to the sky, He fashioned
It into Seven Heavens;
He has full Knowledge of all things.

30. Behold, your Lord said to the angels: "I
Will place a *khalif*[1] on the earth". they said:
Will You be placing one therein who could
Be doing evil there and shedding blood,
While we already sing Your praise and glory,
And only You we hallow?"
"Surely I know", He said, "what you do not know."

31. He now taught Adam all the Names,[2] and set
Them all before the angels, saying:
"Tell me the names of these, if you be right".

32. "Glory to you", they said, "We have no ken,
Except that which You have unto us given,
You are alone the Knower, Full of Wisdom.

33. He said: "O Adam, do inform them,
Of all those names", and when he told them
The names, He said: "Did I not tell you that
I know the truths and secrets of the skies,
And of the earth, and *only* I Know what

---

1. Vicegerent, deputy, representative, successor.

2. The names of all things means the inner nature and qualities of things, which
include "feelings", which are outside the nature of angels.

7

You manifest and all that you disguise.

34.   Behold, We told the angels: "Bow yourselves,
        To Adam"; and they bowed, except Iblees,[1]
        Who in his pride refused, and thus he proved
        To be faithless and thankless.

35.   To Adam We then said: "Go with your spouse
        To live in Paradise,[2] and of its fruits
        Eat to the content of your hearts,
        But do not go near this one tree,[3]
        For then you both will be,
        Harming yourselves and others."

36.   After a time, however, Satan did
        Make them both slip and fall,
        And did bring them out of the very
        Condition they were in, and We decreed:
        "Go hence, descend you all;
        There is to be among you enmity,
        Upon the Earth, you shall abide
        With some provisions for a period.

37.   Then Adam, from his Lord, received some words[4]

---

1. Satan; the word Iblees is derived from a Semitic root meaning
   "being wounded, discarded, and desperate"; compare 'Diabolis'.

2. The Garden of Eden is most probably not a place on the earth,
   because it was after the fall that they were sentenced to live on earth.

3. The tree is not named because there was nothing intrinsically evil in the tree
   itself; a tree was merely chosen for the purpose of a
   trial, and they were duly warned not to violate God's command.

4. Appropriate expressions for asking forgiveness.

Whereby He did redeem him, for He is,
The Great Redeemer, Full of Mercy.

38. We said: "All of you, go down hence,
And when to you will come My Guidance,
Those that My Guidance follow are to have
Nothing to fear, nor ever grieve.

39. But those who do deny and disbelieve
Our Signs,[1] shall be the heirs of Hell,[2]
In which they shall for ever dwell.

40. O Sons of Israel, do call to mind,
The favours that I have on you bestowed,
And to My covenant be true;
And I will keep My covenant with you,
And of Me, only, be afraid.

41. And have belief in what I have revealed,
Which does confirm what, ere this, you received,[3]
And in denying it, be not the first,
And let my revelations not be cheaply priced!
And do fear Me, Me only.

42. Do not disguise the truth by falsehood,
Nor let the truth be covered knowingly.

43. Keep up the prayers, and pay *zakaat*,[4]
And do bow down your heads along

---

1. Revelations.   2. The Fire.   3. Your Scriptures.

4. Regular charity: 2.5% of one's net income according to specific regulations
   to be spent on the needy, etc.

With those who bow before Me.

44. Do you enjoin every good deed,
    Upon the public, but neglect,
    Your very souls, and yet you read
    The Scriptures? Do you not reflect!

45. Nay, seek assistance through
    Patience and prayers; no doubt,
    This is exacting discipline,
    Except to the devout,

46. Who know that they will meet their Lord,
    And that to Him they will return.

47. O Sons of Israel, do pay attention
    Unto the favours that I have before,
    Bestowed on you, and that I blessed you more
    Than any nation;

48. And guard yourselves against the Day
    When not a soul avails another,
    When neither intercession may for her,
    Be sanctioned, nor some compensation,
    Is from her taken, nor unto her given
    Any succour from any quarter.

49. Remember how We saved you from the people,
    Of Pharaoh, who subjected you to dreadful torment:
    Your sons they slaughtered, but they spared your
                                        daughters,
    And this was, from your Lord, a trial vehement.

50. Remember when We opened up the waters,
    To rescue you, and had the followers
    Of Pharaoh drowned before your very eyes.

51. Remember We communed with Moses,
    For forty nights, but in his absence,
    You took the calf to idolize,
    Committing an abhorrence!

52. We did forgive you even then, so now,
    To show your gratefulness, you have a chance.

53. Behold, We gave to Moses then,
    The Book and the Criterion,[1]
    In order that you may have guidance.

54. Recall that Moses to his people said;
    "O people, you have wronged your souls in truth,
    By worshipping the calf, so in repentance,
    Turn to your Maker, and then put to death
    The culprits: that will be for you far better
    In the sight of your Maker;"
    And that He thus redeems you, for He is,
    The Merciful Redeemer.

55. Remember that you said: "O Moses, We
    Will not believe in you until we see
    Allah with our own eyes!" And at that moment,
    The lightning struck you as a punishment,
    While you were looking on without a motion;

---

1. Original: *Al-Furqaan* meaning: "Distinction, and, the standard of judgment between right and wrong, truth and falsehood"; *Porqan* in Aramaic stands for "Salvation".

56.   And then We raised you up again,
          After your death, so that you might
          Show some appreciation.

57.   Behold, We caused the clouds to give you shade,
          And We sent down to you: *manna* and quails,
          Saying: "Do eat of the good things We made
          To be your meals;"
          Beware, they did no harm to Us at all,
          But they did harm to their own souls.

58.   Behold, We said: "Enter this town[1]
          And, as you please, eat of its plenty,
          Pass through the gate with amity,
          Humbly repeating: '*Hitta-toun*'.[2]
          We will forgive you every sin,
          And pour Our bounty,
          On those who do good unto others.

59.   But the transgressors changed the words,
          Spoken to them, so We upon them sent,
          Pestilence from the heavens,
          Because of their infringement.

60.   Recall that Moses for his people's sake,
          Demanded water, and We answered: "strike
          That rock there with your rod", and thereupon,
          Twelve springs from it gushed forth, and so each tribe,
          Knew their own drinking-place, and we did mention:
          "Of Allah's sustenance, eat and imbibe,

---

1. Jerusalem or Jericho.

2. Meaning: "Forgive us", "We repent" or simply "forgiveness".

But do not roam the earth to spread corruption!"

61.   Remember that you grumbled: "O You Moses,
        Patient we will not be at all, we're bored
        With this monotonous food, call on your Lord,
        To give us varied, earthly crops like: beans,
        Cucumbers, garlic,[1] lentils, and fresh onions!"
        "What", wondered he" Exchanging something finer
        For what is surely meaner?!
        Well, go down to some Egypt where you'll find,
        Every thing you demand!"
        To shame and squalor were they thus condemned,
        And did incur the wrath of God; because
        Faithless were they in Allah's Signs[2] and did
        Kill their own prophets for no rightful cause;
        That is because they often disobeyed,
        And did transgress indeed.

62.   Believers,[3] Jews and Christians and Sabeans[4]
        All who believe in God and the Last Day,
        And do good works, leading a righteous life,
        Will be respectively rewarded by
        Their Lord; they'll have no fear, they'll know no grief.

63.   Behold, We made with you a covenant,
        As We above you raised the Mountain:[5]
        "Hold fast to the commands We've to you given
        And bear in mind what they contain,
        This might enable you to self-restain.[6]

---

1. Or "corn" or "wheat".   2. Revelations.   3. In the Quran: or Muslims.

4. Most probably the followers of Prophet John (the Baptist).

5. The Mount Sinai.   6. Be godfearing, virtuous or pious.

64.   Yet, after that, you did forsake it;
      And, were it not for Allah's Grace,
      And His compassion, you would be,
      Ruined and perished long before this.

65.   Surely you've heard of those among you
      Who broke the Sabbath, so to them We said:
      "Be apes, despised and hated".

66.   And thus We made them an example
      To their own folk, and any nation
      That followed, and an admonition,
      For the godfearing people.

67.   Recall that Moses to his people said:
      "God orders you to sacrifice a cow".
      "You mean to have a jest with us?!" They said.
      "Allah forbid", he said, "that I allow
      Myself to be a blockhead!"

68.   "Call on your Lord", they said, "on our behalf,
      To make it plain what kind it is to be."
      He said: "He says that it's a heifer,
      Neither too old, nor very young, but she
      Is of an age between;
      Do, therefore, as you have been bidden."

69.   "Call on your Lord", they said, "on our behalf,
      That He enlightens us as to her dye."
      He said: "He says she is a yellow cow,
      Intensely bright, most pleasing to the eye."

70.   "Call on your Lord", they said "On our behalf,

To specify for us how she should look,
For to us all such heifers are alike,
So that, God willing, make we no mistake!"

71.   He said: "He says that she should be a heifer
      Not ever yoked to plough the earth,
      Nor made to water any tilth,
      Sound, with no blemish whatsoever."
      They said: Now you have brought the truth!"
      And then they offered her in sacrifice,
      Although to it, they were averse!

72.   Also recall to mind: You slew a soul,
      Then you began to disagree about,
      The crime, and it was Allah who let out
      What you were trying to conceal.

73.   Yea, We said: "Strike the body with a piece
      Taken from her."[1] Thus God revives,
      The dead, and lets you see His Signs,
      That you may realize.

74.   But even after that your hearts became,
      As hard as rocks; nay, even harder,
      For there are rocks from which some rivers
      Gush forth, and others which when split asunder,
      Let water out, and others that fall down,
      For fear of God; and God is never
      Unmindful of your deeds.

75.   Do you[2] indeed expect them[3] to believe,

---

1. The sacrificed heifer.   2. Believers, Muslims.   3. The Jews.

As you, when some of them who used to hear,
The Word of God, distorted it on purpose,
After an understanding clear?

76.   Do they not really know that Allah knows,
What they keep secret and what they disclose?!

78.   There are amongst them some unlettered folks,
Who do not know the Book, and so they have to
Depend on lies, guess-work and hoax.

79.   Thus, woe to those who write the Scripture,
With their own hands, and then declare:
"This is from God", seeking some paltry gains,
And woe to them for their distortions;
And woe to them indeed for their
Illicit acquisitions!

80.   They also say: "the Fire is not to touch us
Except for a few days. "say: Have you taken
A pledge from God?-surely God never breaks
His word-or is it that you have just spoken
Something of which you have no ken?!

81.   But truly those committing evil,
Who are beset by sin on every side,
Shall be companions of the Fire,
Wherein they will for long abide.

82.   And those who do believe and do good work,
Shall be companions of the Garden where
They will for long reside.

83.   Behold, from Israelites[1] We took,
       A covenant to this effect:
       Serve none but God; show kindness to,
       Your parents and your kinsfolk,
       And to the orphans and the helpless;
       Be fair to people when you speak;
       And do keep up *salaat*,[2] and pay *zakaat*.
       But then, except a few among you,
       You did backslide, and turned about,
       And even now you're turning back.

84.   Behold, We took another covenant,
       From you: You shall not shed your kinsmen's blood,
       Nor turn each other out from your own towns,
       Which you confirmed, and bore witness to God.

85.   Yet here you are: killing your brethren,
       And driving groups out of their homes,
       And making sinful and aggressive unions,
       Against them, and if they surrender,
       To you, you trade upon their ransoms,
       Whereas it surely was forbidden,
       To banish them at all: Do you not rather
       Believe in one part of the Scripture,
       And disbelieve another?!
       What should then be the retribution,
       Of those among you who behave like this?
       It is in this world's life, humiliation,
       And there shall be for them a graver Torment,
       Upon the Day of Resurrection;

---

1. The Children of Israel.

2. The daily prayers.

And God watches your every action.

86. These people buy this worldly life,
    At the expense of the Hereafter;
    Their punishment shall not be lightened,
    Nor are they helped from any quarter.

87. We did to Moses give the Scriptures,
    And, after him, sent a succession
    Of messengers;
    To Jesus, son of Mary, We had given
    The clearest Signs,[1] and We had even,
    Strengthened him with the Holy Spirit.
    How is it that each time some messenger,
    Unto you comes whose message does not fit,
    Your fancies, then you proudly either
    Call some of them impostors,
    Or some of them you murder?!

88. They say: "Our hearts have been securely sealed;"[2]
    Nay, God has cursed them for their unbelief;
    Little is what they ever have believed.

89. Now that a Book from God has to them come,
    Confirming what's already with them,[3] they
    Reject it, but, till now, they used to pray
    For victory against the disbelievers,
    Before their prophecy had come to pass;[4]
    Thus is God's curse upon the disbelievers.

---

1. Also meaning: "Miracles".   2. Meaning: with the Book of God inside
   our hearts, they will never be penetrated!   3. Their scriptures.
4. The prophecy of the coming of "*that prophet*".

90. Miserable is indeed the price,
For which they sell their souls:
To disbelieve what God sends down,
Out of sheer grudge that God reveals,
It, of His Grace, on whomsoever,
Amongst His servants, as He wills!
Wrath upon wrath have they thus drawn,
Upon themselves; an ignominious
Torment awaits the disbelievers!

91. When they are told: "You shall believe in
What Allah has revealed", they say:
"Our faith is only in what unto us
Has been revealed", and they deny,
Everything sent thereafter, even if
It is the Truth confirming what
They have already got!
Ask them "if that's the case, then why
Did you murder God's messengers?"

92. And surely Moses came to you,
With miracles profound,
But, in his absence, lo, you found,
The calf for worshipping, indeed,
Transgressing every bound!

93. Behold, We made with you a covenant,
And did above you raise the Mount,
Saying: "Hold Firmly unto what
We have unto you granted and obey".
They said: "we hear, and disobey!"
So they were made to drink the calf
Thoroughly, for their unbelief;

Say: Vile indeed is what your faith,
Enjoins you to, if you have faith!

94.   Say: If the Final Home with God, has been
Reserved for you alone, and it's the truth
You speak, then you must long for death!

95.   But they will never long for it, because,
Many a sin they have sent forth;
And God the men of evil actions knows.

96.   Indeed you'll find that they, of all mankind,
Are the most covetous for life, and more
Covetous than the pagans; every one
Of them desires that he'll be living for
A thousand years, but even such long life,
By no means could remove the Retribution,
From them, for God's the Keenest Seer
Into their every action.

97.   Declare: "Whoever is an enemy
To Gabriel: who has, by God's permission,
Into your heart revealed this, which is only,
Of what was sent before, a confirmation,
And Guidance and glad tidings for believers,

98.   "Whoever is to God a foe,
Unto His angels or His messengers
To Gabriel or Michael, lo!
It's God Who is the foe to disbelievers."

99.   Surely We have to you sent down,

Some revelations[1] manifest,
And none shall disbelieve in them,
Except the sinfulest.

100.   And is it not a fact that every time,
They make a covenant, a group amongst,
Them violate it? Nay, among them most,
Choose to be faithless all the same.

101.   And when there came to them a messenger,
From God, confirming what they had with them,
Some groups among the people of the Book,
Cast off the Book of God behind their back,
As if they knew about it nothing ever!

102.   But they accepted what the satans,
Recited of the reign of Solomon;
Yet Solomon was not a faithless pagan!
The disbelievers were the satans, who,
Taught people magic, in addition to,
That which had been sent down in Babylon,
To Haroot and Maroot, the angels twain;
Yet never did they[2] teach a man a lesson,
Without first telling him: "The likes of us,
Are here as trials only, thus,
Never should you your faith abandon";[3]
Yet from them men did learn some charms,
By which they could create division,
Between a husband and his woman;
But certainly they could inflict no harms

1. Or: verses, communications, signs.   2. The two angels.

3. The question of knowledge and science that may be at the service of good
   or evil?

21

To anyone except by God's permission;[1]
Indeed they learned what only hurt them,
Not what would ever profit them;
And they well knew that people in this business,
Would have no portion of the bliss,
In the Hereafter;
Miserable is indeed the goals
For which they sold their souls,[2]
If only they knew better!

103.   Had they but known, had they believed and guarded
Themselves from evil, certainly they would,
Have been by God rewarded,
Far better good!

104.   O you believers, do not say: "*ra'ina*",[3]
But simply say: "*unzurna*",[4] and give ear;
Surely the disbelievers shall be facing,
A chastisement severe.

105.   Neither the people who lack faith,
Among the People of the Book,
Nor the idolaters, would like
That any blissful good is poured
Down to you from your Lord,
But God His Mercy showers,

---

1. The power of evil is, of course, limited to the extent to which God permits.

2. Selling one's soul into slavery to the Evil.

3. This means: "Listen, look or pay attention", but in the dialect of Jewish Arabs, it also meant "Our naughty one"!

4. This also means "Look or pay attention" but it lacks the secondary abusive meaning or derisive pun of the former.

On whom He'll choose;
And God's the Lord of Grace untold.

106.   None of Our revelations,[1]
Do We e'er abrogate,
Or cause to be forgotten,
But We shall substitute,
A better one, or something,
Similar, unto it; do you know not
That God's Omnipotent?

107.   Do you not know that the Dominion
Of heavens and the earth belongs
To God alone, and that besides
Allah, you have no patrons,
Nor any helpers.

108.   Or do you wish to make demands
Of your Apostle in the manner
That Moses was demanded once,
In former times? But whosoever
Changes from Faith to Unbelief,
Has strayed, without a doubt,
From the right route.

109.   Many amongst the People of the Book,
Desire that they could somehow turn you back,
Now that you have believed, unto unfaith:
They burn with jealousy now that the Truth
Has unto them become most plain!
Thus pardon them, leave them alone,

---

1. Or: Signs, miracles, tokens of wonder, and verses.

Till God enforces His intent;
For God's Omnipotent.

110.   And keep up prayers and pay *zakaat*,
You'll find with God, whatever good,
That you have for your souls, sent forward,
For God's the Seer of your every deed.

111.   They claim: "No one enters the Garden,[1]
Unless he be a Jew",[2] or "Christian."[3]
Such is their wishful thinking!
Say: Do produce your proof,
If it's the truth you're speaking."

112.   Of course, whoever does devote himself
Absolutely to God, and leads a life
Of righteous doings, will receive his prize,
From his own Lord; he'll have no fears,
Nor shall he ever come to grief.

113.   The Jewish people say: "The Christians
Have naught to stand upon",
The Christians say: The Jews have naught
To stand upon, and both intone
The Scriptures; while, forsooth,
Those of no knowledge,[4] say the same of both!
Allah will judge about their disputation,
Upon the Day of Resurrection.

114.   Who are more wicked than the men

---

1. Paradise.   2. According to Jews.

3. According to the Christians.   4. The pagans.

Who boycott Allah's mosques,[1] wherein
His name is mentioned, those whose strife,[2]
Is only for their ruin?
Such persons cannot even enter
These places but in constant terror;
Disgrace they shall be meeting in this life,
And awful scourge in the Hereafter.

115.   To God belong both East and West,
Whiche'er direction you are facing,
There is the Face of God, for God's
All-Knowing, All-Embracing.

116.   Some also say: "God has a son adopted!"
He is above such things, He's too exalted;
Whatever is there in the heavens,
And on the earth, to Him belongs,
Obedient to Him are all things;

117.   Originator of the heavens,
And earth is He;
When He decrees a thing,
He merely says unto it: "Be!"
And it's already Being.

118.   And those who have no knowledge say: "If only
Allah to us would speak, or else a token[3]
Would come to us!" In fact, similar kinds
Of statements were by those before them spoken;
Similar are their hearts and minds!
Surely to those with faiths unshaken,

---

1. Places of worship.   2. Zealous effort.   3. A sign, a miracle

We have already shown Our signs.

119.   Certainly We have sent you forth,
With the Truth, as a bearer,
Of tidings glad, and as a warner;
But you shall not be called upon to answer
For the companions of the Blazing Fire!

120.   Neither the Jews, nor any Christian,
Will e'er be pleased with you,[1] unless
You follow their religion;
Tell them: "The only guidance is,
Guidance from God." Were you to acquiesce,
To their desires, despite the knowledge given,
Unto you, then, against God's wrath, you'll find,
Neither a guardian, nor a helping hand.

121.   Those who received the Scriptures,
And do read them and comprehend,
These are sincere believers,
And those who disbelieve them,
Shall be indeed the losers.

122.   O Sons of Israel, remember
How I bestowed on you My favour,
And that I caused you to excel,
All other people;

123.   Be on your guard against the Day
When every soul shall stand alone,
When neither any compensation,

---

1. Mohammad (pbuh)

Is from her taken, nor an intercession
Shall be of any use, nor anyone,
Will be assistance given.

124.   Behold, after His Lord put Abraham
To test with certain words,[1] and he fulfilled them,
He said: "I'm making you for people an Imam"[2];
He asked: And what of my descendants?
"My covenant", said He, "does not embrace,
The ones who would transgress."

125.   And do remember that We made this House,[3]
A place of gathering for humankind,
And a safe sanctuary; do take a place,
Of prayer, where Abraham was wont to stand;
Abraham We enjoined with Ishmael,
To cleanse My House for people who go round
It, or retreat there, or in worship kneel.

126.   Behold, Abraham prayed: "My Lord,
Make this a safe and peaceful land,
And those among its people who have faith,
In God and the Last Day, provide with
Sustenances of every kind."
He answered: "Even those who have no faith,
I'll feed for a short while, then I shall drive,
Them to the chastisement of Fire:
An evil station at which to arrive!

127.   And after Abraham and Ishmael,
Raised the foundations of this House,

---

1. Commands   2. Leader of mankind.   3. The Ka'ba at Mecca.

They prayed: "Our Lord, accept this from us,
You do Hear all and You Know all;

128.   "Our Lord, make us submissive to your Will,[1]
And, from amongst our offspring, raise a nation,
Of true submitters to Yourself,[2]
Show us the ways and rites of our devotion,
And turn to us in kind redemption,
It's You indeed who is Redeeming,
Full of Compassion;

129.   "Our Lord, send forth to them a messenger,
Of their own kind, who shall unto them read,
Your revelations, and instruct them in,
The Scripture and the Wisdom, and indeed,
Purify them, for only You it is,
Who are All-Powerful, All-Wise.

130.   Who would renounce the faith of Abraham,
But fools who cheat their souls with folly? Him,
We'd chosen for Our service in this world,
And in the next, he will be honoured,
To join the ranks of the most righteous.

131.   Behold, His Lord said unto him:
"Be in submission!"
He said: "I'm all submission to,
The Lord of all Creation".

132.   Abraham did the same enjoin,

---

1. Or: Make us Muslims.
2. Muslims.

28

Upon his sons, and so did Jacob:
"O Children mine, Allah[1] has for you chosen
This faith; allow not, therefore, death to rob
You of your life but as submissive men."[2]

133.   You surely were not witnesses to what
Jacob upon his death-bed said!
"What will you serve", he asked his children,
"After I have been gone?", they answered:
"We will be serving Your Ilah,[3]
The very God of your forefathers,
Abraham, Ishmael and Isaac,
The One and Only God; submitters,
We'll be to Him who ne'er go back."[4]

134.   Those people now have passed away,
For them is what they earned,
And for you is what you have earned,
And you are not to answer questions
About those people's actions.

135.   They say: "Follow the faith of Jews or Christians,
And you shall be upon the guided path!"
Say: By no means! The Unitarian faith,
Is that of Abraham; and he was never,
An idol worshiper!"

---

1. El, Il, Elohim in Hebrew as Allah in Arabic and similar words in other
   Semitic languages mean "God the One"; Abraham, Moses, Jesus and
   Mohammad did not speak French, German or English!
2. That is: Muslims, or submitters to the absolute will of the Almighty.
3. God.
4. Or "remain to him sincere muslims".

136.   Say: "We believe in God and what is sent,
        Down unto us, and what has been sent down
        To Abraham, to Ishmael, to Isaac,
        To Jacob and the Tribes, and what was given
        To Moses, and to Jesus and whatever,
        Was given to the Prophets from their Lord;
        And we make no distinction ever,
        Between one of them and another,
        We totally submit to Allah."

137.   Now if they do believe as you believe,
        They'll be on the right course, but if they leave,
        The faith aside, it's they who are in schism,
        And then Allah suffices you against them,
        For he's the Hearer, the All-Knower.

138.   This[1] is indeed God's Baptism,
        And who is surely better than
        God, to baptise? Thus Him,
        Do we worship alone.

139.   Say: will you be disputing with us
        Concerning God? When He is both
        Our Lord and your own Lord! And we
        Shall answer for our deeds in truth,
        And you shall answer yours indeed;
        And we remain to Him sincere in faith.

140.   Will you allege: "Verily Abraham
        Ishmael, Isaac, Jacob and the Tribes
        Were Jews? Or Christians?" And do ask them:

---

1. Islam.

"Who best knows? You or God?" The one who hides
The testimony that he has from God,
Is most unjust; and of your deeds,
Never is Allah Unaware!

141.   Those people passed away; beware!
They shall be recompensed for what they earned,
And for you is the meed for your own deeds,
And you shall not be questioned,
About a single deed of theirs.

142.   The fools among the people are to say:
"What really made them turn away
From the direction of their *qiblah*?"[1]
Tell them: Both East and West belong to Allah;
He guides whome'er He will to the Right Way.

143.   And We have thus[2] made you an *umma*,[3]
Of 'golden mean', that you, for every nation,
May serve as witnesses, and your Apostle,
A witness over you; and the direction,
Of the *qiblah*, that which you used to turn to,
We altered[4] only to distinguish,
The Messenger's adherents true,
From those who turn away in haste;
This was indeed a hard, momentous trial,
Except for those who had been blessed
By Allah's Guidance: God will never,
Let go this faith of yours to waste,

1.*Qibla:* The direction to which Muslims turn in prayer.

2. By granting you a qiblah of your own, as a new community.

3. Community, nation, people.   4. Also "appointed".

For God is unto humankind,
Mercifully Most Kind.

144. Many a time We see you[1] turn your face,
Towards the sky, therefore We now assign,
To you a *qiblah* that you will best like:
you shall, towards the Sacred Shrine,[2]
Your face be turning; thus you ought to turn
Your face to it, no matter where you are,
And surely those who have received the Scripture,
Know that it's rightly from their Lord;
And certainly God is Aware,
Of your every affair.

145. And even if you were to show the People
Of the Book, all the Signs[3] together,
Never would they accept your *qiblah,* nor
Will you adopt their *qiblah*; neither
Will they follow each other's *qiblah*;
And had you to their wishes acquiesced,
After the knowledge that has to you come,
You would have certainly transgressed.

146. The People of the Scripture recognize
This[4] as they know their children,
But certain sects of them the truth disguise,
Even though they surely have the ken!

---

1. Mohammad (pbuh)

2. Or "the Holy Mosque" wherein the Ka'ba is located in Mecca.

3. Or "Miracles".

4. "This ancient place"; "this truth"; or "him" (according to some commentators
who construe the demonstrative pronoun to refer to the holy Prophet).

147. The Truth is from your Lord; therefore be not,
      Ever in doubt.

148. Each person has a destination,[1]
      To which he turns;[2] thus try to race each other,
      In doing righteous works, for wheresoever,
      You be, Allah will bring you all together;
      Everything's under God's dominion.

149. Whatever place you go to, turn your face
      Towards the Holy Shrine, for it's a true
      Bid from your Lord, and God is never heedless
      Of what you do.

150. So from whatever place you come, do turn
      Your face towards the Holy Shrine,
      And where you are, do turn your faces thither,
      That people have no argument against
      You all, except it's from the most unjust
      Among them: yet of them you shall not ever
      Have any fear; fear Me alone,
      And I'll perfect on you my favour,
      That you may be guided aright,

151. Even as We sent to you a Messenger,
      Of your own people to recite,
      To you Our verses, and to purify
      You, and instruct you in the Scripture,[3]
      And in the Wisdom, and to be a teacher
      Of things you'd never known.

---

1. Goal, direction.   2. Or "to which Allah turns him."

3. The Book

152. Remember Me and I'll remember you,
And give Me thanks, and do not be ingrate, untrue.

153. Believers, fortify yourselves,
With patience and with prayer,
For God's indeed with those
Who patiently forbear.

154. And do not say "They're dead" of those
Slain while they did for Allah strive;
Nay, nay! They are alive;
Only you can't perceive.

155. We often test you with some fear and famine,
Some loss of property and lives and crops;
Yet give good tidings to the man,
Who most patiently with them copes;

156. Who says, when some misfortunes on him strike:
"We are of God, and to Him we go back!"

157. Upon such people will be blessings,
And Mercy from their Lord; those are the ones
Upon the guided track.

158. Some symbols are *Safa* and *Marwah*,[1]
Only consecrated by Allah,
Therefore, it shall not be a sin,
Upon observing Hajj[2] or *Umrah*,[3]

---

1. Names of two hills near Mecca.

2. The pilgrimage to the House of God in the appointed season.

3. Paying a visit to the House of God at any other time.

If one goes round about them both;
Be sure that God's the Grateful Knower,
Of those who, with a willing heart,
Perform some righteous part.

159.   Those who conceal the lucid proofs and guidance,
That We sent down, after what in the Scriptures,
We had explained unto the people, will
Surely be cursed by God, and by the creatures,[1]
Able to curse as well;

160.   Excepting those who do repent,
And make amends, and openly,
Declare the Truth, then I relent
Towards them; I am Full of Mercy,
Keen to Accept repentance.

161.   But those who always disbelieved,
And died as disbelievers, shall
Incur the curse of God, of every angel,
And of men, all indeed.

162.   They shall remain accursed for time on end,
Their chastisement shall not be lightened,
Nor shall they be reprieved.

163.   Your deity is one God only,
There is no god but He,
The All-Beneficent,
The Lord of Mercy.

---

1. Angels and mankind.

164.   Behold! In the creation of the heavens,
       And the earth; in the alternation,
       Of Nights and Days; in the ships gliding,
       With what shall profit people, through the ocean;
       In the rain-water God is sending,
       Down from the sky, reviving all dead lands,
       Therein dispersing creatures of all kinds;
       In the manipulation of the winds,
       And in the clouds most humbly[1] driven
       Between the sky and earth: certainly in
       These things are certain Signs,
       For men of reason!

165.   And yet, some people set up idols,
       To rival God, and give the adoration,
       Due unto God to these! whereas the faithful's
       Love of God is the greatest adoration;
       Behold, if these transgressors could now see
       Themselves, as when they face the Retribution,
       They would then know: all Might is God's,
       And Stern is God in retribution;

166.   And then the leaders will declare themselves,
       Clear from their followers, and all their ties,
       Will break asunder, once they witness,
       The scourge with their own eyes.

167.   And those who had been following will say:
       "If only we could get another chance,[2]
       We surely would disown them just as they

---

1. Subserviently, obligingly, obediently.

2. To return to the world!

Did us this Day renounce."
And thus will God their deeds to them display,
As nothing but regrets intense;
And never will they find a way,
Out of the Fire.

168.   O Men, do eat of lawful, wholesome things,
Upon the earth and do not walk abreast
Of Satan's footsteps, for he is,
Your enemy, most manifest;

169.   For he commands you only to
Evil and vice, and does encourage
That you should say of Allah things,
Of which you have no knowledge.

170.   When they are told: "Follow the revelation
Of Allah", they reply: "No, no! We follow
Only the ways of our forefathers!"
What! Even though their fathers had been low,
In wisdom, ne'er upon the right direction?!

171.   The state of disbelievers may be likened,
To the call of a shepherd to the flock:
Nothing they[1] hear but shouts and cries: "They are,
Deaf, dumb and blind, never able to think.

172.   You who believe!
Eat of the wholesome things We have,
For you provided, and give thanks to God,
If Him alone it is you serve.

---

1. The cattle.

173. He has to you forbidden only:
     Carrion, blood, the flesh of swine,
     And consecrated stuff unto a name,
     Other than God's; yet it shall be no sin,
     If one is forced, of them to eat, but never
     Wilfully or exceedingly;
     And God's the Merciful Forgiver.

174. Those who suppress God's revelations in
     The Scriptures, and, for some cheap acquisition,
     Do sell them, fill their bellies with the Fire;
     And God, upon the Day of Resurrection,
     Will not address them, nor is He to ever,
     Purify them; a grievous retribution
     Will be awaiting them.

175. Such people purchase deviation,
     At the expense of Guidance,
     And punishment in place of Pardon;
     What an extreme endurance,
     To face the Fire!

176. For God has now revealed the Book in truth,
     And surely those who cause dissension,
     About the Book, are deeply sunk
     In wicked opposition.

177. There is no righteousness in turning,
     Your faces to the East and West,
     The righteous ones are those who do
     Have faith in God, and in the Last
     Of Days, in angels and the Book,
     And in the prophets of the past,

And out of love for Him, pay out
Of their own wealth, to kith and kin,
To orphans, and the people fraught
With poverty, and the wayfaring alien,
To the beggars, and for the freeing
Of the captives and slaves; who keep up prayers,
And give zakaat, who, in fulfilling
Their pledges are most keen; who are
Patient in pain, adversity and war:
These are sincere believers,
They are the most godfearing!

178.   You who believe, the law of talion,
In case of people slain,[1] is for you written:
A free man for a free man,
A bondsman for a bondsman,
A woman for a woman,[2]
If one is pardoned by the injured brother,[3]
Then he should act by the accepted norms,
And compensate him in a liberal manner;
This is a relaxation from your Lord,
Out of His Ruth, and after this whoever
Exceeds the limits, shall incur
A painful scourge indeed.

179.   O You who have intelligence!
In the law of Retaliation,
There is safety of life for you; perchance,

---

1. That is: "murdered;" not applicable to cases of manslaughter.

2. This is not a third class, but a division in the other two classes.

3. The victim's kin: the term 'brother' is used in its general sense: all men are
   brothers in Islam.

You will guard your salvation.

180.   Prescribed it is to you when death,
       Approaches one of you, who has
       Some property, that he bequeath,
       In manners just and fair, to his
       Parents and next of kin;
       This is a duty on whoever
       Does have a fear of Allah.

181.   If one of those who've heard the will, would ever
       Alter it, he himself shall bear the sin;
       For God is the All-Knowing Hearer.

182.   If one detects, however, an injustice,
       Or wrong-doing by the testator,
       And he effects a settlement amongst,
       The parties, he commits no sinful error;
       God's the Most-Merciful Forgiver.

183.   O You believers! Fasting is to you
       Prescribed, just as it was decreed,
       For those before you, that you may
       Learn self-restraint indeed:

184.   It is of days a certain number;
       But if from 'mongst you any
       Are ill or on a journey,
       Then: other days of the same number;
       And those who could afford it,[1] should
       Effect redemption by the feeding

_____

1. "But have for any reason broken their fast".

40

Of a poor man, and he that's giving
More, of his own free will, he's doing,
Good to himself; yet fasting is for you
Far better, if you only knew.

185. The month of Ramadhan's the one,
In which was sent down Al-Quran:
A guide to humankind, with proofs,
Most clear of Guidance and Furqan;[1]
Thus every one among you who is present,
During this month, shall fast therein,
And anyone who's ill or on a journey,
Fast days of the same number later on:
God wishes for you every ease,
He wishes you no difficulties;
And He desire that you should fast in full,[2]
So, for His guiding you, glorify Allah,
Perhaps you will be grateful.

186. And when My servants question you,[3]
Concerning Me:
Well, I am very near, and I do answer,
The prayers of every single prayer,
Whene'er one calls upon Me;
So let them hearken unto Me,
And do believe in Me, So that they may,
Proceed on the right way.

187. You're now permitted to approach your wives,
On the nights of the fast; they're garments

1. The criterion (to distinguish right from wrong), also "Illumination" and
   "Salvation".

2. The whole month.   3. The Prophet (pbuh).

To you, and garments are you to them too;[1]
God knew that you were faithless to yourselves,
So He relented and forgave your guilts,
And now you may relate with them, and do
Seek that which God has made for your enjoyments.
Thus eat and drink till the white thread of light,
At dawn, is obvious from the dark of night,
And then complete your fast till sunset,[2] but
When you confine yourselves to mosques,[3] do not
Approach your spouses; these are bounds set by,
God, therefore, ne'er be to them nigh!
Allah makes His commands to people plain,
Expecting them to self-restrain.

188. Do not devour each other's property,
For vanities, nor seek to gain access,
Thereby to judges that you may possess,
Unjustly parts of people's property,
While you're aware of this.

189. They ask you of the phases of the moon!
Say: these are timing signs for men,
And for the Pilgrimage;[4] but righteousness
Is not to enter houses from the back![5]

---

1. Men and women are each other's mutual support, comfort, protection as well
   as keepers of each other's secrets.
2. Literal "night".
3. During the last ten days of Ramadhan.
4. Concerning many superstitions connected with the New Moon, which
   continue even to the present day.
5. The pagan Arabs used to enter their houses this way during or on returning
   from pilgrimage.

Righteousness is to be godfearing; thus:
Enter your houses by their proper doors,[1]
And do fear God, perhaps you win success!

190.   Fight in the cause of God with those who fight
Against you, but do not commit transgression;[2]
For God dislikes those who transgress.

191.   Kill them wherever they come face to face,
With you and drive them from whatever place,
They drove you out, for *fitna*[3]
Is worse than carnage;[4]
Yet do not fight them at the Sacred Mosque,[5]
Unless you come therein under attack;
And if they do attack, give them the edge
Of your destructive sword:
The infidels' fitting reward!

192.   But if they cease, go on no further,
For God's the Merciful Forgiver.

193.   The fight goes on until there is no *fitna*,
And God's religion reigns supreme,
But if they cease, fight none except,
The wicked men in the extreme.

---

1. This expression has now turned into an idiom meaning: "Do not beat about the bush", "go about it openly", etc.   2. Or "do not attack first".

3. This word has several meanings: oppression, persecution, suppression, idolatry, sedition, civil discord, trouble-making and trial and temptation. Here it is, most probably "The ruthless persecution of Muslims and the suppression of their beliefs and opinion by the Pagan Meccans.

4. Or "murder".   5. Near or within the precincts of Masjid al-Haraam.

194.   A sacred month should be a sacred month;
       But sacred things are also subject to
       The law of just retaliation;
       Therefore, if they transgress the prohibition,
       'Gainst you, attack them as they have attacked you;
       But still fear God, and in your mind retain,
       That God's with those who self-restrain.

195.   Give generously in the cause of God,
       And do not cast yourselves into perdition,
       With your own hands;[1] but keep on doing good;
       Those who do good are held by God,
       In great compassion.

196.   You shall observe the *Hajj* and *Umrah* only
       For God, but if you are somewhere hemmed in,
       Whatever you can offer, will suffice,
       And ere your gift[2] shall be in place, do not begin
       To shave your heads, but if among you any
       Is ill or has some scalp complaint,[3] atone
       For this by fasting, alms or sacrifice,
       In quieter times; however, if you mean
       To be going from *Umrah* onto *Hajj*,
       Offer the gift that you could manage;
       But if you lack the means, then fast three days,
       During the Hajj, and seven days upon
       Your coming back, making ten days in all;
       This is for those whose homes are not within,

---

1. If the believers do not help with the war effort in the cause of God, but they only hug their wealth, perhaps they will be helping in their own destruction.
2. Sacrifice, offering.
3. (That forces him to cut his hair).

The precincts of the Holy Mosque; and then,
Fear God, and bear in mind that God is Stern
In retribution.

197. For Pilgrimage, some months are set, well known;
He that intends to make his Hajj therein,
Let him abstain from sexual intercourse,
All sorts of wickedness, and rancourous discourse,
During the Hajj; and surely God's Aware
Of all good things you do. Also prepare
Provisions for the trip, but the provision,
Most excellent is certainly to be
God-fearing, thus: you thinking men!
Only fear Me!

198. There shall upon you be no fault,
In seeking bounties from your Lord;[1]
And after you file down from *Arafaat*,
As you approach the Holy Edifice,[2]
Celebrate Allah's praises, and remember
Him that provided you with guidance,
Whereas before this you were all in error.

199. And then return from the location whence,
People return, while asking Allah
For His forgiveness, for indeed,
God's the Most Merciful Forgiver.

200. And once you have performed your rites,

---

1. Trading during the Pilgrimage.

2. Mash'ar al-Haraam located at Muzdalifah, between Arafaat and Mina where the Holy Prophet offered up a long prayer.

Praise Allah as you used to celebrate,
The praises of your fathers, nay, more great,
And more intense shall be His lauding; yet,
Some people pray: "Give us, Our Lord,
All the good things here in this world!"
Such folks will have no portion from,
The world to come.

201. But there are others who would pray:
"Give us, Our Lord, whatever,
Is good in this world, and whatever
Is good in the Hereafter, and do save us
From the chastisement of the Fire."

202. Such people shall receive their proper share
For what they have been earning;
And Swift is God in reckoning.

203. Therefore pass these appointed days,
In celebrating Allah's praise;[1]
And those who leave upon the second day,
Incur no sin, nor those who stay,
Shall be committing any sin,
So long as righteousness will be observed.
Therefore have fear of Allah, and be certain,
That you shall be before Him gathered.

204. There are some men whose view,
About this worldly life[2] may dazzle you,
They call on God to vouch for what
Is in their heart of hearts,

---

1. In Mina.   2. World view, world outlook.

Whereas they are in fact,
Deadliest of opponents.

205. If any of them is in power,
He shall direct his efforts,
To spread corruption in the earth,
Destroying lives and harvests;
But God dislikes corruption.

206. And when it's said to him "fear Allah",
Vanity carries him off unto sin;
Hell is the proper place for such a person,
And it's indeed an evil shelter!

207. And there's a certain type of man,
Who dedicates his life to please
Allah; and Allah's Full of Kindness,
Unto His devotees.

208. O You believers, come into Islam,
Whole-heartedly,[1] and do not follow,
The steps of Satan; for he is,
Certainly your manifest foe.

209. Now if you slip and blunder backwards,
After clear signs[2] have to you come,
Just know that God's
The Almighty, the Wise.

210. Do they expect that God Himself should come,
Down unto them in canopies of cloud,

---

1. In total submission.   2. Or "miracles".

47

With angels in His train, to seal their doom,
When everything is going back to God?

211.   Question the Sons of Israel how many,
A Sign[1] profound have We unto them sent;
But God, to those who waste God's favour, after
It's granted, is Severe in punishment.

212.   Adorned and charming is this worldly life,
To those who have adopted disbelief,
And so they scoff at those who do believe;
But the godfearing will be far above
Them on the Day of Resurrection,
And God bestows on whom He pleases
Abundance of no computation.

213.   Humanity had been a single *Umma*,[2]
And Allah sent forth prophets to deliver,
Both tidings glad and warnings, and with them,
He sent the Scripture based on Truth, in order
To judge disputes between the people; but
Disputes arose among the folks who were
Given it, after they received clear signs,
Because they wanted to oppress each other;
Thus Allah, by His grace, gave guidance,
To those who were believers in that Truth
Which was disputed; for it's God who does
Guide whom He please to the right path.

214.   Did you expect to enter Paradise,

---

1. Or "miracle".   2. Human life began in full Divine light;
    later, Adam's descendants went astray.

Yet, unlike those before you, to be taken
Up with no troubles and afflictions?
But they had been by ills so shaken,
That their apostle and the people,
Who shared his faith, were forced to cry;
"When will the help of God arrive?"
Behold, God's help is always nigh!

215. You're being asked on giving alms;
Answer: Whatever shall be given,
In charity is good: to parents,
To the nearest of kin, the orphan,
The needy and the travelling aliens;
Of whatsoever good you do,
God is the Knower true.

216. Fighting has been enjoined upon you,
Although to you it is not pleasing;
Many a time, you may dislike a thing,
Though it is good for you,
And oftentimes you chance to love a thing,
Though it is bad for you;
You do not know, while God is Knowing.

217. They question you concerning fighting,
During the Sacred Month. Say: Ay,
"Fighting is grave therein, but to debar
People from Allah's path, and to deny
Him, to revile the Sacred Mosque, and drive
Away its dwellers from it, is by far,
The gravest in the sight of Allah, for
Oppression is far worse than murder;

Nor will they cease to fight with you until,
They force you, if they're able, to surrender
Your own religion; but, be warned, whoever
Of you recants and dies an unbeliever,
His works shall bear no fruit at all,
In this world and in the Hereafter;
Such people are the tenants of the Fire,
Wherein they will for ages dwell.

218.   But those who did embrace the Faith,
And those who fled their homes and fought
For Allah's cause, may rightly hope for
Allah's Mercy, for God is Oft-
Forgiving, Very Clement.

219.   They question you about intoxicants,[1]
And games of chance.[2] Answer: "In both of them,
There is great, sinful harm as well as means,
Of profit for the people, but the harm,
Is greater than their profit;" And again,
They ask you "How much should they spend in alms?
Answer: "whatever you could spare!"
And thus does God make clear His signs,
Unto you, so that you may ponder,

220.   Upon this world and the Hereafter.
They also question you concerning orphans.
Say: "In their interest, do the best you could,
And if you ought to be co-partners,
Remember that they are as brothers;

---

1. Wine and all fermented liquor, and, by analogy, any intoxicating liquor or
    drug.   2. Or "Gambling".

God knows the righteous doer from the wicked,
And if Allah had willed, He surely would
Have brought upon you hardships, but God is
The Almighty, the Wise.

221.   *Mushrik*[1] women you shall not wed unless
They will embrace the faith, for certainly,
A faithful[2] bondswoman, is better
Than an idolatress,
Even though she might please you greatly;
Nor shall you wed idolaters unless,
They do embrace the faith, for certainly,
A faithful bondsman is far better,
Than an idolater,
Even though he might please you greatly;
Such people call you to the Fire,
But God invites you, by His Grace,
To the Garden and to Forgiveness;
And He makes plain His signs[3] to humankind,
Perhaps they'll mind.

222.   They question you concerning monthly courses.
Say: "They pollute and harm;[4] therefore remain,
Apart from women in their courses, and,
Approach them not until they're clean again;
But after they have cleansed themselves you may,
Have intercourse with them after the way,
God has for you ordained;

1. Pagan, unbelieving, idol-worshipping.   2. Believing.

3. Revelations, communications, verses.

4. From both the woman's and man's points of view: "in the animal world,
instinct is a guide, man should in this respect be better: he is often worse"!
(Yousuf Ali)

God's Fond of those who turn from sin,
He loves the folks who stay unstained.

223. Your women are your cultivating soils,
Attend them thus as you do with your tilth,
And be producing something for your souls,[1]
Fear Allah and be certain of the truth,
That Him you are to Meet, and carry this
Good news to the believers.

224. Make not the name of Allah, in your swearings,
A means of keeping back from doing good,
Being godfearing or promoting peace,
Amongst the people; surely God,
Hears everything, and Knows all things.

225. God will not take you to account for what,
Is inadvertent in your oaths, but He
Will take you to account for that which is
Intended in your hearts; and God is surely
Forgiving, Most-Forbearing.

226. Those who renounce their wives on oaths,
Shall have to wait four months;
Yet, if they reconcile,
Then God's Forgiving, Merciful.

227. But if they're bent on going through divorce,
Surely Allah Hears all, Knows all.

---

1. This is a clear injunction against perverted ways of intercourse as opposed to
"the manner God has ordained" (v. 222).

228.   The women thus divorced shall guard themselves,
         And wait three menstruations and, if they
         Truly believe in God and the Last Day,
         It is not lawful for them to disguise,
         What Allah has created in their wombs,
         And in this case[1] their husbands would do better,
         To take them back, if they desire reunions;
         And there are rights for women similar
         To those that seem against them, and there is
         For men a certain rank above them;[2] God's,
         The Mighty, the All-wise.

229.   Divorce may be retracted only twice;
         Then either she is kept with honour,
         Or is allowed to go with kindness;
         It is not lawful for you to deny her
         Aught of what you to her have given;
         Unless both parties fear they may transgress,
         The bounds of God; and if you[3] do fear this:
         That they cannot observe the bounds of God,
         There shall be no offence for either party,
         If she should give up something to be free;
         These are the limits set by Allah, thus,
         Do not transgress them, for whoever
         Exceeds the limits set by God,
         Is surely an oppressor.

---

1. In case of pregnancy.

2. Perhaps the difference in economic position makes the man's responsibilities, liabilities and rights a little greater than woman's. The two sexes are on terms of equality in Law, but in certain matters, the weaker party is entitled to special protection (Yousuf Ali).

3. The judges.

230. Thereafter,[1] if he does divorce her;
     He cannot marry her again until
     She has married another man; then if
     He was to give her a divorce, it will
     Be no offence for either of them if
     They reunite, provided that they feel,
     They could observe the bounds ordained by God;
     And these are surely Allah's limits,
     Which He explains to men of wits.

231. And when divorcing women, once they have
     Fulfilled their waiting term, either retain[2]
     Them in a graceful way, or let them leave
     With gentleness; but you shall not retain
     Them merely to harrass or to revenge,
     He that does this, shall his own soul derange;
     Do not make game of Allah's revelations,
     Remember favours He has granted you,
     And what He has sent down, as admonitions,
     Unto you from the Book and Wisdom;
     Be godfearing and bear in mind that Allah
     Is, of all things, the Very Knower.

232. And on divorcing women, once they have,
     Fulfilled their waiting term, do not prevent
     Them from remarrying their husbands[3] when,
     They've come to a benign agreement;
     And this instruction is for all amongst you,
     Who do believe in God and the Last Day;

---

1. After the two divorces mentioned in the previous verse, that is, for the third
   time.   2. Or "allow them to live in the same home amicably."
3. Their former husbands or other persons.

This is for you, of most value and virtue;
And Allah Knows while you know not.

233. The mothers[1] shall give suck unto their infants,
For two whole years, if the men do desire
That suckling is completed, but the father
Of the infant shall bear the maintenance
And clothing of the mother in a manner,
That's just and fair; and ne'er a soul
Is to be charged with more than it can bear;
A mother should not be allowed to suffer,
Because of her own child, nor any father
Because of his own infant, and the same,
Duties shall be upon the father's heir;
Yet if they both decide to wean the child,
Through mutual consent and consultation,
There is no blame upon them, nor shall you
Commit a sin, if you decide to hire
A nursing mother for your children, when
Your payment unto them is just and fair;
Always fear God, and bear in mind that God's,
Of everything you do, the Keen Observer.

234. Widows of those of you who pass away,
Ought to restrain themselves to the extent,
Of four months and ten days, but once they have
Fulfilled their term, no blame shall be on you,
For what they do in lawful manners,
And God is Cognizant
Of everything you do.

---

1. Including divorced mothers.

235. It shall be no offence for you to make
      An offer of betrothal to such widows,
      Or keep it secret in your hearts; God knows
      That you do think of them, but do not seek
      Private meetings and promises, but speak
      Fairly, and make no final, marriage vows,
      Until the term prescribed expires; and always
      Know that God Knows your inner thoughts; thus take
      Heed of Him, and remember too that Allah
      Is Oft-Forgiving, and Forbearing.

236. It is no sin if you divorce the women,
      With whom you have not come together,[1]
      Or you have not yet fixed their dower;
      But for them make provision,
      In a way proper, common:
      The rich according with their greater fortunes,
      And the poor in accordance with their means;
      Binding is this on righteous men.

237. In case you are divorcing them before,
      They have been touched by you, but after
      Fixing for them a dowry, you should pay
      Half of the promised dowry, but they[2] may
      Forego it, or the person in whose power,
      Is laid the marriage tie,[3] decides to pay
      The dowry in full, and it's most proper[4]
      That you[5] forego it; and do not forget
      To be benevolent unto each other;

---

1. The marriage is not consummated.   2. The women.

3. The husband.

4. "Akin to piety", "closer to righteousness".   5. Men, husbands.

56

Whatsoever you do,
God Sees it too!

238. Attend constantly to your prayers,
Especially the Middle Prayer,[1]
And do devote all your attention,
Only to Allah.

239. When you're exposed to danger, pray,
Walking or riding; once you've got
To safety, do remember Allah,
As taught by Him, which you knew not.

240. You, who will die and leave your wives behind,
A will, you shall be making, in relation
To your own wives, for their just maintenance,
For a full year without expulsion;[2]
But if they leave themselves, there is no blame,
On you for any decent, lawful action
They see fit for themselves; and Allah is
The Almighty, the Wise;

241. Women divorced should also be likewise,
Provided for in a suitable manner;
This is incumbent on the people
Who do fear Allah.

242. God thus to you explains
His revelations, that you may
Exploit your brains.

---

1. The Afternoon ('Asr) prayer, according to most commentators.

2. The provision of a year's maintenance with residence.

243.   Did you reflect on those who fled
        Their homes for fear of death, although
        They had been in the thousands; so
        God said to them "You'll all be dead!",
        And then revived them;[1] Bountiful
        Is God to humankind, and yet,
        Most people are ungrateful.

244.   Then fight in Allah's cause and do recall
        That God Hears all, Knows all.

245.   Who is to be the one,
        That lends to God a goodly loan?[2]
        So He will multiply it,
        Many times over to his credit!
        The One who curbs or spreads is God alone,
        And unto Him you shall be coming Home.[3]

246.   Have you not ever heard of what the leaders
        Of the Children of Israel, demanded,
        Of one of their own prophets[4] after Moses?
        "Appoint a king for us", they reprimanded,
        "And we shall fight in Allah's cause!"
        He said: "Is this to mean that you've intended
        Not to fight, if the fighting is

1. This perhaps refers to the exodus of the Children of Israel. Moses ordered
   them to fight against the Philistines, but they showed cowardice and refused.
   Consequently they had to wander in the land for some forty years before a
   "new" generation, brought up in the hardship of the desert life, led them to
   victory.

2. Spending in the cause of God is metaphorically called "a goodly loan", which
   will bring you manifold blessings.

3. Or "returned to him".   4. Samuel.

Ordained on you." "But why should we refuse",
They said, "to fight in Allah's cause,
When we and all our children were evicted
From our own homes?!"
Despite this, when they were commanded
To fight, they all, except a few, declined;
God Knows the people with a wicked mind.

247. Their prophet told them: "God has raised up Saul,
To be a king over you all."
"Ah, how is he entitled", they objected,
"To be our king, when we are better-fitted
To kingship than he is, he is not even
Granted great wealth!" He said: "But God has chosen
Him over you, and He has also gifted,
Him with great knowledge and grand stature;
God grants His kingdom to whomever
He wills, for God's the Ample-Giving Knower."

248. Their prophet further said to them: "A mark
Of his authority is that the Ark
Of the Covenant is to you restored,
Wherein there is *sakeena*[1] from your Lord,
And which contains some relics from the Children
Of Moses and of Aaron,
And it is by the angels borne;
Surely in this there is for you a Sign,
If you are true believers."

---

1. Tranquility, assurance, peace of mind, safety, security and, in this context,
   according to N.J. Dawood, "an echo of the Hebrew word *Shekheenah* (The
   Holy Presence)".

249.   And later when departing with his soldiers,
        Said Saul: "Allah will put you to a test,
        By the side of a river: anyone
        Who drinks from it, unless it is to taste
        A single sip, shall cease to be my soldier,
        My fellow's he who does not quench his thirst;"[1]
        But they, except a smaller party drank
        Their fill of it, and then when he had crossed
        The river with his faithful ones, some said:
        "Our strength to day is not enough against
        Goliath and his troops;" but the convinced
        In meeting Allah, said: "How oft has a small host,
        By God's permission, vanquished bigger armies,
        And God is with the patient, with the steadfast."

250.   And when they faced Goliath and his forces,
        They prayed: "O Lord, bless us with fortitude,
        Make firm our feet, and give us victory
        Over the faithless multitude."

251.   And thus, by Allah's will, they routed them,
        And David put Goliath unto death,
        And God bestowed on him kingdom and wisdom,
        And taught him what He pleased; had it, in truth,
        Not been that Allah checked one set of people,
        By means of others, filled would be the earth,
        With chaos and corruption;
        But Allah's Grace encompasses
        All His creation.

---

1. Following the example of Gideon (Judges, vii); this example was, long after
   wards, followed by Henry V, in Shakespeare's story.

252.   These are God's revelations, and We are,
        Rehearsing them unto you in all truth,
        For you're indeed a messenger.[1]

253.   Some of these messengers We blessed more highly
        Than others: as the one[2] to whom God spoke,
        And some He raised unto a higher rank,
        And We did grant to Jesus, son of Mary,
        Miracles[3] manifest and did support,
        Him with the Holy Spirit; now if Allah
        Had pleased, the people after them[4] would never,
        Despite the signs most clear that to them came,
        Have fought with one another;
        They did, however, disagree: then some
        Of them believed and others disbelieved-
        If Allah had so willed, they would have never,
        Wrangled and fought each other-but, indeed,
        Allah Fulfills what he has Willed.[5]

254.   O You believers!
        Do spend in alms out of the favours,
        We have on you bestowed, before the Day
        Comes when there shall be no transactions,
        No nepotism,[6] and no intercessions,
        And surely those who tread upon the way,
        Of disbelief, engage in evil actions.

---

1. Or "of those who have been sent as Messengers".   2. Or "The ones".

3. Or "signs".   4. After the Prophets.

5. God has granted humankind free will and freedom of choice and action; it
   is not His will to forcibly prevent people from differences.

6. Or "friendship".

255.   Allah! There is no other god but He,
      The Ever-Living Bearer of all beings,
      Not a moment of rest or sleep may seize Him;
      Whatever is there in the heavens,
      And on the earth to Him belongs;
      Who dares to intercede before Him,
      Except by His own leave! He kens
      Absolutely all things that seem,
      As *after* or *before* to humans;
      They cannot comprehend a thing of His,
      Knowledge except that which He please,
      His Throne extends over the heavens,
      And o'er the earth, and holding up the same,
      Him never burdens;
      For He is the Most High, the All-Supreme.

256.   Let there be no compulsion in religion;
      True Guidance now is made distinct from error,
      Therefore whoever now Taghoot[1] forsakes,
      And does believe in God, shall grasp for ever
      A handle most secure that never breaks;
      For God is the All-Knowing Hearer.

257.   God is the Patron of the faithful,
      He leads them out of Darkness into Light,
      But the infidels' patrons are the devils,
      Who'll drive them out of Light into the plight
      Of Darkness; they shall be the inmates
      Of the Hell-Fire, and lasting dwellers!

---

1. Anyone or anything in rebellion against God, and anything worshipped besides God the One, thus: idols, devils, the Satan, leaders, kings, priests or even a state; idol-worship and disbelief are arch-examples.

258. Have you not heard of him¹ who argued,
With Abraham concerning his belief
In God the One, whereas the kingship was
Given to him by God. "He who grants life",
"And causes death", said Abraham, "He is
My Lord." He challenged: "I also grant life
And order death!" And Abraham went on:
"God brings the Sun up from the East,
You try to bring it from the West".
At this, the disbeliever was non-plussed!
Allah does not extend His guidance
To men who are unjust.

259. Or,² of the person who passed by a town,
Fallen down into utter ruination?³
He wondered: "How might Allah bring this back
To life, after its death and desolation?"
At this God took his life and let him be
Dead for a hundred years and then He did
Raise him again, and asked him to reply
Unto the question "How long have you tarried"?
He answered: "I stayed here perhaps a day,
Or even less". He said: "Nay, nay! You tarried
A hundred years! And now, do take a look,
At your own food and drink, there is no mark
Of aging, but look further for your donkey!⁴

---

1. Perhaps Nimrod, an ancient ruler of Mesopotamia.

2. Following the preceding verse, this means "and have you not also heard of...."

3. The Quran in its parables and stories aims at the moral and spiritual lessons
   men may learn; therefore, the persons or places (whether in this case, the
   person is Ezra, Nehemia or Ezekiel, or if the town is Jerusalem) are often
   irrelevant.   4. In fact: its skeleton.

We've done all this in order that We make,
You a symbol[1] for people-Do look further,
At yonder bones, how We set them together,
And cover them with flesh." And now that patent,
Was the Reality to him, he said:
"I do now know that God's Omnipotent.

260.   And also Abraham said once: "My Lord,
Show me how You give life unto the dead."
He asked: "Have you no faith in Me?" He said:
Oh, sure, only my heart to reassure!"
He said: "Well, take four birds, and tame them for
Yourself; and later place, on mountain-tops,
Pieces taken from each bird's corpse."
Then call to them, they'll come to you with speed;
Know then that Allah is
The Mighty, the All-Wise indeed.

261.   The charity of those who spend their wealth,
In Allah's cause is like a grain of corn,
Which brings forth seven ears, each of which born
With hundred grains; and Allah multiplies,
His bounty unto whom He please;
Munificent and Wise is God alone.

262.   People who spend their wealth in Allah's cause,
And then their charity will never follow,
With boasting or reproach, have their reward,
Directly from their Lord;
And they will have no fear, nor any sorrow.

---

1. This verse, among other things, illustrates how immaterial Time is to God's
working.

263.   A kindly word with some forbearance,
        Is better than the alms-giving,
        Followed by nuisance;
        And Allah's Needless, Most-Forbearing.

264.   O You believers, do not spoil,
        Your charitable actions by
        Boasting and doing harm like they,
        Who spend their wealth to show off, while
        Having no faith in God and the Last Day;
        Such men are like a rock with little soil,
        Upon it, then some rain will fall,
        On it, which leaves it bare again;
        They'll from their efforts nothing gain,
        And Allah does not guide the faithless[1] people.

265.   But those who spend their riches with the sole
        Desire of pleasing God and for their souls',
        Certainty may be likened to a garden,
        On elevated ground with fertile soil,
        When heavy rain upon it falls,
        It is to make it doubly laden
        With fruits, and if there is no heavy rain,
        Even a drizzle is sufficient;
        God is of all your actions Cognizant.

266.   Would any of you wish to own a garden,
        Planted with palms and vines and every fruit,
        Watered by flowing streams, then while you grow
        Older, with children not yet strong, astute,

---

1. Or "ungrateful".

A holocaust[1] should strike and burn it down?
Thus Allah makes His revelations plain,
To you, so that you may give thought.

267.   O You believers, you should give, in alms,
Of what is clean and lawful in your earnings,
And of the things We have been bringing forth,
For you out of the earth; do not pick things,
For charity, which aren't of any worth,
Bad things which you yourselves would not accept,
Unless you closed your eyes!
And know that God's All-Rich, Worthy of Praise.

268.   Satan does threaten you with poverty,
And prompts you to commit the evil thing,
And God holds out for you the promise of,
His Pardon and His bounty,
And God's Munificent, All-Knowing.

269.   Wisdom He gives to whom He please,
And He that's given wisdom has indeed,
Attained the greatest wealth but only those,
Who have the common sense, take heed.

270.   Surely God knows of what you give in alms,
Or any vows you make; and the wrong-doers,
Shall have no helpers.

271.   Giving charity openly is fine,
And it will be much better for you yet,

1. Or "a great whirlwind charged with lightning and fire"; this is "the wrath to
   come" in this parable, and the provision against it, is a life of righteousness
   and true charity.

If you give alms to those in need in private,
This will atone for you many a sin,
And Allah, of your every action,
Has Perfect Ken.

272. It is not up to you to guide them,
But God gives guidance unto whom He wills;
Whatever good you give in charity,
It will be good for your own souls;
The charity you give shall only be:
For the seeking of Allah's Pleasure,
And everything you give in charity,
shall be rendered back in full measure,
You'll be dealt with with equity.

273. It's[1] also for the needful men, confined
In Allah's cause, who cannot travel,
To earn their bread, throughout the land,
Therefore, the ignorant take them for people,
Of wealth, as they're modest and self-restrained,
But you can recognize them by their mien;
They never beg importunately from
The other men, and all you spend on them,
Shall be to Allah known.

274. The recompense for those who give in alms,
By day, by night, in private or in public,
Comes from their Lord; they shall not grieve,
Nor ever panic.

275. The swallowers of usury shall rise,[2]

---

1. The charity.   2. (Before God).

Like men whom Satan, by his touch, has made
Insane, because they say that "truly trade,
Is just like usury", but Allah has,
Allowed trading, and outlawed usury;
Henceforth he that respects this admonition
From his Lord and abstains, he is to be
Allowed to keep his previous takings, and
His destiny shall be in Allah's hand;
But those who do return to the affair,
Shall be the inmates of the Fire,
Wherein they will abide for ever.

276.   God curses usury and blesses charity,
He bears no love for the ungrateful sinner.

277.   Those who believe, and do the best of deeds,
Establish prayers and give *zakaat*, receive
Their recompense from their own Lord, and they
Will never fear a thing, nor ever grieve.

278.   You who believe! Have fear of God and waive,
What's still due unto you from usury,
If truly you believe.

279.   But if you do it not, be warned of war,
Declared by Allah and His messenger;
If you repent, however, you may keep
Your capital: do not make suffer,[1]
And you shall not be made to suffer.

280.   But if the debtor is in straitened times,

---

1. "You shall not make the debtor suffer loss..."

Then give him time till he could manage;
Of course if you remit the sum as alms,
That's best for you, if you but had the knowledge.

281.   And guard yourselves against a Day when you
Shall be returned to God, then every soul,
Is paid in full according to his deeds,
And none is to be wronged at all.

282.   You who believe! When you transact a loan,
For any period, you shall write it down,
And an impartial scribe between you should,
Put it in black and white.
No scribe whom God has blessed with such a gift,
Will e'er refuse to write; he ought to write.
And let the debtor be dictating, while
Observing God, his Lord, and not diminish aught
From it at all.
But if a debtor is: mentally feeble,
Or very weak, or verily unable,
To be dictating, then you shall permit
His friend[1] to do the task in fairness,
And call in, two men from among your folk,
For bearing witness,
And if two men be not available,
Then one man and two women you judge fit
For witnesses:
If one of the two women should mistake,
The other may remind her;
And witnesses shall not refuse, whenever
They shall be called upon to witness.

---

1. Or "guardian".

Be not averse to get it written, whether
It shall be small or large, and cite the date,
Of the repayment: this is, in the sight
Of God more just, as testimony stronger,
And nearer to eliminating doubt.
But if it is some goods at hand,
That you exchange between you on the spot,
There is no blame on you, if you do not
Put it in writing, yet you ought to find,
Witnesses for the barters of this kind.
And let no harm be done to either,
The scribe or witness, if you do this,
Guilty are you of wickedness.
Be godfearing, it's God who sends you teachings,
And God Himself has knowledge of all things.

283.   And if you are upon a journey,
And do not find a scribe, then take a pledge,
Into possession; but if any
Of you, entrusts another with a pledge,[1]
Then the trustee should faithfully discharge,
His trust, while having fear of God, his Lord;
A testimony you shall ne'er withhold,
He that it hides, inflicts a sinful damage,
On his own heart, and, of all things you do,
God has full Knowledge.

284.   Whatever is there in the heavens,
And on the earth, to God belongs,
Whether you manifest or hide whatever,
Is in your hearts and minds, He summons

---

1. Merely on trust.

You for it to account; and then he pardons
Whome'er He pleases, and let suffer
Whom He so wills, and God has power,
Over all things.

285. The Messenger has faith in what has been,
Sent down unto him from his Lord, and so
Do all the men of faith; each one believes
In God, His angels, and His Books, as also
In all His messengers: "and We make no
Distinction 'tween a single one of His
Apostles", and they also say: "We hearken
And We obey; our Lord, we seek Your pardon,
For You're the Object of all journeys."[1]

286. God never burdens any soul
Beyond its means; into its[2] credit enters,
Whatever good it earns, but evil deeds shall be against it;
"O Lord, condemn us not if we forget,
Or any wrong commit,
O Lord, lay not on us the burden,
That You on those before us laid,
O Lord, impose on us not more than
We have the strength to bear,
Blot out our sins and grant us Pardon,
And pour Your Mercy over us, You are
The Only Patron we invoke,
Therefore help us against the faithless folk."

---

1. These statements are made by the faithful; it is not for us to make any distinction between one and another of God's messengers, we must honour
them equally, though we know that God in His Wisdom gave them different
missions, ranks and degrees.   2. The soul's.

SURA 3
THE HOUSE OF IMRAN
(AALI-IMRAAN)

In the Name of God, the Beneficent, the Merciful

1. Alif Laam Meem.

2. Allah: there is no God but Him;
    The Ever-Living, the Eternal.

3. In truth has He unto you sent,
    The Book verifying what went
    Before it; Torah and Injeel,[1]
    Did He reveal,

4. As guides in former times for all the people,
    And He sent Al-Furqan;[2]
    For those who disbelieve in
    God's revelations, there shall be
    A grievous scourge; for God is surely
    The Mighty Lord of Vindication;

5. Nothing is ever from God hidden,
    Either on Earth or in the heaven;

6. He is the One who shapes you in the wombs,
    According to His will; there is but He,
    No God at all: The Mighty, the All-wise.

---

1. The Arabic form of the Evangel "good news", which has later come to be
   known also as the Gospel or the New Testament.

2. Distinction between right and wrong, illumination and salvation; see footnote
   to verse 53, Chapter 2.

7.   It's He who has to you revealed the Book,
      Of which some verses are the *muhkamaat*;[1]
      These are the mother verses of the Book,
      And others are the *mutashabihaat*;[2]
      Now those who have unwholesome hearts,
      Are always following the very parts,
      That have been allegorically expressed,
      Seeking mischief and offering their own,
      Explanation of them; but he who best,
      Knows their significance is God alone;
      And those, firmly rooted in knowledge say:
      "In it[3] we do believe, the whole of it,
      Comes from our Lord"; yet none shall pay
      Attention to it but the men of insight.

8.   "Our Lord, now that You've guided us aright,
      Let not our hearts become perverse and show
      To us Your Mercy, for You are indeed,
      The greatest Mercy-Shower;

9.   "O Lord, You will certainly gather all
      Mankind upon a Day most certain,
      For God shall ne'er His promise fail."

10.   Neither the disbelievers' riches nor,

---

1. Meaning "the basic ones"; these refer to the categorical orders of the shari'at
   or the Law, and, in a wider sense the very foundation on which all law rests,
   and briefly the very essence of God's Message.

2. Meaning "the similarly ambiguous ones"; these refer to various illustrative
   parables, allegories and ordinances, tales and stories, and verses of multiple
   meanings; they also refer to such profound, metaphysical matters that are
   beyond human language.   3. The Holy Quran.

Their offspring will be helping them before,
God in the least; they shall, for sure,
Be fuel for the Fire,

11. Following Pharaoh's People's practice,
And those before them, they denied,
Our revelations. Therefore, Allah
Did seize them for their sins; God is indeed,
In retribution Most Severe.

12. Say to the disbelievers: "Soon
You shall be overcome and driven,
All of you, to Gehenna:
It is a most unpleasant haven!

13. "Indeed you have already had a sign,
In the two hosts that met in combat:[1]
One of them battled in the cause of God,
The other was a pagan army that
Saw, facing them, with their own eyes,
Foes twice as many as themselves.
Yes, God will aid and strengthen
With His succor whomever He
Wishes; in this there is a lesson,
For those with eyes to see."

14. Mankind is lured: by lusting after women,
Love for one's children, and the glare of gold
And silver, hoarded high, the glamour
of well-bred horses, cattle, and well-tilled,

---

1. A reference to the battle of Badr where a large, Meccan force fought the
much smaller contingent of Muslims and lost the day.

Productive lands; such are the vanities,
Of the life in this world;
Far pleasanter shall be, however,
A good return to Allah.

15. Say: Let me give you the glad tidings
Of things excelling these: Gardens of Bliss,
With flowing streams, in closest Nearness,
Unto their Lord for the god-fearing;
Therein they will have their eternal dwellings,
Together with their spouses chaste and stainless,
In Allah's boons rejoicing;
God has insight into His servants,

16. Those who do say: "Our Lord, we are embracing
The Faith indeed, therefore forgive our sins,
And save us from the scourges of the Fire";

17. Patient are they and self-controlling,
Truthful, devotedly complying,
Givers of charity, who are,
At early hours of the morning,
For the Pardon of God, imploring.

18. There is no deity but He:
Thus witness Allah and His angels,
And those endued with knowledge, who
Stand firm on justice; and, there is
No God but He, the Mighty, the All-Wise.

19. Religion in the sight of God,

Is certainly Islam.[1]
Those who received the Scriptures,
Did not dissent therefrom,
Till after Knowledge came to them,
When they envied among themselves;
God is most Prompt at computation,
With any who deny His Revelation.

20. Now, if they argue with you, say:
"I have submitted my whole being
To God, and so have my disciples."
And say unto the People of the Scriptures,
As well as to the bookless gentiles:
"Do you submit yourselves to God?",
And if they do submit, they will indeed,
Be rightly guided, if they give no heed,
Your duty then is to convey the Message,
For God is of His servants Most-Informed;

21. To those who disbelieve the revelations
Of God, who slay the prophets in defiance,
Of truth, and kill the men in their own midst-
Who taught them to be just, to them announce
A painful chastisement.

22. These are the people whose endeavours
Shall come to nothing in this world,
Or in the next, and they shall have no helpers.

23. Have you e're looked at those who are,
Given a portion of the Book:

---

1. Absolute submission to His will.

When they are summoned to the judgment
Of Allah's Book, a group of them turn back,
In discontentment;

24.   For they declare: "The Fire of Hell
Shall not be touching us except,
For a few days"! Such forgeries,
Fool them in their religious concept!

25.   What will they do then, when We gather them,
All together upon a Day which is,
Most sure to come, when every soul will be
Paid back in full for every thing it has,
Earned for itself, with no injustice?

26.   Declare: "O God the One,
The Sovereign of all sovereignty!
Kingship[1] You grant to whom You please,
And strip off from this kingship whom You choose,
You raise whom You so please in dignity,
And you abase whome'er You want,
In Your hand lies all Good, all Bounty,
Indeed You are Omnipotent;

27.   "You change the Night into the Day, and merge
The Day into the Night, and You compose
The Living from the Dead, and make the Living,
Be Dead; and You provide for whom You choose,
Without computing."

28.   Believers should not take for friends and helpers,

---

1. Power, rule.

The infidels in preference to believers;
And whoever does this, has no relation
With God, and you should guard yourselves
Against him; and Allah does caution
You all, about Himself alone,
For unto God's the last return.

29.   Say: "Allah knows what's in your hearts,
Whether you hide it or reveal it,
He knows whatever is there in the heavens,
And on the earth, for Allah has full power,
Over all things.

30.   Upon that Day each soul will find before it,
Whatever it has wrought of good, and as to
What it has wrought of evil, it will wish
That there could be, between what it did do,
And its own self, a respite ne'er to end!
God cautions you against Himself, for God's,
Unto His servants, Loving-Kind.

31.   Say: "If you do love God, then follow me,
And God will love you and forgive your sins,
For God is Most-Forgiving, Full of Mercy."

32.   Say: "Do obey God and the Messenger;
But if they give no heed, behold,
God has no love for any disbeliever."

33.   Certainly God had chosen Adam,
And Noah, and the House of Abraham,

And the offspring of Imran[1] from,
Among all earthly men,

34. Offspring, one of the other;
God's the All-Knowing Hearer;

35. Behold, the spouse of Imran prayed: "O Lord,
That which is in my womb, I do commit,
Into Your special service, pray accept it
From me; it's You who Hears, Who Knows indeed."

36. And when she laid her burden down, she said:
"My Lord, I am delivered of a girl,"-
Allah knew best what she brought forth-"but then,
The male could not be as the female;[2]
Mary I'm calling her, and I petition,
Your Own protection for her and her children
From the accursed Satan."

37. Therefore, her Lord accepted her,
With an acceptance Gracious,
And brought her up, a gracious lady,
Under the care of Zacharias;
Now every time that Zacharias entered
Her sanctuary,[3] he found some sustenance,
With her; so he would ask "O Mary, whence
Comes this to you?" And she would answer:
"It comes from God, for God does give to whom,
He pleases without measure."

---

1. The Amramites.

2. For Temple service.

3. A chamber in the Temple.

38.   There and then,[1] Zacharias called upon
       His Lord and prayed: "My Lord, grant unto me,
       From Your Own Self, a goodly progeny,
       The Hearer of all prayers is You alone."

39.   And then as he stood praying in the Shrine,
       The angels called to him and said: "Behold,
       God gives you news of John, who is to be[2]
       The verifier of a Word from God,
       Noble and self-restraining and a prophet,
       Amongst the very righteous."

40.   He said: "My Lord, how shall I have a son,
       When I am overcome by age, and barren
       Has been my spouse?"
       He said: "Thus Allah does whate'er He please."

41.   "My Lord", said he, "will You give me a Sign?"
       He said: "The sign will be that you'll abstain
       From speaking to the people for three days,
       Except by signs, but do remember often,
       Your Lord and celebrate His praise,
       Morning and even."

42.   Behold! The angels said: "O Mary,
       Allah has chosen you and made you pure,
       He has exalted you above the women,
       Of every people everywhere;

---

1. Zacharias and his wife were past the age of parenthood, but now seeing the miraculous growth of Mary, he also prayed for a pure child of his own.

2. A command from God, that is, the word "Be"; either in the case of John or Jesus, God only says "Be" and His divine intention "is already being."

43.   "O Mary, serve your Lord devotedly,
Humbly prostrate yourself and worship with
Those who worship whole-heartedly."

44.   These are some tidings of the Hidden,
That We to you reveal, and you were not,
Present when they were casting down their pens,
To make a choice among themselves, by lot,
Which one of them should be the guardian
Of Mary, nor had you been with them there,
When they about it feuded with each other.

45.   Behold! The angels said: "O Mary,
God sends you the good tidings of a Word,
From Him, whose name shall be Messiah,
Jesus, the son of Mary, who is honoured
Most highly in this world and in the next,
Who is among Our Nearest;

46.   "And he shall speak to people even when
He's in the crib as also in the prime
Of manhood, and he shall be one
Of those in righteousness sublime."

47.   She said: "My Lord, how shall I bear a son,
When I was ne'er touched by a man?!"
He said: "God thus creates whatever,
He wills; when He decrees a thing,
He only says unto it Be!
And it's already Being!

48.   "And He'll teach him the Book as well
As the Wisdom, and the Torah,

And the Evangel;

49. "And send him to the Israelites,
     As an apostle:[1] "
     Indeed I come to you with proof profound
     From your own Lord; I'll make for you, from clay,
     A bird's figure, and into it I'll breathe,
     And then it will, by Allah's sanction, fly;
     I cure the blind, I heal the lepers and,
     Revive the dead, by Allah's leave, and say,
     Unto you what you eat and what you store,
     In your own homes; surely for you in these
     Are certain Signs, if you were true believers;

50. "And I come for the confirmation
     Of what's before me of the Torah,
     And to revoke certain forbidden
     Items, and I do come with a Sign clear,
     From your own Lord, therefore fear Allah,
     And do obey me;

51. "Certainly God the One:[2]
     He is my Lord, He is your Lord,
     Thus worship Him alone,
     This is the Direct Road."

52. After some time, when Jesus felt
     Faithlessness on their[3] part, he said:
     "Who are my helpers in the cause of God?"
     And the disciples said: "We are indeed,

---

1. "Saying:"   2. Allah

3. The Children of Israel.

God's helpers, for in God we have believed;
Bear witness that to Him we have submitted;[1]

53. "Our Lord, we do have faith in what You have,
Sent down, and follow Your apostle; thus
Count us amongst your witnesses!"

54. But lo! They plotted and they planned,
And so did Allah plot and plan,
But God's the Planner Grand!

55. At last, God said: "O Jesus, now I will
Recall your soul and lift you up to Me,
And rid you of the disbelievers' dirt,
And I will cause your followers to be
Above the disbelievers[2] till the Day,
Of Resurrection; finally,
Unto Me you shall all return, and then
I'll judge among you all, regarding
All things you differed in;

56. "And I shall punish those who disbelieved,
With grievous scourge, both in this world,
And in the world to come, and they,
Shall be by no one helped.

57. "But those who do believe and are in practise,
Doers of good, shall be fully rewarded.
Behold! Those who commit injustice,
Are never liked by God indeed."

---

1. Or "have become muslims", in the proper sense of the word.

2. Those who reject you and disbelieve in you.

58.   Thus We recite to you Our signs,
        Together with the wisest warnings.

59.   The case of Jesus, in the sight of God,
        Is just as that of Adam:
        Whom He created out of dust,
        Whom He then thus addressed:
        "Be, and he was!"

60.   The very truth is this,
        Imparted by Your Lord, and thus,
        Be not a cynic doubter.

61.   Now that you have received this knowledge,
        If any argue with you on the matter,
        Say: "Come! Let us gather together:
        Your children and our children,
        Your women and our women,
        The nearest and the dearest,
        To you and unto us, and then
        Pray and invoke the curse of Allah
        On every liar."

62.   This is the very truthful thesis:
        There is no other deity but God,
        And surely God's the Mighty, the All-wise.

63.   Now If they turn away and pay no heed,
        Be sure that God, of evil-doers,
        Has full Knowledge indeed.

64.   Say: "People of the Scripture,
        Let us come to a common proclamation:

We worship none but God, and never
Give Him any association,
And raise no mortal from amongst us,
To be a godly master;
But if they still refuse, then say: "Bear witness
That we to Him surrender.[1]"

65.   O People of the Scripture,
Why do you wrangle over Abraham,
When both the Torah and the Gospel,
Were not revealed till *after* him?
Can't you anything fathom?!

66.   You have already argued over,
Matters you knew something about,
Why should you now contend a thing,
You know nothing about?!
Surely God knows it,
And you know not.

67.   Neither was Abraham Judaic,
Nor yet a Christian, but he was,
A muslim[2] man, monotheistic,
He never was an idol-worshiper;

68.   Surely among mankind the nearest
Of kin to Abraham are those
Who follow him as do this Prophet,
And the faithful, and God's the Patron,
Of all the true believers.

---

1. Or "that we are Muslims".

2. One who submits to the will of God.

69. A party of the people of the Scripture,
    Love to be able to mislead you, but
    None shall they lead astray except themselves,
    Though they may not perceive it.

70. O People of the Scripture, why
    Do you the signs[1] of God deny,
    When you yourselves are witnesses?

71. O People of the Scriptures, why on earth,
    Do you by falsehood clothe the Truth,
    Concealing that which you,
    Know to be True?

72. Another party of the People of the Scripture say:[2]
    "Profess the faith of the Believers[3] in the morning,
    And then reject it in the evening;
    Perhaps from it they'll turn away!"[4]

73. "Believe in none but those who follow
    Your own religion!" Say: true guidance is
    "Allah's Guidance, and that to others,
    May be given the like of what to you
    Has been given; and will they argue
    With you in your Lord's presence?[5] Say:
    In Allah's Hands are plenteous bounties,

---

1. Quranic revelations, the character of the Holy Prophet and other prophetic manifestations.

2. Among themselves.   3. Muslims.

4. That is: "Create doubts in their minds that they may go back on their religion.

5. Those addressed are the Jews of Medina.

86

And He imparts unto whom He will please,
And God's Munificent, All-Knowing;

74.   With His Mercy He overwhelms,
        Whome'er He wills, for Allah is,
        The Lord of boundless Bounties.

75.   Among the people of the Book, there are
        Some who, if trusted with a whole *qintar*,[1]
        They'll pay it back to you intact, and others,
        You cannot trust even with one dinar,[2]
        Who will not hand it back unless you could,
        Over them keep a constant guard!
        This is because they claim that "with the gentiles,
        We ought not to be honest!" Unto God,
        They therefore, knowingly attribute lies.

76.   Nay! Allah only loves the people,
        Who do fulfill their obligation,
        And evil acts repel.

77.   Those who trade off the Covenant of God,
        And their own plighted obligation,
        For a small price, shall have no portion
        In the Hereafter: God will neither
        Converse with them, nor look upon them,
        Nor cleanse them of their error,
        Upon the Day of Resurrection;
        And they shall have a woeful retribution.

---

1. A heap of gold; a *qintar* used to be a talent of 1,200 ounces of gold.

2. Or 'denarius": a small silver coin at that time; in later periods, dinar gold
   coins were also minted.

78.   And there are some of them who twist their tongues,
In imitation of the Scripture, in a manner,
To make you think that what they say is from
The Scripture, when it is not from the Scripture;
They add: "That is from Allah", when it is
Not in the least from Allah; they in fact,
Tell lies 'gainst Allah, by a conscious act.

79.   No man to whom God gives the Scriptures,
Judgment and the Prophetic office would,
To people ever say: "Be worshippers,
Of *me* instead of God!"
But rather: "Be the Lord's devoted servers,
After what you've been taught, and what you studied,
From the same Scriptures;"

80.   Neither would He enjoin you ever
To take the angels or the prophets
For lords and patrons; should He order
You to become infidels after,
You have been Muslims[1]?!

81.   Behold! Allah took from His prophets,
A Covenant: "Certainly you are given
Of Scriptures and of Wisdom, but in time,
A Messenger will come to you to sanction
What you have got, do then believe in him,
And give him help; He further said: "Now then,
Will you affirm this and accept the burden
I lay on you as binding"? They replied:
"Yes, we confirm it"; and God said:

---

1. Believers in and submitters to the absolute will of God.

"Well then bear witness unto this,
I, too, shall be a witness!"

82. He that hereafter breaks it,[1]
Shall wickedly transgress.

83. Do they long after some religion,
Other than that of God, when every soul,
And everything throughout the heavens,
And earth, whether they so intend,
Or not, to Him submit, and they shall all,
Be unto Him returned?

84. Declare: We do believe in everything
Revealed to us, in that which was sent down,
To Abraham and Ishmael, to Isaac,
To Jacob and the Tribes, and what was given
To Moses and to Jesus and the Prophets,
From their own Lord; and no distinction,
Do we e'er make among them, and we are
Muslims[2] to Him alone.

85. Whoever chooses other than Islam,[3]
As his religion, it shall from him,
Not be accepted, and he is to be,
Lost in the world to come.

86. Why should Allah be guiding people who,
Lapse into disbelief, after embracing
The Faith, and after bearing witness that
The Messenger was true, and after facing,

---

1. The Covenant of God.   2. Submitters.   3. Submission to the Almighty.

Most solid proofs? Certainly God does not,
Direct the unjust, the transgressing.

87.   A fitting recompense for them
Is that they shall be under,
The curse of God, and of the angels,
And of mankind together!

88.   And under it they shall remain for ever;
Their chastisement shall not be lightened,
Nor any respite will to them attend;

89.   Save those who even after this repent,
And mend their ways, for Allah is,
Oft-Forgiving, Most Clement.

90.   But those who disbelieve after believing,
And plunge deeper into unfaith,
From them repentance shall not be accepted;
They've gone too far away from Truth.

91.   If it were possible to take a ransom,
And if, any of those who disbelieved,
And died in disbelief, would offer
The whole earth filled with gold, it would indeed
Not be accepted; they shall have to suffer
A woeful torment; and no helper
Would ever to them come!

92.   Never shall you attain true piety,
Until you give, in alms, of what you love,
And God will have full knowledge of,
All you do give in charity.

93.   All food was lawful to the Israelites
        Except what Jacob had forbidden
        Himself, before the Torah was sent down;
        Say: "Fetch the Torah and recite it then,
        If you are truthful men.

94.   If any, after this, invent a lie,
        And unto God attribute it, they must
        Be evil-doers, most unjust.

95.   Say: God proclaims the very Truth:
        Follow the faith of Abraham,
        The solid worshipper of God the One,
        Who never was a Pagan;

96.   Most certainly the very first of shrines,[1]
        For worship, ever built for humankind,
        Is that at Becca,[2] blessedly ordained,
        As a beacon to guide all nations;[3]

97.   In it are lucid signs;
        Even Abraham's Station,[4]
        Whoever enters it, shall be secure;
        People owe it to God to pay a visit
        To the House if they could afford it;
        As for the unbelievers, God, for sure,
        Stands in no need of any creatures!

---

1. Or "houses of worship", or "temples".

2. Ancient name of Mecca meaning "a place of gathering".

3. The original word in Arabic "Al-Aalameen" means: all the worlds, all kinds of
   beings, all nations and all creatures.

4. The spot where Abraham stood for prayer.

98. Say: "People of the Scriptures,
     Why do you disbelieve in,
     God's revelations; surely God's,
     Watching your every action."

99. Say: "People of the Scriptures,
     Why do you block the path of God
     To the faithful, and even seek
     To make it crooked, odd,
     When you know it is straight and true?!
     God is not Unaware of what you do!

100. O You believers, if you listen,
     To some amongst the people of the Book,
     They'll rob you of your faith and take
     You into unbelief again.

101. But how could you go back unto Unfaith,
     When Allah's verses are to you rehearsed
     And His Own Messenger is in your midst!
     Already guided is to the right Path,
     Whoever unto God holds fast.

102. You who believe! Fear Allah as He must,
     Rightly be feared; woe if death overwhelms
     You and you are not Muslims![1]

103. Cling one and all unto the Cord[2] of God,
     Let nothing disunite you, and remember,

---

1. Or: "You are its witnesses."

2. Or "Rope": The simile is that of people struggling in deep water to whom a
   strong rope is stretched out.

With gratitude, God's favour on you when,
You had been enemies to one another,
And He did join your hearts in kindness,
And by His Grace, you are now brethren;
You were upon the slope of an abyss,
And He did save you there and then;
Thus Allah makes His revelations plain,
Perhaps you'll tread upon
The path of Guidance.

104.   And let there be, of you, a nation,[1]
Who call to goodness, advocate what's right
And proper, and forbid what's wrong;
Such people will attain salvation.

105.   Be not like those who split up into groups,
And got involved in wrangles even after,
Receiving clearest proofs; these[2] are to suffer
A dreadful Torture,

106.   On the Day when some faces will be bright,
With joy, and some a darkened, gloomy sight,
Thus will be said, to the grief-stricken lot:
"Recount after believing, did you not?!
Well, taste you then the retribution,
For lack of appreciation."[3]

107.   But those whose faces are,
Brightened with joy, will be,
In God's abundant Mercy,

---

1. An Umma or community.   2. People who cause divisions.

3. It also means: "Because you disbelieved".

Enjoying it for ever.

108.   What we recite unto you in all truth,
Are God's communications,
And God wills no injustice to,
Any of His creations.

109.   To God belongs everything in the heavens
And on the earth, and every single matter,
To God returns.

110.   You are the best community,
Raised up unto humanity:
Enjoining what is just and good,
Forbidding what is wrong and evil,
And you have faith in God;
Had the Followers of the Scripture,[1]
Believed, it would have been for them much better;
There are among them some believers,
But most of them are evil-doers;

111.   They can't inflict upon you serious harm,
Barring some slight annoyance; if they fight,
With you, they'll turn their backs to you and then,
There shall be none to help them in their plight.

112.   Disgrace shall be attending them,
Wherever they are found,
Unless they do abide by God's
Covenant and the people's bond;
They have incurred a wrath from God,

---

1. Here, and in the subsequent verses, the phrase refers to Jews only.

And misery has been on them ordained,
This was because they had denied,
God's revelations, and, with no just ground,
Slew their Prophets, and this they did,
As they rebelled and ravaged every bound.

113.   They are not all alike:
There are among the People of the Book,
Some parties steadfast, upright,
Who chant God's revelations through the night,
And worship Him upon their forelock;

114.   They do believe in God and the Last Day,
And they enjoin what's right and proper,
And they forbid what's wrong and evil,
And, in good work, they vie with one another,
These are indeed among the righteous,

115.   Whatever good they do will never,
Go unrewarded; Allah knows full-well
People who guard against all evil.

116.   As far as disbelievers are concerned,
Neither their riches nor their progeny,
Shall be to them of any use 'gainst Allah;
Surely they will be in the company,
Of the Fire for ever;

117.   Their kind of spending[1] in this worldly life,
May be likened unto a freezing wind,

---

1. The disbelievers' ways of spending their wealth, time, energy, etc.

That strikes and devastates the fields of men,
Who wronged their very souls; nay, not Unkind
Was God to them, but they themselves,
Had done injustice to their souls.

118.   O You who have believed, do not befriend,
People outside your ranks; they spare no pains,
To do you harm, they wish to see you suffer;
Their rank hatred is showing, through what rains,
Out of their mouths; and what their hearts disguise,
Is even worse. Indeed We've made the signs,
Thereof most plain to you, if you are wise.

119.   Lo! You do love them, but they love you not,
Even though you do believe in all the Scriptures,
And when they meet you, they declare:
"We, also, are believers".
But when they are alone, they bite their fingers,
The very tips of them, at you in rage;
Say: "Perish in your rage,
For of all secrets of the hearts,
God has the fullest Knowledge."

120.   They will be grieving, if good fortune calls you,
And they rejoice when something bad befalls you!
However, if you're patient and godfearing,
You won't be injured by their machinations,
For God encircles all their actions.

121.   Recall that morning when you[1] left your household,

---

1. The Holy Prophet.

To post the faithful at their battle-stations;[1]
And God was Hearing all and Knowing all;

122.   Behold! Shaken by trepidations,
Had been two parties of your own,
But God was their Protector; surely,
The faithful always should rely
On God alone.

123.   God had indeed helped you *bi-Badrin*,[2]
And you were *then* some weak and helpless brethren,
Therefore keep on being god-fearing,
That you may show Him some appreciation.

124.   Recall when you unto the faithful said:
"Suffice it not that your own Lord should send,
Down unto you supportive angels,
Of some three thousand?"

125.   Yea! If you do show fortitude,
While fearing God, and they attack
You suddenly, your Lord will back,
You even with five thousand angels,
Who will with foes wreak havoc!

126.   And God designed it for you as good news,
And for your hearts to be further at ease;

---

1. The Battle of Uhud outside Medina.

2. The Arabic phrase means "At Badr"; there was no way of subjecting the word
"Badr" to our rhythm unless I changed it to Badri or Badir; I chose the nice-
sounding, Arabic phrase.

Victory comes, however, only
From God, the Mighty, the Most-Wise.

127.   And that He might cut off a vital flank
Of those who disbelieve, or would abase
Them, so they go back with dishonour,
Frustrated of their purpose.

128.   Nothing is up to you[1] in this affair,
Whether He turns to them in Mercy,
Or shall chastise them, though they are
Men of iniquity,

129.   To God belongs everything in the heavens,
And everything on earth; He pardons
Whome'er He wills; and whom He pleases,
He shall chastise; yet God is Oft-
Forgiving, Full of Mercy.

130.   You who believe, do not engage in usury,
With doubling and redoubling interest,
But be godfearing, that you may be blessed
With real prosperity;

131.   And guard yourselves against the Fire,
Which is prepared for every unbeliever,

132.   And, that you may be blessed by Mercy,
Obey God and the Messenger;

133.   And hasten in the race: to win your Lord's

---

1. The Holy Prophet.

Forgiveness, and a Paradise,
The width of which encompasses
The heavens and the earth, which is prepared
For the godfearing pious,

134.   Who freely give to charity, both in,
Prosperity and in adversity,
Those who restrain their anger and forgive,
Their fellow-men-certainly God does love,
Doers of good unto humanity-

135.   And those who, if they ever fall in sin,
And wrong their souls, they soon remember God,
And ask forgiveness for their sins-who else
But God to pardon sins!-and those who would,
Not, knowingly, persist in any deed,
They've done amiss.

136.   Such are the people whose reward shall be:
Forgiveness from their Lord, as well as Gardens,
With running streams, as their eternal dwellings;
What a fine recompense indeed,
For workers of good deed!

137.   Precedents have been set before you
In days of yore, thus travel in the land,
And look to see what was the end,
of Truth-rejecters!

138.   This is a declaration to mankind,
And for the pious, self-restrainers,
A Guidance and an Admonition.

139. Be not infirm and do not grieve,
      And you shall gain the upper hand,
      If you believe.

140. If you received a wounding blow,
      So did the like of it your foe;
      We bring about such Days[1] to people,
      By turns, so that Allah may know,
      The true believers, and may draw
      Witnesses to Him from your circle-
      Certainly Allah has no amity,
      For workers of iniquity-

141. That God may purify and harden,
      The faithful, and humiliate
      The faithless pagan.

142. Did you expect to enter Paradise,
      Before Allah has proved[2] the men who fought
      For Him, and bore hardships with patience?

143. You used to long for death before you faced it,
      Well, now you've seen it, nay, almost embraced it!

144. Mohammad is no more than an apostle,
      And many an apostle passed away before him;
      Now if he too dies or be slain, would you,

---

1. Ayyaam "days" in Arabic also stands for "battles" or "significant days of victory or defeat".

2. The original Arabic is: "So that Allah may know"; God is, of course, Omniscient; "His knowing" means "not punishing or rewarding us before we have done anything evil or good; for that would have been unjust."

Recant your Faith? And certainly no harm,
Is done to God, if anyone turns back,
Upon his heels this way, for God will duly,
Reward the thankful people only.

145. Nor could a human being ever die,
Save by God's leave, the term is written down;[1]
He who desires the prizes of this world,
To him we'll grant them, and unto the one,
Who's after recompense in the Hereafter,
We'll also grant it; and it is the grateful,
We shall reward in full.

146. Many big groups of men of God have fought,
By the side of their prophets; but they never
Lost heart when meeting with disasters in,
The cause of God, nor did they weakly waver,
Nor did they show a hopeless attitude;
God loves the patient men of fortitude.

147. Their saying was no other than the praying:
"Our Lord, do pardon us our sins,
And our excesses in our actions,
Do make us firm of foot, and help us,
Against the disbelieving factions."

148. Thus Allah granted them the meeds,[2]
Of the life present, and the better
Rewards in the Hereafter;
God loves the doers of good deeds.

---

1. Fixed as by writing, predetermined.

2. Rewards

149. You who believe! If you were e'er to yield
     Unto the unbelievers, they would lead,
     You back to disbelief, and then you shall
     End up in utter loss indeed.

150. But nay! God is your Patron ever,
     And He's the best and only Helper.

151. We will be throwing terror into,
     The hearts of those who disbelieve,
     As they are serving gods and idols,
     Instead of God, for whom God's leave,
     Was ne'er sent down; and thus their dwellings
     Shall be the Fire: What a dismal
     Residence for doers of evil!

152. Surely God did fulfill His promise to you,
     When, by His leave, you were about to slaughter,
     The foe, but then you flinched and did dispute,
     The order,[1] and did disobey it, after
     He brought you to the sight of what you wished;[2]
     And some of you hankered after this world,
     And some among you the Hereafter cherished;
     Thus He allowed you to be overwhelmed,
     That you are put to test; but now He has
     Forgiven you, for Allah is,
     Most Gracious to believers.

153. Remember how you fled to the high ground,

---

1. The Prophet's command to the archers guarding a mountain pass at Uhud, not to leave their post under any circumstance.
2. Victory.

Not even looking at another fellow,
While the Apostle called you from behind!
Thus He granted you sorrow after sorrow,
So that you may not grieve for what you lost,
Nor at what had befallen you;
And God is the Awarest,
Of everything you do.

154.   And then, after this grief, He sent down Peace,
On you, and pacifying slumber,
Overtook some, while others, who were stirred,
By their own selfish whims, began to harbour
Untruthful thoughts concerning Allah-thoughts of
The Days of Ignorance-and so they said:
"Anything of the matter up to us?
Tell them: "The matter wholly rests with God."
In fact they don't disclose to you what they,
Hide in their hearts; they only say:
"Had we had any say in the affair,
Not one of us would have been slaughtered here!"
Say: "Even if you did remain,
In your own homes, those of you who,
Were destined to be slain,
Would surely have gone forth to,
Their own places of rest!"[1]
And all this was by God a test,
To show what's in your breasts,
And purify and harden,
What's in your hearts;
And Allah has the fullest Ken,
Of the innermost thoughts.

---

1. "Graves".

155. Certainly, those of you who ran away,
     Upon the day when the two armies[1] gave
     Battle, were duped by Satan, on account of,
     Some evil they had done; but God forgave
     Their error; surely God's the Oft-Forgiver,
     The All-Forbearer.

156. O You believers,
     Be not like those who disbelieved and said,
     Of their own brethren who had met their deaths,
     Abroad or in a combat: "Had they stayed
     With us, they had not died, or not been killed!"
     God purposed that this, in their hearts,
     Is a sorrow that ne'er imparts!
     God it is who ordains,
     Both Life and Death, and Allah knows the ins,
     And outs of all your actions.

157. And if you should be slain in Allah's cause,
     Or die a natural death, Allah's Forgiveness,
     And Mercy from Him will be better,
     Than all the wealth they could amass.

158. Whether you die or should be slain, however,
     Before Allah shall you be brought together.

159. Thanks to God's Mercy you[2] have been so lenient,
     Towards them; If you had been rough and cruel,
     They would have certainly abandoned you;
     Thus pardon them, implore their pardon, and take counsel,
     With them in the affairs, and once you have decided,

---

1. At the Battle of Uhud.   2. The Holy Prophet.

Then place your trust in God, indeed God loves the people
Who in Him trust.

160.   If God assist you, then there is no power,
Who could defeat you, but if He disown
You, who is there at all who could assist
You after Him; and it's in God alone,
The faithful put their trust.

161.   Prophets may not be cheating in their dealings;
For anyone who makes dishonest gains,
Will have, upon the Day of Resurrection,
To come forth with his gains of crooked means;
Then every soul is to be recompensed,
In full, against its earnings, and there is,
No sentencing unjust.

162.   How could a man who seeks God's Pleasure,
Be likened to the one who draws,
God's Wrath upon himself, whose final
Abode is Hell: the fireside of woes?

163.   All, in the sight of God, will have
Varying grades, for God's the One,
Who has been watching
Whatever they have done.

164.   Certainly God has the believers blessed,
By raising an Apostle from their midst,
To read His revelations to them,
To purify and teach them,
The Scripture and the Wisdom,
Whereas before this, they had been immersed,

In error manifest.

165. What! You have suffered losses once,
Though you'd inflicted losses twice as much,
Before this?! Yet you are exclaiming: "Whence
Was this?" Say: "You have brought this on yourselves";
All things are within God's Omnipotence.

166. And what befell you on the very day,
When the two armies clashed, was by God's leave:
Yea, to distinguish those who did believe;

167. And to expose the hypocrites,
For they were told: "Come, fight in Allah's cause,
Or just defend yourselves".
They answered: "If we knew there would be warfare,
We would have followed you for sure!"
That day they were in truth,
Much nearer to unfaith than Faith,
Uttering with their mouths,
What is not in their hearts,
And God knows best,
Their secret thoughts;

168. These are the very people who,
While they themselves remained at home,
Said of their brethren: "If they had
Listened to us, they would not have been slain!"
Say: "If you speak the truth,
Then, try to ward off your own death!"

169. And you shall not regard as dead,
The fallen in the way of God;

Nay, nay! They are alive, and well-
Provisioned at their Lord,

170. Rejoicing in what God, out of His Grace,
      Has granted them, and they have the good news,
      For those behind who have not joined them yet,
      That they shall have no fear, nor any cause
      For sorrow or regret;

171. They give glad tidings of God's favours,
      And graceful gifts, and that God never
      Fails to reward believers;

172. Those who responded to the call of God,
      And the Apostle, even after having,
      Suffered a setback, those of them, who do
      What's just and right, and are godfearing,
      Shall have a recompense unfailing;

173. Those who, on being warned by many men:
      "People have 'gainst you gathered, throng on throng,
      You better fear them", only grew more strong,
      In their belief, and answered: "God is more than
      Enough for us, oh, what a splendid Guardian."

174. Thus they returned with Allah's grace and blessing,
      Nor had they suffered any harm, they did
      Follow God's pleasure only, and God is,
      The Lord of Grace unbounded.

175. Satan indeed it is that prompts you
      To fear his followers, so you should have,
      No fear of people, but fear Me,

If you believe.

176.   And do not grieve for those of them who hasten,
To unbelief; they won't be harming God one whit;
Thus God intends that they shall have no portion
In the Hereafter; and a grievous torment,
Shall be their lot.

177.   Certainly those who purchase unbelief,
At the price of their faith, will do no harm
To Allah, and a grievous chastisement,
Shall be in store for them.

178.   Let not the disbelievers think that We,
Prolong their days for their own good; We only
Grant them respite that they will make the burden,
Of their own sins more heavy, and they'll have
A punishment disgraceful, grave.

179.   Allah is not to leave the faithful in,
Their present plight; Allah is to distinguish,
The good from evil, nor will God inform,
You of the Hidden; yet, if it's His wish,
He chooses, for this, one of His apostles;
Therefore have faith in God and His apostles;
You will have wages great, unfailing,
If you believe, if you're godfearing.

180.   And let no misers, who withhold the gifts,
God has bestowed upon them, think that it,
Is good for them; nay, for them it is evil:
The wealth they have thus piled up shall be set
Upon their napes on Resurrection Day;

Because the heavens and the earth,
Are Allah's heritage,
And God, of all your actions,
Does have the fullest Knowledge.

181. God heard the very words of those who said:
"Allah is poor and we are rich!" We will,
Surely record this statement, as We did,
Their unjust prophet-killing, and We will,
Declare to them: "Now have a taste,
Of the chastisement that will roast!

182. "This is the consequence of your own works,
And Allah is not in the least,
To His creatures unjust."

183. It's they who said: "God has taken our pledge,
Not to believe the bringer of a Message,
Unless he bring down fire,[1]
That will his sacrifice devour!"[2]
Say: "Other messengers before me came,
To you with most clear signs, and worked the same,
Miracle you are asking for;
Why did you then put them to death,
If you do speak the truth?!"

184. If they reject you, so have been rejected,
Before you, many messengers who came
With clearest signs,[3] with psalms and scriptures,

---

1. From heaven.

2. Some pre-Mosaic laws lay down "a fire from heavens on a sacrifice" as a test
for the credentials of Prophets.   3. Also meaning "proofs and miracles".

And with illuminating writs sublime.

185. Every being shall taste the Cup of Death,
      And only, on the Day of Resurrection,
      Shall you be paid your fullest recompense;
      Whoever then is spared the Fire,
      And is admitted unto Paradise,
      He will have gained his own salvation;
      And the life in this world, however,
      Is nothing but the pleasure of deception;

186. In which you will be surely tried and tested
      Through your possessions and your children,[1]
      And you'll certainly be subjected
      To the insults of those who have been given,
      The Book[2] before you, and the pagans;
      Yet to preserve patiently and to lead,
      A righteous life, shall be indeed,
      One of the greatest resolutions.

187. Behold! God made a covenant with those,
      Who were given the Scriptures,[3] and enjoined:
      "Proclaim these clearly unto humankind,
      And do not e're suppress them". But they chose
      To have them flung behind their backs, and sold
      Them for a sorry price! Behold,
      Too evil is what they have earned!

188. Do not suppose that those who do rejoice,

---

1. Also meaning "your dear ones" or "your own selves."

2. The Scripture.

3. The Jews.

For what they've done, who love to hear the voice
Of flattery for what they have not done,
Nay, think not, that they have the means to bypass
Our torment, and their torment shall be one,
Most grievous.

189.   To God belongs the Kingdom of the heavens
And of the earth, and He has power
Over all things.

190.   In the creation of the heavens and the earth,
And in the alternation of the nights and days,
Surely are many Signs for those who see,
With open eyes;

191.   Those who remember Allah always,
Standing, sitting or lying down,
And who reflect on the creation,
Of heavens and the earth, with prayers:
"Our Lord, You have not brought about all this,
In vain; Your Glory is above and over,
Such things; so, pray deliver,
Us from the scourge of Fire.

192.   "Our Lord, whomever you will cast,
Into the Fire, is disgraced,
For ever, and such wrong-doers,
Shall ne'er have any helpers;

193.   "Our Lord, we heard a crier plead,
For Faith: 'Believe in your own Lord!'
And we believed;
O Lord, forgive us then our sins,

And cover for us every evil deed,
And, after death, make us companions,
Of those who were, righteous indeed;

194. "O Lord, pray grant what You have promised us,
Through your apostles, and disgrace us not,
Upon the Day of Resurrection, for
Never have You a tryst forgot!"

195. And thus their Lord to them responded:
"Never will I let go to waste the labour
Of a worker among you whether,
Male or female, and you are all,
Offsprings of one another;
I will, therefore, forgive the sins of those,
Who left their homes or were therefrom turned out,
And suffered persecutions in My cause,
And fought and died for it, and I, no doubt,
Admit them into Gardens watered by,
E'er-flowing streams"; that is a gift from God,
And under God the richest prizes lie.

196. Let not the easy-going movement,[1]
Of unbelievers in the land, bamboozle
Any of you at all!

197. It's but a brief enjoyment;
Their ultimate abode is Hell,
A resting-place, most evil!

198. But for the people who did fear their Lord,

---

1. Or "Prosperity".

There will be Gardens through which rivers glide,
This is a goodly welcome from their Lord,
And what the virtuous shall find beside,
Allah, is best of all indeed.

199. Behold, among the People of the Scriptures,
Also are those who do have faith in God,
In what to you has been revealed, and in
What was to them sent down; they do indeed,
Bow to God in submission,
And do not sell God's Signs,
For paltry, worldly gains;
For these there is remuneration,
From their own Lord; Most Swift is God,
In Computation.

200. O You who do believe!
Patiently persevere,
Show valour when you strive,
United stand together,
And be godfearing, thus you may achieve
Final salvation.

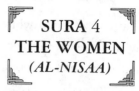

SURA 4
THE WOMEN
(AL-NISAA)

In the Name of God, the Beneficent, the Merciful

1.   O men and women, fear your Lord, the One
Who did create you from a single soul,
And, out of it, produced its mating twin,
And from the twain, He spread the whole
Of men and women;
Therefore, have fear of God through Whom,
you plead with one another,
And heed the fruitage of the womb;[1]
God's over you a constant Watcher.

2.   To the orphans restore their property,
Do not exchange their good things for the paltry,
And cheat them not of their possessions,
By adding theirs to your possession; this
Will surely be a gross injustice.

3.   And if you fear that you may not be able
To treat orphans with fairness, then you could
Marry the widows,[2] who to you seem good:
Two, three or four of them, and if you still,
Fear that you won't do justice to them, then
Take only one, or the bondswomen,

---

1. The original Arabic "Al-Arhaam" also stands, in this context, for "parents",
   "mothers", "kinship" and "ties of relationship".

2. This verse is revealed after the defeat at Uhud when the Muslim community
   was left with many orphans and widows, and some captives; the "widows" are
   the mothers of the orphans.

Who have fallen in your possession;[1]
This way you are more likely
To check iniquity.

4. And you shall freely give the women,
   Their dowers, but if they should choose,
   To give up for you any portion,
   Thereof, you may enjoy it as
   Wholesome and clean.

5. The feeble-minded ones[2] should not be given
   The property which God has to your hand,
   Entrusted, but you should provide therefrom,
   For them, and clothe them, and be to them kind.

6. Go on observing orphans; when you find,
   That they have surely reached the age of marriage,
   And that they their affairs could wisely manage,
   Release their property into their hand;
   Do not consume it wastefully or in a haste,
   Before they grow mature; and let the rich
   Guardian never the orphan's assets touch,[3]
   But a poor guardian may have portions,
   Reasonable for his provisions;
   And do make sure to call in witnesses,
   When you hand over their possessions,
   And God is All-Sufficient in
   Taking account!

---

1. Slave girls captured in war.
2. The incapable of understanding whose interest must be protected and treated
   with special kindness.
3. Claim no remuneration.

7.   There is a share for men in what is left,
Behind by parents and their next of kin;
For women too there is a share in what,
Is left by parents and their next of kin,
Whether it be immense or little,
They ought to have their title.

8.   If relatives or orphans or the poor,
Are present at the hour of distribution,
Provide them, out of it, with something,
And treat them with compassion.

9.   Let them[1] have in their minds the same,
Fear they would have for their own children,
If they had left behind some weaklings; thus,
Fear Allah then and let them be well-spoken!

10.   Those who consume the orphan's properties,
Wrongfully, swallow fire only
Into their bellies;
Inside something, they soon shall be,
That fiercely Blazes!

11.   Concerning your own children, God enjoins you thus:
The male inherits twice the portion of the female;
If there are only daughters, two or more, their total
Portion shall be two-thirds, if there is only one,
Daughter, she gets half of the whole;
Parents shall each receive one-sixth, when the deceased
Has children of his own;
If he be childless, and his parents be his heirs alone,

---

1. The people disposing of an estate.

Then the mother is to receive a third;
If he does have brothers and sisters, then the mother,
Shall have a sixth, and all this after,
The payment of all legacies and debts.
Your parents or your children?! If you only could
Know which would do you more of good!
Surely these are God's laws, and God's
The All-knowing, the Wise.

12.   Of what your wives have left behind, if they are childless,
You shall inherit half; but if they have some children,
Your share shall be a fourth, after the payment of
All debts and legacies;
Your wives will get a fourth of what you leave behind,
If you're without a child; but if you have some children,
Their share shall be an eighth, after the payment of
All debts and legacies;
If a man or a woman whose possession,
Shall be inherited, has neither parents, nor a child,
But has a brother and a sister, they shall each
Receive a sixth; if they are more than that, they shall
Equally share a third, after the payment of
All debts and legacies, without,
Loss to anyone's right;
This is God's ordinance,
And God's All-Knowing, Full of Clemence.

13.   Such are the limits set by Allah;
And he that follows God and His apostle,
Will be admitted into Gardens watered,
By running streams, for ever there to dwell;
And that's the greatest triumph.

14.   But he that counters God and His apostle,
       And goes beyond His limits, shall be sent,
       Unto the Fire therein to dwell,
       For long, and his shall be a shameful torment.

15.   If any woman from among you is accused,
       Of an indecency,[1] do take the evidence,
       Of four to testify against them; if they do
       Bear witness, keep them in their residence,
       Till death takes them away,
       Or God opens for them some way.

16.   And if two persons from among you,
       Commit the same, both shall be disciplined;
       If they repent, however, and amend,
       Leave them alone, for certainly
       God's the Redeemer, Loving-Kind.

17.   God is Responsive to repentance,
       Of those only, who sin in ignorance,
       But soon will turn to God in penitence;
       These are the people God redeems,
       And God's All-Knowing, Wise;

18.   Of no effect is the repentance,
       Of those who go on doing evil,
       Until death comes to them, then say:
       "Now I repent", nor of the people,
       Who die rejecting Faith; for these,
       We have indeed made ready,
       A Torment full of woes!

---

1. Lewdness, whoredom.

19.   O You believers, it's unlawful
       That you by force inherit[1] widows!
       Nor can you treat them harshly that you may,
       Get back parts of the dower given them,
       Unless they have been proven guilty,
       Of manifest adultery;
       Otherwise you shall treat them kindly,
       Even if you dislike them; it may be
       That you dislike a thing, while God
       Has placed in it a lot of good!

20.   And if you have decided to divorce,
       Your wife and take another in her place,
       Do not take back a bit from what you gave her,
       Even if it had been a heap of gold;
       Would you be taking it by slander,
       A sin apparent, bold?!

21.   How could you take it back when you have lain,
       With each other, and made a firm and plain
       Promise of union?!

22.   Marry not women who were in the past,
       Married unto your fathers; what is passed,
       Is the exception; but it was in fact,
       Obscene and odious, and an evil act!

23.   Forbidden unto you, for marriage, are:
       Your mothers and your daughters and your sisters,
       Your aunts, paternal or maternal,

---

1. This forbids the shameful custom, practised among many nations, of heirs
   inheriting the deceased kinsman's widows along with his goods and chattels!

Brothers' daughters and sisters' daughters,
Foster-mothers[1] and foster-sisters,
The mothers of your wives, and your step-daughters
(Brought up with you, and born of wives with whom,
You've lain, but if your marriage with their mothers,
Was never consummated, you are not to blame),
Women who were the wives of your begotten sons,
And two sisters as spouses simultaneously,
Except for what is past; for Allah is
Forgiving, Full of Mercy;

24.   Also women who are already married,
Except captives now owned by you as slaves;
Such is God's ordinance to you, so all,
Women other than those, are to you lawful,
If you, out of your wealth, give them their dowers,
Take them in moral, conjugal relation,
And not in fornication;
And unto those with whom you've sought enjoyment,
Pay their due dowers as an obligation,
But it will not be held against you, if
You come to other terms, and compromise,
Even after your former stipulation,
For certainly God is the Knower, Wise.

25.   Any of you who can't afford to marry,
A free, believing[2] woman, let him marry,
A faithful bondswoman in your possession;
Surely God has, of your beliefs, the fullest Ken.
You are all sprung one from the other one;

---

1. Nursing mothers, who have suckled for you certain periods of time.
2. Muslim.

Thus marry them with the permission,
Of their own guardians, and be fair and proper,
In giving each of them their dower,
Let them be chaste and free from fornication,
Who never take a secret lover;
But, after marriage, if they should be guilty,
Of an indecency, their penalty,
Is half that which free women suffer,
For the sin of adultery.
Such is the law for those of you who fear,
To be committing sins, but self-restraining,
Is best for you, and God is Ever-
Forgiving, Mercy-Giving.

26. God wills to make things to you plain,
And to guide you into the ways,
Of former generations, and to be,
Redeeming you, for God's All-Knowing, Wise.

27. Indeed God wills to show redemption,
To you, but those who only sanction
Lustfulness, like to see you gone astray,
From the right path, too far away!

28. Indeed God wills to lighten things,
For you: for human beings,
Have been created weaklings!

29. O You who have believed!
Do not consume each others' properties,
Illicitly or in frivolities,
Let there be trade among you current,
By mutual consent.

And never kill yourselves, for God,
Is Merciful to you indeed.

30.   But anyone who shall commit this,
        In rancour and injustice,
        Shall soon be thrown into the Fire,
        And that is no hard job for Allah!

31.   If you abstain from greater sins,
        Of which you have been given warnings,
        We will remit your lesser sins,
        And will admit you through a Gate,
        Exalted, great.

32.   Do not covet the favours by which God,
        Made some of you excel some others;
        Rewarded shall be men for what they earn,
        And women are rewarded for their labours,
        Therefore, implore more of God's blessings,
        For God has Knowledge of all things.

33.   To each of you have We appointed heirs,
        To the inheritance that's left behind,
        By parents and by kins; but also give,
        To those to whom was pledged your own right hand,[1]
        Their portion due, for God is Watching
        O'er everything.

---

1. The general meaning is, of course, an injunction for respecting all pledges,
   promises and agreements; the particular meaning refers to bonds and links of
   brotherhood.

34.   Men are indeed protectors[1] of the women,
       Since God conferred upon them certain merits,
       Above the others, and because they ought
       To make them outlays from their means; yea, it's
       The righteous womenfolk, who are devout,
       And always guard the private parts which God,
       Would have them guard; but any on whose part
       You fear disloyalty, you should exhort;
       Next you may send her to a bed apart,
       And scourge her slightly[2] as a last resort;
       But then if she submits, do not go after
       Ways to annoy her, and remember:
       That God's above you, the Most High, the Great.

35.   And if you fear a breach between the twain,[3]
       Appoint two arbiters, one from his people,
       And the other from hers; if the two would,
       Sincerely wish to set things right then God,
       Helps them to get together once again,
       For God's All-Knowing, Most-Aware.

36.   Serve God the One, and do not ever join,
       With him a partner, and be loving-kind,
       Unto your parents, to the near of kin,
       To orphans, and to people badly downed,
       By poverty, and neighbours near or distant,

---

1. The Arabic original *qawwaam* means: one who stands firm in his (or another's) business and protects his interests and looks after his affairs; other translators have used words such as "supporters", "managers," "maintainers", "having authority and responsibility..." and the like to convey the meaning.

2. Any harsh beating, hurt or injury is subject to the Law of Talion.

3. Man and wife.

To colleagues, wayfarers, and to those bound,
Unto your service; surely God dislikes
The egoist, the arrogant,

37. Who're also stingy, and enjoin on others,
Niggardliness, and hide what God has given
To them out of His Grace-We have prepared,
A most disgraceful retribution,
For these ungrateful unbelievers-

38. Who, if they give their wealth in alms, it is
Ostentatious and a public display,
While disbelieving God and the Last Day;
If, for a friend, one chooses Satan,
Lo! He will have the worst companion!

39. What harm would come to them if they
Had faith in God and the Last Day,
And spent in alms of what, by Allah,
They have been given? Surely Allah,
Would have been of them Most-Aware.[1]

40. Not by an atom's weight will God the One,
e'er be unjust to anyone;
Indeed, if one does a good deed,
He is to be repaid twofold,
While He, from His Own Self, will add,
To it a greater rich reward.

41. How will it be then when We raise,
A witness true, from every people,

---

1. If they had done any good.

And call on you[1] to testify
Against these very people?

42. On that Day those who disbelieved,
And disobeyed the Messenger,
Would wish that they were levelled into
The dust of earth, for, over there,
They could not hide a word from Allah.

43. Believers, offer not your Praying,
In a state of intoxication,[2]
Until you know what you are saying!
Nor when you need total ablution,[3]
Until you wash yourselves, except upon
A journey; but in other cases when,
You are unwell, or traveling, or after
Excretion, or an intercourse with women,
And you could not find any water then,
Betake yourself to some clean dust or sand,
And with it wipe your face and hand;
For God's Benignant, Oft-Forgiving.

44. Ponder on those who have been given,
A portion of the Scripture, but they fell,
Into error; they wish to see you in
Error as well.

---

1. The Holy Prophet.
2. Some time after the revelation of this verse, the commandment about total prohibition of intoxicants was sent down (verses 90-91).
3. After sexual orgasm.

45. But God best knows your every enemy,
   God's the Sufficient Guardian, and
   Sufficient succour comes from Allah only.

46. Some of the Jews displace the words and phrases,
   From their points of articulation,
   And say: "We hearken and *asaina*",[1]
   "Let us hear but not listen!",[2] and "*ra'ina*",[3]
   Thus do they mock by desecration
   Of Faith through twisting tongues. But finer,
   And more upright it would have been, if they
   Did simply say: "we hear and we obey",
   "Let us listen" and "look at us"; but God
   Has laid a curse on them for their unfaith,
   Thus only few of them believe in truth.

47. O People of the Scriptures, do have faith
   In verses We sent down, which verify
   The early Scriptures you possess,
   Before We humble you and make you fly
   To exile, or We lay on you a curse,
   As did We curse the Sabbath-breakers;
   What God ordains, always occurs.

48. Idolatry's[4] the only sin that God
   Does not forgive; but other sins than this,
   He will forgive for whom He wills;

---

1. "We disobey": instead of saying "ataina" which means "We obey".

2. Or "we're here not to hear!"

3. This means "look at us", but the Jewish Arabs, with a slight change in intonation, made it sound like a phrase that meant "Our naughty one!"

4. The union of other gods with Him and association of partners with Him.

For he that worships whatsoever less,
Than God, is guilty of devising lies,
Sinfully monstrous!

49.   Let us turn to the people who consider
        That purity's only their own!
        But it is God who purifies whomever,
        He wills, and no one shall be wronged,
        The husk of one date-stone!

50.   Lo! It is lies and falsehoods they invent
        Concerning God, and surely this,
        Is an offense, most evident.

51.   Observe the people who were given,
        A portion of the Scriptures! They believe
        In superstitions[1] and false deities,
        And say of Pagans who do not believe:
        "These are more rightly guided than Believers!"

52.   These are the folks whom God has cursed,
        And you will never find a helper,
        For people cursed by Allah.

53.   Are they given a portion of the kingdom?
        Lo! If they were, they would not spend a damn
        Farthing upon their fellow-men!

54.   Or do they envy others for what God,
        Out of his Grace, has given them?
        Indeed We gave the House of Abraham,

---

1. Or "sorcery".

The Scriptures and the Wisdom,
And did confer upon them,
A mighty kingdom.[1]

55.   Now of them some believed therein;[2]
But others turned away therefrom,
Gehenna's hot enough for them!

56.   Soon We will cast into the Fire,
Those who denied Our revelations:
No sooner will their skins be roasted through,
Than We'll provide them with some other skins,
So that they taste the chastisement in full,
God is All-Wise, All-Powerful.

57.   But those who did believe and did good works,
Soon We shall be admitting unto Gardens,
With ever-flowing streams,
Wherein they will abide for ever,
Wedded to mates of purest nature,
And We will let them be together,
In the shades of their edens.

58.   God certainly commands you to give back
Your trusts unto their rightful owners,
And that to judge with fairness when
Passing judgments on men and women;
Excellent is the counsel God is giving
Unto you all, for God's All-Hearing, Ever-Seeing.

---

1. Such as the kingdoms of David and Solomon.
2. The Holy Qur'an.

59.   You who believe! Obey God, and obey
His Messenger and those entrusted with
Authority among you; should you quarrel
About a thing, refer it unto Allah,
And unto His Apostle,
If you believe in God and the Last Day;
This is the best, and it will settle,
Things finally with truth.

60.   Mark the people who claim they do believe
In revelations sent to you, as well
As in what was revealed before you,
And yet, in their disputes, they seek to settle
Things through the judgment of Satanic powers,[1]
Though they were ordered to deny them all;
Satan intends that they should go astray
From the right path, and very far away!

61.   When they are told: "Come back[2] to what
God has revealed, and unto His apostle,
You see the hypocrites turning away
From you in hatred and ill-will.

62.   And how is it when some misfortune
Befalls them: things of their own doing?
Well, then they hasten to you, ruing:
"We swear by Allah that we meant
Nothing but good-will and appeasement!"

63.   But God well knows the innermost intentions,

---

1. *Taaghoot*: an evil authority, any ungodly rule.

2. For judgment.

Of such people; thus let them be, but do,
Admonish them, and speak to them such words,
That will their souls cut through!

64.　We have sent forth apostles so that men
Should follow them by Our permission;
And had they, when they wronged their souls,
Come to you and implored God's Pardon,
And the Apostle prayed for their forgiveness,
They would have surely found Allah to be
Redeeming, Full of Mercy.

65.　Nay, by your Lord, they cannot be believers,
Until they come to seek your arbitration,
In their disputes and find no hesitation,
In their own hearts 'gainst your judicial orders,
And will accept them with complete submission.

66.　Had We decreed for them: "offer your lives",
Or "leave your homes", only a few of them,
Would have done it; but if they had performed,
What they were told, it would have been for them,
Far better, and would have their faith confirmed;

67.　And if that were the case, We would have given
Them, from Ourselves, a rich reward,

68.　And would have surely guided them,
To the most direct Road.

69.　All who obey Allah and His Apostle
Will be with those whom God has blessed,
Prophets of God, lovers of Truth,

The martyrs and the godliest:
What a fine company in faith!

70. From Allah comes this blessing,
And it's enough that God's All-Knowing.

71. Believers, be alert, and ever
Go forth in groups, or march together.

72. And there are always some who lag behind,
And if you suffer losses in a warfare,
They cheer: "God has indeed been to us gracious,
In that we were not present[1] there!"

73. And when from Allah comes to you a blessing,
They'd say, as though there was no friendly ties,
'Tween you and them: "Would that we'd been with them,
We would have also won a mighty prize!"

74. Therefore let fight in Allah's cause,
Those only who will freely barter,
This worldly life for the Hereafter;
To him who fights in Allah's cause,
Whether he's overcome[2] or conquers,
Soon will We be the richest Granter.

75. And how on earth should you not fight,
In Allah's cause, and for the love,
Of those weak men, women and children,[3]

---

1. This may also be rendered as "martyred".
2. Or "gets killed".
3. In Mecca.

Who in distress are begging God above:
"Our Lord, rescue us from this town,
Whose people are oppressors;
And from Yourself, give us a patron,
And from Yourself, give us some helpers."

76.   Those who believe, fight in the way of God,
But disbelievers fight for Evil's sake,
Thus fight against the friends of Satan,
Be sure that Satan's craft is weak.

77.   Take note of those who had been told:
"At present you fight not, just do your prayers,
And pay *zakaat*." Then order came to fight,
And Lo! Some of them are so full of fears
Of men, as they should be with God, but, nay,
Their fear is even worse than that; they pray:
"Our Lord, why have You ordered us to fight?
Won't You, for this short period, grant us respite?!"
Say: "Trifling are the pleasures of this world,
And the Hereafter is far better,
For those who keep their righteous guard;
Unfairly will you not be treated ever.

78.   Death will catch up with you, no matter,
Where you may be, even though yourselves you hide,
In castles fortified."
Behold, when on them something good does fall,
They say: "This is from Allah", but when some
Evil befalls them, they cry: "It is all,
Your fault."[1] say: All, from God, has come;

---

1. The Holy Prophet's.

What's really with those folks amiss,
They do not fathom any premise?!

79.   Whatever good comes unto you, O man,
It is from God; but what hits you as evil
Is the result of your own doings;
And We sent you as an apostle,
To humankind, and God's own witness,
Suffices for this.

80.   He who obeys the Messenger,
He is indeed obeying Allah;
What of the folks who pay no heed?
We did not send you as their keeper!

81.   "We do obey", their lips articulate,
But when they leave your presence,
Some of them all night meditate
On things adverse unto your utterance;
But God takes note of their nightly ideas!
Thus, let them be, and put your confidence,
In God alone, for certainly God is
Sufficient as an Advocate.

82.   Do they not ever ponder
On the Quran?
Had it been from some other,
Than God the One,
They would have been bound to discover,
Contraries in it by the dozen!

83.   And when they hear some news concerning,
Peaceful or fearful subjects, they divulge

It far and wide; had they reported it
Unto the Messenger and those in charge
Among them, they could pass it on to,
Persons who have the proper knowledge.
Were it not for the Grace of God upon you
And His abundant Mercy, you would all
Have followed Satan save a few.

84.   So you shall combat in the cause of God,
Nothing's imposed on you but your own work,
Thus rouse the faithful to fight on, perchance
God will the disbelievers' power break,
For God's the Strongest in crusades,
And Sternest in taking to task.

85.   Whoever joins in a good cause,
Shall have a share therein,
And whoso joins an evil cause,
Shall share its burden;
It's God who everything controls.

86.   When greeted with a courteous greeting,
Respond with a more courteous greeting,
Or with an equal salutation;
All things enter God's computation.

87.   There is no deity but God the One,
And certainly He'll gather you together,
Upon the Day of Resurrection,
No doubt about it whatsoever;
Who's a more truthful bearer
Of news than God the One?

88. Why on earth are you thus divided into,
    Two groups about the Hypocrites?
    God it is who has cast them off
    For their misdeeds. To those, whom God demerits
    To go astray, would you show guidance?!
    For those whom God lets go astray,
    By no means will you find a way.

89. They only wish that you reject the Faith,
    As they have done themselves, so that you both
    Become alike!
    Therefore take no companions from their rank,
    Unless in Allah's cause they mobilize,[1]
    But if they turn against you, you should seize
    Them and put them to death wherever,
    You find them, and of them you'll never take
    Any as friend or helper;

90. Exempted shall be those who go to people,
    Who by a treaty have become your allies,
    Or come to you with hearts averse to fighting
    Against you or their people. Had it been Allah's
    Will, then He would have made them dominant
    Over you, so they would have taken arms
    Against you;
    Thus if they keep away from you and cease,
    Hostilities and send you signs of peace,
    God bids you not to do them any harms.

91. Another kind of them you'll find who wish,

---

1. This may also be translated: "unless they migrate in the way of Allah",
   referring to those believers who, were able to, but did not emigrate to
   Medina to help the Prophet.

Also to be secure from you, as well
As from their people; but as often as
They are called back unto mischief, they will
Plunge into it headlong; unless these people
Keep distance from you, and ask you for peace,
And cease hostilities, lay hold of them,
And put them to the sword where they be found,
Over such men We have unto you given,
An argument profound.[1]

92.   Believers shall not ever kill each other,
Unless it's done by accident, or error;
If one kills a believer by mistake,
He'll have to free a Muslim slave[2], and pay
Blood-money to the heirs;[3] unless they would forsake
It all as alms. If the victim happens to be,
A Muslim[4] from a hostile tribe, the penalty
Shall be the freeing only of one Muslim slave;
If the victim, however, be a member of,
An allied tribe, blood-money to his family,
Shall be paid *and* a Muslim slave set free.
If one cannot afford it, then he must
Fast for two running months. Such are repenting ways,
To God, and God's Knowing, All-Wise.

93.   Whoever willfully kills a believer,
His recompense is Hell, he will
Abide therein for ever,

---

1. Or "A clear authority to fight them".

2. As expiation.

3. The victim's family.

4. A Believer.

God's wrath he has incurred, and He
Will lay His curse upon him, and prepare
For him a torment most severe.

94.　　Believers, when you go to fight for,
The cause of God, be most discerning,
And to a man who does offer you peace,
Say not: "You're not a Muslim", to be earning
The fleeting booty of this world! Indeed,
It's God Who has abundant gains.
You were before this in the same condition,
Till Allah showered upon you rains
Of grace and bliss; thus be discerning,
For God is Fully Cognizant of all
You're ever doing.

95.　　Equal are not the faithful who, though not,
Handicapped or disabled sit at home,
And those who struggle in the cause of God,
Sacrificing their lives and what they own.
God gives the strivers who give up their lives
And wealth, a higher rank than those who stay
At home. God promises a good reward
To either group, but God exalts the strivers,
Over the sitters with a great reward:

96.　　 High ranks of His own Giving,
Pardon and Clemency;
For God is Most-Forgiving,
And Full of Mercy.

97.　　When angels seize the souls of those who are,
Sunken in sins 'gainst their own selves, they ask:

"How was your circumstance?" They say: "We were
Oppressed upon the earth." Again they ask:
"Was Allah's earth not vast enough for you,
To emigrate therein?!" The final venue,
For them is Hell: what evil fate to come to!

98.   Exempted are the helpless men and women
And children who do not possess the means,
Nor know they any routes or lines;

99.   These are the ones whom God may pardon,
For God's Benignant, Oft-Forgiving.

100.   And anyone who flies in Allah's way, will find
On earth many a place of refuge, and abundance
Of bounties; even he who does forsake his dwelling,
For the sake of God and His Messenger, and thence,
Death overtakes him, shall receive his need in full,
From God, for God's Forgiving, Merciful.

101.   When traveling the road, there is on you no blame,
To shorten prayers, if fearing that there could well be,
Some discomforting action by the disbelievers,
For those who disbelieve are openly,
Most bent upon your enmity.

102.   When you yourself[1] are with them, and you stand,
And lead the prayer for them, do let one section
Of them stand up to pray with you, and let
Them hold their arms, and after their prostration
Is done, let them take their position in the rear,

---

1. The Holy Prophet.

Then let another party come to pray,
With you, who have not yet offered their prayer,
Let them also be on their guard and hold their arms;
For those who disbelieve constantly wish
To see you careless of your arms and baggage,
So that they could assault you in a single rush.
But if, because of heavy rain or being ill,
You're ill-at-ease, upon you there shall be no blame,
If you lay down your arms, while on your guard;
God has for those who disbelieve prepared,
A retribution full of shame.

103.   Once you complete the prayers, you should remember
God, whether you are standing, sitting or reclining,
But once you're free from danger, say your prayer
In full; prayer is indeed a duty binding,
At stated times, on each believer.

104.   In pursuit of these people[1] do not waver;
If you have suffered, they are suffering too,
Just as you do, but you from God expect,
What they may not expect, and Allah knows
Everything, and He is All-Wise.

105.   We have sent down to you the Book in Truth,
That you among men be an arbitrator,
On the basis of what God to you taught,
And that you never plead for any traitor;

106.   You shall implore Allah's Forgiveness:
For God is Oft-Forgiving, Full of Ruth.

---

1. The disbelieving foes.

107. Nor shall you plead for those who wronged their souls,
     For God dislikes the treacherous and the sinful,

108. They seek to hide themselves from men,
     But could they hide themselves from God?!
     He is with them when they utter in secret,
     What He dislikes, and Allah is indeed,
     Encompassing their every deed.

109. These are the sort of men on whose behalf,
     You may well argue in this worldly life,
     But who will plead for them with God,
     Upon the Day of Resurrection?
     Who will, then even give a nod,
     For their protection?!

110. But he that does some evil or does wrong,
     To his own soul, and afterwards shall plea,
     For God's Forgiveness, he will find that God
     Is Oft-Forgiving, Full of Mercy.

111. And he that does a sinful thing, he only
     Hurts his own soul, and Allah knows
     Everything, and He is All-Wise.

112. But he that does commit an error or a sin,
     And lays the blame for it on guiltless men,
     Shall bear the heavy guilt of calumny,
     And of a sinfulness most open.

113. Were it not for God's Grace and Mercy.
     On you,¹ a party of them had decided to,

_____
1. The Holy Prophet.

Lead you astray; in fact they only lead
Themselves astray, nor could they do a harm to you;
For God sent down to you the Book and Wisdom,
And taught you what you never knew,
And great has been indeed,
God's Grace upon you.

114.　There is no good in most of what they say,
In secret talks, except if any would
Exhort to charity and doing good,
Or find between people a peaceful way;
He that does this, seeking God's pleasure,
Gains Our reward of greatest measure.

115.　He that opposes the Apostle after,
The Guidance has been made to him most clear,
And follows other than the faithful's way,
We'll let him on his chosen road to steer,
And let him land in Hell,
A homecoming most evil!

116.　The only sin that God does not forgive:
Is the worship of other gods besides Him,
But He forgives whomever He prefer,
His lesser sins; for worshippers of gods besides Him,
Have surely strayed too far!

117.　Nothing do they[1] invoke, instead of God the One,
But some false goddesses, in fact they only,
Call upon a rebellious Satan,

---

1. The idolatrous pagans.

118.   Whom God has laid His curse upon,
       For he had said: "surely I will attempt,
       To hold the reins of great proportions
       Of your created humans,

119.   "I will mislead them and most surely tempt
       Them with all vain and false desires,
       I'll even order them to slit the ears
       Of cattle,[1] and I bid them to disrupt
       And alter God's creation!"
       Now then, whoever chooses Satan,
       Instead of God, for his protection,
       Ruins himself beyond redemption.

120.   He makes them promises, and he does shape
       In them many a painted, empty hope;
       And Satan's promises are never
       But pure deceptions;

121.   Such people's[2] home is the Gehenna,
       Never will they from it escape.

122.   And those who do believe and do good deeds,
       Will be admitted to the Garden,
       With ever-running streams,
       To dwell therein for ever,
       God's promise is the Truth, and who
       Could be more true in words than Allah?

---

1. A superstitious practice by pagans for dedicating animals to their gods.
2. The followers of Satan.

123. Neither does this[1] depend on your desires,
     Nor on the wishes of the People
     Of the Scriptures: he that does evil,
     Shall be requited with it, and besides
     God, will he find no friends, no aides.

124. But those who do good deeds,
     And they are of the faithful,
     Whether be male or female,
     Will surely enter Paradise,
     Not suffering the least injustice.

125. Who can be better in religion,
     Than one who totally submits to God,
     Does what is good and right and follows,
     The faith of Abraham who trod
     On the right road, and Allah chose,
     Abraham as a friend indeed?

126. All that is in the heavens,
     And all on earth, to God belongs,
     And God encompasses all things.

127. You're being asked again concerning women:
     Say: God enlightens you regarding them,
     And has instructed you already in,
     The Book, concerning orphan girls to whom,
     You do not give their lawful portion,[2]
     While you yourselves desire to marry them,[3]

---

1. This final result.

2. Their rightful portion (of inheritance) or dowers (upon marriage) or both.

3. For greedy purposes.

Also concerning weak and helpless children:[1]
That you stand firm for justice unto orphans;
And there is not a single act of goodness,
Performed by you but Allah kens.

128.   And if a woman fears ill-treatment or
Desertion on her husband's part, the couple
Do better if they reconcile within
A friendly settlement, for peace could well
Be the best thing; avarice is of course,
Present in people's souls, but if you still,
Do what is right and practice self-restraint,
Be sure that God is most Aware
Of your every affair.

129.   Even if you did ardently desire it,
Never would you be able to do justice
Between the wives, but do not be averse,
To one, so that you leave her in suspense,
Certainly if you come to friendly peace,
And self-restraint, you'll find that God's
Forgiving, Full of Kindness.

130.   If the couple decides to separate,
God will, out of His own abundance,
Compensate for them both, for God's
Most Wise, Lord of Munificence;

131.   Everything in the heavens and on earth,
Is God's; and We indeed enjoined on those,

---

1. Verses 1-14 of this Sura.

To whom We gave the Book before, as now
To you: Be godfearing. What if you chose
To disbelieve? Behold, to God belongs,
All things on earth and in the heavens,
God is Needless and Worthy of all praise;

132.   Indeed to God belongs:
Everything on the earth and in the heavens,
With Him you have indeed:
The Most-Sufficient of all guardians;

133.   Were it His Will, O humankind,
He could annihilate your race,
And bring forth others in your place,
God is Able Enough this to command!

134.   If one is after profits of this world,
Let him find it in Allah who possesses
Rewards of both, this and the other world,
For God Hears all, and all He Sees.

135.   O You believers, stand out firm for justice,
And only for the sake of God bear witness,
Even though it may be against yourselves,
Against your parents or your kinsfolk,
Whether the one concerned be rich or broke:
For God's the better Well-Wisher for both;
Thus be not led by lust and passion, lest
You should be swerving from the Truth;
If you distort your evidence, or just,
Decline to give it, know that God's Aware
Of your every affair.

136.   You who believe,[1] have faith in God,
        In His Apostle, in the Scripture,
        That He revealed through His Apostle,
        And in the Scriptures sent before;
        But he that has no faith in God,
        In His angels and Scriptures, nor
        In His apostles, nor in the Last Day,
        Has surely gone far, far astray.

137.   Never will God forgive the people who embrace,
        The Faith, and then renounce it, and again embrace
        Their faith, but once again renounce it, then increase
        In disbelief, nor does he show them any Guidance:

138.   Do give the hypocrites the awful news,
        Of a chastisement full of pains and blues,

139.   For they befriend the disbelievers rather
        Than the believers; do they seek their own
        Honour and dignity with them? But all
        Of honour is with God alone.

140.   You have already been commanded in
        The Scripture: If you hear God's revelations,
        Being denied or ridiculed, you should
        Not sit with them unless some other questions
        May be discussed, or you will be like them;
        Certainly Allah will
        Collect the hypocrites together
        With the pagans[2] in Hell;

---

1. Or "Muslims".

2. The deniers of the Truth, infidels, unbelievers.

141. They're watching you to see in which direction,
     The wind is blowing: If a victory,
     Is granted you by Allah, they declare:
     "Were we not on your side?" And if it be,
     Some happy turn for disbelievers, they
     Shall say:[1] "Could we defeat you not? But we
     Guarded you from the faithful."[2] Well, it's Allah,
     Who will, upon the Day of Resurrection,
     Pass judgment on you all; yet God will never
     Permit the unbelievers to prevail
     Over the faithful.

142. The hypocrites suppose they are
     Deceiving God, but it is He
     Who keeps them in deception!
     When they stand up to prayer,
     They do so sluggishly,
     Just as a public ostentation,
     And with exceptions rare,
     They don't remember God,

143. 'Tween this and that, they always waver;
     For these or those? Loyal to neither!
     When God forsakes a man to err,
     How on earth could you be his guide!

144. You who believe, take not for friends,
     The unbelievers rather than Believers,
     Do you intend to offer God a proof,

---

1. To disbelivers.

2. That is: We were in the ranks of your enemy to protect you if the believers-
   Muslims-were too strong for you!

Most manifest against yourselves?!

145. The hypocrites shall certainly be cast,
Into the lowest pit of Hell, and never
Are they to find a helper;

146. Save for repenters who amend,
And unto God hold fast,
And whose entire religion
Is purely pledged to God the One;
They'll be amongst the faithful,
And the faithful will Allah recompense
With a reward immense.

147. If you believe and render thanks,
Why should God let you suffer torment?
Nay, God's Delighted to Acknowledge thanks,
And He's Omniscient.

148. God does not like the public utterance
Of evil words, except when cried by those,
Fallen victim unto injustice;
And God's the One Who Hears and Knows.

149. Whether you openly perform some good,
Or do it secretly, or you are clement
About an evil done to you, most surely,
God's Pardoning, Omnipotent.

150. The people who do not acknowledge God
And His apostles and desire to draw
A line 'tween God and His apostles, and
They say: "some we believe in, but have no

Faith in others", and it's a middle course
They like to follow,

151.   Surely are these confirmed deniers,
And We've made ready from before,
A most disgraceful torment for
Such unbelievers.

152.   To those who do believe in God and His
Messengers and do not discriminate
Against any of them, We'll give their proper
Rewards, for God's Forgiving and Compassionate.

153.   The People of the Book are asking you
To bring a book upon them from the skies!
Of Moses they had certainly demanded
A thing of more grotesque surprise,
For they insisted:
"Make us see God with our own eyes!"
Therefore We smote them with a thunder-bolt,
For this rebellious thought.
But even after they had seen,
Miracles clear enough,
They took to worshipping a calf!
But after this We did forgive them,
And gave unto Moses authentic Proof;[1]

154.   And at the taking of their covenant,
We lifted over them the Mount.
We warned them to "enter the gate
Humbly". And We told them to note:

---

1. Or "manifest authority and power."

"The Sabbath ne'er to desecrate".
We took from them a solemn covenant.

155.   And yet they broke the covenant,
Rejected Allah's revelations,
And killed the prophets wrongfully,
They even said: "hard laminations
Cover our hearts!" Nay, it is Allah
Who seals them up, because of
Their unbelief. In fact they have no faith,
Except a few.

156.   And for their unbelief to cry,
Against Mary, a monstrous lie;

157.   They even bragged: "We are the people who did kill
Messiah Jesus, Son of Mary, God's apostle!"
Most certainly they did not kill him, nor
Did they crucify him; only there was,
Some likeness them to baffle!
And all the sects who disagree,
Are full of doubts about him, and have no
Sure knowledge of it, but they only
Follow conjectures; it's the very truth,
That they could not put him to death,

158.   But to Himself did Allah raise
Him, for God is the Mighty, the All-Wise.

159.   And one shall not be ever,
A true Believer in the Scripture,
If he will not have faith,
In this before his death,

And he will witness 'gainst them on,
The Day of Resurrection.

160. Many good things that used to be allowed,
We made unlawful for the Jews,
Because of their iniquities,
Because they often hindered,
Others from Allah's avenues.

161. Because they practiced usury,
Although they were forbidden it,
And cheated others of their property;
Therefore, for those of them who disbelieve,
We have prepared a Torment that will grieve!

162. But We shall soon give great rewards to those,
Of them in Knowledge firm and sure indeed,
And those believers who believe in what's
Sent down to you and what has been revealed
Before your time, those who keep up their prayers,
And give in alms, and the sincere believers
In God and the Last Day.

163. We sent Our Will to you by Inspiration,
Just as We sent it unto Noah,
And other prophets after him,
We also sent Our Inspiration
To Abraham, to Ishmael, and Isaac,
To Jacob and to many a Tribal Patriarch,
To Jesus, Job, Jonas and Aaron,
To Solomon, and to David, to whom

We gave the Psalms;[1]

164. And to the messengers We have already
      Mentioned to you, and others whom We have
      Not to you spoken of;
      But Moses: Allah spoke to him Directly;

165. Messengers who did bring good tidings,
      To humankind, as well as warnings,
      So that people, after their coming, should
      Have no excuse to plead, when facing God;
      And God's Almighty, Full of Wisdom.

166. And God bears witness that the revelation
      To you, is sent with His full Ken,
      The angels too bear witness, but enough,
      As a witness, is God Himself.

167. Those who reject belief and hinder men,
      From Allah's way,
      Have really gone too far astray.

168. Never will God forgive the people,
      Who have adopted disbelief,
      And done iniquities as well,
      Nor will He guide them to a way,

169. Except the way to Hell!
      To dwell therein for ever;
      This is a simple thing for Allah.

---

1. Note the conspicuous absence of Moses, the only prophet to whom God
   spoke directly, as mentioned in the next verse.

170.   O Humankind, This Messenger has come,
       To you with Truth from your own Lord,
       Thus do have faith, it will for you be well,
       Yet if you disbelieve, behold!
       Everything in the heavens,
       And on the earth is God's,
       And He's All-Knowing, Wise.

171.   O People of the Book, go not beyond,
       The bounds and limits in your faith,
       Nor say of God anything but the truth:
       Indeed Messiah Jesus, son of Mary,
       Was God's apostle only,
       His Word[1] which He bestowed on Mary,
       And a Spirit from Him. Therefore, have faith,
       In God the One, and never say: "they're *three*"!
       Do put an end to this, it is for your own good;
       God is only One God, to Him be glory,
       Much, much too High is He:
       To be having a son! To Him belongs,
       All that the heavens and the earth contain,
       And He alone is All-Sufficient,
       Everything to sustain.

172.   Never would Christ disdain,
       To be, of God, a servant,[2]
       Nor would His closest angels;
       Those who disdain and feel some arrogance,
       To be His servants, He assembles,
       In His own presence.

---

1. Command, order.

2. Or "to serve and worship God the One."

173. And unto those who did believe and did,
      Good works, He will give their due recompense,
      And He will grant them more from His abundance,
      But He will sternly punish those who were
      Disdainful and too proud; and they shall find,
      Beside Allah, no friend, no helping hand.

174. O Humankind, you now have lucid evidence
      From your own Lord, for it's indeed
      A Glorious Light We have to you revealed.

175. Now those who do believe in God and hold
      Fast unto Him, shall be admitted soon
      To His Mercy and to His graceful Boon,
      And He will guide them to Himself upon
      A very direct Road.

176. And on their legal question from you, say:
      Thus God decrees for you concerning men,
      Who're parentless and childless; when such person
      Dies and he has one sister, she shall gain,
      The half of his inheritance; if first
      She dies and has no children, he would then
      Be the sole heir; if he happens to have two sisters,
      They'll have two-thirds of his bequest.
      But if he have brothers and sisters, then
      Each brother's share is twice a sister's portion.
      Thus God makes things to you most manifest,
      Lest you should go astray; and God's of everything,
      The Knower best.

SURA 5
THE HEAVENLY FOOD
(AL-MAA'IDA)

In the Name of God, the Beneficent, the Merciful

1.　O you believers!
Be faithful to your obligations:
Lawful to you to eat will be all cattle,
Save what you will be told in recitations;
Hunting, however, is forbidden, while
You're in the Sanctified Location;[1]
God surely bids according to His will.

2.　O You believers, do not violate,
The sanctity of Allah's rites,
Neither the Sacred Month,[2]
Nor animals that have been marked for
Sacrifice by the ornamental wreath,
Nor the folks who are making for
The Sacred House, seeking the Grace
And Pleasure of their Lord. But once,
You have put off *ihraam*,[3]
You may again hunt game.
Let not the hatred of some folks who did,
Hinder you from the Sacred Masjid,[4]
Lead you into sin and injustice;
Cooperate in what is good and pious,

---

1. In the Holy Precincts of Ka'ba, or "while in the pilgrimage garment of
   ihraam."

2. The month of pilgrimage, Zul-Hajja, or else, collectively the four sacred
   months of Rajab, Zul-Qa'da, Zul-Hajja and Muharram.

3. The pilgrimage garment.　　　　　　4. Mosque.

But do not help in sin and malice;
For God is Stern in retribution.

3.   Forbidden to you shall be: Carrion,[1]
        Blood and the flesh of swine and whatsoever
        On which a name is breathed other than Allah,
        And animals that have been killed:
        By being strangled,
        By a violent blow,
        By falling from a height,
        Or gored to death, or mangled
        By beasts of prey; unless you have been able
        To slaughter them while not yet still,
        And what was sacrificed on altars;
        Also dividing[2] by divining arrows,
        Is a vile practice full of woes.
        This day the disbelievers must abandon,
        All hope of overcoming your religion;
        Thus fear them not, fear Me alone;
        This day I have perfected your religion
        For you, and surely made complete My Own
        Blessings on you, and I do sanction,
        Islam: your way of life;
        And yet if hunger threatens some one's life,
        And he does eat, with no intention sinful,
        He'll find Allah Forgiving, Merciful.

4.   They ask you what's lawful to them as food.
        Say: Everything wholesome and good,

---

1. Or "dead meat".

2. Division of meat by a sort of lottery or raffle practiced by Pagan mobs;
   division in this way is forbidden as it is a form of gambling.

Is legalised unto you, and that which,
The beasts and birds of prey that you have trained,
As God directed you, may for you catch;
Thus eat of what they catch for you, but mention,
God's name upon them; and fear God,
For Swift is God in computation!

5.   Lawful are to you now all good and wholesome
Items; also the food of those to whom
The Book was given, is unto you lawful,
And lawful is your food to them,
So are the chaste among Believing women,
And the chaste women of the people given
The Book before, provided that you do,
Give them their proper dowers,
That you take them in chaste wedlock, but not to
Fornicate, nor taking as secret lovers;
He that denies the Faith, surely his labours,
Will be in vain, and in the world to come,
He shall be with the losers.

6.   Believers, when you rise to offer prayers,
Do wash your faces, and your hands,
To the elbows, and wipe your heads,
And feet up to the ankles; if, however
You have become unclean,[1] perform a proper
Ablution; if you're ill or on a journey,
Or coming from the prissy, or you had
Intercourse,[2] and could find no water,

1. "Unclean", in such contexts, always means "becoming polluted after
   cohabitation" or a discharge of semen in other forms.
2. Lit "touching women".

Then take some clean, dry soil or sands,
And rub therewith your faces and your hands.
It is not Allah's will to put you through
Hardships, but He intends to purify you,
And to bestow on you His gifts in full,
Perchance you will be grateful.

7.   And keep in mind the favour God conferred,
Upon you and the covenant He bound
You with, when you affirmed: "We heard,
And we'll obey". Thus do piously mind
The fear of God, for Allah is the Knower best,
Of the secrets in every breast.

8.   Believers, be upright for God,
And fair and just in giving witness,
Do not allow your hatred for some people,
To swerve you to injustice;
Be just: for it is next to righteousness,
And be god-fearing, surely God's Aware
Of your every affair.

9.   Allah has promised His forgiveness,
And rich rewards unto the faithful
Who have done deeds of righteousness,

10.   As for the unbelievers
Who treat God's Signs[1] as false,
Surely they will be heirs
Unto the Blazing Furnace.

---

1. Or "revelations".

11.   Believers, call to mind the favour,
        Which God bestowed upon you when,
        He did restrain a group of men,[1]
        Who had determined to deliver
        A paralyzing blow against you all,
        Therefore fear God, and let the faithful
        On Allah be relying ever.

12.   In former times did Allah take,
        A covenant from Jacob's children,[2]
        And in them raised twelve chieftains;
        God said to them: I'm your Companion,
        So long as you observe your prayers,
        Pay the *zakaat*, and will believe in
        My messengers, and honour them,
        And give to God a goodly loan;[3]
        Then I will certainly remit your sins,
        And will admit you into Gardens
        Watered by running streams;
        But if any of you henceforth,
        Adopts the ways of disbelief,
        He shall certainly stray far off
        From the most direct Path.

13.   But then, they broke their covenant,
        And thus on them We laid Our curse,

---

1. In the life-time of the Holy Prophet, the enemies plotted many times to get rid of him and his companions; as the address here is directed towards the Israelites, this incident, which is mentioned by way of introduction, must refer to a plot by the Jews.
2. Children of Israel, the Israelites.
3. That is: spending in the cause of God to be repaid both here and in the Hereafter.

And let their hearts grow hard;
They've taken words[1] out of their place,
And have forgotten major portions,
Of what We did to them rehearse,
Nor will you ever cease to find them,
Barring a few, engaged in some
Deceitful, treacherous case!
You shall, however, disregard them,
And bear with them; for God, of course,
Loves people who are kind to others.

14. From those who say: "We are *Nasaara*",[2]
We also took a covenant,
But they too disregarded some
Parts of their own commandment;
Thus We condemned them to continued
Enmity and innate revulsion
'Gainst one another up to,
The Day of Resurrection;
And God will then inform them of
Their every action.

15. O People of the Scripture,
Now there has come to you Our Own Apostle,
To clarify for you many a matter
Of the Book which you often did conceal,
And plenty more that you did overlook,
Indeed a Light has come to you from God,
Together with a glorious Book,

---

1. Distorting the Scriptures.

2. The Nazarenes (the Christians): In fact the early "Christians" thus called
   themselves; others called them "Christians".

160

16.   With which God guides all those, who seek
        His pleasure, to the paths of peace,
        And leads them, by His will, from darkness
        Unto the Light,
        And He will give them guidance
        Unto the Path most right.

17.   Blasphemous unbelievers are the people
        Who say that "God is the Messiah, son
        Of Mary!" Tell them this: If God the One[1]
        Willed to annihilate Messiah, son
        Of Mary, and his mother, and the whole
        People upon the earth, who would prevent,
        Him from this? God's the Kingdom of the heavens,
        And of the earth and all that 'tween them lies,
        He does create whatsoever He wills:[2]
        For God's Omnipotent.

18.   And both the Jews and Christians make the claim:
        "We are God's sons and His beloved ones!"
        Ask them: why does He then chastise you for
        Your faults and sins?
        Nay, you are also human beings,
        Created by Him; and He pardons,
        Whome'er He will, and whom He pleases,
        He shall chastise; to God belongs,
        The Kingdom of the earth and of the heavens,
        And all that is between; and unto Him

---

1. Allah; also El and Elohim in Hebrew.

2. That is: The miraculous birth of Jesus was merely one of God's countless,
wonderful manifestations, the birth of Adam was even more wonderful!
Therefore, you should not, by calling Jesus, God or Son of God, turn the
miraculous into the ridiculous!

Is the returning of all things.

19. O People of the Scriptures,
This messenger of Ours has to you come,
Explaining things after a long cessation,
Of no apostles,[1] lest you should exclaim:
"None ever came to us to preach or caution!"
Now one has come to you who is,
Both a warner and bearer of good news;
God has absolute power,
Over all things.

20. Recall that Moses to his people said:
"O People mine, remember Allah's blessings,
Upon you: He has raised up prophets
Among you and has made you kings,
And what He has unto you given,
He gave unto no other nation.

21. "O People mine, enter the holy land,
Which Allah has for you assigned,
And do not turn your back, for then
You shall be ruined."

22. They said: "O Moses, in this land,
A race of giants[2] dwells, so we will not
Set foot in it until they're gone,
If they get out, we'll enter it!"

23. But from among that frightened multitude,

---

1. After Jesus Christ (Peace of God he upon him).
2. Or "men of might.

Two men[1] whom God had blessed with His own grace,
Said: "Let's assault them at the proper Gate,
And once you're in, you'll surely be victorious,
But put your trust in Allah, if
You have a firm belief."

24. But they replied: "O Moses, we shall never,
Be going in, so long as they are there,
Thus go, you and your Lord, and fight them,
We will be sitting down right here!"

25. "O Lord", cried he, "I do not have but power,
Over myself and on my brother,
Pray separate us from the million,
Given to vile rebellion!"

26. "Thus", answered He, "the land shall be forbidden,
To them for forty years during which time,
They will, aimlessly roam,
Upon the land, without a home;
So grieve not for a people ridden,
With wickedest rebellion."

27. Recite to them the truthful story
Of the two sons of Adam.
Behold, they each had made an offering,
It was accepted from the one of them,
And not accepted from the other;
The latter said: "I will kill you, most certainly!"
"God has accepted", said the former,
"Only from the godfearing;

1.Joshua and Caleb.

28. "You may extend your hand to kill me,
     But I am utterly averse,
     To your slaughter, for I fear God,
     Lord of the Universe;

29. "I'd rather you should bear my sin[1]
     And your own sins, and thus incur,
     The torment of the Fire, for such will
     Be the reward of every wrongdoer."

30. His selfish soul, despite this, prompted him
     Into the murder of his brother,
     He slew him and he thus became,
     One of those who are lost for ever.

31. Now God dispatched a raven,
     And it began to scratch the ground
     To show him how his brother's corpse,
     Should be a burial given.
     "Oh, woe is me", he groaned,
     "Did I not have the wisdom of this raven,
     To bury my own brother's corpse!"
     Badly was he now riven,
     With sorrow and remorse.

32. It was because of this that We ordained,
     For Jacob's Children that whoever,
     Shall kill a soul, unless it be for murder,
     Or spreading mischief in the land,
     It is as though he slew all humankind
     And that whoever saved a human life,

---

1. The sin of my killing.

It is as though, to all he'd given life;
Indeed Our messengers, with signs of Truth,
Unto them came, yet it did not take long,
Before many of them were doing wrong,
To an extreme degree throughout the earth.

33.   The penalties for those who fight against,
God and His Messenger and do their best
To spread corruption in the land, shall be
Their execution, crucifixion,
Cutting off of the hands or feet upon
Opposite sides,[1] or banishment;
That is to be for them the ignominy
Here in this world, but in the next,
They'll have a greater punishment;

34.   Exempted will be those who do repent,
Before they fall into your power;
Be sure that God's Forgiving, Clement.

35.   O you believers, be godfearing,
And seek the means to win His pleasure,
And strive hard in His cause, perhaps
You'll prosper.

36.   If those who have rejected Faith,
Had all the wealth upon the earth,
And twice as much, to give as ransom,
In order to redeem them from,
The Torment of the Day of Resurrection,
It would not be at all accepted of them;

---

1. Their alternate hands or feet.

And they shall have their grievous retribution;

37. They would keenly desire,
    To get out of the Fire,
    But out from it they shall not come:
    The term of chastisement for them,
    Shall not expire!

38. You shall cut off the hands[1] of thieves,
    Both men and women, for this is
    A recompense for what they did,
    And a deterrent set by God,
    And God's All-Powerful, All-Wise;

39. But people who repent and mend their ways
    After committing an iniquity,
    Shall be pardoned by God, for God is always,
    Forgiving, Full of Mercy.

40. Don't you know that the Kingdom of the heavens,
    And of the earth, to God belongs?
    He punishes whome'er He wills and pardons
    Whome'er He pleases;
    God has power over all things.

41. O You Apostle, never grieve,
    For those who vie with one another
    To disbelieve,
    Be they of those whose lips do mutter:
    "We do believe",

---

1. On various conditions concerning this injunction, one must consult with
   books of Islamic Jurisprudence.

Whereas their hearts do not believe,
Or of the Jews,
Who have good ears for lies,
And always listen to the news
By those who never met you;[1] they distort
Words out of context, and declare:
"If you are given something of this sort,
Take it, if not, beware!"[2]
If God intends to put a man to trial,
You will have no authority at all,
To rescue him against God's will;
These people are the ones,
Whose hearts God will not cleanse,
For them there is humiliation,
Here in this world, and in the next;
They'll have a grievous retribution;

42.   They're eager hearers of everything false,
Imbibers keen of the forbidden!
Thus when they come unto you with some case,
Give them your judgment or pay no attention;
Even if you refuse, they won't, of course,
Be able to distress you, but if you,
Judge between them, then judge with fairness true,
God loves the people who do justice.

43.   Yet how is it that they refer to you,
For a decision, when they have the Torah,
Which does contain the law of Allah?

---

1. Or "who have never so much as come near to" the Prophet.

2. The Jewish scholars told their illiterate people to accept any teaching of the
   Holy Prophet only if it agrees with what they claim to be in the Torah.

Well, with you too, they'll soon be loath,
In fact these people have no Faith.

44.   We it was who sent down the Torah,
In which there is: Guidance and Light,
According to which rulings were the Jews,
Judged by the prophets who had been outright
Submitters,[1] and the rabbis and the Hebrews,
Skilled in the Law, who had been made to look,
After the Book of God and be its witnesses;
Thus have no fear of men, fear Me alone,
And do not sell my revelations for
Some paltry, worldly gain;
Whoever does not judge by that which Allah,
Has sent is certainly an unbeliever.

45.   We made in it[2] for them Our verdict clear:
A life for a life, an eye for an eye,
A nose for a nose, and ear for an ear,
A tooth for a tooth, and for an injury,
Equal retaliation,
Yet if a man, as charity, forgoes it,[3]
This shall for him be goodly expiation;
Whoever does not judge by that which Allah,
Sent down is surely a transgressor.

46.   And after that in their[4] footsteps did We
Send Jesus, son of Mary, as confirmer,
Of the Torah that was revealed already,
And gave him the Evangel, full of right

---

1. The addressees are the Jews.   2. In the Torah.

3. The retaliation.   4. Of the former prophets.

Guidance as well as Light,
Which verified what was there of the Torah,
And was indeed a Guidance and a warning,
For the godfearing.

47.   Thus let the followers of the Evangel,
Judge by what God therein did spell;
Whoever does not judge by that which Allah,
Sent down, is certainly an evil-doer.

48.   And now We send to you this Book in truth,
It verifies what came before it from
The Book,[1] and stands a guardian over it,
Therefore judge them by what from God has come,
And follow not their vain desires to swerve
From all the Truth that you receive;
To each of you We have assigned a law
Together with a way of life; had Allah
So willed, He would have made you all,
A single nation, but it was His will,
To let you prove yourselves in what He gave you,
Therefore, try to excel each other through
Doing good deeds, for in the end,
All of you will to God refer,
Then He shall let you comprehend
The truth of every matter,
In which you differ.

49.   Thus you[2] shall judge[3] among them in accordance,
With Allah's revelations, and shall not,
Follow their low desires; yet do take heed,

---

1. The Scriptures.   2. The Holy Prophet.   3. Or "rule".

Lest they divert you from some parts of what
Has been sent down to you by God; indeed,
If they reject your judgment, do remember,
That it is Allah's purpose them to scourge,
For some of their own sins, and that the number,
Of people who transgress is large.

50.   Are they still longing for the judgments
Of Pagan laws?!¹
Yet, for the firm in faith, whose judgment,
Might be better than Allah's?

51.   O you believers, take not Jews,
Nor Christians for your friends,
They're friends only of one another,
If one of you takes them for friends,
He shall become one of their number,
And God does not with Guidance bless,
The people who transgress.

52.   Yet you see those who have a sickness in,
Their hearts running to woo them; they opine:
"We worry lest a change of fortune bring,
Us some disaster!" Ah, may Allah bring
About a triumph, or a manifest
Event from His own Self, to make them most
Ashamed of what they hid inside the breast.

53.   The faithful will then say: "Are these the men,
Who swore their strongest oaths by Allah,
That they would stand with you?" Lo! All their deeds,

---

1. Lit "the Age of Ignorance".

Are now in vain and they will end in utter failure.

54.   O you believers, if among you some,
        Were to renounce their faith, God would soon raise,
        Another people who do love Him as
        They're loved by Him, humble towards believers,
        Forcefully stern against the disbelievers,
        Keen strivers in the cause of God and fearless
        Of the blaming of any blamers;
        This is the Grace of God and He bestows it
        Upon whome'er He wills, for God is Bounteous,
        And He's the Knower infinite.

55.   Your true *Walee*[1] is only Allah,
        And His Apostle, and Believers,
        Those who set up *salaat*[2] and pay *zakaat*,[3]
        And[4] who bow down as worshippers.

56.   And those who take Allah and His Apostle,
        And the Believers as their guardian,
        Must know that godly leagues will be,
        Victors for certain.

57.   O you believers, never take,
        For friends or guardians those who mock,
        Your Faith or take it for a joke,
        Whether they be among the people,
        Who formerly received the Book,
        Or from among the Pagans; only
        Fear God, if you believe sincerely;

---

1. This word has several meanings: Guardian, master, protector, friend and ally.

2. Regular prayers.   3. Prescribed, Islamic alms.   4. Or "while".

58.   And when you make a call to prayer,
      They mock and take it for a joke,
      This is because they are,
      A feeble-minded folk!

59.   Say to them: "O you people of the Book,
      Do you hate us for any reason,
      Other than that we do believe in God,
      And in the revelations that have been
      Unto us sent, and what was sent before us,
      And for the fact that most of you have proved,
      To be most wicked and rebellious?"

60.   Say: "Shall I tell you who is worse,
      In the matter of Allah's retribution?
      Those upon whom Allah has laid His curse,
      And placed His wrath upon and, in addition,
      Transformed some of them into apes and swine,
      And those who worshipped Satan;
      These are indeed in worse condition,
      And more astray from the Path Even.

61.   And when they come to you they say: "We have
      Embraced the Faith; in fact they do arrive
      Full of unfaith; and full of disbelief
      They surely leave;
      And God's Fully Aware of everything
      They secretly conceive.

62.   You see many of them engaged in,
      Sinful and wicked deeds, and eating
      The fruits of everything forbidden,
      Evil indeed is what they're doing.

63.   Why don't their rabbis and their learned men
       Forbid them from blaspheming, and from earning
       Illicit profits? Wretched is indeed,
       What they have been committing.

64.   The Jews have said: "The Hand of God's tied down!"[1]
       Tied down indeed are their own hands, and they,
       Are cursed for blasphemies they utter; nay,
       His hands are both outstretched, and, at His own
       Pleasure does He in plenty grants. However,
       What's coming to you[2] from your Lord, has further
       Increased rebellion and belief rejection,
       In most of them, and thus We have committed
       Them unto animosity and hatred,
       Until the Day of Resurrection;
       Whenever they ignite the flames of war,
       God puts them out, but they are striving ever
       To spread corruption in the land, and God,
       Has no liking for any evil-doer.

65.   Yet if the people of the Scripture did,
       Believe and led a righteous life, We would
       Surely pardon their sins and give them access,
       To the Gardens of Bliss.

66.   Had they observed the Torah and the Gospel,
       And other revelations to them sent,
       From their own Lord, surely recipient of
       Blessings would have they been both from above
       And from beneath them;[3] though some parties, bent

---

1. The Arabic idiom stands for being "close-fisted, stingy, parsimonious".

2. The Holy Prophet.   3. Both spiritual and material blessings.

On righteousness, are found among them, what
Most of them do, is most malevolent.

67.   O Messenger! Deliver that which was
Revealed unto you from your Lord,
For if you do not, then His Message,
You will not have at all delivered,
And God will guard you 'gainst the crowds,
And God the faithless[1] people never guides.[2]

68.   Say: "O you people of the Book,
You have no ground to stand upon
Until you will uphold:
The Torah and the Gospel,
And whatsoever Was sent down
Unto you from your Lord."
And now the revelations sent
Down to you from your Lord, have made
Many of them more disobedient,
And more unfaithful!
Therefore, you should not grieve,
For a people who disbelieve.

69.   <u>Whoever from among the Muslims,</u>

1. *Kafir* in Arabic means both "an unbeliever" and "a thankless person".

2. As this verse, according to almost all commentators, was revealed to the Holy
Prophet on his way back from the "Farewell Pilgrimage" to Mecca, only
months before his death, it would be very odd of God (!) to order a messenger, who has been delivering the Divine Message, unfailingly, unhesitantly
and continually, for some 23 years, to "Deliver what I revealed to you, or you
haven't delivered the Message!!" Thus, what the Holy Prophet delivered, after
this revelation, must have been of some fateful importance for the future of
the Islamic *umma*.

Jews, Sabians or Christians does believe
In God and the Last Day, and does what's right,
Shall have no fear, nor shall he ever grieve.

70. We covenanted with the Children
Of Israel, and sent them messengers;
Every time an apostle came to them,
Whose exhortation did not answer,
Their souls' many a carnal whim,
They either called him an impostor,
Or simply murdered him!

71. And they presumed there would be no more trial,[1]
And thus they shut their eyes and ears;[2] and still,
God turned to them mercifully, but then
Many of them were blind and deaf again;
And God's the Keenest Watcher of
Their every action.

72. Faithless pagans are people who maintain:
"God? He's Messiah, son of Mary!"
But the Messiah said himself: "O Children
Of Israel! Worship God the One only,
Who is my Lord and your Lord both." Whoever
Joins other gods with God, then God will surely,
Forbid him Paradise, and then the Fire,
Will be his destiny, and none is there
To help the evil-doer.

---

1. Or "punishment".

2. That is: They turned away their eyes from God's Signs and they turned a deaf
   ear to God's Message.

73. And those are also pagans who propose:
    "God is a member of a trinity!"[1]
    Whereas there are no other gods except
    A single Deity;
    If they do not arrest this oddity,
    Most grievously chastised will be,
    The disbelievers of them who,
    Utter such blasphemy.

74. Wont' they just turn[2] to God the One,
    And ask His pardon?
    God's Most Forgiving, Full of Mercy.

75. No more than an apostle was,
    Messiah, son of Mary,
    And many messengers before him,
    Did pass away already,
    His mother was a saintly, truthful woman,
    And each of them was eating as a human!
    Behold! How We explain to them
    The revelations,[3]
    And note! How deeply sunk they are,
    In deviations.

76. Say: "would you serve, instead of God the One,
    Idols and things that may be neither
    Harmful to you nor beneficial?"[4]
    And God is the Omniscient Hearer.

77. Say: "O you people of the Scripture,

---

1. Or "a third of three".   2. "In repentance".

3. Also meaning "signs, miracles and verses".   4. Or "absolutely useless".

Do not transgress the bounds in your religion,
To go beyond the truth, and follow not
The people who had, for their wrong opinion
And fancies gone astray before you, who
Have been misleading many others when,
Themselves had lost the Even Way.

78.   Cursed by the tongue of David, and of Jesus,
Son of Mary, were those who disbelieved,
Amongst the Israelites, because they did
Rebel and every bound exceed;

79.   For they committed evil and did not,
Restrain each other from such hateful wrongs,
Evil was what they used to do indeed.

80.   Today you see a lot of them befriending
The infidels; to evil have their souls
Prompted them in the past, and that is why
They have incurred God's wrath; thus on them falls,
A chastisement abiding.

81.   Had they believed in Allah, in the Prophet
And in what was to him revealed, they would
Not have befriended them at all; in fact,
Most of them are offenders wild.

82.   You will certainly find that Jews and Pagans,
Of all people, are in hostility
To the Believers, the most violent;
And the closest to them[1] in amity,

---

1. "To the Believers."

Are those who say: "We're truly Christians",
Because they bring forth men of piety[1]
In them as well as men of abstinence,[2]
And they are free from arrogance;[3]

83.   And when they hear the revelations,
Sent to the Messenger, you see their eyes,
Flooded with tears as they do recognize
The truth therein; they pray: "Our Lord, do write us
Amongst them who bear witness,

84.   "Why should we not believe in God the One,
And in the truth that now has come to us,
Why should we not be eager that our Lord
Admit us with the righteous?"

85.   And God rewarded them for such a prayer,
With Gardens through which murmur streams,
An endless Life beyond their wildest dreams,
That's the reward for every good-doer.

86.   But people who will ne'er believe,
Those who ever belie Our Signs,
Will certainly become the bosom friends
Unto the Flames!

87.   Believers, do not make unlawful
The wholesome things which God decreed
Lawful to you, but do not cross the limits,

---

1. Or "Pious scholars, priests".   2. Or "Virtuous monks".

3. Not anybody who calls himself a "Christian", but the sincere believers in the
teachings of Jesus Christ who are pious, abstinent and free from arrogance.

For God dislikes the people who exceed.

88.   So eat of the lawful and wholesome things
That God has generously for you provided,
While fearing God in Whom you have believed.

89.   Allah will not take you to task for what,
You inadvertently may say as oaths;
But for your solemn and intended oaths,
He calls you to account; for expiation:
You'll have to feed ten needy men,[1]
With average food you give to your own kin,
Or give them clothes, or free one bondsman;
If none of these you could afford, you must,
Fast for three days. That is the expiation,
For oaths you took and broke; but do be mindful
Of oaths you swear and guard them; thus does God
Explains to you His revelations; would
That you were grateful!

90.   O you who have believed: intoxicants,
Gambling and sacrifices unto stones,[2]
And the use of divining arrows,[3]
Are all abominations, Satan's
Own handiwork! Thus do refrain
From these, perhaps you will attain,
Your own salvations;

---

1. Or "women": that is: "ten persons".

2. Stone altars, columns, slabs and the like on which Pagans sacrificed meat for
idols.

3. Arrows used for division of meat, and for ascertaining lucky or unlucky
moments and for deciding on future actions.

91.   By means of wines and gambling, Satan
       Certainly seeks to stir up enmity
       And hatred in your midst, and to prevent
       You from remembering God, and from the duty
       Of doing prayers; will you not then abstain?

92.   Obey God and obey His Messenger,
       Beware: even if you turn back, you must
       Know that upon Our Messenger, was only
       To make the message manifest.

93.   On those who have embraced the faith and led
       A righteous life, there is no blame for what,
       They used to eat, so long as they continue
       To be godfearing, and maintain their faith and do
       Good works, who then are more godfearing
       And stronger in the faith, then most godfearing,
       While doing their own best for others;
       And God certainly loves the good-doers.

94.   Believers, God will put you to the proof,
       In a small matter of the game, that come within
       Reach of your hands and spears,[1] to see who fears
       Him, even though He is unseen;
       Thus after this whoever may transgress,
       Will face a torment grievous.

95.   O you believers, while you wear *ihraam*,
       You shall not kill a game;
       And anyone who kills a game on purpose,
       His fine shall be killing the same

---

1. Hunting during the Hajj Pilgrimage or in the Holy Precincts.

Number or beast he killed, of cattle,
Decided by two just men of your people,
And brought as offering to Ka'ba;
Or else, he may atone by feeding some
Poor persons or by an equivalent
Fasting, that He may taste the bitter outcome
Of his offense;
God has forgiven what has gone before,
But now for any repetition,
Will God avenge, and God is Mighty,
And Lord of Retribution.

96.   The hunting in the sea and eating,
Of it as food is to you lawful,
It is a good provision for yourselves,
And the people who travel,
But the hunting of land-game,
Is made to you forbidden,
So long as you are in *ihraam*,
Therefore, have fear of God,
Before Whom you shall all,
Be surely gathered.

97.   God the One made the Holy House of Ka'ba,
A mainstay for the humankind, as also
The Sacred Months, the sacrificial offers,
And the garlands that with them go;
All this to help you know that God does know,
Everything in the heavens and the earth,
That God's the Knower of all things in truth,

98.   And that you know that God is both:
Most Strict in retribution,

And Oft-Forgiving with Compassion.

99. The duty of the Messenger is only to
Communicate the Message,
And of whatever you disclose or hide,
Allah has perfect Knowledge.

100. Tell them: Equal are not evil and good,
Although the numeral abundance,
Of evil makes upon you an impression,
Thus, you, men of intelligence,
Be godfearing, perhaps you win salvation.

101. O you believers, question not about
Matters, which if to you made plain,
Would only cause you pain,
And if you ask about them when,
The Reading[1] is being sent down,
They'll be to you made known;
But God has let them pass, for God
Is Oft-Forgiving, Most-Forbearing;

102. Indeed some people in the past,
Were used to asking of such matters:
They ended up becoming unbelievers![2]

103. Never did God ordain such things as
Baheeras, Saa'ibas, Waseelas,

---

1. The Quran.

2. As some merely fractious questions asked of Moses by some Jews which
showed they had no faith.

Or *haams*;[1] it is indeed the unbelievers,
Who have, concerning Allah, forged such lies;
Most of them are certainly most unwise!

104.   When it is said to them: "Come to the law,
Sent down by Allah, and to His Apostle",
They say: "the ways we found our fathers on,
Are quite enough for us". What if their fossil
Fathers knew nothing and had gone,
Far, far astray?!

105.   You who believe! Look after your own souls,
If you yourselves are rightly guided,
No hurt could come to you from those who stray,
You'll all to Him return, and it is God,
That will inform you of all things you did.

106.   Believers, when the time of death draws nigh,
To one of you, let two fair-minded men,
Of your own people act as witnesses,
When you will make a will; if overtaken
By death upon your journeys, call two people,
Outside your own;[2] and for alleviation

---

1. These are all names of various, superstitious practices by Arab Pagans:

a) A *baheera* was a she-camel which had given birth to five young ones; her ear was slit and let loose to roam.

b) A *saa'iba* was a she-camel (or a he-camel) dedicated to idols in gratitude for the fulfillment of a vow.

c) A *waseela* was a he-goat, the first of twins (the other of which was a she-goat): The first born young ones used to be sacrificed in the name of pagan deities, except a *waseela*!

d) A *haam* was a he-camel which begat ten young ones; (stallion-camel freed from work).   2. Non-Muslims.

Of any doubts, detain them, after prayers,
To take an oath by God, by the assertion:
"We will not take a price for this at all,
Even if it involves a near relation,
And we will never hide this evidence,
Due to Allah, for then we'll have committed
A gross offense."

107.　But if it is discovered that the two,
Have been dishonest, then two others,
From among those who have been victimized,
Shall stand up in their place, and each one swears
By God: "My witnessing is much more true
Than the witnessing of those two;
Beyond the truth I have not trespassed
For surely then I would be most unjust."

108.　Thus will it be more proper for them,
To give the truest evidence,
Or fear that other oaths be given,
After their oaths; therefore, fear God and listen;
For God does not show Guidance,
To sinners always in rebellion.

109.　The Day will come when God will summon
The messengers and ask: "How has the Message
You carried, been received?" They answer:
"About it we possess no knowledge,
You are indeed the perfect Knower,
Of everything unknown".

110.　Behold, God will then mention:
"O Jesus, son of Mary, let's remember,

My favour on you and upon your mother,
I did support you with the Holy Spirit,
And you did speak with people when you were,
Still in the crib, as well as in adulthood,
I gave you then instructions in the Scripture,
In Wisdom, in the Torah and the Gospel,
And you, by My permission, shaped the figure,
Of a bird from some clay, and then you breathed
Into it, and it, by My leave,
Became a bird alive;
And you, by My permission, healed,
The blind men and the leper,
And you revived the dead when I so willed,
And then I saved you from the Children
Of Israel, though you had brought them many
A veritable Sign,
When those of them who disbelieved, were caustic:
'These are most plainly magic!'

111.   "Behold, it was My inspiration
To the Disciples: 'do have faith in Me,
And My Apostle;' and they did confess:
'We have believed, so You bear witness
That we are Muslims[1] now in truth.'

112.   And the Disciples once demanded:
'O Jesus, son of Mary, could your Lord,
To us send down a tray of food from heaven?
"Have fear of God", he reprimanded,
"If your belief is even."

---

1. Total submitters to the will of God.

113.   "We wish to eat of it", they said,
       "Only our hearts to strengthen,
       And know for sure that you have spoken
       The very Truth, and that we may,
       Ourselves, be witnesses therein."

114.   So Jesus, son of Mary, did thus pray:
       "O Elohim, our Lord, send down to us a tray,
       Of heavenly food that it may mark a feast,
       For all of us, from the first to the last,
       And be another Portent from your own,
       Give us our daily bread, for You alone,
       Are the Provider Best."

115.   God answered: "surely I will send it down,
       To you, but from now on if anyone,
       Among you disbelieves, a retribution,
       I will inflict upon him which on no one,
       Did I inflict in any nation.

116.   Then God will say:[1] "O Jesus, son of Mary,
       Did you say to the people ever:
       "Worship me and my mother
       As deities along with Allah?"
       "Glory to You", "he'll answer" I would never,
       Say what I had no right to say;
       Had I said so, You would have surely known,
       You do know what is in my mind, but I,
       Never know what's in Yours, for You're alone
       The very Knower of all things unknown;

---

1. On that Day.

117. "I told them only what you had enjoined,
On me to say: serve God the One, my Lord,
As well as your own Lord, and I did watch,
Over them, whilst with them was my abode,
And ever since You took me up to You,
You've been the Watcher over them indeed,
For everything is always by You Witnessed;

118. "Surely they're all your bondsmen,
It is for You: them to chastise,
Or pardon them; You are the One,
Who's Mighty, and All-Wise."

119. Then God will say: this is the very Day,
When truth will benefit the truthful ones,
For this, they will for ever dwell in Gardens
With many a flowing stream,
While God's well pleased with them,
And they're well pleased with Him;
This is the greatest of all gains;

120. The Kingdom of the heavens,
The earth, and what they all contain,
Belong to God alone,
And over everything He reigns.

SURA 6
LIVESTOCK
(AL-AN'AAM)

In the Name of God, the Beneficent, the Merciful

1. Praise be to God, Who brought about
    The heavens and the earth and made
    The Darkness and the Light,
    Yet those who disbelieve, have strayed
    To set up equals with their Lord;

2. He it was who created you from clay,
    Then He decreed a stated term; and yet,
    With Him there is another stated term;[1]
    But you are still in doubt.

3. And He is God in both
    The heavens and the earth,
    He knows your secrets and the truth,
    Of what you publicly declare,
    And He's Informed of your every affair.

4. Yet never has a single revelation,
    Of the Signs of their Lord, unto them[2] come,
    But they have turned back in aversion.

5. Now as they have denied the very Truth,
    That came to them, soon will they learn,
    The consequences of their scorn.

6. Do they not note how many generations,

---

1. "For the Resurrection".   2. The disbelievers.

We have destroyed before them? Generations
We let be dominant throughout the earth,
As We did not for you;[1] We sent them oceans,
Of rain from heavens, and immense streams,
We made roll at their feet, yet in their sins,
We did destroy them, and then in their wake,
We woke up other generations.

7.   Even if We had unto you sent down,
A Book inscribed on actual parchment,
And they could have touched it with their own hand,
The unbelievers would have surely spurned:
"This is nothing but plain enchantment!"

8.   They also say: "why has no angel,
Been unto him sent down?"[2] Why, had We sent
Down an angel, their fates would have been sealed,
And they would never, after its descent,
Have been reprieved;

9.   And even if We meant to send an angel,[3]
We should have certainly made it a human,
And thereby made a further contribution,
To their present confusion!

10.   Other apostles have indeed been mocked,
Before you, but the ones who ridiculed,
were by the very thing they mocked,
Ultimately encircled.

---

1. The people of Mecca.

2. To support him in some supernatural ways.

3. As Our messenger.

11.　　Say: Travel through the land,
　　　　And see what was the end,
　　　　Of people who rejected faith;

12.　　Say: 'Who is it that owns,
　　　　All that's on earth and in the heavens?"[1]
　　　　Say: "All belongs to God the One,"
　　　　Who has ordained compassion
　　　　Upon Himself, but He will gather,
　　　　You all upon the Day of Resurrection,
　　　　Concerning which there is no doubt whatever,
　　　　But he that forfeits his own soul,
　　　　Will ne'er be a believer.

13.　　All beings in the space of Nights and Days,
　　　　Are His, and He's the One Who Hears and Knows.

14.　　Say: "should I take as guardian-lord of mine,
　　　　Any but Allah, the Originator,
　　　　Of heavens and the earth, and the Sustainer
　　　　Of all, Himself sustained by none?"
　　　　Say: "Verily I have been bidden
　　　　To be, of those who do surrender
　　　　Themselves to Him,[1] the first; and cautioned:
　　　　Ne'er should you be an idol-worshipper!"

15.　　Say: "I do fear the torment of a dreadful Day,
　　　　If I my Lord should ever disobey:

16.　　"Whoever on that Day will be,

---

1. The Meccan pagans had chosen not to answer this fundamental question, as either way they would, logically, be in trouble!　　　　2. Muslims.

Delivered from it,[1] will receive
His Mercy, and that is a blissful,
Victory to achieve.

17.   "For the afflictions brought on you by God,
There is, except through Him, no treatment,
And when you're blessed by Him with some good fortune,
Remember He's Omnipotent.

18.   "He reigns supreme over His creatures,
He is alone the Wise, the Cognizant."

19.   Say: "In a testimony,
What thing is the most weighty?"
Then say: "Let Allah be the witness,
Between you all and me,;
And this Quran[2] has been revealed
To me that I thereby may preach,
You, and whoever it could reach;
Dare you to testify indeed,
That there are other gods besides
Allah?" Say: "I for one shall plead,
To no such things!" Say: "He's alone
The Deity, and I disown
All your idolatry."

20.   The people whom We gave the Scriptures to,
Do know this[3] as they know their children,

---

1. The Torment.   2. This Reading.

3. The fact that there is only One God; the pronoun may also stand for "him",
   and in that case, as some commentators think, it refers to Mohammad
   (pbuh), the Messenger of God.

Those, therefore, who do not believe it,
Are authors of their own perdition.

21. And who's more wicked than
The man who forges lies
Concerning Allah, or denies
His revelations?[1] Never
Will the wrong-doers prosper.

22. And on the Day when We will gather,
Them all together, We shall question
The *mushriks*:[2] Where are now those other
Partners of Us, in your opinion?!

23. Then, as there will be nothing else to try,
They'll say: "By Allah, Our own Lord, we swear,
We did not worship idols ever!"

24. Behold! How they will be against themselves,
And how the fabricated gods, will march
Away from them, and leave them in the lurch!

25. Some of them seem to listen to you, but
They do not understand it,[3] or We have
Placed veils upon their hearts, and made their ears
Unfit to hear;[4] and they do not believe,

1. Or "Signs".

2. The Idolaters, those who set up other gods besides God the One.

3. The pronoun "it" may mean: "The Quran", "The recitation of the Quran" or
   "what you say".

4. As a consequence of their evil obduracy, their faculties have been dulled, but
   God ascribes the final cause to Himself, for nothing ever takes place without
   God's will or order.

In any of our Signs, although
They see them all; and thus they only argue
With you, whene'er they come to you;
Such unbelievers even make the statement:
"Oh, these are tales of times most ancient!"

26. And they forbid it unto others, as
They keep away from it themselves,
They are preparing for their own perdition,
Though of it they have no cognition!

27. Would that you could see their condition,
When they are made to face the Fire,
Lamenting: "Woe to us, if we could only
Go back, we would not be denying ever,
Our Lord's Communications, and would be
Each one, a true believer."

28. Nay! What they had concealed, has now
Become most clear to them, but though,
They should return, they would, for certain,
Relapse to what they were forbidden;
They are incorrigible liars!

29. They used to say: "There is no other life
But this, the very present worldly one,
Nor are we to be ever raised
To life again!"

30. If only you could see those people,
When they'll be brought before their Lord!

He would ask them: "Is this not real?"[1]
And they would say: "Yes, by Our Lord!"
So He would say: "then taste Our Scourge
For that which you did not acknowledge!"

31.   Losers indeed will be the ones who did
        Deny that they would ever meet their Lord;
        And when the Hour's[2] upon them unawares,
        They will exclaim: "Alas, we have indeed
        Wasted our worldly life." And now they'll carry
        Their loads of sins upon their backs: behold,
        What evil loads they have to carry!

32.   And the life of this world is nothing more,
        Than idle plays and sport, and pleasures vain,
        And certainly the Home in the Hereafter,
        Is best for people who restrain;
        Will you not ever ponder?!

33.   We surely know that you are saddened by
        What they are saying, but you should then know
        It is not you[3] they are denying, no!
        God's Signs it is the wicked folks deny.

34.   Other apostles have been called impostors,
        Before you, but they bore with fortitude
        All rejections and every persecution,
        Until Our help and victory ensued;

---

1. Or "The Truth", "The Reality".

2. The Hour of Doom.

3. The Holy Prophet.

There are, to God's Decrees, no challengers,[1]
And you already have some information,
About those messengers.

35.   And if you find it hard to tolerate
Their detestation, could you dig a chasm
Deep down into the earth or raise a ladder
Up to the sky, some miracle[2] to bring them?!
Had God so Willed, he would have given
Them Guidance, one and all; therefore, be not
Ignorance-stricken!

36.   Those who do hear, will certainly respond;
And the dead will be raised by God,
And brought back to Him in the end.

37.   They still object: "why has no miracle
Been sent down to him by his Lord?"
Say: "Surely God could well afford
To send down any miracle!
But many of these people know,
Nothing at all;"

38.   All animals that move upon the earth,
And all the creatures flying on their wings,
Are also species like yourselves; all things
We rendered perfect by the Book[3] in truth;
And to their Lord shall be their final wendings;

1. Or "changers".

2. Or "a Sign".

3. According to the Book of Creation, the Grand Scheme or Predetermination of
the courses of their lives.

39. But deaf and dumb are people[1] who deny
    Our Signs, they are in total darkness; yea,
    Whom Allah Will, He leaves to go astray
    And whom He Wills, He guides on the Right way.

40. Ask them to think: "If any great misfortune,
    Sent by Allah befalls you, or the Hour
    Suddenly overtakes you, will you call on
    Any other but Allah?
    Answer, if you are truthful men!

41. "Undoubtedly you call on Him alone-
    And if He please, He will remove the evils,
    About which you implored Him-while you do
    For a moment, forget your idols."

42. Other apostles did We send before
    Your time, to many nations,
    And then We seized them with afflictions
    And hardships, that they might
    Humbly make invocations.

43. If only they implored when they were struck
    By Our calamity! But their hearts were
    Hardened, and Satan made their foul exploits,
    Seem to them fair.

44. And when they had indeed forgotten
    Our Admonition, then We left the gates
    Of all good things unto them open,

---

1. Contrary to beasts, birds and fish, men who have a free will and possess the
   power to discern, could certainly understand the Message that All Nature
   proclaims.

But, as they were rejoicing in Our gifts,
We seized them all, when they were unaware,
And lo! They were in absolute despair!

45. Thus were the wrong-doers, adverse
To justice, totally uprooted; praise
Be unto God, Lord of the Universe.

46. Say: "Think if Allah takes away,
Your hearing and your sight, and sets
A seal upon your hearts,
Which deity but Allah may,
them unto you restore?"
Behold! How We Our signs[1] explain
Over and o'er again, and they ignore
Them in disdain!

47. Say: "Think, if Allah's chastisement should fall,
Upon you unawares or openly,[2]
Will it not be the wicked only
Who perish one and all?"

48. For We are sending Our apostles only
As bearers of good tidings and conveyors
Of warnings; thus the people who believe,
And mend their ways, will have nothing to fear,
Nor will they ever grieve.

49. But those who treat Our revelations
As false, shall have to suffer Torment,
A consequence of their transgressions.

---

1. Also: verses, revelations.   2. After warning or announcement.

50.   Tell them: "I do not claim that I possess
        The treasures of the Heavens,[1] nor do I
        Know the Unseen[2] nor do I ever claim
        To be an angel; only I obey
        The revelations sent to me." And say:
        "The blind, the seer: are they to be alike?
        Do you not ever think?"

51.   And preach with this[3] to those who truly fear,
        Their summoning before their Lord, when they
        Will find no guardian, nor an intercessor
        But Him, in order that they may
        Take the godfearing way.

52.   And do not drive away the people who,
        Call on their Lord, mornings and evenings,
        In pure devotion unto Him alone;
        You'll not answer for them by any means,
        Neither are they to blame for you a grain,
        If you, therefore, drive them away, you will
        Yourself be one who has committed evil.

53.   In fact, We in this way make some of them,
        A means of testing others, so they'll scorn:
        "Are these the people from amongst us whom
        God has favoured?![4] Is it not God alone,

---

1. Literally: "of God".

2. Or "telling what is hidden, the future events, etc. as soothsayers, fortune-
   tellers and the like often do."

3. The Quran, the Revelations.

4. The Meccan Pagans said that none but the lowest stratum of society, consist-
   ing of slaves, servants and the like, had accepted Islam.

Who does know best the thankful.

54. So when believers in Our revelations,
Unto you come, say: "Peace[1] upon you all;
Your Lord has for Himself laid down a law
Of Mercy, so that if one of you will,
In ignorance, commit an evil,
But after that repents and mends his ways,
He'll find Him Pardoning and Merciful.

55. Thus do We make Our revelations clear,
So that the way the guilty travel on,
Will be laid bare.

56. Say: "I'm forbidden e'er to worship,
What you invoke instead of God the One";
Say: "I will never follow your desires,
For if I did, I'd go astray, and then,
I would receive no Guidance."

57. Say: "From my Lord I have some solid proof,
But you deny Him; and I have no power,
To hasten what you challenge me to bring;[2]
Command and Judgment do belong to Allah;
He does communicate the Truth,
And He's the best Decider ever.

58. Say: "Were it in my might to hasten on,
What you demand, the matter would be past
'Tween you and me at once, but it is God,

---

1. *Salaam* in Arabic and *Shalom* in Hebrew.
2. God's Scourge upon the Pagans.

Who knows the evil-doers best;

59.   He has the Keys of all that's Hidden,
       None has Knowledge of them but He,
       He knows all things on land and in the sea,
       Never a leaf will fall without His Ken,
       Neither is there a grain down in the depth
       Of darkness in the earth;
       Nor anything from A to Z,
       But it is in a Glorious Book recorded.

60.   He it is who recalls your souls by night,[1]
       Knowing full well what you have done by day,
       And He does bring you back to life each dawn,
       That you a term allotted spend away;
       Then you shall all to Him return,
       And then He'll let you know about
       Everything you have wrought!

61.   He reigns supreme over His creatures,
       And over you He sets some keepers;
       At length when death to your direction veers,
       Our messengers will take your souls away
       Without delay.

62.   Then shall they be sent back to God the One,
       Their Master True; beware, to Him alone,
       Belongs the judgment, and beyond imagination,
       Is the speed of His Computation!

63.   Say: "who may save you from the lurking,

---

1. When you are sleeping like the dead.

Perils of land and sea when you're invoking
Him humbly and in secret: 'If He will,
Save us from this, we will be truly grateful!'"

64.   Say: "It is God who saves you from them,
And from other afflictions, and you still
Set up idols besides Him."

65.   Say: "He is Able to afflict you with
A retribution from above your heads,
Or from beneath your feet, or clothe you with
Dissension, and to make you feel the dreads,
Of the harshness of other factions!"
Behold! How We repeat Our revelations,
Perhaps they'll notice!

66.   Yet your own people have rejected this,[1]
Although it is the very Truth;" declare:
I'm not in charge of your Affair;

67.   "Every prophecy has its own set time,
And you shall soon the consequences witness.

68.   Meanwhile when you see men engaged,
In scoffing at Our revelations,
Withdraw from them until they get engaged,
In other themes; and if Satan's temptations
Make you forget, then after recollection,
Soon quit your sitting with a throng,
Ever engaged in doing wrong.

---

1. The Quran.

69.   The righteous shall on no account,
        Be held accountable for these;[1]
        Reminding them, however, might
        Help them refrain from evil ways.

70.   You shall avoid the people who have taken,
        Their faith for sport and pastime, and have been
        Deceived by the life of this world; however,
        Remind them with it, lest a soul should ruin
        Itself by its own actions; then he'll find
        There is no guardian and no intercessor,
        Along with God, and even though he offer,
        Every plausible ransom, none would ever,
        Be accepted from it; such folks have earned
        Their own damnation by their deeds: for drinking
        They'll have some boiling fluid stinking,
        Plus a most painful retribution,
        For faith-rejection.

71.   Say: "shall we call, instead of God, on things
        Which have no use at all, for or against?
        Are we to turn upon our heels, now after
        Being guided by God, like those possessed
        By Devils, who do wander here and there
        With a bewildered spirit, while their closest
        Friends call: 'come to us on the right direction.'"
        Say: "Allah's guidance is the guidance true,
        And we have been commanded to submit to
        The Lord of the Creation,

72.   To keep up prayers and be godfearing, for

---

1. The unbelievers.

Before Him, is your final Congregation.

73. He is the One who did create the heavens,
     And the earth in all truth, and on the Day,
     He utters Be, that Day's already there,
     His word's the Truth, and His shall be the Sway,
     As ever, on the Day the Horn is blown,
     Knower is He of all: known or unknown,
     For the All-Knowing Wise is He alone.

74. "How could you worship images as gods?"
     Said Abraham unto Azar, his sire,
     "In my opinion, you and all your people
     Are in manifest error."

75. Thus was it that We showed to Abraham,
     The Kingdom of the heavens and the earth,
     So that he may be one with the most firm
     Belief in truth:

76. When the night fell, he saw a glaring planet,
     "Maybe this is my Lord", he said. But when
     It set, he said: "I love not gods that set!"

77. Then, when he saw the rising, shining Moon,
     He said: "Is this my Lord?" But when it too,
     Faded, he said: "Indeed if the Lord true,
     Does not guide me, I'll surely go astray".

78. And when he saw the rising, blazing Sun,
     He said: "It's greater than the other two,
     So it's my Lord." But when it went its way,[1]

---

1. "When it also set".

He made a proclamation: "O my folk,
I do denounce all idols you invoke!

79.   "I am devoting my devotion wholly,
Unto the One who broke apart the heavens,
And earth into existence, and I'll never,
Worship idols and icons."

80.   And when his folks engaged in arguments
With him, he said: "Do you come to dispute
With me concerning God, while he has shown
Guidance to me? Nay, of those idols mute,
You join with Him, I have no fear, for nothing
Happens unless Allah be willing;
Everything falls indeed
Within the Knowledge of my Lord,
Will you not e'er take heed!

81.   "How could I fear your idols? Is it not,
You who should fear for joining gods and icons,
As partners unto God, without His sanction!
Which side is more deserving of salvation,
If you are men of kens?

82.   "Those only who have faith and do not taint,
Their faith with idol-worship, shall attain
Salvation surely, for they are already
Upon the guided terrain."

83.   Such was the argument with which We furnished,
Abraham 'gainst his people; We do raise
To an exalted rank whome'er We wish;
Your Lord is the All-Knowing, the Most-Wise.

84. And We bestowed upon him then,
    Isaac and Jacob,
    We gave Our guidance to all three,
    As We had guided Noah long before them,
    And from among his progeny:
    David and Solomon and Job,
    Joseph, Moses and Aaron,
    Whom We rewarded as benevolent men,

85. And Zacharias, John and Jesus,
    Elijah too, all good men pious,

86. And Ishmael, Elisha, Jonas, Lot,
    And every one of them We brought
    To leading ranks among the nations,

87. So did We favour with distinctions,
    Some of their fathers, children, brethren;
    We chose them all and guided them,
    Unto the right Direction.

88. This is God's guidance, which He gives,
    To whom He wills among His creatures;
    If they had fallen into serving idols,
    Ruined would have been all their labours.

89. Such were the men upon whom We bestowed
    The Book,[1] the Wisdom[2] and the Prophethood,
    Yet if these people[3] are to disbelieve,

---

1. Or "the Scriptures".
2. Or "The judgment, Authority".
3. Their descendants, this generation.

In them? Behold! We most certainly would[1]
Entrust with them a throng who do believe.

90.   These were the ones whom God had guided,
Thus follow in their footsteps and remind:
"For this I ask from you no recompense,
This is but a Reminder[2] to mankind."

91.   No just evaluation do they make,
Of God the One, when they allege: "God never
Revealed a thing unto a human being!"
Say: "Who then has revealed the Scripture
That Moses brought, with Light and Guidance,
For humankind? That which you often scatter
On separate scraps, revealing some of it,
While hiding much?! Whereas therein you were
Taught knowledge, neither you nor your forefathers
Ever possessed. To these people, just mention: "Allah";[3]
Then leave them to enjoy their foolish chatter!

92.   And this too is a Book We have sent down,
Bringing blessings and verifying what,
Was sent before it, and for you to warn,
The Mother-Town[4] and the people about;
Those who believe in the Hereafter
Surely believe in this; they are
The ones who never lose a prayer.

93.   And who could be more wicked than the man,

---

1. It may also mean: "We have already entrusted....".

2. Or "an admonition, a message".

3. A world of meaning is implied in this one word!   4. Mecca.

Who fabricates falsehoods concerning Allah,
Or claims: "I am receiving revelations,"
When he receives no revelation ever,
Or says: "I can reveal the like of what,
God has revealed?" If only you could see
The wicked people in the throes of death:
When angels, hands outstretched, shall say: "Come ye,
Yield up your souls, today you are to be,
Recompensed with a shameful retribution,
For all the matters false and odd,
You did attribute unto God,
And for your contempt of His Revelation."

94.   "And now you have returned to Us, alone,
As We created you at first; behind
Your backs you left what We for you provided;
Nor any intercessors do We find
Along with you, the ones you had considered,
Having some shares in your affairs!
Broken are all the ties that used to bind
You then, and all your fancies are in tatters!"

95.   God is the Splitter of the seeds and stones,
The One Who causes them to germinate,
He's the Producer of the living from,
The dead, and the dead from the living,
Such is Allah! How could you deviate!

96.   He Splits the darkness into Dawn,
He has the Night for rest ordained;
And the times of the Sun and Moon,
Have been by Him determined;
Such is the ordinance of God the One,

The Mighty, the All-Knowing.

97.   And He it was Who made the stars to guide you,
      During the darkness of the land and sea;
      Truly We make Our revelations plain,
      For those who know enough to see!

98.   And He it was Who did produce you from,
      A single being, later to be lodged,
      In the loins and entrusted with the womb;
      Our Revelations are most clearly messaged,
      For men of understanding.

99.   It's He Who sends down water from the heavens,
      Then We bring forth thereby all kinds of plants;
      From it; We then produce the matter green,
      And from this every manner of rich grain,
      Palm-trees with hanging clusters, various gardens
      Of grapes and olive groves and pomegranates:
      Similar yet dissimilar in traits,
      Do feast your eyes with their abundant burdens,
      As they develop and as each one ripens!
      Behold, in these are truly Signs
      For true believers.

100. Yet they regard the Jinn as Allah's partners,
      Though He created them, and also, out of
      Their ignorance, attribute sons and daughters
      To Him! Glory to Him, He's far above
      Their imputations;

101. Initiator of the Excellence,
      Of the heavens and earth is He; so whence

Is He to have a son of any sort,
When He has never had a consort?!
He has created everything; He has,
Knowledge of everything there is.

102.　Such is then God the One, your Lord,
There is no deity but He,
He has created everything,
Therefore worship Him only,
He's in control of everything.

103.　No mortal eyes could see Him,
But He encompasses all visions,
He's the Knower beyond
Conceivable precisions.

104.　"Eye-opening proofs have now unto you come,
From your own Lord; whoever now will use
His sight, it is for his own good, and those
Who are unto them blind, will surely lose,
And I am not to be your keeper;"

105.　Thus We repeat Our revelations
In different ways; let them allege:
"You have been given lessons!" Yet,
We make them plain for men of knowledge.

106.　You shall follow what is to you revealed,
From your own Lord; there is no God but He,
And disregard the Pagans, let them be!

107.　Had Allah pleased, they would have never prayed
To gods beside Him, and We have not made,

You a keeper over them, neither
Are you their guardian ever.

108.   Do not revile the idols they have joined,
With Allah, lest they should, in ignorance,
And out of spite, be blasphemous to Allah;
We have indeed let the performance,
Of each people seem pleasant in their eyes,
But they will all unto their Lord return,
And He will let them know how much their deeds,
Would for them earn!

109.   They swear their strongest oaths by Allah
That if a miracle[1] unto them comes,
They will believe in it[2] for certain.
Say: "Only God could bring forth miracles;
But what will make you[3] know that if,
A miracle did come to them, they would
Not go on with their disbelief?!"

110.   And since they have made up their minds
Not to believe in it at all,
From the first instance, We have turned,
Their hearts and eyes out of control,
Thus We leave them to stumble and to fall,
In their rebellion, like the blind.

111.   Even if We sent down to them the angels,
And made the dead to speak with them, and rallied,
All things before their very eyes, they still

---

1. Sign   2. The prophethood of Mohammad (pbuh)
3. The Muslim community.

Would not believe, unless God had it willed;
But most of them are senseless, heedless people.

112. Likewise We have assigned to every prophet,
Some enemy: Satans 'mongst men and jinn,
Inspiring one another with most varnished,
But vain, discourses aimed at man's deception;
Yet if your Lord had e'er so wished,
They would not do this, therefore leave them in,
The loneliness of their own fabrication;

113. And let the hearts of those who have no faith
In the next world, incline to what they say,
Let them delight in them, and let them earn,
From them what ill they may.

114. "Should I be seeking, as a source of law,
Other than Allah, when it's He Who sent
Down unto you this Book with all its details?"
And those given the Book are cognizant
That it was sent down from your Lord in truth,
Never then harbour any doubt.

115. And the Word of your Lord is perfect,
In truthfulness and justice; nothing
Shall abrogate His Words, and He's
The Hearer, the All-Knowing.

116. If you obey most people in this land
They will lead you astray from Allah's Way,
For nothing do they follow but
Conjecture, and whate'er they say
If falsehood based on lies!

117.   It is your Lord certainly Who best knows
The people who from His way go astray,
And those remaining on the guided way.

118.   So you shall eat from that on which the name
Of Allah has been mentioned, if you are
Believers in His revelations;

119.   And why should you not eat of that upon
Which God's name has been mentioned: plain
Has He already made all prohibitions,
Except under extreme conditions;
Many people, led by their low desires,
Mislead others through ignorance; indeed,
Your Lord is Most-Aware of those,
Who the limits exceed.

120.   Eschew all sin: open or secret sins,
Sinners will surely get the recompense,
For their own earnings!

121.   Eat not of that on which the name
Of God has not been mentioned; wicked
Is this indeed; surely the satans,
Always inspire their every friend,
That they should with you all, contend;
But if you follow them, you could,
Indeed become one of the Pagans!

122.   If one was dead[1] and We did grant him life,
And made for him a light with which he would

---

1. "Dead" in this parable means "dead spiritually".

Move among people, could he be compared
To one who's in a darkness deep, and could
Never emerge from it? That's how the deeds,
Of disbelievers in their eyes seem good!

123. That is how We allow in every town,
Its notables to be its criminals,
To plot and scheme therein, but they are not
Plotting and scheming but against their souls;
Though they may not perceive it.

124. And when a revelation to them comes,
They say: "We won't believe in it until
We too receive the likes of what was given
To Allah's Messengers!" Whom Allah will
Entrust His mission with, is only known
To Him! God's humiliation shall befall
Those guilty sinners soon, and they will suffer
A grievous Torment for their planning evil.

125. Whomever Allah wills to guide, He opens,
His bosom to Islam,[1] and whom He wills
To send astray, his chest He renders narrow
And tight, as if one were to try uphills
To reach the sky! Thus Allah lays
His curse on disbelievers.

126. Whereas most straight is this:
Path of your Lord; indeed,
We've made the Signs most plain
For people who take heed.

---

1. Absolute submission to God the One.

213

127. They shall be dwelling in the Home of Peace[1]
     Nearest unto their Lord, and He will be
     Their friendly Guardian, as a recompense
     For works of piety.

128. Upon the Day when He all of them summons,
     It's mentioned: "O you of the race of Jinns,[2]
     You did exploit great multitudes of humans!"
     And then, their human allies add: "Our Lord,
     Mutual was the profits we adored,
     But lo! We reached the limit of the period
     You had for us appointed."
     He'll say: "Thus, Hell is your abode,
     Wherein you shall for good abide,
     Unless Allah will order otherwise;"
     Surely your Lord is the All-Knower Wise.

129. Thus do We match the wicked to be comrades
     Of one another in their evil deeds.

130. "O Congregation of the Jinns and humans!
     Did messengers of your own kind not come
     To you, bringing to you my revelations,
     And warning you about the outcome
     You'll meet with on this Day?"
     "We do witness against ourselves", they say.
     The worldly life deceived them, and this Day
     They are to witness 'gainst themselves,
     That they were disbelievers.

---

1. Heaven, the place of perfect peace and true happiness.

2. These are the satans of Jinns.

131. This is because your Lord would never
    Destroy communities in an unfair
    Manner, when their inhabitants
    Are really unaware.

132. Ranks and rewards they will acquire,
    According to their deeds;
    Your Lord is never Unaware
    Of any of their deeds.

133. Your Lord is Needless, Full of Mercy,
    If He pleases, He may have you destroyed,
    And make whome'er He wills,
    You to succeed:
    Just as He raised you from the seed
    Of other peoples.

134. All that has been unto you Promised,
    Will come to pass, and you may not
    Escape them in the least.

135. Say: O My folk, do all that's in your power,
    And I will do my best, and you'll know soon,
    Which one of us will reach the Final Boon!
    Surely the wicked shall not prosper.

136. Out of Allah-provided crops and cattle,
    They set aside for Him, a portion:
    "This is for God and that is for our idols!"
    They say, in their pretentious demonstration.
    Behold! Their idols' share does not reach Allah,
    But Allah's portion goes unto their idols;
    Their decisions are truly evil!

137. Likewise the idols of the Pagans have
     Made the killing of their own children
     Seem, unto most of them, a proper thing,
     In order to mislead them into ruin,
     And further muddle their religion;
     Had God willed, they would not have been
     Doing this; thus you leave them to,
     Their own false fabrications.

138. They also say: these cattle and those crops,
     Are now forbidden, of them none may eat,
     But whom we choose-so they assert-
     Then there are other animals they treat
     As consecrated, neither to be ridden,
     Nor burdened, and some beasts on which God's name
     Is not pronounced: all this is evil claim
     Against Him; soon shall they be scourged,
     By Him for what they've forged.

139. They also say: what's in the wombs[1] of certain
     Livestock will only be allowed unto Our men,
     Forbidden is it to our wives;
     Yet if it be still-born then all therein,
     Are to be partners!
     Soon will He punish them for such portrayals,
     For He's All-Knowing, Wise.

140. Losers indeed are those who foolishly,
     In utter lack of knowledge, kill their children,
     Who have also forbidden,
     What God gave them for their provision,

---

1. In their bellies: their offspring.

216

Ascribing unto God some falsity!
They've gone astray indeed:
No guidance did they ever heed.

141.   It's He indeed Who has produced
Paradises of plants:
Of trellised vines and trees untrellised,
The palms, the olives and the pomegranates,
Similar yet dissimilar in taste,
Eat of their fruits when they bear fruits,
And give away what's due of them and just,
Upon the day of harvest,
And do not be a waster by excess,
For God dislikes those who transgress;

142.   Among the animals unto you given,
Are those for slaughter and the beasts of burden,
Eat of what God has set as your provision,
And follow not the steps of Satan,
For he's to you a foe most open.

143.   Of the eight kinds of cattle, males and females,
First take two pairs of sheep and goats, and question:
Has He of these forbidden you the males,
The females, or what's in the wombs of females?!
Tell me with knowledge if you're truthful men!

144.   Then take two pairs of camels and of oxen,
And ask: Has He of these to you forbidden,
The males, the females or the young within
The females' wombs?! Perhaps you all did witness,
When God enjoined you this!
Who is indeed more wicked than the man

Who, in his ignorance, invents such lies
Concerning Allah to mislead the others,
Surely God never guides the evil-doers.

145.   Say: "In the revelations sent to me,
I find nothing forbidding men to eat
As food except dead meat,[1] or running blood,[2]
Or flesh of swine-that's an abhorrent meat-
Or any flesh profanely slaughtered in
The name of any gods but God the One;
But if a man is forced to eat, without
Transgressing bounds or being wilful,
He'll surely find that God is Oft-
Forgiving and Most Merciful.

146.   And We forbade the Jews all animals,
With undivided hoofs, and of the oxen
And sheep, We made the fat unlawful,
Except what's carried on their backs, or in
Their entrails or what is attached to bones;
This was a punishment for their rebellions;
Indeed We are the Truthful.

147.   And if they still reject you, say: "Your Lord
Possesses boundless Mercy,
But never will His wrath be turned aside,
From a people sinfully guilty."

148.   The idol-worshippers will soon be saying:
"Had Allah willed, we would not have been serving

---

1. Carrion, animals that die of themselves.

2. Not trapped within the meat.

Idols at all, neither we nor our fathers,
Nor would We have forbidden anything;"
Thus did their ancestors deny the Truth,
Until they had tasted Our dreaded Wrath.
Say: "Have you any knowledge that you could,
Bring it forth unto us and lecture?!
Nay, nothing do you follow but conjecture,
And nothing do you preach but falsehood."

149. Say: "The conclusive proof belongs,
To God alone;
Had He so willed, He'd have, to all of you,
His guidance shown."

150. Say: "Bring your witnesses to prove that God
Has this or that forbidden;" but if they
Themselves unto it swear, you shall not swear,
With them; nor are you ever to obey
The vain desires of those who have denied
Our revelations, those who disbelieve in
The life to come, and set up gods beside,
Their Lord as equals.

151. Say: "Come you all, and I will tell you what,
Your Lord has really made upon you binding:
i) You shall not serve besides Him any other,
ii) You shall be to your father and your mother
Benign and full of honour,
iii) You shall not kill your children from the fear
Of poverty; We are, to you and to them, the Provider,
iv) You shall not to indecencies draw near,
Whether open or hidden,
v) You shall not kill a soul-which God indeed,

219

But in the course of justice, has forbidden-
These are the things which He on you enjoins,
That you may use your brains!

152.　vi) And you shall not approach the property,
　　　　Of orphans, save in a most righteous manner,
　　　　Until they reach maturity,
　　　vii) And you shall give the fairest weight and measure-
　　　　No soul are We to burden ever, with more than it can
　　　　　　　　　　　　　　　　　　　　　　　　　　bear-
　　　viii) And you shall always speak for justice, even
　　　　　If it affects your closest kinsmen,
　　　ix) And you shall all fulfill God's covenant;
　　　　This does He make on you incumbent,
　　　　That you may notice and remember;

153.　And know:
　　　x) This is My Path, the very straight one.
　　　　Thus follow it, and do not follow,
　　　　Other byways, for they'll take you away
　　　　From His Right way;
　　　　That's what He does on you enjoin,
　　　　That you may be godfearing and restrain.

154.　In former times We gave the Book,
　　　Unto Moses, a perfect code,
　　　For those who would do right,
　　　Detailing everything, also a guide,
　　　And blessing, that his people might
　　　Believe the Meeting with their Lord.

155.　And now We have sent down this Book,
　　　Which has a blessing of its own;

Thus follow it, and be godfearing,
That Mercy to you may be shown:

156.   Lest you should say "The Book had been
Unto two groups[1] before us sent,
And so we could not be acquainted
With what they taught or learnt."

157.   Or lest you claim: "Had the Book been revealed
To us, we would have been indeed,
Better guided than both of them!"
Now that the clearest proof has come,
Unto you from your Lord, who can
Be more oppressive than the man,
Who disbelieves God's revelations,
And turns away from them?
Soon, with the harshest of Our retributions,
Shall We chastise the very men who did,
Turn away from Our revelations,
Because they turned away from them.

158.   Are they expecting that the angels,
Or God Himself, or certain Signs
Sent by your Lord, will visit them?!
Upon the Day when some such signs
From God should come, no benefit
Will faith have for the persons
Who had no faith before, or did not do,
Any virtuous deeds, in virtue
Of their own faith; nay, it's too late!
Say only: "wait, we too will wait."

---

1. Jews and Christians.

159.   You have nothing to do with those who split
    Up their religion and become sectarian;
    With Allah only is their case, and later
    Will He declare to them what they have done.

160.   He who has done a righteous deed,
    Shall be repaid tenfold,
    But He who has committed evil,
    Shall have an equal evil for reward,
    Injustice shall be done to none indeed.

161.   Say: "verily my Lord has guided me,
    To the Straight Path, to the Ever True Faith,
    The creed of Abraham, who was in truth,
    Upright, and never did He
    Next to God, set another party!"

162.   Declare: "surely my prayers and my devotions,
    My life and death are all for God the One,
    The Lord of all creations,

163.   "The peerless One; all this has been
    Commanded to me, and I am,
    The first embracer of Islam."[1]

164.   Say: "what! should I be seeking any lord
    But God the One, Who is the Lord of All?!
    Each soul shall reap the fruits of its own deeds,
    None is to bear the burden of another soul;
    You will be, in the end,
    All to your Lord returned,

---

1. The first "Muslim", submitter to the absolute will of the Almighty.

And He will then for you resolve
All upon which you did contend."

165.   He it is Who has made you viceroys
Of Earth, and some of you has He exalted
In rank above the others, that He may
Try you through gifts that He to you has granted;
Your Lord is certainly Most Swift,
In retribution, yet He's also Oft-
Forgiving, Full of Mercy.

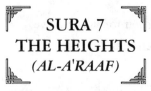

SURA 7
THE HEIGHTS
(AL-A'RAAF)

In the Name of God, the Beneficent, the Merciful

1.   Alif Laam Meem Saad.[1]

2.   Unto you is a *book* sent down;
Therefore, let there be, in your heart,
No reservation[2] on its part:
You may thereby exhort and warn,
And let it serve as a reminder,
Unto every believer.

3.   Follow what has been from your Lord,
To you revealed,
And follow not patrons beside Him,
How seldom you take heed!

4.   Lo! Many habitations
We Have destroyed: Our scourge did take
Them, of a sudden, when they were
Asleep or wide awake.

5.   And when Our scourge upon them fell,
These were the only words they spoke:
"Indeed we were transgressors foul!

6.   Certainly We will question people,
To whom Our messages were sent,
And surely We will question each apostle;

---

1. A.L.M.S.   2. Or " straitness" or "difficulty".

7.   And knowingly We will recount,
      Their story unto them in full,
      For We were never absent!

8.   That Day, with truth, will be the Weighing Out,
      Then those whose weights[1] are heavy will
      Attain salvation,

9.   And those whose weights are light,
      Find their souls in perdition,
      For having wronged Our revelations.

10.   Upon the earth We placed you and did give,
      You power, and prepared for you the means
      And sustenance therein to live;
      Yet small is your appreciation!

11.   We it was Who effected your creation,
      And We designed your frame and face,
      And We then bade the angels:
      "Before Adam, yourselves abase".
      And they all did themselves abase,
      Except Iblees,[2] who would not be,
      One to go down upon his knee!

12.   "What has prevented you from bowing down",
      Said He, "when I commanded you to do so?"
      "Nobler am I than he", he said, "You did
      Create me out of fire, and him? Oh, lo!
      You have created, out of mud!"[3]

1. "Whose scale of good deeds."   2. Satan, Diabolis.

3. Thus Satan commits the triple crime of arrogance, jealousy and rebellion
   against God.

13.   He said: "Begone from here;[1] this is no place
       To be so proud in. Thus get out,
       Henceforth you'll be debased."

14.   "Grant me a respite", he requested,
       "Until the Day of Resurrection".

15.   He said: "Respite is granted".

16.   He said: "Because You have led me astray,
       I will certainly lie in wait for them,[2]
       Along Your own right way;

17.   "Then I will surely spring upon them from
       Everywhere: from before them and behind,
       And from their right and left, and You will find,
       No gratitude in most of them."

18.   "Begone from here", said He, "Henceforth you will
       Be an outcast despised, and, with you all,
       You and your followers, I'll fill
       The pit of Hell;

19.   "As for you Adam and your spouse,
       In Paradise[3] you'll dwell,
       And eat of everything you will;
       Only do not go near this Tree,
       For then transgressors shall you be."

20.   But Satan cunningly seduced them both

---

1. From "The Garden" or "Paradise".   2. Mankind.

3. The Garden.

In order to reveal their nakedness,[1]
Which was to them until then hidden.
He said: "Your Lord has certainly forbidden
You from this Tree that you do not progress
To be two angels, or become immortal."

21.   He also swore an oath unto them both:[2]
"I am your well-wisher in truth!"

22.   Thus by deceit he brought about their Fall:
After they both had tasted of the Tree,
Their nakedness was to them visible,
And they began to fasten hurriedly
On them the leaves plucked from the Garden.
And then their Lord called out to them:
"Did I forbid you not that Tree,
And did I not inform you both that Satan,
Was your sworn enemy?"

23.   They both replied: "Our Lord!
We have certainly been unjust,
To our own souls; if You do not
Pardon us, if we are not blessed,
With Your own Mercy, we shall be
Surely among the lost."

---

1. Or "shame"; our first parents were innocent in matters material as well as
   spiritual, but the faculty of choice given to them could raise them above the
   angels, for they had the capacity of evil too, and when they fell, they realized
   the evil.

2. Contrary to other Books and their centuries-old sexist literature, nowhere in
   the Holy Quran is the blame for the Fall put on Eve: they both had the faculty of choice and free will, and both of them were deceived.

24. He said: "well then, go hence,
    Yet some of you will be to others,
    As enemies. And on the earth will be
    Your dwelling and your sustenance,
    For an appointed time,

25. There you shall live and die and thence
    You shall be taken out, at last.

26. O You children of Adam!
    We have provided you with raiment,
    That you will clothe your nakedness,
    And use as items of adornment;
    The best to wear, however, is the garment
    Of righteousness;
    This is one of the Signs of God,
    Perhaps they will take heed.

27. Children of Adam, do not let
    Satan seduce you in the same
    Manner he got your parents out
    Of Paradise: to let them see their shame,
    He stripped them of their godly raiment,[1]
    Most certainly he and his minions,
    See you from whence you cannot see them;
    We made these Satans the companions,
    Of those who have no faith at all.

28. Whenever they commit indecencies,
    They say: "we found our fathers doing these,

---

1. As all men are warned against a similar attack of the Devil, what Adam and
   Eve are wearing before the Fall, is the divine clothing of piety which Satan
   tries to remove.

And it was Allah who enjoined us thus"!
Say: "God does not enjoin indecencies,
Do you to God attribute what,
You know nothing about?"

29.   Say: "What my Lord is advocating
Is justice; thus do turn to Him wherever,
And any time, you will kneel down in prayer,
And call upon Him, dedicating
Unto Him your devotion ever;
Just as He did initiate you,
Back unto Him, shall you go too.

30.   Some He has guided, and some others,
He's justly left to go astray:
This is because they've chosen satans,
Instead of Allah, as their patrons,
Yet they think they're on the Right Way!

31.   Children of Adam! Wear,
The best and cleanest of your raiments,
And the nicest of your adornments,
At every time or place of prayer;
And eat and drink, but do be moderate,
For He does not like the intemperate.

32.   Query: "Who has prohibited
Beautiful clothes and viands healthful,
That Allah for His creatures has provided?"
Say: "They are also for the faithful,
In the life of this world, but purely
Theirs, on the Day of Resurrection;
Thus We explain, for men of knowledge,

Every communication.[1]

33.   Declare: "My Lord's only forbidden,
    Indecencies, open or hidden,
    Committing sins and wrongful violence,
    Serving idols for which no license,
    Has Allah granted, and pronouncing
    Something on God when you know nothing!

34.   A space of time is fixed for every folk,
    And when it's going to expire,
    None is able to put it back,
    Or forward, even for an hour.

35.   Children of Adam, when apostles,
    Of your own people, to you come,
    Reciting unto you My revelations,
    Those that refrain, for fear of Allah, from
    Evil and mend their ways, will have:
    Nothing to fear, nothing to grieve;

36.   But those who will reject and scorn
    Our revelations haughtily shall be
    The inmates of the blazing Fire,
    Wherein they will remain for ever.

37.   Who is more wicked than the one,
    Who forges lies concerning Allah,
    Or treats His Signs[2] as false? Such people
    Receive their destined shares, until
    Our angels come to take their souls,

---

1. Revelation, sign, verse.   2. Revelations.

And ask them: "where are now your idols,
Those whom you used to call upon,
Instead of Allah?" And they answer:
"They've left us in the lurch!" And then
They'll be admitting that they had,
Indeed rejected God.

38.   And He shall say:
"Enter the Fire, and join the nations
Of Jinns and humans who did pass away,
Before you." Then as generations,
Enter it, each will curse the one that passed,
Before it, and when all are joined, the last
Of them will say about the first:[1]
"Those very people, Lord, led us astray,
Give them a double Torment of the Fire."
"Doubled it will be for you all,"[2] He'll answer,
"Although you may not be aware!"

39.   And now the first will say unto the last:
"No better have you been than we; thus taste
The chastisement for which you did your best!"

40.   For those who have denied Our revelations,
And scorned them haughtily, the gates of heaven
Shall never open;
And they shall not enter the Garden,
Until the passing of the camel,

---

1. Or "each succeeding party will say about the preceding one."

2. For two crimes: Their own sins and the sin of setting an evil example for
   succeeding generations.

Through the eye of the needle!
Such is Our retribution
For those guilty of sin;

41.   A patch of Hell will be their couch,
      Which is by fire blanketed;
      Thus do We recompense the wicked.

42.   The heirs of Paradise are those who did
      Believe and led a righteous life; in there,
      They will abide for good; We never burden,
      A soul with more than it can bear;

43.   All hatred in their hearts We take away.
      Rivers shall roll beneath them, and they'll say:
      "Allah be praised for guiding us to this,
      Had it not been for Allah's guidance, never
      Would we have found the Path;
      Our Lord's apostles did come with the Truth."
      Then they shall hear: "This is the Paradise
      Which you possess through your good labour."

44.   And the inmates of Hell are thus addressed
      By the people of Paradise:
      "All that our Lord unto us promised,
      We found to be the truth; now have you, too
      Found your Lord's promise to be true?"
      They'll answer: "Yes!" Then from their midst,
      A crier will say this: "Surely God's curse,
      Will be upon the workers of injustice,

45.   "Who had debarred the Path of God,
      To other people, and did what they could

To make it crooked, and who never
Believed in the Hereafter."

46.   And there shall be a screen between the twain,[1]
But on the heights,[2] shall stand a group of men,
Who recognize each person by his face,
Who tell the candidates of Paradise:
"Peace be upon you!"
-This is before they[3] through it[4] pass,
While loving to go through,

47.   And when they turn their eyes towards
The inmates of the Fire, they petition:
"Our Lord, let us not ever be
Together with such wicked men."

48.   Then the men on the heights shall cry to those
Whom they will, by their tokens recognize:
"It seems that your amassing
Riches and property,
And other things that made you haughty,
Availed you nothing!

49.   "And, by the way, are those,[5] the very
Men whom you swore that Allah's Mercy
Would never touch: 'Enter the Garden where

---

1. The two groups of the blessed and the damned.

2. Some translators have translated this as "the purgatory".

3. I take "they" as the righteous people about to enter Paradise, not the "men on
the heights", as some suggest.

4. The Gate of Paradise.

5. The blessed people about to enter Paradise.

You'll know no fear, no sadness, no despair?"'[1]

50. Later the inmates of the Fire,
Will beg the people of the Garden:
"Do let us have some of your water,
Or little of what has been given
To you by God". They answer: "God has both,
Unto the infidels forbidden,

51. "Those who had taken their religious faith,
Merely for making fun and being gay,
And were beguiled by the life of this world;"
Them, therefore, We'll forget Today, as they
Forgot the meeting of this Day of theirs,
And, of Our revelations, were deniers.

52. And We have now unto them brought a Book,
On Knowledge based, and We have made it well-
Defined, it is a Guidance and a Mercy,
For the believing people.

53. Do they now wait for its fulfillment?[2]
But, on the Day, it is fulfilled,
The people who forgot it in the past,
Will say: "The truth was brought to us indeed
By the apostles of our Lord; are there

---

1. In this and the previous verse, according to one interpretation, the 'men on the heights' are reproaching the damned in a sarcastic manner; in this light the meaning of this verse may become clear: "Those who you swore would never receive God's Mercy were addressed: 'Enter the Garden....'! There are some other interpretations for this verse.

2. The final realization of all the prophecies in the Book.

Now any intercessors who would plead,
On our behalf? Or could we be sent back,
To lead a life other than what we lived"!
Lo, certainly their souls were lost, and all
Their false inventions were of no avail.

54. Your Lord is God the One Who, in six Days,[1]
Created all the heavens and the earth,
And then ascended His Own Throne; He lays
The veil of Night upon the Day; and both
Are made to follow one another always;
The Sun, the Moon, the stars: in subjugation
Are serving His command; what is created,
Is His and under His command; Exalted
Is God the One, the Lord of all creation.

55. Humbly and privately invoke your Lord,
For He dislikes those who commit transgression.

56. And do not ever spread corruption,
On earth after it is set straight,[2]
And call on Him with hope and fear,
For God's Mercy is always near,
To the doers of good and right.

57. It's He Who sends the winds as heralds,
Of the glad tidings of His Mercy,
And when they have brought up the heavy clouds,
We drive them to dead lands, and let them be
Raining thereon, and with it We bring forth,
All kinds of fruits; thus from the state of death,

---

1. Or "periods".   2. Well ordered by God.

We raise to life; perchance, you meditate!

58.   By the leave of its Lord, the good soil will
        Produce abundance of its fruit and plant,
        And the soil which is bad and sterile,
        Puts out things poor and scant;
        Thus We explain Our signs and numerate
        Them for the people who appreciate.[1]

59.   Noah We sent to his own people,
        And he said: "O my people, worship God,
        You have no God but Him; indeed I fear,
        For you the torture of a Day of Dread".

60.   But the chiefs of his people cried: "Indeed,
        We see most clearly that you are,
        In obvious error!"

61.   He said: "My people, I am not in error,
        But I am sent forth as a messenger,
        By the Lord of the Worlds,

62.   "My Lord's messages I deliver,
        To you, I am your well-wisher,
        And I, of Allah, know,
        That which you do not know;

63.   "What! Do you wonder that an admonition
        Should come unto you from your Lord,

---

1. The parable extends to both the physical and spiritual worlds: The Guidance
   and Mercy of God descend and fertilize souls hitherto spiritually dead, but
   they evoke no response in some souls which have chosen evil.

Through a man from your midst, and that he should
Warn you all, so that you might guard,
Against all evil, to receive compassion?"

64.   But they rejected him as an impostor;
We finally delivered him together,
With his companions in the Ark, and drowned
Those who denied Our revelations, for
They were indeed a people blind.

65.   And unto 'Aad,[1] We sent their brother, Hood;
He said: "My people, worship God; indeed,
There is no God but He; will you not ever
Restrain yourselves and fear?"[2]

66.   The Pagan chiefs among his people said:
"We see that you are foolishly in error,
And we do think that you're a liar!"

67.   He said: "My people, I am not in error
Foolishly, but I am a messenger,
From the Lord of the Worlds;

68.   "And I do unto you deliver
All the messages of my Lord,
And I'm your most sincere adviser;

69.   "What! Do you wonder that an admonition
Should come unto you from your Lord,
Through a man from your midst, and that he should
Be warning you? Remember that He made

---

1. An ancient people of Arabia.   2. Or "be godfearing".

You heirs of Noah's people, and He gave you
A stature far greater than any nation,
Therefore remember Allah's every favour,
That you may prosper."

70. They answered: "Have you come to make us
Worship Allah alone, and give up all
The gods our fathers used to worship?
Well then, let what you threaten us with, fall
On us, if you are truthful."

71. He said: "You have incurred the curse,
And wrath of God already; and,
You now dispute with me about,
Some names you and your fathers coined,
For which no sanction came from Allah?!
Thus you just wait; I too,
Will wait along with you!"

72. Finally We, through Our Own Mercy,
Delivered him and all his company,
And We cut off the roots of those,
Who had taken our Signs[1] as lies;
Certainly they were not believers.

73. And to Thamood,[2] We sent their brother, Saalih;
He said: "My people worship Allah,
There is no deity but He; and now,
From your own Lord, has come to you,
A most clear proof: This she-camel of Allah,
Will be for you a Sign; so, leave her

---

1. Or "revelations".   2. Some ancient people of North Arabia.

To graze at will in Allah's land,
And do not touch her with an evil hand,
Lest a chastisement full of woes,
Arrest you in its claws!

74. "And do remember that He made you heirs,
After the 'Aad, and let you settle in
The land, to set up mansions on the plains,
And hew out houses in the mountains;
Therefore, remember Allah's favours,
And do not roam the earth to spread corruption."

75. But the chiefs of his tribe were full of pride,
And thus addressed the faithful from amongst,
Those they oppressed: "Do you believe in earnest,
That Saalih has been sent forth by his Lord?"
They answered: "surely we have faith
In the Message he has been sent with."

76. The arrogant derided: "But we don't
Believe in what you have believed in!"

77. Later on they did kill the she-camel,
And so they did insolently rebel
Against their Lord's command, and did thus urge:
"O Saalih, do bring down your threatened scourge,
If you happen to be a true apostle!"

78. Consequently an earthquake shocking,
Did overtake them, and the morning,
Found them all lying prostrate, lifeless,
Each in his dwelling!

79. And then he turned away from them lamenting:
    "O people mine, indeed I did convey,
    The Message of my Lord to you; I gave
    You good advice, but you did have no love
    For counsellors who show the way!"

80. And do remember Lot who warned his people:
    "What! You're committing an abomination,
    Never, before you, practiced by the people,
    Of any nation?!

81. "You gratify your lusts with men,
    Instead of women! Lo, you've gone beyond
    Every limit and bound."

82. The only answer by these people was to shout:
    "Let us evict them from our town; out, out!
    These are the gentlemen who mean
    To stay most chastely clean!"

83. At last We rescued him together,
    With all the people to him bound,
    Except his wife, who was of those,
    Who did get stuck behind.

84. We then some Rain[1] upon them rained!
    Behold! what was the end,

---

1. In sura 11, verse 82 and sura 15 verses 73-74, the shower is expressly stated
   to have been "of stones", and that there was a "terrible blast" in addition to
   the shower of stones.

Of those who grossly sinned!

85. And to the folks of Midian,
We sent Shuaib, one of their brethren,
He said: "My people, worship God the One,
You have no deity but Him alone,
And now clear proof, from your own Lord,
Has to you come: thus you should give
Full measures and just weights, and not defraud,
Others out of their rights,
Nor spread corruption on the earth,
After it has been set aright,
This is better for you, if you have Faith;

86. "And do not lie in wait in every path,
Seeking to threaten those who do have faith,
And to debar them from the Path of Allah,
And do not seek to make it crooked;
Remember when you were a few in number,
And He did multiply you; and consider
The fate of those who were corrupt and wicked;

87. "Now if there is a group among you who,
Believes in that with which I have been sent,
And still another group who disbelieves it,
Then let us keep on being patient,
Until Allah decides between us,
For He's the Best to issue Judgment."

88. But the chiefs of his tribe, puffed up with pride,
Said: "O Shuaib, come back unto our fold,
Or We will surely drive you out from this,
City of ours, with all your faithful horde!"

He said: "Though we already have abhorred?!"[1]

89. "We would be forging lies against our Lord,
     If we returned to your religion after,
     God has from it delivered us, nor could we
     Be going back to it by any manner,
     Unless Allah, Our Lord, so wills: our Lord's
     Knowledge embraces everything, and we,
     Have put our trust in God. 'Our Lord, do judge,
     With truth between us and our people; surely
     You are the Best and Most Benevolent Judge.'"

90. But the infidel leaders of his tribe,
     Threatened: "You folks, if you subscribe
     To Shuaib's way, you'll surely end in
     Losses and ruin!"

91. Consequently an earthquake shocking,
     Did overtake them, and the morning,
     Found them all lying prostrate, lifeless,
     Each in his dwelling;

92. The men who called Shuaib a liar perished,
     As if therein they never flourished,
     The men who called Shuaib a liar; suffered
     The greatest loss, and vanished.

93. Therefore, he from them turned away,
     Sighing: "O people mine, I did convey,
     My Lord's messages unto you, and gave
     You good advice; and how could I now grieve

---

1. "Though we already abhor your creed!"

For people who did not believe!"

94. Each time We sent a prophet to a town,[1]
We did afflict its people with distress,
And hardship that they might show humbleness,

95. And then We substituted welfare,
In place of their adversity,
But when they gained prosperity,
They cheered: "Our fathers also had,
Their share of fortune and calamity!"[2]
And thus Our vengeance them afflicted,
When they had least expected.

96. Now if the people of those towns,
Had but believed and kept from evil,
We would have showered them with the boons
Of heaven and the earth; but then, their will,
Was to deny the Truth, and hence,
As a result of their own actions,
We took them with Our vengeance.

97. Lo! Were the people of the towns secure,
That We would not be smiting them by night,
As they were lying down.

98. Or could the people of the towns be sure,
That We would smite them not, in broad daylight,
When they were having fun?

---

1. Community, habitation, city.

2. They meant "these changes have nothing to do with God, the coming of
prophets or 'our own' behaviour and beliefs!"

99. Perhaps they felt secure,
From Allah's machination?!
But none may feel secure,
From Allah's secret plans except
Those doomed to ruination.

100. Has it not still become most plain,
To generations who the earth inherit,
After their former occupants:
That, if We please We'll surely hit,
Them also with Our scourge, and seal
Their minds so that they could not hear it.[1]

101. Such were the stories of the towns,
We have to you related:
Unto them all, with clearest Signs,
Came their apostles, but they did
Have no faith in what they had once rejected;
Thus Allah seals the minds of disbelievers;

102. In most of them, for any covenant,
We found no faithfulness; evil-doers
Were most of them and disobedient.

103. Moses We raised then, after them, and sent
Him, with Our Signs to Pharaoh and his chiefs,
But they reviled them; thus, behold the fate,
Of practisers of mischiefs!

104. "O Pharaoh", Moses said, "I am

---

1. That is: "They have reached a point when they absolutely do not listen to any advice".

A most certain apostle from,
The Lord of all the Worlds,

105. "Upon me it's incumbent that I never,
Say aught concerning Allah but the Truth,
Indeed I bring to you undoubted Signs,
From your own Lord; thus let the Sons
Of Israel with me depart."

106. He said: "If you have brought some Signs,
And you do speak the truth,
Then show them forth."

107. So he threw down his rod, and lo!
It was a serpent, on the go!

108. Then he drew out his hand, and in the sight,
Of all beholders, it was shining bright!

109. At this the chiefs of Pharaoh's people cried:
"A skilled magician is this man indeed!

110. "His plan it is to drive you out,
Of your own land!
What do you, therefore, recommend?"

111. The others said: "Let's keep them in suspense,
Him and His brother, then let's send,
Men to the cities to collect,

112. "And bring up to your presence,
All sorcerers select."

113.   And so the sorcerers to Pharaoh came,
        And said: "Are we to handsomely avail
        Ourselves of your reward, if we prevail?"

114.   He answered: "Yes, and you shall certainly
        Be some of courtesans most near to me!"

115.   They then said: "O you Moses, do you cast,
        Or do you want us to be throwers first?"

116.   He said: "Do cast!" And when they threw their wiles,
        They did bewitch the people's eyes,
        And really struck into them panic,
        With a fantastic show of magic.

117.   We now to Moses spake:
        "Throw down your rod!" And lo!
        It presently did swallow,
        All their devices fake!

118.   The Truth was thus established,
        And what they faked, just vanished;

119.   They were, in this affair, thus vanquished,
        And suffered much humiliation;

120.   And the magicians fell upon their knees,
        In adoration;

121.   They cried: "We now believe in
        The Lord of the Creation,

122.   "The Lord of Moses and of Aaron."

123.   Pharaoh now yelled: "what! you believe in him
    Before I've given you permission?
    This is indeed a plot you have contrived,
    In order to drive out a settled nation,
    From their own habitation,[1]
    But soon I'll let you know enough:

124.   "I'll have your hands and feet cut off,
    On the alternate sides, and then will I,
    All of you crucify!"

125.   They said: "We'll then be only,
    Back to our Lord more quickly;

126.   "But you intend to wreak upon us vengeance
    Only because we have believed the Signs
    Of our own Lord, when they were to us shown;
    O Lord of ours, do grant us patience,
    And let us die as *Muslims*."[2]

127.   And then the chiefs of Pharaoh's nation,
    Enquired: "will you leave Moses and his folk,
    At liberty to spread corruption,
    Throughout the land, and to forsake
    You and your gods?" He said: "Let's slaughter,
    Every young man of them and spare the daughters,
    Over them we have domination.

128.   Moses advised his people: "Let's implore
    God for assistance and show fortitude;

---

1. Or "to overthrow the existing order".

2. Believers in submission to God Almighty.

Surely the earth is God's and He will give it,
To whom He chooses from the multitude
Of His own creatures;[1] and the happy end,
Belongs to those who have restrained.[2]

129. They said: "we were oppressed before you came,
And since you've come, our plight's the same."
He said: "Perhaps your Lord will ruin,
Your enemy and make you rulers in
The land; but He will certainly observe,
How you behave."

130. We had afflicted Pharaoh's people
With droughts and shortages of crops,
That they might heed the admonition.

131. And yet, whenever some good things befell them,
They claimed: "We have deserved this", but when evil
Afflicted them, they did ascribe it to,
The ill omens of Moses and his people;
In fact their evil omens were ordained,
By God, but most of them were never able
To comprehend.

132. They said: "Regardless of the type of signs,[3]
You bring to us to charm and to deceive,
Never will we in you believe!

133. And so We plagued them with the evil flood,[4]

1. Or "His servants."

2. The god-fearing, the righteous, those who guard against evil.

3. Or "Miracles".

4. Or "storm or typhoon" accompanied by hailstones, an epidemic, etc.

Followed by locusts, insects,[1] frogs and Blood:[2]
Signs lucid, self-explained; yet they maintained,
Their arrogance: what sinful people bold!

134.   Of course each time a plague befell them,
They begged: "O Moses, pray unto your Lord,
On our behalf in virtue of His promise,
Unto you; if you lift from us the Menace,
We will believe in you and send the Children
Of Israel with you away."

135.   But when We did remove the evil burden,[3]
From them, according to a term that they,
Had to fulfill: Behold!
They broke their word!

136.   Therefore Our vengeance came on them, and We
Did drown them in the sea:
Our Signs they had denied as sham,
And had not been forewarned by them!

137.   And then, a people who had been oppressed,
We made inheritors of both the eastern,
And western portions of a land We blessed;
The promise of your Lord unto the Children
Of Israel was thus fulfilled, because
They had endured with fortitude; We then
Razed to the ground: What Pharaoh and his people
Had built to raise up to the heaven!

---

1. The Arabic word stands for small insects like louse, small fly, mosquito, weevil and the like.

2. The water turning to blood.   3. The plague.

138. We took the Israelites across the sea,
And while they were upon their journey,
They came across a people zealously
Devoted to their idols; so they pressed:
"Do make for us a god, O Moses, just
Like unto gods these people have!"
He said: "Most foolishly you folks behave!

139. "The cult these people follow is in ruin,
And everything they do is false and vain;"

140. He further said: "This is most odd!
Should I be seeking for you any god,
Other than Allah, Who has blessed and held
You far above the nations of the world?"

141. Behold, We rescued you from Pharaoh's people,
Who had subjected you to torments dreadful,
And used to slay your sons and spare your women;
And certainly in this there was a trial,
From your own Lord, most fateful.

142. We promised Moses that We would be meeting
Him after thirty nights, and added ten,
More nights, bringing it up to forty nights;
Moses had charged his brother Aaron:
"Deputize me among my nation,
Do what is right, and never follow
The path of those who spread corruption."

143. When Moses came at the appointed time,
And when his Lord addressed him, He implored:
"My Lord, reveal Yourself to me, I like

To look at You." He said: "You can't afford
To set your eyes upon me, but you may,
Look at the mountain yonder, if it stay
Firm on its base, then you shall see me soon!"
And then His Lord Himself did manifest,
To the mountain and crushed it to fine dust,
And Moses fell down in a swoon!
When he came to, he said: "Glory to You,
I turn to You,[1] and I will be the first,
Of those who do believe in You."

144.   He said: "O Moses, you I've chosen,
Of all mankind and honoured with My Own
Messages and my Words, thus do take hold,
Of what I gave you and made known,
And do remain a grateful servant."

145.   And We inscribed for him upon the Tablets,
Admonition of every kind and explanation
Of everything, and said to him: "Hold fast
To these, and do enjoin your nation,
To follow by the best in these instructions;
I shall be showing you the habitations,
Of those who were the wickedest;"

146.   And, from My revelations, I will turn
Away the arrogant who do behave
Unjustly on the earth: even if they see,
All kinds of Signs, they won't in them believe,
And if they see the direct path of guidance,
They won't adopt it as a path, but when

---

1. "In repentance."

251

They see a crooked way, they, there and then,
Take it as theirs; this is the consequence
Of their rejection of Our Signs,
And disregarding them in every sense.

147.   Totally vain shall be the doings,
Of people who reject Our signs,
And the Meeting of the Hereafter.
Do they expect to be rewarded aught
Except as they have wrought?

148.   In Moses' absence did his folk,
Out of their jewels, made a calf,
A ruddy body with a lowing rough!
Lo! Did they not see that it neither spoke
With them, nor could they ever it invoke,
To guide them in the way? And yet the throng
Took it for worship, and did awful wrong;

149.   Later when they regretted and found out
That they had erred most surely, they confessed:
"Unless our Lord redeems us with His Mercy,
And Pardons us, we'll certainly be lost".

150.   When Moses, full of wrath and grievance,
Came back unto his people, he had cried:
"Most evil was your doing in my absence!
Could you not wait with patience,
For the Commandment of your Lord?"[1]

---

1. Or "Did you make haste to bring on the Judgment of your Lord?"

And he threw down the tablets,[1] and took hold
Of the head of his brother;
While being dragged, he cried: "Son of my mother,
Indeed these people overpowered me,
They almost killed me, therefore do not make
My enemies over me happy,
And count me not among the throng
Who have committed wrong!"

151. He prayed: "O Lord!
Forgive me and forgive my brother,
And let us into Your Compassion enter,
For You're the Most Merciful ever."

152. Certainly, those who made the calf a god,
Incurred the wrath of their own Lord and shame
In the life of this world; thus We requite
People who make their faith a sham.

153. But those who have committed sins
And have indeed repented later,
And kept their faith, will find your Lord,
Forgiving, Merciful, thereafter.

154. Moses took up the Tablets,
After his anger was alloyed:
Guidance and Mercy was inscribed on them,
For those who reverence and fear their Lord.

---

1. Or "put them down angrily"; we are not told that the Tablets were "broken"!
On this point and on the point that Aaron actually helped with the making
of the Calf, the Holy Quran differs from the Old Testament: no man of God
could descend so low as to help with idolatry!

155.   Moses then chose, out of his people,
       Seventy men to come unto Our meeting,
       And when the earth was shaking under them,
       He prayed: "My Lord, if You were willing,
       You could have long ago destroyed them,
       Along with me; would You now be destroying
       Us all for what some fools among us did?
       You only set that test to lead astray,
       Whome'er you will, and to give guidance,
       To whom You please; You are our Guardian only,
       Do forgive us and bless us with Your Mercy:
       You, Forgiver, Par Excellence;

156.   "And do for us ordain
       What is good in this world,
       And in the coming world,
       Indeed we turn to You alone."
       He said: "My retribution shall
       Fall on the ones I will,
       But My Mercy encompasses all things,
       And I will specially ordain it,
       For those who do refrain from sins,
       Who give in charity and alms,
       And are believers in Our Signs."

157.   The followers of the Apostle,
       The gentile[1] Prophet, who is mentioned,
       In their own Torah and Evangel-
       He who enjoins on them what's just,
       And does forbid them to do evil,
       Who makes lawful all wholesome things,

---

1. Original Arabic "Ummi".

And does prohibit all that's foul,
Who has released them from their burdens,
And things imposed on them like shackle-
And those who have in him believed,
And honoured him and gave him aid,
And have the Light, sent with him, followed,
All these people will certainly succeed.[1]

158.   Say: "O Mankind, I am a Messenger,
To all of you from God the One, to Whom
Belongs the Kingdom of the heavens
And of the earth, there is no God but Him,
And it is He Who life and death ordains;
Therefore believe in God and His apostle,
The gentile Prophet, who believes in God
And His commandments. Follow him,
So that you may be rightly guided."

159.   Of the people of Moses were, of course,
Some men who preached the Truth, and in its light,
Acted aright.

160.   Now We divided them into twelve Tribes,
Each a distinct community, and when,
His thirsty people asked for water, We
Directed Moses through Our inspiration:
"Do strike that rock with your own rod",
And, thereupon, twelve springs did flood,
Out of it, thus, unto each Tribe,
It became known where to imbibe;
We further shaded them with clouds,

---

1. Or "attain salvation."

And sent to them *manna* and quails:
"Eat of the pure and clean provision,
We have unto you given";
They did no harm to Us by any deed,
But their own souls they harmed indeed.

161.   Behold, they had been told: "Enter this town,
And as you please, eat of its plenty,
But do go through the gate with amity,
Humbly repeating "Hittatoun";[1]
We will forgive your every sin,
And, on the pious, pour Our bounty.

162.   But the transgressors of them changed the word,
Spoken to them, so We upon them sent
A pestilence from heavens,
For their infringement.

163.   Ask them about the city,[2]
Which stood close by the sea,
Whose people broke the Sabbath:
On the days of their Sabbath, all the fish,
Appeared before them in abundance,
And on week-days did they just vanish!
Thus, for their acts of disobedience,
Them did We test and punish.

164.   Also behold! A party of them once,
Objected to some others, saying: "why
Do you keep preaching to some people whom,

---

1. This means: "Forgiveness, Forgiveness", "Forgive us" and the like.
2. Eylat, on the Red Sea.

Allah will soon destroy or crucify
Most sternly?" They replied: "we must acquit
Ourselves before your Lord, and hope they may
Their evil doings quit."

165. Therefore, when they forgot the warnings,
They had been given, We delivered,
Those who'd forbidden evil, and We seized
The evil-doers with a torment dreaded,
For it was surely evil what they did,

166. Thus when they, in their insolence,
All prohibitions had transgressed,
We said to them: "Be apes,
Despised, disgraced!"

167. And then, behold, your Lord also decreed
That He, until the Day of Resurrection,
Shall be raising people against them to
Oppress them cruelly; the retribution
Of your Lord is most swift, but certainly
He is Forgiving, Full of Mercy.

168. We have dispersed them on the earth,
In multitudes; among them some,
Were righteous people and the others,
Were not so, and We tested them,
With blessings and misfortunes,
So that they might desist from sins.

169. And then another generation,
Succeeded them who did inherit,
The Book, but, in this nether world,

They grabbed the vanities of it!
They blithely say:
"We'll be forgiven anyway!"
Thus, they shall always do the same,
If worldly gains should come their way.
Did they not ever make a solemn pledge,
Writ in the Book, of which they have good knowledge,
To tell of Allah nothing but the Truth?
Surely the Home of the Hereafter is,
Far better for the righteous, self-restrainers;
Do you not understand the aftermath!

170. But We shall never let go waste,
      The prize for people who hold fast
      Unto the Book, and keep up prayers,
      They are surely the good-doers.

171. Behold! We raised the Mount above their heads,
      As if it had been an umbrella-
      They feared that it was falling down on them-
      And said: "Take hold, with strength and valour,
      Of what we've given you, and bear in mind,
      What is therein, perchance you do fear Allah."

172. Behold! Your Lord did summon all the children
      Of Adam's offspring to be bearing witness,
      Upon their souls by asking: "Am I not
      Your Lord?" They all said: "Yes, we do bear witness;"
      Lest, on the Day of Resurrection,
      You claim: "we weren't aware of this;"

173. Or say: "It was our ancient fathers
      Who were indeed idolaters,

And we only followed their creed;
Will You destroy us for the deed
Of some falsehood-inventors?!"

174. Thus do We make Our revelations plain,
So that they might to the right path return.

175. And tell them of the man[1] to whom We sent
Our revelations, but he turned away
From them, and therefore Satan quickly went
After him, and he badly was astray;

176. If We had willed, We would have him exalted
Therewith, but he did cling unto the ground,
And chased his lusts; the likeness of a dog:
He's lolling out his tongue, whether you hound,
Him, or pay no attention to him! That's
The likeness of the people who reject
Our Signs; rehearse to them this parable,
Perhaps they will reflect.

177. Terrible is the tale of those,
Who did reject Our Signs;
They were only unjust,
To their own souls.

---

1. This is most probably a contemporary figure of the time, but his name is not
mentioned: a practice followed, almost always, by the Holy Quran and the
Traditions in such cases. The parable is, however, most clearly about 'the
knowledgeable bad type' who, despite their knowledge of Revelations
succumb to temptations of avarice, personal lusts and carnal desires, as dogs
who look for nothing but the means of filling up their bellies and gratifying
their animal lusts.

178.　The one whom Allah guides, is rightly guided,
　　　Whom He deprives of this, is surely lost.

179.　Multitudes of the Jinn and of the men
　　　We have brought forth for Hell, for certain!
　　　For they have minds with which they don't
　　　Discern a thing, and they have eyes,
　　　With which they do not see, and ears,
　　　With which they do not hear; indeed,
　　　They are like cattle, nay, less guided!
　　　Such are the heedless humans.

180.　Allah has Names, Most Excellent,
　　　Call upon Him therewith, and shun
　　　The people who pervert His Names;
　　　For what they do, they'll be requited soon.

181.　Among Our creatures, there are those,
　　　Who preach the Truth, and in its light,
　　　e'er act aright.

182.　As for the people who reject
　　　Our revelation, We will lead them
　　　To ruin, step by step, from whence
　　　They cannot fathom;

183.　Respite I grant them, but,
　　　Effective is My stratagem!

184.　Do they never reflect on things?
　　　By no means is their friend,[1]

---

1. Or "compatriot", "companion": The Holy Prophet.

Unsound of mind;
He's just a giver of plain warnings.

185.   Do they not ever ponder on
The Kingdom of the heavens and the earth,
And everything in God's creation,
Or on the fact that their own Hour,
May well be drawing near?
Lo! After this, in what *hadeeth*,[1]
Will they have faith?!

186.   Whomever Allah leaves in error,
No one could guide, for He abandons
Them, so that they may blindly wallow
In their own sins.

187.   They question you about the Hour of Doom:
When will it come?
Say: "None knows it except my Lord, and only,
He will disclose it at the proper time;
Fatefully heavy it will weigh upon
The heavens and the earth; all of a sudden,
Will it unto you come;"
They question you as if you were,
The person, of it, most aware!
Tell them: "Its knowledge is with God alone,
Though this, to most men, is not known."

188.   Say: "over any good or harm,
Even for my own self, no power,
Do I have, save by Allah's will;

---

1. Message, announcement, news, tradition, revelation.

Surely, had I the knowledge of
What is hidden, I would have gained
Abundant good, and nothing grave
Could touch me! Nay, I am a Warner,
Only, and a good-tidings bringer,
To people who believe.

189.   Allah it was Who did create you from,
A single being, and he made his mate
Of the same kind, in order that he may
To her incline. So when they copulate,
She will be bearing first a burden mild,
Carried about with ease, but as the load
Gets heavy, both will pray to God, their Lord:
"We're thankful folks, grant us a goodly child."

190.   Yet when He does grant them a goodly child,
They set up partners to Him in return
For what He gave them; but exalted is,
God far above the idols they retain.

191.   Odd is indeed their worship of some gods,
Who cannot cause any creations,
And are themselves some fabrications,

192.   They could never give help to others,
Nothing are they but helpless idols!

193.   If you invite these folks[1] to the right way,
You will they not obey,
So it will be for you no different,

---

1. The Pagans or their human idols.

Whether you call them or keep silent!

194. Verily those whom you invoke,
Instead of God, are creatures like,
Any of you, thus let them hear your prayer,
And, if you're truthful, they should answer!

195. Do they have legs with which to walk,
Do they have hands with which to hold,
Do they have eyes, so they behold,
Do they have ears, so they could hark?
Say: "call your partner-gods; then make
Against me, every plot or trick:
Give me no break!

196. "Certainly my Protector's God the One,
Who has sent down this Book,
And He befriends and guards
The righteous folk;

197. "And those to whom you pray,
Instead of Him, could in no way,
Be helping you; those idols
Can't even help themselves!"

198. And if you call them unto the right way,
They won't be hearing what you say!
They seem to be towards you looking,
But they do not behold a thing!

199. Adopt the way of pardon and forbearance,
Enjoin what's good and right, and turn away
From men of ignorance;

200. And if certain suggestions,
Inspired by Satan tempt your soul,
Do seek refuge in God, for He's,
The Hearer who Knows all.

201. When Satan tempts the people who restrain,
They only should remember God, and lo!
They'll be seers, again.

202. But their own brethren[1] drag them into error,
They are never relaxing their endeavour.

203. When you do not bring them a revelation,[2]
They prattle: "Why, could you not patch up *one*?!"[3]
Tell them: "I only follow what my Lord
Sends down to me by Inspiration:
Lights of insights from your own Lord,
Guidance and Mercy for believers;

204. When Al-Quran is thus being rehearsed,
Listen to it in peace and silence,
Perhaps you'll be with Mercy blessed;

205. And do remember your own Lord,
Deep in your soul with humbleness,
And reverence, mornings and evenings,
Let not your voice be loud in prayings,

---

1. Their misguided kinsmen who believe in false idols as explained in verse 198
and verses before this; it's only the remembrance of God that protects the
righteous from Satan's temptations.

2. Arabic original is ayat meaning: verse, revelation, sign and miracle.

3. One new verse!

And never be amongst the heedless.

206.   Surely the Nearest to your Lord,
Are not too haughty to adore Him,
They celebrate His praise indeed,
And fall upon their knees before Him.

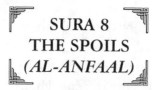

SURA 8
THE SPOILS
(AL-ANFAAL)

In the Name of God, the Beneficent, the Merciful

1.   They question you about the spoils of battle.[1]
        Answer: "The spoils shall be at the disposal
        Of God and His Apostle;
        Thus be godfearing, and set all relation,
        Aright among yourselves,
        And do obey Allah and His Apostle,
        If you are true believers.

2.   For, true believers are indeed the people,
        Whose hearts are filled with awe and veneration,
        When God the One[2] is mentioned,
        Whose faith is further strengthened,
        When a verse of His revelation,
        Is unto them rehearsed,
        Who only in their Lord, put all their trust,

3.   Who steadfastly keep up their prayers, and spend[3]
        Of what we have for them provisioned.

4.   Such are the truly faithful:
        For them there shall be, with their Lord,
        Exalted ranks of dignity, as well
        As Pardon and provisions noble.

---

1. The spoils of the Battle of Badr, A.D. 624.

2. Allah.

3. "In the cause of God".

266

5.   Remember when your Lord had willed
     That you should leave your home to struggle
     For truth, surely reluctant were some parties,
     Among the faithful.

6.   After it had become most clear, they still
     Argued with you about the truth,[1]
     They looked like people being driven,
     With open eyes, to certain death!

7.   Behold! Allah had promised you that one,
     Of the two hosts, would fall to you, and you
     Wanted to fight the one unarmed;[2] Allah
     Wanted to show the option proper[3] through
     His words, and to root out the disbelievers,

8.   That He may manifest the Truth and show
     The falsehood of the false, although
     It was distasteful to the sinners!

9.   Behold! In answer to your supplication
     For help, your Lord, proclaimed: "Unto your aid,
     I send a thousand angels in succession."

---

1. The right course.

2. This a Quranic report of discussions among Muslims before they went out of
   Medina to fight. It was decided not to fall upon the unarmed Quraish caravan
   returning from Syria to Mecca that promised much booty, but to attack the
   well-armed Quraish army of 1,000 men coming from Mecca, by the poorly-
   equipped Muslim force of some 300 men; by God's help they routed the
   stronger force of the Pagans. Therefore, comments by some 'analysts' that
   Mohammad (pbuh) was planning to attack the caravan for booty, is biased
   rubbish.

3. Or "to establish the Truth."

10.   Allah gave it[1] purely as a good news,
    And that your hearts might be at ease,
    For victory shall come from Allah only,
    Certainly God's Most-Powerful, All-Wise.

11.   Behold! He covered you with godly calm,
    As a protection, and did, from the sky
    Send down water on you to purify
    you and to take away the Satan's grime
    From you, to reassure your hearts thereby,
    And to strengthen your foothold.

12.   Behold! your Lord inspired the angels:
    "I am with you: thus you make steadfast
    The faithful; terror I shall cast,
    Into the hearts of the infidels;
    Then smite them hard upon the napes,
    And strike off all their finger-tips!"

13.   They suffered for their active opposition,
    To God and His Apostle; for the people,
    Who act against Allah and His Apostle,
    Grievous shall be God's retribution.

14.   Thus will they hear: "Have a taste of it now;
    The chastisement for disbelievers, though,
    Shall be the Fire."

15.   O You believers! When you do encounter,
    Disbelievers in marshalled battle order,
    Never turn back to run away;

---

1. Or "made this promise".

16.   Whoever turns his back upon such day,
    Unless it be for some tactical reason,
    Or to regroup with his own squadron,
    He shall indeed incur the wrath of Allah,
    And his abode shall be Gehenna;
    That is an evil destination!

17.   It was not you, but God, who slew them,
    And when you threw, it was not you who threw,
    God was the One who threw; yea, it was rather,
    A gracious test He put the faithful through,
    God's the All-Hearing Knower.

18.   Thus it is; and it's also God who weakens,
    The unbelievers' clever plans.

19.   If you[1] were praying for a victory,
    Ordained,[2] you now did witness one ordained!
    If you desist, it will be for you best,
    But if you were to turn back, you shall find,
    Us there to do the same, and not the least
    Good, will your forces to you be, no matter
    How large their number is, for Allah
    Is surely with the faithful.

20.   O you believers do obey
    Allah and His Apostle,
    You've heard his Message well,

1. The addressees are the Meccan unbelievers.
2. The original Arabic word means: victory, decision and judgment. Before they marched for the fight, the Quraish Pagans held the curtains of the Ka'ba and prayed: "Grant victory to the better of the two parties, the one that is in the right."

Thus from him never turn away.

21.   Be not like those who claim: "We hear",
And give no heed to what they hear!

22.   The vilest creatures in the sight of God,
Are those who never reason, and become,
Like people deaf and dumb.

23.   If God had found in them some good,
He would have surely made them listen;
But as they are, even if He did make
Them hear, they would have, with disdain,
Turned away from it.[1]

24.   O You believers, answer
The call of Allah and His Messenger,
When he does call you to that which will give,
You life, and know for sure,
That God comes in between a man
And his own heart,[2] and that to Him alone,
You'll have to gather.

25.   And guard against the sort of mischief,
Which shall not smite the evil-doer,[3]
Among you in particular,
And know that God's in chastisement Most Tough.

26.   And call to mind when you had been a band,
Petty, and persecuted in the land,

---

1. The truth, the Message.   2. Desires, affections.

3. Or "the unjust, the transgressors".

Fearful of being cast off by the mob;
But then He gave you refuge and He strengthened
You with His help, and gave you for provision,
Good and pure things, so that you may
Show some appreciation.

27.   O You who have believed, never betray,
The trust of God and His Apostle, neither
Be knowingly unfaithful to the trusts,
Under your power.

28.   Do know that your possessions and your children,
Are but a trial and temptation,
And that it's only God with Whom you find,
Rewards of greatest estimation.

29.   O You believers, if you do fear God,
He'll bless you with salvation,
He'll cleanse you of your sins,
And give you His Forgiveness,
God is certainly in possession
Of bounties endless.

30.   Remember how the unbelievers,
Plotted against you,[1] and attempted
To capture you or have you killed,
Or banish you! They always plotted,
But Allah too had His own scheme:
God's the Plotter Supreme!

31.   And when Our revelations were to them

---

1. The Holy Prophet.

Rehearsed, they cried: "we have heard them before,
And if we wished we could invent the like;
Nothing are they but tales of yore!"

32.   Behold! They used to cry: "O Allah, if
This be the truth from you indeed, then rain
Upon us showers of stones from heaven,
Or smite us with some grave affliction!"

33.   But Allah was not to chastise them, whilst
You[1] had been living in their midst,
Neither would Allah punish men,
If they were seeking pardon.

34.   Now do they not deserve to be chastised
By Allah, when they bar the very,
Way to the Sacred Mosque? They have no right
To be its guardians; nay, no men could be
Its guardians but the truly righteous,
Although most of them do not know this.

35.   Their praying at the House[2] was only:
To whistle and to clap their hands;
"Now taste the chastisement for what,
Your faithlessness demands!"

36.   The unbelievers spend their wealth in blocking
The path of God, and will they further spend;
But their attempts shall turn into remorse
For them, and they'll be losers in the end;
The disbelievers shall once more assemble,

---

1. The Holy Prophet.   2. Ka'ba.

To be driven to Hell;

37.   Then God will separate the wicked from,
The good and just; and pile the wicked on,
Top of each other in one heap, and cast,
The whole into Gehenna; surely fallen
Shall they be and for ever lost.

38.   Tell those who disbelieve: if they desist,
They'll be forgiven for their past,
But if they will persist, let them reflect,
Upon some former folks whose doom
Is a determined fact.

39.   Fight against them then till there be no room,
For persecution, and religion be
For Allah unreservedly,
But if they cease, then surely God sees through
Everything they may do.

40.   But if they turn their backs and pay no heed,
Then you should know that God the One,
Is your Patron indeed:
What an excellent Parton,
And what a splendid Helper!

41.   And know that out of spoils of war you gather,
A fifth must be assigned to Allah
And His Apostle: for his kith and kin,
For the orphans, the needy and the traveller,
On foot and needful, if you do believe in
God, and in What We sent down to Our servant,
On that day of victory, when the two

Hosts met in combat: God's Omnipotent.

42.   Behold! You had been on the nearer side,
        Of the vale, but they were encamped upon
        The farthest side, meanwhile the caravan,
        Was on the lower ground. If you had made
        A prior pledge for this,[1] you would indeed
        Have not engaged there, but then Allah willed
        To execute the plan He had ordained,
        Whereby the destined people died, and those
        Destined to live were saved;
        Verily God's the Hearing One Who Knows.

43.   Behold! God showed them to you in your dream,[2]
        As small and few, if He had to you shown,
        Them as a greater force, you[3] would have been
        Disheartened, and discord would have been sown
        Among your ranks but Allah from such doubts,
        Did save you; for He Knows all secret thoughts.

44.   And when you met, He made them, in your eyes,
        Look a small band, and made you, in their eyes,
        Seem less than what you were, so that He might
        Accomplish something that He had ordained:
        Every affair is unto God returned.

45.   Believers, when you face a hostile force,
        Be steadfast and remember God most often,
        And triumph you'll perhaps embrace.

---

1. To fight at this battlefield.   2. The Holy Prophet's dream.
3. You believers.

46.   Obey Allah and His Apostle,
    And never with each other quarrel,
    For then you shall lose heart,
    And all your power shall depart;
    And steadfastly preserve, for God
    Is with the steadfast, patient people.

47.   And do not be like those who marched,
    Out of their homes in exultation,
    And made a public showing off,
    And who actively cause obstruction,
    Upon the path of God; but God
    Encompasses their every action.

48.   Recall that Satan made their deeds
    Adorned to them, and said: "No one
    May conquer you to day, and I
    Will be at hand to help", but when,
    The two parties had come within
    Each other's sight, he turned upon
    His heels and said: "I'm surely clear
    Of you because I do see certain,
    Things you do not see, and I surely fear
    Allah, for Allah's retribution,
    Is most severe!"

49.   Remember that the hypocrites,
    And people of malicious hearts,
    Often opined:
    "Their Faith has made them blind!"
    But nay, if one on God relies,
    He'll find that God's Mighty and Wise.

50.   If only you could see the angels when
        They seized the souls of disbelievers:
        They smote them on their faces and their rears,
        And said: "soon will you taste the ire
        Of the chastisement of the Blazing Fire!"

51.   "This is the consequence of what
        Your hands have sent forth in the past,
        For God is to His creatures,
        Not in the least unjust."

52.   Just like the Pharaoh's people,
        And those before them: They denied
        God's revelations, and thus Allah,
        For their own sins, had them destroyed;
        For God's All-Strong, and Stern
        In retribution.

53.   This is because Allah will ne'er withdraw,
        The grace He has bestowed on any nation,
        Unless they change what's in their souls;
        Hearing is He, Full of Cognition.

54.   Just like the Pharaoh's people,
        And those before them: They denied
        The revelations of their Lord,
        So, for their sins, He had them all destroyed;
        We surely drowned the Pharaoh's people,
        They were wicked indeed.

55.   The vilest creatures in the sight of God,
        Are the thankless rejecters of the Truth,
        Who have never believed,

56. Those you made treaties with, and who are ever
    Breaking their league, and have no fear of Allah.

57. Thus if you capture them in battle,
    Discriminate between them and the men,
    Who follow them, so that the others,
    May take a lesson.

58. If you're suspecting treachery,
    From any group, then throw their treaty,
    Back to them but in a fair manner,
    For God dislikes a treacherous party.

59. Let not the disbelievers hope
    That they could get away with it;
    Nay, they cannot escape.

60. Muster against them all the forces,
    And fighting squadrons[1] you could mobilize,
    To strike terror into the hearts of foes
    Of God and your own enemies, and those
    Besides them, who are not unto you known,
    But whom Allah well knows;
    And whatsoever you expend in aid
    Of Allah's cause, shall be to you repaid
    In full and you shall not be wronged.

61. But if they do to peace incline, you must,
    Also incline to it, and put your trust
    In God, The Hearer and the Knower Best.

---

1. Or "horses".

62. And if deceiving you is their intent,
    God will be for you All-Sufficient;
    It's He Who strengthened you with help indeed,
    And with the people who believed,

63. And it is He Who did unite their hearts:
    Not if you were to give away the whole
    Wealth of the earth, could you unite their hearts,
    But God united them in heart and soul;
    In Might Exalted is He, and All-wise.

64. O Prophet, God and those who follow you,
    Of the faithful, are all-sufficient for you.

65. O you Prophet, rouse the faithful to fight;
    If there are, of you, twenty steadfast men,
    You are to overcome two hundred,
    And if there are, of you, a hundred, then
    You'll rout a thousand unbelievers,
    These people have not any ken.[1]

66. For the present, however, Allah makes,
    Your burden lighter for he is aware
    That you're still weak:[2] Thus as it is, a hundred
    Of your men, steadfast patient, may well dare
    To fight and overcome two hundred,
    And if a thousand of such men are there,
    They shall, by Allah's will, defeat two thousand;

---

1. They don't know what they are fighting for and, hence, have no "morale".

2. At the Battle of Badr, devoted Muslims won through against odds of more
   than three to one.

For God's with those who steadfastly forbear.

67.   It is not fitting for a prophet to
Be seeking captives ere he has
Battled and he has won the day:
Yet you people[1] look for the passing ware,
And the gain of this world, but God desires,
For you the world to come, and Allah is,
The Almighty, the Wise.

68.   Had it not been for an ordainment,
Gone forth from God already, you would have
Incurred a grievous chastisement,
For what you had got hold of.[2]

69.   Therefore, enjoy the good and lawful things,
You gained as spoils in action,
And be godfearing, for He is indeed,
Oft-Forgiving, Full of Compassion.

70.   O Prophet, say to those you've taken captive:
"If Allah finds some goodness in your hearts,
He'll give you something far, far better
Than what from you departs,[3]
And bless you with His Pardon; surely
God's Oft-Forgiving, Full of Mercy."

71.   But if they venture to betray you,
Know that they did show treachery,

---

1. The Prophet's followers

2. Taking captives for later ransom and not fight on to the end.

3. Or "is taken away from you".

To God already, but He gave you,
Triumph over them and mastery,
For God's the Knower Wise.

72. Those who believed and fled their homes,
Risking their property and lives,
To fight in Allah's cause,
And those who gave them shelter and support,
Are certainly each other's friends and allies;
However, you do not owe such support,
And guardianship to those who have believed,
But have not had to flee their homes,
Until they leave their home; yet if they plead,
For help in Faith, it is on you incumbent,
To help, except it be against the tribes,
With whom you have a treaty; Cognizant
Is Allah of your every deed.

73. In fact the disbelievers are,
Each other's friends and allies; if
You will not do the same, there will,
Be everywhere much mischief,
And great corruption.

74. Those who embraced the Faith and left their homes,
To fight in Allah's cause, and those who did,
Give them refuge and help, are true believers,
They'll have Pardon, and a Provision splendid.

75. And those who did embrace the Faith,
At later dates, who left their homes to fight,
Along with you, are also of you; yet,

Kindred by blood do have their prior right,[1]
To one another, in the Book of God,
And God has Knowledge of all things indeed.

---

1. Believers are brethren in faith, but only blood relations are the inheritors of
   one another; earlier some of the believers had made arrangements of mutual
   inheritance on the basis of their religious Brotherhood,

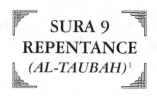

SURA 9
REPENTANCE
(AL-TAUBAH)[1]

1.   God and His Messenger declare,
Immunity to the idolaters,
With whom you are by treaties bound;

2.   You[2] may now freely go about the land,
For four more months, but you should be aware
That you could not escape from Allah, and
That Allah will disgrace the Truth-rejecters;

3.   God and His Messenger also declare,
Upon this Day of Greater Pilgrimage,[3]
To all the people: "God and His Apostle
Dissolve all bounds to the idolaters;
Thus now, if you repent, it will be better,
For you, but if you give no heed, beware!
You won't escape from Allah's Power!
So, give the tidings of a woeful scourge,
Unto the Faith-rejecters,

4.   Except for those idolaters, with whom
You made agreements, who did never
Fail you in aught, nor did they ever,

---

1. The only chapter in the Quran without the invocation of "*In the Name of God, the Beneficent, the Merciful*"; some commentators believe it is really the continuation of the previous chapter "*the Spoils*", and others give other reasons for this omission. This sura is also called Immunity (*Baraa'at*).

2. The Pagans, the idolaters.

3. The 10th of Zil-Hajjah, the Day of Sacrifice, as opposed to the Lesser Hajj or "*umrah*".

Aid anyone against you; with them,
Keep faith until their treaties run their terms;
God surely loves the self-restrainers.

5.   And when the sacred months are over,
Fight the idolaters unto the finish,
Where're you find them, or arrest them,
Besiege them, or do lie in ambush,
For them through every stratagem;
Yet if they do repent and take to prayer,
And pay *zakaat,* then let them go their way;
God is indeed Forgiving, Full of Mercy.

6.   Yet, if a pagan asks you for asylum,
Do grant him that, in order that he may,
Listen unto the Word of God; and then,
Help him attain his place of refuge,
For they are folks devoid of knowledge.

7.   God and His Messenger repose no trust,
In the idolaters' agreements, save
The ones with whom you made a treaty at
The Sacred Mosque;¹ so long as they behave
Justly with you, keep faith with them, for God,
Does love the righteous, self-restrainers.

8.   Nay, they cannot be trusted, seeing
That once they come by an advantage,
Over you, they will honour neither
Kindred allegiance, nor a pledge!

---

1. The Banu Hamza and the Banu Kinaana pagan tribes who swore their treaty
   near the Sacred Mosque, and faithfully observed it.

The while their hearts are not consenting,
They seek, by what their tongues allege,
To please you; most of them, however,
Are wicked, evil-doers.

9.   They barter Allah's Signs,
For trifling gains,
And they do turn away
The people from His way;
Evil indeed are all their doings.

10.   In a believer, they do not respect,
Either the ties of kinship or agreements,
These people have in fact,
Transgressed all limits.

11.   Yet if they do repent and keep up prayers,
And pay *zakaat*, they shall become your brethren
In faith; We make the Revelations,
Most clear to thinking men.

12.   But if they break their oaths, and slander,
Your Faith, after their covenant,
Then fight the ringleaders of Unbelief,
Because their oaths are not to them important:
That thus they e're could be kept off.

13.   What! Won't you fight against such folk,
Who broke their solemn oaths, and schemed
To banish the Apostle? Those who aimed
At you the first aggressive stroke?
Are you of them indeed afraid?
But if you are believers, hark!

God is more rightful to be feared!

14.   Fight them, and, at your hands, will Allah,
      Chastise and humble them, and He'll allow
      Your triumph over them, and He'll relieve
      The hearts of people who believe;

15.   And He'll remove the hatred in their hearts,
      God turns in Mercy unto whom He please,
      And God is All-Knowing, All-Wise.

16.   Do you suppose you would be left alone,
      Before it has been unto God made known,[1]
      Which one of you do most devoutly struggle,
      And for their friends will not take anyone,
      But God and His Apostle and the faithful?
      God's Most-Aware of all you've done.

17.   It ill becomes the Pagans to become,
      Visitors of God's temples or maintain
      Them ever, while they're sunk in disbelief,
      Against themselves! Their works are all in vain,
      And in the Fire they shall abide for ever.

18.   Those only may become the servers,
      And visitors of Allah's temples,
      Who do believe in God and the Last Day:
      A prayerful man who pays *zakaat*, and trembles,
      At nothing but the thought of God; he may
      Be one guided to the Right Way.

---

1. As God is not bound by Time, this means: "Before you prove yourselves to Him, through your deeds and devotions."

19.   Are you making the man who gives a drink
To the pilgrims and guards the Sacred Mosque,
As equal to the one with faith in God,
And the Last Day, who fights for Allah's sake?
They are not equal in the sight of God,
And Allah guides not a wrong doing folk.

20.   Those who embraced the faith and fled their homes,
And struggled in the cause of Allah, risking,
Their lives and their possessions, have indeed,
In Allah's sight, the highest ranking;
It's they who shall undoubtedly succeed;

21.   Their Lord does give them tidings glad
Of His own Mercy, of His pleasure,
And of the Gardens to be theirs,
Whose blessings last beyond all measure,

22.   Wherein they will abide for endless ages;
For certainly it's only God who could,
Provide the greatest wages.

23.   O You who have believed, do not befriend,
Your fathers and your brothers if they place,
Unfaith above Belief, for he who does
Befriend them, surely does injustice.

24.   Say: If your fathers and your sons,
Brothers and spouses and your kins,
The property which you have gained,
The trade you fear to be declined,
And homes of which you are so fond,
Happen to be unto you dearer,

Than Allah and His Messenger,
And fighting in His cause, then wait around,
Till God materializes His Command;
For God does not with guidance bless,
The wicked people who transgress.

25. You have been helped by God on many a field,[1]
     As well as in the Battle of Hounain,[2]
     When your tremendous numbers made you vain,
     But this availed you nothing, and the land,
     For all its breadth, about you straitened,
     And, tails between your legs, you fled!

26. But Allah sent down His *sakeena*,[3]
     On His Apostle and upon believers,
     And He sent down the hosts you could not see,
     And He punished the disbelievers;
     That was the disbelievers' penalty.

27. Yet, after this will God again,
     Turn unto whom He will in Mercy,
     God's Full of Pardon and Compassion.

28. O You believers!
     Unclean are the idolaters;
     Allow them not then to come near,

---

1. More specifically: Battle-field.

2. A valley between Mecca and Taa'if, the battle was fought in 630 A.D., the Muslim Army of 12,000 strong, was attacked from mountain hideouts by 4,000 Meccans!

3. Divine tranquillity, spirit of repose, peace, calm; cf. Hebrew *shekheena* "The Holy Presence."

The Sacred Mosque, after this year;[1]
And if you have a fear of poverty,
God will enrich you, if He wills,
Out of His Bounty;
For God is All-Knowing, All-Wise.

29.   Amongst the people who were given
The Scriptures, fight with those who neither,
Believe in God, nor in the Final Day,
Nor do they hold forbidden,
What God and His apostle have so bidden,
Who follow not the truthful Way,
As their religion, till they come to pay
Tribute[2] with full consent, and in subjection.

30.   Jews labelled Ezra[3] as a Son of Allah,
While Christians claim that the Messiah
Had been the Son of God! Such wrongs
Are uttered by their tongues,
In the footsteps of ancient pagans![4]
On them be God's eternal curse,
How could a man be so perverse!

---

1. After this pilgrimage, their last.

2. Jizyah in Arabic: A poll-tax levied from non-Muslim subjects of an Islamic state in place of a variety of taxes and alms, etc. that Muslims have to pay.

3. "Uzair" in Arabic: There is historical evidence that some Jewish sects used very exaggerated language concerning him and others almost deified him. The Holy Quran mentions this only here in connection with the Christian doctrine, but it never blames the Jews for this in other chapters; thus the Jewish nation as a whole is never accused of having held such beliefs; they are always addressed as a monotheistic people.

4. Taking men for gods or sons and daughters of God was not a new thing. Almost all ancient mythologies of ignorant, primitive peoples have foibles of

31. They take their rabbins and their monks,
    And the Messiah, son of Mary,
    To be their gods, instead of Allah,
    Though bidden to worship One God only!
    There are no gods but He;
    Exalted is He far too high
    Above what they besides Him deify.

32. Emitting puffs from mouths, these people
    Mean to blow out God's Light!
    But God's making His Light more lustrous,
    Despite the disbelievers' hate.

33. He it is Who has sent His Messenger,
    With Guidance and the true religion,[1]
    To overcome the other ways of life[2]
    No matter how it may disgust a pagan!

34. O You believers, certainly there are,
    Many rabbins and priests who dispossess
    Men, of their wealth, in falsehood, and debar
    Them from the Way of God, those who amass
    Silver and gold and spend not in God's cause,
    Shall be given a torment full of woes,
    Do give them the good news!

35. Upon the Day when these[3] are to be heated,
    In the Hell-fire, and then with them their foreheads,

---

this kind.

1. The original Arabic word *deen* means a "way of life", especially 'a just way of life'; the root meaning of the word in ancient Semitic languages is "judgment".

2. Or "every other religion".   3. Their treasures of precious metals.

Their sides and backs are branded, they shall hear:
"These are the precious hoards,
That you for your own selves did treasure,
Now taste your treasure!"

36.   The count for months, ordained by Allah in
    His Record, has been twelve, since He created
    Heavenly bodies and the earth, and four,
    Of these are sacred:[1] that's the steadfast method;
    Thus do not sin against yourselves regarding
    Them,[2] and do fight the pagans all year round,
    As they attack you all year round;
    Be sure that God's with the godfearing.

37.   The *nassi* practice[3] is another instance
    Of disbelief, whereby the disbelievers,
    Are led astray: One year they violate it,[4]
    But make it sacred in the coming years,
    In order that they make up for the months,
    Which God had sanctified, and thus they further
    Violate that which Allah had made sacred!
    To them the foulness of their deeds seem fair!
    For God does not His guidance spread,
    Over the Faith-deniers.

38.   What's wrong, O you embracers of the Faith?
    Weighted down were you to the earth,

---

1. Forbidden.   2. These months.

3. Postponement of sacred months: The pagans added or deducted a month to
   the four forbidden months to attack an enemy! The question of a solar astro-
   nomical year as against the lunar Islamic year does not arise here.

4. A certain sacred (forbidden) month.

When you were asked to "march in Allah's cause"!
Do you prefer this earthly life of yours,
To the Hereafter? Yet, of little worth,
Are all the comforts of the worldly life,
Compared to what is to come forth.

39.   If you do not set out to fight, He will
Inflict on you a painful scourge, and bring
Other men in your place; you never harm Him,
For God has power over everything.

40.   Will you not help him[1] out? It is no matter:
God did support him when he had been driven
Out by the infidels, he with another;[2]
And in the cave, he said to his companion:
"Do not despair; surely with us is Allah;"
Then God sent down upon him His *sakeena*,
And strengthened him with hosts unseen,
He rooted out the pagans' platform,
And Allah's word was most supreme:
For God's Almighty, Wise.

41.   Whether scarcely equipped or thickly steeled,
March on to combat in the cause of God,
Sacrificing your wealth and lives;
Best is this for you, if you realize!

42.   If there had been immediate gains in sight,

---

1. The Prophet.

2. This refers to the Prophet's flight from Mecca accompanied only by Abu Bakr,
his devoted disciple; Ali had volunteered to sleep in the Prophet's bed to face
the unsheathed swords of the plotters.

Upon an easy trip, they would indeed,
Have followed you, but this[1] was hard and long;
Yet they will swear by Allah: "If we could
Do it, we would have with you marched along!
They are certainly self-destroyers!
And God well knows that they are liars!

43.   God pardon you! Why did you grant them,
Exemption, ere you came to recognize
The truthful ones, and when you'd known
The people telling lies.

44.   Those who believe in God and the Last Day,
Will never ask your leave for veering,
From striving with their property and lives,
And God knows the godfearing!

45.   Those only ask you for such leave,
Who disbelieve in God and the Last Day,
Whose hearts are centers of uncertainties,
And who will thus in doubts for ever sway.

46.   Had they intended to come out, they would,
Have certainly prepared themselves for war,
But God disliked their marching forth, and thus,
Caused them to stay behind: as if they were,
Bidden to: sit around among the sitters!

47.   Even if they had marched along with you,
They would have not been an addition,

---

1. The expedition to Tabook, a place near the frontier of Arabia, in Syria, then a Byzantine province.

Only a burden, they would hurry through
Your ranks, seeking to sow sedition,
And some among you would unto them listen,
But Allah knows the evil-doers.

48.   Indeed, before this, they had sought
To stir up mischief: they reversed
Matters for you, till Truth arrived,
And what prevailed, was God's behest,
To their disgust.

49.   Some of them say: "Grant us exemption,
And do not draw us into trial."
Behold! These people have already fallen
Into a trial; and the fire of Hell,
Will certainly surround the infidel.

50.   It grieves them when some good befalls you,
But if you meet with some affliction,
They boast: "Lucky we'd taken care already;"
And then they walk away in exultation!

51.   Say: "Nothing will befall us save,
What Allah did for us ordain,
He is our Patron, and the faithful,
Should put their trust in Him alone."

52.   Say: "what could you for us await except,
One of the twain, both of which are quite fine?[1]
But what we do await for you is whether,

---

1. Victory or martyrdom.

God shall bring down on you His bane,
Direct from Him or through our power?[1]
Thus wait, because we, too,
Will wait around with you."

53. Say: "whether you shall give in charity,
Willingly or unwillingly, it will
Not be accepted from you, for you are,
Indeed a wicked people."

54. The very reasons why their contributions
Are not accepted from them are: That they
Do not believe in God and His Apostle,
And that they come reluctantly to pray,
And when they spend for God, they grudge and grumble.

55. Let Not their riches nor their children
Excite your admiration: Allah wills,
To turn these into means of retribution,
For them, in this world's life, and that their souls
Depart in faith-rejection!

56. They swear by God that they're indeed of you!
But they are not; these people are
Only afraid of you!

57. If they could find some shelter or a hole,
Or any secret place, therein to hide,
They would run into it like mad!

58. There are among them some who criticize

---

1. At our hands.

You[1] with respect to *sadaqaat*;[2]
If they are given parts thereof, they will,
Be really happy in their heart,
But if they have no portion, lo!
They're full of rage and woe.

59.   Would that they had been satisfied,
With what God and His Messenger
Have given them and would have said: "For us,
God is sufficient, and soon Allah,
Will give us out of His abundance,
And so will His Apostle; surely
We're eager for God's providence."

60.   Charities[3] shall be only for the poor,
The needy, and collectors of such alms,
Those recently won over to the Truth,
For the bondsmen's and debtors' ransoms,
And in the way of God[4] as well as for,
The traveling aliens;
That is an ordinance from God, and God's
All-Knowing and All-Wise.

61.   And there are some among them who molest
The Prophet by asserting: "He believes,
Readily what he hears!" Say: "It is best
For you that he does listen, he believes

---

1. The Holy Prophet.   2. *Sadaqaat* embraces all charities including zakaat (which is a regular, obligatory charity usually 2.1/2 per cent of merchandise and 10 per cent of the products of the earth).

3. *Sadaqaat*.   4. "In the Way of God" is a general term which implies all those good works that please God. In this context, however, many Muslim scholars believe that it stands for *Jihaad*.

In Allah and he trusts the faithful,
And he's a blessing for the people,
Among you who embraced the Faith in truth,
And those who wrong and injure God's Apostle,
Shall face a torment painful.

62. They swear by God before you all,
That they might please you, but it is,
More just if they be pleasing Allah,
And His Apostle, as sincere believers.

63. Aren't they aware that people who oppose
God and His Messenger, surely incur
The Fire of Hell for ever,
Which is the worst dishonour?!

64. The hypocrites now worry lest a *sura*,
Concerning them should be sent down that would,
Plainly expose what's in their hearts;
Say: "Go on mocking", surely Allah
Will bring to light all that you dread.

65. And if you question them they'll promptly say:
"Oh, we were merely commenting as ever,
In jest and play!"
Ask them: "were you not mocking Allah,
His revelations and His Messenger?"

66. Make no excuses: for you have indeed,
Denied the Faith after you had believed,
Now even if we pardon some of you,
We will surely chastise the others,
For they are guilty sinners.

67.   The hypocrites, both men and women
       Are all alike: they advocate what's evil,
       Prohibit what is good, and always tighten
       Their purses' strings; Allah they have forsaken,
       So He forgot them too; the hypocrites
       Are evil doers of no limits!

68.   The Fire of Hell is what God promises
       Unto the hypocrites, both men and women,
       And to the disbelievers, they will dwell
       Therein for ever, and this retribution
       Suffices them, for God has laid His curse
       Upon them, and their scourge shall be unbroken.

69.   You[1] are like those before you, but they were
       Surely far stronger than you, and did gather
       Greater riches and had more children,
       And they rejoiced in their material portion;
       And now are you rejoicing in your portion,
       Just as the men before you; and like them,
       You have engaged in idle, vain discussion;[2]
       Fruitless were all their actions in this world,
       And vain shall they be in the life to come,
       Totally lost were all these folks of old.

70.   Have they not heard a thing of those,
       Who've gone before? The fate of Noah's
       People, of Aad, and of Thamood,[3]
       Abraham's people and the dwellers

---

1. The hypocrites are being directly addressed.

2. Rejection of the Truth, blasphemy.

3. Names of ancient, Arabian people.

Of Midian, and the Cities Ruined?[1]
To all did come their messengers,
With lucid Signs; thus Allah did
Them no injustice: they themselves
Wronged their own souls.

71.   And the believing men and women,
Are friends and allies to each other,
They advocate what's just and proper,
Prohibit evil and keep up the prayer,
Pay their *zakaat*, and do obey
God and His Messenger; it's they
Who will be by God's Mercy blessed,
For God's the Mightiest, the Wisest.

72.   God promises the faithful men and women,
Gardens watered by running streams, wherein
They shall abide for good, and goodly mansions
In everlasting Eden Gardens,
But Allah's Pleasure is the greatest bliss:
That is indeed the Grand Success.

73.   O Prophet, struggle hard against
The unbelievers and the hypocrites,
And be most firm with them; the pits
Of Hell shall be their homes, most wretched
Shall be their journey there indeed!

74.   They swear by Allah that they never did
Utter a word of blasphemy, although
They did; thus they went back to unbelief,

---

1. Sodom and Gomorrah.

After embracing Islam; and they also,
Tried hard to do what they could not attain,[1]
In fact no vengeance could they entertain
Except that God and His Apostle made
Them prosper through His graceful, bounteous aid![2]
Yet if they do repent, it will be better,
For their own selves, but if they give no heed,
God will, both in this world and the Hereafter,
Punish them sternly; and, throughout the land,
They'll find no friend, and no one ever,
Who would extend to them a hand.

75.   Amongst them some had made a promise
        To God that "if He gives us from His bounty,
        We will be large in giving charity,
        And lead the life of the most righteous";

76.   But when He did bestow His graceful bliss,
        Upon them, they became most niggardly,
        And turned away,[3] totally heedless.

77.   Thus as a consequence of breaking
        Their pledge with God and telling lies,
        He let hypocrisy be lurking
        Deep in their hearts until the rise,
        Of the Day when they meet Him.

1. A reference to plots by the Hypocrites of Medina against the life of the Holy
   Prophet.

2. The small town of Medina had, within the short period of nine years of the
   residence of the Holy Prophet there, become the central city of Arabia and
   the greatest center of commercial activity, and some of the conspirators were
   among the richest people of Medina!

3. From their pledge.

78.   Do they not know that Allah knows
        Their secrets and their secret counsels,
        And that God is the Very Knower,
        Of things beyond all veils;

79.   Those who reproach the open-handed faithful
        For their benevolence, and then ridicule
        The poor that give all takings of their chore,
        Will find God scoffing at them, and a woeful
        Torment shall be for them in store.

80.   Whether you ask forgiveness for such people,
        Or not, it is the same, even if you implore
        Forgiveness for them seventy times, God will
        Not pardon them, for they rejected God,
        And His Apostle; Allah does not guide
        People immersed in evil.

81.   Those who were left at home were very glad
        Not to have gone with God's Apostle,[1]
        Because they did not like to struggle
        In Allah's cause with their own wealth and lives;
        They said: "Fighting in such heat is not wise!"
        Tell them: "Much hotter is the Fire of Hell!"
        If only they could realize!

82.   Let them now laugh and cheer a little,
        Many a tear shall roll down from their eyes:
        Their own misdeed's requital.

83.   Henceforth, when Allah brings you to a group

---

1. In the Tabook expedition against the Romans.

Of them, and if they ask for your permission
To march with you, say: "you will not with me,
Ever be marching, nor shall fight an enemy
Along with me; surely on that first mission,
You had been very pleased to sit at home,
Therefore sit on with those who must keep home!"

84.   You shall not offer prayer for any,
Of them that dies, nor shall you e're attend
Their burial; they have indeed rejected
God and His Messenger, and met their end
While they still sinned.

85.   Let not their riches and their children
Ever excite your admiration;
It's Allah's Wish to punish them by means
Of these things in this world, and let their souls
Depart as disbelieving pagans.

86.   Each time a *sura* is sent down that states:
"Have faith in God and strive and fight along
With His Apostle, then the rich and strong
Among them ask you for exemption,
And supplicate: "Give us permission
To stay behind with those who must remain!"

87.   They are content to stay at home,
As women who remain behind;
Their hearts and minds are sealed,
They cannot comprehend.[1]

---

1. That is, they are not only cowards, but fools; they don't even understand their
   own interest: if the enemy got the better of their brethren, they would themselves be crushed.

88.   But the Apostle and the men who share
        His Faith, eagerly strive with all they own,
        And their own lives; many good things await them,
        Salvation shall be theirs alone;

89.   God has prepared them Gardens,
        Watered by flowing streams,
        Wherein they shall abide for eons;
        That is the greatest of all wins!

90.   And there were some among the Bedouins,[1]
        Who, making up excuses came to claim
        Exemption; therefore those who had been false
        To God and His Apostle sat at home!
        Soon will a grievous chastisement afflict
        Those of them who rejected Faith in fact.

91.   On the disabled there shall be no blame,
        Nor on the sick, nor on the people
        Who lack the means to help,[2] provided
        They are sincere to God and His Apostle;
        Against the righteous there shall never be
        A cause of blame; And God's Forgiving
        And Full of Mercy.

92.   Nor any blame on those who to you came,
        Requesting mounts, and you had to proclaim:
        "I cannot find you mounts!" and they went back,
        With their eyes overflowed with tears of grief,
        That they had naught to spend for their belief!

---

1. Arabs of the desert, or Arabs dwelling outside Medina.

2. To contribute to the war effort.

93.   The real offenders are the rich who have,
    The means, and still request you for permission
    To stay with women who remain behind;
    God has indeed set seals upon their mind,
    They have no knowledge, no cognition!

94.   They do apologize to you when you,
    Come back to them; say: "do not fabricate
    Any excuses, we cannot believe you;
    God has informed us of the proper state
    Of things concerning you already; now
    Allah and His Apostle will watch over
    Your deeds: then you'll be taken to the Knower
    Of the Hidden and Open, and He then
    Will tell you what you've done!"

95.   They will be swearing soon in Allah's name,
    When you come back to them that you may turn
    Aside from them; therefore leave them alone:
    For they are certainly unclean[1]
    And Hell will be their destination
    For what they ceaselessly have done.

96.   They will take solemn oaths before you,
    To please you, but, if you are pleased
    With them, certainly God will never,
    Be with the wicked people pleased!

97.   In disbelief and in hypocrisy,
    The desert Arabs are immovable,
    And the most likely to ignore the laws,

---

1. Or "an abomination".

And bounds that God sent down to His Apostle;
But God is the All-Knowing, the All-Wise.

98.   Some of these Arabs think that what they spend,
For the cause is a kind of penalty!
They even wait for a calamity,
To hit you all; but they will in the end,
The worst calamity incur,
For God is the All-Knowing Hearer.

99.   Yet there are those among these Arabs,
Who do believe in God and the Last Day,
And take their contributions as a means
Of nearing God and the Apostle's prayings,
Indeed they shall be taken closer, aye,
Soon will Allah admit them to His Mercy,
For God is the Forgiver, Full of Mercy.

100.   As for the vanguards of *muhajireen*,[1]
And the *ansaar*[2] as well as those who followed
Them in good deeds, God is with them most pleased,
And they're well-pleased with Him: God has allowed
Them to be occupants of Gardens,
Watered by flowing streams, for them prepared,
Wherein they shall abide for eons:
That is the greatest of all wins.

101.   Not only some among the desert Arabs,
Around you, but some from among Medinan
People are hypocrites: each one is in,

---

1. The Holy Prophet's early followers who fled with him to Medina.
2. The Holy Prophet's followers and supporters in Medina.

The craft of double-dealing, some magician,
You do not know them, but to Us they're known,
Twice will We give them chastisement,
And after that they shall be sent,
To bear the greater Torment.

102.   Yet others have confessed to being sinful
For having mixed evil with acts of goodness,
So God may turn to them again in Kindness,
For God's the Oft-Forgiving Merciful.

103.   In order that you cleanse and purify them,
Take alms out of their properties, and offer
Prayers for them, for your prayer will bring
Them peace, God is the Hearing Knower.

104.   Do they not know that God accepts
Repentance from His servants,
And takes their charities, and He
Is the Redeemer Full of Mercy?

105.   Tell them: "Do as you will: for God beholds
Your doing, and so will His Messenger,
And the believers; then you shall return
To Him Who is, of all secrets, the Knower,
Whether open or hidden, and He will
Tell you concerning all your deeds.

106.   There are others who wait for Allah's
Judgment: them either He'll chastise,
Or turn to them in Mercy; God's
The All-Knowing, Most Wise.

107.   And there were others who set up a mosque[1],
         To spread mischief, and practice disbelief
         And cause disunity among believers,
         And headquarters for one[2] who was in strife,
         With God and His Apostle from before;
         Now they will surely swear:
         "Nothing but good did we desire!"
         But God bears witness that they are
         Absolute liars!

108.   You shall never set foot in it;
         It's worthiest for you to pray
         In the Mosque[3] that was founded
         On righteousness from the first day,
         Wherein are men who love to be,
         Kept purified, and Allah loves the souls
         Who purify themselves.

109.   Who will be better placed? The man
         Who founds his building on:
         The hallowed fear of God,
         And His good pleasure? Or the one
         Who builds his house upon the brink,
         Of a collapsing, hollowed bank,
         So that it will with him fall down
         Into the fire of Hell?
         Certainly Allah will not guide,
         The wicked, unjust people.

1. A mosque built by some hypocrites in Quba, about 3 miles to the south-east of Medina.

2. Abu Amir "Raahib" (the Monk): so surnamed for his association with Christian monks.   3. The original "Mosque of Righteousness" was built by the Holy Prophet himself in Quba.

110. The building they have raised will never,
     Cease to create suspicion in their hearts,
     Unless their hearts shall be cut into parts,[1]
     And God's The Wise All-Knower.

111. God purchases indeed, of the believers,
     Their lives and their possessions in exchange
     For Paradise: they fight in Allah's cause,
     Kill and get killed. Such is His truthful pledge
     In the Torah, the Gospel, and the Quran.
     And who's more faithful to his promise than
     God the One? Thus be happy with the bargain
     Which you have made, and that's the greatest gain.

112. So do repenters, worshippers and praisers,
     Activists, kneelers, and prostrators,
     Advocators of justice and forbidders
     Of evil, and observers of God's laws;
     So give the faithful this good news.

113. It is not for the Prophet or the faithful,
     To ask forgiveness for the Pagans,
     Even though they should be their kinsmen, after
     It's to them plain that they will be companions
     Of the consuming Flames.[2]

114. And Abraham's asking forgiveness for,
     His sire was owing to a pledge he had
     Unto him made, but after he did realize,
     That he had been an enemy to God,

---

1. That is "until they die".

2. This is usually understood to refer to the prayer for those who die unrepen-
   tant or those who actively oppose Faith to the last.

He did dissociate himself from him;
A tender-hearted, patient man indeed,
Was Abraham.

115.   God lets not any people go astray,
When He has guided them, until He's made
Most clear to them what to avoid;
God is fully Aware of everything.

116.   To God belongs the Kingdom of the heavens
And earth; it's He Who life and death ordains;
You have, except for Allah,
Neither a guardian, nor a helper.

117.   Certainly God did turn in Mercy to
The Prophet, the *muhajirs* and *ansaar*,
Who stood by him during the hours of need,
When the zeal of some groups well-nigh turned sour;
But then He turned to them, for He was Full
Of Pity to them, and Most Merciful;

118.   So was He to the Three[1] whose case had been
Put off:[2] the spacious earth seemed to close in
On them, and their own souls were like a burden
Upon them, but they knew for certain:
There was no refuge but in God alone;
Thus He did turn to them, so that they might
Repent; for He's the Merciful, Redeeming One.

---

1. Three of the faithful who failed to obey the Holy Prophet's summons in the Tabook affair out of human weakness; they later repented.

2. "The acceptance of their repentance was delayed.

119.   Be god-fearing, O you the Faithful,
        And stay among the truthful.

120.   Neither the people of Medina, nor
        The Arabs of the neighbourhood shall ever
        Remain behind[1] the Messenger of Allah,
        Nor shall they their own lives to his prefer:
        For nothing shall they do or suffer
        That will not be recorded in their favour,
        As a good deed, whether it's thirst or hunger
        Or any effort in the cause of Allah,
        Or any step they take to raise the ire
        Of pagans or some gains that they acquire
        From enemies; nay; Allah never would
        Fail to reward the people who do good.

121.   Nor do they spend anything for the cause,
        Be it little or much, nor do they chance
        A daring journey, but it's credited
        To their account, that God may recompense
        Them with the best rewards for what they did.

122.   And it is not required that all,
        The faithful shall go forth at once;
        A band from every group shall stay
        And deepen their own cognizance,
        Of the religious Faith and, when their people
        Come back, give them caution and guidance,
        So that they guard against all evil.

123.   Believers, fight those unbelievers who,

---

1. When he mobilizes for war.

Have come too close to you, and let them find
You firm and stern, and know that Allah is
With the godfearing who have been restrained.

124. Each time a *sura* is revealed,
Some of them question: "which of you
Has had his faith by it increased?!
It will surely increase the faith
Of those who do have faith,
And they'll have joy in truth.

125. But for the people in whose hearts there is,
A moral sickness, it will multiply,
Their evil doubts, so that they shall remain
In Unbelief until they die.

126. Do these people not ever notice
That they are tried, every year once or twice?
Yet, they neither turn in repentance,
Nor ever learn a lesson from this!

127. Each time a *sura* is sent down, they glance
At each other, as if to question:
"Anyone seeing you?" And then,
They turn away! Allah has turned His grace
Away from them, for they are senseless men.

128. There has now come to you a Messenger,
One from amongst you, who does grieve
If you fall into loss and sinfulness,
Who is solicitous for your success,
And merciful and full of kindness,
To people who believe.

129.   But if they give no heed, say: "Allah
        Suffices me, there is no God but He alone,
        In Him do I rely, who is the Only
        Lord of the Glorious Throne."

SURA 10
JONAH
(YOUNUS)

In the Name of God, the Beneficent, the Merciful

1. Alif Laam Raa.[1] These are the verses of
    The Scripture, Full of Wisdom.

2. Does it amaze the people that We sent
    Our revelation to a man[2] among them:
    To warn the people and to give the tidings
    Glad to the faithful that they have a firm,
    Merited footing with their Lord?!
    "This man's a skilled enchanter"!
    The disbelievers claim.

3. Surely your Lord is Allah who did fashion
    Heavens and Earth within six Days, and then,
    His Throne ascended to ordain
    All things in His Dominion;
    There is no one with Him to intercede,
    Save after His permission:
    Such is Allah, your Lord indeed,
    Thus worship Him alone! Will you not heed
    The Admonition?

4. All of you shall to Him return: most certain,
    And truthful is the Promise made by God;
    He is the One who did begin Creation,
    And He will bring it back, so that He would

---

1. A.L.R.

2. Mohammad (pbuh).

312

Justly reward the faithful who have done
Good works, and let the ones who disbelieved,
Have drinks of Boiling Water and infliction,
Of painful torment for their Truth-rejection!

5.   It's He alone who gave the Sun and Moon,
His splendoured radiance and her lustrous light,
Measuring out her mansions, that you might,
The count of years and computation learn;
Allah did not create all this for aught
But to display the Truth;[1] He does explain,
His Signs[2] in full for knowing men.

6.   In the rotation of the night and day,
And what has Allah in the heavens,
And on the earth, created, there are Signs,
For righteous men.

7.   For those who don't expect to meet Us,
And find their satisfaction,
In the life of this world,
And those who, pay no heed,
Unto Our Revelation,

8.   The ultimate abode shall be the Fire,
In recompense of their own action;

9.   Those who believe and do good works,
Shall, through their faith, be guided by no less,
Than their own Lord; beneath them streams will flow,
In the Gardens of Bliss;

1. That is, for a serious end, to manifest the Divine Unity.

2. Or "revelations".

10.   Their prayer therein will be:
      "Glory to You, O Lord", their salutation:
      "Peace[1] be to all", and, of their hymns,
      The burden: "Praise be unto Allah,
      The Lord of all Creation."

11.   If Allah were to speed up evil for
      Mankind just as they seek to hasten good;
      Surely their fate would have been sealed before;
      But We let those who never hope,
      To have a Meeting with Us, grope
      Along in their rebellious mood!

12.   When some affliction touches man, he calls,
      Us, standing, sitting or upon his side,
      Yet after We remove from him his trouble,
      He passes on, as though he never cried,
      To Us, when he was in affliction!
      Thus does what they are doing seem,
      Fair to wrongdoers in the extreme!

13.   We put an end to many generations,
      Before you, for their vile transgressions,
      After they had rejected their apostles,
      Who came to them with lucid Signs;
      Thus do we punish peoples
      Guilty of sins.

14.   And then We made you their successors in the land,
      And We shall be observing how you act!

---

1. Salaam, shalom.

15. And when Our revelations, self-explaining,
    Are unto them rehearsed, those who reject,
    The Meeting with Us, say: "Give us a Reading
    Other than this, or change its text!"
    Say: It is not for me to change a thing,
    About it of my own accord,
    I follow what is unto me revealed;
    Surely if I would disobey my Lord,
    I should myself be fearful of the Torments
    Of that Day of Events!

16. Say: If God did not will, I'd never
    Recite it unto you, nor ever
    Would I have made it known; indeed,
    I dwelt amongst you for a whole
    Life-time, before it was revealed;
    Do you not use your minds at all?!"

17. And who could be a greater wicked sinner
    Than one who forges lies concerning Allah,
    Or falsifies His revelations? Surely,
    Such criminals shall never prosper.

18. Instead of God, these people worship idols,
    That neither harm nor help them; they allege:
    Those things shall intercede for us with God!
    Do you presume you give to God some knowledge
    He lacks on Heavens and the earth?! Glory to Him;
    Exalted is He over any image,
    That they set up with Him

19. There was a time when all mankind,
    Was a single nation indeed,

But they amongst them disagreed,[1]
And had it not been for a Word,
Already uttered by your Lord,
The matter would have been between them
Decided, for their causing discord.

20.   They also say: "Why has he not been given
A miracle[2] from his own Lord?" say: "It is only
God who has knowledge of the Hidden;
Thus wait,[3] for I am surely,
Waiting along with you."

21.   No sooner do We show Compassion,
To people, after some misfortune,
Has touched them down, than they begin
To scheme against Our revelations!
Say: "God's the Swiftest Schemer;" and behold!
Our messengers[4] keep a full record,
Of all your machinations.

22.   He it is Who enables you to travel,
By land and sea; thus you embark the ships:
As you set sails, rejoicing some fair breeze,
Suddenly violent winds begin to rage,
Against you, and the billows start to surge,
From every side upon you, and you realize
That you are being overwhelmed; henceforth,
You call on God, in your sincerest faith:
"If You deliver us from this, we will
Ever be truly thankful!"

---

1. "On recognition of the Reality".   2. Or: a Sign.

3. "For any signs of Miracles in the future".   4. Angels

23.   Yet once He does deliver them, behold!
       They soon begin transgressing in the land,
       Without a right! O Men, your vices bold,
       Only corrupt your souls: a brief command
       Of worldly joy, and, in the end,
       You are to Us returned! And then,
       We'll let you know what you have done!

24.   Indeed this worldly life could well be likened,
       Unto the produce of the earth: We do
       Send down rain-water from the skies to blend
       With earthly crops of every hue,
       Providing man and beast with food,
       Until the earth puts out its golden raiment,
       Decked out in beauty and beatitude,
       And hopeful tenants think that they could now
       Reap every profit from it; lo!
       Our Scourge comes down upon it, by
       The night or by daytime to lay
       It waste, as if it never had been teeming,
       Only there yesterday!
       Thus do We make Our revelations plain
       Unto reflecting men.

25.   God is inviting to the Home of Peace,[1]
       He guides whome'er He please to the Right Way.

26.   Rewarded shall be those who did good works,
       With goodness in abundance, and no face
       'Mong them is smeared by the soot of disgrace.
       They will be the companions,
       Of Paradise,

---

1. Paradise.

Wherein they shall abide for eons!

27. The punishment for those whose acquisition
    Was only evil shall be equal evil,
    Abasement shall embrace them, and they will,
    Against God's wrath have no protection,
    And every face shall be a gloomy sight,
    As if it had been coated by a fraction
    Of the murkiest night;
    They are the inmates of the Fire;
    In it, they shall remain for ever.

28. And on the Day We gather them together,
    We shall declare to the idolaters:
    "Keep to your places, you and all your partners!"
    And so we'll have them stand in separate rows,
    And then their idol-partners shall be saying:
    "Behold, it was not us at all
    That you were serving;

29. "God is an All-Sufficient Witness,
    'Tween you and us, that we were utterly,
    Of your worshipping, heedless."

30. It's there and then, that every soul,
    Shall see what it has sent ahead!
    All shall be sent back unto God,
    Their rightful Lord; and their invented
    Falsehoods shall leave them in the lurch!

31. Say: "Who provides for you from skies and earth?
    Or, who controls the hearing and the seeing?
    And who brings forth the living from the dead,

And brings the dead forth from the living?
Who is ordaining Everything?"[1]
They will say "God".
Say: "Will you not then be godfearing?"

32.   And such is Allah, your true Lord;
So, what is there, after the Truth,
Except: going astray?
Now, whither are you turned away?

33.   Therefore, the previous Word,
Of Your Lord, was the utter Truth,
Regarding evil-doers, that:
Never would they embrace the Faith.

34.   Ask them: "Could any of your idols,
Originate creation, out of nothing,
And keep renewing it?" Say: "Allah
Originates creation, out of nothing,
And keeps renewing it; indeed you are,
Amazingly misled!"

35.   Ask them: "Could any of your idols guide,
Unto the Truth?" say: "It is God alone
Who guides unto the Truth. Now is the One,
Who guides to Truth, more worthy to be followed,
Or he that cannot guide, and is in need,
Himself, of guidance? What's the matter then,
That you cannot decide?"

36.   Most of them follow nothing but conjecture,

---

1. "Directing the universe".

Yet guesswork is no substitute for Truth,
And God is, of their doings, Most Aware.

37.   And this Quran[1] could not have been composed,
        Except by God the One, by any;
        Nay, it's a confirmation of that which
        We have been sending down already,[2]
        As well as an elucidation,
        Of the Book,[3] it undoubtedly comes from,
        The Lord of the Creation.

38.   Are they still saying: "It's his own invention?"
        Say: Then produce a *sura* like it,
        And call on your false gods to help you,
        If what you say be true!

39.   But nay! They are rejecting that, about which
        They have no comprehensive knowledge,
        Nor has, as yet, its clear interpretation[4]
        Visited them. Likewise Our revelation,
        Has been denied in many a former age;
        Behold! What was the awful destinies
        Of those who worked iniquities?!

40.   Some of them shall believe in it,
        And some shall not come nigh belief;
        Your Lord best knows the ones,

---

1. Or "Reading".   2. The Scriptures, the Torah.

3. The Book: God's revelation throughout the ages is one; the Quran confirms,
   fulfills, completes, and further explains the one true revelation, which has
   been sent by the One True God in all ages.

4. Also meaning: "elucidation", "final realization"; "consequences".

Engaged in mischief!

41. And if they call you an impostor, say:
"My deeds are mine, and what you do is yours,
Accountable you shan't be for my deeds,
Nor shall I be accountable for yours."

42. Some of them to you lend an ear,
But could you make the deaf,
Who do not mind, to hear?

43. And some of them keep looking at you;
But could you show the way unto the blind,
Even though they have no sight?

44. Never is God unjust unto mankind,
It's men who are to their own souls unjust.

45. And on the Day He gathers them together,
They feel as if they had not tarried,
But, of a day, an hour;
They surely recognize each other;
Those are to be the losers who denied,
Meeting with Allah, and were never
Righteously guided.

46. Whether We let you witness some of what
We've Promised[1] them, or take your soul before this,
Their ultimate return shall be to Us,
And God, to what they do, shall be the Witness.

---

1. The scourges they were threatened with.

47.   There is a messenger for every *umma*,[1]
        And, once the messenger is come, a just
        Judgment is passed on them, and they are not
        Wronged in the least.

48.   And they still ask:
        "When will this Promise come to pass,
        If it's the truth you speak?"

49.   Say: "I have for myself no power,
        To harm or profit; and all things on Allah's
        Pleasure depend; there is for every *umma*
        A term appointed; when their term expires,
        They can't postpone or bring it forward,
        Even for a single hour."

50.   Say: "Note! His scourge may fall on you by night
        Or during daylight: what on earth is it,
        The guilty sinners want to expedite?!

51.   "Only when it has overtaken you,
        Will you believe in it? "'Ah, now indeed?!
        But, in your unbelief, you had demanded,
        It at full speed!'"

52.   Transgressors shall be also told:
        "Now taste the everlasting torment;
        Did you, for what you have been doing,
        Expect no punishment?!"

53.   And they still seek to be informed;

---

1. Community, nation, people, multitude.

"Is it really the truth?!"
Tell them: Aye, by my Lord!
It is the truth indeed,
It cannot be at all avoided.

54. And to redeem himself, each person,
Who was unjust, would fain give all
The wealth upon the earth in ransom,
If he possessed it; and they will
Declare their deep repentance when,
They see the Torment, but the Sentence
Is passed upon them in all fairness,
None shall be dealt with with injustice.

55. Take note! To God belongs,
All on the earth and in the heavens,
Take Note! God's Promise is
Certainly true; and yet,
Most of them know it not!

56. He it is Who gives life and takes it,
And unto Him you shall be taken back.

57. O Humankind! An Admonition from
Your Lord has now unto you come,
It's a Healer of hearts, and for the faithful,
A Guidance and a Blessing;

58. Say: In God's Grace and in His Mercy,
They ought to be rejoicing,
That is indeed far better,
Than what they are amassing!

59.   Say: "Have you ever noted this that you,
      Out of what God, for your provision,
      Has given you, have made some things unlawful,
      And some things lawful!"
      Ask them: "Did God give you permission,
      Or do you only unto God ascribe
      Your own invention?!"

60.   And what will those, who have invented,
      Falsehoods concerning Allah, mull
      Over the Day of Resurrection?
      Certainly God's Most Bountiful,
      Unto mankind; yet most of them,
      Happen to be ungrateful.

61.   We're keeping watch on everything
      You are engaged in, every portion
      Of any Reading you're reciting,
      And each and every work you undertake;
      For not an atom's weight in Earth or Heaven,
      Nor aught that's less than this or greater,
      Lie hidden from your Lord's attention,
      All is on record in a lucid Book.

62.   Behold! The friends of God indeed,
      Dread naught, nor are they ever grieved!

63.   Such people are believing and godfearing,

64.   For them there are glad tidings, both
      In the life of this world, as well
      As in the life henceforth:
      There is no changing in the words of God:

A great felicity indeed!

65. Let not their words, make you have sorrows;
Power and Honour wholly rest with God,
He is the One Who Hears, Who Knows.

66. Behold! All creatures in the heavens,
And on the earth belong to God;
What do they follow, those who do invoke,
Deities they have joined with God?
They follow nothing but some guess-work,
Nothing they preach but falsehood!

67. He it is Who ordained the night,
That you therein might rest, and gave
The Day, discriminating light;
Surely in this are Signs for people
Who would hearken aright.

68. They say: "God has a son begotten!"
Glory be to Him; He is purely Needless;
All that the heavens and the earth contain,
To Him belongs. What evidence for this,
Have you at all? Have you really betaken,
Yourselves to say something concerning God,
Of which you have no ken?!

69. Tell them: "There shall be no salvation,
For those who forge, concerning God,
An untrue attribution."

70. Some fleeting pleasures have they in this world,
And then to Us is their return,

And We shall make them taste a Torment stern,
Because of what they disbelieved.

71. And now recount to them the tale of Noah;
     Behold, he told his people: "O my folk!
     If my abode with you, and what I spoke,
     Of the communications sent by Allah,
     Was to you grievous-and in Allah,
     I put my trust-then on me make,
     All your designs and muster
     All your false gods, and do not ever
     carry out plottings in the dark:
     Make up your minds about me any way,
     And don't delay!

72. "And if you turn your backs on me, remember:
     Never have I from you demanded
     Rewards, for my reward is ever
     With Allah; and I was commanded
     To be a *Muslim*."[1]

73. But they rejected him, and thus We saved
     Him and the others with him in the Ark,
     And made them the successors, and We drowned
     Those who denied Our revelations; hark!
     What was the final end,
     Of those who had been warned!

74. And after him, We raised up many
     A messenger, to their own clans,
     They came to them with clearest Signs,

---

1. A submitter to the will of God Almighty.

But they would not believe the very
Truth that they had before rejected!
Thus it is that We do indeed,
Set seals upon the hearts of any
People who do the bounds exceed.

75.   Then after them we sent up Moses,
And Aaron unto Pharaoh and his party,
Together with Our Signs, but they, with scorn,
Treated them; for they were a people guilty.

76.   So when the truth from Us was to them shown,
They cried: "This is some magic plain!"

77.   "What!" Moses said, "The Truth upon you does descend,
And you are asking whether it is magic?!
But sorcerers are losers in the end."

78.   They answered: "Have you come to us to turn
Us all away from what we found our fathers,
Doing, so that you twain may rule the land?!
Nay, never will we be in you believers."

79.   And Pharaoh added: "Bring unto my presence,
All sorcerers of highest competence."

80.   And when the sorcerers arrived,
Moses told them: "Throw down,
Whatever you wish to throw down."

81.   And after they had their devices thrown,
Moses said to them: "What you have produced
Is sorcery, and it will be reduced,

To naught by God, for God does not condone
The work of mischief-makers."

82. And by His Words will Allah verify,
The very Truth, although the guilty sinners,
Over it, into rage and hatred fly!

83. All told, only some youths from his own folk,
Believed in Moses, for they feared that Pharaoh,
And their own chiefs would torment them; indeed
Pharaoh was mighty in the land; but lo!
He did all bounds exceed.

84. Moses also advised: "O people mine,
If you have e're in God believed,
And if you follow still your Muslim creed,[1]
Then put your trust in Him alone."

85. They said: "In Allah do we put our trust,
Our Lord! Do not make us a trial-subject,
For the unjust;

86. And save us through Your Ruth,
From folks who have no Faith!

87. We then revealed to Moses and his brother:
Provide some dwellings for your folk,
In Egypt, and in your own houses make,
Places of worship, and establish prayers,
And give good news to the believers.

---

1. Absolute submission to the will of the Almighty.

88.   And Moses prayed: "Our Lord, You have bestowed
    On Pharaoh and his princes pomp and wealth,
    In the life of this earth;
    And they are, O our Lord,
    Misleading people from your Road,
    Destroy their wealth, O Lord, make adamant
    Their hearts, so that they would, in unbelief,
    Remain, until they shall behold,
    The chastisement of pain and grief."

89.   He said: "Your prayer is heard, and now you both,
    Follow the direct path,
    And walk not in the path of those
    Who do not know the Truth."

90.   We took the Sons of Israel,[1]
    Safely across the sea,
    While Pharaoh and his force pursued them,
    Ruthless in enmity,
    Until, nigh being drowned, he cried:
    "I do admit there is no deity,
    But the One Whom the Sons of Israel,
    Believe in, so I am a Muslim[2] real!"[3]

91.   "What! Now? And hitherto you've been,
    A rebel bold, sunk in corruption?!

92.   "Thus this day We preserve you in your body,
    So that you shall become an omen,

---

1. Or "Children of Israel".   2. A true believer in the absolute will of
the Almighty.

3. This was death-bed repentance! The body, however, was saved from the sea,
and presumably, according to Egyptian custom, it was embalmed.

To all posterity;
Yet there are always many men,
Who do not heed Our signs."[1]

93.   At length, We settled Israel's Children
In an excellent dwelling-region,
And did provide them with some bounties wholesome.
Lo! They fell into schisms only after
The Knowledge[2] had been to them given!
Surely your Lord will judge between them,
Concerning their lasting dissensions,
Upon the Day of Resurrection.

94.   Now if you were in doubt regarding,
What we are to you sending down,
Enquire from those who have been reading
The Scriptures from before you;
For certainly the very Truth has now
Come to you from your Lord, so never
Be a disputing waverer!

95.   Nor should you ever join the people,
Denying Allah's revelations, for
You shall certainly be a loser!

96.   Verily those 'gainst whom your Lord's decree,
Has been pronounced, shall not believe,

97.   Even if every Sign is to them shown,
Till they behold the Torment grave.

---

1. The Divine reply.   2. Divine knowledge given to
them through Moses to judge between Right and Wrong.

98.   Surely there has not been a nation,
      Save Jonah's folk, who did embrace,
      The faith this way, and they were saved;
      When they[1] believed: The Torment of Disgrace,
      We spared them in this life, and gave them
      Provisions for a given space.

99.   And if your Lord had pleased, surely all dwellers
      Upon the earth, would have believed,
      Without exception; what! Will you now force,
      Men to become believers?!

100. Believing is not up to any soul,
      Unless it is with God's permission,
      And He does cast Abomination
      On those who do not use their common sense.

101. Say: Look at what is in the heavens,
      And on the earth! Nay, neither Signs,
      Nor warners will enlighten,
      The unbelieving humans.

102. What can they wait for but the evil fate,
      Of those who have before them gone?
      Say: wait and see, for I am one,
      Of those who, with you, wait!

103. At length, We'll save Our messengers,
      And those who do believe; it is indeed,
      Binding on Us to save believers.

------

1. The people of Jonah's: he was sent to the Assyrians.

104. Say: O you people, if you are uncertain,
    About my Faith? Know that I do not ever
    Worship the things you serve, instead of Allah!
    I only worship Allah, God the One,
    Who is to take your souls; and I was bidden
    To "be a true believer";

105. And ordered: "dedicate yourself in all,
    Uprightness to the Faith, and be not ever,
    An idol-worshipper;

106. "And never call, instead of God, upon
    Idols that, neither harm, nor have a use;
    For if you were to do so, you would then,
    Be one who works injustice."

107. Should God afflict you with some trouble,
    No one could do away with it, but He,
    And if He should intend to do you good,
    There won't be any to repel His bounty;
    He gives unto His creatures as He will,
    And He's Forgiving, Full of Mercy.

108. Say: "O Mankind! The Truth has come indeed,
    Unto you from your Lord; now whosoever
    Is guided, does he so, for his own good,
    And he that strays, will take himself to error,
    And I am surely not your keeper!"

109. Thus follow what is unto you revealed,
    And patiently preserve until the Time,
    When God shall make His judgment known,
    For He's the Judge Supreme.

SURA 11
HOOD[1]
(HOUD)

In the Name of God, the Beneficent, the Merciful

1.   Alif Laam Raa;[2] this is a Book with verses,
     Firmly rooted in Wisdom,
     Which is set forth with clearness, from
     The All-Informed, Most Wise:

2.   Serve none but God the One; indeed I am
     From Him to you a warner,
     And a glad-tidings bearer;

3.   Do ask forgiveness of your Lord, and turn
     Unto Him in repentance; and abundant,
     Goodly provision, till a destined term,
     He'll let you have for your enjoyment,
     And He'll bestow His graceful favours,
     On all the Grace-deservers;
     But if you were to turn away,
     Surely I'd fear for you the torment
     Of a most fateful Day!

4.   Unto Allah is your return,
     Over all things He's Potent.

5.   Behold! They cover up their breasts,
     That they themselves from him[3] may hide!

---

1. The prophet sent to an ancient, Semitic people of Arabia, the 'Aad.

2. A. L. R.

3. The Holy Prophet.

Now surely, when they use their garments,
Does He not know what they reveal and hide!
Certainly He's Aware of what's inside
Their breasts and hearts.

6. There is no moving creature in the earth,
Whose livelihood does not on God depend,
He knows its lair and den, its womb and tomb,
Everything's in a lucid Record[1] penned!

7. While Throned above the waters,[2] He created
The heavens and the earth, within six Days,
So that He may for you make manifest,
Which of you would excel in their own ways;[3]
Now when you tell them: "After death you shall,
Surely be raised to life again",
The disbelievers would be sure to say:
"That will be magic plain!"

8. If We put off their chastisement until,
A time appointed, they are sure to say:
"What on earth causes this delay?!"
Behold! The Day it shall on them befall,
Nothing turns it from them away:
Then by the very thing they ridiculed,
They shall be utterly encircled!

---

1. The word *Kitaab*, that also occurs in the first verse of this chapter, has many meanings in Arabic, among them: Book, writing, record, decree, command and ordinance.

2. Of the nature of that mater or, perhaps, the fluid state of the matter, none has any knowledge (see the same in Genesis).

3. Or "works, actions".

9.   If We give man a taste of Our Own Mercy,
      And then from him withhold it, he will surely,
      Despair and be ungrateful;

10.   And if We let him taste some favour,
      After afflictions touch him, he shall cheer:
      "Gone are my sorrows from me", and he will
      Be joyous, boastful!

11.   Not so are those who keep up patience,
      And do good works; for them there shall be,
      Forgiveness and rich recompense.

12.   You may be tempted to omit a part
      Of what is unto you revealed,
      Or be deeply distressed at heart,
      Because they often moan:
      "Why has no treasure been to him sent down?
      Why has no angle him accompanied?"
      You're only an admonisher at large,
      And God has all things in His Charge.

13.   Or are they saying: "He has forged it[1] ?"
      Say: "Then, ten *suras,*[2] like it, forge,
      And call to help whome'er you may, save God,
      If it's the truth that you allege!"

14.   And now if they to you do not respond,

---

1. The Holy Quran.   2. Chapters; the challenge is not
to produce something to equal the Quran in point of poetry or rhetoric, but
in the importance of its contents: Divine Unity, absolute submission to the
will of God, the certainty of the Resurrection, etc.

Then you should know that it has surely come,
With Allah's knowledge, that there is no God,
But He; will you then not embrace Islam?[1]

15.   To those who choose this worldly life,
And all its glitter, We reward their actions,
Therein in full, and they'll have their deserts,
Without the least reductions!

16.   But then these are the men who, in Hereafter,
Shall be rewarded only with the Fire!
Fruitless is everything they wrought,
And what they've done, has come to nought!

17.   Are they[2] the same as those who have in hand,
From their own Lord, clear evidence,
Recited by a witness[3] from Him, and
Preceded by the Book of Moses,
A Mercy and a Guidance?
Such folks believe in it,[4] whereas
Those of the Factions[5] who reject it,
Shall be consigned unto the promised Flames!
Thus have no doubts about it: it's the Truth,
From your Lord, but most men will have no faith.

18.   And who is more unjust than those who forge
Lies against God? Such people shall be floored,

---

1. Or become 'Muslims', those who submit to the Will of God.
2. The worldly men of the preceding verses.
3. The Quran.
4. The Quran
5. The partisans of idolatry.

Before their Lord, and witnesses shall say:
"Those are the men who lied against their Lord."
Shall not God's curse be on the wrong doers,[1]

19. Who, from the path of Allah, hinder others,
And seek to make it crooked, and do not
Believe the life to come a jot!

20. Never shall they escape upon the earth,
Nor have they any patrons to protect,
Them from God's wrath;
Doubled shall be for them the chastisement
For they would neither hear, nor see the Truth.

21. These people surely forfeited their souls,
And what they forged misled them further,

22. Undoubtedly the greatest losers,
They'll be in the Hereafter.

23. And those who did believe and did good works,
In dedication to their Lord, they are,
The heirs of Paradise,
And in it they'll abide for ever.

24. These two distinctive types resemble,
Men who are blind and deaf, and men
Who could well see and listen;
Can they at all be equal?
Will you not learn a lesson!

---

1. The unjust, the oppressors.

25.   Noah We sent to his own people:
        "I am to you indeed,
        A plain admonisher,

26.   "Serve none but God the One;
        I fear for you the punishment upon,
        A Day most woeful."

27.   The chiefs of those, amongst his clan,
        Who had no faith, retorted: "We
        Consider you only a man,
        Just like ourselves, nor do we see,
        Amongst your followers except,
        The lowliest of us, the most inept!
        Nor do we see that any of you bears,
        Any advantage over us; in fact,
        We take you as some liars!"

28.   He said: "Do think! O people mine,
        What if my Lord, a lucid Sign,
        Unto me sent, and did bestow,
        On me His special Grace, although
        To you obscure; could we compel
        You unto it against your will?

29.   "O people mine! I ask you not for riches,
        Only of Allah is my recompense;
        But no! I'll never drive away the ones,
        Who have embraced the faith and hence,
        Are certain that they'll meet their Lord,
        But I do see you are in ignorance;

30.   "And, O my people, if I drive them off,

Who is to help me in God's presence?
Do you not comprehend such simple stuff?!

31.   "I tell you not that with me are the Treasures
        Of God, nor do I know of the Unseen,
        Nor do I claim to be an angel, nor
        Shall I e'er say to those you reckon mean:
        'Allah shall never grant you any good'-
        Of what is in their souls, Allah Knows Best-
        And I would surely be of the unjust,
        If so I did."

32.   They said: "O Noah! You have been already
        Challenging us and arguing too much!
        Now do upon us bring the such-and-such
        Threat you have promised, if you really
        Are one who speaks the truth."

33.   He said: "It's Allah who shall bring it down,
        If He so wills, and Him you shall not weaken;

34.   "If God intend to let you go astray,
        My counsel shall not profit you a mite,
        Although I fain would counsel you aright;
        He is your Lord, and, in the end,
        You shall be unto Him returned."

35.   -Do they still say: "He's forged all this himself?"
        Say: "If I've forged it, on me be my crime,
        Yet I am clear of all the sins,
        For which you are to blame"-

36.   And unto Noah then it was revealed:

"None of your folk, shall any more believe,
Save those who have believed already,
Thus, at their doings, do not grieve!

37. "And build the Ark, under Our Watchful Eyes,
According to Our inspiration, and:
Don't plead with me for those who have been most,
Unjust, for they shall all be drowned!"

38. And he began to make the Ark,
But then the chiefs of his own folk,
Whenever they were passing by,
Made fun of him. He said: "Do mock,
If you so will, for soon we too,
Even as you laugh at us, shall laugh at you!

39. "For soon you'll come to know on whom,
The shameful Torment shall descend,
And o'er whose heads shall loom,
The torment of no end."

40. At length when Our command did come to pass
And all the fountains of the earth gushed forth,
"Embark therein, one pair of every genus",
We said, "and your own folk-save those whose death
Was marked already-and the faithful true";
Yet those who shared his faith were but a few!

41. And then he said: "Embark her; in
The name of Allah, be its roving,
And its repose; surely my Lord,
Is Oft-Forgiving, Mercy-Giving.

42.   As she was moving on with them amid,
      Mountainous waves, Noah called to his son,
      Who kept aloof: "Embark with us, my kid,
      And be not with the heathen".

43.   He said: "I will betake myself for refuge,
      To some high mount to save me from this deluge!"
      He cried: "None is secure from God's Command,
      This day, unless His Mercy be a shield."
      And, at this time, billows between them rolled,
      And he was one among the people drowned.

44.   And then the Word went forth:
      "Swallow your water, O you Earth!
      And cease your rains, O heavens!"
      The water thus receded,
      The matter was decided,
      And *she* came down to rest,
      Upon Mount Joudi's"[1] breast,
      And the announcement rang:
      "Gone are the people who did wrong!"

45.   Noah had called unto his Lord and said:
      "My Lord, my son is of my kith and kin,
      And surely true has been your promise,
      And You're the Judge Supreme."

46.   "Noah", He said, "He is no more a kinsman,
      But an embodiment of evil-doing;
      Therefore, do not ask me about
      That of which you know nothing;

---

1. One of the mountains which divide Armenia on the south from Mesopotamia.

I give you counsel lest you will,
Into ignorance fall."

47.   He said: "My Lord! I seek Your refuge,
From asking You the things,
Of which I have no knowledge,
Pardon me and on me have Mercy,
Or I'll be lost, most certainly."

48.   "Noah", He said: "Do go ashore with peace,
From Us, and blessings be on you and on,
The peoples springing from your own companions;
There shall be also many a nation,
On whom We shall bestow provision,
But then they shall incur upon themselves,
Our most painful affliction."

49.   What We reveal unto you now, are some
Tidings of the Unkenned,
Neither you, nor your people ever had,
Before this, of them learned;
Therefore be patient, as, for the godfearing,
There is a goodly End.

50.   And unto 'Aad We sent their brother,[1] Hood.
He said: "Serve Allah, O my folk, indeed,
Other than Him, you have no God,
Nothing you're serving now but falsehood!

51.   "My brethren, I demand no recompense,
For this from you, for my reward is only

---

1. Their compatriot.

With Him who has created me;
Do you not use your common-sense!

52. "My people, seek forgiveness of your Lord,
Then turn to Him in full repentance,
And He will make the skies above you,
Pour rain upon you in abundance,
And give you ever much more power;
Only do not renew your vile offense."[1]

53. They said: "O Hood, you have to us brought forth,
No proof of mission, and we won't forsake,
Our gods for your talk's sake,
Nor have we in you any faith!

54. "All we can say is that some of our gods,
Have smitten you with madness!"
He said: "Now I take God to witness,
And you should witness too,
That I am absolutely through
With your idol-worshipping business,

55. "Idols instead of God?! Conspire then,
Against me, all of you together,
Give me no respite!

56. "I've put my trust in God for ever,
He is my Lord, and He's your Lord,
There is no single living creature,
That's not held in His Grasp; only the Road,
Trod by my Lord, is truly Right.

---

1. The worship of idols.

57.   "And if you turn away giving no heed,
I'll have indeed conveyed to you the message,
I was sent with; and then my Lord shall bring
Other men in your place; and you, no damage,
Do unto Him! My Lord indeed,
Keeps Watch on everything."

58.   Thus when Our Judgment came to pass,
We did deliver, through Our Blessing,
Hood, and the ones who shared his faith,
We saved them from a Torment, most distressing.

59.   Yea, such were Aad! They openly denied,
The Portents of their Lord, and disobeyed
His messengers, but did the bidding,
Of every despot, proud, depraved.

60.   And therefore, by a Curse they were pursued,
In the life of this world; so will damnation
Be theirs upon the Day of Resurrection;
Behold! The Aad disowned Their Lord,
Behold! Gone are the Aad,
The horde of Hood!

61.   And to Thamood We sent their brother Saalih,
He said: "O people mine, do worship Allah,
You have no other God but Him, it's He
Who fashioned you out of the earth, and then,
Made it a place for you to live in,
Therefore ask His forgiveness, and do turn
Unto Him in repentance; surely ever
My Lord is Nigh, Ready to answer."

62.   They said: "O Saalih, in you we had placed
Great hopes till now! Do you forbid us
To serve the gods our fathers worshipped?!
And now indeed We have the most suspicious,
Disquieting doubt of what you're calling us."

63.   He said: "My people, do consider this:
If, from my Lord, I have some confirmation,
And He's bestowed on me His special blessing,
Now if I disobeyed Him, who'd be saving
Me from Allah? You'd hasten my perdition!

64.   "And, O My people, this she-camel
Of Allah, is to you a lucid Sign,
So let her graze at will in God's own land,
And in no way be unto her malign,
Lest a torment be for you near at hand."

65.   And yet, they hamstrung her, and killed her!
At this, he warned: "You only have three days,
To be delighting in your homes, and this
Promise is certainly to realize."

66.   And when Our Judgment came to pass,
We did deliver, through Our Grace,
Saalih and those who shared his faith,
From that Day of Disgrace;
Surely your Lord is Mighty, Full of Strength;

67.   It only took a dreadful Blast,
And the unjust, were lifeless bodies,
Prostrate in their abodes:

68.   As if therein they never gaily lived!
       Beware! Thamood denied their Lord,
       Lo! Perished were Thamood for good.

69.   And long ago, Our message-bearers went,
       To Abraham with some good tiding,
       "*Salaaman*",[1] said they unto him,
       "*Salaamun*",[2] answered he to them,
       And did not tarry long to bring,
       For them a meal of roasted calf;

70.   But when he saw their hands not stretching to it,
       He deemed it strange, and felt of them some fear;
       They said: "fear not!
       We're sent unto the tribe of Lot."

71.   And now his wife who had been standing there,
       Some cycle did she feel inside her:
       And so We gave her the glad tidings,
       Of Isaac's birth, and that of Jacob,
       From Isaac's loins.

72.   She cried out: "Woe is me! Am I to give
       Birth to a child when I'm so old a woman,
       And this, my husband, even an older man!
       This is indeed something unheard of!"

73.   They said: "Are you amazed at Allah's ways?!
       God's Mercy and His blissful Grace,
       Has been on you, O people of the House;[3]

---

1. Peace be upon you.   2. Peace be upon you too.

3. Abraham's Household.

Glorious is He, Most Worthy of all Praise."

74.   And when all fear left Abraham,
After the tidings glad had to him come,
He did begin to plead with Us a lot,
For the sake of the folk of Lot!

75.   For Abraham was certainly forbearing,
Soft-hearted and godfearing.

76.   "O Abraham! Abandon this!
Your Lord's command's already there!
And no one could avert the Torment
That them shall overpower.

77.   Our messengers now came to Lot;
He was, on their account, in sorrow,
And lacked the strength to help; he thought:
"This is indeed a day of woe!"

78.   And soon, his people, long addicted,
To practicing Abominations, came
Rushing to Him. he warned: "O people,
These are my daughters, they are lawful,
And pure for you; therefore fear God, and shame,
Me not by wronging guests of mine;
Is there among you no straight-minded man?!

79.   They said: "we have no longing for a daughter
Of yours, and, of that, you've been well-aware,
And you do know what we are after!"

80.   He cried: "I wish I had the power,

347

To set you right, or could resort
To some unshakable support."

81. They[1] said: "O Lot! We are indeed,
The message-bearers of your Lord,
Never will they upon you raise a hand;
Therefore, depart with all your household,
In the dead of the night, and do not let,
Any of you turn round to look behind,
Except your wife, who would, and will be met,
By the same scourge that shall the others grind;
Their destined Hour is when the Morn shall sigh;
Ah! Isn't Morning drawing nigh?!"

82. And when time came for Our command,
To be fulfilled We turned it[2] upside down,
And hard clay-stones upon it rained,
Mound after mound:

83. Bearing the Tokens of your Lord;
Such scourges are not ever far,
From the transgressors bold!

84. Unto the folk of Midian,
We sent Shu'aib, their brother,[3]
He said: "O people mine,
Do worship God, you have no other,
Godhead but Him; and do not ever,
Give weights or measures short,
Although I see that now you prosper,

---

1. The angels.   2. Their habitation, their towns.

3. Their compatriot.

I fear for you indeed the Torment,
Of a Day that shall overpower;

85.   "O people, give full weight and measure,
In all justice, and do not undervalue,
By finding faults, the things to people due,
And do not spread corruption in the land;

86.   "The gift of God, the residue,
Is best for you, if you are faithful,
But I am not a guardian over you."

87.   They answered: " O Shu'aib! Does your *salaat*[1]
Enjoin you that we should abandon gods
Our forefathers were wont to serve, or that
We can't do what we like with our own goods?
Surely you are the most forbearing,
Sagacious man we've got!"

88.   He said: "Consider this, O people mine,
If I have, from my Lord, a lucid Sign
And if He has with good provision,
Supplied me, and if my intention,
It has been not to follow you in what,
I have to you forbidden, do I mean
Aught but your own amendment,
As far as lies in me?
And my success[2] depends on God entirely,
On Him do I rely, and to Him only

---

1. I have not used the usual translation "prayer" for *salaat*, because I believe the
   word here has a wider meaning such as: creed, belief, religion and the like.

2. Also implying the earlier meaning of this English word: "result or outcome".

Do I return continually;

89. "And, O my people, do not let your strife
Against me, bring on you the doom that struck,
The clans of Noah, Hood and Saalih's folk;
Nor is the tribe of Lot from you far off![1]

90. " And ask forgiveness of your Lord, and to Him
Turn with remorse; surely my Lord is Full of
Mercy and Love."

91. They said: "Shu'aib! We do not understand,
Most of what you are saying, but we see,
How powerless you are amongst us,
And had it not been for your family,[2]
We would have stoned you unto death;
Any way, you will not prevail against us!"

92. He said: "O people! Is my family
More reverent to you than God? And you
Cast Him behind your backs, with negligence;
Surely my Lord encircles all you do.

93. "O people! Do whate'er you can,
And I will do all in my power;
You will know soon who is disgraced
By punishment, and who's the liar;
Be on the watch, for I am too,
Watching along with you!"

94. And when Our judgment came to pass,

---

1. In both geographical and chronological senses.   2. Or "tribe, clan".

We rescued people We had Graced:
Shu'aib and those who shared his faith;
Seized were the wicked by a dreadful Blast,
And the morning found them as lifeless bodies,
Prostrate in their abodes,

95.   As though in them they never lived!
Behold! The Midians perished,
Even as did Thamood!

96.   Of old We sent forth Moses, with Our Signs,
And, with authority most manifest,

97.   To Pharaoh and his nobles;
But they all followed the behest,
Of Pharaoh; surely Pharaoh's biddings were
Unrighteous, most unfair.

98.   Upon the Day of Resurrection,
He shall be standing at the head,
Of his own folk, and he'll be leading,
Them to the Fire; and most wretched
Is the manner they shall be led!

99.   A curse fell on them in this world,
And cursed they all shall be upon
The Day of Resurrection;
Evil's the Gifts they will be given!

100.   We are giving you some accounts,
About many a town,[1]

---

1. Also meaning: clans, nations, communities.

Some of them are still standing, while
Some were mown down.

101.   Nay, We did not do unto them injustice,
But they themselves were to their souls unjust;
And the false gods they served, instead of God,
After the judgment of your Lord was passed,
Profited them no whit, and they could add,
Aught to their lot, but more perdition!

102.   Such is the retribution of your Lord,
When He visits upon a sinful nation,
Indeed His scourge is stern and full of pain;

103.   And certainly there is in this a Sign,
For those who dread the scourge of the Hereafter,
That is the Day when all mankind,
Are to be brought together,
That is a Day that will be witnessed![1]

104.   And We shall not delay it,
Its term has been already fixed.

105.   When that Day comes, no soul shall speak a word,
Except at God's behest,
And then, some people shall be damned,
And others blessed.

106.   Now those who have been damned are thrown,
Into the Fire; and in there they could only,

---

1. It also means: A Day when all sorts of witnesses shall be heard before God's
Judgment-Seat.

Heave sighs and sob, and wail and moan!

107.   And while the heavens and the earth endure,
They shall therein remain,
Unless your Lord will otherwise ordain,
For He's the Great Fulfiller of His wills;

108.   But those who have been blessed,
Shall be residing in the Garden,
The while the heavens and the earth shall last,
Unless your Lord, will else ordain;
Endlessly are they recompensed!

109.   Therefore, be in no doubt concerning what
Those people serve:
They blindly worship what, before them,
Their fathers used to serve,
And we'll requite them in full measure:
Nothing less than what they deserve!

110.   We gave Moses the Book before this,
But then they disagreed about it,
And, had it not been for a Word,
Already uttered by your Lord, their fate
Would have been long before decided;
These people also strongly doubt it![1]

111.   And certainly your Lord will be rewarding
Them in full measure for their works,
For He is Most-Informed of what they're doing.

---

1. This Book, the Holy Quran.

112. As you have been commanded,
Thus firmly stand in the straight Path,
Yourself and all who share your faith,
And do not e'er attempt transgression,
Surely He watches o'er your every action.

113. Do not lean ever in the least,
Upon the men who are unjust,
Lest you shall end inside the Fire;
You have no patron, but for Allah:
There is, but He, no helper!

114. And keep up prayers at the two ends,
Of days, and early parts of nights,
Surely good deeds do make amends,
For sins and wrongs; and this reminder
Is for the thoughtful man who minds;

115. And practice patience; surely God
Does not allow a loss of wages,
To the doers of good.

116. If only there had been many more men
Of righteousness among the nations,
Before you, who would preach against corruptions,
Throughout the land! But there were only few,
And from among them some We had to rescue!
The wrong-doers, however, did pursue,
Their own selfish and worldly pleasures,
And turned themselves into unbridled sinners.

117. Your Lord would not have tyrannously,
Destroyed those Townships, had their populations,

Been aiming at the right direction;

118. Your Lord, if He so willed, could certainly,
      Have made mankind a single nation,[1]
      But now they'll never cease to differ!

119. Save those on whom your Lord has Mercy;
      He has created you for this,[2] indeed.
      The Word already uttered by Your Lord,
      Must be fulfilled: "I'll fill Gehenna,
      With *Jinns* and humans, all together!"

120. Everything We relate to you concerning,
      The stories of the messengers is meant
      To brace your heart, and by them to reveal,
      To you the Truth, and an admonishment
      And a reminder to believers.

121. Thus say unto the unbelievers:
      "Do act according to your state,
      And we shall do the same;"

122. "And wait! Surely we also wait."

123. Everything hidden in the heavens,
      And on the earth is God's, the whole
      Of the Affair to Him returns;[3]
      Thus worship Him, and never fail
      To put your trust in Him; your Lord is not,
      Of what you do, Heedless at all!

---

1. Umma.   2. To enjoy freedom of choice and action.

3. Or: shall be to Him returned.

SURA 12
JOSEPH
(YOUSUF)

In the Name of God, the Beneficent, the Merciful

1. Alif Laam Raa,[1]
   These are the verses of the Book,
   Explicit and profound.

2. A Reading[2] We sent down in Arabic,
   Perchance you understand.

3. As We reveal unto you this Quran,
   We shall be telling you a story,
   The finest of the fine;
   Whereas before this,
   You were among the heedless.

4. Now Joseph said unto his father:
   "O Father mine,
   I saw eleven stars, the Sun and Moon;
   Lo! They were all before me kneeling down!"

5. He said: "My little son,
   Tell not your vision to your brethren,
   Lest they against you something evil plan;
   For certainly is Satan,
   As open enemy to Man.

6. "This means that you, your Lord Will choose,
   And teach you to interpret dreams,

---

1. A.L.R.   2. Quran means "reading", recitation", "declamation".

356

And shall complete His blessed Grace,
Upon you and on Jacob's House,
As He perfected it, some decades back,
For your forefathers Abraham and Isaac;
For your Lord is the All-Knowing, All-Wise."

7.   Indeed in Joseph and his brothers,
        Are Signs for the enquirers.

8.   Now they[1] complained that "Joseph and his brother,[2]
        Are much more loved than us by father,
        Whereas we're stronger and of greater number;
        Our father clearly is in error!

9.   "Let us kill Joseph or to lands remote,
        Take him and cast him out,
        That thus your father's favour,
        Only to you is given,
        And after that you shall be righteous men!"

10.   "Do not kill Joseph", one among them[3] said,
        "But if you mean to rid of him, instead,
        Let's put him down into the well's recess,
        So that he may be found and hoisted,
        By caravans that pass."

11.   So said they: "O Our father!
        Why do you not with Joseph trust us?
        We are the very people,

---

1. The ten half-brothers.   2. The one full-brother, Benjamin.

3. The eldest brother, Reuben, or the fourth son of Jacob and Leah, Judah:
   according to different traditions.

Who surely wish him well!

12. "Send him with us tomorrow that he may
Enjoy himself and play,
And we shall guard him well!"

13. He said: "It grieves my heart to see him march
away with you, I worry lest a wolf
Should eat him up when you are not on watch."

14. They said: "With us? Such strong and numerous group?
Then if the wolf could eat him up,
We must be weaklings of no hope!"

15. And thus they took him with them and conspired
To cast him down into the well's recess;
(And We into his heart[1] inspired:
"Indeed of this affair of theirs,
You shall remind them all, when you,
They cannot recognize.")

16. And they returned at night, and facing,
Their father, said, with tearful eyes:

17. "O Father ours, we went off racing,
And posted Joseph by our merchandise,
Then came the wolf and ate him up;
But you, although we speak the truth,
Shall have in us no faith!"

18. They also brought his falsely-blooded shirt!

---

1. Joseph's.

"Oh, no!", Said he, "your egos made the matter
Appeal to you as good and proper;
Thus welcome will be Patience,
And 'gainst what you report,
It shall be God's assistance,
That should be sought.

19.   Now came a caravan who sent ahead,
       Their water-man, and he his bucket delved.
       "Rejoice, I've got a lad", he cried aloud,
       Thus as a piece of chattel, him they hid;
       And God was Cognizant of what they did.

20.   And then they sold him for a paltry price:
       For a few coins of Dirhams;
       To them he was no prize!

21.   Now the Egyptian buyer told his wife:
       "Do use him kindly; may he bring us gain,
       Or maybe we adopt him as a son."
       Thus in that land did We establish Joseph,
       And taught him to interpret dreams,
       For God is Master of His own Affair;
       Although most men are not aware.

22.   And when he had become mature of age,
       We gave him Cognizance and Knowledge;
       For thus do We reward the righteous men.

23.   But now the mistress in whose house he lived,
       Desirous of seducing him, all doors,
       Securely closed, and thus she craved:
       "Come on, I'm yours!"

"Oh, God forbid!", Said he, "Indeed my Lord
Has given me a fine abode;
Surely the evil-doers won't be saved."

24.   But still she made for him, and to her whim,
He might have given in, had he not seen,
His Lord's authentic Sign.
Thus did We turn aside from him,
Indecency and evil, since he was,
One of Our servants chosen.

25.   So they each other raced up to the door,
And clinging to him from behind,
His shirt she tore;
And at the door they found her husband.
Lo! Thus she spoke:
"What is the penalty for one who meant,
To do some ill against your folk,[1]
But prison or some torment sore?!"

26.   He said: "Nay, it was she who tempted me."
And a witness from her own family,
Did thus advise:
"If from the front, his shirt is torn, then she
The truth is telling, and it's *he* who lies;"

27.   "But if his shirt is rent behind, then he
The truth is telling, and it's *she* who lies."

28.   So when he[2] saw his shirt was rent behind,
Thus did he state:
"This is a cunning of you womankind,

---

1. Also meaning: family or wife.   2. His lord, the Aziz (the Egyptian prince).

Indeed your guile is great.

29. "O Joseph, on this keep your tongue;
O Woman, ask forgiveness for your sin,
For surely you are in the wrong."

30. Now ladies in the city let it loose:
"Aziz's wife is seeking to seduce
The young boy in her house;
He has inflamed her breast with love and lust,
We do believe that she is clearly lost!"

31. On hearing of their evil talk, the wife,
Sent for them and prepared a banquet for them;
And gave each one a knife;
Then ordered him to come before them.
As soon as they on him set eyes,
Amazed and full of praise,
They cut their hands, and shouted in surprise:
"Oh, God preserve us! This is not a mortal,
But just a gracious angel."

32. "This is the one on whose account," she claimed,
"You have me harshly blamed!
Oh, yes, seducing him I keenly tried,
But he my will denied;
Now if he doesn't gratify my will,
He shall be into prison thrown,
And held in wretched scorn."

33. My Lord!", he said, "I'd sooner go to jail,
Than give in to their invitation,
Unless you from me turn away their guile,

I may incline to their temptation,
And be a fool!"

34.   And now in answer to his supplication,
His Lord did turn away from him their wiles;
He is indeed the One who Hears, who Knows.

35.   Thus they resolved, despite the signs
That they had seen,
To imprison him for a while.

36.   Now two young men with him to prison came.
Said one: "I dreamt that I was making wine",
And said the other: "I saw in my dream,
That birds were nibbling at the bread,
Which I was taking on my head;
Tell us the meanings foreordained,
We see you are a goodly man refined."

37.   "I can", he said, "inform you of the ration,
That you receive for your provision,
Before they're brought into your vision;
This knowledge is a part of what my Lord,
To me bestowed, as I did leave,
The faith of people who did not believe
In Allah,[1] and the life to come denied.

38.   "And I follow the faith of my forefathers,
The faith of Abraham, Isaac and Jacob;
We never any partnership ascribe,
To Allah, it's a gift that God did grant

---

1. God the One.

Unto us, and to all mankind,
Although most people are ingrate.

39.   "My two companions of the prison-fetter!
Are miscellaneous Masters better
Than God the One, the Mighty?!

40.   "What you besides Him serve are only names,
That you and your forefathers coined,
With no authority of God;
To God belongs all judgment and command,
And He did give you no command,
To worship aught but Him alone:
This is the steadfast, right religion,
But most men do not comprehend.

41.   "My fellow-prisoners, of you one,
Shall serve his king with wine,
The other shall be crucified,
And birds shall nibble at his head;
That's what has been decreed,
About that which you two enquired."

42.   Then to the one he knew was to be freed,
He said: "Unto your lord do mention me."
But Satan caused him to forget to mention
This to his lord; thus he remained in prison,
For several years.

43.   Now said the king:
"I dreamt of seven, fleshy kine,
Who were completely eaten,
By other seven, skin and bone;

And seven, greenish ears of corn,
And other seven, dry and barren.
Expound to me my dream, O barons,
If you indeed interpret dreams."

44.   "Some dreams confused!", did they suggest,
"And we are not well-versed,
In exposition of such dreams!"

45.   But, of the twain, the one who was released,
Remembering at last,
Said: "I will tell you what it means,
But let me go after it first."

46.   "O Joseph, man of truth, to us explain,
Regarding seven, fleshy kine,
Who were completely eaten.
By other seven, only skin and bone,
And seven, greenish ears of corn.
And other seven, dry and barren;
That I may to the folks return
And them accordingly inform."

47.   He said: "You shall be sowing,
For seven, continuous years,
But all that you are reaping.
You should leave in their ears,
Except a little for your eating.

48.   "And after that, you shall be facing,
Hardship of drought for seven years,
Which eats away all that you have been saving,
Already for these years,

Except a little for your keeping.

49.   "And then shall come a year of rain profuse,
      In which the people shall be pressing juice!"

50.   "Bring him before me", said the King.
      Yet when the envoy to him came,
      He said: "Go back unto your lord and ask him,
      What was the story of the dames,
      Who cut their hands?!
      Certainly my lord knows about their frames."

51.   He asked the dames: "What were your schemes,
      When you persuaded Joseph to bow down,
      Unto your whims?
      "Oh, God forbid!", they cried,
      "No evil of him have we known"
      Aziz's wife did then confess:
      "Now truth has come to light,
      I lusted after him and tried
      To make him acquiesce,
      He speaks the truth indeed;

52.   "From this my lord will know I did not once,
      Play him false in his absence,
      And surely God shall never guide,
      The treacherous people's guile.

53.   "Yet I do not absolve myself of blame:
      The human ego is to evil prone,
      Excepting those on whom my Lord,
      Mercy has shown;
      He is the Oft-Forgiving, Merciful."

54.   The king then said: "Bring him before me now,
    I shall appoint him as my special aide;
    And, after speaking with him, he did vow:
    "As from today, you shall be highly placed,
    With us, in perfect trust,"

55.   "Set me over the treasuries of the land",
    Said he, "I'll be an overseer, shrewd and sound."

56.   Thus We established Joseph in the land,
    And he did govern as he pleased;
    Our Mercy We bestow on whom We will,
    And the reward of the good-doing people,
    We will not let be perished.

57.   Indeed the recompense in the Hereafter,
    For the believers and the self-restrainers,
    Shall be far better.

58.   Now Joseph's brothers had arrived, and were,
    Led unto him: them did he recognize,
    But of him they were unaware.

59.   After he had, with their supplies,
    Provided them, he said:
    "Bring me your brother on your father's side,
    You see that I give measures to the fullest,
    And that I am a generous host;

60.   "But if you do not bring him to me, then,
    From me, you shall receive no corn,
    Nor shall you near me come again."

61.   They said: "We go to get him from his father,
    We're certainly go-getters!"

62.   Then he said to his servants: "Put their coins,
    Into their bags, so that they shall them find,
    When they are back with their own clan;
    Perchance they will return."

63.   Thus when they went back to their father,
    They said: "O Father ours, for us no longer,
    There shall be any corn, unless our brother,
    You send along with us ; we then the measure,
    Will have and him we'll guard with utmost care."

64.   "Shall I entrust you with him", he replied,
    "As once before, I did entrust,
    You with his brother?
    But, then, it's God who is the Keeper Best,
    And He's the Lord of Mercy Ever."

65.   And now when they their bundles opened,
    They found their coins to them returned;
    "Father", they cried, "what more can we be after?
    Our assets have been unto us returned,
    And now we shall be able further,
    To buy foodstuff for our own people,
    And while We take care of our brother,
    We shall receive an extra load of camel;
    Oh, that's an easy measure."

66.   He said: "I will not send him with you all the same,
    Unless a solemn oath you'll take in Allah's name,
    That you shall bring him back to me, unless it be,

Out of your hand completely."
And when the solemn oath they took, he added:
"God is the Witness over what we said."

67.   He then advised: "My sons,
Enter you not all by one gate,
But go through different ones;
Yet I cannot avail you aught
Against what comes from God The One,
Indeed to God belongs all judgment,
On Him do I rely, and let reliant men,
Rely on Him alone."

68.   And when they entered as their father bade,
It did not profit them at all,
Against the plan of God;
This was an eagerness in Jacob's soul,
That he thus satisfied;
And he possessed the knowledge which We had,
Unto him given; yet most men,,
Have not that sort of ken.

69.   And now when they into his presence came,
Joseph his brother seated with himself,
And whispered: "I'm your brother, yes, the same!
Therefore, do not despair,
At their affair!"

70.   So after giving them provision.
He had a drinking-cup inserted,
In his full-brother's saddle-bag.
And next, a crier after them called out:
"O You in caravan, behold!

You are a band of robbers bold!"

71.　They turned around and asked:
"What is it that you've lost?"

72.　"The drinking goblet of the king,
And for him, who shall it return,
There is a camel-load of grain,
And to this I have sworn."

73.　"By God", they said, "you must have known,
That we have not come to this land
To spread corruption,
And we are not of thieves a band."

74.　They said: "Then what shall be the reprimand
Of this, if you are proven to be liars?"

75.　"He in whose bag", they said, "it shall be found,
Himself into a bondsman shall be turned;
That's how we punish the transgressors."

76.　So he began to search the bags of others,
Before his brother's:
At last he brought it out from his
Full-brother's sack!
-Thus We contrived for Joseph's sake,
As he his brother could not take,
According to the canon of the King;
We raise to higher ranks the ones We please,
But over and above each one who knows,
Is one, more knowing.

77.   They said: "Now if he did commit a theft,
         So did a brother of his in the past!"
         Yet Joseph kept it secret in his heart,
         And did not let them know, but thought:
         "You're in a dreadful plight! And God knows best
         About what you assert."

78.   They said: "O Prince!
         He has a very aged father,
         So take, one of us, in his place,
         Since we see that you are a doer,
         Of good and full of grace."

79.   "Oh, God forbid", he said, "if we should bind,
         A person other than the one,
         With whom our goods we find;
         For, then, we would be unto justice blind."

80.   Thus when they of him did despair,
         They went aside in order to confer;
         The eldest said: "Have you the oath forgot,
         You gave our father in the name of God?
         And that, in former times, you failed,
         Concerning Joseph?! Therefore I shall never,
         Forsake this land until my father,
         Shall give me leave, or God makes known,
         Unto me His decision,
         Since He's the Judge Supreme.

81.   "Go back unto your father and declare,
         "O Father ours, your son has stolen;
         Of what we know, we only witness bear,
         We could not guard against the hidden;

82.   "And ask the townsfolk with whom we remained,
    And ask the caravan with us returned,
    Indeed we speak the truth."

83.   "Oh, no!" Said he,
    "Your egos have upon you played a game,
    And, therefore, Patience is most seemly,
    God may, unto me, just the same,
    Together bring them all;
    For Cognizant and Wise is He alone."

84.   And then he turned away from them, to moan:
    "My Joseph! Woe is me, oh, wail!"
    And then his eyes went white with grief,
    And silent sorrow pressed his soul.

85.   "By God", they said, "will you not cease
    Remembering Joseph, till your health,
    Is ruined, or you meet your death!"

86.   He said: "I only, of my grief and pain,
    To God complain,
    And I do know, from God the One,
    Things unto you unknown.

87.   "Now go, my sons, and seek some information,
    Of Joseph and his brother,
    And never give up hope in God's Compassion;
    Surely of God's compassion none despairs,
    Except the disbelieving, truth-deniers.

88.   Now when they came back to his presence,
    They said: "O Prince!

We and our folks are stricken by distress,
And little money have we brought with us,
But pray give us full measure,
Show us charity at your pleasure,
For God will recompense
People who give in alms!"

89. He said: "Do you remember,
All that you did to Joseph and his brother,
When you were foolishly in error?

90. "You Joseph?! Are you he! Himself?! They cried.
"Yes, I am Joseph!" He replied,
"And here's my brother at my side!
God has bestowed on us beneficence,
For when one leads a life defying evil,
And perseveres with patience,
God never fails to recompense the people
Showing benevolence."

91. "We swear by God, that God", they said,
"Has chosen you above us and indeed,
We have been sinners."

92. He said: "There is today on you no blame,
God will forgive you, since He is,
The Merciful Supreme;

93. "Now take this shirt of mine,
Then cast it on my father's face.
He shall his sight regain!
Then you and all your folks,
Shall unto me return."

94. Now, when the caravan had travelled forth,
Their father faintly uttered:
"I smell the scent of Joseph's breath!
No! Think me not a dotard!"

95. "By God". they said, "you are indeed,
In your illusion old!"

96. Then came the bearer of the tidings glad,
And it[1] upon his face he laid,
And forthwith, he his sight regained!
"Did I not tell you", he explained,
"That certain things, through God, I know,
That are to you unknown?"

97. They said: "O Father, pray for us implore
Forgiveness of our sinful doings, for,
We have been wrong indeed."

98. He said: "I'll ask my Lord for your forgiveness,
For He is Oft-Forgiving, Mercy-Giving.

99. Thus when they came to Joseph, he embraced,
His parents and thus phrased:
"Welcome to Egypt! if God will,
You will be safe and well."

100. He lodged his parents on the throne,
And others, to him, on their knees fell down.
Then said he: "O My father, do behold!
This is the meaning of my vision old,

---

1. The shirt.

It was completed by my Lord,
Indeed he has to me been kind:
When He released me from the prison,
And brought you from the desert, after Satan,
Between me and my brethren,
Had sown dissension;
Surely my Lord has loving-grace
To whom He please;
For He Knows all, He is All-Wise.

101.   "My Lord! You granted me dominion,
And taught me to interpret dreams,
O You, Designer of the Heavens,
And of the Earth; You are my Guardian in,
This world, and in the one to come,
Make me to die a Muslim,[1]
And join me with the just."

102.   This, that We have to you rehearsed,
Is of the tidings of the Hidden World,
And you weren't there when they resolved,
On their affair, and wicked plans evolved.

103.   And though you keenly strive,
Most men shall not believe.

---

1. Muslim, or Mushlim in Semitic languages are derived from the root, "salama"
or "shalama", giving us other derivatives such as "salaam", and "Shalom" in
Hebrew, they all mean: "submission to the will of the Almighty" and "believing in the absolute unity of God, the Creator of all and every thing". All people so believing are, therefore muslims. This may, incidentally, shed light on
what Jesus Christ (pbuh) actually   said, in his own Semitic vernacular at the
beginning of the Sermon on the Mount: "O Ye Believers!, or "O Ye peace-
makers?!" F.N.

104.   And for this you do not envisage,
        Rewards of them, of any kind,
        It is simply a message,
        To humankind.

105.   Lo! Many are the Portents in the Sky,
        And on the earth, which they pass by,
        And, at them, close their eye.

106.   And most of them believe in God,
        If they could worship other gods,
        Besides the One!

107.   Are they securely certain that a pall,
        Of God's extensive chastisement shall not,
        Upon them fall?
        Or that the Hour[1] shall not upon them rush
        Without a call?

108.   Declare: "This is my Path,
        I call you all to God,
        I and my followers,
        With certainty of insight;
        And glory be to God, that I am not,
        Among the idol-worshippers!"

109.   Never before you,[2] have We sent but mortals,
        Chosen out of the locals,
        Who did receive Our revelations;
        Do they not travel through the land?

---

1. Doomsday.

2. Mohammad (pbuh).

Have they not seen how was the end,
Of those who lived before them?!
Far better is the Home of the Hereafter,
For every righteous, self-restrainer;
Do they not ever ponder?!

110.   And when at length Our messengers despaired,
And thought that they were looked upon as liars,
Our help came down to them, and We then saved,
Those whom We pleased, but guilty sinners,
Did not escape Our retribution.

111.   Indeed in their account, there was a Lesson,
To men of understanding,
It was no fabricated fiction,
But confirmation of the Scripts preceding,
And of all things, an explanation,
And, to the faithful, and believing,
A Guidance and a Blessing.

SURA 13
THUNDER
(AL-RA'D)

In the Name of God, the Beneficent, the Merciful

1. Alif Laam Meem Raa;[1]
   These are the verses of the Book; and what
   Is to you, from your Lord, sent down
   Is just the Truth; and yet,
   Most men believe it not.

2. God is the One Who raised the heavens,
   Without a pillar to be seen,
   He did then mount His Mighty Throne,
   And tamed the Sun and Moon,
   And made each one to run,
   For an appointed term upon,
   A course its own; He does ordain
   The whole Affair, and He makes plain
   His revelations,[2] making you assured,
   About a Meeting with your Lord.

3. And He it is Who spread the planet Earth,
   And placed upon it mighty mountains,
   And running rivers; and all fruits and plants
   On it, He made of mating twains;
   And over Days He drew the veil of Nights;
   Behold, in these are certain Signs in fact,
   For people who reflect.

---

1. A. L. M. R.
2. Or "signs".

4.   And in the land, there are adjoining regions,
And there you find: gardens of vines,
Cornfields and groves of palms,
Single and clustered over,
Watered with the same water;
Yet some of them We have made better,
As food than other;
Surely in these are certain Signs
For those who ponder.

5.   If ever you may wonder,
Then wondrous is their exclamation:
"After we turn to dust and powder,
Are we to be existing further,
In a renewed creation?!"
Such are the people who deny their Lord:
Their necks are to be bound in chains;
And they shall be companions
Of the Hell-fire; and they shall dwell
In there for eons.

6.   They bid you hasten evil,
Rather than good! yet numerous
Were the examples of the grievous
Punishments for the former people;
Surely your Lord is Most Forgiving
Unto all people, notwithstanding,
Their cases of transgression;
But He is also Most Exacting,
In Retribution.

7.   The disbelievers also often chide:

"Why has his Lord no sign[1] unto him given?"
You are a warner only, and each nation,
Has its own guide.

8.   God knows what every female bears,
      What's happening in every womb,
      Whether they fail or will be in full bloom;
      Everything with Him is by measures.

9.   Of the Unseen and of the Seen,
      Only He knows, the Greatest, Most Supreme,

10.   It's the same whether you shall whisper
      Or speak aloud, or, in the cloak of night,
      Cover yourselves, or walk in broad daylight;

11.   Unto each person is assigned a range,
      Of angels close before him and behind,
      O'er him to watch by God's command;
      Indeed God does not change the plight
      Of a people unless they change
      Themselves from the inside;
      But once He shall decide,
      On causing retribution to a band,
      None could avert it, nor beside,
      Him, will they find a helping hand;

12.   It's He Who lets you see the lightning,
      Which fill you both with fear and hope,
      And Who the laden clouds brings up.

---

1. Miracle.

13.   The thunder celebrates His praise,
        So do the angels, of His holy fright;
        He flings the thunderbolts to smite
        With them, whome'er He please,
        While they dispute concerning God;
        And He chastises with all might.

14.   The truthful prayer is due to Him alone;
        And those whom they, beside Him, call upon,
        Shall ne'er to them respond:
        It is as if a man would stretch his hand,
        For water, and demand that it should rise
        Upon his mouth; it will not do! Likewise,
        The disbeliever's prayer,
        Dies out into thin air!

15.   All beings in the heavens and on earth,
        Prostrate themselves to Allah, be they willing,
        Or forcedly, together with their shadows,
        Morning and evening.

16.   Say: "who's the Lord of heaven and the earth?"
        Answer: "it's God he One."
        Say: "why then do you take, along with
        Him, patrons who do not have power even
        To be of help or harm to their own selves?
        Say: "Are the blind equal to those with sight?
        Could darkness be the same as light?
        Or have they fabricated partners
        To God, who have created something like,
        Allah's Creation, and they both
        Appear to them alike?!"
        Say: "Allah has created everything,

And He's the One, the Overpowering;"

17.   He sends down water from the sky, and fills
Channels and river-beds to overflowing,
So that the torrents bear the swelling foams,
Along with them, much like the scums that surface,
When metals have been molten in the furnace,
For making ornaments and various vessels;
God makes, by such similitude,
The truth distinct from falsehood:
As to the foam, it will be quickly gone,
And that which is of use to man,
Shall be remaining on the earth;
Such are some parables by God set forth.

18.   For those, who do respond,
To the call of their Lord,
There shall be fine reward,
But the rejecters of His call,
Had they at their disposal all
The wealth on earth, and as much more,
They would surely give it up for
Their ransom! As their reckoning is evil,
And Hell is certainly their Home,
A resting-place most awesome!

19.   How can the one who knows for sure,
That what to you your Lord does send
Is nothing but the truth, be like
The man who is unto this blind?
Only the men of insight will,
Bear this in mind,

20.   Those who fulfill their pledge with God,
And do not break the covenant,

21.   Those who shall join together,
What God has bidden to be joined,
Who fear their Lord, and dread the terror
Of an ill judgment;

22.   And those who, for the Pleasure of their Lord,
Endure with fortitude,
Attend unto their prayers,
And, out of what We have on them bestowed,
Give alms, in private and in public,
And do repel evil with good;
These shall enjoy the Glad Abode,[1]

23.   Gardens of Eden,[2] which they'll enter,
Together with the upright men and women,
Amongst their own forefathers,
Their spouses and their children;
And angels come from every Portal,
To wish them well:

24.   "Upon you be *salaam*![3]
For all you patiently endured,
How blissful is this final Home."

25.   But those who break their covenant with God,
After having their word unto it plighted,

---

1. In the Hereafter.

2. Or "perpetual Bliss".

3. Shalom: Divine tranquillity and peace.

Who cut asunder things that God has made
Imperative to be united,[1]
And who do spread corruption in the land,
A curse shall be upon them laid,
And they shall have an Evil End.

26. God gives abundantly or sparingly,
Of His provisions unto whom He's willed,
And they rejoice in the life of this world,
Yet this world's life is just a flotsam,
Compared unto the life to come!

27. The disbelievers still protest:
"Why has his Lord not given him a sign?"[2]
Say: "Allah leaves in error whom He wills,
And those who do unto Him turn,
In penitence, He guides unto Himself,

28. "Embracers of the faith, whose hearts
Are set at rest by God's remembrance;
Surely by God's remembrance,
The heart is set at rest;

29. "Boundlessly blessed are those who do have faith,
And do good works; their journey's end,
Shall be the finest."

30. Thus[3] have We sent you to a nation,

---

1. All those social and civil relations that are conducive to the correct and right
   conduct of collective human life.

2. Or "miracle".

3. That is: without giving you the Sign they demand.

Whom many nations did precede,
That you may to them read
Our Revelation;
But still they disbelieve in Al-Rahmaan![1]
Say: He's my Lord, no God is there but He,
On Him do I rely and in Him,
My sole resort, shall be.

31.   "What if a Reading[2] could have moved the mountains,
Or cleft the earth asunder, or compelled
The dead to speak?"[3] But nay! All things
Happen as God has willed.
Are the believers still in doubt that God,
Had He so pleased, could certainly have guided
All humankind to the right road?
And now, because of what they do,
The disbelievers shall continue,
Having repeated cataclysms,
Or they[4] will crouch close to their homes,
Until the threat of Allah comes to pass,
For God shall never fail His promise.

32.   Many a messenger has been before you,
Mocked at indeed, but then I always gave
Respite to people who did not believe;
At length I seized them; and unpleasant
Was surely My repayment!

---

1. The Most Beneficent.   2. (As this Quran).

3. This is addressed to the believers who thought that a Sign would make the
   disbelievers to embrace the Faith! Every Sign was shown to such people by
   many of God's prophets, and they still denied the Truth!

4. The cataclysms, the misfortunes.

33.   What! Are they setting up some partners,
        Along with God: the Ever-Present Watcher,
        Of every soul to mark its gains?
        Say: "Give their names!
        Perhaps you mean to let Him Know
        Of some unknown-to-Him-earth news!
        Perhaps you play some verbal games!"
        But, nay! The fact is that their foul devising,
        Appear to disbelievers very pleasing,
        Yet they have surely been debarred
        From the right Road;
        And there is none to show the way,
        To those whom God lets go astray;

34.   For them there is a torment in
        This world's life, but the retribution
        In the Hereafter is more grievous;
        Who could, 'gainst God, be their protection?

35.   Here is a picture[1] of the Paradise,
        To the god-fearing promised:
        Beneath it, rivers flow for ever,
        Its foods and fruits are never missed,
        Eternal is that shaded shelter!
        This is the End for self-restrainers,
        But the End of the disbelievers,
        Shall only be the Fire.

36.   Those unto whom We have already
        Given the Book, rejoice
        At what is unto you sent down;

---

1. Or "likeness".

But there are also men who voice-
From 'mongst the Factions[1] -
Their disbelief in certain sections;
Say: "I've been only bidden:
To worship God the One,
And none to join with Him in Godship;
I do invite to Him alone,
And unto Him is my return."

37.   It is with this instruction that We sent
        It as an Arabic commandment;
        Now if, unto their whims, you should succumb,
        After the knowledge which has to you come,
        You would not find a guardian,
        'Gainst God, and none for your protection.

38.   We have already sent before you, other
        Apostles, and We have unto them given,
        Consorts and children,
        Yet it was not within the power,
        Of any messenger to show a Sign,
        Without God's sanction;
        For every term, however,
        Decrees were Written down.[2]

39.   God abrogates or keeps entire,
        Whate'er He does desire;
        His is the ageless Mother-Book.

40.   Whether We let you watch the execution,

---

1. The infidel parties, the confederates, or any other groups.
2. Or "there has been a Book".

Of what we're holding out to them, or take
Your soul to Us, your only mission,
Is to convey the Message, and on Us
Shall be the Calculation!

41. Do they not see how We invade the land,
By shrinking its outlying borders;
For when Allah decrees a thing,
None may reverse His orders,
And Swift is He at reckoning;

42. Those who have gone before them also planned,
But the whole Planning is in Allah's Hand;
He Knows the deeds of every soul, and soon,
The unbelievers come to know for whom,
Will be the boon of the Good Home!

43. The disbelievers claim:
"You are not an apostle true!"
Say: "God's Sufficient as a witness,
'Tween me and you, and those who do,
Some knowledge of the Book[1] possess.

---

1. Of the nature of divine revelations in general.

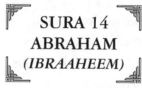

SURA 14
ABRAHAM
(IBRAAHEEM)

In the Name of God, the Beneficent, the Merciful

1.   Alif Laam Raa;[1] a Book have We sent down,
To you that, by their Lord's permission,
You bring men, out of darkness into light,
Into the right Path of the One: in Might
Exalted, Worthy of all Admiration,

2.   The very God to Whom belongs,
Whatever is there in the heavens,
And all on earth; and woe to people
Who disbelieve, because they will
Receive a torment terrible.

3.   They are the ones who love this worldly life,
Above the life to come, and turn away,
From Allah's path, and seek to make it
Look crooked; these are surely far astray.

4.   We never sent a messenger,
But with the tongue of his own tribe,
In order that he might describe
Everything plainly, yet it's Allah
Who will let be in error,
Whom He wishes, and guides whomever,
He so desires;
He is the Mighty, the All-Wise.

---

1. A. L. R.

5.   Of old did We send Moses with Our Signs,
     Saying: "Bring out your folk from darkness
     Into the light, and tell them of the lesson,
     Of Days of God;"[1] there are great Signs in this,
     For every patient, thankful person.

6.   Behold! Moses his people thus addressed:
     "Remember Allah's favour to you when,
     He rescued you from Pharaoh and his henchmen,
     Who had subjected you to tough affliction,
     And slew your sons and spared your women;
     In this was a tremendous test,
     At your own Lord's behest!"

7.   And call to mind! Your Lord did make it known:
     If you give thanks, I will on you bestow
     Much more, but if you are ungrateful,
     My chastisement is to be full of woe!

8.   Moses then added:
     "If all of you and every multitude,
     Upon the earth, will show ingratitude,
     Allah shall still be Free of Need,
     And Ever-Praised, indeed;

9.   "Have you not heard the news of those,
     Before you gone: the tribes of Noah,
     Aad and Thamood, and others after them?
     None knows of them but Allah!
     Their messengers, with proofs of mission,

---

1. In divine history, these are days when God shows a people special Mercy or afflicts them with special punishment.

Came unto them, but they gave them the edge,
Of their tongues, saying: "We deny the Message
That you have brought, and certainly about,
What you invite us to, we are in doubt,
And have a great suspicion!"

10.   "What!" said their messengers, "you have some doubts,
Concerning God, the Author of the heavens
And earth? He only calls you to Himself
That He may pardon you your faults and sins,
And respite you till an appointed time!"
They still said: "you are mortals like ourselves,
Your purpose is that we do keep aloof,
From what our fathers used to worship;
Bring us, therefore, some solid proof."

11.   Their messengers told them: "We are indeed,
Mortals, just like yourselves, but Allah shows
His Grace, among his servants, unto those
Whom He so wills; it is not in our hand,
To bring you proofs except by God's command;
And, therefore, true believers put their trust
In God alone;

12.   "And why should we not put our trust in God,
After He has our ways unto us shown;
And We will bear with patience every hurt,
You may on us exert;
Surely the faithful, trustful men,
Rely on God alone."

13.   And now the folk who disbelieved,
Their own apostles, threatened:

"We will most surely banish
You from our land,
Or else you must return
To our religion!"
But then their Lord to them revealed:
"Surely the wicked We shall cause to perish!

14.   "And We will surely let you settle,
After them in the land;
This is for those who dread to stand,
In front of My tribunal,
And fear My retribution."

15.   Then they[1] implored for help, and thus,
The fate of all the proud, rebellious,
People was nothing but frustration;

16.   Hell is before them, and for drinking,
They're given some hot water stinking;

17.   They have to sup it, but could scarce,
Swallow it or inhale,
And Death, on every side,
Them shall assail;
Yet they won't die: only they will confront,
A lasting, grievous Torment.

18.   The deeds of those who their own Lord deny,
Are like the ashes scattered by the gale,
On a tempestuous day;
Their works shall be to them of no avail;

---

1. The messengers; some commentators interpret this verse differently.

This is being: farthest astray!

19. Do you not see that God has based,
    The Creation of heavens and the earth,
    Upon the Truth?[1]
    And that He could, if He did wish,
    Remove you and have you replaced,
    By a creation fresh;

20. And this is not for God a matter,
    Of any labour!

21. When all mankind shall be to God presented,
    The weak shall say unto the arrogant:
    "Surely we followed you; will you not then,
    Relieve us of some part of Allah's torment?"
    They say: "If God had guided us, we would
    Have surely guided you; now it's indeed,
    All the same if we wail and weep,
    Or be patient; there's no escape."

22. And Satan will thus argue,
    When Judgment is already passed:
    "What God had to you promised,
    Was certainly a promise true,
    Some promises did I make too,
    But I had been deceiving you!
    Yet I had on you no dominion,
    I only to you made the call,
    And you answered me all;
    Therefore, do not blame me, but blame

---

1. That is, for a serious purpose: to manifest the Divine Unity.

Your very selves! I cannot be an aider,
To you, and you can't help me either!
Indeed I never shared your claim,
That I was ever:
With God the One a partner!"
Thus the unjust, the wrongful,
Shall face a scourge most painful.

23.   But those who did believe and did good works,
Shall be admitted into Gardens,
Watered by running streams,
Their ever-lasting dwellings,
By their own Lord's permission,
Wherein *Salaamun*[1] is their salutation.

24.   Have you noted to what God likens,
A godly word?[2] To a good tree, whose root
Is firmly fixed, and to the heavens,
Reach up its branch and shoot,

25.   Yielding its fruit, by the permission,
Of its own Lord, in every season;
And God sets forth such parables to men,
That they from them may learn a lesson.

26.   The likeness of an evil word, however,
Is certainly that of an evil tree,
With roots pulled up from the face of the earth,
Lacking solidity.

---

1. Upon you Peace!

2. Divine word, Divine Message or God's true Religion; in a more general sense:
   any word of truth, of goodness or kindness.

27.   God will establish true believers,
       With the Word that is firmly fixed,
       Both in this world and in the next,
       But Allah lets all the transgressors,
       Remain in error;
       For Allah executes His Pleasure.

28.   Have you not ever thought of those who did,
       Repay God's grace with unappreciation,
       And drove their people with them into,
       The House of Ruination,

29.   Known as Gehenna? They will surely reach it,
       But it's a wretched station!

30.   They have set up as equals unto God,
       Idols of falsehood that they would mislead,
       Men from His Path! Tell them: "Enjoy yourselves,
       Your final Home is in the Fire indeed!"

31.   Say to My servants, those who do believe:
       To keep up prayers, and be expending,[1]
       In private and in public, out of what,
       We have to them supplied, ere the descending
       Of the Day, when there shall be no occasion,
       For trading or befriending!

32.   God is the One who did create the heavens,
       And the earth, and it's He Who, from the heaven,
       Sends down the water that brings forth the fruits
       And crops for your provision;

---

1. In the cause of God.

He has subjected ships into your service,
So that they sail the seas by His permission;
And He subjected unto you the rivers,

33.   And made subject to you the Sun and Moon,
In their courses as constant movers,
And nights and days rendered He your domain,

34.   And He does grant you everything you need:
Were you to reckon up God's favours,
You'd fail to number them indeed,
But men are most unjust and thankless creatures!

35.   Remember Abraham who prayed:
"My Lord, make this[1] a city
Of safety and security,
And save me and my sons
From serving icons;

36.   "Many a man have they[2] misled already,
But whosoever follows me, shall be
Truly of me; but those who turn against me?
Surely You are Forgiving, Full of Mercy;

37.   "Our Lord! Verily have I settled some,
Of my offspring in an unfruitful valley,
Yet nigh Your Sacred House; our Lord, that they
May keep up prayer: thus fill the hearts of many
People with love towards them, and apportion
To them abundant fruits that they may be

---

1. Mecca.

2. The idols, icons and false deities.

Showing appreciation;

38.　"Our Lord, You truly know what we conceal
　　　And whatsoever we reveal,
　　　For naught on earth or in the heaven,
　　　Is ever from God hidden;

39.　"Praise be to God who, in the cul-de-sac
　　　Of my old age, made the donation
　　　To me, of Ishmael[1] and Isaac;
　　　My Lord is certainly the Hearer,
　　　Of every prayer;

40.　"My Lord, make me and my posterity,
　　　People who keep up prayer,
　　　And, O my Lord, accept my prayer;

41.　"Our Lord, forgive me and my parents,
　　　And the faithful, on the Day when accounts
　　　Are to be taken."

42.　Think not that Allah is regardless
　　　Of the deeds of the wicked; rather,
　　　He gives them respite till a Day,
　　　When eyes shall stare in horror;

43.　They hasten forward, fearfully annoyed,
　　　Their heads uplifted, and their eyes,
　　　Fixed in a mental haze,
　　　With every heart, a hopeless void!

---

1. The name in Hebrew means: "God will hear".

44. Thus warn[1] mankind about the Day,
    When Chastisement shall to them reach,
    And when the evil-doers will beseech:
    "Our Lord, do grant us a delay,
    Only a while, and we will answer,
    Your call, and follow every messenger!"
    "What! Are you not the ones who used to swear
    That never will your power wear away!"

45. "And yet you had been dwelling,
    In the homes of the peoples,
    Who were unjust to their own souls,
    And what had been our dealing
    With them, was unto you made plain:
    We held them up unto you as examples."

46. Indeed they plotted cunning plots, but God
    Did master all their plottings,
    Even though their plots had been so mighty as
    To move the mountains.

47. Think not, therefore, that God will fail His
    Promise to His apostles: for He is
    The Mighty Lord of All-Revenge!

48. On the Day when the Earth shall change
    Into a different earth, and heavens,
    Into new ones, they[2] shall before Him range,
    Before Allah: the One Who Ever-Reigns;

---

1. "O Mohammad" (pbuh).
2. The humankind.

49.   And on that Day, you'll see the guilty
        Together linked in chains,

50.   Their garments are of liquid pitch,
        Their faces jacketed in flames;

51.   Thus does God recompense each soul,
        According to its worldly gains;
        Most Swift is God at reckonings

52.   This is a Message for mankind,
        So that they may thereby be warned,
        And that they know for certain that there is,
        Only one God, and that the wise,
        Will possibly bear it in mind!

SURA 15
THE ROCKY TRACT
(AL-HIJR)[1]

In the Name of God, the Beneficent, the Merciful

1.   Alif Laam Raa;[2] these are the verses of
   The Book, and a Reading that clears;

2.   Many a time will the unfaithful
   Wish that they too had been submitters.[3]

3.   Let them be eating, drinking, merry-making,
   And fooled by wishful thinking,
   It won't be long before they know!

4.   Never did We destroy a town,
   Whose record was not clearly taken down;[4]

5.   No nation can bring forward or delay,
   Its fatal day!

6.   And now they say: "O you[5] to whom
   The Message is sent down!
   You are indeed insane![6]

7.   "Why don't you bring to us some angels,

---

1. The city of the ancient, Arabian people called Thamood, north of Medina, on the old highway to Syria.

2. A.L.R.

3. "Muslims": true believers in God who 'surrender' to the will of the Almighty.

4. Or "whose term was not ordained".

5. The Holy Prophet.   6. Or "possessed by the Jinn".

If you are of the truthful ones?"

8.   But We do not send angels down,
      Except with justice;[1] in that case,
      They would have been no respite given.

9.   Verily it is We Who have revealed,
      The Message, and Ourselves indeed,
      Will be its guardian.

10.   And certainly to ancient peoples,
      Before you, we did send apostles;

11.   But every messenger who to them came,
      Was made a victim of derision;

12.   Thus do We let it enter,
      Into the hearts of hardened sinners:[2]

13.   In it they won't become believers,
      Though the example of the men of yore,
      Has gone before.

14.   And even if We were to open,
      To them a gateway unto Heaven,
      So that they could ascend
      Into it hours on end,

15.   They would certainly say:
      "Our eyes were dazzled, nay!
      We're an enchanted folk!"

---

1. To execute justice and prompt punishment.   2. "To do the same."

16.   It's We Who authored constellations,
Throughout the heavens,
And decked them out for those who look;

17.   And We have been their guardians
From all accursed satans;

18.   Save such as try to steal a hearing,
But then they'll find a meteoroid,
After them blazing!

19.   Also the earth did We spread forth, and set
Upon it mountains firm, and in it let,
Everything grow in proper balance;

20.   And We therein provided sustenance,
For you and for the other creatures,
For whom you may not be providers.

21.   Not a thing is there but its treasures,
Are in Our hand, and it We do not send
Down but in settled measures.

22.   And We send forth the fertilizing winds,
And from the skies We send down rains,
Providing you with water; but not you,
Could be their guardians![1]

23.   Surely it's We Who life and death ordain,
And it is We Who will as Heirs remain!

---

1. Or "their storers".

24. And known to Us are those among you,
    Who hasten forward,
    And known to Us are those who lag behind.[1]

25. And it's your Lord Who will certainly gather
    Them all together;
    For surely He's the Wise, the Knower.

26. Indeed We made the humans from
    Some dried-up clay of blackish loam
    Wrought into form.

27. The race of Jinns We did create before,
    Out of intensely heated, smokeless fire.

28. Behold! Your Lord said to the angels:
    "I'll now create a human from
    Some dried-up clay of blackish loam
    Wrought into form;

29. "So when I shall have brought him to perfection,
    And breathed into him of My spirit, then
    Fall down before him in prostration."

30. Therefore the angels did prostrate themselves,
    All of them in the congregation,

31. Except Iblees,[2] who did refuse
    To be with those who bent their knees!

---

1. Or "those who've gone before and those who come later."

2. The epithet of the Satan (Diabolis) meaning: the rejected, wounded, or stoned
   one; an outcast.

32. "O You Iblees", said He "What's wrong,
    Why are you not with the prostrating throng?"

33. He answered: "It does not behoove me to
    Bow down in worship to a human whom
    You have created from:
    Some dried-up clay of blackish loam,
    Wrought into form!"

34. "Begone then hence", He said, "you are rejected,

35. "And curse shall be upon you,
    Until the Day of Doom."

36. "My Lord," he begged, "reprieve me then,
    Until the Day they'll be raised up again."

37. He said: "Granted are you a respite,

38. Until a Day of prefixed date."

39. "My Lord," he said, "Since You beguiled me,
    I shall seduce them all by making,
    Everything on the earth to them fair-seeming;
    Surely I'll cause them all to deviate!

40. "Except, among Your servants, those
    Who are most purely Yours."

41. He said: "with Me this is a right direction,

42. "For you shall have no domination,
    Over My servants, save the strayers,

Who will become your followers."

43. And surely for them one and all
    The promised place is Hell;

44. To it are seven Gates, and every band
    Of them, shall be to one assigned.

45. But 'mid Gardens and Fountains will,
    The righteous self-restrainers dwell:

46. "Enter therein in peace, secure."

47. And We'll remove all hate and rancour,
    From their bosoms: they'll sit as brethren,
    On raised couches, facing each other,

48. No weariness therein shall touch them,
    Nor will they be ejected from it ever.

49. Inform My servants that I am in truth,
    Most-Pardoning and Full of Ruth.

50. And that My chastisement,
    Shall be a grievous chastisement.

51. Now tell them of the guests of Abraham:

52. Behold, they went into his home,
    And said: "Shalom;"[1]
    "We are afraid of you!", he said.

---

1. Salaaman "peace upon you".

53. "Be not alarmed", they answered," for We come,
    To give to you the tidings glad
    Of a son blessed with wisdom.[1]

54. He wondered: "What! you bring me such good message,
    In my old age?
    Of what then are you giving me the news?"

55. They said: "We do announce to you,
    The tidings of a true affair,
    And you ought not to be among
    Those who despair."

56. He said: "Of course not, strayers only,
    Ever despair of their Lord's Mercy;"

57. And then he added: "O you messengers,
    Are you on an important mission?"

58. They said: "We have been sent unto a nation,
    Deeply in sin;

59. "Except the folk and followers of Lot-
    Them We shall rescue, all the lot,

60. "Except his wife, who has been destined,
    To be with those who stay behind-"

61. So when the messengers,
    came to the House of Lot,

---

1. That is: Isaac.

62.   He said: "you're surely strangers,
        Unto me quite unknown!"

63.   They said: "yes, but We've come to you about
        Something your people doubt,

64.   "And unto you we bring the truth;
        And we are truthful men indeed;

65.   "So take your kinsfolk in the dead of night,
        Walk in the rear yourself, and do not let,
        Any of you turn round, but travel straight,
        Wither you have been bidden."

66.   And this decree We made unto him known
        That they were going to be overthrown,
        To the last man, by the next morn.

67.   Now many people of that town,[1]
        In lustful joy, unto him came!

68.   "Surely these are my guests", said Lot,
        "Therefore, disgrace me not,

69.   "Fear God and put me not to shame!"

70.   They said: "Have we not it forbidden,
        That you should no one entertain?!"

71.   He pleaded on: "Here are my daughters,[2]

---

1. At the news of the arrival of some handsome young men at Lot's house!

2. This is Lot's final plea to save them while he knows that those ruffians have

If you are bent on doing aught."

72.   Verily, as you[1] live, they sought,
      In wild intoxication,
      After their blind perversion.

73.   And so at dawn,
      A dreadful Blast above them rang,

74.   Whereby We turned them[2] upside down,
      And did upon them fling,
      Baked clays as hard as stones.

75.   Surely in this are certain Signs,
      For those who see by Tokens;

76.   And they've been lying by,
      An often-trodden highway![3]

77.   And surely in this there are Signs,
      For true believers.

78.   The Dwellers of the Forest,[4]
      Also transgressed;

79.   Thus We exacted retribution

---

no feeling for marrying women.

1. (You, Prophet Mohammad).   2. The towns.

3. The high road from Medina to Syria.

4. Original: The companions of al-Aika, the community of Prophet Shu'aib,
   whose capital was Midian; the Aika people could perhaps be a neighbour of
   the Midianites.

From them, and they are both[1] upon
A road still trodden, open.

80. Denied had been Our messengers in fact,
Also by Dwellers of the Rocky Tract;[2]

81. We sent to them Our revelations,
But they drew back from them;

82. They used to hew their houses,
In the mountains, to feel secure;

83. But then a dreadful Blast
Seized them at early morning,

84. And what they had achieved,
Availed them nothing!

85. And We did not create the skies
And what between them lies,
But for a worthy end,
And certainly the Hour is coming,
Thus be forgiving and most kind;

86. For certainly your Lord is ever,
The Great Creator, the All-Knower;

87. And unto you We have already granted,

---

1 The twin towns of Sodom and Gomorrah, and the territory of Aika, the
Sylvans.

2. The Companions of Al-hijr in the territory of Thamood, to the north of
Medina, on the old highway to Syria.

The Seven Pairs,[1] and Al-Quran the Grand.

88. Never envy certain good things,
We have to certain classes given,
Nor ever grieve at their condition,
But spread your tender wings,
On those who do believe.

89. And say: "I am
Only a Warner plain."

90. For We'll come down upon;
The breakers-up,

91. Who dealt with Al-Quran,
As shredded scrap!

92. We, by your Lord, most surely will,
Take account from them one and all,

93. Concerning what they've done.

94. Thus openly profess what you are bidden,
And turn away from every pagan,

95. Surely We shall suffice you,
Against the scoffers,

96. Who set up other deities,
Along with Allah; soon shall they,

1. Or "the seven oft-repeated verses"; most commentators believe these to
be the seven verses of Sura 1.

Know the realities!

97.   We do know that your heart has been distressed,
        By what they have expressed;

98.   Therefore, give glory to your Lord,
        And celebrate His praise, and be,
        of those who go before Him,
        Upon the knee.

99.   And serve your Lord till when,
        To you shall come:
        That which is certain.[1]

---

1. *Al-yaqeen*, lit. *certainty*, is here generally understood to mean "death".

SURA 16
THE BEES
(AL-NAHL)

In the Name of God, the Beneficent, the Merciful

1.   Allah's command shall come to pass,
    Thus do not seek to hasten it!
    Glory be to Him, He is far above,
    The partners they beside Him posit.

2.   He sends down, by His own behest,
    The angels with the Spirit,[1]
    Unto such of His servants as He please,
    Bidding them: "Give the warning: that there is
    No God but I; therefore fear Me alone."

3.   His truth to manifest,
    Did He create the heavens and the earth;
    He's far above what they beside Him posit.

4.   Man He created from a tiny seed;
    Lo! An opponent[2] open,
    Has he become indeed!

5.   And the cattle did He for you create:
    Warmth you derive from them and other
    Benefits, and of them you eat.

6.   You have in them a sense of beauty when,
    You bring them home, and when you once again,

---

1. Inspiration of His Command.

2. Challenger, disputer, contender.

Will drive them out to pasture.

7.   They also bear your heavy burden,
To far-off lands, which you could never
Reach, but with lots of travail,
Truly your Lord is Kind and Merciful.

8.   He also gave you horses, mules and asses,
To ride upon, and for adorning uses;
And He creates a lot,
Of things that you know not!

9.   Of God it is to show the Way,
But some do from it turn away,
Certainly, if He ever wills it,
All of you He could guide aright.

10.   It's He Who sends down water from the heaven,
For you to drink, and grows the vegetation,
Of use for food and forage;

11.   Thereby He brings forth corn and herbage,
Olives, palm-trees, and grapes, and every other
Order of fruits for you; surely there are,
Some Signs in this for those who ponder.

12.   He's made for you subservient,
The night and day, the sun and moon;
So are the stars, by His command,
Subjected; surely there's a Sign
In this for those who understand.

13.   And surely there are signs for men who muse,

In all the things He has for you created,
Upon the earth, of various hues.

14. And it is He Who did to you subject,
The seas from which you eat fresh meat, and take
From it to wear many an object,
For ornaments, and see the ships that rake
Through them, that you may of His bounties seek,
And that you might give thanks.

15. And He has set up mountains firm upon,
The earth to be for you the stable marks,
As well as streams and paths, that you
go not askew;

16. Yea, by many landmarks as these,
Guided are men, as by the Pleiades.[1]

17. Is He: He the Creator,
Like those who have created nothing?
Do you ever consider?!

18. If you would reckon up God's favours,
Never could you show them in numbers;
Aye! God's Forgiving, Merciful.

19. And He does Know everything you conceal,
And all that you reveal.

20. What they call on, instead of God, did not

---

1. This is the meaning of *al-najm* as singular; if we take it as a plural, it would
mean "the stars".

Create a thing, they are themselves,
Created beings;

21. Dead and lifeless are they, not knowing when,
They shall be raised again!

22. Your God is one God only: But the hearts
Of those who have no faith in the Hereafter,
Are given to denial, and they are,
Puffed up with pride as ever.

23. Undoubtedly God knows what they
Reveal and what they hide,
Surely He has no love for men,
Puffed up with pride.

24. For when it's said to them: "What is it
Your Lord has sent?"
They answer: "Oh, some fables ancient!"

25. For this, upon the Day of Resurrection,
They'll have to bear not only their own burdens,
Totally, but the burdens of the people,
Whom they, in ignorance, misled; how evil,
Indeed, shall be their burdens!

26. Such evil plans were also plotted,
By former generations,
But God attacked their building,
At its foundations,
And so the roof fell on them from
Above; and whence they did not look
For it, the Chastisement them overtook!

27.   Then, on the Day of Resurrection,
He'll bring them to disgrace, and say:
"Where are My partner-idols,
The subjects of your disputation?"
Those granted knowledge will declare: "Today
All shame, all evil falls,
Upon the infidels,

28.   "Whose lives the angels took away,
While doing wrong to their own souls;"
And then they proffer the submission:
"We aren't the conscious doers of those fouls!"
Nay! Allah Knows what you have done.

29.   "Therefore enter the gates of Hell,
You shall for ever there abide;
Dismal indeed is the Abode,
Wherein the haughty are to dwell!"

30.   To the godfearing it is said:
"What has your Lord unto you granted?"
They answer: "What is best". There is indeed,
For good-doers, some goodly meed
In this our present world, but best,
Will be the Mansion of the next;
Certainly blissful is the dwelling,
Of the godfearing;

31.   Gardens of Eden they shall enter,
Beneath them rivers shall be flowing,
All they wish for, they find in there,
That's God's reward for the godfearing;

32.   They're those to whom the angels shall announce,
      When they receive their souls, as pious,
      Purified folk, "On you be peace,
      Do enter Paradise,
      It's for what you have done,
      A recompense!"

33.   Are they[1] then waiting for the angels
      To come upon them, or an edict,
      From your Lord takes effect?[2]
      Thus was the manner of the former peoples!
      So God was not to them unjust at all,
      But they did wrong to their own souls;

34.   Therefore, the ill which they had done,
      On them recoiled:
      The very thing they used to ridicule,
      Them overwhelmed!

35.   They who have joined false deities with God,
      Argue: "Had Allah pleased, then neither,
      We nor our fathers would have worshipped aught,
      But Him, nor should we have forbidden ever,
      A thing without His order!"
      Such was also the custom,
      Of those who went before them!
      But then, is the apostles' duty other
      Than: the clear Message to deliver?

36.   Indeed, in every people,

---

1. "The ungodly".

2. That is: "until death comes to them or some Punishment in this life".

We raised a messenger who did,
Say: "Worship God and eschew Evil;"
Among these people some were guided,
By God, and there were some whose fate,
It was to deviate!
Now you may travel through the land,
And see what was the end,
Of the rejection band!

37.   No matter how devotedly you[1] try
To guide them, God will not show guidance,
To those whom He has left to go astray,
None shall they have for their assistance.

38.   They swear by God with their most sacred oaths,
That "Allah will raise none after their death!"
Nay! It's a binding pledge on Him in truth,
Though most men know it not forsooth,

39.   So that He may clear up to them the subject,
Of what they do dispute about,
And let the disbelievers know that they
Are liars without doubt.

40.   Whenever We decree a thing,
We only say unto it: "Be",
And it's already Being!

41.   To those who after persecution did,
Forsake their country for the sake of God,
We'll give a goodly station in this world,

---

1. The Holy Prophet.

But surely greater shall be their reward,
In the next life; but do they know!

42. They're those who persevere with gusto,
And put their full trust in their Lord.

43. Never have We, before you,[1] sent but men,
To whom We gave Our inspiration,
So, if you[2] lack the knowledge,
Ask the People of Invocation;[3]

44. They came with proofs and signs and scriptures,
And unto you We sent this Admonition,
That you make clear to men what has in fact,
Been sent to them: perhaps they will reflect.

45. Do the people who evil plots devise,
Really feel safe that Allah will not cause,
The earth to cleave beneath them?
Or that some scourge is not to seize them,
From whence they could not fathom!

46. Or that He will not strike them while,
They're in the midst of some day-to-day business,
And they shall be completely helpless!

47. Or that He will not let them be,
Suffering a slow, destructive process?
But then your Lord is Kind and Full of Mercy.

---

1. The Holy Prophet. 2. Idolaters, pagans.

3. Jews and Christians or any wise men qualified to have an opinion on divine
Scriptures.

48.   Do they not see how everything
        God has created, turns its shadow,
        Right and left, in obeisance to
        Allah, while casting down more low!

49.   All in the heavens and on earth,
        From animals unto the angels,
        Do make obeisance unto Allah,
        They're free from condescending ills!

50.   They fear their Lord Above them all, and do
        Whatever they are ordered to.

51.   And God has said: "take not two gods,
        For He is one God only;
        So none shall you revere but Me."

52.   Everything in the heavens
        And all on earth to Him belongs,
        And Judgment is for ever His indeed;
        Will you then any other God,
        But Allah heed?!

53.   You have no blessing but it is,
        From God alone,
        And soon, when trouble touches you,
        To Him you cry and moan!

54.   Yet no sooner has He removed your hardship,
        Than some of you, revert to idol-worship,

55.   Renouncing all We have unto you given!
        So then enjoy yourselves, for soon,

The truth shall be unto you known.

56.   They ignorantly set apart,
    For their idols some allocations,
    Out of what We have to them given,
    As their provisions!
    By God, you shall be taken to account,
    For your inventions.

57.   Daughters do they assign to God!
    To Him be glory!
    But for themselves they choose
    That which they fancy.[1]

58.   Thus when the tidings glad is given,
    To one of them about a baby girl,
    Coal-black will go his face, and stricken
    With sorrow, is his soul!

59.   And then, because of this ill tiding,
    Given him, goes he into hiding
    From the folks: should he be disgraced,
    And keep her or bury her in the dust?!
    Behold! their judgment is most evil!

60.   Certainly evil are the ways,
    Of people who do not believe
    In the hereafter, but the ways
    Of Allah are uniquely brave,[2]
    For He's the Mighty, the All-Wise.

---

1. An allusion to the prejudice of idolatrous Arabs for male offspring.

2. Excellent, admirable.

61. Were God to scourge men for their wrongs and crimes,
    He would indeed upon it[1] leave,
    No animate creature alive;
    But He respites them till appointed times;
    And once their doom is come, they'll have no power,
    To put it back, or take it forth an hour!

62. To God they have attributed what they,
    Themselves like not,
    And then their tongues utter the lie:
    That theirs shall be the finest lot!
    No doubt the Fire, shall be theirs,
    They'll be the first sent into it!

63. By God, We have before you sent apostles
    Unto nations in their own age,
    But Satan made their evil actions seem
    Fair to them, thus he is today their liege,
    And they shall have a chastisement extreme.

64. And We have sent to you this Book,
    Only that you may further make,
    Clear many a controversy,
    To them, and as a guide and mercy,
    Unto the faithful folk;

65. For God from heavens sends down rain,[2]
    And by it brings the earth to life again,
    After its death; there is in this indeed,

---

1. Upon the earth.

2. Both material and spiritual meanings of the word "rain" may be considered: water from the skies and blessings and guidance from the heavens.

A Sign for people who do listen.

66.   You even have a worthy lesson in
       The cattle: from the stuff within their bellies,
       Between the cud and blood, We give you milk,
       Pure and pleasant, to drink with ease.

67.   And from the fruits of palms and vines likewise,
       You get intoxicants and wholesome food,
       And in this too there is a good
       Sign for the wise.

68.   Behold! Your Lord inspired the bees:
       "Set up your hives upon the hills,
       And in the trees, and in the cells,
       That people will erect,

69.   "Then feed on every fruit you may select,
       And humbly follow your Lord's ways and byways."
       Thus comes out from their wombs a drink,[1]
       In different hues, that surely plays
       A healing role for men; indeed there is
       A Sign in this for those who think.

70.   God has created you, and, by and bye,
       Will He cause you to die;
       And some among you will He carry on,
       To an abject old age,
       When after having knowledge,
       Nothing is to you known;
       Omniscient and Omnipotent,

---

1. Or "a fluid".

Is God alone.

71.   And, in the matter of provisions,
       God has to some amongst you given
       More freely than to others; yet the ones
       Amply given, deny their bondsmen,
       A portion equal in advantage;
       What! Aren't these boons from God,
       Do they not this acknowledge?!

72.   And it was God Who gave you spouses,
       Of your own species,[1]
       And through your spouses, did bestow
       Upon you children and grand-children,
       And granted you wholesome provision;
       What! Will they still believe in falsehood,
       And be ungrateful to the boons of God?!

73.   They worship worthless things, instead of God,
       Which would on them confer,
       No benefits from heavens or the earth,
       Nor do they have the power.

74.   Compare[2] nothing to God the One,
       All ken is God's and yours is none!

75.   Allah sets forth the parable: a bondsman
       Helpless, under his lord's dominion,[3]

---

1. From amongst yourselves or your own race. 2. Or" do not coin similitudes".

3. The bondsman, and the dumb in the following verse, represent idols of any
   sort that men set up, whether powers of nature or deified men and heroes, who
   have no power of their own, but are all subject to the Will of God the One.

And a man blessed from Us with plenty,
And who does freely give to charity,
In private and in public;
Shall they be held alike?
All praise is due to Allah, though
Most of them do not know.

76.   And God sets forth the clear example,
Of two men: one of whom is deaf and dumb,
Unable to perform a thing, and is,
Unto his lord a burden awesome:
Send him where'er he will on errands,
He does return with empty hands!
The other is a person who commands
Justice and is upon the Direct Path;
Shall they be held alike in truth?!

77.   All the secrets of heavens and the earth
Are known to God the One,
And the Command of the Last Hour,
Is as the twinkling of an eye, or even
Much less in time; yes, surely God has power,
Over all things.

78.   And God it was who brought you out of,
Your mothers' wombs, devoid of knowledge,
And gave you ears and eyes and brains,[1]
Perhaps His Grace you will acknowledge.

79.   Do they not ever look up at the birds,
That are in mid air governed? None sustains

---

1. Original: "hearts": literally the seat of thoughts and emotions.

Them there but God; certainly for the faithful,
In this are Signs.

80. And it is God who gave you homes,
Wherein contentedly to dwell,
And of the skins of cattle, made
Tents, light to carry, when you travel,
Or on the day you stop to settle,
And, from their wool and fur and hair,
Has He for you prepared,
Household goods and provisions fair,
Far a short while.

81. And from the things that He has made,
God has for you provided shade,
And formed the mountains as your haunts;
And to protect you from the heat,
He granted you the proper garments,
And coats of mail to guard you, in
Your violent engagements,
And thus does He fill up the measure,
Of His abundant gifts toward you, that
You may unto His Will surrender.

82. But if they turn away and pay no heed,
Your mission then shall be indeed,
The Message plainly to deliver.

83. They fully recognize God's favour,
Then they disown it; for the greater
Part of them, are the thankless;

84. But one Day We shall raise a witness,

From every nation, and then no permission,
Shall be unto the disbelievers given,[1]
And they cannot solicit favour.

85. And after those who have done wrong,
Behold their torment, it shall neither
Be lightened for them, neither will they be
Granted a respite ever.[2]

86. When those who unto God gave partners see
Their "partners", they will say: "Our Lord, these are
The partners whom we called upon instead
Of You," but then they will declare:
"Most surely you are liars!"

87. And on that Day, they will display,
Total submission unto God, and each
And every deity they had invented,
Shall leave them in the lurch!

88. To those who were themselves infidels,
And did obstruct the path of God, We will
Inflict torment upon torment,
For their mischief and evil.

89. And on the Day when We shall raise a witness,
In every nation from amongst themselves,
To testify against them, We shall bring
You[3] too to testify against these folk,[4]
For unto you have we sent down the Book,

---

1. "To make excuses and argue back!" 2. Or "nor will God deign to look
upon them." 3. The Holy Prophet. 4. The Meccan pagans.

Clearly explaining everything,
A guide and mercy, and good news,
To those who unto God submit themselves.[1]

90.   Justice does God enjoin, and doing good,
And giving charity unto the kindred,
And He forbids: every indecent deed,
Wickedness and transgression,
Perhaps you will pay heed!

91.   Fulfill your covenant with Allah, after
You've made a covenant; and after,
You've sworn to an affair,
Break not your oaths, but be aware:
God it is you have made your guarantor,
And God is certainly Aware,
Of everything you're working for!

92.   And do not, like a woman who unravels,
The yarn that she has firmly spun, abuse
Your oaths as means of cheating other peoples,
When finding that there is a nation[2] whose
Might's greater than another nation;
God's making trials of you by means of these,
And lo, upon the Day of Resurrection,
He will clear up to you indeed,
All that in which you disagreed.

93.   Had Allah willed, He could have surely made,
You all a single nation, but He leaves

---

1. Original "Muslims".   2. Or "faction" or "group".

In error whom He will, and whom He please
He will certainly guide;
And you shall have to answer many questions,
Concerning all your actions.

94.   Therefore make not your oaths a means,
Of mutual deception,
Lest after being firmly fixed,
Your foot may slip, and you shall taste
Of evil for debarring others from
The path of God, and retribution
For you be awesome.

95.   And barter not away the covenant
Of God for trifling prices, for the payment
That is with God, if you but knew,
Is surely best for you.

96.   What you possess, passes away, whereas
What is with Allah, will for ever last,
And We shall certainly reward the steadfast,
According to their doings, nay, their finest!

97.   Of men or women, those who do what's right,
And do believe, We'll surely let delight,
In a pure life, and recompense with meeds,[1]
Meet for the finest of their deeds.

98.   And so, upon reciting Al-Quran,
Do seek refuge with God from Satan,
The Damned, Rejected One.

---

1. Rewards

99.   No power could he wield,
       'Gainst those who have believed,
       Whose trust is merely in their Lord.

100.   But only has he power over people,
       Who take him as their patron,[1]
       And those who join some partners,
       Unto Him, as the pagan.

101.   Whenever We elaborate upon,
       A former verse by verses coming later,
       And only Allah knows what He sends down,
       They cry out: "You're[2] a fabricator!"
       Nay! Most of them possess no ken.

102.   Tell them it is communicated by,
       The Holy Spirit, from your Lord,
       With every truth, to fortify
       Those who believe, and to afford
       Muslims a guide and tidings glad;

103.   And We are most aware of what they're saying:
       "He's being tutored by a human being!"
       But the tongue of the hinted[3] is exotic,
       And this: well-versed and fluent Arabic!

---

1. Alternative interpretation: "who turn away from Him (God)".

2. The Holy Prophet.

3. Not Salman the Persian, who embraced Islam at a later date in Medina; perhaps the pagans hinted at one of the Christian slaves, who were among the most devoted, early converts to Islam; and how could they be the authors of the sublime themes of the Holy Quran?!

104.　As for the people who do not believe in,
　　　God's revelations, surely God will never,
　　　Be guiding them, and a sore punishment
　　　They'll certainly incur.

105.　It will be only those who have no faith,
　　　In Allah's Signs who do resort to falsehood;
　　　Liars are they indeed;

106.　Anyone who recants his faith in God,
　　　After belief-save someone who was forced
　　　Unto it and his heart was full of faith-
　　　And he who opens to unfaith his breast,
　　　Shall certainly incur the wrath of God,
　　　And a most grievous torment next.

107.　That is because they love this worldly life,
　　　Beyond the next, and Allah will not give
　　　Guidance to people who do not believe.

108.　Those are the ones whose hearts,
　　　Their hearing and their eyesight,
　　　God has already sealed,
　　　Heedless are they outright!

109.　Undoubtedly they shall become,
　　　The losers in the life to come.

110.　To those who left their homes and fled,
　　　After tormenting trials, and later struggled,
　　　And steadfastly preserved, your Lord will be,
　　　But nay, your Lord has been already,
　　　Most Forgiving and Full of Mercy.

111.   Some Day will every soul,
Come for itself to plead,
And every soul is to be recompensed,
In full for every deed,
And no injustice shall be noticed.

112.   God cites the instance of a city,
Of undisturbed prosperity,
With its provisions coming from
Every side, and in plenty;
But then it turned ingrate to Allah's boons,
And so God let the people taste the pains,
Of draughts and insecurity,
For their own doings.

113.   And, from among them, an apostle came
To them, but they rejected him; at last,
Our chastisement did overtake them,
For having been unjust.

114.   Eat, therefore, of the lawful, wholesome things,
God has for you provided, and observe
His favours with gratefulness, if it is,
Him only that you serve.

115.   He has only to you forbidden:
Carrion, blood, the flesh of swine,
And whatsoever has been slain,
On which a name but God's was bidden;
Yet if a man has been constrained
To have of them, not being willful,
Nor going to excess, he'll find
Allah Forgiving, Merciful.

116. And say not with a lie upon your tongues:
     "This is lawful, this is forbidden",
     For in this way, you will invent
     A lie concerning Allah, and whoever
     Forges such lies of Allah, shall not prosper.

117. Ah, paltry profit!
     And lo! The painful torment for it!

118. And to the Jews, We have prohibited,
     What We already unto you narrated;
     But We did them no wrong: They were the ones,
     Who wronged themselves.

119. To those who had, in ignorance, committed
     Evil, then later did repent and mend,
     Their ways, your Lord was verily Forgiving,
     And Full of Mercy in the end.

120. Abraham was indeed a paragon
     Of piety, obedient unto Allah,
     A truly faithful man who never
     Worshipped an idol or an icon.

121. Grateful was he in truth,
     For His beneficence;
     He chose him and did show him guidance,
     To the Right Path.

122. And, in this world, We gave him happiness,
     And, in the world to come, he shall be,
     Amongst the righteous.

123. We have, moreover, unto you revealed:
"Follow the ways of Abraham, the faithful,
Who never served an idol."

124. And, as regards the Sabbath, it was meant,
Only for those who now dispute it![1]
Surely your Lord will make a judgment,
Upon the Day of Resurrection,
About their lasting disputation.

125. You shall invite to the Way of your Lord,
With wisdom and with kindly exhortation:
Do reason with them in the kindest manner,
Surely your Lord knows best who is astray,
From His Own Way, and He is Most Aware,
Of those who yield unto His guidance.

126. And if you punish, let your punishment,
Be correspondent to the hurt and harm,
That has been done to you, but for the patient,
It shall be best if they show patient calm.

127. Thus do be patient,[2] but your patience comes
Only from God; and ne'er be grieving
Over them, nor distress yourself about
Their sly intriguing.

128. Certainly God is with the self-restrainers,
And those who render good to others.

---

1. Jews and Christians.
2. "You, The Holy Prophet".

SURA 17
THE NIGHT JOURNEY
(AL-ISRAA)[1]

In The Name of God, the Beneficent, the Merciful

1. Glory to Him who made His servant,
   Go from the sacred shrine,[2] by night,
   To the Temple more distant,[3]
   Whose precincts We have blessed;
   That we to him make manifest,
   Some of Our signs; He is alone,
   The Hearing, Seeing One.

2. And We to Moses gave the Book,
   And made it unto Jacob's Children,
   A guidance, so they do not take,
   Besides Me, any guardian;

3. They are the progeny of those we took,
   Along with Noah, in the Ark,
   He was a truly grateful servant.

4. And in the Book we had decreed,
   To Jacob's Children: You shall twice,
   Make mischief through the land; indeed
   You'll be most insolently arrogant.

5. When the first warning came to pass,
   We sent against you those, from 'mongst
   Our creatures of the mighty prowess,[4]

---

1. Another name for this Chapter is "Bani Israail" (The Israelites).

2. Mecca.   3. Jerusalem.   4. The Assyrians.

Who even sacked the very inmost
Parts of your homes, and thus the Promise
Was utterly fulfilled.

6.　　But then we made you over them prevail,[1]
And multiplied your wealth and children,
To be a numerous band again:

7.　　"If you do good, you've done good for yourselves,
And if it's evil that you do, the evil
Is only 'gainst your very souls."
Thus when the second Promise came to pass,
Others[2] we sent to bring you face to face,
With grief and sufference, and to enter
The Temple, as done by the former,
And utterly destroy whatever fell,
Into their power.

8.　　Perhaps your Lord will show compassion
On you, but if you do renege, we will
Revenge again; and We've made Hell,
For those who disbelieve, a prison!

9.　　Verily this Quran will guide,
Unto that which is most upright,
And to believers who do good,
Does give the tidings glad,
That their reward is to be great,

10.　　And threatens those who disbelieve,
In the Hereafter, with the grave

---

1. Over Sennacherib.　　　　　　2. The Romans.

Chastisement that we have,
For them got ready.

11. Yet man for evil prays as eagerly,
As he for goodness prays: man is indeed,
Heedlessly hasty!

12. Night and Day We created portents twain:
The Night-portent, We have deprived of light,
And the Day-portent, We have rendered bright,
To help you seek your Lord's provision,
And learn the yearly computation,
And timing calculation;
Everything We have made distinctly plain.

13. And We have bound the fate of every man,
About his neck, and We'll confront him,
Upon the Day of Resurrection,
With a book spread wide open.

14. "Read your recorded scroll:
Sufficient will be your own soul,
To work out your account this Day!"

15. The guided man does yield to guidance,
For his own good, and he that goes astray,
Shall err at his own soul's expense;
No bearer bears the burden of another;
Nor have We e'er chastised,
Ere had We an apostle raised.

16. When We decide to bring a town to ruin,
We give Our warning first to those,

Of them who're leading easy lives,
Then if they do persist in sin,
Thus is the Word against them proven,
And to the ground will We it raze!

17. How many nations since the time of Noah,
Have We destroyed! Of the sins of each servant,
Of his, your Lord is Well-Informed,
And Most Observant.

18. To those who choose this quickly-passing world,
We'll quickly grant what We have willed,
And unto whom we please, but, also, Hell
Have We for them prepared, and they'll be taken,
Into it, scorned, forsaken.

19. But those who wish for the Hereafter,
And strive for it, as true believers,
With all their souls, then surely their endeavours,
Shall be approved.

20. We grant the bounties of your Lord,
To all, both these and those;[1] to none
Shall be denied the bounty of your Lord.

21. See how we have exalted some
Above the others; yet the life to come,
Has greater honours, and it's hence,
Greater in excellence.

22. Do not associate with Allah,

---

1. Both groups, the just and the unjust (as explained in the last two verses).

Another deity, for then,
You shall incur disgrace and ruin.

23.   Your Lord decrees that you should worship none,
But Him alone,
And to show kindness to your parents,
If one or both of them will reach,
Old age with you, and never say so much,
To them as fie! Neither reproach,
Them, but address them ever,
In terms of love and honour,

24.   And treat them with submissiveness,
Tenderness and compassion,
And pray: "O Lord, bestow on them Your Mercy,
As they in childhood cherished me."

25.   Your Lord is best Aware of what
Is in your hearts; and if you're righteous:
Surely to those who turn to Him,
He is Most Gracious.

26.   Fulfil your obligations to the near of kin,
The needy and the travellers,
Yet be not wasteful squanderers.

27.   Brethren to devils are the wasteful,
And Satan was unto his Lord,
Ever ungrateful;

28.   And if you turn away from them,
While seeking mercy from your Lord,
For which you hope, then you could speak to them,

At least a kindly, gentle word.

29.   Do not be miserly, nor prodigal,
For then you shall be either blamed
Or left in destitution.

30.   Your Lord provides abundantly,
Or sparingly, to whom he please,
He knows His servants best, and He
Them closely Sees.

31.   You shall not kill your children
For fear of want; it's surely We
Who grant provisions both to them
And you; it's certainly
A heinous crime to kill them.

32.   Do not come close to fornication,
It is a gross indecency,
Evil indeed, is such direction.

33.   Do not take life, which Allah has forbidden,[1]
Unless it be by right; If anyone,
Is slain unjustly, We indeed have given
His heir[2] the right of retribution;
But let him not the proper bounds exceed,
In seeking vengeance,[3] for he shall indeed,
Receive protection.

34.   Do not approach the property

---

1. Or "made sacred".   2. Or: next of kin or guardian.

3. In the matter of taking life.

Of orphans, save with good intention,
Until they reach maturity.
And keep your pledges; for, no doubt,
Each pledge is to be asked about.

35.   And give full measure, when you measure,
And use an even balance, when you weigh,
That is the fairest way,
And in the end, far better.

36.   And do not follow what you do not know;
Surely the ears, the eyes and hearts,
And all such human parts,
Are to go through a probing thorough!

37.   And do not proudly walk upon the land,
Never would you the earth asunder rend,
Nor could you rival mountains grand!

38.   Evil is all this, odious to your Lord.

39.   These are some precepts of the Wisdom which,
Your Lord has unto you revealed,
Thus never take to worship any gods,
Along with God, for then you will indeed,
Be thrown, despised and helpless,
Down into the Abyss.

40.   What! Has your Lord bestowed upon you sons,
And for Himself adopted daughters from,
Among the angels?! Surely what you utter,
Is blasphemy[1] most awesome.

---

1. Original: "speaking a big word" against God.

41. Moreover, We have varied this Quran,
    So that they may be warned; instead they run,
    Further and further from it in aversion.

42. Say: "If, as they assert, there had been other
    Deities with Him, they would then endeavour
    To seek an access of their own,
    Unto the Master of the Throne?!

43. Glory be to Him; He is Most Exalted
    And Far Above the falsehoods they intone!

44. The heavens seven and the earth and those,
    Who dwell therein, do celebrate His praise,
    There is no single being who is not,
    Chanting His glorifying hymns;
    And yet their kind of glory-giving,
    You do not recognize;
    Surely he is Benignant, Most Forgiving.

45. And when you are reciting Al-Quran,
    We place a hidden curtain,
    'Tween you and those who have no faith in,
    The life to come,

46. And coverings upon their hearts we cast,
    And make them hard of hearing, lest
    They understand it; therefore when
    You make a mention of the One,
    And Only Lord of yours in Al-Quran,
    They turn their faces in disgust.

47. Only do We know best,

Of what they hear when they unto you listen,
And of their private conversation when,
The wrongdoers assert: "This man
You follow is possessed!"[1]

48.   Behold, what designations they apply
Unto you, but they've gone astray,
And they shall never find the way!

49.   They also say: "What! When we are reduced
To rotten bones and dust,
Shall we be really raised again,
Into a new creation?!"

50.   Answer: "Most surely, even
If you were stones or iron,

51.   Or some created matter which you reckon,
Hardest to bring to life again!"
At this they'll say: "Who is to bring us back?"
Answer: "The very Being who did bring
You firstly into being!"
Yet they will shake their heads at you, and clack:
"When is this, when?!" Reply:
"Perhaps it's drawing nigh."

52.   Upon that Day, He'll call you forth,
And you shall answer Him with praise,
And you will think: "We, in this phase,
Have tarried but a little while!"

---

1. Or: "bewitched", "spell-bound", "deprived of reason".

53. And tell My servants: you should utter
Only that which is best of all;
For Satan sows dissension 'mongst them;
Satan is certainly a sworn
Enemy unto man;

54. It is your Lord who knows you best,
He'll show you Mercy, if He please,
And, if He will, He'll punish you;
But We've not sent you[1] to dispose
People's affairs.

55. Your Lord has perfect ken of all things in,
The heavens and the earth; We surely did
Give higher gifts unto some prophets than
To others, and We gave the Psalms to David.

56. Say: "Pray to those you deify besides Him!
They cannot do away with any harms
For you, nor can they even change their forms."

57. In fact all those they call upon,
Themselves are seeking means and ways,
Of nearing Him,[2] they vie with one,
Another in this, and they always
Crave for His mercy, and do dread
His scourge; for your Lord's scourge indeed,
Is something to be dreaded!

58. And there shall be no habitation,

---

1. Mohammad (pbuh).

2. Most probably an allusion to the saint-worship of the Christians.

Which We will not annihilate,
Or punish with a torment great,
Before the Day of Resurrection;
This has already been decreed,
In the Eternal Record.

59.　　And nothing hinders Us from sending Signs,[1]
Except that they have been rejected by
The former generations:
Unto Thamood We sent the female-camel,
It was a Sign, most visible,
Yet she was made a prey of violations;
Whereas We only give the Signs,
By way of warnings.

60.　　Behold, We told you that your Lord encircles
All humankind; and it was only as a trial,
For men, that We ordained the Vision,[2]
You saw, and showed you the Accursed Tree,[3]
Mentioned in the Quran.
Thus do We warn them but it only,
Helps to increase their insurrection.

61.　　And now recall: We did command the angels,
"Bow down to Adam", they all bowed; but, nay!
Iblees did not. He said: "Should I bow down
Before the one You made of clay?!"

62.　　He added: "Since You evidently have,
This man above me honoured, if You do,

---

1. Or "miracles".　2. Either the Holy Prophet's *Mi'raaj* or some other vision.
3. The Tree of Zaqqoom.

Respite me till the Day of Resurrection,
I'll surely bring his future generation,
Under my sway, all but a few."

63.   "Begone!" said He. "Hell is the recompense
For you and those who follow you,
It is an ample recompense!

64.   "And now, with your alluring voice,
Whome'er of them you can entice,
Muster against them all your force,
Your cavalry and infantry,
And share with them in wealth and progeny,
And to them, what you fancy, promise;"
So Satan promises them only,
What is deceitful, false.

65.   "Indeed you'll have no dominance
Over My servants true;"[1] because your Lord,
As a protector, shall suffice.

66.   Your Lord's the One Who does propel,
The ships for you across the seas,
That you may profit of His bounties;
Surely He is to you Most Merciful.

67.   Now when misfortunes seize you out at sea,
All those you call on, fail you, all but He!
Yet when he brings you safely back to land,
You keep away from Him; ungrateful
Is man most certainly!

---

1. Satan may only delude by false counsel and false promises; men are free to choose.

68.   Will you then feel secure that He,
Shall not allow some tract of land,
To swallow you, or send a deadly wind,
Against you, charged with sand?
Then you'll have no one to give you a hand.

69.   Or do you feel secure that, when again,
He sends you back a second time,[1] He will
Not smite you with a devastating gale,
To get you drowned for being thankless, while
There shall be none to question Us
Concerning this?!

70.   Surely We honoured Adam's Children,
And blessed them with conveyance,
On land and sea, and gave them,
Good and pure things for sustenance,
And raised them by a special excellence,
Above the greater part of Our creation.

71.   There is the Day when We shall summon,
All human beings led by their *imams*;[2]
Then those who shall be given,
Their books[3] in their right palms;[4]
These people read their books again, again:
Nay, they have not been wronged a grain.

72.   But those who here were acting as the blind,
Blind shall they be in the Hereafter, nay,
The most misguided from the Way!

---

1. "Back to sea".   2. Leaders.

3. Records.   4. Or "hands".

73. They nearly tempted you away from what,
    We to you sent; they wanted you to bend,
    And fabricate some falsehood in Our name,
    And, in that case, they would become your friend!

74. Had We not made you firm and stable,
    You would have nearly leaned to them a little.

75. Had you done that, We would have let you taste
    A double retribution both,
    In your own life and after death,
    And you would then find no one to assist
    You 'gainst Our wrath.

76. Their purpose was to scare you off the land,
    And send you into exile;
    But in that case, they would have not survived,
    After you but a little while;

77. Such was Our way with all the messengers,
    That We, before you, sent, and you shall find,
    That Our way never changes.

78. Keep up the prayers, from when the sun goes down,[1]
    Moving towards the falling of the night,
    Besides the Reading[2] at the dawn;
    Indeed the morning recitation,
    Receives its own Attention.[3]

---

1. From the highest point at noon.

2. The recitation of Quranic verses: the morning prayer.

3. Lit. "has its witness" or "is witnessed".

79.   And keep awake a portion of the night
        To do some prayer beyond what is incumbent,
        Perhaps your Lord shall raise
        You to a glorious rank of praise;

80.   And say: "My Lord, do make me enter
        In everything with honour,
        And let my exit be
        The truthfulest departure,
        And grant me from Yourself
        Support and power."

81.   And say: "The Truth has come and Falsehood,
        Has perished; surely Falsehood,
        Was bound to perish!"

82.   We're sending down in this Quran,
        What is for the believers,
        A healing and a blessing;
        Although it causes nothing
        But loss to the transgressors.

83.   When We bestow the human being
        With boons, He turns remote and arrogant,
        But when some evil seizes him,
        He turns despondent!

84.   Say: "Everyone behaves
        According to his disposition;
        Surely your Lord best knows,
        Who's on the right direction."

85.   They question you about the Spirit,[1]
       Answer: The spirit is an ordinance,
       Come from my Lord; but what of knowledge,
       You're given, is of no significance.[2]

86.   And if We pleased, We could have taken back,
       That which We sent to you by inspiration:
       And then you would have found no guardian,
       Your cause with Us to undertake;

87.   But it's a Mercy from your Lord;
       His grace to you is great indeed.

88.   Declare: "If all the humans and the Jinns,
       Banded together to produce the like
       Of this Quran, they would certainly fail
       To bring its like, even if they did back,
       Each other in this travail!"

89.   We have in this Quran, for humankind,
       Cited examples of all kind,[3]
       Nevertheless, the greater part of men
       Insist on irreligion.

90.   And they say: "We will, by no means,
       In you have any faith,
       Unless you cause a fountain,
       To gush forth for us from the earth;

---

1. The immaterial soul of man, or, according to some commentators, the nature of Revelation.

2. Or "very little".   3. Or "all manners of argument".

91.   "Unless you have a gorgeous garden,
      Of palms and vines, with streams
      Meandering therein;

92.   "Unless you get the welkin,[1]
      To fall upon us broken,
      As you do so surmise;
      Or bring down Allah and the angels
      Before our very eyes;

93.   "Unless you own a mansion,
      Luxurious, golden;[2]
      Or you ascend unto the heaven;
      Even then we will not believe,
      In your ascension,
      Unless you send to us a scripture,
      Which we could read!!"
      Say: "Glory to my Lord! Am I indeed,
      More than a human messenger?"

94.   Whenever Guidance came before the people,
      Nothing prevented them from faith, but saying:
      "Has Allah sent a human being,
      As an apostle?!"

95.   Say: "If the earth was peopled by the angels,
      Walking upon it free of danger,[3]
      We would have sent to them from heavens,
      An angel as their messenger."

96.   Say: "God suffices as a witness,

---

1. The Sky.   2. Made of gold.   3. Or "as safe settlers".

450

'Tween me and you; for He best Knows,
His creatures, and He always Sees."

97.   Whomever Allah guides, he is
The guided one, and whom He sends
Astray, you'll never find for him,
Besides Him, any friends;[1]
And on the Day of Resurrection,
We'll gather them, upon their faces,
Blind will they be, and dumb and deaf,
Their destination will be Hell:
Each time it may cool off,
We will the flames rekindle!

98.   This is their recompense, because
They did reject Our revelations,
And said: "After we shall have been reduced
To bones and dust,
Are we then to be raised
As new creations?!"

99.   Can't they imagine that the very God,
Who did create the heavens and the earth,
Is Able to create the like of them?
Only He has for them set forth,
A doom which is undoubtedly to come;
Yet the wicked consent to naught,
Except unfaith!

100.   Say: "If you were possessors of my Lord's
Treasures of Mercy, you would have for certain,

---

1. Or "protectors", "guardians".

Kept them unspent through fear of spending;"
How niggardly, how covetous are men!

101.   To Moses did We give nine lucid Signs,
Question this from Israel's sons;
When he came to them, Pharaoh thus addressed:
"O Moses, I believe you are possessed!"

102.   He said: "You do well know that all of these,
Have only been sent forth,
By the Lord of the heavens and the earth,
As Signs to open eyes;
O Pharaoh, I believe you to be lost![1] "

103.   Thus he[2] decided to remove them,
From the face of the earth, but then,
We drowned him side by side of all his men!

104.   And after him, We told the Children
Of Israel: "Do settle in this land;
And when the final promise comes to pass,
Well' gather you as a collected[3] band.

105.   In truth have We revealed it,[4]
And it is truthfully sent down,
And We have made you an apostle,
To give good tidings and to warn.

---

1. Doomed to perdition.   2. Pharaoh.

3. Or "assorted" or "mingled"; commentators differ as to the exact interpretation
of this verse, and, as I adhere to none, I let it be as it is.

4. The Holy Quran.

106.　This is a Reading unto which We gave,
　　　Distinctive features, that you may recite,
　　　It to the people at some intervals;
　　　Thus We release it in the portions right.

107.　Say: "Whether you believe or not believe it,
　　　Those who have been already granted,
　　　Knowledge, fall down upon their faces in
　　　Prostration, when it is to them recited;

108.　And say:[1] 'Glory be to our Lord, indeed
　　　The promise of our Lord has been fulfilled.'"

109.　And while they in prostration weep,
　　　Their humbleness becomes more deep.

110.　It's the same whether you call on
　　　Allah or Al-Rahmaan:
　　　His are the beautifulest names;
　　　And when you're praying, do not raise
　　　Your voice, neither silently pray,
　　　But seek between extremes,
　　　A moderate way.

111.　And say: "All praise is due to God the One,
　　　Who never takes unto Himself a son,
　　　Who has no partner in His Kingdom, nor
　　　Does He e'er need a helper due to weakness."
　　　Thus magnify Him for:
　　　His matchless Greatness and Uniqueness!

---

1. "Those granted Knowledge".

SURA 18
THE CAVE
(AL-KAHF)

In the Name of God, the Beneficent, the Merciful

1.   Praise be to God the One,[1] who sent the Book,
To His servant,[2] and in it did not make,
A thing distorted, fake;

2.   It's very straight, so that he may give warning,
From Him, about a dreadful scourge,
And to the good-doing believers, bring
The tidings glad of an excellent Wage,

3.   In which they would for ever bask;

4.   And caution those who reckon:
God has a son begotten!

5.   Of this, in fact, they have no knowledge,
Nor did their fathers! It's a grievous word,[3]
Emitted from their mouths; what they allege,
Is surely false, absurd.

6.   And yet if they deny this Message,
Ought you to bring yourself unto the verge
Of death, out of vexation, for their sake?

7.   We certainly have made whatever,

---

1. Allah.   2. Mohammad (pbuh).

3. To speak "big" or "grievous" words against God, means "uttering
blasphemies".

There is on earth as ornament and glitter,
For it, so that We put to test,
Who will, in doing good and proper,
Excel the rest.

8.   And certainly we'll make a waste,
Of all that's on it, with no herbage.

9.   Perhaps you thought the Sleepers of the Cave
Of *Warraqeem*,[1] had been, amongst Our Signs,
A case extreme, some story brave?!

10.   Behold! The young men who had taken refuge,
Inside the cavern, prayed: "O Lord, award
Us mercy from Yourself, and guide us out
Of our ordeal to the right road!"

11.   Therefore, We struck and sealed their ears,[2]
Inside the cave, for many years;

12.   And then we did awaken them again,
To see which of the parties twain[3] could reckon
The time they had been there abiding.

13.   We now narrate to you their truthful tiding:

1. I take "warraqeem" as the name of the valley or the mountain, in which the
   cave of the Seven Sleepers-thus known to the Christians-was situated;
   Warraqeem could have been understandably rendered into Arabic script as
   "wa-al-raqeem" (pronounced "warraqeem") and thus translated into: "and the
   Inscription".   2. Lulled them to a deep sleep.
3. Commentators identify 'the two parties' differently: "two grouplets among the
   Companions of the Cave", or simply "amongst them"; I kept to a literal
   rendering of the original.

They were young men, most faithful with their Lord,
Whom We did strengthen by Our guiding;

14.   And in their hearts We did put courage,
When they stood up and said, "Our Lord He is,
The Lord of heavens and the earth, and homage
We pay, besides Him, to no deity,
For that is surely speaking outrage,

15.   "These folks of ours have taken other gods,
Instead of Him, while they do not present
Any clear argument in their support!
Who's more unjust than people who invent
Falsehoods concerning God?[1]

16.   "Now that you have forsaken them,
And what they have been serving, save
Allah, betake yourselves for refuge
To such and such a cave:
Your Lord will give you of His mercy,
And cause the course of your affair
To run in safety."

17.   One might have seen the rising sun descend,
Unto the Cave's right hand, and when it set,
Went past them on the left,[2] and they remained
Inside a roomy space: This was indeed,
One of the Signs of God, for He will let
Whom He may wish, be truly guided,

---

1. Having expressed their faith (in verse 14 and 15), The Companions (Sleepers) of the Cave take counsel among themselves (in verse 16).

2. We may suppose that the Cave was facing north.

And whom He sends astray, shall find,
No guiding friend, no patron kind.

18.   One might have thought they were awake, whereas
They were asleep: We turned them on their right,
And on their left sides, and their dog, with paws
Outstretched, lay at the threshold. In full flight,
One would have turned from them, if one had come
Upon them suddenly; surely their sight
Would have filled any heart with fright.

19.   And, from this stage, We raised them up again,
And they, between them, raised some questions:
"How long have you remained in this condition?"
One of them asked. "We have tarried a day,
Or maybe of a day, some portion,"
Answered the others. Some said: "Nay,
It is your Lord who surely knows
How long we have been in repose.
Now let us send one of your men to Town,
Taking this silver coin of yours, to look,
Who has some wholesome food, and bring it back,
For our provision, yet he must
Behave with gentle caution, lest
Your whereabouts should be made known;

20.   "For if they find you out, they will
Stone you to death indeed,
Or force you back into their creed,
And then you will, for ever,
Be faring ill!"

21.   And thus did We let people know of them,

That they might learn that Allah's promise will
Always come true, and that the Hour of Doom,
Will surely come.
Later when they[1] concerning this event,
Carried, amongst themselves, some argument:
Some said: "Let's build for them a building simple,
For it's their Lord who knows about them best,
But those who in the end imposed their will,
Opined: "certainly over them we must,
For worshipping, erect a temple!"

22.   Soon will some people say that they were three,
And that their dog had been the fourth,
Others shall say that they were five,
And that the dog had been the sixth-
They only guess at the unseen of Heaven!-
And others say that they were seven,
And that the dog had been the eighth.
Say: "It's my Lord alone,
Who knows about their number best,
And it will not, save to a few, be known.
Thus argue not about the matter, rather
Heed the occurrence manifest;[2]
And question none of them about it.

23.   And do not say of anything at all:
"Surely tomorrow I will do it",

24.   Unless it's added: "If God will",

---

1. The fellow citizens of the Companions of the Cave.

2. Meaning: "take the actual divine phenomenon into consideration, and do not
   bother over its details.

And if you happen to forget, recall
Your Lord at once, and say: "Perhaps
My Lord guides me to the right cause,
Even more close than this."

25. Some also say: "They stayed inside the Cave
Three hundred years," and some to it add nine!

26. Say: "None but Allah knows how long,
They did in there remain;
To Him are known all the unseen,
Of heavens and the earth; His Sight
Is clear, His Hearing Keen!
They have, but Him, no patron,
And He does not let any party
Bear part in His authority."

27. Recite then what has been to you revealed,
Of the Book of your Lord; There is indeed
None who could change His words, and never,
Except in Him, you'll find a shelter.

28. And keep yourself[1] content with those who call
Upon their Lord, morning and evening,
Seeking His Presence, and let not your eyes,
Wander far from them, craving
For the attractions of this world;
Nor follow those whose hearts We have allowed
To be, of Our remembrance, heedless,
Pursuing only their own whims, whose business,
In Life, is nothing but excess!

---

1. Mohammad (pbuh).

29.   Proclaim: This is the Ruth come from your Lord,
Therefore, let him who please, accept it,
And him who wishes so, reject it;
We have prepared, however,
For the iniquitous, a Fire,
Which, like curtains of a pavilion
On fire, shall hem them in.
And if they beg for some relief:
Water, as hot as molten brass,
Showers on them that will roast their lips:
What evil stuff for drinks,
What an ill resting-place!

30.   The faithful who did right and good,
Must be most certain that We would,
Ne'er let the wage of those who raced,
After good deeds, go waste.

31.   They shall deservedly be living,
In the Gardens of Eden,[1]
With streams beneath them flowing;
They'll be adorned with bracelets golden,
Attired in garments made,
Of fine green silk and rich brocade,
Upon high thrones reclining;
Blissful is their reward,
Excellent their abode.

32.   And now narrate for them the episode,
Of the two men: On one We had bestowed,
Two spacious gardens of grape-vines,

---

1. This means "Eternal pleasure, delight or bliss" in Hebrew.

With lands for tillage in between,
And palms outside in circling lines;

33. Both vineyards yielded fruits in volume:
They never failed to bloom;
We also made a gushing river,
There to meander.

34. He had an ample crop collection,
And, in the course of conversation,
He bragged to his companion:
"More do I have than you of wealth,
And greater are my men and children!"

35. Having thus harmed his soul, he did
Enter his paradise and added:
"I do not think that this will end;

36. "And I don't think the Hour of Doom,
Shall ever come!
And even if I be returned,
Unto my Lord, there I will surely find,
A grander version of this kind!?"

37. Rebuking him, his neighbour said:
"What! Have you no faith in the One,
Who from some dust, and later from,
A tiny drop of semen,
Created you, and fashioned you,
Into a perfect man?!

38. "As far as I'm concerned,
My Lord is Allah, God the One,

And with my Lord, I am
Associating none.

39. "And, when you went into your garden,
Wherefore did you not say: 'whatever
Allah may please?' For none but God
Has any power?
Also, if you regard me less than you
In wealth and children,

40. "Perhaps my Lord shall grant to me,
Something far better than your garden,
And yet, a thunderbolt He may from heaven,
Let fall on yours to turn it into
A desert fruitless, barren,

41. "Or drain its waters deep into the ground,
Never to be re-found!"

42. And something did encompass
His paradise:
He now wakes up and sees;
All that he spent on it was gone,
As all his vines, upon their trellises,
Were tumbled down!
So he begins to wring his hands, and wails:
"Oh, woe! I wish I had no idols[1]
Ever worshipped, instead of God."

43. Indeed he had no host to help him,
Instead of God, nor was himself,

---

1. Man's idols are his wealth and property and what he lusts after.

Able to change the cataclysm.

44.   In such ordeals, only from God,
      The True one, comes protection,
      He is the best bestower of reward,
      And best for one's salvation.

45.   Set forth to them this simile,
      Of the life in this world: when We
      Send down rain-water from the sky,
      The earthly herbage multiply;
      But soon they turn into stubbles dry,
      That winds will blow away!
      And it is only God who over
      All things holds sway.

46.   Ornaments only of this worldly venue,
      Are wealth and children,
      Whereas good deeds of lasting value,
      In your Lord's vision,
      Are of the best results, and for you,
      The best ambition;

47.   Upon the Day when We remove the mountains,
      And you shall see the earth as levelled plains,
      When We will bring together all mankind,
      And leave of them no single soul behind,

48.   They shall be ranged before their Lord in ranks:
      "Now you have come back to Us, just
      As We created you at first;
      Although you thought that We would never,
      Realize Our promised get-together!"

49.   And then the Book shall be laid open,
And you shall see the guilty, full of awe,
Of that which is therein, declaring: "woe,
To us! What book is this? It has not aught,
Left unrecorded, small or great!"
And they shall find before them what they've done;
And yet, your Lord shall be unjust to none.

50.   Behold! We ordered angels to prostrate,
Themselves to Adam, and they all bowed down,
Except Iblees, one of the Jinns; and thus
He did the order of his Lord transgress.
What! Will you ever take as patron
Him and his progeny, instead of Me,
Although they are to you the enemy?
What sad exchange,
For the ungodly!

51.   I never made them witnesses
Of the creation of the heavens
And of the earth, nor did they ever
Witness their own creations,
Nor did I ever those misleaders,
Take as my aiders!

52.   And on that Day, He'll say: "Do call
On those you joined with Me in Godhood!
And they shall call them, but they never would
To them respond; and there, We'll make perdition
To serve between them as partition!

53.   The sinners then shall see the Fire,
And they will know they are about,

To be into it thrown, and in there,
Never find a way out!

54. We have indeed in this Quran explained,
Everything by examples for mankind,
But man's inclined, at all events,
To hostile arguments!

55. And now that Guidance is to people come,
Nothing at all is to prevent them from,
Embracing Faith, and asking for forgiveness
From their own Lord, unless they wish to wait
For the likes of the ancient peoples' fate,
Or, at close range, the Chastisement to witness.

56. Messengers do We only send,
As bearers of glad tidings,
And bringers of grim warnings,
But those who have no faith intend,
With vain contention, to defeat
The Very Truth, and always treat
My Signs and what I warn,
With ridicule and scorn.

57. Who could be then more wicked than the man,
Who, when reminded of the revelations,
Of his own Lord, avoids them and forgets
His previous actions?
We have indeed set on their hearts some wrapping,
And have deprived them of their sense of hearing,
So this they shall not understand; and while
In this condition, if you were to call,
Them unto Guidance, they could never then

Be guided to the right direction.

58. Nevertheless your Lord is Most-Forgiving,
And Full of Mercy; were He willing,
To punish them for what they did,
He would have brought their Torment forward,
But there's a time for them ordained,
From which no refuge will they find.

59. We did annihilate those cities,
For being sunken in iniquities,
And yet before their final plight,
We'd set for them a term of respite.

60. Behold! once Moses told his page:
"I will not stop until I reach the spot
Where the two seas converge; if not,
I am prepared to spend an age
Upon this voyage!

61. But when at last, they came unto the land,
Between the two, their fish escaped their mind
And it escaped into the sea,
Softly its way back did it find!

62. Now after they had gone farther along,
He said to his attendant young:
"Let's have our meal, we suffer from fatigue,
Marching league after league."

63. He said: "Ah! When we rested by the rock,
I did forget the fish, and Satan made me,
Forget to speak of it, and it slipped back,

Most strangely to the sea."

64. He said: "This was indeed the very aim,
We have been seeking, thus they did
Go back the way they came."

65. And there they found one of Our servants,
One to whom we had given,
Our special Grace, and taught him
Something of Our Own Ken.

66. Moses said unto him: "Am I allowed
To follow you, that you, for guidance,
Teach me of that which is on you bestowed?"

67. He said: "But surely you could not,
With me have patience;

68. "And how could you be patient with
Matters beyond your cognizance?!"

69. He said: "You shall, God willing, find me patient,
Nor will I be in any matter,
Unto you disobedient."

70. He said: "well, if you're bent on coming,
After me, then you shall not question,
Me of a thing until I have myself,
To you about it spoken."

71. Therefore, the two set out,
Until they were aboard,
A ship: A hole in her he bored!

"What", cried he" Have you made a hole
To drown her inmates all?
Now certainly you have
Committed something grave!"

72. "Did I not tell you", said he, "that you couldn't
With me be patient?"

73. He said: "Pray blame me not for what
I had forgotten, and do not
Take me to task on that account."

74. Therefore they journeyed on until they ran
Into a youth: He killed him there and then!
He cried: "What! Have you slain
A harmless boy, of nought to blame?
You did, no doubt, commit a crime!"

75. "Did I not tell you", said he "that you couldn't
With me be patient?!

76. He said: "If after this, I ever question,
A thing from you, you may not let me
Be your companion, for there shall be none,
To blame at all, but me!"

77. Therefore they journeyed on until they came,
Across the people of a certain town,
They asked them for some food, but they would like
No guests to entertain!
Later they noticed in that town,
A wall, on point of falling down:
Now he did put it right.

He said: "If you so wished, you could exact
Some payment for this goodly act."

78.   He said: "well, now it's time for separation,
'Tween you and me; so I make you aware,
Of the meaning and explanation,[1]
Of things you could not bear.

79.   "As for the boat, it did belong,
To some poor men who toiled along
The sea, and thus I did, at will,
Damage it, as there was a king,
Coming behind them, who was taking,
Forcibly every vessel.

80.   "As for the youth, his parents both,
Were true believers in the Truth;
We feared he'd bring them unto grief,
Through insolence and unbelief.[2]

81.   "So we desired that, in his place,
Their Lord might bless them with a son,
Better than him in virtue,
With more filial compassion.

82.   "As for the wall, it had belonged to two,
Orphan boys in that town, whose father,
Had been a righteous man, and under
It lay a treasure, and your Lord had ruled
That after they had grown to manhood,

---

1. Also meaning: "interpretation", "significance".
2. Also meaning: "ingratitude", infidelity".

They should dig out their treasure, and it would
Serve as a Mercy from your Lord;
And all this, I have not been doing,
Of my accord;
This certainly is the significance,
Of that which you could not behold,
With steadfast patience."

83.   You're also being questioned,
        Concerning Zul-Qarnain;[1]
        Say: I shall now recite to you,
        About him, something plain.

84.   We did his might establish in the land,
        And gave him means to every end.

85.   Thus he set out upon a course;

86.   Until he reached the limit,
        Where the sun set:

---

1. "The two-horned: this is the title of the great ruler or King. To identify the
historical figure (if at all necessary), we must consider the characteristics of
Zul-Qarnain in the light of the story as given in the Quran: an ancient ruler
whose conquests spread from East to the West, who was just and righteous,
and worshipped God who had given him his power. Such characteristics could
only fit Cyrus the Great of Persia, who is known in history to have possessed
the required conditions, and the Old Testament testifies that Cyrus united the
Kingdoms of Persia and Media, brought about the downfall of Babylon and
the liberation of the Israelites, like a "two-horned ram" (Dan. 8, 3-20).
Alexander of Macedonia, a polytheistic pagan or an insignificant Hymarite
King, as some commentators have suggested, do not fit the Quranic descrip-
tion by any stretch of imagination.

He found it setting in some waters black,[1]
And quite near by he found some folk.
We called: "O Zul-Qarnain!
Either chastise these people,
Or be to them benign!"

87.   He said: "We certainly shall punish
Committers of iniquities,
Then they are sent back to their Lord,
And He'll subject them to a Torment
Of gravest agonies.

88.   "But for the faithful who will do good works,
There shall be rich rewards, and we'll impose
On them no heavy tasks."

89.   Then he set out upon another course,

90.   Until he reached the limit where the sun,
Was rising, and he saw it rise upon,
Some folk for whom We had not made,
Against it any shade.

91.   He left them as they were!
Of course, of his restricted power, We
Were perfectly Aware.

92.   Then he set out upon another course;

93.   He marched until he came between,

---

1. If Zul-Qarnain was Cyrus, then the place would be the Western limit of Asia Minor, and the "black waters" would be the Aegean Sea.

The mountains twain,[1]
And there he found a human horde,
Who hardly understood a word.[2]

94.   "O Zul-Qarnain", they seemed to beg,
"Certainly Gog and Magog,[3]
Are evil for this land as plague,
Could we be paying you a tribute,
So that you build a dam and clog,
'Tween us and them, the route?"

95.   He said: "What God has granted me,
Is good enough; so you can only
Be helping me by manual labour,
And I shall build, as barrier,
A solid dam, 'tween you and them,

96.   "Come bring me blocks and sheets of iron".
And after he had filled the glen,
'Tween the two palisades, he said:
"Now blow the bellows", and he added,
When it was red as fire:
"Bring up to me the molten lead,
All over it to shower;

---

1. Most probably near Derbent in the Caucasus.

2. That is: their language was foreign to Zul-Qarnain.

3. It has nearly been established now that they were the wild tribes of Central Asia known by different names: Tartars, Mongols, Huns and Scythians; according to Ezekiel (chapters 38,39) they originally inhabited the territories of Meshech (Moscow) and Tubal (Tubalsek), and, according to Josephus, they were the Scythians and their territory spread to the north and the east of the Black Sea.

97.   "Now this they[1] could not scale,
      Nor in it bore a hole."

98.   "This," said he, "is a blessing from my Lord,
      Yet when the Promise of my Lord is realized,
      All this is by Him pulverized;
      And my Lord's Promise is the Truth indeed."

99.   Yes, on that Day, We'll let them dash
      Like billows one over another,
      And when the Trumpet shall be blown,
      We'll bring them all together;

100. And on that Day, Gehenna shall be drawn,
      Close to the sight of disbelievers,

101. Whose eyes were closed to My reminders,
      Whose ears could not afford to hear!

102. Lo! Did the unbelievers really,
      Think they could take, as patrons dear,
      Any servants of Mine, beside Me?!
      Surely We have prepared Gehenna,
      To entertain the unbelievers!

103. Say: "Shall we tell you who have lost,
      Their labour most?

104. "They are the people whose endeavours,
      In the life of this world, have gone

---

1. "The enemies", "the barbarians", it is known that strong bulwarks had been
   built in the southern regions of Caucasia against the barbarian invaders from
   North Eastern and Central Asia.

Astray, and yet they think they've done
Good through their labours!"

105. These are indeed the disbelievers,
In the Signs of their Lord, and in His Meeting:
Wasted shall be their every action,
And, on the Day of Resurrection,
No weight we set up for their rating!

106. Gehenna shall be their requital just,
Because they disbelieved, and held,
My Signs and messengers in jest.

107. But those who did believe, and did good works,
Shall find their own delightful bliss,
In the Gardens of Paradise,

108. They shall therein for ever live,
Never wishing from there to move!

109. Say: "If the ocean could be flush
With ink, to write the words expressed by,
My Lord, the ocean would go dry,
Ere the words of my Lord, would finish,
Even though we brought one like it,
It to replenish!"

110. Say: "I am but a mortal like you all,
Only it has been unto me revealed
That your God is: One God alone;"
Thus whosoever hopes to meet his Lord,
Let him work righteousness, and join,
In his Lord's worship, none.

SURA 19
MARY
(MARYAM)

In the Name of God, the Beneficent, the Merciful

1. K.H.Y.'A.S.[1]

2. Here's an account of your Lord's goodness
   Unto his servant, Zacharias;

3. Behold! He called upon his Lord,
   In a low voice,

4. And said: "My Lord, my bones have brittled,
   And my head is aflame with hoariness;
   But never have I prayed to you, my Lord,
   With ill success;

5. "But I have fears now for my kinsmen,
   After me, for my wife is barren;
   So, pray give me an heir, out of your Grace,

6. "Who may inherit me and be an heir
   To Jacob's House;[2]
   And make him one, my Lord, a choice,
   Of Your own pleasure."

7. "O Zacharias, do rejoice,
   We shall be giving you a son,

---

1. Kaaf Haa Yaa 'Ain Saad.

2. The inheritance of the Children of Jacob is the inheritance of the Divine
   blessing of prophethood.

Whose name is to be John,[1]
A name unto no person
Before him given."

8.   He said: "My Lord, how shall I have a son,
When, barren is my spouse, and I have come,
To the old age of impotence."

9.   "It is to be so, all the same",
The answer came,
And says your Lord:
"This is to Me an easy thing,
Just as I brought you into being,
In former times, when you were nothing."

10.   "My Lord", said he, "will you give me some Sign".
"The sign will be", The answer came,
"That for three nights, though in a healthy frame,
You shall with none converse."

11.   So he went to his people from the shrine,
And made it known unto them, by a sign,
That they should celebrate God's praise,
Mornings and evenings.

12.   John was inspired: "You shall observe,
The Scripture with a firm resolve."
Wisdom We granted him while yet a child,

13.   And tenderness of heart and purity,
From Our Own Self; he was a man of piety;

---

1. Arabic Yahya (Hebrew: Yohanan, meaning: "Jehova has been Gracious").

14.   And to his parents, dutifully mild,
        He knew no arrogance,
        Nor disobedience.

15.   Peace[1] was upon him on the day
        When he was born,
        And on the day he passed away;
        And Peace shall be upon him when,
        He shall be raised to life again.

16.   Now mention Mary in the Book:
        When she abandoned her own folk,
        And to an eastern place,[2]
        Herself betook,

17.   And she hung down a veil,
        Herself from them to screen;
        And now We sent to her Our spirit,[3] in
        The semblance of a perfect male.

18.   She said: "I fly for refuge to Al-Rahmaan,[4]
        From you, unless you be a righteous man."

19.   He said: "I am indeed an envoy,
        Sent by your Lord to grant you,
        A most pure boy."

20.   She said: "How shall I bear a son,

---

1. "Salaam" in Arabic, and "shalom" in Hebrew.

2. Probably to a private eastern chamber of the Temple in Jerusalem.

3. An angel.

4. The Most Beneficent, or the Most Merciful.

When I was ne'er touched by a man,
Nor have I been an unchaste woman?"

21.   "It is so willed", said he,
"And says your Lord" This is to Me,
An easy thing, and We intend
To make a Sign of him to humankind,
He is a Mercy from Ourself,
And it's a matter foreordained."

22.   So she conceived him, and with him retired,
Unto a distant place;[1]

23.   And pains of childbirth drove her to the trunk,
Of a palm-tree; she cried:
"Would that before this, I had died,
And been in sheer oblivion sunk!"

24.   Now from beneath her, cried to her a voice:
"Do not despair; your Lord for you has let,
A streamlet run beneath your feet;

25.   "And shake the trunk of this palm-tree, and ripe,
Fresh dates will drop down in your lap,

26.   "Therefore, refresh your eyes,[2] and drink and eat;
And should you come across a man,
Say: "I have vowed to Al-Rahmaan,
A fast of silence, so today, I will
Not speak at all with any human."

---

1. Probably to Bethlehem about 6 miles south of Jerusalem.

2. Literal: "cool your eye": An idiom meaning "comfort yourself and be glad."

27. At length, she brought him to her people;
    They cried: "O Mary, surely you have done,
    Something most horrible!

28. "You, Lady virtuous![1]
    Your dad was not a man of wickedness,
    Nor was your mother's morals loose!"

29. But she did merely point,
    Towards the infant;
    "And, how on earth" They gibed,
    "Could we speak with a babe,
    Still in the crib?!"

30. But it[2] did cry: "I am God's servant,
    The Scripture did He to me grant,
    And prophethood on me ordained,

31. "His Blessing is on me wherever,
    I may be, and He has enjoined,
    Upon me prayer, and giving to the poor,
    As long as I shall live,

32. "And to be kind to her that gave
    Birth to me; and He has not made
    Me insolent, depraved;

1. Literal: "you, sister of Aaron": such idiomatic expressions are abundant in
Arabic, as well as in some other languages; also both Mary and Elisabeth,
    mother of John, belonged to the priestly family of Aaron. Some Western
    scholars (!) have charged Mohammad (pbuh) that he confused Miriam,
    Aaron's sister with Mary mother of Jesus! The baseless charge does not
    deserve further comment.
2. The infant Jesus.

33.   "And Peace on me upon the day
When I was born, and on the day I die,
And Peace shall be upon me when
I shall be raised to life again;"

34.   And such is Jesus, Mary's son;
The very truth in which they differ.

35.   It shall not be for God the One,[1]
That He beget a son!
Glory be to Him: He's above this:
When he decrees a thing,
He only to it says:
"Be", and it is already "Being".

36.   "And God the One is certainly my Lord,
Your Lord as well; thus worship him,
That is the Direct Road!"[2]

37.   In spite of this, the Sects[3] began to differ
Among themselves; but woe to disbelievers,
When they witness that Great Day's horrors!

38.   How clearly they shall see and hear,
The Day when they before Us shall appear!
Today, therefore, are the offenders,
In clearest error.

---

1. Allah.

2. Another quotation from Jesus; this is cited to tell the Christians that Jesus
   also taught the same doctrine of Oneness of God as taught by all other
   prophets.

3. The numerous sects of the Christians.

39. As they are now in utter heedlessness,
    And do persist in unbelief, forewarn,
    Them of the Day of Absolute Distress,
    When matters shall have been determined;

40. For it is We who will inherit,
    The earth and all there is upon it,
    And they are all to us returned.

41. And, in the Book, mention Abraham too:
    He was a prophet, one most true.

42. Behold, he said unto his father:
    "Dear father, why are you a server,
    To things which do not see nor hear,
    And for you have no use whatever?!

43. "Father! Some knowledge came to me in truth,
    Which never reached you, therefore, follow me,
    And I shall guide you to an even Path;

44. "O Father mine, do not serve Satan,
    For Satan has indeed rebelled,
    Against Al-Rahmaan;

45. "O Father mine!
    I fear lest you incur the retribution
    Of Al-Rahmaan, and will become
    A Satan's minion."

46. He said: "How dare you shrink, O Abraham,
    From gods of mine? If you do not forbear,
    I'll have you stoned for sure!

Begone from me for a good while!"

47.   "Peace be on you", said he, "I shall implore
        My Lord for your forgiveness; for
        He's always been to me Most Gracious.

48.   "And I withdraw from you, and what you call on,
        Instead of God the One,
        And I shall call upon my Lord alone;
        My prayings to my Lord perhaps,
        Won't be with ill success."

49.   So when he left them and the deities,
        Which they, instead of Allah, worshipped,
        We granted him Isaac and Jacob,
        And made each one of them a prophet,

50.   And We, of Our own Grace, on them bestowed,
        And made them known upon all tongues of truth.
        And caused them to be highly praised.

51.   And make a mention in the Book of Moses:
        He was a chosen one, and he was both,
        Made an apostle and a prophet;

52.   We called upon him from,
        The right side of the Mountain,[1]
        And made him nearer come,
        For a communion;

53.   And, through Our Grace, We let him profit,

---

1. Mount Sinai; Arabic: The Toor.

From the aide of his brother, Aaron,
Himself a prophet.

54.   And, in this Book, do mention Ishmael,
Surely he was unto his promise truthful,
And he was an apostle and a prophet,

55.   And he enjoined upon his people,
Praying and alms-giving;
And he was to his Lord well pleasing.

56.   And mention, in this Book, Idrees,[1]
Who was a prophet, highly righteous.

57.   And We did raise him to a lofty place.

58.   These are some from among the prophets,
Upon whom God bestowed His Grace,
Descendants of the seed of Adam,
And of the people whom We had,
Aboard with Noah, carried,
And of the seed of Abraham,
Of Israel, and of all those,
Whom We guided and chose:
Whene're the revelations of Al-Rahmaan
Were unto them rehearsed, they fell upon
Their knees in adoration, with wet eyes.

59.   But after them the generations,
Who followed, missed their prayers;
And yielded unto their temptations;

---

1. Most probably: Enoch; "idrees" means "The most learned".

Soon shall they, therefore, meet Perdition!

60. But those who do repent,
Embrace the Faith, and do what's right,
Shall be admitted unto Paradise,
Without the least injustice,

61. In the Gardens of Everlasting Bliss,[1]
Which was Al-Rahmaan's promise,
Unto His servants for their faith,
In the Unseen; because His promise,
Shall come to pass in truth.

62. There they shall hear no nonsense,
But only words of Peace,
And they receive their sustenance,
Morning and evening;

63. Such is the Paradise,
Which We give, as inheritance,
To Our god-fearing servants,

64. "We[2] ne'er descend but by the bidding
Of your own Lord; to Him belongs,
What is before us, what's behind us,
And whatsoe'er between them lies;
And never does your Lord Forget a thing;

65. "The Lord of heavens and the earth,

---

1. Gardens of Eden.

2. A statement by Gabriel and other Message-carrying angels; This is a
paragraph in parenthesis.

And all that is between them; thus,
Do worship Him alone, and be
Most patient in His service;
Do you know any being worthy
Of the same Name as He?!"

66.   Man wonders also: "What! Once I am dead,
Shall I be raised to life again?!"

67.   Is Man forgetting that We did,
Create him firstly when,
He had been nothing?

68.   Thus, by your Lord, We'll surely summon these,
Together with the devils,
Then we shall bring them forth to Hell's
Vicinity, upon their knees,

69.   And then We will pluck forth from every sect,
Those who were most defiant,
Against the Most Beneficent;[1]

70.   For it is We who do know well,
Who does deserve to burn in Hell;[2]

71.   And of you there is not a single person,
But will go down to it;[3] That is a verdict
Of your own Lord, indeed a must;

---

1. Al-Rahmaan.

2. Original: "in it, therein"

3. Going through Gehenna; even the godfearing, on their way to Paradise, shall
have to pass by or over the Fire.

72.   And then We shall deliver those,
        Who feared,[1] and leave behind the most unjust,
        Upon their knees!

73.   Now when Our revelations manifest,
        Are unto them rehearsed, the disbelievers
        Address the faithful: "say which party,
        Between us, is positioned best,
        Which is the better company?!"

74.   Behold! We have annihilated,
        Before them, many generations,
        Who were far richer in provisions,
        And, to the eye, more splendid.

75.   Say: "as for those who choose to be in error,
        To them Al-Rahmaan surely gives a respite,
        Until they witness what they have been promised:
        Either some scourge at present or the Hour;
        Then they shall find out who is worst-
        Off, in an evil plight,
        And who's weaker in power?!

76.   But God augments the guidance,
        Of the already guided;
        And righteous deeds of lasting merit,
        In your Lord's sight, shall earn,
        A better guerdon, and result
        In excellent return.

77.   Now, have you come across the man,

---

1. The godfearing, the pious.

Who does reject Our revelations,
Yet boasts: "I shall continue to be given,
Riches and children?!"

78. What! Has he been informed of the Unknown,
Or has he ever made a covenant,
With Al-Rahmaan?!

79. Nay, by no means! We certainly write down,
Whate'er he claims, and We shall only lengthen,
For him, the retribution,

80. Everything he is claiming as his own,
He leaves behind for Us, and he shall come,
Before Us all alone;

81. These people have, instead of God, set up
Many a deity,
That they might bring them,
Power and dignity!

82. By no means! They shall soon disown their worship,
Not only that, but they'll[1] become
Adversaries to them.

83. Do you not know that, over disbelievers,
We have appointed devils,
Who constantly incite them unto evils;

84. Thus do not be with them impatient,
For certainly their days We number,

---

1. The idols, or deities.

85. Up to the Day, when We shall gather,
    The righteous, in the presence,
    Of Al-Rahmaan, with the due honour;

86. And We shall herd the guilty unto Hell,
    Like hordes of thirsty cattle!

87. No one shall have the power of intercession,
    Save those who have, from Al-Rahmaan,
    Received permission.

88. They also say that Al-Rahmaan,
    Has a begotten son!

89. "Now you have certainly come up with
    The worst abomination:

90. The heavens could have been asunder cloven,
    Thereat, and Earth to pieces broken,
    And mountains crumbled down,

91. At their report that Al-Rahmaan,
    Has got a son!

92. By no means shall it be befitting
    The Most Beneficent that He,
    Should be a son begetting!

93. There is none in the heavens,
    And in the earth, but shall be present,
    Before Al-Rahmaan, as a servant.

94.   He has indeed encompassed them, and made,
       Of them the strictest calculation,

95.   And everyone shall come to Him alone,
       Upon the Day of Resurrection;

96.   The God of Mercy[1] shall vouchsafe,
       His love and kindness,
       To those who did believe and led a life,
       Of righteousness,

97.   Thus We have made it[2] easy in your tongue,
       So that you give thereby glad tidings,
       To the god-fearing, and due warnings,
       Unto a nation given,
       To obdurate contention;

98.   And We, before them, have destroyed,
       Many a generation;
       Can you search out one of them somewhere?
       Or do you from them hear,
       The faintest whisper?!

---

1. Al-Rahmaan, The Most Beneficent.
2. The Holy Quran.

SURA 20
TAA HAA[1]

In the Name of God, the Beneficent, the Merciful

1.   Taa Haa;

2.   Certainly We have not sent down,
      Unto you this Quran,
      To put you in affliction;

3.   Nay, it's an Admonition,
      To the god-fearing men,

4.   Surely it is a revelation,
      From the One Who created
      The earth and the high heavens,

5.   The All-Merciful One,[2]
      Who's firmly mounted,
      Upon His Throne.

6.   Whatever is there in the heavens,
      What is on earth, what is between them both,
      And whatsoever is beneath the earth,[3]
      Belong to Him alone.

7.   Every secret is to Him known,
      As everything more hidden:
      Thus, you need not your voices louden!

---

1. T. H.

2. Original: Al-Rahmaan: Beneficent, Merciful, God of Mercy.

3. Or "soil".

8.   Yea, God the One:
        There is no God but He, and every
        Excellent Name is His!

9.   Now, have you ever heard the story,
        Concerning Moses?

10.   Behold! Some fire he espied;
        He told his folk: "Do stop for I behold,
        A fire, haply I will bring a brand,
        Therefrom, or at the fire, find
        Some kind of guide."

11.   And when he went up thereabout,
        A voice called out:
        "O Moses!

12.   "I am your Lord, for sure,
        Thus put your shoes off, for you are
        Upon the sacred vale of Toowa,[1]

13.   "You I have surely chosen;
        Therefore heedfully hearken,
        Unto the inspiration given;

14.   "Verily I am Allah,
        There is no God But I,
        So worship Me alone,
        And, keep up prayer,
        Me to remember;

---

1. The valley just below Mount Sinai, where subsequently he was to receive the
   Torah.

15.   "Know that the Hour of Doom[1]
      Is sure to come,
      I am about to make it manifest,
      So that each soul is recompensed
      According to its labour.

16.   "Thus let not those who disbelieve therein,
      Who only follow their own lust and wish,
      Turn you aside therefrom,
      And make you perish!

17.   "But now, O Moses, what is this,
      In your right hand?"

18.   "Oh, it's my staff", he did respond,
      "I do upon it lean,
      With it, I beat down leaves,
      For my own flock of sheep,
      That I for many uses keep."

19.   He said: "O Moses, cast it down!"

20.   So he did cast it down, and lo!
      It was a serpent on the go!

21.   "Pick it up now", said He "and do not panic!
      We shall in no time change it back,
      Into its former make;

22.   "And put your hand close to your arm-pit,

---

1. The Hour signifies both the Resurrection and, very often, the doom of people:
   the hour of the departure of their glory and power.

And it comes out resplending white,
But still unharmed shall it remain:
And that's, another Sign,

23. "And soon We'll show you, of Our Signs,
Some greater ones.

24. "Go to Pharaoh, for certainly,
He has all bounds transgressed."

25. "My Lord", he said, "Then pray,
Expand for me my breast,

26. "And make my mission light,

27. "And from my tongue remove the catch,

28. "That they may understand my speech,

29. "And from amongst my kin, appoint
For me a wise assistant,

30. "Aaron, my brother,

31. "And by him fortify my power,

32. "And let him share my mission,

33. "That we glorify You most often,

34. "And We remember You most often,

35. For You have certainly of us,

Been Most Observant."

36. "O Moses", said He "granted,
     Is your request;

37. "Indeed, another time, did We confer,
     On you a favour in the past;

38. "Behold! By inspiration to your mother,
     We thus informed her:

39. "Put him¹ into a chest,
     And then cast it into the river,
     But it the river is to cast
     Onto the bank, and there he will
     Be taken up by one who is,
     Both My foe and a foe of his;
     Then I made you an object of,
     My very love:
     That you are brought up under My,
     Own watchful Eye.

40. "Behold, your sister went and said:
     'Shall I direct you unto someone
     Who'll nurse him?!' Thus did We return,
     You to your mother, so that glad
     Will be her heart, no longer sad;
     And when you killed a certain man,
     We saved you from the trouble,
     And then We tried you with another trial;
     Thus you for many years remained,

---

1. The infant Moses.

Among the folks of Midian,
And now you have, O Moses,
Come along hither, as,
Had been ordained;

41. "You I have, for My mission,
Moulded and chosen.

42. "Go now, you and your brother,
Supported by My Signs, and never,
In My remembrance be too slow;

43. "Go both of you to Pharaoh,
For he has gone too far,
Even as a transgressor,

44. "But speak unto him, each
Of you, with gentle speech,
Haply he may take heed,
Or fear the Lord indeed."

45. They said: "Our Lord, we surely dread,
Lest he break forth against us,
Or act with all injustice."

46. He said: "Fear not, I am indeed,
With you, I hearken and behold;

47. "So go you both to him and say:
'We are apostles of your Lord,
Thus let the Israelites depart,
With us, and stop their harm and hurt,
A Message from your Lord, we bring you,

And peace be on the people who
Follow the guided road;

48.   "Indeed We were informed by revelation
That people who reject and give no heed,
Will surely taste the retribution;'"

49.   He asked: "Who then, O Moses,
Is the Lord of you two?"

50.   "Our Lord", he said "is He Who gave creation,
To every thing, and He did guide them too.

51.   He asked: "What is then the condition,
Of any former generation?"

52.   "The knowledge of that, properly recorded,
Is only with my Lord", he said,
"There is no erring or forgetting
On the part of my Lord;

53.   "It's He Who made the earth a bed
For you, and traced out paths for you therein,
And sent down water from the heaven;"
Thereby did We produce all sorts
Of herbs and plants,

54.   For you to eat and feed
Your own cattle, indeed;
Signs are in these, for those
With acumen endued;

55.   From it¹ have We created you,
        And We will send you back into the same,
        And out of it We'll bring you forth,
        A second time.

56.   Surely We showed unto him² every Sign,
        But he rejected all, and did decline;³

57.   He said: "O Moses, have you not come back,
        To drive us from our country with your magic?!

58.   "Then, We will certainly confront you
        With magic, strong as yours, so make
        Between us and yourself a tryst,
        That none of us may break,
        At some location fairly placed."

59.   He said: "Let us set your encounter,
        For the day of the Public Feast,⁴
        And let the people gather,
        After the sun is well advanced."

60.   So Pharaoh did withdraw to bring together,
        His craftsmen, then he came back thither.

61.   Moses warned them:
        "Woe to you, if you ever forge,
        Any falsehood 'gainst Allah, for
        He'll then destroy you by a scourge;
        Surely they who have forged such lies,

---

1. The earth.   2. Pharaoh.   3. "To believe".

4. Most probably a great day of Temple Festival in ancient Egypt.

Have always been the failures."

62. Thus they disputed over their affair,
Among themselves, but kept the matter,
Secret by speaking in a whisper.

63. They said: "These men are only two magicians,
Who do intend to drive you from your land,
And, through their sorcery, to put an end,
To your esteemed traditions;

64. "Therefore, let us concert our plans,
And come in a united stand,
And this day shall be well for him,
Who'll gain the upper hand."

65. They called: "O Moses, either you will cast,
Or we will cast down first?"

66. "Nay!" said he, "You be first;" and lo!
Their ropes and rods, through their enchantment,
Did seem to him as though:
They were quickened to movement!

67. And Moses was, inside him, filled with awe.

68. "Fear not", We said, "for it is you who will,
Come out triumphant;

69. "And throw down what you're holding,
In your right hand: it will devour
What they have wrought, for surely what,
They've wrought is a magician's plot,

And no magician ever,
However skilled, will prosper."

70. Consequently, all the magicians fell
Down in prostration on their knees,
Saying: "We're now believers in the Lord,
Of Aaron and of Moses!"

71. He[1] cried: "Do you in him believe,
Before I give you leave?!
Surely this man must be your chiefest one,
Who taught you magic, therefore I shall have,
Your hands and feet cut off upon
Opposite sides, and crucify you on,
Trunks of the palms, and you shall learn,
Surely which of us is more stern,
In chastisement, and lasting longer!"

72. They answered: "We cannot prefer you over
The miracles[2] to which We have been witness,
And o'er the One who did create us,
Therefore, decide what you decide; however,
It's only in this worldly life you could,
Make some decisions;

73. "We now believe in our own Lord,
That he may pardon us our sins,
And the magic you forced us to;
Better is God, And He remains."

74. Indeed for him who comes before

---

1. Pharaoh.   2. Or "clear tokens".

His Lord laden with sin,
There shall be Hell, and surely he,
Shall neither die nor live therein!

75.   But the people who come before him, as
Believers, having done good works,
Shall reap the highest ranks:

76.   Dwelling for ever in the Gardens
Of Eden with their running streams;
For those who purify themselves,
Such is to be the recompense.

77.   We it was Who revealed to Moses:
Set forth at night, in company
With My servants, and strike for them,
A passage dry across the sea,
Fear not that you'll be caught,
And have no dreadful worry.

78.   And Pharaoh, with his cohorts followed,
them, but the whelming billows rolled,
And they were overwhelmed!

79.   Instead of guiding, Pharaoh had,
His own people misled!

80.   O You: Children of Israel!
We saved you from your foes, and made
With you a covenant upon the right
Side of the Mount,[1] and on you rained
Manna and quail:[2]

---

1. Original: Al-Toor; Mount Sinai.   2. Original: Salwa.

81.   "Eat of the pure provision,
    We have unto you given,
    And go not to excess therewith,
    Lest you incur My wrath;
    For he on whom My wrath my fall,
    Ruined is he in truth.

82.   Certainly I am Most Forgiving,
    To those who do repent, believe again,
    Conduct a righteous living,
    And guided shall remain.

83.   "O Moses, what has made you hasten,
    Ahead of your own people hither?"[1]

84.   He answered: "They are on my track,
    I rushed to you, my Lord, to seek
    Only Your pleasure."

85.   "Behold!" Said He "We put your people,
    Unto a test, while you had been away,
    And the Samiri[1] has indeed,
    Led them astray!"

86.   Thus Moses, full of wrath and in distress,

1. Perhaps "without the 70 elders who were to accompany him": Exodus
xxiv. 14.

2. He may have been an Egyptianized Hebrew, as *shemer* in old Egyptian means
"a stranger, a foreigner"; we also read in the Old Testament (1 Kings, xvi.
21) that Omri, King of Israel (903-896 B.C.) bought a hill from Shemer, and
built the new city of Samaria upon it; therefore, the translation of the word
"Samiri" into "Samaritan", (as some translators have done) for a person who
lived long before Samaria was built, is obviously wrong.

Went back unto his folk,
And cried: "O People, did your Lord not make
To you a gracious Promise?
Was the time[1] to you long to pass?
Or you intended to provoke,
'Gainst you, the anger of your Lord,
That you the promise with me broke?!"

87.   They said: "We have not, of our own accord,
Failed in the pledge with you, but we were loaded
Down with the ornaments of people, thus
We made a casting of them, and it had,
Been the Samiri who suggested this;

88.   "And then he for the people made
The body of a calf that mooed,
And people said: 'This is your god,
The god of Moses, but it did
Escape his mind!'"[2]

89.   Verily did they not consider,
That it could not return an answer,
Nor could it hurt or help them ever?

90.   And Aaron had already warned them:
"My people, by this you are being
Put to a test, for your God only,
Has been the God of Mercy,[3]
Thus follow me and do obey my bidding."

---

1. "Of my absence".

2. They allege: Moses is searching for a god on the Mount, but he has forgotten that his god is really here!

3. Original: Al-Rahmaan "the Most Merciful, the Most Beneficent."

91.   They had answered: "We, by no means,
Will cease devotion unto it until,
Moses to us returns."

92.   He shouted: "What prevented you, O Aaron,
After you saw that they had gone astray,

93.   "That you did not follow my way?
Did you indeed my order disobey?"

94.   "O Son of my own mother," Aaron pleaded,
"Seize me not by my beard, nor by my head,
Indeed I feared that you would come and say:
'You rent the Israelites asunder,
And did not contemplate my order.'"

95.   He cried: "And what about your very
Motive in this, O You Samiri?"

96.   He answered: "Something I had witnessed,
That others did not see: a fistful,
I did get hold of, of the dust,
From the footprints of that *rasool*,[1]
And then I threw it in the cast,
Thus was I prompted by my soul!"[2]

97.   "Begone then" , said he "for your doom,
Even in this life is to say: *no touch*,[3]

---

1. Messenger, apostle, envoy, and an angel of God.

2. The Samiri, in his unblushing effrontery, evades the main issue and invents
confusing falsehoods.

3. A curse: "you shall be plagued with leprosy" or "you will become a social

And there shall be for you a promise,
That will not fail at all, and now do watch
Your god to which you were a devotee,
Indeed we'll burn it and dispatch,
The ashes to the sea."

98.   Your only deity is God the One,[1]
There is no god but He, Who in His ken,
Embraces everything.

99.   Thus do We unto you[2] narrate,
Some news of times already flown,
And We are surely giving you
A Message[3] from Our Own;

100.   Those who to it pay no attention,
Shall bear a very heavy burden,
Upon the Day of Resurrection;

101.   And under it shall they remain
It is indeed an evil burden
Upon the Day of Resurrection;

102.   On the Day when the Horn is to be blown
When We summon the terror-stricken[4] sinners,

103.   They will be commenting in whispers:

---

leper the rest of your life"; an untouchable.

1. Allah.   2. The Holy Prophet.

3. Or " A Reminder, "an Admonition".

4. Also meaning "blear-eyed", "eyes dimmed with terror", "blue-eyed" and
"blind".

"We tarried not longer than ten?"[1]

104.   We know full well what they shall say,
When their own fairest arbiter maintains:
"You've not tarried above a day!"[2]

105.   Now they ask you about the mountains?![3]
Tell them: My Lord shall scatter them like grains,
Most finely milled,

106.   And turn them into flattest plains,

107.   A vast you'll see: unholed, unhilled;

108.   That Day they all will follow,
The Summoner,[4] who marches straight,
Onwards, and low shall be their voices,
In fear of Al-Rahmaan,
Nor shall you hear a sound except,
The light footfall of people tramping on.

109.   Upon that Day no intercession,
Shall profit, save by him who has
From Al-Rahmaan, received permission,
Whose words receive His sanction;

110.   He knows their future and their past, whereas,

---

1. Ten days.

2. Faced with eternity they will realize that their life on this earth, or the interval between death and Resurrection was very brief: ten days? One day? or less?

3. The fate of mountains.   4. This could be the Angel Israfil.

They'll never comprehend him knowledge-wise.

111.   Hung down shall be their heads before,
         The Ever-Living, the Eternal One,
         And he who bears the burden of injustice,
         Shall be indeed undone!

112.   But he who did good deeds as a believer,
         Shall fear no wrong or any loss whatever.

113.   Thus have We sent to you this Reading,
         In the Arabic tongue, and admonition
         Of various sorts have We therein set forth,
         Perhaps they fear or it may, to reflection,
         In them, give a new birth.

114.   Exalted then be Allah,
         The King, the True One;
         And with regard to Al-Quran,
         Be patient while its Revelation
         To you is not complete; but pray:
         "My Lord, increase my ken."

115.   Of old We made a covenant,
         With Adam, but it did escape his mind,
         Indeed in him, We did not find,
         A resolution adamant.

116.   Behold, We said unto the angels:
         "Prostrate yourselves to Adam",
         They all went down upon their knees,
         Except Iblees; he did refuse;

117.   Just then We warned: "O Adam, this
        Is certainly an enemy,
        To you and to your spouse,
        Let him not therefore drive you out
        Of the Garden of Paradise,
        For then you'll be in great distress;

118.   "For here it is unto you granted,
        That you shall never hunger,
        Nor need yourselves to cover,[1]

119.   "You shall not suffer thirst therein,
        Nor feel the scorching sun."

120.   But Satan whispered evil unto him,
        And said: "O Adam, shall I lead
        You to the Tree of Immortality,
        And a Kingdom that never fails indeed?"

121.   At last, they both did from it eat,
        And so their nakedness became,
        Apparent to the other mate;
        And they began to clothe the same,
        With the leaves from the Garden;
        And thus his Lord did Adam disobey,
        And went astray.

122.   Later His Lord was to him gracious:[2]
        He turned to him to guide his way;

---

1. Or "nor be unsheltered".

2. Or "chose him out of His grace."

123. And said: "Go hence, you both together,
   Some of your offspring are to be
   Enemies unto one another;
   Yet guidance from Me will,
   Come unto you hereafter;
   And those who do follow My guidance,
   Will not fall into error,
   Nor be unhappy ever.

124. But He who disregards My Admonition,
   Shall lead a life distressed and straitened,
   And on the Day of Resurrection,
   We'll raise him blind.

125. He says: "My Lord, why have You raised me blind,
   Whereas before this, I was blessed with sight?"

126. He'll say: "Thus is it, for Our Signs did come
   Unto you but you did forget them,
   And this Day you shall be forgotten!"

127. Thus do We punish those who have transgressed,
   Beyond all bounds, and never did believe,
   In the Signs of their Lord; the chastisement
   Of the next world will surely grieve,
   More woefully and be more permanent.

128. Could this not be to them a lesson:
   How many generations,
   Have We destroyed before them,
   And now they walk amidst the ruins,
   That used to be their habitations;
   Indeed in these are Signs,

For men of reason.

129. Had there not been a Word,
      Already uttered by your Lord,
      That fixed a predetermined term,
      Their fate would have by now been sealed!

130. Thus bear with what they say with patience,
      And celebrate your own Lord's praise
      Before the sunrise,
      Before its setting, and do praise,
      Him in the watches of the night,
      And in the hours of the day,
      That you may please.

131. And do not cast an envious look upon,
      What We have granted unto certain parties,
      Of splendours of this worldly life, for We
      Are only trying them by these!
      The portion that your Lord provides,
      Is better and, for long, abides.

132. Enjoin the prayer upon your folk,[1]
      And strictly persevere therein,
      We do not ask you for provision,
      For We Ourself give you provision;
      And it is Righteousness that will,
      The final issue win!

133. They say: "If he could only bring us from,
      His Lord a marvellous Sign!

---

1. Both family members and followers.

But have they not received sufficient proofs
In Pages pristine?[1]

134.   Had We destroyed them by some chastisement,
Before this,[2] they would certainly have roared:
"O Lord, if you had only to us sent,
A messenger, we would have surely followed
Your revelations, ere we had to face
All this shame and disgrace!"

135.   Say: "Everyone of us is waiting, so
You also wait, and soon you'll come to know
Who follows the right road and who,
Is on the guidance true.

---

1. Earlier Scriptures, Books and Scrolls.

2. Before the revelation of the Holy Quran, or before the Holy Prophet himself

SURA 21
THE PROPHETS
(AL-ANBIYAA)

In the Name of God, the Beneficent, the Merciful

1. The Hour of reckoning is drawing nigh,
   For the people,[1] yet, sunk in disregard,
   They turn away.

2. No fresh warning does ever from their Lord,
   Come to them, but they to it only,
   Hearken in mockery,

3. With hearts set on some trifling play;
   And such wrongdoers whisper 'mongst themselves:
   "Is he more than a mortal like yourselves?
   What! You have eyes to see, and yet you may,
   Accede to sorcery?!"

4. Say: "My Lord is Aware of every word,
   That, in the heavens or on earth, is spoken,
   For He is the All-Hearing
   Possessor of All-Ken.

5. "Nay", say they, 'it's[2] of dreams a medley,
   Nay, he has made it up; but nay,
   He is a poet only; anyway,
   Let him bring us a Sign
   As messengers in days gone by!"

6. Before their time, none of the towns,[3]

---

1. This may indicate both the people of Mecca, and mankind in general.

2. The Quran and its revelations.   3. Or "habitations".

That We annihilated, did believe;
Will these men then believe?

7.   Never, before you, have We sent but men,
To whom We gave Our revelation;
Question the People of the Scriptures,
If you do not have any ken;

8.   Nor did We give them bodies,
Which could dispense with food,
Nor did they live for good!

9.   Then We Our promise unto them fulfilled,
And We delivered them and whom We willed,
And We did put an end,
To people breaking every bound.

10.   And now We have sent down to you a Book,
Which will you all, for your own good, Remind;
What, will you still not understand?!

11.   Numerous are the guilty habitations,
That We have broken down, and later,
Replaced with other nations!

12.   Now, when they felt Our vengeance coming,
Lo! They were from it running![1]

13.   "Flee not, but come back to your luxuries,
And to your homes wherein you lived in ease,

---

1. Compare Christ's saying in the present Gospel of St. Matthew (iii:7): "O generation of vipers, who has warned you to flee from the Wrath to come?"

Perhaps you shall be questioned!"

14. "O woe to us", they wailed and moaned:
    "We have been doing wrong indeed."

15. Their lamentation came not to an end,
    Until We made them like a corn-field mown,
    As ashes in extinction.

16. For We did not create the heavens and the earth,
    And all that is between them, for Our recreation!

17. Were it Our wish to take a pastime,
    We would surely find it within
    Ourself; nay, thus do We not function!

18. Nay, We will hurl the Truth at Falsehood,
    Until the former smites the latter,
    And lo, it vanishes; but woe to you,
    For falsehoods that you utter.[1]

19. To Him belong all beings in the heavens,
    And the earth; and those in His presence,
    Worship Him with no arrogance;
    Are they wearied? Nay, by no means!

20. They glorify Him night and day,
    Nor do they intermit or stay.

21. What! Have they taken earthly gods,
    who could raise up the dead?!

---

1. "Concerning God."

22. Had there been other gods in either,[1]
Instead of God the One, then both would suffer
Chaos, and certainly collapse;
Thus glory be to God alone,
The Lord of the High Throne,
Above their utterances false!

23. He can't be asked concerning any act,
It's they who shall be asked in fact.

24. Perhaps they've taken other gods[2] beside Him?
Say: "Bring your proof; whereas this Admonition
To the people about me, is the same
As those given to every generation,
Before me; nay, they mostly do not know
The Truth at all, so they pay no attention.

25. We never sent a messenger,
Before your time, unto whom We,
Had not revealed: There is no God but I,
Thus worship Me."

26. And yet they claim that Al-Rahmaan,[3]
Has taken to Himself a son!
Glory be to Him! Nay, such person,
Among His servants is an honoured one.

27. Such beings never speak a word,
Till He has spoken,
And they do nothing but,

---

1. The heavens and the earth.   2. "For worship."

3. The God of Mercy, the Most Beneficent.

What He has bidden;[1]

28.   He knows what is before them and all that,
Has been behind them, and they could not ever
An intercession offer, save for whom He please,
And even then, they tremble for His fear;

29.   If any of them should declare:
"I am a god beside Him,"
We will reward him with the Fire,
Thus do We punish an offender.

30.   Let those who disbelieve consider this:
The heavens and the earth were both a mass,
Most solid,[2] which We did asunder cleave,
And then by means of water, We gave life
To everything; will they still not believe!

31.   And on the earth We set up mountain ranges,
Making it stronger with such elevations,
And hewed out highways wide between them,
That they may follow right directions,

32.   We also made the heaven,

---

1. The true prophets of God never say or do anything before they receive God's command. This is also the teaching of our exalted prophet, Jesus Christ, as reported in the Gospel of St. John (xii. 49-50): "For I have not spoken of myself, but the Father which sent me, He gave me a commandment, what I should say, and what I should speak... even as the Father said unto me, so I speak." If rightly understood, "Father" has the meaning of "the Creator, Sustainer and Cherisher", not Begetter or Progenitor in a paganistic, biological sense!

2. Or "closed up", "joined together as one", "a closed stuff".

A roof, guarded, strongly upholden;
Yet, from its Signs, they turn aside.

33.   And He it is Who brought about,
The night, the day, the sun, and moon,
Each swiftly swims along,
The orbit of its own.

34.   Never have We, in former times,
Granted abiding life unto a man,
So if you should now die,
Shall they, for good, remain?!

35.   Every soul is to taste of death, and We
Test you with good and evil turns,
By way of trial, and each one of you,
Finally unto Us returns.

36.   When seeing you,[1] the disbelievers,
Receive you with their scoffs and sneers:
"Is this the very man who is at odds,
With all your gods?!"
And they themselves profane
The name of Al-Rahmaan!

37.   Man is innately hasty;
But soon I shall be showing you My Signs,
Thus ask me not to hasten things.

38.   They also ask: "when will this threat[2] fulfill,
If you are truthful?

---

1. The Holy Prophet.   2. The threatened Punishment.

39.   Had those who disbelieve but known
        The time when they could not defend,
        Their backs or faces from the Fire,
        When no one will to them extend,
        A helping hand!

40.   But it shall come on them all of a sudden,
        And they'll be stunned,
        Then they could not avert it,
        Nor are they respited.

41.   Other apostles have, before your time,
        Been ridiculed, but those who at them scoffed,
        Were hemmed in by the very thing
        At which they scoffed!

42.   Say: "Who could guard you, night and day,
        From Al-Rahmaan?" But nay, they still,
        From their Lord's warning turn away.

43.   Perhaps they have some gods beside Us,
        Who could defend them? Those who have no power
        To help themselves, nor could they ever,
        Protect these folks against Us.

44.   Yes! To these people and their fathers,
        We gave provisions that they could attain
        Old age; but don't they ever notice
        That We come to a land and straiten
        It on all sides? Are they the ones,
        To be the winners?!

45.   Say: "I am only warning you upon

Authority of Revelation;"
The deaf, when they are warned, however,
Hear not the call of Admonition.

46.　　Yet when touched by the slightest breath
Of your Lord's wrath,
They surely cry: "O woe to us,
Offenders have we been in truth!

47.　　Just balances We shall set up,
Upon the Resurrection Day,
No soul is to be wronged; and deeds,
Shall We bring forth to weigh,
Even as weightless as a mustard-seed;
Sufficient are We at accounts indeed!

48.　　Of old We did to Moses and to Aaron,
Grant Al-Furqan,[1] a Light and a Reminder,
For the god-fearing men,

49.　　Who do revere their Lord, although unseen,
Whose worry for the Hour, is most keen.

50.　　And now We have sent down
This hallowed Message,
Will you it not acknowledge!

51.　　Of old We gave to Abraham,
His right direction, for of him,
We had a perfect knowledge.

---

1. Meaning: Criterion (of right from wrong), Illumination, a statute book and
Salvation.

52.   Behold! He told his father and his folk:
    "What on earth are these images,
    To whom you pay such zealous homages?"

53.   They said: "We found our fathers
    Worshipping them in earnest."

54.   He said: "Then both, you and your fathers,
    Have been in error manifest!"

55.   They asked: "Have you come unto us in earnest,
    Or are you one of those who jest?"

56.   He answered: "Nay, your Lord in truth,
    Is the Lord of the heavens and the earth,
    He did create them all, and unto this,
    I am a witness;

57.   "By God, I will employ some clever tricks,
    Against your idols, once you've turned your backs."

58.   Therefore he broke them into fragments,
    But left the biggest one intact,
    That they may it contact![1]

59.   They cried out: "Who has done this to our gods?
    He must be wicked for a fact."

60.   Some said: "We heard a young man speak of them,
    They call him Abraham."

---

1. "For inquiring".

61. They said: "Bring him before the people's eyes,
    So that they may bear witness."

62. They questioned: "Was it you, O Abraham,
    Who has unto our gods done this?"

63. "Why!" answered he," their big chief here has done it,
    Do question them,[1] if they can use their tongue?

64. At this, they turned unto themselves and thought:
    "Certainly we are in the wrong!"

65. But soon they somersaulted in their thought,
    Saying: "You know quite well that these
    Things do not utter aught."

66. "What!" said he, do you worship then,
    Such things, instead of God, that neither
    Benefit you, nor harm you ever?

67. "Ah, fie on you and what you worship,
    Instead of God! Do you not ponder?"

68. Thus they cried out: "Let us burn him alive,
    To help our gods, if we should really strive."

69. We said: "O Fire, be cool to Abraham,
    And keep him safe!"

70. Later they sought to force on him a strife,
    But We did make them losers grand!

---

1. The shattered idols.

71.   We did deliver him and Lot,
    And brought them to the land,
    Which We have blessed for all mankind.

72.   Later we gave him Isaac,
    And Jacob, for a grandson,[1]
    Each one of them We made,
    A righteous person.

73.   And We also made them *imams*,[2]
    Who guided[3] at Our own behest,
    And We revealed to them to always,
    Do their own righteous best,
    To keep up constant prayers,
    And to expend in alms;
    They did serve Us in earnest.

74.   And unto Lot:
    We gave wisdom and ken,
    And saved him from the townsmen,
    Who wrought abomination,[4]
    Because they were, for certain,
    An evil, wicked lot;

75.   And We admitted him into Our mercy,
    He was indeed a righteous person.

76.   Of old did Noah Us invoke,
    And so We answered him and did,

---

1. The original also means: "an additional gift."   2. Leaders, guides.
3. "Others".   4. Evil doings, filthiness.

Deliver, from a great disaster,
Him and his kinsfolk;

77. And We assisted him against a nation,
Who had denied Our Signs as fabrication;
A people were they truly evil,
And so We drowned them all.

78. Behold! David and Solomon,
Once gave a judgment,
About a field on which the sheep
Of certain folks had grazed all night:
And We were witnessing their judgment;

79. So We to Solomon gave insight
Into it, though We had bestowed
On both of them wisdom and knowledge.
The hills and birds We had subdued,
To celebrate Our praise with David;
And We it was who all this did!

80. And it was We who taught to him the skill,
Of making coats of mail for you to shield,
Your selves in battle;
Are you not grateful?

81. For Solomon We made the raging wind,
Race, at his bidding, to the land,
On which We had bestowed Our blessings,
We are the Ever-Knower of all things.

82. Subjected to him were some devils,[1]

1. Or: "satans", "demons".

Who dived for him into the deep,
And did some other works beside, yet We,
A Watchful Eye did o'er them keep.

83.   And tell of Job; behold,
He cried unto his Lord: "Extreme
Harm has afflicted me indeed,
But You're the Merciful Supreme."[1]

84.   So We responded to him and did lighten
All his distressful, trying burden,
And gave him back his kith and kin,
And of the same, doubled the number:
A Grace from Us, and a Reminder,
To all and every worshipper.

85.   And mention Ishmael,
Idrees[2] and Ezekiel,[3]
Who were most patient all,

86.   And We admitted them into Our grace,
For they were truly righteous.

87.   And there was Jonah:[4]
Behold, he went away in anger,
Imagining We had no power,
Over him; but then soon he did invoke

---

1. Or: The Most Merciful.

2. Most probably: Enoch.

3. The Quranic spelling is "Zul-kifl", and most commentators take it as the Arabized form of Ezekiel.

4. The original is Zul-noon: "The man of the fish."

Us in the depth of dark:
"There is no God but You, to You be glory,
Indeed I've been an evil-doer stark."

88. So We responded to his prayer,
And saved him from that grief;
For thus do We deliver,
The people of belief.

89. And there was Zacharias;
Behold, he called upon his Lord:
"My Lord, leave me not childless,
Although there is no better-
Than-you inheritor."

90. So We answered his prayer, and gave him John,[1]
And made his wife for him most proper;[2]
For they did surely vie in goodness,
And used to call upon us ever,
With love and fear, and were before Us,
In perfect humbleness.

91. And mention her[3] who kept her chastity,
And into whom We breathed of Our Own Spirit,
And made her and her son a beacon[4] lit
For all humanity.

92. Indeed this very Brotherhood,[5]

1. Quranic original: Yahyaa; Hebrew: Yohaanan (meaning: Jehova has been Gracious).

2. "For child-bearing".   3. Mary.   4. A Sign.

5. The original word is Umma which has several meanings: "Community, the people of the same beliefs, race, nation, religion, and a way of life.

Of yours, was e'er a single one,[1]
And I have been your only Lord,
Thus worship Me alone.

93.   And people rent asunder this concern,[2]
Among them; yet to Us they all return.

94.   And so whoever will do righteous deeds
As a believer,
His effort shall not be disowned, for We,
Write them down in his favour.

95.   There is a ban on any nation,[3]
That We destroy to rise again,

96.   Until Gog and Magog[4] go on the rampage,
And will swarm down from every point of vantage;

97.   Then the true promise shall draw nigh; and lo!
The disbelievers' eyes will stare in awe:
"O woe to us, of this we have been heedless,
But nay, we've been transgressors most impious."

98.   Your own persons[5] and what you have been humble,
Unto, instead of God, shall be the fuel,

---

1. A single umma.

2. "The unity and amity among them."

3. Or: "people", "habitation", "population", "town" and "land".

4. The appearance of such wild and lawless tribes who will break their barriers
and swarm through the earth, is one of the prognostications of the approaching Judgment.

5. "You, disbelievers".

For the Gehenna: which you surely enter.

99.   Had these been gods, they would not come to it,
But now they shall abide therein for ever;

100.   Sobbing and groaning is their lot in there,
And they'll be hearing nothing farther!

101.   But they for whom has favour
From Us, gone forth before,
Shall be from it kept far.

102.   They shall not hear the faintest,
Sound of its[1] ire,
And they'll delight for ever,
In what their souls desire;

103.   The Greatest Terror[2] shall not grieve them;
Instead, the angels are to greet them:
"This is your day, the very day,
Which you were promised."

104.   We shall roll up the heavens on that Day,
As written scrolls are rolled; as We began,
The first Creation, so will We again,
Reproduce it; this have We promised
And We'll bring it about.

105.   Before this, in the Psalms,[3] We wrote

---

1. Hell's

2. The mighty terror of the Day of Judgment.

3. Psalms xxv. 13, and xxxii. 29.

As in the previous writ:[1]
"My righteous servants shall,
The earth inherit."

106. In this indeed there is a message,
      For those who pay Us faithful homage.

107. And We have sent you only,
      Unto all peoples, as a Mercy.

108. Say: "It has been revealed to me,
      Surely your God is one God only,
      Will you therefore bow to His Will?"[2]

109. And if they heed not and turn back,
      Say: "I have warned you all alike,
      And I do not know whether that event,
      You're threatened with, is nigh or distant,

110. "It's only He Who has the ken,
      To tell the truth of what is spoken,
      And He knows of your hearts the hidden;

111. "Nor do I know if it[3] may be a trial
      For you, and so you will be given,
      Provisions for a while."

---

1. Pentateuch: Exod. xxxii. 13.

2. That is "become Muslims" or "be muslims" in the proper sense of the word: Submitters to the Will of the Almighty God.

3. "This delay" or "respite".

112.　Say: "O My Lord, judge with your truth; indeed
　　　Our Lord is Al-Rahmaan,[1] to Whom our pleas,
　　　For succour are directed,
　　　Against your blasphemies."

---

1. The Beneficent, God of Mercy.

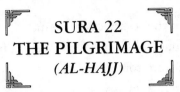

SURA 22
THE PILGRIMAGE
(AL-HAJJ)

In the Name of God, the Beneficent, the Merciful

1.   O People, be god-fearing;
Surely the shaking[1] of the Hour,[2]
Shall be a most tremendous thing;

2.   Upon that Day you shall behold,
Suckling mothers abandon,
Their suckling babes, and pregnant women,
Cast down their burden;
And you shall see men rocking like the drunk,
Although they are not drunken;
Such is the awesome panic,
At God's forbidding scourge.

3.   And yet there are some people who engage,
In arguments concerning Allah,
Despite their lack of knowledge,
And follow every mutinous fellow,
Inspired by Satan,[3]

4.   On whom it is decreed:
Whoever him befriends,
Certainly he shall then mislead,
And guide him to the torment of the Flames.

---

1. Or "quaking," "earthquake" and "convulsion".

2. The Last Hour, the Judgment.

3. Or "every rebellious satan".

5.   O People, if the resurrection[1] seem,
        To you a doubtful thing? Well, We did first
        Create you from some dust,
        Later on, from some sperm,
        Then from a leech-like clot,
        Then from an embryonic germ,
        Partly shapen, partly yet not;
        Let things be to you manifest:
        And, in the wombs, then We let rest,
        What We ordain, till a set term,
        And bring you forth as babes after a time,
        And let you grow and reach your prime;
        Then, some of you shall be deceased,
        And some live on unto an abject age,
        When, nothing gleams of your own former knowledge!
        You also see the earth: dried up and barren,
        But then We send upon it rain,
        And it begins to stir, and does get swollen
        And generates all kinds of radiant herbage.

6.   It's thus, for God's the Truth,
        He it is Who revives the dead,
        And He possesses power,
        Over all things indeed.

7.   The Hour of Doom is sure to come,
        There is no doubt of it, and God,
        Will raise the folks of every tomb.

8.   And yet there are some people who engage,
        In arguments concerning God, who lack,

---

1. Or "life after death".

All knowledge, and they have received
No guidance, nor a lustrous[1] Book;

9. They haughtily turn back to lead astray,
Others from Allah's way;
Disgrace is for them in this world,
And on the Day of Doom,[2] we'll make them taste,
The retribution hottest:

10. "This is due to your handiwork of old!
Because Allah is not unjust
To His Own creatures in the least."

11. And there's the type of man who worships,
God, as it were, upon condition:
If good befalls him, he is reassured,
But when he's tried by an affliction,
He thoroughly turns back: a forfeiter,
Is he of both this world, and the Hereafter,
That is the manifest perdition!

12. Instead of God, he calls on what may neither
Harm him, nor profit him; this is the farther,
And greater deviation.

13. He calls upon him who would sooner,
Harm him than help: the lord is evil,
And evil is the vassal!

14. But surely Allah will admit,

---

1. Or "enlightening", "illuminating", "lucid".

2. Day of Resurrection.

Into Gardens with running streams,
Those who believe and do good works,
For God does what His pleasure deems.

15. Whoever thinks that God will not assist
Him ever in this world or in the next,
Let him ascend unto the heavens,
By some device, then let him be at rest,
And let him see if his maneuver,
Could really take away the very
Thing that has made him angry![1]

16. And thus do We reveal it[2] in the form
Of clearest verses; and to whom
God pleases, He shall give direction.

17. Surely upon the Day of Resurrection,
Allah will judge between the Muslims,[3]
The Jews, the Sabi'ites,[4] the Christians,
The Magians,[5] and those who joined some idols
With God; for God's the Witness of all things.

18. Do you not see how unto God,
Bow down, all in the heavens,
And all on earth, along with,
The sun and moon, the stars and mountains,

---

1. I spent days studying almost everything interpreters have written to explain
this verse, and having found all of them unsatisfactory, I stuck to a literal
translation.

2. The Holy Quran.   3. Original "Those who have believed".

4. Most probably: The followers of prophet John; also "Sabians".

5. The Zoroastrians.

The trees and beasts and countless men,
Of whom many deserve the retribution?
And he whom God abases, none may raise
To honour; surely Allah does,
Whate'er He please.

19. The two antagonists[1] always dispute
    About their Lord with one another;
    As to the disbelievers: cut and tailored
    Shall be for them garments of Fire,
    And on their heads shall be poured down,
    Some Hellish shower;

20. Their skins shall roast, and all that is,
    Inside their bellies shall be melted,

21. Meanwhile they will be belted
    By whips of iron;

22. Whenever they, from grief, would fain
    Escape from it, they shall be turned
    Back into it: "you do not leave
    The chastisement of being burned!"

23. But God will bring in those who did believe,
    And did things that were righteous, into Gardens,
    Watered by running streams,
    Adorned they'll be therein with bracelets golden,
    With pearls, and with their raiments silken;

24. To them the purest words are spoken,

---

1. The believers and the disbelievers.

In guidance, to be further guided on,
The road of the Most Praised One.

25. We shall afflict a painful punishment,
On those who disbelieve and do prevent
Men from God's Path, and from the Sacred Mosque,
Which We appointed to all men alike-
For any visitor or resident-
And those who wrongfully incline,
It to profane.

26. Behold! To Abraham We showed the site
Of the House, and announced: "Do not unite
A thing with Me in worship, and do cleanse
My House for those who compass round it,
Or stand in prayer, or go upon their knees;

27. "Proclaim the Pilgrimage among all men:
Let people come to you upon their feet
Or on the camels thin and fleet,
From every distant path of plain or mountain,

28. "That they may witness benefits
For them provided, and make mention
Of Allah's name, on stated days,
Over the cattle He has given,
Unto them that they eat thereof, and feed,
The indigent, the ones badly in need;

29. "Then let them bring their cleansing[1] to a close,

---

1. That is, by removing the superfluous growth on one's body such as nails, hair,
beards, etc.

Fulfill their vows, and circumambulate
The Ancient House."

30.   That shall be so; and thus whoever
Reveres the sacred rites of Allah,
Best shall he fare in his Lord's sight;
Lawful are made for you the cattle,
Except what We to you recite,[1]
Thus shun the filth of every idol,
And shun all statements false, unreal;

31.   Be dedicated wholly unto Allah,
And worship none besides Him, for whoever
Associates to God a partner,
Is like a man who falls from heaven,
Who is then snatched by birds of prey,
Or girdled by the wind and blown away,
To some abyssal region.

32.   That is a fact; and they who hold in honour,
The rites of God: this surely sprouts
From the piety of their hearts;

33.   There have been benefits for you in them,[2]
Till the appointed time:[3]
But then their place of sacrifice,
Shall be about the Ancient House.[4]

---

1. Or "already recited to you."

2. The livestock dedicated for sacrifice.

3. "For sacrifice."

4. Meaning: Mecca.

34.   We have decreed for every umma,[1]
      Some rituals, so that they mention,
      The name of God over the cattle,
      He's given to them as provision;
      Because your God is only God the One;
      Thus do submit to Him alone,
      And give good news unto the humble,

35.   Whose Hearts, when God is mentioned, tremble
      With awe, to those who keep their resignation,
      When they encounter an affliction,
      Who do keep up their prayers, and from the bounty,
      We have supplied them, give in charity.

36.   The sacrificial camels have We made,
      For you a part of Allah's rites; much good,
      You have in them, therefore make mention of
      The name of God over them, as they would
      Stand in a row; and later when
      They've fallen over on their side, you could
      Eat of them all, and feed the needy,
      Both the silent and those who would
      Be asking with humility;
      Thus did We bring them under your subjection,
      Perhaps you'll show appreciation.

37.   By no means may their flesh or blood,
      Be reaching God!
      Nay, it's your piety that could,
      Go up to Him; thus have We made them
      Subject to you, perhaps you would,

---

1. Community, people, nation.

Glorify God for guiding you aright;
And give good news to people who do good;

38. Certainly God defends the faithful,
Surely God has no love at all,
For the unfaithful, the ungrateful.

39. Permission to fight back,
Is now given to people
Who've come under unjust attack,
And have been wrongfully oppressed,
Verily God is Powerful enough
Them to assist,

40. People expelled unjustly from their homes,
Only because they utter: "God the One's
Our only Lord".
If God had not repelled some men by means
Of others, they would surely have destroyed,
All cloisters,[1] churches, synagogues and mosques,
Wherein the name of Allah is most often,
Upon the lips of men;
And surely Allah helps the people,
Who help His cause, and God's indeed
The Mighty, the All-Able;

41. The people who, if We establish them,
Throughout the land, will keep up prayer,
And pay *zakaat,* and advocate whatever
Is righteous and forbid what's evil;
And unto God all issues shall be final.

---

1. Or "monasteries".

42.　　　And now if they reject you? Well, so did,
　　　　Before them, Noah's people, and the people
　　　　Of the Aad and Thamood,

43.　　　Abraham's folks and Lot's,

44.　　　As also did the Midianites;
　　　　Moses had also been denied,
　　　　But unto those who disbelieved,
　　　　We gave a respite, and We seized
　　　　Them in the end, and terrible
　　　　Had been My disapproval!

45.　　　How many are the wicked towns,
　　　　We have destroyed, whose roofs are now
　　　　Laid low in ruins,
　　　　How many desolate, deserted wells,
　　　　And well-built, lofty castles?!

46.　　　Have they not ever journeyed through the land,
　　　　And used their minds[1] to think and understand,
　　　　Or learned something by hearing with their ears?
　　　　Nay! It is not the eyes that have gone blind,
　　　　But it's the blindness in the hearts
　　　　Inside their breasts!

47.　　　And they ask you to hasten on the scourge,
　　　　But surely God fails not in threats He's spoken;
　　　　And a Day with your Lord is like,
　　　　A thousand years of what you reckon!

---

1. Original "hearts".

48.   And many were the habitations,
       To whom, in spite of their transgressions,
       I gave a respite, then I seized them;
       And unto Me are all the destinations.

49.   Say: "O You men, I am to you,
       Only a Warner open,

50.   "Those who believe and do what's right,
       Will win Our pardon,
       Together with a rich provision;

51.   "But those who strive to counter,
       Our revelations,
       Shall be companions,
       To the most flaming Fire!

52.   There was no messenger or prophet,
       Sent by Us in the past, with whose
       Intention, Satan did not try
       To interfere, but Allah nullifies,
       All Satan's interjections, then
       God does affirm His revelations,
       For God is the All-Knowing, the Most-Wise;

53.   Thus does He make what Satan has
       Suggested just a test for those,
       Who in their hearts have a disease,
       And those whose hearts have hardened;
       The wicked have certainly fallen,
       Into perversion of no end;

54.   But those who have been given,

Knowledge do know that it's[1] the Truth
Sent by your Lord, and so they may
Believe in it, and then their humble faith
May acquiesce their hearts; and surely
God guides the faithful to the direct Path.

55.   But those who disbelieve will never,
Cease to be doubting it, until the Hour,
Suddenly comes upon them or until,
The torment of the Day of Gloom,
Will o'er them loom.

56.   Upon that Day shall Allah reign supreme,
And He Himself will judge between them:
Thus those who did believe and did what's right,
Enter the Gardens of Delight,

57.   And those who disbelieved and treated
Our revelations as some lies,
Will certainly be granted,
A chastisement that humbles!

58.   And those who fled their homes in Allah's cause,
And afterwards were slain or died,
For them will surely God provide,
The best of sustenance, for Allah
Is the Supreme Provider ever;

59.   Surely He will be bringing
Them in, with an arrival,
That is, to please them well;

---

1. The Holy Quran.

God is All-Knowing, Most-Forbearing;

60.   That was their case. And anyone
       Who makes exact reprisal
       For injury afflicted on him,
       And is oppressed for this as well,
       He will be helped by God, for God's
       The One Who Pardons and Forgives.

61.   That is because it's God who merges
       Nights into Days and also changes
       Days into Nights, and that He is
       The One Who Hears and Sees;

62.   That is because God is the Truth, and what
       They call upon, but Him, is vanity,
       Certainly only God is the Most High,
       And the Almighty.

63.   Do you not see that God sends down
       Water from clouds, and on the morrow,
       The earth wakes up all clad in green;
       Gracious is God, the Knower Thorough.

64.   Whatever is there in the heavens,
       And everything on earth, are His, and He's
       The Needless One, Worthy of Praise.

65.   Do you not see that God has put
       Under you everything that's found
       Upon the earth, and ships that sail
       Across the seas by His Command?
       And He withholds the heaven, lest it fall

Upon the earth, unless it be His will;
Verily God is very Kind,
And Merciful, unto mankind.

66. And He it is Who gives you life,
And then will let you die, and later,
Shall bring you back to life; man is
Indeed a thankless, truth-denying creature!

67. We have ordained for every nation,
A way of worship and devotion,
That they observe; thus let them not
Dispute with you about this question;
But bid unto your Lord, for surely,
You are upon the right Direction.

68. And if with you they argue,
Say: "God knows better what you do;

69. "And God shall judge between you,
Upon the Day of Resurrection,
Concerning what you differ in."

70. Do you not know that Allah knows,
All that the Sky and Earth possess?
All is recorded in a book, and this,
For God, is something effortless.

71. And yet, along with God, they worship idols
For which He sent no sanction whatsoever,
And that of which they have no knowledge; surely
Such wrong-doers shall have no helper.

72. And when Our revelations plain,
    Are unto them rehearsed, you notice,
    In disbeliever's faces, much disdain;
    From springing on the people who rehearse
    Our verses, scarce could they refrain!
    Say: "Shall I tell you something worse than this?
    The Fire of Hell! That is indeed God's promise;
    That is the destination worse.

73. O People, here's an aphorism,
    So listen to it carefully:
    Those idols you invoke, instead of God,
    Could not create even a fly,
    Though they should all assemble for this ploy,
    And if the fly should snatch away
    A tiny thing from them, they'd have no power,
    To take back from it aught!
    How weak indeed are both:
    The seeker and the sought!

74. Of God's true worth and glory,
    They have no estimation; surely
    God is All-Powerful, All-Mighty.

75. Of men and of the angels,
    Does Allah choose apostles,
    Indeed God Hears and Sees.

76. He knows what is before them,
    And what has been before them,
    And all affairs return to God.

77. O you believers!

Bow down, prostrate yourselves and worship
Your Lord, and do every good deed,
In order to succeed.

78.   And strive in Allah's cause: a striving
Worthy of your devotion;
He's chosen you and laid no burden
Upon you in religion:
It is the Faith of Abraham,
Your own forefather, and he's given
To you the name of Muslim,
Before this[1] and in this one,[2]
That the Apostle[3] be a witness,
To you, and you a witness to all men;
Therefore keep up *salaat*[4] and pay *zakaat*,[5]
And do hold fast to God the One,
It's He Who is your Patron,
Oh, what a Gracious Patron,
Excellent Helper next to none!

---

1. In former scriptures.
2. In the Holy Quran.
3. The Last Prophet, Mohammad (pbuh).
4. Regular prayers.
5. The legal alms, poor-rate, obligatory charity.

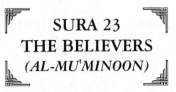

SURA 23
THE BELIEVERS
(AL-MU'MINOON)

In the Name of God, the Beneficent, the Merciful

1.   Final salvation is indeed,
       For true believers,

2.   Who, with humility,
       Perform their prayers,

3.   And who, regarding idle words,
       Are strict refrainers,

4.   And who in paying their *zakaat*,[1]
       Are active givers,

5.   And who of their own modesty,[2]
       Are scrupled guarders;

6.   -Save with their spouses or the ones,
       Whom they possess in proper bond,
       For with them they commit no sins,

7.   But if they were to go beyond
       Limits as these, seeking their lusts,
       They'll be transgressors-

8.   And who are faithful to their trusts,
       And who are truthful covenanters,

---

1. Obligatory alms, poor-rate.

2. Carnal desires, sexual passions, private parts.

9.   And who do strictly keep unto their prayers;

10.   Those are indeed the heritors,

11.   Inheriting the Paradise,
As permanent abiders.

12.   Surely it was some mud quintessence,
That We created people from;

13.   Later We made each one a sperm,
To place in an enclosure firm,

14.   And then We changed that drop of sperm
Into a leech-like clot, and turned the clot
Into an embryonic germ,
And bones did We create out of this germ,
And let the bones with flesh be dressed,
And thus a new creation We produced;
Blessed be thus God, the very
Creator of the Best!

15.   But after this you'll surely pass away,

16.   And then be raised again upon the Day
Of Resurrection.

17.   Certainly We created heavens seven,
Above your heads, and We will never,
Neglect Our own Creation.

18.   And water from the Heaven,
Do We send down unto a measure,

And then We cause it in the soil to settle,
And certainly We have the power
For its withdrawal;

19.   And by it We have let be grown
Gardens of palms and groves of vines,
Which give you plenteous fruits,
Whereof man dines;

20.   Also a tree that springs,
Upon Mount Sinai, and brings
Forth oil as well as relish
For people who so wish.

21.   And even in the beasts you have
A telling lesson, for We give
You drinks of what's within their bellies,
And from them you also derive,
Numerous benefits, and of their meat,
For food you eat;

22.   And on them and upon
Ships are you borne.

23.   Noah We sent unto his people,
And he said: "O My folk, be serving
Allah, you have no God but Him,
Will you not be god-fearing?"

24.   But then the unbelieving chiefs amongst
His people cried: "He's nothing but a mortal
Like all of you, he fain would raise himself,
Above you, for if it had been God's will,

Surely He would have sent an angel;
Nay, never did We hear before,
Of this from our own sires of yore!

25.   "He is a man possessed, insane,
Thus, for a time, leave him alone!"

26.   He prayed: "My Lord, do give me succour,
Against their calling me a liar."

27.   So We revealed unto him: "Make the Ark,
Under Our watchful eye, to correspond
With Our instruction, and when Our command
Comes, and the earthly fountains shall outbreak,
Do take on board two pairs of every kind,
Together with your folk,
Save those of them 'gainst whom the word,
Has been already spoke;
And do not plead with Me about the rest:
The wicked people who transgressed,
For they shall certainly be drowned!

28.   "And once you have embarked,
You and those with you, on the Ark,
Say: "Praise be unto God,
Who saved us from the wicked folk",

29.   And say: "My Lord, help me to disembark,
With every blessing, for You are indeed
The Best to let us disembark."

30.   In this were certainly many a Sign,
And surely tests do We to man assign.

31. And after them We raised up,
    Some other generations;

32. To each of them We sent
    Apostles of their own,
    Saying: "Do worship God alone,
    You have no other God but Him,
    Will you from evil not refrain?"

33. But then the unbelieving chiefs amongst
    Their people, who denied the Meeting
    Of the Hereafter, whom We had supplied
    With plenty in this present living,
    Said every time: "He is a man just like
    Yourselves, he eats of what you eat,
    And drinks of what you drink,

34. "If you obey a mortal like yourselves,
    You will indeed be losers!

35. "Oh, does he threaten you that once you're dead,
    And turned to dust and bones,
    You shall emerge from tombs?!

36. "Away with what you're threatened with, away!

37. "There is no life beyond this worldly one,
    We only live and die,
    Never to rise again!

38. "He is only a man who forges lies
    Concerning God, and we are not believers
    In what he does allege."

39. He[1] prayed: "My Lord, help me against this charge,
    Of being called a forger."

40. "Yet in a little while", He said,
    "They'll be awakened to lament!"

41. The Blast[2] surprised them then in justice,
    And We made them as rubbish
    Floating upon a torrent;
    Thus did the wicked perish!

42. Then other generations,
    We raised up after them;

43. Neither too early, nor too late, may nations
    Reach their appointed time.

44. Then We sent Our apostles in succession;
    Oft as a messenger came to a nation,
    They did reject him as a liar,
    And so We made them follow one another,
    And We made them the subjects of some tales;
    Away then with the peoples
    Who had no faith embraced!

45. And We sent Moses later on,
    Together with his brother Aaron,
    With Signs from Us and mandate manifest,

46. To Pharaoh and his nobles; but they waxed,

---

1. The prophet concerned.

2. Or the Shout "of the destroying angel".

most proud, for they were haughty men.

47.   "What!" they derided, "Are we to believe in,
Two mortals like ourselves,
Whose tribe have been our slaves?!"

48.   So they rejected both of them,
And thus incurred destruction.

49.   Later We gave the Book to Moses,
To lead them to the right direction;

50.   The Son of Mary and his mother,
We made a Sign, and gave them shelter,
Upon some lofty terrain quiet,
Watered by many a streamlet.[1]

51.   O You apostles,
Enjoy everything good and pure,
And do what's right and proper,
For surely I am All-Aware,
Of all your doings.

52.   And this your umma,[2] is
A single umma certainly,
And I, I am your Lord, and thus,
Only fear Me.[3]

---

1. Mary retired to such a place in seclusion, and she and her child rested there until it was time for her to go to her people with the baby Jesus.

2. Community, religion, nation, congregation, brotherhood.

3. All prophets form one Brotherhood, their messages and teachings are one, and they serve the One True God, and their duty is to Him alone.

53. But men then rent this great concern,
    Into many a wrangling faction,
    With every party overjoyed with
    Its own peculiar fraction!

54. Therefore leave them alone,
    In the deep error of their own,
    Until a certain time!

55. Ah, do they really think that since,
    We gave them children and abundance,

56. We help them hasten unto every blessing?
    Nay, they do not have any understanding!

57. Only the people who are awed,
    With the fear of their Lord,

58. And who are true believers,
    In the Signs[1] of their Lord,

59. And those who join no partners in
    The worship of their Lord,

60. And those who give what they do give in alms,
    With hearts filled with the dread,
    That they'll go back unto their Lord,

61. Those are indeed the people who themselves,
    Hasten after the charitable best,
    And in them try to be foremost.

---

1. Or: revelations.

62.   Never will We burden a single soul,
        Beyond what it could bear,
        And with Us is a book,[1] that tells the whole
        Of every fact; and so they will,
        Never receive a deal unfair.

63.   And yet their hearts are plunged in error
        Concerning this,[2] and they do many other,
        Wrong things, apart from this, as ever.

64.   Until when We shall seize the affluent,
        Among them with the Chastisement;
        Lo! They will cry for succour!

65.   "Do not in supplication cry this Day,
        Any succour from Us? No way!

66.   "My revelations used to be recited
        Unto you, but you always did,
        Turn back upon your heels, and went away,

67.   "Puffed up with pride, and yet about it,[3]
        Discoursing gibberish by night!"

68.   What is it? Do they never ponder
        Over the word?[4] Or do they wonder,
        Why something is unto to them given which,
        Did not their ancient fathers reach?

---

1. The record that shows exactly what each soul has done and thought.

2. The rejection of Faith and denial of future Life and Judgment.

3. The Holy Quran.

4. The Word of God, or any spoken message.

69. Or, don't they recognize their own
    Messenger, and they therefore,
    Must him disown.

70. Or do they claim: "In him there is a Jinn!"[1]
    Nay, nay! The truth is that he has
    Come with the Truth,
    But the majority of them,
    Do loathe the Truth!

71. But if the Truth had followed in the train
    Of their desires, the heavens and the earth
    And all that is therein, would, of a truth,
    Have been in ruin!
    Nay, We have brought to them
    Their own Reminder,
    And they pay no attention
    To their Reminder.

72. Perhaps you ask them for some wages?!
    But nay, far better is the recompense
    Of your own Lord, for He is the Provider
    Par excellence!

73. Indeed you've been inviting them,
    Unto a right Direction,

74. But those who lack conviction,
    About the life to come, will ever,
    From that direction wander.

---

1. That is: he is "Possessed" or "mad".

75. And if We on them take compassion,
    And do relieve them from their present trouble,[1]
    They would persist in their rebellion,
    Wandering blindly into evil.

76. We have already seized them with
    Some torment, but before their Lord,
    They have not been submissive,
    Nor have they Him implored;

77. Until We open onto them a gate,
    Leading into a dreadful chastisement;
    Lo! They shall be therein most desperate!

78. But He's the One Who did for you create,
    Hearing and seeing, feeling and discerning;[2]
    How often do you these appreciate!

79. And He's the One Who settled,
    You on the earth, and unto Him,
    You'll be assembled;

80. And He's the One who life and death ordains,
    And brings about the alternations,
    Of nights and days; why don't you use your brains!

81. Nay, nay! They only parrot,
    What their forefathers said;

82. They say: "what! After we are dead,

---

1. According to most commentators, the reference is to a severe famine in Mecca. 2. Original: "hearts".

And turned to dust and bones,
Shall we be resurrected?!

83. "We have been promised this before,
We and our fathers; yet it's nothing
But fables of the folks of yore!"

84. Ask them: "Whose is the earth, and every being,
That is therein, if you have known?"

85. They will say: "God's" Say: "Why
Do you not ponder then?"

86. And say: "Who's the Lord of the heavens seven,
And the Lord of the Glorious Throne?"[1]

87. They will say: "God!" Say: "Why
Aren't you god-fearing men?

88. Ask them: "Who is it in Whose Power,[2]
Is the Sovereignty of all things,
Who gives protection to all beings,
And none against Him could be ever
Protected? Say, if you do know."

89. And they will say: "All's in God's Hand."
Say: "why are you then so spell-bound?!"

90. The truth We have unto them brought,
But they are truth-deniers:

---

1. Or "The Mighty Dominion".
2. Original: "Hand".

91.   Never has God a son begotten,
        Neither is there with Him another god,
        Else every god would take away whatever
        He had created,[1] and, of them, some would
        Have tried to lord it over one another!
        Glory be unto God the One,
        Above their attributions;

92.   The Knower of the Hidden and the Open,
        Is He: too High for their associations.[2]

93.   Pray: "O My Lord, if you will let me witness
        That which they have been warned against![3]

94.   "My Lord, pray place me not amongst,
        People who were unjust!"

95.   Surely Able are We to make you witness,
        That which they have been warned against.

96.   You just repel their evil with
        That which is best,
        We are Better-Informed of
        What they suggest.[4]

97.   And pray: "My Lord, in You I seek,
        Refuge from promptings of the satans,

---

1. That is: would establish a different kingdom.

2. To suppose that God has a son or family or partners and companions, is to
   have a low idea of God, who is high above such relationships.

3. The Punishment and its infliction.

4. "Against you, the Prophet".

98. "And, O My Lord, in You I seek,
    Refuge that none[1] my presence gains.

99. When one of them[2] is overtaken
    By death, he supplicates: "My Lord,
    Pray send me back again,

100. That I may then do righteous good,
     In the things I ignored!"
     "Nay, by no means!" Indeed, he is ad-libbing
     An empty word!
     Behind them now is a partition,[3]
     Until the Resurrection.

101. And when the Horn is blown:
     No ties there shall be to their kith and kin,
     Upon that Day, nor any conversation.

102. Then those whose scales[4] are heavy shall attain,
     Bliss and salvation,

103. And those whose scales are light, will surely gain
     Loss and perdition!
     Gehenna's their eternal Station!

104. The Flames shall fleece their faces, and therein
     They'll only scream and writhe with pain:

---

1. "Of the satans".
2. "Of the wicked".
3. Barrier or a bar "between their souls and the worldly life."
4. Balances of good or evil deeds.

105. "Were not my revelations
Unto you read,
Which you always rejected?"

106. They will say: "O Our Lord, bad luck
Betrayed us, and we thus became
An erring folk,

107. "Now, O Our Lord, bring us forth hence,
And if we e'er unto a sin go back,
We shall indeed be wicked thence!"

108. He'll answer: "stay therein with ignominy,
And stop addressing Me!

109. "Surely among My servants was a party,
Who prayed: 'Our Lord, we do believe,
So do forgive us, and relieve
Us with Your Mercy; Certainly
You are the Merciful Supreme;

110. "But them you did disdain,
With every sort of mockery,
So much so that you did forget
All messages from Me,
And did laugh them to scorn;

111. "This Day certainly will I recompense
Them for their patience and endurance,
These are they who have won the day!"

112. And He will ask: "How many years
Have you on earth resided?"

113. They will reply: "We must have tarried
A day, or of a day a portion,
But question those who kept the computation!"

114. He'll say: "short was the time you tarried,
If you had known indeed!

115. "Did you then really think that We
Created you in vain,
And that you should be never brought
Back unto Us again?"

116. Therefore exalted be
Allah, the rightful Sovereign,
There is no God but He,
Lord of the Noble Throne;

117. Therefore, if one invokes, together
With God, another deity,
And has no proof of its divinity,
He'll have to give account unto His Lord,
And those who disbelieve shall never,
Attain prosperity.

118. Now pray: "My Lord, do pardon, and let fall
Rains of Your Mercy, for you are:
Most Merciful of all!

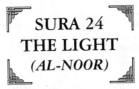

SURA 24
THE LIGHT
(AL-NOOR)

In the Name of God, the Beneficent, the Merciful

1.   This is a *sura*[1] which we have sent down,
And sanctioned, and therein some revelations,
Have We sent down most plain, so that you may
Receive an admonition:

2.   Every woman and every man,
Guilty of fornication,
Shall be a hundred lashes given;
When you believe in God and the Last Day,
Let not compassion for them sway,
You from fulfilling God's religion,
Do let a party of the faithful,
Witness their retribution.

3.   The fornicator shall not marry but,
A fornicatress or idolatress,
As for a fornicating slut,
None shall she marry but,
A fornicator or idolater;
Such unions are forbidden,
To true believers.

4.   They who defame virtuous women,
And fail to bring four witnesses,
Fourscore of stripes they shall be given,
And ne'er their evidence again,

---

1. Chapter of the Quran.

Will be accepted, for such men
Are surely evil-doers;

5.   Save those who do repent thereafter,
And mend their ways, for God's
The Most Forgiving Mercy-Granter.

6.   And those accusing their own wives,[1]
Who have no witness but themselves,
Let them each swear by God four times,
That he is of the truthful ones;

7.   And by the fifth that Allah's curse,
Shall be on him, if he is false.

8.   But *she* averts the punishment from her,
If she, also four times, by God shall swear,
That he it is who is a liar,

9.   And then by the fifth oath,
She shall invoke on her God's wrath,
If *he* did speak the truth.

10.   Woe, if god's Grace and Mercy
Were not on you! But surely God's
Redeeming, Wise.

11.   Those who advanced the slanderous lie,[2]

---

1. Or "spouses."

2. This is an allusion to the slander against the Holy Prophet's wife 'Aisha, who
was left behind, upon a return journey to Medina, and was brought back, the
following day, by a Muslim who found her.

Were but a group amongst yourselves;
Yet you should not regard the matter,
As evil for you, for it serves,
A goodly purpose: every person,
Who did take part in this, shall suffer,
His portion of the sin, and for the One,
Among them who in this affair,
Did have the greatest share,
Will be a torment sore.

12. Why did the faithful men and women,
Upon hearing of the event,
Not have in them the good opinion,
To say: "This is a falsehood evident?"

13. Have they produced four witnesses,
To prove it? As they have not brought
Witnesses, surely liars shall they be
In Allah's sight!

14. So, but for Allah's Grace towards you,
And His Compassion, in this world,
And in the next, a painful scourge,
Would certainly have come upon you,
For that in which you were involved,

15. When you did with your tongues allege,
And uttered with your mouths a tale
Of which you had no knowledge!
You took it as a trifling matter, while
In God's sight, it had been most vile!

16. And when you heard it, did you ever cry:

"It is not right of us to speak of this,
Oh, God forbid! This is indeed too gross
A calumny?!"

17.   God warns you not to lend your ears,[1]
Ever unto the like of this again,
If you be true believers.

18.   And God has made His revelations plain,
To you, for God's All-Knowing, Wise.

19.   Those who delight in spreading scandal,
Among the faithful, shall be vexed,
By a most painful chastisement,
Both in this world and in the next:
God knows and you know not.

20.   Woe if God's Grace and Mercy
Were not upon you! Surely God is kind,
And Full of Mercy.

21.   O You Believers! Be not followers,
Of Satan's footsteps, for whoever
follows the steps of Satan, will
Be commanded by him, to enter
Upon all things indecent, foul and base;
And were it not for Allah's Grace,
And Mercy on you, not a single
One of you would be cleansed for ever,
For it is God alone who purifies
Whome'er He pleases, and it's Allah,

---

1. Or "not to go back to..."

Who hears, Who knows.

22. And let not graceful men of better means,,
    Among you, swear that they would by no means,
    Give to their kindred, to the poor, and those
    Who left their homes in Allah's cause,
    Nay, they should rather pardon and forbear;
    Do you not wish it heartily,
    To be pardoned by Allah?
    Allah Who is Forgiving, Full of Mercy?

23. Cursed shall be those who charge with slander,
    Imprudent women yet believing, chaste,
    Both in this world and in the next;
    Great is the Torment they'll go under:

24. Upon the Day when their own tongues,
    Their hands and feet witness against
    Them of their wrongs.

25. Upon that Day will God repay,
    Their recompenses just,
    And they shall come to know that God:
    He's the Truth manifest!

26. Women impure,[1] shall be for men impure,
    And men impure, for the women impure,
    The women pure for men of purity,
    And men of purity for women pure,
    Innocent are indeed the latter,
    From what accusers utter,

---

1. Or: "indecent", "immoral", "unclean".

For them there shall be Pardon,
And a noble provision.

27.   O You believers, enter not the dwellings,
Of other men, until you have the kind
Permission of the inmates ascertained,
And have extended to them greetings;
This is for you the best of doings,
Perhaps you will bear it in mind!

28.   And if you find no one therein,
Do not go in until you're given
Such a permission,
And if you're told to go away,
Then, go away;
This is a purer manner for you,
And God's Aware of what you do.

29.   There is no sin upon you, if you enter
Houses that are not dwelling places,
Which serve for you some other useful matter;
God knows whatever you disclose, and He's
Aware of what you shelter.

30.   Say to believing men that they
Ought to restrain their gaze,
And to observe their modesty:
More righteous then shall be their lives;
Certainly God is Most Aware of
All their affairs.

31.   Say to believing women, too, that they
Ought to restrain their gaze,

Safeguard their modesty, and ne'er display
Their ornaments-except what normally
Thereof appears;[1]
And that they ought to draw their veils
Over their breasts, and ne'er display
Their finery, except before:
Their husbands, their own fathers,
Their husband's fathers, their own sons,
Their step-sons, their own brothers,
Their womenfolk, and slaves in their possession,
Or male attendants free of sexual passion,
Or children who have not yet known
Carnal knowledge of women,
And that they should not strike their feet together,
Lest they reveal a portion,
Of their ornaments hidden;
And, all of you, believers, turn to Allah,
Perhaps you'll win salvation.

32.   And you shall take in marriage union,
The single men and women in your midst,
And the good-doing ones amongst,
Your bondsmen and bondswomen;
And if they are in poverty,
God surely will provide for them,
Out of His bounty,
For God is Ample-Giving, and All-Knowing.

33.   Let those who can't afford to marry live,
In continence, till God, out of His bounty,
Gives them provision;

---

1. Hands and faces.

If some of those in your possession,
Shall ask for deeds of liberty,
Grant them the deeds, when you are certain,
Of good in them, and give some property,
To them, of that which God has to you given;
And do not ever force your maidens,
To prostitution for some worldly gains,
As they desire to keep their chastity;
If anyone compels them, Allah then,
Witnessing their compulsion,
Will be to them[1] Forgiving,
Full of Compassion.

34.   And now we have to you sent down,
        Clear revelations, and examples,
        Concerning those before you gone,
        And to god-fearing peoples,
        An Admonition.

35.   God is the Light of Heavens and the earth,
        A likeness of His light is as a niche,
        Wherein there is a lamp-the lamp is placed,
        Inside a crystal, yet a crystal which,
        Is like a star, resplendent, shining forth-
        Lit from a blissful olive-tree that's nursed,
        On the most friendly, sun-bathed site[2]
        Whose oil shines out, although no fire
        Did it ignite: Light upon light!
        Unto His light does God direct whomever,
        He will, and parables, for human beings,

---

1. The maidens thus forced.

2. The literal meaning of the Arabic idiom is: "Neither Eastern, nor Western."

Are coined by God, for God does know all things.

36.   It's[1] found in temples God has sanctioned,
    To be exalted, that His name be mentioned,
    Therein, and that His praise be sung
    Morning and evening,

37.   By men who shall not be distracted,
    Either by trade or merchandise,
    From God's remembrance, from observance
    Of prayers, and payment of the stated alms,[2]
    Those who do dread the Day when hearts shall pound,
    And petrified shall be the eyes;

38.   So that Allah rewards them for,
    Their finest works and doings, and increases,
    It to them, from His bounty, more and more;
    For God provides for whom He pleases,
    In boundless measure.

39.   The deeds of disbelievers may indeed,
    Be likened to a mirage in a plain,
    The thirsty man takes it for water,
    Till when he reaches there, he finds it vain;
    And he shall find that only God is there!
    Who pays him his account amain,
    For Prompt is God in reckoning.

40.   Another likeness for them[3] is the darkness,
    In a deep sea when she is covered,

---

1. His Light.   2. Zakaat.

3. The disbelievers, with regard to their deeds.

By billows riding upon billows,
Above which is a heavy cloud,
Layers of darkness over darkness,
If one would stretch his hand, he scarcely could
See it! And he to whom Allah does not
Give light, will ne'er have any light.

41.   Have you not ever seen
How all, throughout the heavens,
Are praising God, as on this terrene[1] ;
So do the very birds in columns,
When on the wing? To each is known
The mode of prayer and praise its own,
And God is Cognizant of everything,
They may be doing.

42.   The Kingdom of the Heavens and the Earth
To God belongs,
And unto God is all, final returns.

43.   Have you not ever seen,
How Allah drives the clouds,
Then makes them join together,
Then piles them up in massive crowds,
When you shall notice rain,
From their midst pouring down?
And he sends down the heavy hails,
Out of the clouds, massive as hills,
That He makes fall on whom He please,
And whom He will, He spares;
The brightness of His lightning wellnigh,

---

1. Earth.

Darkens the eye!

44.   It's God who alternates the Day and Night;
        In this there is indeed a lesson,
        For men of insight.

45.   And God created every beast from water:
        Some of them creep upon their bellies,
        Some walk upon two legs, yet others,
        Walk upon four; what He may please,
        Does God create, for He has power
        Over all things.

46.   Certainly We have now sent down,
        Enlightening verses plain,
        And God will guide, whome'er He may,
        To the Right way;

47.   For there are those who parley:
        "We do believe in God and His Apostle,
        And we obey," yet, after this, a party
        Of them do turn away, such people
        Aren't truly faithful.

48.   When they are called to God and His Apostle,
        That he may judge between them, lo!
        Parties of them withdraw;

49.   But, if the right be on their side
        Submissively and quickly,
        Will they towards him stride.

50.   Is there a sickness in their hearts?

Are they harbouring doubts?
Or do they fear that God and His Apostle,
Might their affairs unfairly settle?!
Nay, nay! In fact these are themselves
Wrong-doing people.

51.   The sole response by true believers,
When they are called to God and His Apostle,
That he may judge between them, is:
"We've heard, and we obey"; these are the people,
Who'll be the final winners.

52.   Yea, only those shall be successful,
Who do obey Allah and His Apostle,
Who are god-fearing, and about their duties
To Him, most careful.

53.   They[1] swear their strongest oaths by God that if,
You give the word, they will come out in force;
Say: "Do not swear: obeying is the worthy thing,[2]
And God is Most-Aware, of course,
Of all you're doing."

54.   Say: "Be obedient unto God and do,
Obey the Messenger, but on him still,
Even if you turn away, shall be the burden,
Of his own duties, and you must fulfill,
The duties placed on you; surely you will,
Be rightly guided, if you show obedience,
To him; and nothing rests on the Apostle,

---

1. The Hypocrites and similar wavering people.

2. Or "of more worth", "more reasonable", "recognized" and "well-known".

But plain Conveyance.[1]

55. Allah has promised unto those amongst you,
Who do believe and do good deeds, that He
Will make them masters in the land, just as
He made others before them, and that He
Will certainly make firm the Faith,
He chose for them in truth,
And that He'll change their fears to safety;
Thus let them only worship Me,
And serve no one beside Me;
Wicked are they indeed,
Who, after this, deny Me.

56. Therefore keep up your daily prayers,
Pay the prescribed poor-rate,[2] and be
Obedient to the Messenger, perhaps
You will be granted Mercy.

57. Think not that disbelievers ever,
Escape the Wrath upon the earth,
Their sure abode shall be the Fire,
Evil it is to end in there!

58. O You believers!
Your bondservants and those among your children,
Who have not come of age, may ask permission
To come to you, on three occasions:
Before the morning prayer, and at mid-day,
When you have laid aside your clothing,

---

1. Clear delivering "of the message".
2. Zakaat.

And after prayings of the evening;[1]
These are for you three non-intrusions.[2]
At other times, it is not wrong, however,
That you or they attend to one another;
Thus God His revelations clarifies,
For God's All-knowing, Wise.

59. But when they come of age, do teach your children,
Like their elders to ask for your permission;
Thus God His revelations clarifies,
For God's All-Knowing, Wise.

60. There shall be no offense for elder women,
Expected not to ever marry, when
They lay aside their outer garments,
Without showing their ornaments;[3]
Yet it is better for them if they chose
To check themselves, for Allah Hears and Knows.

61. There is no blame upon the blind,
Nor any blame upon the lame,
Nor on the ailing person any blame,
To eat with you,[4] nor on yourselves,
To eat at your own houses,
Or at the houses of your mothers,
Or at the houses of your brothers,
Or at the houses of your sisters,

---

1. Al-'Ishaa.

2. Three times of privacy.

3. Or "not making a wanton display of their body."

4. Instructions that do away with certain tribal traditions and superstitions prevalent in Arabia and elsewhere.

Or at the homes of your paternal uncles,
Or at the homes of your paternal aunts,
Or at the homes of your maternal uncles,
Or at the homes of your maternal aunts,
Or at some place whose keys, are in your hands,
Entrusted, or the houses of close friends;
Nor shall it be a sin whether you eat,
Together or apart;[1]
However, when you enter houses, greet
Each other with a salutation godly,
Blessed and pure and goodly;[2]
And God His verses thus explains,
That you may use your brains.

62. Those only are sincere believers,
Who do believe in God and His Apostle,
And who, whene'er they are upon affairs,
With him, of value to the congregation,
Never leave him without permission,
Certainly they who ask your leave,
Are those who do believe,
In God and His Apostle;
Thus when they ask for your permission,
For some affair of theirs,
You may give leave to those you sanction,
While asking God's forgiveness for them then,
For God is Oft-Forgiving, Full of Pardon.

63. Do not address the Messenger,[3]

---

1. & 2. Instructions that do away with certain tribal traditions and superstitions prevalent in Arabia and elsewhere.

3. The Holy Prophet.

Among yourselves, in the same manner,
That you address each other;
And surely Allah knows a person who,
Withdraws to screen behind another!
Therefore let those who disobey his order,
Beware, lest an affliction imminent
Befalls them, or they'll have to suffer
A grevious chastisement.

64.   Behold, whatever is there in the Heavens,
And on the Earth, to God belongs,
All your conditions are unto Him known,
And on the Day they are to Him returned,
He'll tell them what their deeds have earned;
The Knower of all things is God alone.

SURA 25
THE CRITERION
(AL-FURQAAN)[1]

In the Name of God, the Beneficent, the Merciful

1.   Blessed be the One who has sent down the Furqaan
To His servant, so that he can,
Be a warner to humankind,

2.   The One to Whom belongs the Kingdom
Of Heavens and the Earth, who has begotten
Never a son, nor in His kingdom,
Has He a partner; and He is the One,
Who did create all things, and then ordained
Them all in due proportion;

3.   And still they set up gods beside Him,
Who have created naught, for they themselves,
Have been created, and possess no power
To do evil or good for their own selves,
Nor over Death or Life have they a thread
Of power, nor could they raise up the dead.

4.   The disbelievers say:
"This is indeed a fraud,
That he has in collaboration
With other men devised!"
In truth it's they who have put forward,
Injustice mixed with falsehood.

---

1. One of the names of the Holy Quran, as also of the Scriptures meaning: The criterion of right and wrong, distinction or discrimination, and salvation.

5.   "These are some ancient tales," they add,
"And he has got them written down, for being
Read out to him, morning and evening!"

6.   Say: "He has sent it down Who Knows
The Secret of the Skies and Earth, and is
Oft-Forgiving and Mercy-Giving.

7.   They also cry: "What an apostle is this?
Foodstuff he eats and walks the streets!
Why has no angel been sent down to him,
To help him with his warning threats?!

8.   "Why is he not a treasure given,[1]
Or made to own a garden,
For his provision?"
The wicked folks have also taunted:
"You follow but a man enchanted!"

9.   Just see what kinds of epithets
They unto you apply!
Surely they err, and cannot find a way.

10.   Blessed be the One Who, if He please,
Can give you better things than these:
Gardens watered by flowing streams,
And even lofty mansions.

11.   The fact is that they disbelieve the Hour,
And We have, for deniers of the Hour,
Prepared a flaming Fire!

---

1. Or "thrown down on him".

12.   When she[1] shall see them from afar,
    They'll hear her raging cries,
    And deep, fiery sighs!

13.   And then when, bound together, they are thrown,
    Into it through a narrow space,
    Remorsefully shall they therein bemoan;

14.   "You don't lament this Day for once,
    Infinite times you'll have to moan!"

15.   Say: "Which is better, this[2] or Paradise
    Of immortality that is the promise
    Made to the righteous?
    That is their recompense as well as
    Their final progress;

16.   They'll be therein for good abiding,
    And having everything they may desire:
    That's on your Lord a promise binding.

17.   And on the Day when He shall gather
    Them all, together with whatever,
    They served, instead of Allah, He shall say:
    "Has it been you who led astray
    All these creatures of Mine,
    Or did they go astray upon their own?"

18.   They answer: "Glory be to You; it was
    Not proper for us to take other patrons,

---

1. The Fire, the blazing Gehenna.
2. This state of affairs in Hell.

Than You, but you bestowed upon them,
And on their fathers good provisions,
Till they forgot the Admonition,[1]
And ended in perdition."

19. "Indeed they have now made you liars,
In what you claim,[2] and they cannot prevent
A thing, nor give you any help."[3] Whoever,
Of you does wrong, a grievous chastisement,
Shall he be made to taste.

20. Never have We sent, in the past,
Apostles who did not have food, and went
Not walking in the streets; and We do test
You through each other; could you then be steadfast?
Your Lord is Most-Observant!

21. And those who do not hope to Meet Us, say:
"Why are no angels sent to us, and why
Could we not see Our Lord?" They are indeed,
Too haughty, and they shamelessly exceed!

22. The Day when they behold the angels,
Holds no good news for criminals!
"Pray quarter, quarter!"
Shall be the only thing they utter.

23. But We shall only look at what
They really did perform,

---

1. Or: "Reminder", "Remembrance", "Scriptures".

2. "Of ascription's of divinity to them".

3. This is God's statement to the idolaters.

And We shall render them[1] as dust,
Flung about in a storm!

24. But the inmates of Paradise,
Shall on that Day be in a place,
Far happier, and better tidings,
Shall they be hearing.

25. Upon that Day, the heavens shall be rent
Asunder into clouds,
And angels shall be sent
Down in their crowds;

26. Upon that Day, the Kingdom shall be rightly
Under the God of Mercy's Sway,
And for the disbelievers it shall be,
The hardest Day!

27. And on that Day the wicked bite their fingers,
And say: "Oh! Would that I had taken
The same path as the Messenger's!

28. "Oh, woe is me! Would that I had not chosen,
So and so for a friend,

29. "Surely it was due to him that I turned
Aside from the Reminder after,
It reached me; and most surely Satan
Is humankind's betrayer!"

---

1. That is, their actions shall be of no weight in the Divine Scale on the stormy
Day of Resurrection.

30.   And then the Messenger will say: "My Lord,
      Indeed my people treated this Quran,[1]
      As something obsolete, forlorn."

31.   Thus have We an adversary assigned
      To every prophet from among,
      The sinners always doing wrong;
      Your Lord, however, is Sufficient,
      To guide and give a helping hand.

32.   The disbelievers argue: "Why was not
      The whole Quran sent to him all at once?"
      But in this manner We do strengthen
      Your heart thereby, and therefore, in a sequence,
      Well-phrased and gentle, We rehearse it.

33.   No sooner do they come to you,
      With any argument or question,
      Than We provide you with the truth,
      And the best explanation;

34.   The people who shall be, upon their faces,
      Unto Gehenna driven,
      Are certainly in the worst plight, and straying
      Farther from the direction even.

35.   To Moses, heretofore, We gave the Law,[2]
      And chose for him his brother, Aaron,
      As Minister.[3]

---

1. Or "this holy Reading".

2. The Book, the Scriptures, Divine instructions.

3. Helper, aide, counsellor or one authorized to conduct religious worship.

36.   And then We said: "Go, both of you, to those
        Who treat Our Signs as lies";
        These folks We subsequently,
        Annihilated utterly.

37.   It was the same with Noah's people:
        As they denied their messengers, We drowned
        Them all, and turned them, for mankind,
        Into a Lesson; surely for the sinful,
        Have We prepared a torment painful.

38.   So was indeed the case,
        With the Aad and with the Thamood,
        And those who dwelt at Raas,[1]
        And many generations,
        Who did between them pass:

39.   Each one of them We warned by some
        Examples, and We did destroy each one,
        And sent them all unto their doom.

40.   Surely these people have passed by the town,
        On which was rained a fatal rain;
        Have they not really seen it? Aye!
        They only hope not to be raised again!

41.   When they see you, they scoff at you and jeer:
        "Is this the man whom God has chosen
        To be His messenger?!

---

1. Most probably the people of Prophet Shu'aib who dwelt at a place or town of
   this name.

42.   "He had well-nigh led us astray
       From our own gods, had we not been
       In their service most adamant!"
       Soon when they face the chastisement,
       They shall find out who's really been
       From the Path most astray!

43.   Do you not see the man who has
       Taken his lusts and ego for a god?
       Could you be over him a guardian?

44.   Do you suppose most of them could
       Hearken or understand? Indeed,
       They are like beasts, but, when astray,
       They go much farther from the way!

45.   Have you not noticed how your Lord
       Lengthens the shade?
       If He had pleased, He would have made
       It motionless, but then We did
       Make the Sun be its guide;

46.   And then We draw it in unto Ourself,
       With an indrawing mild.

47.   And He it is Who has ordained the Night
       To serve you as a garment and the Sleep
       For resting and repose, and made the Day
       To rise up and recoup.

48.   And it is He Who sends the winds,
       The vanguards of His rain of blessings;
       And water very pure We then,

Send down from heaven;

49.   We then revive with it dead lands,
        And quench the thirst of all Our creatures,
        The multitudes of brutes and humans;

50.   We do present the same phenomenon
        Before them often, so that they take heed,
        Most men, however, do go on
        Being thankless indeed.

51.   In every city could We raise
        A warner, if We please.

52.   Thus give not way unto the disbelievers,
        But with this[1] fight them, and do call
        For the hottest *Jihaad*[2] of all.

53.   And it is He Who has sent rolling
        The waters of two seas[3] adjoining:
        The one is fresh and sweet, the other
        Saltish and bitter,
        And He has made between them some partition,
        An insurmountable obstruction.

54.   And it was He Who from the water,
        Created humans, and He did
        Give them, of blood and marriage, kindred;
        Over all things your Lord has power.

1. The Holy Quran.   2. Doing one's utmost in the cause of God.

3. Or "rivers, lakes, separate bodies of water": these (sweet waters) have their
   sources in rain, and they eventually join the oceans (salty waters); this is a
   regular water-cycle: they mingle and yet they remain separate.

55.   They still, beside God, set up idols,
        Which do not harm or profit them; indeed,
        Helpers of evil are the infidels,
        Against their Lord.

56.   And We have sent you only
        To bring glad tidings,
        And give them warnings.

57.   Say: "I am asking for it no reward,
        From you but this: that any man who will,
        Could take the way unto his Lord.

58.   Now put your trust in Him, the One
        Who: Ever-Lives and Never Dies,
        And celebrate His praise;
        The faults and sins of His own creatures,
        He fully knows;

59.   Within six Days He did alone,
        Create the skies, the earth and all that lies
        Between them; then, He did ascend His Throne;
        He is the Merciful:[1] concerning Him,
        Ask of the Wise![2]

60.   But when it's said to them: "Bow down
        Before the Merciful," they wonder:
        "Who is the Merciful? Shall we
        Bow down to what you order?!"
        And this only increases their disdain.

---

1. Al-Rahmaan, the God of Mercy. God is also known as the Merciful in the Scriptures.   2. Those who have such knowledge.

61.   Blessed be the One who's placed;
        The constellations in the heavens,
        And set a glowing Lantern in their midst,
        And made a Moon that brightly shines.

62.   And it is He Who has designed the Night
        And Day to follow one another,
        For those who do decide to ponder,
        Or to appreciate.

63.   And the Merciful's servants are the people
        Who walk upon the earth in humbleness,
        And all that they will say is "peace",[1]
        Unto the ignorant who them address,

64.   And those who pass the night
        In the worship of their own Lord,
        Standing and prostrate,

65.   And those who pray: "O Lord,
        Ward off the punishment of Hell from us,
        For its torment is endless,

66.   It is indeed an ill abode,
        And evil resting place!

67.   And those who, when they give in alms,
        Are not extravagant, nor niggardly,
        But keep the mean between extremes,

68.   And those who never call on other gods,

---

1. Original: *salaaman.*

Along with God, nor ever slay a soul,
Which Allah has forbidden,
Save in the course of justice,
And who commit not fornication,
And he who does this, surely will
Meet the reward of wickedness,

69.   Doubled shall be to him the retribution,
Upon the Day of Resurrection,
Living therein for ever in disgrace,

70.   Except the people who repent, embrace
The faith, and do what's right, for verily
Allah will change their sins into good things,
For God's Forgiving, Full of Mercy.

71.   And he that does repent and does what's right,
He'll be a true repenter in God's sight.

72.   And those who bear not witness
To what is false, and if they pass
By something vain or useless,
They pass it on with nobleness,

73.   And those who, when the revelations from
Their Lord, are unto them reminded,
Do not react to them as though they were
Made deaf, or blinded!

74.   And those who pray: "Our Lord, do realize
Whatever in our spouses and our children,
Shall be the comfort of our eyes,
And turn us into leaders,

For the god-fearing, self-restrainers."

75. Such are the people who shall be rewarded
With the High Places,[1] for their toleration,
And they therein are to be met with
Welcome and Salutation,

76. They will therein abide for good,
What a serene abode,
What a good Station!

77. Declare: "If you are not on Him to call,
Little would care my Lord for you at all,
You have rejected Him already, thus
The Unavoidable shall come to pass!

---

1. Lofty palaces in Paradise.

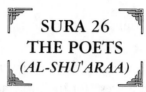

SURA 26
THE POETS
(AL-SHU'ARAA)

In the Name of God, the Beneficent, the Merciful

1. Taa Seen Meem.[1]

2. These are the verses of the Book,
   Of clarity extreme.

3. Perhaps you'll[2] fret yourself to death,
   That they do not embrace the Faith!

4. Were it Our will, We could send down
   A Sign unto them from the heavens,
   Before which they would bend their knees!

5. They have already turned their backs upon
   The new warning unto them given
   From Al-Rahmaan,

6. And treated it as false, but soon
   The truth of what they used to scorn,
   Shall on them dawn.

7. Have they not ever looked
   At the earth to admit
   The plentitude of noble plants,
   We have produced in it!

8. Verily in this is a Sign, and yet,

---

1. T.S.M.   2. The Holy Prophet.

Of them the greater part,
Will not embrace the Faith;

9.   And certainly your Lord is both,
Almighty and Compassionate.

10.   Behold! Your Lord did call on Moses:
"Go to the wicked folk,

11.   "The folk of Pharaoh; see if they,
Will take the righteous way?"

12.   He said: "My Lord, in sooth I fear,
Lest they will treat me as a liar,

13.   "Nor is my breast broadened enough,[1]
And in my speaking I do stammer,
Thus Aaron should be sent for;

14.   "They also have a charge[2] against me,
And I do fear that they may slay me."

15.   He said: "Certainly not, go both of you,
Together with my Signs; surely We too,
Are with you and will hearken,

16.   "Thus go to Pharaoh, and proclaim:
We are on a prophetic mission,
By the Lord of Creation,

---

1. Original "my breast will be straitened"; Moses thus begs God to give him
more spiritual power through His Grace.

2. The charge of murdering an Egyptian in the past.

17.   That you send forth the Children
      Of Israel along with us."

18.   He said: "Did we not bring you up among us when
      You were a child? And did you not, for certain
      Years of your life, among us dwell?

19.   "And still you did commit what you have done,
      You are certainly most ungrateful!"

20.   He said: "I did that when I was misguided,

21.   "Then out of fear of you, I fled;
      Now has my Lord unto me granted,
      Wise judgment, and appointed
      Me an apostle;

22.   "And how about the favour
      You have unto me given,
      That you have turned the Children
      Of Israel into your bondsmen?!"

23.   Then Pharaoh asked: "And what is this:
      'The Lord of all Creation'?"

24.   He said: "It means the Lord of heavens,
      The earth and all that is between them;
      Would that you had been certain!"

25.   He[1] said to those around him: "Oh, do listen!"

---

1. Pharaoh.

592

26.   And he went on: "Your Lord, also the Lord,
        Of your fathers of old."

27.   "This messenger sent to you",[1] he opined,
        "Is certainly out of his mind!"[2]

28.   Yet he added: "He is the Lord of East and West,
        And everything that does between them rest,
        If only you could understand!"

29.   Now he did threaten: "If, but me
        You serve another deity,
        I'll have you thrown among the ones
        Who rot in dungeons!"

30.   He challenged: "What! Even if I should bring
        You some convincing proof!"

31.   He said: "If you speak truth, forth with the thing!"

32.   Thus threw he down his staff,
        And lo! It was a serpent true to life;

33.   Then he drew out his hand,
        And lo! It radiated white,
        In the beholders' sight.

34.   "This fellow is a skilled magician,"
        He warned his noblemen around,

---

1. "Addressing his chiefs and courtiers".

2. Or "possessed, bedevilled".

35. "He means to drive you from your land,
By the means of the magic of his hand,
Therefore, what is it that you counsel?"

36. They said: "Let's put him and his brother
Off for a while, and send a summoner
To every town,

37. "To bring unto your presence,
Every magician of renown."

38. Thus all magicians were collected
Upon a solemn day selected,

39. And it was said unto the people:
"Here you will all assemble?

40. "Yes! And we'll follow the magicians' way,
After they win the day".

41. When the magicians came, they said to Pharaoh:
"Are we to be the gainers
Of prizes if we gain the day?"

42. "Surely", said he, "and, in that case, you may
Even be honoured 'mongst my nobles."

43. Now Moses said to them: "Do throw,
What you have got to throw!"

44. Thus they cast down their cords and sticks,
And blithely hailed: "By Pharaoh's kudos,
We will certainly be victorious!"

45. And now, Moses threw down his rod,
    And lo! It swallowed up,
    Their every cheating odd!

46. At this, all the magicians fell
    Down in prostration,

47. And cried: "We now believe in
    The Lord of all Creation,

48. "The Lord of Moses and of Aaron."

49. He shouted: "You in him believe,
    Before I give you leave?!
    In teaching magic unto you,
    He must have surely been your guru!
    But soon you shall find out:
    I'll have your hands and feet
    Cut off from left and right,
    And then will have you crucified
    Without a doubt."

50. They said: "That's to us now of no concern,
    For surely, to our Lord, we shall return,

51. "Indeed we hope that all our sins,
    Will, by our Lord, be pardoned since,
    We are the first embracers of the faith."

52. To Moses then did We reveal: "Go forth,
    By night together with My servants, for
    You'll be pursued for sure."

53. And Pharaoh, on the other side,
    Sent heralds, to the towns, who cried:

54. "These people[1] are a scanty nation,

55. "Yet they have always been against us,
    Engaged in agitation,

56. "But we are much more numerous,
    And do have prior information."[2]

57. Thus did We cause them to abandon,
    Every fountain and garden,

58. Their treasures and their splendid dwellings.

59. Thus was it; and We made such things,
    The heritage of Jacob's Children.

60. Therefore, at sunrise did they them pursue,

61. And after the two hosts had come
    In one another's view,
    The company of Moses were thus shaken:
    "We're surely overtaken?!"

62. "No", said he, "by no means
    Surely my Lord is at my side,
    And me shall He soon guide.

---

1. The Israelites.

2. Or: "we are forewarned, vigilant."

63.   And We revealed to Moses then:
"Do strike the sea with your own staff";
Thereby she was asunder cloven,
And each disjointed part came off,
Like a gigantic cliff.

64.   And then We made the other party also
Get closer thither;

65.   Moses We did then save together,
With all his men,

66.   And let the others drown!

67.   Indeed in this there is a Sign;
Yet most people have not believed.

68.   Your Lord is verily,
The Mighty God of Mercy.

69.   And now recite to them,
Some news on Abraham;

70.   Behold, he asked his father and his folk:
"What is it you invoke?"

71.   They said: "We worship idols and we'll ever,
Remain devoted to them with all fervour!"

72.   He asked: "Could they hear you at all,
When you upon them call?

73.   "Are they to you of any benefit,

Or can they hurt?"

74. They said: "Well, no! But We all saw
Our fathers and forefathers doing so!"

75. He said: "You've never then been thinking
Over what you're invoking?!

76. "You and your ancient sires?

77. "Surely to me they are adversaries;
The only Lord of all Creation,

78. "Is He Who has created me,
And then He has directed me,

79. "The One who gives me food and drink,

80. "Who heals me when I'm sick,

81. "Who causes me to die,
And later brings me back,

82. "And who, I hope, will be Forgiving,
My sins, upon the Day of Reckoning,

83. "My Lord, do grant me wisdom,
And join me with the righteous people,

84. "Let me have a good name,
With later generations,

85. "Place me amongst the heirs,

Of the Garden of Bliss,

86.   "Forgive my father, for he was
        Among the erring ones,

87.   "And put me not to shame,
        Upon the Day when every-one
        Is raised again,

88.   "The Day when wealth or children,
        Shall nothing whatsoever gain,

89.   "Those only shall be saved who will,
        Bring hearts to Allah, free of evil."

90.   Then Paradise is closer drawn,
        To the god-fearing, self-restrainers,

91.   And Hell shall lay wide open,
        Before the erring strayers,

92.   And they'll be asked: "where are the idols,
        To whom you used to be the servers,

93.   "Instead of God? Could they be helpers
        To you or even help themselves?"

94.   Then into it,[1] they shall be cast:
        The seducers and the seduced,

95.   And all the Satan's[2] host.

---

1. Hell.   2. Original: Iblees "the outcast, the wounded one."

96. As they wrangle therein together,
    They shall thus utter:

97. "By God! We were in plainest error,

98. "In holding you¹ as equals
    With the Lord of the Worlds,

99. "Those who misled us were the ones,
    Totally steeped in sins;

100. "And now no intercessor do we find,

101. "Nor any caring friend,

102. "We would be surely true believers,
     If we could be returned!"

103. Indeed in this there is a Sign,
     But most of them are not believers.

104. And yet your Lord is surely
     The Mighty, Full of Mercy.

105. The clan of Noah also treated
     Their messengers as liars,

106. When their own brother to them said:
     "Have you of God no dread?

107. "To you I bring a Message,

---

1. Devils, satans, false leaders, and personified evil fancies.

Most faithfully,

108. "Therefore fear God and follow me,

109. "And I am asking for this no rewards
      From you, for my reward comes only
      From the Lord of the Worlds,

110. Therefore fear God and follow me."

111. But they retorted: "Shall we
      Believe on you when only,
      The lowest and the meanest fellows,
      Have been your followers?!"

112. He said: "I have no knowledge of
      What they have really done,

113. "Only unto my Lord,
      Must their account be given,
      Would that you understood this truth!

114. "But I am not the one to drive away
      Those who embrace the faith,

115. "I am a person only charged
      With warnings manifest."

116. They threatened: "O You Noah, do desist
      Or you'll undoubtedly be stoned!"

117. "My Lord", he then intoned,
      "My people, certainly,

Have now denied me,

118. "Judge You therefore between,
Me and them rightly,
And save me and the faithful
Who are with me."

119. Thus We delivered him and every person
Who had been his companion
In the Ark fully laden,

120. And afterwards We drowned
All those who stayed behind.

121. Indeed in this there is a Sign,
But most of them are disbelievers!

122. And yet your Lord is certainly,
The Mighty, Full of Mercy.

123. The Messengers had been denied,
Also by tribe of Aad;

124. When their own brother, Hood, unto them said:
"Have you of God no dread?"

125. "To you I bring a Message,
Most faithfully,

126. "Therefore fear God and follow me,

127. "And for this I am asking no rewards,
From you, for my reward comes only,

From the Lord of the Worlds;

128. "What! You erect a lofty mansion,
On every hill and mountain,
Only for pleasures wanton?!

129. "And raise many a massive structure,
As though you could abide for ever,

130. "And when you exercise your-power,
You lay your hands on men most harshly,

131. "Therefore fear God and follow me,

132. "Fear Him Who has unto you given,
Plenty of what you know,

133. "Who did abundantly on you bestow,
Livestock and children,

134. "And many a spring and garden;

135. "Indeed I fear for you the chastisement
Of a Day grievous, vehement!"

136. They said: "Whether you warn or warn us not,
We do not care a jot!

137. "Such threats are empty claims,
Since ancient times!

138. "None shall us ever penalize!"

139. Thus they rejected him, and We
     Destroyed them utterly;
     In this indeed there is a Sign,
     But most of them shall not be faithful,

140. Yet certainly your Lord is
     The Almighty, the Merciful.

141. Another people who denied
     Their messengers were the Thamood,

142. When their own brother, Saalih, to them said:
     "Have you of God no dread?

143. "I bring to you a Message,
     Most faithfully,

144. "Therefore fear God and follow me,

145. "And for this I am asking no rewards,
     From you, for my reward comes only,
     From the Lord of the Worlds;

146. "Do you suppose you will be left for ever,
     In safety, with no fear,
     Amid all things around you here?

147. "Amid gardens and fountains,

148. "Cornfields and palm-trees laden
     With fruits and flowers?

149. "To happily hew out,

Your houses in the mountains,

150.   "Therefore fear God and follow me,

151.   "And follow not that which is ordered,
By the extravagant unbridled,

152.   Who spread corruption in the land,
And nothing ever mend."

153.   They said: "Certainly you're a man bedevilled!

154.   "Naught are you but a mortal,
Just like us, therefore, if you tell
The truth, then bring a Sign."

155.   "This camel", said he, "is to be the Sign:
One day, she is to have her water portion,
And one day, you shall have your portion;

156.   "And touch her not with evil, not at all,
Lest the chastisement of a dreadful Day,
Upon you fall."

157.   But they hamstrung her, and upon the morrow,
They had to wake up unto woe and sorrow,

158.   For the chastisement had by then
Them overtaken!
Indeed in this there is a Lesson,
But most of them have been unfaithful,

159.   And yet, your Lord is certainly

The Almighty, the Merciful.

160.　Lot's people also did
　　　Their messengers deny,

161.　When their own brother, Lot, unto them said:
　　　"Have you of God no dread?

162.　"I only bring to you a Message,
　　　Most faithfully,

163.　"Therefore fear God and follow me,

164.　"And for this I am asking no rewards
　　　From you, for my reward comes only
　　　From the Lord of the Worlds;

165.　"What! Of all people,
　　　You go unto the males?!

166.　"And leave the ones whom has your Lord
　　　Created as your mates;
　　　You have indeed transgressed all limits!"

167.　They said: "O Lot, if you do not desist,
　　　Out of this town, shall you be cast!

168.　He said: "Your ways and doings,
　　　I certainly detest:

169.　"My Lord! Rescue me and my kinsfolk,[1]
　　　From what these people work."

---

1. Also meaning "followers".

170. Thus, him and all his folk We saved,

171. Save for a woman old,[1] who stayed
     To be amongst the doomed;

172. We then annihilated all the rest:

173. A rain on them We rained;
     Dreadfully fatal was the rain,
     To those who had been warned.

174. Indeed in this there is a Sign,
     But most of them are not believers;

175. And yet your Lord is certainly,
     The Mighty, Full of Mercy.

176. Apostles were also rejected by
     The Aikah[2] tribe;

177. Behold! They were admonished by Shu'aib:
     "Will you not be god-fearing?

178. "I bring to you a Message,
     Most faithfully,

179. "Therefore fear God and follow me,

---

1. Lot's wife.

2. Meaning "the Sylvans" or "the forest dwellers": Prophet Shu'aib is sent, as
   other *suras* show, to both the Midian and Al-Aikah peoples. Shu'aib is most
   probably the Jethro and Hobab of the Old Testament, and Al-Aikah must
   have lived in the neighbourhood of the Midianites.

180.　　"And for this I am asking no rewards,
　　　　From you, for my reward comes only
　　　　From the Lord of the Worlds;

181.　　"Give measures full, and never be,
　　　　One of those who subtract,

182.　　"But weigh with scales exact,

183.　　"And do not cheat the others,
　　　　Of what is rightly theirs,
　　　　And stop committing evil in the land,
　　　　As practiced by corrupters,

184.　　"And fear the One Who did create you,
　　　　And all the people in the past."

185.　　They said: "We really think you are possessed!

186.　　"Naught are you but a mortal just
　　　　Like us, and we do deem you ever,
　　　　To be a liar,

187.　　"But if you happen to be truthful,
　　　　Do make a fragment of the sky
　　　　Upon us fall!"

188.　　He said: "It is my Lord who's Most Aware,
　　　　Of your every affair."

189.　　Thus they rejected him, and did incur
　　　　The Retribution of the Darkened Day,

1. Or "The Day of Overshadowing Gloom": Perhaps a shower of ashes and

Which was the torment of a day,
Vehement, full of horror.

190.   Indeed in this there is a Sign,
       But most of them do not believe,

191.   And yet your Lord is certainly
       The Mighty, Full of Mercy.

192.   Indeed is this[1] a Revelation,
       From the Lord of Creation,

193.   The Trusted Spirit[2] brought it down,

194.   Upon your heart, that you may warn,

195.   In the Arabic language plain;

196.   The same had been foretold,
       In the scriptures of old;

197.   Has it not been to them a Sign,
       That to the learned 'mongst the Children,
       Of Israel it has been known?

198.   Had We revealed it to a foreign man,

199.   And had he it to them recited,
       They would have not believed therein;

---

cinders accompanying a volcanic eruption.

1. This Book: The Holy Quran.
2. The Holy Spirit or Gabriel.

200. Thus[1] do we make it enter
     Into the heart of every sinner,

201. But they will not believe it till
     They see the woeful chastisement,[2]

202. That comes upon them on a sudden
     When they shall not perceive;

203. And they will say: "could we receive
     Any respite at all?!"

204. What! Will they seek to hasten
     Our retribution?

205. Think! If We do bestow on them their fill
     For many years,

206. And then the scourge unto them promised
     Shall come on them at last,

207. Will their enjoyments be at all,
     Unto them of any avail?

208. Never have We destroyed a nation
     Which did not have its warners first,

209. Forewarning them: never are We unjust;

210. Neither is this[3] brought down by satans,

---

1. "Through the medium of the Arabic language."
2. "Until it is too late."   3. The Holy Quran.

211. For them it's never meet,[1]
     Nor do they have the might,

212. Indeed they have been kept
     From hearing it.[2]

213. Thus never any other gods should be,
     By you, along with Allah, idolized,
     For then you'll find yourself among,
     The ones to be chastized.

214. Now warn your nearest kinsmen,

215. And kindly spread your wings,
     Over the faithful who,
     Follow your warnings

216. But if they disobey you, say:
     "I am clear of your doings."

217. And put your trust in Him who is,
     The Merciful, the Lord of Power,

218. Who sees you when you stand in prayer,

219. And your every demeanour,
     Amongst the worshippers,

220. Surely it's He Who is
     The Hearer, the All-Knower.

---

1. Suitable, fitting, proper.
2. Comp. Sura 37-7, 8.

221.   Shall I tell you on whom the satans,[1]
       Tend to descend?

222.   They do descend upon all persons,
       Who've often lied and sinned;

223.   They whisper hearsay into ears,
       But most of them are liars.

224.   As for the Poets,[2] they are followed,
       Only by erring strayers:

225.   Have you not noticed:
       That they are in confusion,
       And that they go this or that way,
       According to the situation?!

226.   And that they always say
       What they have never practiced!

227.   Not so are those who do believe,
       And do good works, and oft remember
       Allah, and who defend themselves,
       When they're oppressed;[3] but every member
       Of the transgressing party will
       Soon come to know what for an evil
       Fortune, he'll have to suffer!

---

1. Or devils, Jinns, evil influences.

2. These are faithless poets who used their art in the service of Evil.

3. But arts, and poetry in this case, may also be used in the service of religion and righteousness.

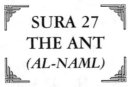

SURA 27
THE ANT
(AL-NAML)

In the Name of God, the Beneficent, the Merciful

1. Taa Seen;[1]
   These are verses of Al-Quran,
   A Book of glorious sheen.

2. A guidance and good news,
   For the believers,

3. Who do attend unto their prayers,
   And pay the stated alms, and firm,
   Is their faith in the life to come.

4. And unto those who have no faith,
   In the Hereafter, have We made,
   Their deeds most pleasing, and they thus
   Wander on like the blind indeed;

5. A grievous chastisement is to be theirs,
   And in the life to come they shall be
   The greatest losers.

6. Surely you are receiving the Quran,
   From the All-Knower, the Most-Wise.

7. Behold! Thus Moses spoke unto his household:
   "I do descry a fire; let me bring
   You some tidings from it, or just get hold,

---

1. T.S.

613

Of a few blazing brands to fight the cold."

8.   And when he came to it, a voice:
Cried out: "Blessed is He who is in,
This fire, and He who is about it,
And glory be to God,
The Lord of all Creation,

9.   "O Moses! Surely I, am God the One,[1]
The Lord of Might and Wisdom,

10.   "Now do throw down your rod!"
And when he noticed that it was in motion,
As though it were a snake, he took,
To his heels, never looking back!
"O Moses! Fear not! No apostles near
Me ever fear;

11.   "Even if one does wrong, but then he will,
Substitute good in place of evil,
Surely I'll be Forgiving, Merciful;

12.   "Now put your hand into your bosom:
Shining shall it come forth, yet free from stain,
One of miracles nine,
To Pharaoh and his nation,
Badly are they sunk in transgression."

13.   But when Our Signs most manifest, he took,
Unto them they did mock:
"Ah, this is obvious magic!"

---

1. Allah.

14. And though in their own souls they were convinced
That they were true, yet in their vice and pride,
They obstinately them denied;
Behold and make a note:
What was the mischief-makers' fate!

15. Unto David and Solomon We gave
Knowledge; and they were often saying: "Praise
Be to Allah Who graciously did raise,
Us over many who believe,
Among His servants.

16. And Solomon succeeded David;
He said: "O Men, We have been taught
The speech of birds and are endued
With everything; and this is nought
But a manifest Grace indeed.

17. To Solomon had once been summoned
His hosts of Jinns and men and birds,
And they were marched in many a band,

18. Until they reached the Valley of the Ants;
A she-ant cried: "O you antkind, do rush
Into your homes, lest Solomon and hosts,
Though not antagonists, all of you crush!"

19. Hearing her words, he was amused and smiled,
And prayed: "Do stir me up, my Lord,
To render thanks for favours You have showed
To me and to my parents,
And to do righteousness that may
Well please You; and by Your own Mercy,

Admit me 'mongst your righteous servants."

20.   And he reviewed the birds and wondered:
        "Why do I not behold the lapwing?
        Where on earth is it hiding?

21.   "If it does not a clear explaining,
        Unto me bring,
        I will give it a torment hard,
        Or even have it slaughtered."

22.   But it tarried not long; it came and said:
        "I've got some news, out of your ken,
        For I have brought to you from Sheba,
        Some news most certain!

23.   "Therein I found a woman,
        Who has the royal diadem
        Of reigning over them,
        And she does have the most splendid throne;

24.   "I found her and her nation bowing down,
        Instead of God the One, before the Sun,
        But, in their eyes, has Satan
        Made their doings look fine,
        He has thus led them off the Way,
        And so they've gone astray,

25.   "From the worship of God the One,
        Who brings forth what is hidden,
        Upon the earth or in the heaven,
        And Who does know what men¹ disguise,

---

1. Original: you.

616

And whatsoever they disclose,

26.   "Allah: there is no God but He,
        And he is certainly the Very
        Lord of the Glorious Throne."

27.   He commented: "We'll soon
        Discover whether what you utter
        Is true or you're a liar;

28.   "Fly out with this my letter,
        And let it drop before them,
        Then turn away from them,
        And wait their answer."

29.   "O Nobles! Down to me has been," she said,
        "A noble letter thrown in truth,

30.   "It is from Solomon, and it is headed:
        'In Allah's Name, Benefic, Full of Ruth,

31.   'Set not yourselves against me,
        By condescension,
        But do come unto me,
        In all submission.'"[1]

32.   She asked: "O chiefs, do counsel me in this
        Affair of mine, for I make no decision,
        If you do not it witness."[2]

---

1. Or "as submitters to the Will of the Almighty."
2. That is: "without your concurrence and confirmation."

33.   They said: "We are a nation of great might,
      Given to battles vehement,
      But the ultimate judgment,
      Rests in your hand,
      Thus only tell us what
      You will command!"

34.   She pondered: "Kings when they invade a land,
      They devastate it, and shall make the grand,
      And the mighty amongst its people, most
      Abased of all; thus is done at their hand;

35.   "Therefore, together with sending a present,
      I'll with them correspond,
      And wait to find out how they will,
      To my envoys respond."

36.   Now when the envoy came to Solomon,
      He¹ cried and said: "Fie! Do you mean
      To help me with some property?! Yet what,
      Has God unto me given,
      Is far better than all you've got;
      Do you still glory in your gift?!

37.   "Go back to them, for surely we shall come
      To them with forces they cannot withstand,
      And we'll be driving them therefrom,
      In dishonour, while most contemned!"

38.   He asked: "O chiefs, before they come,
      Unto me in submission, which one
      Of you will bring to me her throne?"

---

1. Solomon.

39. The staunchest of the Jinn replied: "I will
Bring it to you before you end this council,
For this I am certainly strong and faithful."

40. But one who had the knowledge of the Book,
Said: "I will, in the twinkling of an eye,
Bring it to you." And when he saw it set,
In front of him, said he: "This is of my
Lord's favours that He may assess
If I am grateful or a person thankless;
Indeed he who is grateful,
His gratefulness is for his soul,
And as for him who is ungrateful?
Truly my Lord is Needless, Bountiful."

41. Now he advised: "Let us be casual
With her about he throne: we will see whether
She is upon true guidance or
She has not been guided ever."

42. So after she arrived, they did solicit:
"By the way, is your splendid throne,
Something like this?" "It seems that this is it!
Said she, "indeed We had already known,
And did thus unto truth submit."[1]

43. In fact what she did worship,
Instead of God, had been an obstacle[2]
To her, for surely she belonged
Unto an unbelieving people.

1. While on the way, she must have been informed about the disappearance of
her throne and, therefore, recognized Allah's true prophet in Solomon.

2. Or "prevented her, led her astray."

44.   Now she was told to step inside
        The lofty mansions,
        And when she saw them she surmised
        That there were ponds, and bared her shins;
        But he informed: "This is a palace
        Paved with smooth glass."
        And now she said: "My Lord, I've sinned
        Against my soul; yet I have joined,
        With Solomon, in his submission,
        To God, the Lord of all Creation."

45.   And to Thamood, We sent their brother, Saalih,
        Who warned: "Serve none but Allah;"
        But lo! They turned into two factions,
        Harshly opposing one another.

46.   He said: "My people, if you do not plead
        For God's Pardon that may be you are given
        Mercy, why do you have to hasten,
        Evil rather than doing some good deed?

47.   They said: "We only auger some ill omens
        Concerning you and your companions!"
        He answered: "What you auger as your ill,
        Depends on Allah, but you are a people
        Surely on trial."

48.   And in that town there was a nine-man band
        Of chiefs who spread corruption in the land,
        The kind who naught do right or mend.

49.   They plotted: "Let's, by Allah, take an Oath,
        That we, by night, will surely fall on both,

Him and his family, and We could then
Declare unto his patron:[1]
"We witnessed not his kindred's death,
And We do speak the truth!"

50. And so they planned a plot,
We also planned a plot,
But they knew not.

51. Behold! What was the end;
Of plots they planned,
Them and their folks We wiped
Off the face of the land!

52. And for their wicked sins,
Those are their homes, the empty ruins,
Verily in this is a Sign,
For those who understand!

53. But We delivered those who did believe,
And had themselves restrained.

54. Then there was Lot;
He warned his people: "What!
Committing such indecency,
Of which the evil you do see!

55. "Going lustfully unto men,
Instead of women!
Ignorant folks are you for certain!"

---

1. Original also meaning "heir" or "the avenger of blood", and in the present
case, perhaps "the chief of Prophet Saalih's tribe."

56. His folk's response was only to opine:
     "Let us banish Lot's household from your town,
     They do, forsooth, mean to remain,
     Piously clean!"

57. Thus We delivered him and all his people,
     Except his wife, whom We ordained,
     To lag behind among the doomed;

58. So We upon them rained,
     An evil rain, meant only for
     People already warned.

59. Say: Praise be unto God the One,
     And peace upon his servants
     Whom He has chosen;
     Is God better or those vice-regents,[1]
     They with Him join?

60. Is it not He Who made the heavens,
     And earth, and sent down water from the skies
     Whereby We raise delightful gardens?
     It is not possible for you to cause
     One tree to grow! A god with God? Nay, nay!
     They are people badly astray!

61. Is it not He Who made the earth so firm
     A station, and let run therein the rivers,
     And raised upon it solid mountains,
     And placed a barrier between two waters?[2]

---

1. Partners, associates and false gods joined with the Almighty.

2. Or: Two bulks of water, two seas, etc.

What! Other gods with God? But no!
Surely most of them do not know.

62.   Is it not He Who answers calls,
From the distressed, when they in truth,
Cry to him, and relieves the ills,
And makes you heirs upon the earth?
Another god with God?! In fact,
Very little do you reflect!

63.   Is it not He Who guides you in the darkness
Of the land and the sea, and sends the winds,
As heralds of His coming mercy? What!
Another god with God?! The idol-gods
They join with God are nought as to His Height;

64.   Or is it not He Who initiates
Creation, then He'll cause its repetition,
And Who supplies you with your life's provision,
Out of the heavens and the earth? So what's
The meaning of a god with God? Say: "If
You speak the truth, do bring your proof!"

65.   Say: None but Allah, either in the Heaven,
Or in the earth knows of the Hidden,
Nor do they have the slightest notion
Of the advent of Resurrection.

66.   In fact their[1] knowledge fails to fathom
The issue of the life to come:
Now they're in doubt about it,

---

1. The disbelievers'.

Now they are blind about it![1]

67. The disbelievers say: "How odd!
After we and our fathers old
Have into dust been turned,
Shall we be reawakened?!

68. "The same was promised in the past
To us and to our parents,
Surely nothing are these
But stories of the ancients!"

69. Say: "Travel in the land
And see what was the end
Of the wicked who sinned!

70. "And do not ever for them grieve,
And never be distressed at plots
That they conceive."

71. "If you do speak the truth", they further press,
"When is that promised threat,
Coming to pass?"

72. Announce: "Perhaps a part of what
You do wish to be hastened,
Is near you, close behind!"

73. Indeed your Lord, to humankind,
Has been Most Gracious, but most people,

---

1. The unbelievers, who are generally materialists, often go through such mental stages with regard to the next world.

624

Are never grateful.

74. Surely your Lord well knows,
All that they in their breasts conceal,
And all that they disclose.

75. There is no secret in the heaven
Or earth, but is already in
A Book most plain.

76. Surely does this Quran explain
Most of the things wherein the Children
Of Israel between them disagree;

77. And surely it's a Guide and Mercy,
Unto the faithful.

78. Verily, by His Wisdom,
Your Lord will judge between them:
He is the Mighty, the Omniscient.

79. Therefore, only in Allah put your trust,
For on your side's the truth most manifest.

80. You cannot make the dead to hear;
Nor could you make the deaf to listen
Unto the call, when they decide
Backwards to hasten!

81. Neither are you a guide unto the blind,
Out of their errors; you will get to listen
Only the people who believe Our sings,

Who then accept submission.[1]

82.   And when the Word has been fulfilled,[2]
       Against them, We'll to them bring forth,
       A monstrous creature[3] from the earth,
       Who shall converse with them; indeed,
       The people[4] in Our Revelation,
       Did not have any faith.

83.   Upon that Day, from every nation,
       Will We assemble some collection,
       Of those who did reject Our Signs,
       In separated lines;

84.   And when all present, he shall say:
       "Did you reject My revelations,
       Because you had no comprehensive
       Knowledge of them? Or for your actions
       You had some other motive?!"

85.   And then the Word against them is fulfilled,[5]
       For their own wickedness indeed,
       And nought have they to plead.

86.   Do they see not that We,
       Ordained the Night,
       That they may rest in it
       And the Day with its gift of Light?

1. To the will of the Almighty, thus becoming muslims in the general sense of
   the word.
2. That is the Decree or Sentence ending the respite given to mankind.
3. One of the Signs of the approaching Doom.
4. The unbelievers.   5. Or "Doom shall light upon them."

Herein are Signs in truth,
For people who have faith.

87.   On the Day when the Trumpet shall be blown,
Everyone in the heavens and all men
Upon the earth, shall be with terror seized,
Save those whom God has not so pleased,
But all shall come before Him in
Perfect submission.

88.   And mountains that you think are firm and solid,
Shall pass away, the passing of a cloud;
It is a handiwork of God who's made
Everything to perfection; Most Aware
Is He of your every affair;

89.   Those who did good, shall be rewarded
With what will be far better,
And they shall be secure,
From the Day's terror.

90.   And those who've brought with them
Records of their own evil,
Are to be flung headlong,
Into the Fire of Hell!
Shall you not be rewarded
Exactly as you did!

91.   "For me, I only have been ordered,
To serve this City's Lord,
The One Who has it hallowed;
His is everything; and I am
Ordered to be a muslim,

92.   "And to be chanting the Quran;
       Whoever is thus rightly guided,
       For his own soul, has he been guided,
       And unto those who are in error,
       Do say:[1] "I am only a warner."

93.   And Add: "To God be praise,
       He'll soon show you His Signs,
       Which you shall recognize;
       Surely your Lord is Most Aware
       Of your every affair."

---

1. This shows that the preceding verse is also meant to be spoken by the Holy
   Prophet.

SURA 28
THE NARRATION
(AL-QASAS)

In the Name of God, the Beneficent, the Merciful

1.   Taa Seen Meem.[1]

2.   These are the verses of the Book,
In clarity supreme.

3.   We will relate to you with truth,
Parts of the history related to
Moses and Pharaoh, with the view
Of doing good for men of faith.

4.   Now Pharaoh turned into a grand,
And haughty tyrant in the land,
He made his folk into many a caste:
One group of them he viciously depressed,
Putting their sons to death but sparing daughters,
He was indeed one of the most
Corrupting, evil-doers.

5.   And We intended to be Gracious to the folk,
Oppressed and weakened in the land, and make
Them leaders of the faith, and give them honours,
To be the Heirs;[2]

6.   And grant them power in the land,

---

1. T.S.M.

2. Heirs to "the land promised to them".

And let Pharaoh, Haamaan[1] and their great host
Be witnesses of what they dreaded most,
To suffer at their hand.

7.   And so We did reveal unto the mother
Of Moses: "Give him suck, but if you ever,
Feel that he is in danger:
Do put him down the river,
And do not fear or fret, for We
Shall bring him back to thee;
And We'll make him a Messenger."

8.   Thus was he picked up by
The family of Pharaoh,
That he might be a foe,
And cause them lots of sorrow!
For Pharaoh, Haamaan and their host,
Had been in sinfulness engrossed.

9.   So Pharaoh's wife did thus advise:
"Oh! What a sight for our sore eyes,
For both of us; nay, him you will not slay,
Perchance he'll bring us luck, or else we may
Even adopt him as a son;"
Little they knew what they had done!

10.   And Moses' mother was then, in her soul
And heart, feeling dreadfully empty,
So much so that she almost did unveil
The child's identity,

---

1. Not to be confused with Haman of the Old Testament (Esther III, 1), the
   minister of Xerxes, King of Persia, which is perhaps a Hebraized form of a
   Persian name.

But We girt her up in the liver,
That she became a firm believer.

11.   So she said to his[1] sister: "Follow him";
And she did watch him from afar,
And they were not of this aware.

12.   We had already caused him to refuse,
The breasts of any foster-nurse;
Until she came and said: "shall I propose
To you the people of a house,
Who may well rear him up for you, and will
Attend unto him well?"

13.   Thus We restored him to his mother,
So that she might in him rejoice,
And not be grieving any further,
And that she'd know that Allah's promise,
Is truth; though most of them are not aware.

14.   And when he reached an adult age,
And grew to manhood, We on him bestowed
Wisdom and Knowledge;
The good-doers We thus reward.

15.   One day he went into the town,
At a time when not many people,
Had been about,[2] and there he found
Two men engaged in violent quarrel:

---

1. A sister of Moses.   2. Either the time of noontime siesta or at
night time; and perhaps, as he was a member of the Royal Family, he was
visiting the city privately and eluding the guards.

One of them was of his own party,
And the other was of the enemy;
The one of his own party then appealed
To him for help against the enemy,
And Moses struck him with his fist,
And he was killed!
"This was a work of Satan", he expressed,
"For he's an enemy indeed,
And a misleader manifest."

16.   He prayed: "Forgive me, O my Lord,
For I have sinned against my soul;"
And He forgave him, for He is,
The Most Forgiving, Merciful.

17.   "My Lord", he added,
"For this favour you did
On me bestow, I'll never be
The helper of the wicked."

18.   The next day he was in the town again,
Fearing and on his guard; and lo, the man,
Whom he had helped the day before, cried out
To him for help! "You are without a doubt,
An erring, trouble-making person[1] !"

19.   Yet, when he was about to lay
Violent hands on him who was
Their common foe, he cried: "O Moses!
Me too, you want to slay,
As the poor soul you did in yesterday?!

---

1. The speaker is Moses.

To be a tyrant and to oppress,
Is certainly your only purpose,
And you do not intend to be
One who makes peace!"

20.   Now from the city's further end,
A man came rushing up and cautioned:
"O Moses, of a truth, the nobles
Have been consulting in a band,
To slay you, thus: take to your heels,
I do advise you as a friend."

21.   So forth he went from it in fear and caution,
And prayed: "My Lord, deliver me,
From the oppressive nation."

22.   And, when in the direction
Of Midian, he set forth,
He prayed: "Perhaps my Lord
Will guide me to an even path."

23.   And when he reached a well of Midianites,
At it a multitude of men, he found,
Watering flocks, and saw beside them,
Two maidens being shoved around;
He asked: "What is your matter?"
They said: "Until the shepherds scatter,
We cannot water, and too old indeed,
Is our own father."

24.   So he for them their cattle watered,
And back unto the shade retired,
And then he prayed: "My Lord, I stand

Badly in need of any good,
You might unto me send."

25.   Now one of the two maidens, walking
Bashfully, came to him to say:
"You are, invited by my father,
For watering for us, he likes to pay
You some reward." And when he went to him,
And unto him narrated his narration,
"Fear not", said he, "for you have run away
To safety from a wicked nation."

26.   One of the damsels said: "O father mine,
Employ this man, for certainly the best
Of those you could employ, shall be a man,
Who is both strong and honest."

27.   "I shall give you the hand in marriage,
Of one of these, my daughters twain,
On the condition that you shall remain,
For eight returns of pilgrimage,[1]
As my own hired hand;
But if you will, you may do ten,
However I do not intend,
To place you under any burden,
And, Allah Willing, you shall find,
That I'm an upright man."

28.   He said: "Let it be so 'tween you and me,
Whichever term I may fulfil, there shall be,
Unto me no injustice,

---

1. For eight years.

And unto what we say,
Be God the Witness.

29.   After Moses fulfilled his obligation,
And was, with his own folk, on an excursion:
Lo! A fire, did he descry,
On the side of Mount Sinai.
"Tarry, for I have seen some fire,
Perhaps I bring you news from there,
Or burning firebrands,
To warm our hands."[1]

30.   And when he came up unto it, a Voice,
From the bush in the right side of the valley,
In hallowed ground, called out: "O Moses, truly
I am Allah, the Lord of Universe:

31.   "Now do throw down your rod!" So when,
He saw that it was moving like a snake,
He turned and fled, not looking back!
"O Moses, do come forward,
And do not be afraid,
For you'll be safe indeed;

32.   "Now put your hand into your bosom,
It shall come out brilliantly white,
And still unharmed, and gather up
Your courage 'gainst all fright;
These shall be, from your Lord, two lucid proofs
To show to Pharaoh and his chiefs,
For surely they have been engaged in

---

1. Original: "That you may warm yourselves".

Some wicked mischiefs."

33.   "My Lord", he said, "I have most surely,
    Killed one of them, thus truly,
    I fear that they will kill me,

34.   "My brother Aaron is more fluent
    In speech than me; send him to stand by me,
    And verify my argument,
    For I'm afraid they will deny me!"

35.   He said: "Your arm We'll strengthen with your brother,
    And shall bestow on both of you such power
    That none may equal, and you two,
    Shall have the upper hand, so will whoever
    Will follow you."

36.   When Moses did, however, to them come,
    With Our undoubted Signs, thus did they speak:
    "Nothing is this but some,
    Magic deceptive, fake!
    Never have we the like been told
    By our fathers of old!"

37.   And Moses said: "My Lord best knows on whom
    He has bestowed His guidance, and whoever
    May gain the happy end of the Abode;
    But certainly the wicked shall not prosper."

38.   But Pharaoh said: "O Chiefs, I have not known,
    Of any god[1] for you but me alone;

---

1. Original: Ilah.

O Haamaan, kindle kilns for bricks of clay,
And build for me a tower that I may
Mount up unto[1] the god of Moses,
For certainly I think he is,
One of the liars!"

39.   Aye, he behaved most proudly and unjustly,
He and his hosts throughout the land,
They thought that they should never be
To Us returned.

40.   But We did seize on him and all his host,
And cast them down into the sea;
Do take a look and see,
The end of those who were unjust!

41.   And We made them[2] *Imams*,[3]
Who call unto the Fire!
And on the Resurrection Day,
They'll have no helper!

42.   We laid our curse upon them in this world,
And they'll be shamefully dishonoured,
Upon the Day of Resurrection.

43.   After We had annihilated,
Many a former generation,
We gave the Book to Moses, to
Enlighten men and give direction,
And be a mercy, that perhaps

---

1. "To take a look or obtain knowledge of..."
2. Them "and the likes of them".   3. Leaders.

They give it some reflection.

44.   And you[1] were not upon the western side,[2]
        When We were giving the commandment
        To Moses, nor were you a witness
        Of this event.[3]

45.   But since, We have been raising up,
        Many more generations, and their days,
        Were made prolonged; nor did you dwell
        Among the Midianites to publicize
        To them Our revelations; but it was,
        We Who did then apostles raise.

46.   Nor were you on the slope of Sinai,
        When We called out; but you're a Mercy from,
        Your Lord that you may warn a people,
        To whom no warner had before you come,
        Perhaps they'll give it some reflection;

47.   And should not say, if a disaster shall
        Befall them for their previous deeds, "Our Lord,
        Why have You not sent to us an apostle,
        Your revelation would have we then followed,
        And would have been believers."

48.   And now that, from Our very presence,
        The Truth has to them come, they question:
        "Why is he not given the like,

---

1. The Holy Prophet.   2. Of the Mount (or the Valley of Tuwa).

3. Note that "seventy of the elders of Israel" were summoned along with Moses
   for the covenant to follow the Law.

Of what was unto Moses given?!"
Do they not cry: "Two kinds of magic![1]
Each backing up the other!"
Do they not say: "We will believe in neither?!"

49.   Say: "Bring you then a book from God,
That is a better guide,
Than either of these two,
And I may follow it,
If what you say be true."

50.   But if they give you no response,
Be sure they are the slaves of their caprice;
And who is more astray than one who'll trace
His lusts and whims, without God's guidance;
For Allah does not guide
Those who transgress.

51.   And now We have certainly made
The Word to come to them, perhaps
They will it heed.

52.   Those unto whom We gave
The Book[2] before this[3] surely
In it believe.

53.   And when it is to them recited,
They say: "We do in it believe,
For it's the Truth come from our Lord,

---

1. Moses was called a sorcerer by the Egyptians, and Mohammad (pbuh) was similarly accused by the Meccan pagans, as the Quran confirmed the Message of Moses.   2. The Scriptures.   3. The Quran.

Submitters[1] were we ere it we receive."

54.   Twice shall they be rewarded for
        Their steadfast patience, and because,
        Evil did they repel with good,
        And out of what We had provided,
        For them, they spent in alms.

55.   And when they come across some idle talk,
        They turn away from it, and say: "Our deeds,
        Shall be for us, and for you, your own deeds,
        Peace be upon you, but we do not seek
        The ways of the ignorant folk."

56.   Surely you[2] cannot guide the ones you love,
        It's only God Who, in the light of
        His will, gives guidance, and the Most-Informed
        Is He of those who shall receive
        Guidance to be reformed.

57.   They say: "If We follow your kind of guidance,
        We shall be driven from our land!"
        What! Have We not for them established,
        A sanctum safe, unto which every kind,
        Of tribute fruits, the very gifts from Us,
        Are ever brought? But most of them,
        Will not this understand!

58.   And have We not annihilated
        Many communities,
        That led a life of wanton ease!

---

1. "To the will of the Almighty: muslims".   2. The Holy Prophet.

Behold the dwellings that were theirs:
Ruins rarely inhabited;
And it is We again Who are the Heirs!

59.   But never did your Lord destroy,
A habitat before He sent
Apostles to its mother-town,
To read to them Our revelations;
Certainly We are never bent,
On the destruction of a town,
Unless its people do employ
Their life-time in transgressions.

60.   And everything you have been given,
Is merely for this life's provision,
And worldly, ornamental glitter,
But that which is with God is better,
And far more lasting; do you ever
Upon this ponder?!

61.   Are they the same: the one to whom We have
Promised a gracious promise,
Which he is surely to possess,
Like one to whom We only gave
This worldly life's ease of provision,
But then upon the Day of Resurrection,
He will be summoned for interrogation.

62.   And on the Day when He will to them call:
"Where are those others who, in your opinions,
Were My companions?!"

63.   And they, on whom the sentence shall be,

Justly pronounced, will say: "Our Lord,
These are the people whom we led astray:
But our misleading them was due, indeed
To the fact that we were ourselves astray;
So we absolve ourselves before You; nay,
It was not we whom they adored!"

64.   And it is said: "Do call upon your idols";
They call on them, but there is no reaction;
Then they shall see the Punishment, and wish
That they had been upon the right direction.

65.   And on that Day, He'll call them,
And question them: "What sort of answers,
Did you give to My messengers?"

66.   The tidings on that Day shall dull and blind,
And they wish, of each other, naught to find!

67.   But those who did repent and did believe,
And did good works, may hopefully receive
Salvation in the end.

68.   Your Lord creates, and chooses, as He will,
Choosing is done by no one else,
Glorified is He, and Exalted,
Above their idols false.

69.   Your Lord does know what they conceal
Within their breasts and all that they reveal;

70.   And He is God the One,[1]

1. Allah.

No gods are there but He,
All praise is due to Him alone,
In this and the next world,
His is the Sovereignty,
And to Him will you be recalled.

71.   Say: "Only think if Allah should enshroud
You with a long, undying night,
Until the Day of Resurrection,
What gods but God would bring you light?
Won't you then hearken?"

72.   Say: "Think again, if God should make the day,
For you a lengthened one until the Day
Of Resurrection, who's the god but God,
Able to bring you night in which to lay
Your heads down? But, could you behold?"

73.   It was out of His mercy that He made
For you the night that you therein relax,
And the day that you seek some of His bounty,
Perhaps you render thanks.

74.   And on the Day when he will call to them:
"Where are those others who, in your opinions,
Were My companions?!"

75.   We'll surely draw a witness from each nation,
And say: "submit your proof"! And they shall then
Know that the truth belongs to God alone,
And that the gods of their invention,
Will surely them disown.

76.   Now Korah was a man of Moses' clan,
       And arrogance he showed to every one;
       And we had unto him already given
       Treasures of which the keys would have weighed down
       A company of sturdy men!
       Behold! His people did to him thus caution:
       "Do not exult, for Allah doesn't
       Love the exultant;

77.   "And seek by means of all that God
       Upon you has bestowed,
       To win the very last Abode;
       Do not neglect your portion in,
       This world, and do abundant good,
       As Allah has to you so Gracious been,
       And do not spread corruption in the land,
       For God is not, to mischief-makers, Kind."

78.   He answered back: "All this I have attained
       Through my own learned merit!"
       Did he not know that God had ruined
       Before him many peoples, who in might,
       Were far above him, and in magazines
       Of wealth much bigger? Surely of their sins,
       The guilty men shall not be questioned![1]

79.   And once he went forth to his people in
       His finest, worldly glitter,
       And lovers of this present life did utter:
       "Oh that we had the like of what is given
       Unto Korah! He is indeed a lucky man!"

---

1. "Not asked to give any explanations for their sins, for God is All-Knowing."

80.   But Those with gifted knowledge said: O woe
        To you! Certainly Allah's recompense
        Is far better for people who believe,
        And do good works, and none shall it achieve,
        But people who preserve with patience."

81.   At last, We caused the earth to swallow him
        Together with his mansion:
        And without God, no host could help him,
        And he himself could make no motion!

82.   Now the same folk, who only yesterday,
        Had yearned for his position, came to say:
        "Aha! It's only God who amplifies
        Or straitens whatsoever he supplies,
        To whom He pleases of His creatures;
        Had He not shown us any favours,
        He would have caused the earth to rend asunder
        Under us also! Surely never,
        Will the ungrateful prosper!"

83.   As for that future Mansion,
        We will assign it to whoever,
        Does not covet self-exaltation,
        Upon the earth, nor spreads corruption;
        The Final happy ending,
        Belongs to the god-fearing.

84.   The recompense for him who brings,
        With him good deed, shall be beyond,
        What it merits, and he who brings,
        Evil with him: such sinners find,
        That they shall be requited,

Only for what they did.

85.   He Who has made the Quran binding
On you, will most certainly bring,
You back to the Home of Return;[1]
Declare: "My Lord is perfectly Aware,
Who is it that did truly earn
Guidance and who's in clearest error."

86.   Never had you expected that the Book
Would be sent down to you; it is however,
A Mercy from your Lord; thus never give
A helping hand to those who disbelieve.

87.   And let them not divert you from
God's Signs, after they have been,
Revealed to you and bid
Men to your Lord, and never join
Those who have added gods to God!

88.   Invoke no deity,
Along with God the One,
There is no god but He;
But for His Image, everything,
Shall perish and come to an end,
His is the Sovereignty,
And unto Him you'll be returned.

---

1. "Place of Return", "Final End" or "Destination"; according to different interpretations: either Mecca or Paradise."

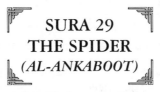

SURA 29
THE SPIDER
(AL-ANKABOOT)

In the Name of God, the Beneficent, the Merciful

1.   Alif Laam Meem.[1]

2.   Do people think that once they manifest:
"We have believed", they shall be let alone,
And not be put to any solid test?

3.   We put to proof all those before them,
This way it will most surely be made known,[2]
To Allah who had been the true believers,
And who had been the liars.

4.   Or do the evil-doers reckon:
They shall escape Our scourge?
Ill do they judge!

5.   For those who hope to meet with God,
God's term is surely coming;
And He's the Hearing, the All-Knowing.

6.   Whoever strives for God with might and main,
He surely strives for his own soul,
God's Rich Enough to be dispensing with,
His own created beings, all.

---

1. A.L.M.

2. Original: "So God will certainly know..": Surely God is All-Knowing, but for the purpose of rewarding or punishing, it will not be fair to reward or punish prior to any deeds!

7.　　And We will most certainly cleanse,
　　　The faithful who did good, of faults and sins,
　　　And We will grant them meeds[1]
　　　For the best of their deeds.

8.　　We have enjoined on man to show
　　　Kindness unto his parents, but
　　　If they contend with you to join,
　　　Others with Me of whom,
　　　You lack knowledge,[2] obey them not!
　　　Unto Me shall be your return,
　　　And then of what you've done,
　　　I shall you all inform.

9.　　And those who did believe and did good works:
　　　We will most certainly admit them,
　　　To the company of the righteous folks.

10.　　There are some men who say: "We do believe";
　　　Yet when they suffer in the cause of God,
　　　They will equate men's persecution,
　　　With Allah's retribution;
　　　But if there come a triumph from your Lord,
　　　They surely say: "Weren't we with you indeed!"
　　　Beware! Does Allah not know best
　　　What's in humankind's breast?!

11.　　Yes, Allah does the faithful recognize,
　　　And He the hypocrites well knows.

---

1. Rewards.

2. "You are uncertain about, or have no authority for their worship."

12. The unbelievers say to the believers:
"Follow our way, and we shall bear
The burden of your sins!"
Not true! They could not bear
Even their own sins,
Only they are absolute liars.

13. Indeed they shall be bearing their own burdens,
And other burdens piled upon their burdens:
For inquisition shall be made of them,
Upon the Day of resurrection,
As to their fabrication.

14. We sent Noah to his community:
A thousand years less fifty,
Had he with them remained,
At last the Deluge overtook them,
While they did wrong and sinned.

15. But him and his companions of the Ark,
We rescued and made it a landmark,
To all mankind.

16. Abraham too; he thus addressed his folk:
"Serve God the One and fear Him; this for you,
Will be the best, if you but knew!

17. "Indeed you're only serving helpless idols,
Instead of Allah, and inventing lies;
Surely those things you worship,
Instead of God, could give you no supplies;
Seek, then, your sustenance from God alone,
Serve Him and give Him thanks, for unto Him,

Shall you return;

18.   "But if you should reject-
And nations have before you been
Rejecters of this fact-
The function of the messenger is only:
To preach the message openly."

19.   Do they not see how God originates
Creation, and that He keeps this renewing?
That is indeed for Allah
An easy thing.

20.   Say: "Travel through the earth
And see how Allah has brought forth,
Created beings; later Allah
Creates them with a second birth;
Over all things has God,
Power, in truth;

21.   "Whome'er He wills, He will chastise,
And mercy He will show to any
Person He pleases;
And unto Him shall be your final journey.

22.   "Neither on earth, nor in the heavens,
Shall you be able to escape His reach,
Nor do you have, apart from God,
A patron or a helper to beseech!

23.   "And those who disbelieve in Allah's Signs,
And in His meeting, surely will despair
Of My Compassion, and they shall,

A painful scourge incur."

24. And yet the only answer from his folk,
     Was the outcry: "kill him or burn him at the stake!"
     But Allah saved him from the fire! Lessons
     Are in this for the faithful persons.

25. And he had warned: "You've taken helpless idols,
     Instead of God, out of love and affection,
     Between yourselves,¹ in the life of this world,
     But, on the Day of Resurrection,
     Some of you shall deny the others,
     And some of you will curse the others,
     And the Fire, shall be your lasting Home,
     And you shall not have any aiders."

26. And Lot was one who did have faith in him.
     And now he² said: "I surely leave my home,
     For my Lord's sake, for it is He alone,
     Who is the Mighty, Full of Wisdom."

27. Then We bestowed upon him of Our Grace,
     Isaac and Jacob, and We did ordain
     Prophethood and the Scripture
     In his descendants to remain;
     We granted him his own reward,
     In this worldly domain,
     And he shall be, in the next world,
     With the righteous indeed.

28. And Lot: Behold, he did his people caution:

---

1. Or "as a bond of union in common worship".   2. Abraham.

"You are committing an abomination,
Never, before you, done by any nation;

29. "Do you go even unto males,
Attack them on a public path,
And do all kinds of vice and evil,
In your orgies?" But all his people,
Answered was: "Bring down Allah's wrath
Upon us, if you speak the truth!"

30. He cried: "My Lord, help me against this nation,
Sunk in corruption."

31. And when Our emissaries paid a visit
To Abraham with the good tidings,[1]
They also said: "We are indeed intent on,
Liquidating the people of this town;[2]
Its folks are sunk in wrong-doings."

32. He said: "Therein is Lot"; they said: "we know
Full well who therein dwells; we will deliver
Him and his family, except his wife,
She'll be of those who linger!"

33. And when Our emissaries went to Lot,
He grew, on their account, rather concerned,
For he was powerless to guard them;
But they said: "Fear you not, and be not saddened,
As you and your dependents we'll deliver,
Except your wife, who is of those who linger;

---

1. Concerning Isaac's birth in his old age.
2. Sodom.

34.   "We're bringing down a Scourge from heaven,
    Upon the people of this town;
    Evil has been what they have done!"

35.   And We have left of it a lucid Sign.
    For people who discern.

36.   And to the Midianites there was,
    Shu'aib, their own compatriot;
    He said: "O people mine, do worship God,
    Expect the Latter Day, and so do not,
    Be spreading evil in the land,
    As the corrupt."

37.   But they denied him: Thus a mighty Blast,[1]
    Assailed them, and at morn they were in dust,
    Of lifelessness in their own dwellings!

38.   So were the Aad and the Thamood:
    Already is this made most manifest
    Unto you by the ruins of their buildings,
    For Satan so adorned their doings
    That to them foul resembled fair!
    And thus he drew them from the direct road,
    Keen-sighted though they were;

39.   So were Korah, Pharaoh and Haamaan:
    With lucid proofs of mission did,
    Moses come to them, and they still
    Behaved with arrogance most sordid,
    Upon the earth; and there had been no way

---

1. "Preceding a devastating earthquake."

For them to get away!

40.   Every one of them did We seize
For what they sinned:
On some We sent a violent Wind,[1]
Some did We silence by a thundering Shout,[2]
Some others We let crumble underground,[3]
And some of them We drowned;[4]
Surely it was not God Who did them wrong,
But they did wrong to their own souls.

41.   The people taking to themselves
Patrons instead of Allah may,
Be likened to the spider who,
Makes a house out of webs; but nay,
The frailest of all pied-a-terres,
Shall be the spider's;
Would that they could this realize!

42.   Verily Allah knows:
All that they call upon besides Him,
He's the Almighty, the All-Wise.

43.   We set forth such similitudes,
For the attention of mankind,
Although the knowledgeable only,
Will use their mind.

44.   God has created, for a rightful end,[5]
The heavens and the earth,

---

1. The case of the Aad.   2. The case of the Thamood.

3. The case of Korah.   4. The case of Pharaoh.   5. Original: in Truth.

Surely there is a Sign in this,
For men of faith.

45.   Recite out of the Book the portions
Already unto you revealed,
And keep up prayers, for prayers indeed
Help you avoid abominations
And every vulgar deed;
Surely the greatest thing
Is God's remembrance; and All-Knowing
Is God of all your actions.

46.   And, with the People of the Scriptures, never
Dispute but in the finest manner,
Save with such of them who transgress;
And say: "We do believe in whatsoever
Has been sent down to you and unto us,
Our Allah and your God is One,
And We ourselves to Him surrender".[1]

47.   And thus have We to you sent down the Book;
So do the People of the Scriptures
Believe in it, and of these people,[2]
Some have also believed in it; rejecters
Of Our communications only are:
People who have no faith whatever.

48.   Never had you before it,[3]
A book[4] recited,
Nor had you ever penned

---

1. Or "we are Muslims".   2. The Arab Pagans.

3. The Quran.   4. Books of revelation.

A single line with your own hand,
Else would the falsehood-mongers,
Have surely doubted.

49. Nay, these are clearest verses[1] in
The breasts of those who are endowed,
With knowledge; none will e're indeed
Deny Our Signs but evil-doers.

50. They also say: "Why has his Lord no Sign,[2]
Unto him given?"
Say: "Signs belong to God alone,
I am only a Warner plain."

51. Suffice it not for them that We have sent,
Down unto you this Book for recitation
To them? Surely in this, for true believers,
Is Mercy and an Admonition.

52. Say: "God's witness enough between me
And you; He knows all that is in the heavens,
And on the earth, and those who, in vain things,
Believe and disbelieve in God, shall be
The losing persons.

53. They challenge you to hasten
The scourge; but had there not been
A season fixed for it, the scourge
Would have upon them fallen;
But it will come to them for certain,
When they watch not, all of a sudden.

---

1. Or: revelations, signs. 2. Or: miracle.

54.   They challenge you to hasten,
      The Torment; but Gehenna
      Already has been closing in
      On every disbeliever!

55.   On the Day when Our Punishment surrounds,
      Them from above and from beneath their feet,
      He shall address: "Now taste the fruit
      Of your own doings."

56.   O Servants Mine,
      You who embraced the Faith,
      Truly vast is My earth;
      Thus worship Me alone.[1]

57.   Each single soul shall have to drink,
      The cup of death, and in the end,
      They will be all to Us returned.

58.   Those who believed and practised righteousness,
      Shall certainly be placed
      In palaces of Paradise,
      Beneath which whisper streams,
      To dwell therein for endless times,
      Excellent is the recompense,
      For practisers of righteousness,

59.   Who did preserve with patience,
      And only on their Lord had placed

---

1. That is: You may, under certain circumstances, have to leave your home and
country, but never abandon God-worship.

Their full reliance.

60. How many living creatures
     Do not bring forth their own provision!
     God it is Who provides for
     Them and for you, and He's the One
     Who Hears and Knows all things.

61. Now if you ask them: "Who created
     The heavens and the earth, and who did laws,
     Upon the sun and on the moon, impose?
     They'll surely answer: "Allah!"[1] How then,
     Could they devise the lies?!

62. It's God who lavishes supplies,
     On whom among his creatures,
     He pleases, or will give by measures
     Restricted to them; God is Most Aware
     Of everything, of each affair.

63. And if you ask them Who it is that sends
     Down water from the heavens, and thereby,
     Quickens the lifeless lands?
     "God it is!" Shall they certainly reply!
     Thus say: "Praise be to Allah!" yet,
     Most of them do not comprehend it.

64. Indeed this worldly life's no more,
     Than a pastime and pleasures vain,
     The Final Home: that's life for sure;
     Would their knowledge this much attain!

---

1. God the One.

65. Lo! When they have embarked upon a ship,
    They call on God, in all sincere devotion,
    But when He brings them safe to shore,
    Behold, they allocate a share,
    For others in their worship!

66. Well, let them be ungrateful unto all,
    We've given them, and let them revel,
    A while in wanton ease,
    Soon will they come to realize!

67. Do they not see that We have made
    This sacred sanctuary safe,
    While all around them people
    Are caught in dreadful strife?
    Will they then still believe in Falsehood,
    And not believe the Grace of God?

68. Who is more wicked than the man who forges
    Against Allah a lie,
    Or does the truth, when it's already
    Unto him come, deny?
    Is there not an abode in Hell
    For the infidel?!

69. But those who struggle in Our cause,
    We'll surely guide them in Our ways,
    And the doers of any righteous deed,
    Have God with them indeed.

SURA 30
THE ROMANS
(AL-ROUM)[1]

In the Name of God, the Beneficent, the Merciful

1. Alif Laam Meem.[2]

2. The Romans have been overcome,

3. In an adjacent clime,[3]
    But after being beaten,
    Soon shall they overcome,

4. Within a few years' time;
    Whether Before or After,[4] all command,
    Is only in God's hand:
    And the faithful upon that day,
    Shall be heartily gay,

5. In Allah's aid;[5] He helps the people,
    According to His will,
    For He's the Almighty, the Merciful.

6. This is God's promise, and His promise,

1. By "Roum", in Arab and Persian literature, is meant the Eastern Greco-
   Roman (Byzantine) Empire set up in 476, with Constantinople as its capital.
2. A.L.M.   3. Land, a region of the earth.   4. God is not subject to Time!
5. The Persian armies occupied Syria and Asia Minor and advanced to Chalcedon
   in 608; in 613 and 614 Damascus and Jerusalem were taken by a Persian
   general, and soon after, Egypt was conquered. This Revelation came to the
   Prophet in the year 615 or 616. Then, in 624 the tables were turned and the
   Persians suffered many defeats that resulted in a peace treaty between the
   powerful Persian and Roman Empires.

Allah shall never fail,
This is, however, not
Known by most people.

7.   They only know the outward,
Of the life in this world,
Too negligent are they to fathom
The life to come.

8.   Do they not e'er reflect within themselves,
That God did not create the skies,
The earth, and what between them lies,
But for a truthful aim,
And an appointed term?
Yet multitudes of people are deniers
That they shall Meet[1] the very Lord of theirs!

9.   Have they not ever journeyed through the land
To contemplate the fateful end,
Of those before them gone?
Greater than them were they in might,
And they broke up the land, and built
On it much more than these[2] have done!
And to them came their own apostles,
With proofs of mission lucid, strong:
Therefore it was not God who did them wrong,
But they themselves did wrong to their own souls.

10.   Then evil was the end of those,
Who did evil by treating Allah's
Revelations as lies,

---

1. "At the Resurrection."

2. Those who dwell there now or the pagans of Mecca.

Issues to laugh at and despise!

11.   God it is Who originates creation,
        And continues its reproduction,
        And then He shall you all,
        Unto Himself recall.

12.   And on that Day, after the Hour is come,
        The guilty shall be with despair struck dumb.

13.   None of their partner-gods indeed,
        Shall for them intercede,
        In fact they shall deny that any god,
        They had unto Him added!

14.   And on that Day, after the Hour
        Is come, aye, on this day, they scatter,[1]
        One from another.

15.   Then those who did believe and practised righteouness,
        Shall find themselves in perfect happiness,
        In a flowery mead of bliss.

16.   But disbelievers who were treating
        Our revelations and the Meeting,
        Of the next life as fabrication,
        Shall be brought forth to Retribution.

17.   Therefore to God give glory, when
        You reach the evening,
        And when you rise at morn;

---

1. Or "will be separated".

18.   In the heavens and on the earth,
Praise be to Him alone,
And praise Him when the sun declines,
And later in the afternoon.[1]

19.   It's He Who, from the dead,
Brings forth the living,
And from the living,
Brings forth the dead,
And He revives the dormant earth;
Thus is it that you also,
Shall be brought forth!

20.   One of His Signs is that He did,
Create you out of dust, and then,
Behold! You are now human beings,
Numerous by multiplication.

21.   And of His Signs is that He has
Created for you spouses,
From your own species,
That you may live with them in peace,
And He has put between your hearts,
Love and merciful kindness;
Herein are Signs in fact,
For people who reflect.

22.   And of His Signs are the creation
Of the heavens and of the earth,
And the variety found in
Your tongues and colours; in all truth,

---

1. Original order: "in the late afternoon and when the sun declines".

Herein are Signs for learned men.

23.　　And of His Signs are yet your sleep,
　　　　And your obtaining of His bounties,
　　　　By night and day; surely in these,
　　　　Are Signs for those who hearken deep.

24.　　And of His Signs is that He shows you
　　　　The lightning as a source of fear and hope,
　　　　And He then sends down water from the heavens,
　　　　And the torpid earth by it quickens;
　　　　Surely in this are Signs to men who keep
　　　　Using their minds.

25.　　Another of His Signs is yet the standing
　　　　Firm of the heaven and the earth,
　　　　Just at His bidding;
　　　　Thus when He calls you, by a single call,
　　　　Lo! From the earth shall you be all,
　　　　Coming instantly forth.

26.　　Whatsoever is in the heavens,
　　　　And on the earth, to Him belongs,
　　　　All are under His Domination.

27.　　Aye, He originates creation,
　　　　And He causes its reproduction,
　　　　And all this does He with most ease;
　　　　The most exalted attributions in
　　　　The heavens and the earth are His,
　　　　He's the Almighty, the All-Wise.

28.　　To you does He set forth an instance,

Drawn out from your own lives:
Have you a partner from among your slaves,
Who shares the wealth We have on you bestowed,
Fairly and squarely, with yourselves?
Do you fear them as you fear one another?
Thus do We make Our revelations plain
For people who do ponder.

29.   Nay! But the wicked do, unwittingly,
Follow their low and lustful idols[1] ;
Who will then guide the man whom God has left
Astray? None is to be their helpers.

30.   Thus set your face towards the Faith,
Upright,[2] in which nature, was wrought
Mankind by God; there is no alteration
In God's creation;
This is religion true and right, but nought
Is the knowledge of many men.[3]

31.   Turn wholly unto Him, fear Him alone,
Keep up the prayers, and do not be a man,
Who joins some gods with God the One,

32.   Or of the men who split up their religion,
And grew into many a faction,
Each group rejoicing in
Their petty acquisition!

---

1. That is: "they worship idols conjointly with God."
2. Or: "as a true believer in pure devotion to God alone".
3. Or :"the greater part of mankind."

33. When trouble touches men, they call upon
    Their Lord most penitently, then,
    After He lets them taste His Mercy,
    Behold! Parties of them begin to join
    Some other gods with their own Lord!

34. Well, let them be ungrateful unto all,
    We've given them and let them revel,
    A while, in wanton ease,
    Soon will they come to realize!

35. Have We sent down to them a mandate,
    That speaks in favour of the idols
    That they with Him associate?

36. When We make people taste of Mercy,
    They are thereat exultant,
    But when, through what they have already
    Committed, some calamity
    Befalls them, lo! They grow despondent!

37. Do they not see that God enlarges
    Provisions unto whom He chooses,
    Or, as He wills, restrains?
    Truly in this are Signs,
    For true believers.

38. Thus give unto the near of kin
    Their rightful portion,
    As to the needy and the traveller,
    Of no fixed station;
    This will be best for those who seek
    God's very pleasure,

And it is they who surely prosper.

39.   Whatever you put out at usury,
    For an increase through others' property,
    Shall not increase with Allah,
    But what you give in charity,
    Only to win God's very pleasure,
    Will let you have, many times over,
    Of any bounty.

40.   God it is Who created you, and then
    Provided you with daily bread,
    Then He shall cause you to be dead,
    And then He'll give you life again,
    Could any of your idol-gods
    Do any of such deeds?
    Glorified is He and Exalted
    Above what they have ever
    With Him associated.

41.   Corruption in the land and sea is brought
    About by what the hand of man has wrought;
    He so ordains it that they may
    Taste somewhat of the fruit of what
    They've done themselves, in order that
    They stop going astray.

42.   Say: "Travel in the land,
    And see what was the end
    Of those in older days!
    The greater part of them had joined,
    With God the One, some idols."

43.   Thus set your face towards the upright Faith,
Ere the Day come which none could ever,
Its coming hinder, 'gainst the will of Allah;
Upon that Day they shall be,
Parted in twain:

44.   The unbelievers who shall bear,
Their own burden of disbelief,
And the righteous who did prepare
Through their good deeds for their relief,

45.   That He may then reward the faithful,
Who led a righteous life, in full,
Indeed He has no love,
For those who unbelieve.

46.   Another of His Signs is that He sends,
As heralds of the tidings glad,[1] the winds,
Both that he may give you a taste
Of His Mercy, and that the ships
May glide at His behest,
And that you seek of His benevolence,
And render thanks perchance!

47.   We have before you sent apostles,
Unto their peoples,
And they did go to them with lucid Signs;
And while We did chastise the guilty ones,
It was on Us incumbent to assist
People who had the faith embraced.

---

1. "Of rain".

48.   It's God Who drives the winds that raise
    The clouds, and He then, as He please,
    Spreads them throughout the skies,
    And breaks them into fragments,
    And from their midst you shall behold,
    Rain falling down, and of His servants,
    He pours it down upon whomever,
    He pleases; lo! They shall be filled
    With joy and pleasure;

49.   Even the people who before,
    It was sent down unto them, were
    Dumb with despair.

50.   Then just behold the tokens of God's blessings:
    How He a fresh life to the dead earth brings;
    This very God's the Quickener of the dead,
    For He has Might over all things.

51.   Yet if, instead, We send a blast,
    And should they see their tilth turn yellow,
    They would, after that, surely grow,
    In their unfaith, more steadfast!

52.   Indeed you cannot make the dead to hear,
    Nor make the deaf to listen to the call,
    When they withdraw and do not heed at all;

53.   Nor could you lead the blind away,
    From their going astray[1] ;
    None shall you make to listen save,

---

1. "Those who do not want to see!"

Those who do in Our Signs believe,
For they have then embraced Islam.[1]

54. It was Allah Who did create you from
A state of weakness, and after the weakness,
He gave you strength, and then after that strength,
Gave you gray hairs and weakness;
He brings into creation what He Will,
And He's the Knowing, the Most Able.

55. And on the Day whereon the Hour,
Shall come, the guilty ones will swear,
That they tarried not but an hour!
Thus were they fooled for ever.

56. But those with knowledge and with faith endued,
Will say: "You have been tarrying indeed,
Until the Day of Resurrection,
As was by God decreed:
And this, it is the Day of Resurrection!
Of which you had no recognition!

57. But, on that Day, their pleas shall not avail
The wicked, nor will they be granted goodwill.

58. We have most certainly set forth for men,
All sorts of arguments in this Quran,
Yet when you bring to them a single verse,
From it, the disbelievers say with scorn:
"Vanities are indeed what you rehearse!"

---

1. Or " have submitted to the will of the Almighty."

59. And it is thus that Allah sets,
    A seal upon the hearts of people
    Who will not know at all.

60. Therefore be patient, for indeed
    God's promise is the truth,
    And it will never be unsettled by
    Those who have no firm faith.

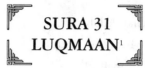

SURA 31
LUQMAAN[1]

In the Name of God, The Beneficent, the Merciful

1.   Alif Laam Meem.[2]

2.   These are the verses of the Book of Wisdom,

3.   A Guidance and a Mercy to the people,
      Who do good every time,

4.   Who keep up prayer and pay *zakaat*,[3]
      And do have a most firm
      Faith in the life to come.

5.   They rest on guidance from their Lord:
      They shall achieve success supreme.[4]

6.   There are some men who purchase idle tales,
      That they may, in their ignorance, mislead
      Others from Allah's path, and turn it[5]
      To scorn and mockery indeed;
      For these, there is a chastisement,
      Shamefully vehement.

7.   And when Our verses are rehearsed to them,

---

1. A sage in Arab traditions; many instructive apologues are credited to him,
   similar to Aesop's Fables in Greek tradition.

2. A.L.M.

3. Alms-tax, poor-rate or impost, paid by Muslims according to certain rules of
   the Law.

4. Final salvation.   5. The invitation to the Path of God.

They turn back feeling most disdainful,
As if they heard them not or had their ears,
Filled up! Thus, of a torment painful,
Give them the news!

8.   But for the people who believed
And led a life of righteousness,
There will be Gardens full of bliss,

9.   Wherein they shall abide for always:
For it is God's true promise,
And He's the Mighty, the Most-Wise

10.   With no pillars that can be seen,
Did He create the heavens,
And put upon the earth,
Well-rooted mountains,
Lest it[1] should with you sway; and He,
Over it scattered animals,
Of every kind; then from the skies,
We send down rain, and thus on it give rise,
To every kind of useful species.

11.   Yes, such is God's creation!
But then show me of what, the others
Than He, have been creators?
Ah! The wicked are surely in
A manifest delusion

12.   Of old We granted wisdom to Loqmaan:
"Be thankful unto God, for any man,

---

1. The earth.

Who thanks, will render thanks for his own soul;
And those who are ungrateful?
Well, God does not have any Need,
He is the Highly Praised indeed."

13. "My dearest son", said Loqmaan, when
He was admonishing his son:
"In worship never join a thing,
With Allah, for idolatry,
Is a most grave iniquity."

14. -"Respecting his own parents, We
Already have on man enjoined.
The mother carries him in travail
Upon travail, while being pained,
And it shall take years twain
Before he could be weaned.
Behold! To Me be grateful, and,
To your own parents, for you will,
Be finally to Me returned;

15. "Yet if they did importune you to join
With Me some things of which you have no ken,
Obey them not, but keep company kind,
Towards them in this world, and follow men
Whose way shall only turn to Me; and when,
You have to Me returned, I will inform,
You of all things you did perform-"

16. "My little son! God will indeed,
Bring every thing to light:
Though it be but the weight,
Of a grain of the mustard-seed,

Hidden inside a rock, or if it loomed
In the high heavens or it was entombed
In earth's dark womb; for God is ever
The Subtle Knower;

17. "My dearest son, keep up your prayer,
Enjoin what's right and proper,
Forbid evil, and bear,
What shall betide you with submission;
These are affairs of dauntless resolution;

18. "Be not a swollen-headed buster,
With men, nor walk the earth in haughtiness,
For Allah has no loving-kindness,
For any self-conceited boaster.

19. "But walk in humbleness; and make your voice
Less blaring: surely the most hideous
Of voices is the braying of the ass!"

20. Do you not ever see that Allah has,
All that the heavens and the earth contain,
Put under your domain,
And made His bounties flow unto you in,
Ample measures, seen and unseen?[1]
Yet some are there among the people,
Who, in respect of Allah, wrangle,
But they possess no knowledge, nor a guidance,
Nor an illuminating bible.[2]

---

1. Also meaning "outwardly and inwardly, or body and soul."

2. A book, a scripture.

21. And when they're told to follow
    What Allah has sent down,
    They say: "Nay, nay! We only follow
    What we have found our fathers on!"
    What! Even if it's Satan bidding them
    Unto the torment of the Raging One!

22. The people who submit themselves to God,
    And lead a life of doing righteous good,
    They will have certainly laid hold
    On a handle most firm, for unto God
    Shall all things finally unfold.

23. Let not the unbelievers' unbelief,
    Bring you to any grief;
    To Us is their return, and then,
    We shall inform them of
    What they have done;
    Certainly God Knows best
    What's deep in every breast.

24. We let them, for a little while,
    Amuse themselves and cheer,
    Then shall We force them into
    A chastisement severe.

25. Now if you ask them: "Who created
    The heavens and the earth?" They do
    Answer: "Allah". Say: "then to Allah,
    All praise is due!"
    Nay, most of them do not know ever.

26. Everything in the heavens,

And on the earth, to God belongs,
The Needless One, ever and always,
And the Worthy of endless praise.

27. If all the trees that are upon the earth,
Were to become pencils and pens,
And if He would the seas replenish,
With seven other inky oceans,
The Words of Allah would not finish,
For God's the Mighty, the All-Wise in truth.

28. Both your creation and your resurrection,
Is in no wise but as a single soul,[1]
And God' the Hearer Who Sees all.

29. Do you not see that Allah changes
Nights into Days, and also merges
Days into Nights, that He has tamed
The Sun and Moon each of which voyages,
Along a course already timed,
And that God is the All-Aware
Of your every affair?

30. This is because: God is the Truth,
And whatsoever else,
Beside Him is invoked, is false;
God's the Most High, the Great in truth.

31. Do you not see how ships sail through
The seas by Allah's blessings,
That He may show some of His Signs?

---

1. Or "a single person, an individual".

For certainly herein are Signs,
For all the patient, grateful persons.

32.   When waves, like giant shadows, them surround,
They call on God with all devotion;
But when He brings them safely onto land
Some of them halt 'tween two opinions[1] ;
Yet none reject Our revelations,
But the perfidious, thankless ones.

33.   O People! Be god-fearing,
And dread the Day when father
Shall not atone for son,
Nor shall a son atone
For his own father in the least;
Surely God's promise shall come true;
Thus let not this world's life deceive you,
Nor ever let the Arch-Dissembler,
Trick you concerning Allah.

34.   Certainly it is God alone with whom,
Is the knowledge about the Day of Doom;[2]
He sends down rains; and He does know
What is in every womb;
No soul will ever know
What he shall earn the morrow,
No mortal knows upon which clime,[3]
He'll be breathing for the last time;
God only is All-Knowing,
Informed of everything.

---

1. "Between idolatry and Islam" or "falter between right and wrong".
2. The Hour.   3. Land.

678

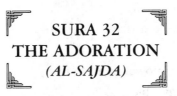

SURA 32
THE ADORATION
(AL-SAJDA)

In the Name of God, the Beneficent, the Merciful

1.   Alif Laam Meem.[1]

2.   The revelation of this Book wherein,
There is no doubt, is from
The Lord of all Creation.

3.   Now do they say: "It is his fabrication?"
Nay, it's the truth from your own Lord,
So that you may forewarn a nation,
To whom no warner had, before you, come;
Perhaps they will be guided
Unto the right Direction.

4.   Allah is He Who did create the heavens,
The earth and what between them lies,
Within six Days; and then He held the reins
Of power, on His Throne;[2]
Save Him, therefore, you have no patrons;
And none for you to intercede!
Will you not then take heed?

5.   He does administer the universe,
From Heaven to the Earth; and in the end,
It all shall unto Him ascend:
Within a Day whose space,

---

1. A. L. M.   2. Or "ascended His Throne of authority"
or "established Himself on the Throne".

Is, as you reckon years, one thousand;

6.   Such is the Knower of all things,
Visible or invisible,
The Almighty, the Merciful,

7.   Who fashioned, in the finest way,
Everything He created, and began
To bring forth man from clay,

8.   And then He made his progeny,
From the quintessence of some fluid,
Common and puny;

9.   But He shaped him in due proportion,
And breathed into him of His Spirit,
And gave you ears and eyes and minds[1] ;
What little thanks do you give for it!

10.   They still say: "What! When we are lost,
And hidden deep under the dust,
Shall our creation be renewed?!"
Yea, what they are denying is indeed,
The Meeting with their Lord!

11.   Tell them: "Your souls are to be duly taken
By the Angel of Death, to whom was given,
The charge of you, and then you'll be returned
Unto your Lord."

12.   If only you could see the guilty,

---

1. Or "hearts, brains".

When they're before their Lord, with heads hung low,
Imploring: "O Our Lord, we do see now,
And we do hear, pray send us back,
And we'll be doing righteous work,
We now believe with certainty!"

13.   Had We so willed,
We would have surely guided every soul,[1]
But then the spoken Word of Mine:
"I'll fill the pit of Hell,
With multitudes of Jinns and men",
Shall be fulfilled.

14.   Thus "Taste the recompense of your forgetting,
The Meeting of This Day of yours,
Surely we, too, shall now forget you:
And you, for former deeds of yours,
Shall taste the torment unrelenting.

15.   Only such men believe Our Signs,
Who, when of these is made a mention,
Fall down in adoration,
And celebrate the glory of their Lord,
And are never puffed up with pride,

16.   Who draw away their bodies from the calms
Of soft divans, to call upon their Lord,
In fear and hope; and give in alms,
Of what We have on them bestowed.

---

1. Surely He could have created a world in which there would have been no choice and no free will, but that was not His Will and Plan.

17.   No mortal ever may imagine,
    What pleasing Favour We have hidden
    For these:[1] only a recompense,
    For what they've done.

18.   Behold! Could he who is a true believer,
    Be likened unto an unbridled sinner?
    Nay, nought shall be unfairer!

19.   The faithful who were leading righteous lives,
    Will surely take up residence,
    In the Gardens of Paradise:
    It is a happy recompense
    For their own doings.

20.   But the unbridled sinners' haven,
    Shall be the Fire: so oft as they,
    Decide, from it, to get away,
    Back into it shall they be driven,
    And it is said to them: "Do taste
    The torment of the Fire, which you used
    To call a lie at best!"

21.   And We shall surely let them taste the Torment,
    Nearer at hand,[2] before the greater Chastisement,[3]
    Perchance they will be turning to repent.

22.   And who's more wicked than the man who is,
    Reminded of the Signs of his own Lord,

---

1. The righteous believers.

2. In this world.

3. In the Hereafter.

And yet, he turns away from them? Indeed,
We shall, from the transgressors proven,
Exact due retribution.

23. We heretofore did give the Scripture,[1]
To Moses: thus be not uncertain,
As to his Meeting;[2] and We made it
A guide for Israel's Children.

24. And We appointed from among them,
Imams[3] to guide, by Our Command,
So long as they preserved with patience,
And did Our Signs certainly understand.

25. It is indeed your Lord alone,
Who shall decide between them on
The Day of Resurrection,
Concerning what they differed in.

26. Does it indeed teach them no lesson,
That We, before them, have destroyed
Many a nation; and they won't avoid,
Setting their feet on their remains,
When they go to and fro? Certainly Signs,
Are in this; will they never listen?!

27. Or have they never noted how We drive
The rain to barren lands and make them thrive,
Producing crops which feed their cattle and themselves?

---

1. The Book of the Law.

2. "With Us".

3. Leaders.

Do they then have no eyes?!

28. They question: "When is this Decision,
     If you are truthful men?"

29. Tell them: "On the Decision Day,
     The faith of pagans[1] shall not gain
     A thing for them, nor shall they any
     Respite be given."

30. So stand aloof from them, and wait,
     For they too have to wait!

---

1. The disbelievers, the infidels.

SURA 33
THE CONFEDERATES
(AL-AHZAAB)

In the Name of God, the Beneficent, the Merciful

1.   O Prophet, be God-fearing,
And follow not the ways,
Of the infidels and the hypocrites;
For God is the All-Knowing, the All-Wise.

2.   But follow what is unto you revealed,
From your own Lord, God is indeed,
The Most Informed of all your doings.

3.   And put your trust in God, for God's Enough
As a Disposer of affairs.

4.   God has not made for any man
Two hearts within his breast,[1] nor does
He change the wives you *ziharize*,[2]
Into your mothers, neither has,
He made adopted sons as your own sons;
These are some empty words you verbalize!
God only speaks the truth,
And He does guide to the right Path.

5.   Name them after their fathers: this will be
Fairer with God, but if you know not who,

---

1. That is "two inconsistent attitudes" such as: serving God and Mammon, Truth and Falsehood, etc.

2. The evil Arab custom of divorcing a wife by pronouncing: "From now on you are like my mother", but still keeping her as a bound slave; see also sura 58, verses 1-5.

Their fathers are, regard them as your brethren
In Faith, and as your comrades true[1] ;
If you have been therein in error,
There is to be no crime in you,
Unless it was heart-felt and purposeful;
Yet, Forgiving is God and Merciful.

6.   Nearer of kin unto the faithful is
The Prophet, than they are to their own selves,
And like their mothers are his wives;
And blood-relations, in the Book of God,
Have better claims to one another than
Other believers and the ones who fled[2] ;
But to your closest friends, do every good,
For this is also written in the Book.

7.   Behold! A covenant We took,
From every prophet, and from you,
From Noah, Abraham and Moses,
And Jesus, son of Mary; it was too
Severe a Pledge We from them took;

8.   That He may ask the truthful men
About their truthfulness,
And to prepare for the infidels,
A punishment most grievous.

---

1. The original is "mowla" meaning: "friend, companion, associate, master, lord, and patron".

2. Original "Muhajirs": The Muslims who fled their home to go to Medina and struggle in the cause of God, and in the early Medina period, there was a bond of brotherhood between its inhabitants and the Migrants, which entitled them to inherit one another!

9.   O you believers, call to mind the goodness
    Of God to you when armies came against
    You, and We then let loose a violent blast,
    Upon them and the hosts you could not witness;
    For God was Seeing all your doings:

10.   When they assaulted you from every side,[1]
    When eyes with fear were petrified,
    And hearts were leaping unto throats,
    And you began to entertain some thoughts,
    Vainly diverse concerning God;

11.   And there it was that the believers,
    Who had been shaken horribly, were tried,

12.   When all the hypocrites,
    And those with ailments in their hearts,
    Alleged: "What God and His apostle,
    Promised were nothing but deceits,

13.   When parties of them said: "O men of Yathrib,[2]
    You cannot make a stand, so do go back!"
    And a band of them asked the Prophet's leave,
    Saying: "Our homes could come under attack!"
    Whereas they had not been exposed at all:
    They only meant to run away!

14.   And if an entry on them had been made,[3]
    From the outlying parts of it,[4] and then,

---

1. Original: From above you and from below you.

2. The former name of Medina.

3. "By the enemy".   4. The city.

They had been asked to make sedition,
They would have certainly obliged; indeed,
They would not have it much delayed!

15.   And surely they had made a pledge,
With God before:
That they would not turn back; and pledges
With Allah must be answered for.

16.   Say: "Flight is not to do you any good,
If it is flight from death or slaughter;
And even then, you shall not be allowed,
But for a little while, to gaily loiter!"

17.   Say: "Who is it that will,
Screen you from God, if it's His Will,
To bring upon you evil,
Or if He opts to show you Mercy?
Nay, they shall find, apart from Allah, none,
To help them or to be their patron.

18.   Of the impeding elements[1] among you,
God has the fullest Ken,
And of the other people who,
Say unto their own brethren:
"Come to our side", also of they,
Who seldom join the fray;

19.   Covetous of you are they only: thus
When there is danger, you shall see them eyeing
You up, with rolling eyes, like one who faints,

---

1. Those who hinder others from fighting in the cause of God.

From fear of dying!
But when the fear is past and nought is wrong,
They shall assail you with a cutting tongue,
Covetous of the better in the spoil!
No faith have these, and, therefore, God shall bring
Their deeds to be of no avail;
And that's for God an easy thing.

20.   They thought that the Confederates would never
Withdraw; and certainly if now the legions,
Of the Confederates should come again,
They'd fain be in the desert with the Bedouins,
Asking for news concerning you from there!
And even if they did stay in your midst,
They'd surely fight the least.

21.   In the person of God's Apostle,
There is indeed the finest model,
For all who look forward to God,
And to the Final Day, and mention
Allah most often.

22.   When the faithful saw the Confederates,
They said: "This is what God and His Apostle
Promised us, and what God and His Apostle
Did speak, has come to realization";
And this only increased them in
Faith and submission.

23.   Amongst believers you have men
Who are most truthful to the vow
They have with Allah taken:
Of them some have fulfilled their vow,

And there are others who await it[1] now,
And have not e're been shaken;[2]

24.   So that God may reward the truthful
For truthfulness, and sternly punish
The hypocrites, if it will be His Wish,
Or turn to them in Mercy, for:
God's Oft-Forgiving, Merciful.

25.   And it was Allah Who drove back,
The unbelievers, in their rage,
And they did not win an advantage;
With God shall not the faithful lack
A thing in any fight;
For God's the Strong, the Full of Might.

26.   And those among the People of the Book,[3]
Who had extended help to them,[4] He took,
Down from their fortresses, and did such tremors,
Thrust in their hearts, that some with swords you struck,
And some you took as prisoners.[5]

27.   And He did make you heirs unto their land,
Their dwellings and all their belongings,
And to a land on which you never trod;
For God has Might over all things.

28.   O Prophet, say unto your spouses:
"If it be that you love this present life,
And its adornments, come, I will provide,

---

1. "Their fulfilment of the vow."   2. "In their devotion."
3. The Jews.   4. The enemy.   5. Or "captives".

For you, and will then send you off,
In the most handsome manner;

29. "But if you favour Allah and His Messenger,
And the eternal home in the Hereafter,
Then Allah will have certainly prepared,
For well-doers of you, a great reward."

30. O consorts of the Prophet!
Should anyone of you be guilty,
Of an open indecency;
The chastisement for her shall be,
Twice over; and for Allah,
This is an easy matter.

31. But then of you whoever is devoted
To the service of God and His Apostle,
And does what's right and proper,
Her recompense shall We redouble,
And We will have prepared for her,
A sustenance most noble.

32. O consorts of the Prophet,
You are not as the other womenfolk:
If you fear God, then in your talk,
Do not be too complaisant, lest
Men of unwholesome heart, should lust
After you. Utter words, discreet and just;

33. And do stay still inside your houses,
And, when in public, don't,
Make a show of your fineries,
In the way they were wont,

In former Times of Ignorance;
But keep up prayers, pay the poor-rate,
And show complete obedience,
To God and His Apostle: Allah,
Only intends, O Ahl-al-Bait,[1]
To keep away abomination,
From you, and purify you ever,
In purest fashion;

34.   And recollect what is recited,
Unto you in your houses, of
God's Revelations and of Wisdom;
Surely God is the Most Pervasive
Knower, and All-Aware.

35.   Indeed Allah will have prepared
Forgiveness and a rich reward,
For the submitters,[2] men and women,
For faithful men and women,
For the devoted men and women,
For the truth-speaking men and women,
For patient men and women,
For humble men and women,
For those who give in charity,
Both men and women,
For those who fast, both men and women,
For those who guard their chastity,
Both men and women,

---

1. Meaning: "Members of the Household": This, according to most commentators, includes the Holy Prophet's wives, his daughter Fatima, his son-in-law
Ali and his grandsons Hassan and Hussain.
2. Or "Muslims".

And for all men and women who
Remember God most often.

36.　And it is not for the believers,
Men or women, to have an option,
In a matter, when God and His Apostle,
Have on it made their own decision;
And those who disobey,
Allah and His Apostle, shall
Into manifest error stray.

37.　Behold, you did say to the one who had
Received God's grace, whom you did also favour:[1]
"Retain your wife and be god-fearing", while
You did hide in your heart what Allah
Would later bring to light;
And you feared men, whereas a greater right,
Has Allah to be feared! Then after Zaid,
His union with her duly dissolved,
Did We ordain that you should gain her hand,
For marriage, that it may no longer be,
A fault in the believers to betroth
The wives of their adopted sons, and only
After they have dissolved their ties in truth;[2]
Certainly God's command:
Must be performed, unquestioned.

38.　In the Prophet there is no blame,

1. This is Zaid son of Haritha, among the first to accept Islam, a slave, freed by
the Holy Prophet who loved him as a son and gave him in marriage his own
cousin Zainab; the marriage, however, turned out to be an unhappy one.

2. That is: after the *Iddat*, or period of waiting after divorce, was duly
completed.

In what has God for him ordained,
Such was the way of God with those
Who have before you gone; for God's
Command is a decree determined;

39.   Those who conveyed the messages
Of Allah, and feared Him, and none
Feared they but God the One;
God's certainly Sufficient
For calling to account.

40.   Nay! Mohammad is not the father
Of any of your men,
He is God's Messenger,
And the Seal of the Prophets,
And, of all things, God has full Ken.

41.   O you believers, do remember,
Allah most often,

42.   And celebrate His praise,
Morning and even;

43.   He it is Who sends blessings on you, as
Do His angels, that He may bring you out
Of utter darkness into light,
And He is Merciful,
Unto the faithful.

44.   Their salutation on the Day they meet Him,
Is to be "peace!" indeed,
And He will have prepared for them,
A generous meed.

45.　　O Prophet, We have surely sent you
　　　　To be a witness, and a bearer
　　　　Of tidings glad, and as a warner,

46.　　And one who summons unto Allah,
　　　　By His permission,
　　　　As a Torch of Illumination.

47.　　Give the good news then to believers
　　　　That they shall be the glad receivers,
　　　　Of greatest boons from God;

48.　　Thus never yield to disbelievers,
　　　　Or to the Hypocrites, and disregard,
　　　　Their insolence; but put your trust in God,
　　　　For only God is your Sufficient Guard.

49.　　O you believers, when you marry,
　　　　Faithful women, and then divorce them,
　　　　Before you touch them, there shall be,
　　　　No iddat in their case to reckon,
　　　　But you should give them some provision,
　　　　And gracefully release them.

50.　　O Prophet, lawful to you have We made,
　　　　Your wives whose dowers you have duly paid,
　　　　And those, under your hand, out of the slaves
　　　　Whom Allah granted you as captives;
　　　　And the daughters of your paternal uncles,
　　　　Daughters of your maternal uncles,
　　　　Daughters of your paternal aunts,
　　　　Daughters of your maternal aunts,

Who fled with you;[1] and any faithful woman,
Who allocates her soul unto the Prophet,
If the Prophet would marry her; this privilege,
Is purely yours, not for the men of faith at large;
For them We do know what We have assigned,
As to their wives, and bondswomen that they possess,
That you may in this matter not be blamed,
For God is Oft-Forgiving, Full of Kindness.

51.   You may put off whome'er you will,[2]
And may receive whome'er you please,
And you may bring back one of those,
Whom you had set aside; in these
Decisions, you shall not be blamed;
Thus will it be more proper to provide
Them with what they desire, and to avoid
Their grief and satisfy them with whatever,
You may to each of them accord; and Allah
Knows what is in your hearts; for God is ever
Knowing and Most-Forbearing.

52.   Hereafter you are not permitted
To marry other women, nor to change
Your present wives for others, though
Their beauty be to hearts a challenge,
Captives and bondswomen[3] excepting;
And God is Watchful over everything.

---

1. "To Medina".   2. This verse, according to most interpreters, allows the
Prophet to do justice, as he best judges, in his personal relations with his wives
and handmaidens, almost all of whom were married to him, after the estab-
lishment of his Prophetic office, for other considerations than conjugal ones.

3. Original: "Those that thy right hand may possess."

53.   Believers, enter not the Prophet's quarters,
        Unless permission has to you been given,
        To have a meal, and not ahead of time,
        For the service; but you may enter when
        You are invited, then when you have taken
        Your meal, disperse without engaging in
        Familiar talks: this gives the Prophet trouble,
        And he would be too shy to bid farewell;
        But Allah is not shy to say the truth!
        And when you ask the ladies for a certain
        Thing you need, ask them from behind a curtain;
        This will surely be purer, both
        For your own hearts and theirs;
        Never ought you to be a source of trouble
        Unto Allah's Apostle,
        Nor should you ever, after him,
        Marry his widows: for this surely would,
        Be grievous in the sight of God.

54.   Whether you hide a thing or bring,
        It to the light, God has full Knowledge
        Of everything.

55.   There shall be nothing sinful if
        They[1] be unveiled before their fathers,
        Before their sons, before their brothers,
        Their brothers' sons, their sisters' sons,
        Their woman-friends or those who are
        In their possessions;
        Yet be god-fearing, ladies,
        Certainly God everything Sees.

---

1. The spouses.

56. Indeed God and His angles send
     Blessings upon the Prophet, thus,
     O you believers, also bless him,
     And salute him in perfect peace.

57. Verily, people who affront,
     God and His Messenger,
     The curse of God is on them in
     This world and the Hereafter,
     And He will have prepared for them
     A most disgraceful torture.

58. And those who shall affront,
     Believing men and women,
     For nothing they have done,
     Certainly will they bear the burden
     Of slanderous imputation,
     And an explicit sin.

59. O Prophet, tell your wives and daughters,
     And to the spouses of the faithful,
     That they should let their *Jalaabeeb*,[1]
     Lower and closer fall;
     This is more suitable than being spotted;
     This way they shall not be molested;
     And God is Oft-Forgiving, Merciful.

60. But surely if the Hypocrites,
     And men of evil, tainted hearts,

---

1. This is the plural form of *Julbab* or *Jilbab* meaning: a veil, garment, over
   -garment, a long gown, or a cloak covering the neck and bosom.

And rabble-rousers of the Town,[1]
Will not be ceasing, of their own,
Certainly shall We raise
You 'gainst them, then their days
Of staying in it, as your neighbours,
Are to be numbered;

61.　A curse shall they have on them, and wherever,
They're found, they shall be seized and slaughtered.

62.　Such was the Way of God with those
Who have before them passed,
And you shall find no changes in
The Way of Allah in the least.

63.　Men question you about the Hour of Doom,[2]
Tell them: "Its knowledge is with God alone":
And what on earth could make you comprehend,
That the Hour, may not be nigh at hand?!

64.　Allah indeed has laid a curse
On every disbeliever,
And has got ready for him
The Blazing Fire,

65.　Therein they shall abide for ever,
No Patron will they find, nor helper;

66.　On the Day when their faces,
Shall be rolled in the Fire,

---

1. Original: Al-Madina, the city.

2. Original: The Hour.

They will lament: "Oh, woe to us,
Would that we had obeyed,
Allah, and if we only did
Obey His Messenger!"

67. They'll also say: "Our Lord! Indeed we followed
Our leaders and our chiefs, and it was they
Who did lead us away,
From the right Road!

68. "O Lord, give them a double chastisement,
And lay a curse on them most vehement!"

69. Believers! Be not like the people,
Who slandered and affronted Moses,
But God did clear him of the calumnies,
They spoke: he was with God, a man of Scruple.

70. Believers! Be god-fearing, and do utter
What's straight and proper;

71. That He may for you bless your doings,
And overlook your sins;
And he who follows God and His Apostle,
Shall win the greatest wins.

72. We did offer the Trust unto the Heavens,
Unto the Earth, and to the Mountains,
But they refused to bear the burden,
Being afraid from it, and man,
Undertook it! Indeed, he's been
Very unjust, extremely foolish!

73. Therefore will God certainly punish
The Hypocrites, both men and women,
And the polytheists, both men and women;
And He will mercifully turn to
The faithful men and faithful women,
For God is Oft-Forgiving, Merciful.

SURA 34
SHEBA
(SABAA) [1]

In the Name of God, the Beneficent, the Merciful

1.   Praise be to God, to Whom belongs,
Everything in the Heavens,
And what the Earth contains,
And praise is also His
In the Hereafter, for He is,
The All-Informed, All-Wise.

2.   He knows what goes into the earth, and what
Proceeds from it, and what is to descend,
From heaven, and what will to it ascend;
He is the Merciful, the One Who Pardons.

3.   The unbelievers say: "The Hour of Doom
Shall ne'er upon us come!"
Say: "surely, by my Lord,
Knower of the Unknown,
It will upon you come for certain;
Nothing the weight of the minutest mote,
Upon the earth or in the heaven
Is ever from Him hidden;
Neither is there anything less, or aught
Greater than this, which is not there,
In a most lucid Register;

4.   "That He may recompense,

---

1. This is the city of Sheba, in Yemen, said to have been three days' journey from the city of San'a.

702

The folks who did believe,
And did good works: Forgiveness,
And a provision generous,
Shall they receive.

5.   And for the people who were striving,
Against Our revelations,
There shall certainly be a series,
Of painful, wrathful retributions.

6.   And those who have been given Knowledge see,
That what has been to you sent down,
From your Lord, is the very Truth,
And that it surely guides unto the Path,
Of the All-Mighty, the Most-Praised One.

7.   The unbelievers say in ridicule:
"Shall we show you a man[1] who will foretell
That when you will be in disintegration,
As scattered specks of dust, you shall be then
Raised in a New Creation?!

8.   "Is he inventing lies concerning God,
Or has some Jinn inside him made him mad?"
But nay! Those only who have not believed
In the next world, will surely have incurred
The Chastisement, for they have badly erred!

9.   Have they not ever pondered on
The past and future of the Heaven,
And of the Earth? Were it Our pleasure,

---

1. The Holy Prophet.

We would allow them to be swallowed
Up by the earth, or let a parted measure,
From the Sky fall on them! Herein indeed,
There is a Sign for every servant,
Who opts to be repentant.

10.   Of old did We bestow on David,
Gifts, of Our special boons:
"O you mountains and birds,
Echo his praising words";
And We did make the iron in his hand,
Easy to bend:

11.   "Make coats of mail and set the linking rings,
In place; but do what's righteous in all things,
For I am Watching all your doings."

12.   To Solomon did We subdue the wind:
A month's journey it scudded in the morning,
And a month's journey in the evening;
We also made to flow for him a fountain
Of copper molten;
And of the Jinns, by the Command,
Of his own Lord, were some who worked,
In his presence; should any of them veer
Away from Our command, We made him,
Taste of the torment of Sa'eer[1] .

13.   They for him made whate'er he fancied:
Grand buildings, images and basins,
As large as water tanks and built-in cauldrons;

---

1. The blazing Fire.

"Give thanks, by your own deeds, O Sons of David!"
But, of My servants, those who do,
Give thanks, are very few!

14.   Yet, when We had his death decreed,
        Nothing showed them that he had died,
        But a Worm of the earth that gnawed his staff!
        And the Jinns came to know, when he fell off,
        That if they knew a thing of the Unseen,
        They would have not continued,
        In the wretched torment of servitude.[1]

15.   In former times there was a Sign,
        For folks of Sheba in their homeland:
        They had been situated 'tween
        Bountiful paradises twain,
        One on the left, and one on the right hand:
        "Eat of your Lord's provision,
        And give Him thanks; pleasant is the abode,
        And Most-Benignant is the Lord!

16.   Lo! They were heedless; so upon them,
        We did unloose the flood of 'Arim,[2]
        And We replaced their paradises twain,
        With *gardens* bearing only bitter fruit,
        Some tamarisks and fewer plants of lote!

17.   Such was Our retribution on them,

---

1. Presumably the Jinns looked upon their work as a Penalty.

2. "Dams or Embankments"; it may have been a proper noun, or may simply
   mean the great earth-works lined with stone, which formed the ancient
   Ma'arib dam, of which traces still exist in Yemen.

For their ingratitude;
Do We any but the ungrateful
In punishment include?

18.   We had already placed:
Between them[1] and the cities We had blessed,[2]
Prominent habitations,
And stages for their journeys,
Set up in due proportions:
"Do travel through these ways,
In safety, nights and days."

19.   But they still craved: "Our Lord, do place,
Longer distances 'tween our journey-stations[3] ;"
They only wronged themselves when they thus sinned;
Therefore We made their fate a legend,
And let them be dispersed among the nations;
Truly in this are Signs for every soul
That is patient and grateful.

20.   Certainly in their case, Iblees,[4]
Did justify his case!
For they became his followers,
All but a group of true believers;

21.   Yet he did not on them have any power:
Only We meant to set aside whoever
Had faith in the Hereafter, and make known,

---

1. "The people of Sheba" in Araby Blest (Arabia Felix).

2. The prosperous cities in Mesopotamian Kingdoms, and in Syria and Egypt.

3. "Fewer journey-stages" that only the people of Sheba could monopolize.

4. Satan, the Devil.

Those who of it had doubts; your Lord alone,
Is of all things the Keen Observer.

22.   Say: "call upon those idols¹ whom you fancy,
Instead of Allah: They do not control a feather,
In the heavens and on the earth,
Neither have they a share in either,
Nor has He from among them any helper.

23.   And intercession has no application,
Before Him, save for the person for whom,
He has given permission;
And not before their hearts have been relieved,
From terror,² shall they say: "What says your Lord?"
And they³ shall say: the very Truth,
For He is the Most High, the Great indeed.

24.   Say: "Who supplies you with provisions,
Out of the heavens and the earth?"
Say: "Yea, it's God! Then it is certain
That We and you could not be both,
Upon the guided Way,
Surely one group is most astray!"

25.   Say: "You shall not be questioned of our sins,
Neither shall we be questioned of your doings."

26.   Say: "We'll be brought together by our Lord,
And then He will in justice judge between

---

1. Any object of worship whether men as Lord, Saints, Prophets, or things such
   as: Self, Money or Power.

2. "Upon the Day of Judgment".   3. Apparently "the angels".

Us, for he is the Knowing Judge Most Keen."

27.   Say: "Show me those you have united
With Him as partners!
Nay! He is God the One,
The Mighty, the All-Wise.

28.   And We have sent you forth,
Unto the whole mankind,
To give them tidings glad,
And warn and reprimand,
Nevertheless most people,
This do not understand.

29.   And they say: "If you speak the truth,
When will this Promise,[1]
E'er come to pass?"

30.   Say: "You have the appointment of a Day,
Which, even for a single hour,
You shall not hasten or delay!"

31.   And those who disbelieve proclaim:
"Never are we to be believers in,
This scripture,[2] nor in those that came,
Before it!" Only if you could behold,
When the wicked are set before their Lord:
Throwing back, on each other, words of blame!
The weak shall say to the arrogant leaders:
"But for you, we had been believers".

---

1. Or "the Threat".   2. The Quran, the Reading.

32.   The arrogant will answer the oppressed:
"What! Was it we who kept you from
Guidance when it had to you come?!
Nay, you yourselves transgressed."

33.   And still the weak hit back and say:
"Nay! It was your intrigues by night and day,
That made us to deny belief in God,
And to set up for Him some counterparts!"
And when they see the Chastisement, they would,
Repent in their regretful hearts!
Then we'll put yokes and fetters
Upon the necks of disbelievers;
Shall they not be rewarded
For what they did?

34.   And never have We sent a Warner,
To any town whose rich and mighty men,
Did not declare: "In sooth, we'll never
Believe your apostolic mission!"

35.   They always say: "We are the more abundant,
In wealth and sons; for us there is no torment!"

36.   Say: "Surely does my Lord enlarge,
And straiten His provision,
To whom He pleases, but most men,
Do not this e'er acknowledge."

37.   Neither your riches, nor your children,
Shall bring you nearer Us in station,
But they who do believe and do what's right,
Shall have rewards that will be multiplied,

For their good deeds, and shall, in peace, reside,
Each in a lofty Mansion.[1]

38.   But those who try to undermine Our Signs,
Shall be consigned to painful Retribution.

39.   Say: "My Lord surely amplifies or trims,
Provisions to His creatures as He wills,
And whatsoever you may spend in alms,
He, in His recompense, redoubles,
For He's the Best Provider of provisions.

40.   And on the Day He brings them all together,
He will then ask the angels:
"Was it you that these people
Used to worship as idols?"

41.   "Glory be unto you", they answer,
"It's You Who is our Lord and Patron,
Not these! Nay, certainly they were,
Worshippers of the Jinn,[2]
It was in them indeed,
That most of them believed."

42.   Upon that Day you'll have no power,
Either to help or harm each other,
And to the wrong-doers we'll say:
"Do taste the Torment of the Fire,
You used to call a lie."

---

1. Or "pavilions in Paradise".

2. The Jinns also represent "forces of evil" and "evil leaders among men".

43.   Now when Our lucid verses are rehearsed,
      Unto them, they suggest:
      "This person's sole intention is to swerve,
      You from what your forefathers used to serve!"
      And they have also charged:
      "Nothing is this[1] but falsehood forged."
      And, of the Truth, after it came to them,
      The disbelievers urged:
      "Nothing is this but magic manifest!"

44.   No scriptures have We given them to learn,
      Nor sent to them, before you, one to warn;

45.   Peoples before them were rejecters;[2]
      And these have not received a tenth,
      Of what We had bestowed on those!
      Yet when they did reject My messengers,
      Ah! How did I, of them, dispose!

46.   Say: "One thing unto you do I suggest:
      Do rise up once for Allah's sake, in pairs,
      Or singly,[3] and reflect within yourselves,
      That your fellow-townsman[4] is not possessed:
      A warner only is he, to you sent,
      Before a dreadful Torment."

47.   Say: "I demand of you no wages,
      Do keep them for yourselves; my wages

---

1. The Quran.   2. "Of the Truth".

3. Careful and heart-felt reflection is, preferably alone, or a teacher is necessary
   to appraise the higher Truths; a crowd mentality is not the best for such
   perceptions.   4. The Holy Prophet.

Come from Allah alone;
And He is Witness to all things;"

48.   Say: "Verily the One Who brings,
Forth all truth is my Lord:
The All-Knower of the Unknown."

49.   Say: "Truth is come, and Falsehood,
Shall vanish, and it would
Not come back any more;"

50.   Say: "If I err, to my own loss,
Shall I be erring, but if I,
Follow the right direction, it is only
Because of what My Lord reveals to me;
For He's the Hearer, Ever-Nigh."

51.   If only you could see them when they tremble,
When no escape is possible,
And they are taken from a place
Very accessible!

52.   And they shall say: "We now in Him believe!"
But how, when something is so out of reach,
Could they now it receive?!

53.   Whereas they had already disbelieved,
The Faith, and when they all had been,
At a position very far indeed,[1]
They used to sneer at the Unseen!

---

1. The Earth.

54.　And so between them and what they desire,
　　　Is placed a barrier, as brought about,
　　　Against the likes of them before:
　　　They, too, were in disturbing doubt.

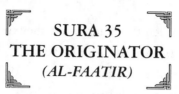

SURA 35
THE ORIGINATOR
(AL-FAATIR)

In the Name of God, the beneficent, the Merciful

1. Praise be to God the One, the Maker
   And the Originator of the heavens,
   And of the earth, Who made the angels
   As messengers with pairs of wings,
   Two, three, and four; He makes additions,
   To the Creation as He Wills;
   Power has Allah for all things.

2. What God, out of His Mercy, lays
   Open for man, none could withhold,
   And what He does withhold, no others,
   Could grant thereafter; and, behold!
   He's the All-Mighty, the All-Wise.

3. O Men! Do bear in mind God's favour,
   Unto you; is there some creator,
   Other than Allah, Who provides you,
   With gifts of heaven and the earth?
   There is no God but He: whence are you then,
   Diverted from the Truth!

4. And do they treat you as a liar!
   Well, other messengers were labelled,
   As impostors before you, but
   All things shall be to God recalled.

5. O Men! God's promise is most surely true,
   Therefore let not this worldly life deceive you,

Neither allow the Arch-Deceiver,
To be deceiving you in Allah.[1]

6. Certainly Satan is your enemy,
    Thus treat him as an enemy!
    He only calls his party to adhere
    To him that they may also be
    Inmates of the Sa'eer![2]

7. For those who disbelieve, there is
    A dreadful punishment,
    And for believers who do good,
    Pardon and rich repayment.

8. What! Are there men whose evil deeds,
    Are so alluring in their eyes,
    That they consider them as good!
    But Allah leaves in error whom He pleases,
    And whom He chooses, He will guide.
    Thus do not spend your soul for them in sighs:
    For God is Cognizant of all their doings.

9. And God it is Who sends the winds,
    Which raise the clouds aloft, and then,
    We drive them on to the dead lands,
    And thus revive the earth,
    After its death:
    So is to be the Bringing Forth![3]

---

1. Respecting God.

2. The Blazing Fire.

3. The Resurrection.

10.   If you are seeking might and glory,
All might and glory is in Allah only,
The goodly words to Him ascend,
And righteous doings help its upward flight,
But a chastisement grievous, shall await,
Those who have always vice and evil planned,
Yet plans of such, shall end in nought.

11.   God has created you from dust, then from
Some germ of life, and then He made you pairs,
Of males and females; yet no woman bears,
Or does bring forth, without His knowledge;
No aged man is granted length of days,
Nor is a part diminished from one's age,
But is already in a Book,
All this God does truly with ease.

12.   Nor are two seas[1] ever alike:
The one is sweet and fresh and good to drink,
The other salty, pungent, yet you get,
Fresh meat from both, and ornaments to deck
Yourselves; and you see ships and smacks,
Ploughing the waves that you may seek,
Of His Bounty, and may give thanks!

13.   The Night He makes merge into Daylight,
And wraps the Daylight by the Night,
He has subdued[2] the Sun and Moon,
Each runs a course, ordained, in tune;
Such is Allah your Lord, His is the Kingdom,

---

1. Great masses of fresh water including inland lakes, rivers, etc.
2. "To His laws".

And those you call upon, instead of Him,
Do not control a tiny atom!

14.   When you upon them call,
They will not hear your prayer;
And even if they heard, they could
Never your invocation answer!
And on the Day of Resurrection,
They shall disown your venture
Of taking them into Association;[1]
And none, except the All-Aware,
Could bring you information.[2]

15.   O humankind, you are but paupers
In need of God; and He,
Is God the One, the Needless,
But of all praise, the Worthy.

16.   Were it His will, you would,
Be an obliteration,
And He would bring about,
A new creation!

17.   Nor will this be for God,
A mighty operation!

18.   No burdened[3] soul shall bear the burden,
Of the others, and if a soul, heavily laden,
Cries out for help, even his near of kin
Won't come along to ease his load of sin;

---

1. "With God".   2. "Concerning what you've done."
3. Sinful.

You[1] shall but warn the people
Who fear their Lord unseen,
And regularly do their prayer;
And those who have been purely clean,
Have purified themselves for their own good,
For the final returning is to God.

19.   Alike are not the blind,
And people with keen sight,

20.   Neither darkness and light,

21.   Nor the shade and the heat;

22.   Nor are the living and the dead;
Allah will certainly make whom,
He pleases hearken, but you cannot make
Hearers out of men in their tomb;

23.   For you are only charged with warnings,

24.   Verily We have sent you with,
The Truth: a bearer of good tidings,
And as a warner, for there never,
Was a nation unvisited,
By its own warner.

25.   And if they treat you as a liar,
So did the folks before them treat
Their own apostles when they came,
To them with clearest Signs and brought

---

1. The Holy Prophet.

Them scriptures and the lucid Book.[1]

26.   And in the end I struck
Those who rejected Faith,
And devastating was My wrath!

27.   Do you not see that God sends down
Rainwater from the heavens;
And that with it, We then produce,
The fruits of varied hues,
And that there are, upon the mountains,
All kinds of streaks: white track, red track,
Other colours, and that of raven black?

28.   And men and beasts and cattle are likewise,
Of various hues;
But of His creatures only those
Who have the knowledge are god-fearing;
Indeed God is All-Mighty, Oft-Forgiving!

29.   Those who rehearse the Book of Allah
And do attend to their *salaat*,[2]
And out of what We have unto them given,
Give out in alms, openly or in secret,
Could certainly hope for a trade
That shall not ever fade!

30.   For He will pay them their full need,
Nay, He will give them even more,
Out of His Grace, for He's indeed,

---

1. The Torah or the Evangel, or the Book of God in the general sense.

2. Regular prayers.

Oft-Forgiving, Most Ready for
Divine Appreciation.

31.　　And what We have by Inspiration,
　　　Sent to you of the Book, that is the truth,
　　　Confirming what has come before,[1]
　　　Certainly, of His creatures, is God both,
　　　The Most Aware and the Seer in depth.

32.　　And finally We have given the Book
　　　As heritage to such, as We have chosen,
　　　Among Our servants, but of them there are
　　　Some who injure their souls; some other men,
　　　Among them keep unto a middle course,
　　　But there are some who do, by God's permission,
　　　Excel in deeds of goodness:
　　　This is indeed His highest bliss;

33.　　Into Gardens of Eden shall they enter
　　　They shall be decked therein,
　　　With golden bracelets, and with pearls,
　　　And garments silken,

34.　　And this is what they utter:
　　　"Praise be to God Who has removed,
　　　From us all sorrow, for Our Lord,
　　　Is Forgiving, Ready to Offer,
　　　Divine Appreciation;

35.　　"Who, by His Grace, has lodged us in
　　　An everlasting Mansion,

---

1. The previous scriptures.

Wherein no toil shall ever reach us,
Neither weariness touch us.

36.　　But for the disbelievers,
There is the Fire of Hell; it does not end,
For them, so they should die, nor shall
The Chastisement be to them lightened;
Thus do We retribution deal
On every thankless infidel.

37.　　And they therein shall cry for help and howl:
"Oh pray, Our Lord, take us out of this hell!
Righteousness will we work, and naught
Of what we ever wrought!"
"Did We prolong your days not long enough,
So that whoever might be warned therein,[1]
Would mind the warning, and We did send off
A warner unto you! Thus taste and taste,[2]
No helping hand is lent to the unjust!

38.　　Truly God knows the Hidden, both
Of the heavens and of the earth;
Surely Aware is He of what is hidden,
Inside the breasts of men.

39.　　He it is Who appointed you[3] as His
Vicegerents in the earth,
Therefore the unbelievers' lack of faith,
Shall only work against themselves,
And for the unbelievers, their unfaith,

---

1. In the world.　　　2. "The torment".

3. Mankind.

Gains, with their Lord, nothing but wrath[1] :
The unbelief of unbelievers
Is only an addition,
Unto their own perdition!

40.   Say: "Look upon those gods and idols,
You call upon, instead of God the One!
Show me what portion of the earth has been,
By them created? Or have they a share in[2]
The heavens? Or did We give to them[3] ever,
A book from which they have such sanctions?
Nay, the wrong-doers promise one another,
Nothing but mutual deceptions.

41.   Surely it's God Who does hold fast,
The heavens and the earth that they,
Pass not away; were they to pass away,
None could, after Him, hold them fast,
Surely He is Forbearing and Forgiving.

42.   They used to swear their strongest oaths by God,
That if a warner to them came, they would,
Certainly yield to Guidance more
Than any nation in the world;
But when a Warner[4] did unto them come,
They only turned away in hatred,

43.   And acted proudly in the land,

---

1. Also: disgust, hatred.

2. "The creation of".

3. The idol-worshippers and polytheists.

4. The Holy Prophet.

And every plan of evil planned!
But evil plans only recoil,
Upon their authors; thus what end,
Are they awaiting, but the fates,
That overtook the ancients?
No changes shall you ever find in
The ways of God, yea, you shall find,
In God's Way, no diversion!

44. Have they not ever journeyed in the land,
To see what was the final end,
Of those who lived before them: far,
Greater than these, in power?
Naught is there in the heavens,
Or on the earth that might,
Escape God's Power, for He is
The Ever-Knowing Lord of Might

45. If God were to chastise mankind,
According to what they deserve,
No living creature would He leave
Upon its[1] back, alive;
But for a stated term, He gives them respite,
So when their Hour will arrive,
God will surely have all his creatures,
In His Keen Sight.

---

1. "The Earth's".

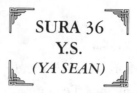

SURA 36
Y.S.
(YA SEAN)

In the Name of God, the Beneficent, the Merciful

1.   Ya Sean.

2.   By the Wise Reading,[1]

3.   You are a messenger in truth,

4.   Upon the Right Direction treading,

5.   Together with the revelation
Of the Mighty, the Full of Ruth;

6.   That you may warn a nation,
Whose fathers were not ever warned,
And thus in heedlessness remained.

7.   Most of them have already proved the truth
Of the Sentence,[2] and they do not embrace the Faith;

8.   Certainly We have put their necks in chains,[3]
Reaching up to the chins,
Therefore they cannot bow their heads!

---

1. The Quran.

2. Or "God's Word" already pronounced: "I shall certainly fill Hell with you
(Satan) and all those who follow you" (S. 38, v. 85 and other places).

3. The result of disbelievers' wilful disobedience is now described in a series of
metaphors, and results and punishments are attributed to God.

9. And We have set up bars and barriers,
   Before them and behind them, and have We,
   Shrouded them further in a veil,
   That will not let them see!

10. It is the same unto them whether,
    You warn them or you warn them not,
    They will not be believers ever.

11. Indeed you'll only warn the man
    Who heeds the Admonition,
    And has a fear of Al-Rahmaan[1] ;
    Do cheer such people then,
    With the tidings of Pardon,
    And a rich retribution.

12. We it is Who revive the dead, and We,
    Write down the works that they before them send,
    And all the traces which they leave behind;
    For everything do We record,
    In a Most Lucid Code.[2]

13. And cite to them a parable:
    There was a town unto whose people,
    Were sent apostles:

14. Behold, We sent unto them two,
    But they denied them as impostors,
    So with a third We strengthened them,

---

1. The Most Merciful.

2. Original: "in the clear prototype", that is, the Preserved Table, on which all
   the actions of mankind are written down.

They said: "We're truly Messengers[1] ."

15. They said: "Indeed, you're only men
Just like ourselves, and Al-Rahman,
Has sent down nothing;
You're simply lying!"

16. They said: "It is our Lord who has full ken,
That we are sent to you upon a Mission,

17. "And our assignment only
Is to convey it plainly."

18. They said: "In fact we augur ill from you,
Therefore, if you will not desist, we will
Have you stoned, or a grievous punishment,
Will upon you from us befall!"

19. They said: "Only from your own selves,
Will come your augury of ill;
Lo! You will not be warned!
Nay, you're the sort of people
Who are in evil drowned[2] !

20. Then from the fringes of the town,
Came a man[3] in a haste to plead:
"O You my people,[4] do obey

---

1. "Of God."   2. Or "the unbridled transgressors".

3. He is perhaps an enlightened, resigned man of God who knows that when
God's messengers declare a people as "drowned in evil and transgression",
then God's Scourge would become imminent.

4. The identity of the man, the people or the town is irrelevant: this is a parable

These messengers indeed!

21. "Follow the men who do not ask
Of you any reward,
And who are rightly guided,

22. "And what reason have I if I should not
Worship the One Who brought me into being,
And unto Him you'll be returning?

23. "Should I be taking other gods beside Him,
Whose intercession, if the God of Mercy[1]
Be willing to afflict me, would avail
Nothing, nor ever could deliver me!

24. "Indeed I will have fallen,
Into the clearest Error then;

25. "Indeed in your true Lord have I believed,
Thus hear me and pay heed."

26. Thereafter[2] when he was addressed:
"Do enter into Paradise!"
He sighed and said: "Would that my people knew,

27. "For what my Lord's Pardon and Grace
Has been on me bestowed, and why
I was given an honoured Place!"

---

about the oft-repeated story of mankind to whom many a God's messenger
has been sent.

1. Al-Rahmaan, the Merciful.

2. "After his death"; perhaps it is implied that this godly and righteous man
suffered martyrdom at the hands of the wicked disbelievers.

28. And after him, We did not send a host
    Against his people out of heaven,
    Nor was it needful for Us to come down!

29. Nay! There was but a single blast,[1]
    And lo! They were for ever lost!

30. Woe to My creatures! There has never,
    Come unto them a messenger,
    But they received him only with,
    Ridicule and humiliation.

31. See they not how many a generation,[2]
    We have destroyed before them, who will never
    To them return?

32. But all of them, gathered together,
    Will be brought back to Us in turn.

33. The very Earth when it is dead,
    Should be to them a Sign:
    We give it life again, and from it,
    We do bring forth the grain;
    Which they shall use for food;

34. And We have placed upon it gardens
    Of palms and grapes; and We made fountains
    And springs, to flow forth in it,

35. That they thereof, eat of the fruit,

---

1. Or "a Shout".

2. "Including their own former generations.

Which was not made by their own works;
Should they not then give thanks?

36.   Glory be to the One,
Who did create in pairs,
Everything that the Earth produces,
Of their own humankind, and others:
Things and beings beyond their ken!

37.   Another Sign to them may be the Night,
When We withdraw from it the Day,
Lo! They'll be in the dark outright!

38.   And the Sun hastens on an orb
Appointed for it; that's the measure
Fixed by the Mighty, the All-Knower;

39.   As for the Moon, We have for it ordained
Stations, until it wanes, and in the end,
Is like a palm-branch, withered, thinned.

40.   It is not given to the Sun
To overtake the Moon,
Nor does the Night outstrip the Day:
Each does in its own orbit sway.

41.   Another Sign to them is that We carried,
Their offspring in the fully-laden Ark,

42.   And that We made for them the like of it,
Upon which they embark;

43.   And We can drown them, if We please,

And then there shall be none to ease
Their plight, nor will they ever be
Rescued by any,

44.   Unless through Our Own Mercy,
And that they haply entertain
Themselves for just a time!

45.   And when they are advised: "Beware of
What's before you and what will be behind,[1]
So that Mercy you may obtain;"

46.   But nay! They turn aside from any Sign,
Of their Lord's Signs, that you may to them bring.

47.   And when it's said to them: "Give alms of what
God has on you bestowed," the unbelievers
Say to the faithful: "Shall we be the feeders
Of those whom God could feed, had he so willed?
In error manifest are you indeed!"

48.   They also say: "If you are truthful,
When will this promise[2] be fulfilled?"

49.   Nothing should they be waiting
For, but a single Blast,
Which will assail them, just
As they will be disputing.

50.   Neither shall they make a bequest,

---

1. Man's doings and their consequences, past and future.

2. Or: Threat of punishment.

Nor will they ever be retreating
To their own families!

51.   And when the Trumpet shall be blown,
Lo! From their tombs unto their Lord,
Shall they be rushing forward,
As if they had been drawn;

52.   "O woe to us!" Shall they now moan,
"Who roused us from our sleeping place?"
"It's what Al-Rahmaan promised" says a voice,
"And to its truth had the apostles sworn."

53.   It will not be more than a single Blast,
When lo! They all will be brought up before Us;

54.   On that Day, not a soul, will, in the least
Suffer any injustice:
You shall be certainly rewarded,
Commensurate with what you did.

55.   This Day the residents of Paradise,
Will be absorbed in their own joys of Bliss,

56.   Reclining, each on a lofty divan,
Together with his spouse,
In shades that please,

57.   Therein shall they have fruits divine
And whatsoever they desire,

58.   And Peace[1] shall be the word,

---

1. After describing the various, perhaps symbolic, blessings of Paradise, it is

From a Merciful Lord!

59.   "But separated shall you be this Day,
        O you, guilty of sins!

60.   "Did I not have a covenant with you
        O Adam's sons,
        Not to be serving Satan,
        Who was your open enemy,

61.   "But to worship Me only,
        For this was the Right way;

62.   "But now has he certainly led astray,
        Amongst you legions!
        What! Could you never
        Have used your Reasons!

63.   "This is indeed the very Hell
        Which you were promised!

64.   "Embrace it and endure its heat today,
        Because you did in faithlessness insist!"

65.   Upon that Day we'll set a seal upon
        Their mouths, but make their hands to speak to Us,
        And let their feet be bearing witness,
        Of everything they've done.

66.   If it had been Our Will, We would,
        Have surely blotted out their eyes,

---

summed up in a single word: *salaam.*

732

And let them race upon some path;
But how would they be vision-wise?[1]

67.   And if We pleased, We would transform
Them as they stand, then they would neither
Be able to go onward or return.[2]

68.   We cause to be reversed in nature,[3]
Any person whose days We lengthen,
Do they not ever on this ponder?

69.   We did not tutor him in poetry,
Nor would it for him have been fitting;
And this[4] is naught but a Reminder,
And a Reading[5] enlightening,

70.   That it may give a warning to the person,
Who is really alive,[6]
And that just sentence[7] could be passed against
People who disbelieve.

71.   Do they not even see the cattle,
That We, among the things, Our hands,
Have fashioned, did for them create,
Which are completely in their hands?

---

1. If they had no sight or intelligence, man's relative free-will and the power of choice would become irrelevant.

2. That is: either in physical form, as trees, or in spiritual qualities as the angels, when there would be no possibility of human-like progress.

3. That is: stooping through age and being reduced to an abject state of constitution.   4. The Quran.   5. Original: a quran.

6. "Not spiritually dead!"   7. Original: The Word.

72. Tamed have We made them for them,
    On some they ride, and some they eat,

73. And many other uses for them,
    In them are found, and even drinks,
    They get from them, will they not then
    Give any thanks?!

74. Nay, they have set up other gods,
    Instead of God the One, and hope
    That they may give them help!

75. Although they are unable to provide,
    Them with support of any sort,
    They're always in their presence,
    Like an army on full alert!

76. Therefore let not their statement grieve you,[1]
    We do know what they say and do,
    In secret or in public.

77. Does man not see that We indeed,
    Created him out of a tiny seed!
    Yet lo! He is as ever,
    An open caviller!

78. For Us He makes up some comparison,[2]
    And does forget his own creation,
    That's why he questions: "Who will give
    Life to some bones, decayed and rotten?!"

---

1. The Holy Prophet.

2. Or "strikes out a likeness for Us".

79.   Say: "He shall give them life again,
        Who brought them into being
        For the first time, for He's of all
        Creation, the All-Knowing;

80.   Who even grants you fire from,
        Green trees: when lo, a flame,
        From it you kindle!

81.   Is the One Who has brought about,
        The heavens and the earth, not Able
        To re-create the likes of them?
        Yea! He is the Supreme
        Creator, of Unbounded Skill.

82.   When He intends a thing,
        He only orders it to be,
        And it's already being!

83.   Thus glory be unto Him in Whose hand,
        Is the Kingship of everything,
        And you'll be all to Him returned.

SURA 37
RANGED IN ORDER
(AL-SAAFFAAT)

In the Name of God, the Beneficent, the Merciful

1. By Organized Arrangers,

2. And by Repellers of Infringers,

3. And by Reciting Messengers:[1]

4. One only is your God, in truth,

5. Lord of the Heavens and the Earth,
   And what between them lies,
   And the Lord of the Points of sunrise;

6. We have adorned the lower heaven,
   With the beauty of constellations,

7. Which also guard against all rebel satans:

8. Who cannot to the Highest Council listen,
   For they'll be darted at from all directions,

9. And driven off, then given,
   A lasting retribution;

10. If one, however, does eavesdrop, he will
    Be followed by a flaming missile.

---

1. No translation would do justice to these pithy, meaningful oaths; most commentators, however, believe them to be the names of certain Orders of angels.

11.   Now question their[1] opinion:
        Which was the harder task, their own creation,
        Or other beings We created? Aye,
        We did create them of some sticky clay!

12.   But while you marvel, they just mock,

13.   And when they are reminded,
        No warning do they take;

14.   And when they see a Sign,
        They turn it unto mockery,

15.   And cry: "This is no other than
        Clear sorcery:

16.   "What! When We have been dead,
        And turned to dust and bones,
        Shall we be raised to life,

17.   "Our fathers also, of the olden times?!"

18.   Say: "Yes! you shall, only you will,
        Be held to many shames!

19.   A single cry[2] it is to be,
        And lo! They all begin to see!

20.   "Oh! Woe to us!" They shall then say,
        "This is surely the Judgment-Day!"

---

1. The Meccans'.
2. Or "a Blast".

21.   "Yes! It's indeed the Separation-Day,[1]
       Which you had called a lie;

22.   "Gather together all the wrong-doers,
       And their companions[2] and the idols,
       To which they used to pray,

23.   "Instead of Allah, and show them the way
       Unto the Blazing Hell;

24.   "And let them halt a while,
       To answer one more question:

25.   "What is with you the matter,
       Why aren't you helping one another?"

26.   Nay, on that Day they will,
       Themselves surrender;

27.   And some of them the others will approach,
       Only them to reproach!

28.   They'll say: "you did employ your power,
       Us to deceive."

29.   They answer: "Nay, it was indeed,
       You who did not believe!

30.   "And over you We did not have a hold,
       Oh, no! You were a bunch of sinners bold;

---

1. Or "The Day of Decision," or "The Day of Sorting Out."
2. Or "comrades" meaning "their demons".

31. "And thus the Sentence of our Lord is passed,
    Against us which we'll have to taste;

32. "And if you were by us misled,
    Well! We had also been misled!"

33. Therefore in Punishment shall they,
    Be partners on that Day;

34. Thus do We surely treat the wicked!

35. For when it was to them remarked:
    There is no deity but God, they did
    Puff themselves up with pride,

36. And only countered: "Rot!
    Shall we forsake our gods,
    For the sake of a crazy poet?!"

37. Nay! He has brought the Truth and does confirm,
    The message of God's every prophet.

38. You will certainly taste
    The grievous chastisement.

39. And you are not to be rewarded
    Except for what you did.

40. But Allah's servants,
    The purified, the chosen,

41. Shall have a well-prepared provision,

42. And feast on fruits; and they'll be held
In honour and distinction,

43. Inside delightful Gardens,

44. Reclining face to face upon
Couches and thrones,

45. From the water of Ma'in Fountain, cups
Will be among them handed round,

46. As white as crystal, which delight the lips,
Of the drinkers on end!

47. The drink will not their senses dull,
Nor shall it them befuddle.

48. And with them shall be bashful maidens,
With dreamful eyes of the gazelles,

49. With fair and tender skins,
Like sheltered egg-shells.

50. And some of them will turn,
To others with some questions:

51. One from among them says: "I used to have
An intimate companion,

52. Who often asked: 'Do you really believe in,

53. "Us being brought to judgment when
We're dead and turned to dust and bones?!'"

54.   He says[1] :"Would you like to look down?"

55.   For he had looked and seen him writhing,
        In the midst of the Blazing;

56.   And he now cries: "By God, you[2] nearly did
        Land me in Ruin!

57.   "But for the favour of my Lord,
        I, too would have certainly been
        Among those taken in!

58.   "Now will we never visit any death,

59.   "After the previous death?
        And are we going to be safe
        From any torment?"

60.   This is certainly the achievement,
        Mighty, supreme!

61.   Therefore, let every worker work,
        For the sake of this and its like!

62.   Aren't these delights more welcome
        Than the Tree of Zaqqoom?

63.   We've made it for the wicked people,
        Truly a trying doom:

---

1. "To those around him."

2. Addressing the condemned friend.

64. For it's a tree that comes up,
    From the Hell's Bottom,

65. The produce it brings forth resembles,
    The heads of Devils;

66. And yet they eat from it in volumes,
    And with it fill their wombs;

67. And they will have thereon to drink of some,
    Boiling, hellish amalgam;

68. Then shall they surely be returned,
    To Hell for a repeated round!

69. Surely these people also found
    Their own fathers on the wrong road,

70. Therefore they hastened on and followed
    Their footsteps like the blind.

71. Many a generation went astray,
    Of the ancients, in the same way,

72. Despite the fact that We had sent
    Warners among them.

73. Thus note what was the fateful end,
    Of those who had been warned,

74. Except of votaries of Allah's bond.

75. Noah did call upon Us, and We were,

Most Gracious to respond.

76.   So, from the great calamity,
       Him and his folks, We saved,

77.   And thus We made his progeny
       The people who survived,

78.   And We preserved for him the praise
       Of later generations;

79.   Salutation shall be to Noah,
       Among the nations.[1]

80.   Thus do We recompense,
       The men of righteous actions

81.   He was indeed a servant,
       Faithfully to Us bound;

82.   Whereas the rest We drowned.

83.   And Abraham had been in truth,
       One who followed his[2] faith;

84.   Behold! He did approach his Lord,
       Humbly and of his own accord.

85.   And lo! He asked his father and his folk:

---

1. The story of Noah and the Flood is found, in some form or other, among all
   nations of the world.

2. Noah's.

"What on earth are these things that you invoke?!

86.   "Invented gods, instead of God the One,
        This sort of falsehood do you seek?

87.   "And how about the Lord of all Creation,
        What do you really think?!"

88.   And then towards the stars,
        He took a look,

89.   And said: "Indeed I'm sick"[1]

90.   So they all in aversion,
        Did on him turn their back;

91.   And now he shifted his attention,
        Unto their idols, saying:
        "Do you not eat a thing?

92.   "What ails you that you do not speak?"

93.   Then he upon them fell, and struck,
        Them, strikes to break.

94.   Now people to him hurried back.

95.   He cried out: "Do you really serve,
        Something you carve,

96.   "When it was Allah Who created you,

---

1. "Of all your idol-worshipping, its ceremonies and sacrifices".

And all your handiwork!"

97. They cried: "Let us prepare a pyre,
And cast him in the blazing fire!"

98. And[1] They against him plotted,
But We made them the ones
To be humiliated.

99. He said: "Indeed I must now fly
Unto my Lord, for certainly,
He will be guiding me:

100. "Grant me, my Lord, a son,
An upright, honest one."

101. Therefore We gave him the good tiding,
Of a boy, meek, abiding.

102. Now after he had grown enough,
With him to work,
He said: "My little son,
What do you think:
I did see in a dream that I must offer
You as a sacrifice!" He said: "My father,
You should do as you have been bidden,
You'll find me, if God please, a patient one!"

103. Now that both of them had submitted,[2]
And he had laid him down upon his forehead,

---

1. After the failure of the 'fire' scheme.

2. "To the Will of God."

104.   We did cry unto him: "O Abraham!

105.   "You have already,
       Fulfilled the dream indeed,
       See how We recompense,
       The people of good deed."

106.   This was indeed a lucid trial,

107.   And so We ransomed him,[1]
       With a sacrifice noble.[2]

108.   And We bestowed on him the praise,
       Of later generations:

109.   On Abraham be peace and salutations!

110.   Thus do We recompense,
       The doers of virtuous actions;

111.   He was indeed one of Our faithful servants;

112.   Then We gave him the tidings glad of Isaac,
       One of the most virtuous prophets;

113.   And We bestowed our blessing,
       Both on him and on Isaac;
       And some among their offspring,
       Were good and righteous folk,
       But there were others most unjust,

---

1. The boy.

2. A fine sheep or ram brought to them by an angel.

To their own souls.

114.   Moses and Aaron had We surely blessed;

115.   Both of them and their nation,
We rescued from the great oppression;

116.   We helped them, so they were victorious,

117.   And We gave to them both the Scripture,
A clarifier glorious;

118.   And guided them unto the right direction.

119.   And We preserved for them the praise,
Of every later generation;

120.   On Moses and on Aaron,
Be peace and salutation;

121.   Thus do We recompense,
Men of virtuous action,

122.   They were true servants both,
Profound of faith.

123.   Among the messengers,
Was certainly Elijah;

124.   Behold, he warned his people:
"Have you no dread of Allah?

125. "You are invoking Baal,[1] hence,
     You have forsaken the Creator
     Par Excellence,

126. God the One, your own Lord and Lord,
     Of your fathers of old?!"

127. But they did treat him as a liar,
     So they will be brought up to Answer;

128. Except the purified and chosen
     Servants of Allah.

129. And We preserved for him the praise,
     Of every later generation,

130. Upon Elijah,
     Be peace and salutation!

131. Thus do We recompense
     Men of virtuous action;

132. A most believing servant,
     Of Ours was he, no doubt.

133. And Lot was also an apostle;

134. Behold, We rescued him and all his people,

135. Except a woman aged,
     Who stayed with those who tarried;

---

1. The sun-god worshipped in ancient Syria, the chief god of the Phoenicians.

136. And the others We then destroyed.

137. Indeed you still pass by,
     Ruins of theirs during the day,

138. Even by night in fact;
     Will you then not reflect?!

139. Jonah was also an apostle;

140. Behold! He ran off like a slave,
     Unto a laden vessel,

141. And then his lot he had to brave,
     In casting lots, but he did fail,
     And was then cast away.

142. And he was swallowed by a whale;[1]
     But it was he himself to blame!

143. And if he had not been the same,
     Person who glorified and praised,[2]

144. He would have in its belly tarried,
     Till the Day when the dead are raised.

145. At last We threw him on a vacant shore,
     While he was gravely sore;

146. And let a gourd-tree to grow,

---

1. Or: a big fish.
2. Or: "who celebrated the glory of God.

Over him, to fruition;

147. And afterwards We sent him to a nation,
Of a hundred thousand or more;[1]

148. And they believed; therefore We let them,
Live in comfort until a time.

149. Now question their[2] opinions:
Whether your Lord has only daughters,
And they have sons?

150. Or if We did create the angels-
While they were witnessing-as females?!

151. It is a falsehood of their own invention,
When they declare:

152. "God has begotten children",
They are certainly liars bare!

153. Has He some daughters chosen,
Rather than sons?!

154. What is with you the mater?
Could you not ever reason?!

155. Will you not ever learn a lesson?

156. Perhaps you have some solid proof?

---

1. The ancient, prosperous city of Nineva of the Assyrian Empire.
2. The Meccans'.

157.   Then do present your scripture, if
       It be the truth upon your lips.

158.   They also fabricate some kinships
       Between the jinns and Him! Whereas the jinns,[1]
       Already know that they would be brought up,
       To answer questions.

159.   God is indeed far glorified,
       Above their imputations;

160.   Yet Allah's truly purified
       Servants have no such notions.

161.   Neither you, nor your idols,

162.   Could make a soul, concerning Him,
       Fall into trials,[2]

163.   Save those who cause themselves to be
       Going into the Blazing Fire;

164.   "Each single one of us,
       Has its appointed status,

165.   "Indeed we range ourselves in order,

166.   "And we're the singers of His praises ever!"[3]

---

1. Or: "angels", according to some commentators.

2. Or; "temptations".

3. This verse and the two (or the five) preceding one, according to most commentators, are spoken by the Arch-angel Gabriel.

167. They[1] used to make such comments:

168. "Had we received an Admonition,[2]
     From our own ancient parents,

169. "We would certainly have been God's
     Purified, chosen servants!"

170. But now they in it[3] disbelieve!
     Soon are they going to conceive!

171. Surely Our Word already has gone forth,
     To Our servants the messengers,

172. That they shall certainly be succoured,

173. And that Our hosts will surely be the winners.

174. Thus disregard them for a while,

175. And just behold them, for they will,
     Also have to behold![4]

176. Do they indeed intend to urge
     Us to speed up Our scourge?

177. Dreadful shall be the morning of the men,
     Who were forewarned already when,

---

1. The infidels, the pagans.
2. Or: "a revelation", "a scripture", "a reminder".
3. The Quran.
4. "Their doom" or "see how you shall fare".

It[1] shall descend upon their courtyard!

178. Thus let them be and disregard,
Them for a while;

179. And just behold them, for they will,
Also have to behold!

180. Glory be to your Lord, the Lord of
Grandeur and Power: far above
Their imputation,

181. And on the messengers,
Be peace and salutation,

182. And praise be unto Allah,
The Lord of all Creation.

---

1. The scourge, the vengeance.

SURA 38
SAAD[1]

In the Name of God, the Beneficent, the Merciful,

1. Saad;
   By the Quran,[2] well-versed in Admonition;[3]

2. In sooth the disbelievers have been steeped
   In arrogance and in contention.

3. How many generations did We bring,
   Before them, to destruction!
   They all cried out for Mercy, but the time,
   Had lapsed to seek salvation!

4. And now they wonder that a warner from,
   Among themselves to them has come,
   And thus the disbelievers claim:
   "He is a perjuring magician!

5. "Has he made all the gods into one God?
   That's something really odd!"

6. The chiefs among them then direct them thus:
   "Do walk away, and steadfastly remain,
   Firm to your gods; this is surely against you,
   A clear design;

---

1. The Arabic letter "Swaad".
2. Or: The Reading.
3. Also meaning: "remembrance", "praising God", "teaching", "message" and
   "devotional exercises".

7.   "We did not hear the like of this,[1]
In the preceding creed:[2]
It is a forgery indeed!

8.   "What! From among us,[3] only unto him,
Was sent the Admonition?!"
Surely They are in doubt concerning
My Admonition,
certainly they have not yet tasted
My painful retribution!

9.   Perhaps the treasures of the Mercy of,
Your Lord, the Mighty, the Magnanimous,
Happens to be in their possession!

10.   Or does the Kingdom of the Skies,
The Earth and what between them lies,
Belong to them? If so, let them ascend,
By any means to reach that end!

11.   A little host of the confederates,[4]
Shall over there be put to rout![5]

12.   Others before them had the truth denied:
The clan of Noah and the tribe of Aad,
And Pharaoh, lord of the *owtaad*,[6]

---

1. The Message of Monotheism.
2. The Christian religion in which the pagans found a plurality of gods too!
3. That is: "there are more important men than Mohammad."
4. The parties of the Quraish clan who had allied themselves against the Holy
   Prophet.
5. That is: "No combined forces of Evil could ever frustrate God's Purpose."
6. "Stakes", "Spikes"; thus: Pharaoh, "lord of the stakes," or "the impaler."

13. So did Thamood, the tribe of Lot,
    And the Companions of the Wood,[1]
    These were confederates,[2] were they not!

14. All of them charged the messengers with falsehood,
    Therefore, My chastisement was truly just.

15. These people[3] also should await
    A single mighty blast,[4]
    Wherein[5] there shall be no delay;

16. And yet they say: "Our Lord, before the Day
    Of Reckoning should come,
    Hasten our share of Doom!"

17. Put up with everything they say or bid,
    And call to mind Our servant, David,
    A man of mighty hand,
    Who always to Us turned.

18. Indeed We made the mountains join,
    With him in laud and praise,
    At even and at sunrise,

19. Also the birds in throngs,
    Attended to his hymns;

---

1. Or "the Dwellers of the Forest", most probably: the Midianites.
2. That is: "united in their rejection of the prophets and the truth.
3. The pagans of Mecca.
4. "Shout", "cry" or "trumpet blast".
5. "At the appointed time".

20. His Kingdom did We strengthen,
     Blessed him with wisdom,
     And granted him the vision
     To make a clear decision.

21. And have you heard the story
     Of the litigants twain? Behold,
     Over his private chamber,
     They climbed, sudden and bold;

22. When they did thus burst in on David,
     And he was of them terrified,
     They said: "Be not afraid,
     We are two litigants, of whom,
     One wronged the other: pray decide,
     With truth between us, and do not
     Be in the least unfair, and guide
     Us to the right direction:

23. "This man's my brother and his ewes
     Are ninety-nine,
     And I, of ewes, have only one,
     And yet he says: 'Let her also be mine,'
     And in debating his demand,
     He has on me the upper hand!"

24. He said: "Surely he has been most unjust,
     Asking to add your one-ewe to his ewes;
     Lo! Many are the partners who abuse,
     One another, save those who have embraced
     The faith and do what's right, but these,
     Are very few indeed!"
     Yet now David perceived:

That We had put him to a test!
Therefore he asked his Lord for Pardon,
Fell down and bowed himself, and often
Besought to be forgiven.

25. Therefore We did forgive his lapse,[1]
And most certainly he shall be to Us,
In Nearness, at a pleasant, final place.

26. O David! Truly have We made you
A Vicegerent upon the earth,
Therefore judge between men with truth,
And follow not your passions, lest
They should mislead you from God's Path;
Indeed there is a grievous retribution,
For those who go astray from Allah's Path,
Because they have indeed forgotten,
The Day of Reckoning;

27. For We did not create the heavens,
The earth and all between, for nought;
That is the disbelievers' thought!
And Woe to every disbeliever,

---

1. The Quranic parables have nothing to do with the scandalous tales in the Bible wherein all sorts of heinous crimes are attributed to the chosen, purified prophets of God, as in chapters xi and xii of Samuel 2, where David is accused of adultery, fraudulent dealing with a faithful servant and his murder! In fact, according to what some evil hands have inserted in the Bible, almost all the members of the Holy House of Jacob are described as rough hooligans, liars, thieves, murderers and adulterers; may the hands, who wrote such stuff, be in the Fire of Hell for ever! The Quranic parable suggests that an idea may have come to his mind as a human being which was removed after "the two" appeared to him and he did, as a man of God, immediately repent.

When he is in the Fire!

28. Shall We treat those who do believe,
And do what's righteous, and the spreaders
Of mischief on the earth alike?
Are the god-fearing self-restrainers,
As the unbridled sinners?!

29. This is a Book in blessings decked,
That We have unto you revealed,
That men upon its verses may reflect,
And men endowed with wits, take heed.

30. We then to David granted Solomon:
Most excellent a servant,
And truly penitent.[1]

31. Behold! Some horses of the highest breeding,[2]
Were brought to him one evening;

32. Then he said to himself: "truly I love
The earthly goods just on account of
Remembering my Lord"-Now they[3] had been
By the curtain of darkness hidden:

33. "They all shall be to me brought back!"
And he began to give soft strokes[4]

---

1. Or: "one who loved to turn himself Godward.

2. Or "swift of foot coursers," "prancing chargers".

3. The horses: "following a race or a parade."

4. Here some translators, taking another meaning of the original verb: "to sever, to slash", into consideration, have rendered the verse into: "He severed the legs and the necks of the horses because they had drawn his attention away

Of hand upon their legs and necks.

34. And still We did put Solomon to test:
    We placed a corpse[1] upon his throne,
    Whereupon back to Us he raced!

35. He prayed: "My Lord, forgive me;
    Give me a Kingdom that shall, after
    My time, not be inherited by any,
    You are indeed the greatest Granter,
    Of every bounty."

36. Thus We subjected unto him the wind;
    It gently ran at his command,
    Wheresoever did he it send;

37. And the devils, divers of them,
    Builders and divers,

38. And others bound in fetters;

39. "Free gifts are these from Us,
    Therefore give freely or withhold:
    Your books shall not unfold!"

40. And most certainly he shall be to Us
    In Nearness, at a pleasant, final place.

41. Commemorate Our servant Job, behold!

---

from God! This account has no basis and does not befit Solomon.
1. Or "a lifeless body", "a phantom".

Calling upon his Lord, he did complain:
"Satan has been afflicting me
With much distress and pain".

42. "With your foot only stamp:
Here is[1] a place for washing,
And water to imbibe,
Cool and refreshing."

43. And to him We gave back his kith and kin,
And made them twice as many, as a blessing
From Us, and for commemoration,
To the intelligence-possessing!

44. "Take in your hand a bunch of twigs therewith
To strike, and do not break your oath!"[2]
Indeed We found him patient,[3]
Most excellent a servant,
Who always turned to Us in truth.

45. Mention also Our servants Abraham,
Isaac and Jacob, surely men
Of might and vision.

---

1. Here Job's recuperative process begins: he strikes the earth or a rock with his foot, and a fountain or fountains gush forth, to clean his body, to drink and to refresh his spirits.

2. Apparently Job's wife was impatient, and he must have said in his haste to the woman that he would, say, give her a hundred stripes; he is now told to correct her with only a wisp of grass to show that he was gentle and humble as well as firm and constant.

3. Similar words are, previously in this sura, spoken of David and Solomon; patience and active faith, are also a form of service. So Milton in his Sonnet: "They also serve who only stand and wait."

46. Surely We purified them all,
    With this one purity:
    The keeping in their minds
    Of the Home of Eternity.

47. Certainly in Our sight they are amongst,
    The chosen of the best.

48. And also mention Ishmael,
    Elisha and Ezekiel,
    For they were all amongst
    The just, the best.

49. This is an Admonition;
    Surely the self-restrainers,
    Shall, to a pleasant place,
    Be the happy returners:

50. Gardens of Eden,
    Whose gates shall stand,
    Unto them open,

51. Therein they will recline at ease;
    And fruits and drinks can they demand,
    Therein in plenty as they please,

52. And for companions,
    There will be bashful maidens,
    Of their own age, like twins.

53. Such is the Promise
    Unto you made,
    To be upon the Day of

Accounts fulfilled.

54.   Yes! This is Our provision,
      And it will never end.

55.   That's for them; but the lawless evil-doers,
      Shall to a place most wretched be returned:

56.   Yea, unto Hell, wherein they shall be burned;
      What a dismal resort!

57.   It is all theirs: so they shall have to taste,
      Some boiling fluid with another coldest,[1]

58.   And other putrid things of kindred sort!

59.   "Here is a rushing throng,
      Who'll be thrown in with you headlong,
      No greetings for them there!
      For promptly shall they be
      Plunged in the Fire!"[2]

60.   They say:[3] But that goes for you too,
      There'll be no welcome for you either;
      But it was you who brought this,
      Upon us! What a wretched station!"

61.   They also say: "O Lord, increase the portion

---

1. Also meaning: "filth, gore, festering blood".

2. These lines are probably spoken by the leaders of evil whenever other groups
   of sinners are brought forward.

3. The followers of the bad leaders.

Of the punishment in the Fire,
Twofold, for those who brought this on us!"

62.   And they will ask each other: "Curious,
It is, is it not, that We witness
Not any of the men We used to
Number among the vicious,[1]

63.   Whom we did treat with utter scorn?!
Or is there something with our eyes amiss?!"

64.   Certainly this shall come to pass:
All this controversy together,
Of the companions of the Fire.

65.   Say: "I am but a warner,
And there's no God but God the One,
The Most Supreme in Power,

66.   The Lord of heavens and the earth, and all
That is between, in Might Exalted,
The Ever-Pardoner."

67.   Say: "It's[2] the most important news,

68.   "Which you do heedlessly refuse!

69.   "Indeed I had no information,
Of the High Council's[3] disputation;

---

1. By this they mean: "the believers"!

2. The prophetic Message.

3. Or; "the exalted (celestial) chiefs".

70. "Only I am informed by revelation,
    That I am to give warnings,
    Public and open."

71. Behold! Your Lord said to the angels:
    "I will create a man from clay,

72. "So when I fashion him and breathe
    Into him of My Spirit, pray
    Fall down before him in prostration

73. Thus the angels went on their knees,
    All together:

74. Except Iblees! He was too proud, and thus,
    Became a disbeliever.

75. He called out: "O Iblees!
    What makes you bow not unto whom
    I have created with My hands?
    Are you puffed up with pride,
    Or do you think you are a god?[1] !"

76. He said: "I am more excellent than he:
    Me have You made of fire, and of mud,
    Have You created him!"

77. He said: "From hence go forth:
    You are an outcast[2] now, in truth;

78. "Surely My curse will be upon you,

---

1. Or: "A being of exalted, lofty merit".   2. Also meaning: "stoned, rejected".

Until the Day of Judgment is in view.

79. He begged: "My Lord, give me then respite,
Until the Day of Resurrection!"

80. He said: "you are respited,

81. "Till the Day of the time appointed."

82. He said: "Then, by Your Might and Glory,
I will certainly all of them seduce,

83. "Save those servants of Yours amongst them,
Purified by Your Grace!"

84. He said: "That's true, and Truth I tell:

85. "Most certainly I will fill Hell,
With you and those of them who would
Follow you, one and all!"

86. And now declare: "I ask of you no wage,
For this and I am no pretender;

87. "Of a truth, it's[1] but a Reminder,
To all nations at every age,

88. And you will certainly after a time,
Come to realize its Message.

---

1. The Quran.

SURA 39
THE MULTITUDES
(AL-ZUMAR)

In the Name of God, the Beneficent, the Merciful

1.   The revelation of this Book is from
     God, the Almighty, the All-Wise.

2.   We have sent down the Book to you in truth,
     Thus worship God in the devoutest ways.

3.   Is not devoutest worship only due,
     To God the One?
     Yet those who take some other patron,
     Beside him, reason thus:
     "We serve them only that they bring us
     Nearer to God the One!"
     Certainly God will judge between them
     In that wherein they differ,
     And surely Allah will not guide
     The lying, thankless disbeliever.

4.   If God had willed to take a son,
     He would have chosen whomsoever,
     He pleased, out of His own creation;
     But praise be to Him: He is God the One,
     The Most Supreme in Power;

5.   He did create in truth,[1]
     The heavens and the earth;
     He makes the day be covered by the night,

---

1. That is: "for a serious purpose".

And lets the night be covered by the day,
And He controls the sun and moon, that they
Follow their course each for a stated era;
Is He not the Almighty, the Forgiver?

6.   He did create you all,
Out of a single soul,
From whom He later formed its mate;
And He sent down of cattle eight
Head but in their own pairs.[1]
In the wombs of your mothers,
Does He create you by creation in
Succession, under curtains three;[2]
Such is Allah, your Lord, the whole Dominion,
To Him belongs: there is no God but He;
How have you turned so heedless!

7.   Suppose you do not render any thanks,
Yet surely God is Rich and Needless,
Without you: but He, with ungratefulness,
In his own creatures is not pleased,
And He'll be pleased, if you are grateful;
No soul will have to bear the burden
Of another: for later you shall all,
To your own Lord return, and then He will,
Inform you of your deeds; indeed full Ken,
Has He of everything in every breast.

8.   When man is by some ill distressed,
He calls upon his Lord and turns,
Unto Him in repentance, yet,

1. Pairs of the four domesticated cattle: Oxen, Camels, Sheep and Goats.
2. Or: Triple darkness.

As soon as through His grace, he earns
Some favour from Him, he'll forget
What it was that he did implore,
His help for it before;
He sets up peers with God, to lead astray,
The others from His way.
Say: "Do enjoy your thankless unbelief,
A little further,
You shall certainly be one of
The inmates of the Fire!"

9.   Far from this is the man who meditates,
During the hours of the nights,
Prostrate or standing in devotion,
Who's heedful of the life to come,
While hoping for his Lord's Compassion!
Say: "Shall the people who have knowledge be,
Considered equal to the unenlightened?"
Only, the men endued with understanding,
Will this Warning attend.

10.   Say: "O My servants who believe!
Do fear your Lord,
There shall be good for those who do,
Good in this world,
And Allah's earth is surely broad;
And those who patiently preserve
Shall have a measureless reward."

11.   Say: "I have been commanded to
Worship God with a dedicated
Devotion only unto Him;

12.   "And I have also been commanded
        To be the first and foremost Muslim."[1]

13.   Say: "certainly I fear the chastisement,
        Of a most fateful Day,
        If I do not my Lord obey."

14.   Say: "It is God I worship with my own,
        Sincere devotion unto Him alone.

15.   "And you may serve whate'er you like beside Him!"
        Say: "Certainly the losers will they be,
        Who lose their souls and their own family,
        Upon the Day of Resurrection:
        Now is not this the clearest ruin?

16.   Layers of Fire will burn above them,
        And floors of it, beneath them,
        With this does God alarm His servants:
        "Fear Me then, O My servants!"

17.   But there shall be good news for those,
        Who shun the worship of *taghoot*,[2]
        And turn to God: Thus give good news,
        To My creatures devout,

18.   Who hearken to the Word and follow
        The best in it: those are indeed,
        The guided ones by God, and they,
        Are the men with insight endued.

---

1. One who surrenders himself to the Will of the Almighty.

2. Satanic powers.

19. But him on whom the sentence of
    Torment is justly due,
    One who's in fact already in the Fire,
    Could you attempt to rescue?

20. But those who fear their Lord,
    Will surely dwell in storied Mansions,
    Set up for them, with streams,
    Running beneath them; surely this
    Is Allah's promise,
    And God His promise ever sanctions.

21. Do you not see how God sends down
    Water from heavens,
    And guides it through the earth to form
    The springs and fountains,
    And brings forth by it crop of varied hues,
    Then it withers, and you see that it turns
    Yellow, and then He lets it crumble,
    Into some stubbles; certainly a lesson,
    There is in this, for men of ken.

22. When, for reception of Islam,
    One's heart is by God broadened,
    He will follow a Light from his own Lord;
    Thus woe to those whose hearts are hardened,
    Against God's message; surely they,
    Have gone too far astray.

23. God has sent down the finest Message,
    In the form of a Book, whose content
    Repeats itself and is consistent:
    The skins of those who dread their Lord,

Shiver thereat, but then, at God's remembrance,
Their skins and hearts become most pliant;
This is certainly Allah's guidance:
By it He guides whome'er He pleases,
And for the man whom God lets go astray,
There shall be none to show the way.

24.   Is there a man who will ward off,
The torment of the Retribution,
By shielding his own face against it,
Upon the Day of Resurrection?!
For to the evil-doers it is said:
"Do taste the fruit of your own action".

25.   People before them had the truth rejected,
But then Our scourge upon them came,
From whence they least expected.

26.   Thus God gave them a taste of humiliation,
In the life of this world, but greater
Shall be the retribution
In the Hereafter;
Did they have no cognition!

27.   In this Quran[1] have We indeed,
Set forth for humankind,
Similitudes of every kind,
Perhaps they will take heed:

28.   A Reading sent in Arabic, untwisted,
And free from crookedness,

---

1. Or: "Reading".

To the intent that they perhaps,
Guard against wickedness[1] !

29.   God sets forth an example:
There is a bondsman who belongs
To several masters[2] e'er at odds,
And there's another who belongs,
Safely[3] to one: would it be fair,
To hold the two alike? So praise
Is due to God the One, but these,
People are mostly not aware.

30.   You[4] shall certainly die,
They too shall pass away,

31.   And then you will, upon the Day
Of Resurrection, fall into discord,
With one another, in the presence
Of your own Lord!

32.   Thus who will be more wicked than the man
Who forges lies concerning God,
And treats the Truth after it has,
Unto him come, as falsehood?
Ah, is there not a Home in Hell,
For every infidel?!

33.   But he who brings the Truth,

---

1. Or: "be god-fearing, restrain oneself, guard against evil."

2. Or "partners" and "associates": surely an implied allusion to the deities
   worshipped by the idolaters.

3. Or "Wholly".   4. The Holy Prophet.

And he who does in it have faith:
These are the dutiful,
Among the faithful.

34.   Whatever they desire,
        Awaits them with their Lord:
        Such is the recompense
        Of those who practice good,

35.   And Allah shall indeed write off
        The worst of what they did,
        And for the best of what they did,
        Render them their reward.

36.   Is God not All-Sufficient,
        For His own servant?!
        Yet they would like to scare you off,
        With their own lowly idol-stuff!
        There shall be none to show the way,
        For those whom God allows to stray!

37.   But he whom God will guide aright,
        Shall be misled by none;
        Is God not of Exalted Might,
        And to chastise, the Ablest One?

38.   And if you ask them who created
        The heavens and the earth, they would
        Certainly answer: "God!"
        Say: "Think this now: If Allah wills
        Afflictions for me, could the deities
        You call upon, instead of Allah, ever
        Be removers of His calamities,

Or if He wills to show me Mercy,
Could they[1] remove His Mercy?"
Say: "God the One suffices me;
The trustful people do rely,
Upon Him only."

39.   Say: "O My people, you may try
All in your power, so will I,
And in the end you'll know:

40.   "Whom does a shameful torment follow,
And unto whom is to be due,
A punishment that shall continue!

41.   We have sent down the Book for humankind,
To you in truth;[2] therefore, whoever
Is guided by it, benefits his soul,
And whoso goes astray, he'll only err,
To his own loss; and you are not at all,
Their overseer ever.

42.   It's God Who takes the souls at death,
And the souls of the living, while asleep;
The souls of those upon whom death has been
Decreed, shall He then keep,[3]
But the others He shall send back until,
A term appointed; and in this, in fact,
Are Signs, for people who reflect.

---

1. The original word in Arabic is in feminine gender, alluding to the female
   deities the pagans worshipped.
2. That is: "for a truthful purpose."
3. That is: "keeps back from returning to life".

43. And do they take others as intercessors,
    Along with Allah?
    Say: "What?! You know they have no power,
    And no intelligence whatever!"

44. Say: "Intercession is with God the One,
    Wholly and altogether,
    The Kingdom of the heavens and the earth,
    Belongs to Him, and you shall be hereafter,
    To Him returned.

45. When God the only One, is mentioned,
    The hearts of those who have no faith,
    In the Hereafter, will be loath!
    But when some deities are mentioned,
    Beside Him, lo! They're filled with mirth!

46. Proclaim: "O God, the Author of the heavens,
    And of the earth, the Very Knower,
    Of all the hidden and the open, You
    Will judge concerning whatsoever,
    Wherein Your own creatures did differ.

47. Now if the wicked did possess the wealth,
    Of all the earth, and as much more therewith,
    Certainly they would offer it for ransom,
    That they might be let off the awesome,
    Pain of the punishment, upon
    The Day of Resurrection;
    For God will show them certain things,
    That they had never reckoned on:

48. As all the evils of their own misdeeds,

Will reappear to them, and what[1] they did deride,
Shall be encircling them on every side!

49.   When trouble hits a man, he cries to Us,
        But afterwards, when We have favoured,
        Him with a blessing from Us, he declares:
        "This is a grant that I deserved!"
        But nay! It is only a trial; yet
        Most of them know this not.

50.   The same was said by those who flourished,
        Before them, but their deeds,
        Had nought accomplished;

51.   And their own evil deeds recoiled
        Upon them; and the wicked from among,
        These people[2] will likewise encounter
        The evil consequence of doing wrong,
        Surely they shall be overpowered!

52.   Do they not know that it is God Who gives,
        To whom He will, supplies and ample means,
        Or straitens them; for the believers,
        Surely in this are Signs.

53.   Say: "O My servants who have acted,
        Extravagantly 'gainst your souls!
        Despair not ever of God's Mercy, since
        God does forgive all sins:
        The Gracious Pardoner is He,

---

1. The promised Fire.
2. The Meccans, this generation.

And Full of Mercy.

54.   Therefore, return unto your Lord,
And purely unto Him submit,
While the punishment has not yet,
Upon you come, for you will then
Be helped by none.

55.   And follow thus this finest Revelation,
Sent down to you already from your Lord,
Before the chastisement upon you come,
Of a sudden, when you are off your guard!

56.   Lest any soul should say: "O Misery!
For my neglect of duty unto God,
Surely I was a man who did deride,"[1]

57.   Or say: "Had Allah guided me,
I would have been god-fearing, surely!"

58.   Or, after he has had a glance
At the Punishment, say: "If only
I was given another chance,
Of the good-doers would I be!"

59.   But nay! My revelations came
To you, but you denied them as untruth,
You were too arrogant, and thus became
One who opposes faith.

60.   And on the Day of Resurrection,

---

1. "That is: derided the faithful and their Faith".

You shall see how the faces of the people,
Who lied of God, shall he completely soiled;[1]
Is there not an abode in Hell,
For the arrogant people!

61.　But God shall save the self-restrainers,
For what they have achieved,
Evil shall never touch them now,
Nor will they e'er be grieved.

62.　Allah is the Creator of all things,
And He has charge of all affairs indeed;

63.　His are the Treasures[2] of the heavens,
And of the earth, and losers are the ones,
Who in God's revelations disbelieved.

64.　Say: "Are you bidding me to worship
Some other things, instead of God the One,
You foolish men?!"

65.　Whereas it has already been revealed,
To you, and unto those before you that:
"If you associate[3] a thing with God,
Vain is to be everything you have worked at!
A loser shall you be without a doubt.

66.　Nay! Worship only God the One,
And be a thankful person.

---

1. "By sinfulness, tarnished by sin", or "by the flames of Hell".

2. Or: the Keys.

3. "Join partners with God the One", "Associate other deities with Allah."

67. But they have not valued the value
    Of God, such as is to Him due;
    For on the Day of Resurrection,
    The whole earth will be in His grip,
    And the heavens will be rolled up,
    In His right hand: all adoration,
    Be unto Him! He's surely far Exalted
    Above what is to Him associated.

68. And as the Trumpet will be blown,
    All who are in the heavens,
    And all on earth shall swoon,
    Save those whom God not thus ordains,
    And it will then be blown again,
    And lo! They will be all arising,
    To be around them gazing!

69. And then the Earth[1] is to be radiant,
    With the light of her Lord,
    The Book shall be laid down, and prophets
    And witnesses shall be brought up, and Judgment,
    Will be given with equity,
    Between them all, and none shall be
    Dealt with unjustly.

70. And every soul will be repaid in full,
    For everything it did fulfill;
    For of what men have done,
    Knows He perfectly well.

71. And then by multitudes,

---

1. This is a new Earth in the new Universe of the Light and Glory of God.

The disbelievers shall be driven
Towards Gehenna; when they come,
Near it, its Portals to them open,
And its Porters shall say to them:
"Did no apostle of your own,
Ever come unto you, reciting
Your Lord's communications,
And warning you against the Meeting,
Of this Day set for you?"
They shall only say: "This is true!"
And thus,[1] the Word[2] of Punishment,
Proved true against the disbelievers!

72. It will be said: "Do enter
The Portals of Gehenna,
Therein to dwell for ever;
Evil is the abode
Of the most proud!

73. But those who feared their Lord, will then be driven,
In multitudes towards the Garden;[3]
And when they come near it, its Portals open,
And its Porters shall say: "All hail!
Well have you fared; do enter,
To dwell therein for ever!"

74. And they shall say: "To God be praise,
Who has to us fulfilled His promise,
And made us, of this earth, the heirs,

---

1. That is: "But for those who rejected their prophets."

2. Also meaning: Decree or Sentence.

3. Or: Paradise.

That we may dwell in Paradise,
Wheresoever we please."

75.   And you shall see the angels,
Circling the Throne, singing the praise
Of their own Lord; and judgment is
Pronounced on them with justice,
And you shall hear the words:
"All praise belongs,
To God the One,
Lord of the Worlds!"

SURA 40
THE BELIEVER
(AL-MO'MIN) [1]

In the Name of God, the Beneficent, the Merciful

1. Haa Meem. [2]

2. This Book has been sent down through God,
    The Mighty, the Knower Supreme,

3. The Pardoner of sin, Acceptor of repentance,
    Severe in chastisement, and Lord of influence,
    There is no God but He, and unto Him,
    Shall be the last deliverance!

4. None but the disbelievers shall dispute
    God's revelations,
    Let not, therefore, their prosperous dealings in
    The country lead you [3] into some deceptions.

5. Before them, [4] Noah's people were deniers,
    And, after them, some other godless factions; [5]
    Each nation schemed against their own apostle,
    To lay a hand on him, and with false notions,
    Did they dispute with him to render null
    The Truth, thus I did lay My hand on them,
    And awesome were My retributions!

---

1. Also named "The Pardoner or Forgiver" (Al-Ghaafir).

2. H.M. 3. The Holy Prophet. 4. The Meccan pagans.

5. Original: Ahzaab (parties, allies, confederates) is, in the plural form, almost
   always used for hosts and bands of evil, who reject the Truth and deny the
   prophets sent by God.

6.   Thus is it that the Word of God:
       That the infidels are to be
       The Inmates of the Fire, was
       Fulfilled most certainly.

7.   The bearers of the Throne, and those
       Around it, celebrate the praise,
       Of their Lord, and in Him have faith,
       And ask forgiveness for believers:
       "Our Lord, You have embraced all things in Ruth,
       And Knowledge; do grant pardon unto those,
       Who turn to You[1] and follow your true Path,
       And shield them from the blazing Flames!

8.   "Bring them, Our Lord, into the Gardens
       Of everlasting Bliss,
       Which was to them Your promise,
       As well as to the righteous ones,
       Among the fathers, and the spouses,
       And the descendants of them,
       You are in Might Exalted, Full of Wisdom!

9.   "And keep them from all ills,
       And any whom You keep from ills,
       Upon this Day, You will have surely
       Bestowed upon him Mercy,
       And that's the great felicity!"

10.   "Greater is God's aversion of you",
       Shall a voice to the disbelievers cry,
       "Than your aversion to yourselves, when you

---

1. "In repentance".

Were called unto the Faith,
And yet you did deny."

11. They shall say: "Twice have you, our Lord,
Given us death,[1] and twice,
You've given life to us,
But now we do our sins confess,
Is there no way that we escape this?!"

12. "This has befallen you because,
When God alone was called upon,
You disbelieved, but when some partners,
Were joined to Him, you did believe anon!
Now judgment is, at any rate,
With God, the High, the Great."

13. It's He Who lets you see His Signs,
And from the sky sends you supplies,
But of this only those take heed,
Who often turn to Him indeed.

14. Thus call on God while being
Purely sincere in His devotion,
Despite the disbelievers'
Severe aversion;

15. Exalted is He in His attributes,
And He's the Lord of the High Throne,
He does send forth the spirit[2] at his own

---

1. Non-existence, or existence as clay without life, is equivalent to death; from this "first death" state, man was given true Life on this earth.

2. The spirit "of inspiration".

Behest on whom He chooses of His servants,
That he may of the Day of Meeting
The people warn;

16. The Day whereon they all rise up,
    When naught about them shall be hidden
    From God; and Who shall reign supreme,[1]
    On that Day? The Almighty, God, the One!

17. On that Day every soul is paid
    For what it earned; and none
    Shall be unjustly treated;
    Lo! God is Swift to reckon!

18. Thus warn them of the e're-approaching Day,
    When hearts shall leap up to the throats,
    To choke them; when the evil doers find
    No friends compassionate, nor any sorts
    Of intercessors in command!

19. He even knows the treachery of the eyes,
    And whatever the breasts disguise!

20. And it is God Who judges with the truth,
    And those others they call upon, instead
    Of Him, cannot decide a thing; it's God
    Only Who Hears and Sees indeed.

21. Have they not ever travelled,
    Across the land,
    To see what was the end,

---

1. Or: "whose is the Kingdom?"

Of people who before them dwelled:
Greater than these were they in might, and in,
What of them has remained,
Throughout the land; yet Allah did
Seize them because they gravely sinned,
And, there was no one vis-a-vis
Allah them to defend!

22.   That was because there came to them,
Their messengers with Signs most bright,
But they rejected them, so Allah
Took them in Hand; for Full of Might,
Is He and Stern in retribution.

23.   We did, of old, send Moses with Our Signs,
And clear authorization,

24.   To Pharaoh and Haamaan and Korah;
But they all cried: "A sorcerer,
Who is also a liar!"

25.   And when he did the truth convey,
To them from Us, they ordered: "Slay
The sons of those who do believe,
As he, but let their daughters live!"
But bound to fail has always been,
The stratagem of those who disbelieve.

26.   Pharaoh had said:
"Let me put Moses to the Sword,
And let him call upon his Lord,
I fear that he may change your faith,
And spread corruption in the earth!"

27. And Moses said: "I do take refuge in
     My Lord, Who is also your Lord,[1] concerning
     Every arrogant man who has no faith in
     The Day of Reckoning."

28. And a believing man of Pharaoh's kinsfolk,
     Who had been hiding his belief, thus spoke:
     "What! Will you slay a man because he says,
     'My Lord is God the One', and lucid Signs
     Has he unto you brought from your own Lord?
     And if he be a liar, then his lies,
     Upon him will recoil,
     But if he happens to be truthful,
     Then some of what he warns, may fall
     Upon you; surely Allah will not guide,
     Those who rebel and lie, at all.

29. "This day the kingdom, O my people,
     Is yours, and you do have the upper hand,
     Throughout the land, but who, from Allah's vengeance,
     When it befalls on us, shall us defend?"
     Pharaoh said: "I would only have you sense,
     What I see, and I only guide you,
     To the right avenue."

30. The faithful man still said: "My folk,
     Truly I fear for you the like,
     Of what upon the Factions[2] fell,

1. What Moses preached was the Gospel of Unity: that the God of Moses, the
   God of Pharaoh, of Israel and Egypt, the Lord of all the Worlds, was God the
   One: El, Il and Allah in Semitic languages.

2. Or "Parties", "Confederates": Those who rejected God's message and his
   prophets.

31.   "Fates similar to those that overtook,
The folk of Noah, of the Aad as well
As the Thamood, and others after them;
Yet injustice does Allah never will,
To His creatures at all;

32.   "And, O my people, for you have I fears
Against the Day of Cries and Tears!

33.   "The Day when you shall all be made to
Retreat,[1] when there will be no saviour,
To rescue you from Allah!
For anyone whom God will leave in error,
None may be guiding ever!

34.   "And, long before this, Joseph did
Come unto you with lucid tokens,
But you did never cease to doubt
The message he had to you brought,
And when he died, you said: 'By no means,
Will Allah send another Messenger,
After him! 'Surely Allah leaves in error,
Every transgressing, chronic doubter!

35.   "Those who dispute about the Signs of God,
With no authority unto them given,
Are surely held in great dislike by God,
And by the men of faith; thus is it then,
That Allah sets a sealed-up covert,
On every haughty, contumacious heart."

---

1. "After the Judgment, into Hell".

36.　　And Pharaoh said: "O Haaman!
　　　　Build me a lofty tower,
　　　　And raise for me the means,

37.　　"The ways and means to reach the heavens,
　　　　And mount unto the God of Moses,
　　　　Far I do think that He's a liar!"
　　　　Thus was the evil of his doings,
　　　　Made to seem fair in Pharaoh's eyes,
　　　　And he was hindered from the right direction;
　　　　Yes, Pharaoh's scheming only ended in
　　　　His total ruin.

38.　　And the man who believed had also said:
　　　　"O people mine! Follow me that I may,
　　　　Guide you to the right way;

39.　　"O My people! This worldly life,
　　　　Is nothing but a passing pleasure,
　　　　It's the Hereafter that's the Mansion,
　　　　Abiding beyond measure."

40.　　"For those of evil deeds, the recompense,
　　　　Shall be its like, but those who have done good,
　　　　Both men and women, and who do believe,
　　　　Shall enter Paradise,
　　　　Wherein they will receive,
　　　　Their boundless, blissful livelihood.

41.　　"How strange, my people, is this matter:
　　　　That I do call you to Salvation,
　　　　And unto me, your invitation,
　　　　Is to the Fire!

42.   "You call upon me to blaspheme
Against Allah, and, those of whom,
I have no ken, to join with Him!
While I invite you to the Being,
All-Mighty, Most-Forgiving?

43.   "Undoubtedly the deities you call,
Me to, may in no way be called upon,
Either in this world or in the Hereafter,
For our return shall be to God the One,
And rebels will be Inmates of the Fire.

44.   "Soon shall you be recalling,
What I unto you recommend,
And I will my affair to God commend,
Far surely He is Most Observant,
Of the affairs of every servant."

45.   So Allah saved him from the evil plans.
That they devised against him, and the woe
Of the chastisement did encompass
The court of Pharaoh;

46.   Before the Fire,
They are presented,
Morning and evening,
And on the Day wherein the Hour
Is brought about: "Do bring
In the people of Pharaoh
To be gravely tormented."

47.   Behold! with one another, when in Hell,
They'll be contending, and the weak shall tell,

The arrogant: "We were your followers,
Will you ward off from us a little
Of these Hell-Flames?"

48.   The arrogant shall answer:
"We're all in it together;
And God has given judgments
Already for His servants."

49.   Also, the dwellers of the Fire,
Say to the Keepers of Gehenna:
"Implore your Lord, so that He may
Lighten our scourge for just a day!"

50.   They say: "Did not your own apostles ever
Come unto you with clearest arguments?"
They answer: "Yes!" They say: "Then go on praying,
But disbeliever's prayer, at all events,
Shall go astray!"

51.   Surely We shall extend, in this world's life,
Our help to Our apostles and to those,
Who do believe, and We shall do likewise,
Upon the Day when witnesses arise;

52.   The Day whereon the wrong-doers' excuse
Shall be unto them of no use;
But theirs, will be a Curse,
And theirs, will be an evil Place.

53.   In former times We granted Moses
The Guidance, and We made the Children
Of Israel, be heirs unto the Scripture:

54.   A Guidance and Reminder,
       To understanding men.

55.   Therefore have[1] patience,
       For true is Allah's Promise,
       And ask forgiveness for a sin,
       And sing your own Lord's praise
       Evenings and mornings.

56.   The hearts of those who tend to quarrel
       With Allah's revelations,
       With no authority at their disposal,
       Are only filled with proud ambitions,
       To which they shall never attain;
       Thus seek refuge in God alone,
       He is the Hearer and the Seer in truth;

57.   Lo! The creation of the heavens and the earth,
       Was certainly far greater than
       Creating man!
       Most men, however, of this have no ken.

58.   But certainly the sighted and the blind,
       Are not alike, nor those believers,
       Who do what's right and the wrong-doers;
       Little is it that you do mind!

59.   The Hour of Doom,
       Is sure to come,
       There is no doubt of it,
       But most people believe it not!

---

1. The verb is in singular: The addressee is the Holy Prophet.

60. And says your Lord: "Do call upon Me,
    I'll Hear you all and Answer;
    They who disdain My service, will
    Surely enter Hell in dishonour.

61. God is the One Who has ordained,
    For your resting, the night,
    And made the day to give you light,
    God is Most Bountiful to humankind,
    But most people are most ingrate!

62. Such is Allah your Lord,
    Creator of all things,
    No God is there but He;
    Whence are your strayings?!

63. Thus is it that the people who gainsay
    God's revelations always go astray.

64. It's Allah who has made the earth,
    For you a place of rest,
    Built up the Heaven as a ceiling,
    And shaped your forms the finest,
    And feeds you with the best and purest;
    Such is Allah your Lord,
    So blessed is God the One, the Lord
    Of every World;

65. He is the Living One,
    There is no God but He,
    Thus call upon Him only,
    Giving Him pure devotion,
    Praise be to God, the Lord,

Of all Creation.

66. Say: "I have been forbidden,
    To worship what you call upon,
    Instead of God, when lucid Signs
    Have come unto me from my Lord,
    And I am also bidden,
    That I submit myself unto the Lord
    Of all Creation.

67. He it was Who created you
    From the dust of the earth,
    Then from a small life-germ,
    Then from a clot of blood, then forth
    He brought you as an infant, then
    Let you reach your full strength,
    Then you may reach old age, but some
    Of you shall meet an early death:
    So that you reach your own appointed term,
    And that perhaps you use your wisdom.

68. It's He Who life and death ordains,
    When He decrees a thing
    He only to it orders:
    "Be", and it is already being!

69. Do you not see the people who,
    Always about God's Tokens argue?
    How turned away[1] are they indeed!

70. They who reject the Book and pay no heed,

---

1. "From Reality".

To the Message We sent with Our apostles:
Soon shall they come to know!

71.   When on their necks are shackles,
        And chains to drag them, lo,

72.   Into some fetid fluid boiling,
        Then to be cast into the Blazing;

73.   Then shall they be reminded:
        "Where are those others whom you did
        Set up for worshipping,

74.   "Instead of Allah?" They shall say:
        "They have forsaken us, but, nay,
        Indeed We used to pray to nought!"
        Thus God lets disbelievers go astray;

75.   "You suffer this because:
        You did rejoice on earth,
        Unjustly in untruth,
        And insolence had been your cause!

76.   "Enter Gehenna by its gates,
        Therein for ever to abide,
        Evil indeed is the Abode,
        For anyone who arrogates!"

77.   Thus persevere in patience,
        For true is Allah's promise,
        And whether We will let you witness,
        Part of the evil consequence,
        With which they have been threatened,

By Us, or whether We will take your soul,
Before that, to Us shall they be returned.

78.   Surely We have before you sent apostles:
Of them are those We have unto you mentioned,
And others whom We have not to you mentioned,
But no apostle could work miracles,
Except by God's permission;
And after the command of Allah came,
Judgment with truth was given,
And at this juncture the refuters
Became the losers.

79.   God is the One Who granted you the beasts,
So you may ride on some and eat from others,

80.   You find in them assorted interests,
And certain projects that you , in your breasts,
Cherish, you may effect through them; and on,
Them and on ships you shall be borne.

81.   Moreover does He let you see His Signs;
Which then, do you deny, of Allah's Signs?

82.   Have they not ever travelled,
Across the land,
To see what was the end,
Of people who before them dwelled
Greater than these were they in might
And in what of them has remained,
Throughout the land; yet, of no weight,
Was to them all they earned.

83. For when their own apostles to them came,
     With clearest Signs, they, in what they possessed
     Of knowledge had exulted, but the same
     Thing that they scoffed at, them encompassed!

84. And when they did behold Our vengeance,
     They cried: "We now believe in God alone,
     And all those things we used to worship once,
     Instead of Him, we now disown!"

85. But Their belief, when they had witnessed
     Our vengeance, was to them of no avail:
     Such has been Allah's way with His own creatures,
     Since ancient times, therefore the disbelievers,
     Did there dismally fail!

SURA 41
THE WELL-EXPLAINED
(FUSSILAT)[1]

In the Name of God, the Beneficent, the Merciful

1. Haa Meem,[2]

2. Revealed by the Benefic,
    The Merciful Supreme.

3. A Book, of verses well-explained,
    As a Reading in Arabic,
    For the people who understand;

4. A herald of glad tidings,
    And charged with warnings;
    But most of them do not pay heed,
    And, therefore, they hear not indeed.

5. They even claim: "Under some coverings,
    Have we our hearts disguised against your teachings,
    And there is deafness in our ears,
    And between us and you, a curtain hangs!
    Do what you please and we do our own things!"

6. Declare: "I am a mortal only,
    Like you; it is revealed to me,
    By inspiration that your God
    Is One God only, therefore be,
    On the right road to Him, and plead
    For His Pardon;" and woe will be the fate

---

1. This chapter is also known as "Haa Meem Sajda". 2. H.M.

Of people who Associate;[1]

7.   These never pay any *zakaat*,[2]
Nor have they faith in the Hereafter.

8.   But those who do believe,
And do what's right and pleasant,
Shall certainly receive
A recompense incessant!

9.   Say: "what! Do you indeed deny the One
Who did create the Earth within two Days,
And peers and equals for Him raise?
For Him, Who is the Lord of all Creation!

10.   And He has set up mountains,
Towering above the earth and He bestowed
Blessings on it, and in four Days,
Did everywhere distribute food,
Alike for all who seek.

11.   He then applied Himself unto the Sky,
Which was only as smoke,[3]
And said to it and to the Earth:
"Come together, with pleasure or dislike!"
"We come willingly", said they both.

12.   So He did form them, in two Days,
Into the Universes seven,

---

1. The polytheists, those who join partners with God the One.

2. The regular Islamic alms, the poor-rate, obligatory charity, etc.

3. Gas or Vapour.

And He made known in every heaven,
What was its own affairs;
And We adorned the lower heaven,
With brilliant stars, and with some guards;
Such was the measured drawing,
Of the All-Mighty, the All-Knowing.

13. And if they turn away and pay no heed,
Say: "I have warned you of a scourge[1] indeed,
Like the scourge of the Aad and the Thamood;[2]

14. When their apostles came,
To them on every side,
Preaching: "Serve none but Allah",
They simply said:
"If our Lord had so pleased,
He would have certainly sent down,
Some angels, so we do disown,
Whatever is with you sent down!"

15. Unjust and proud had been the men of Aad,
Throughout the land, against all truth and reason;
They used to boast: "Who is in prowess more
Mighty than we?!" Did they never envision
That God Who had created them, was more
Mighty than them in prowess? And in fact,
They did Our Signs roundly reject.

16. Thus We let loose on them a furious blast,
Upon ill-omened days, to make them taste,

---

1. Also: Thunderbolt or tempest.
2. Ancient peoples in Arabia.

The torment of disgrace in this world's life,
But the next world's chastisement is more rife
With shamefulness indeed; and none is there
To help them ever.

17. And, as to the Thamood,
We had vouchsafed them guidance,
But they loved blindness better
Than being guided, hence,
The scourge of an abasing torment,
Seized them for their performance!

18. But We delivered the believing,
And the god-fearing.

19. The Day will come when God's adversaries,
Are brought together in their throngs
Towards the Fire;

20. At length, when they are there:
Their ears, their eyes and their own skins will bear,
Witness against them of their doings;

21. And they shall ask their skins: "Oh, why
Do you against us testify?"
"We're made to speak by God", they shall reply,
"Who gives to all things tongues!
And He created you for the first time,
And taken back will you be unto Him;

22. "You could not hide yourselves so that
Your ears, your eyes and skins would not
Be witnessing against you; yet,

You did suppose that Allah knew
Not many of the things you used to do!

23.   "In fact, this very thought of yours about
Your Lord, has brought you to destruction,
And you woke up to find yourselves,
Among the people of perdition!"

24.   Now if they will endure with patience,
Their lasting Home shall be the Fire,
And if they beg for pardon, they shall not
Be of the people to receive a favour.

25.   And We'll assign to them companions,[1]
Most intimate, for it was they who did
Make their present, past and future states
Seem fair and right to them; and thus the Word,[2]
Uttered about the former generations,
Of Jinn and men has been against them proved;
For they are now most surely lost.

26.   "Do not listen to this Quran[3] at all",
The unbelievers recommend,
"But boo and chatter when it's read,
And you will gain the upper hand!"

27.   Certainly, therefore, will We cause
The unbelievers to go through,

---

1. The same satans who urged them to Evil: evil company in Hell as opposed to
pleasant, congenial companionship in Paradise.

2. Or: Sentence.

3. Or: Reading.

A grievous chastisement, and recompense
Them for the evil deeds[1] they used to do:

28. It is the Fire;
Fit penalty for Allah's foes,
Wherein they shall abide for ever,
It is a punishment for those
Who wittingly denied Our Signs.

29. And those who disbelieved, will say:
"Our Lord, do show us those among the Jinn,
And men who did lead us astray:
Under our feet we'll crush them, no,
We'll render them the lowest of the low!"

30. To those who say: "Our Lord is God the One",
And, further, straight and steadfast stand,
The angels shall descend:
"Fear not at all and never grieve,
But do rejoice as you receive
The tidings glad of Paradise,
To you already promised.

31. "We are your guardian-friends
In both this life and in the next,
Yours is to be therein your soul's desire,
And yours shall be whatever could be asked,

32. "As gifts of Bliss most bountiful,
From the Forgiving One, the Merciful."

---

1. Or: "for the worst of their doings".

33.　　And who is more benign in speech
　　　　Than he who summons men to God,
　　　　While he himself does what is good,
　　　　And says: "Most certainly I am,
　　　　A Muslim[1] ."

34.　　Good and evil are not alike;
　　　　Repel evil with something better,
　　　　And lo! He shall become a bosom friend,
　　　　Who used to be your long-time hater.[2]

35.　　Yet none attain to this except
　　　　People who persevere in patience,
　　　　And none is granted it except,
　　　　The highly favoured with benevolence.

36.　　And yet if some incitement,[3]
　　　　Is made to you by Satan,
　　　　Take refuge then in God the One;
　　　　He's the All-Hearing, the Omniscient.

37.　　Among His portents are the Night and Day,
　　　　And the Sun and the Moon,
　　　　Therefore do not go down upon your knees,
　　　　To the Sun and the Moon!
　　　　But bend in adoration unto God,
　　　　Who did create them, if it's Him alone,
　　　　You wish to worship.

---

1. Submitter to the absolute will of the Almighty.

2. Or: "he between whom and you was enmity".

3. "To discord".

38.   No matter if they are, for this, too proud,
      For those about your Lord do glorify
      Him night and day;
      Yet of it are they never wearied

39.   And of His Signs is this:
      You see the earth drooping and still,
      Yet whenever We send down water,
      Upon it, it will stir and swell,
      Certainly, He Who gives it life,
      Is the Giver of life unto the dead,
      His might extends over all things indeed.

40.   Those people who with obloquy,
      Disown Our revelations,
      Aren't hidden from Our observation;
      Does he who shall be cast into the Fire,
      Fare better than the one who'll be secure,
      Upon the Day of Resurrection?
      Do what you like: but He sees through,
      Everything you may do.

41.   Nor those denying Our Reminder,
      After it came to them[1] ; it[2] is for ever
      A scripture full of power;

42.   No falsehood may approach it now,
      By any means from any side,
      Since it's a Revelation from
      The One All-Wise, Most-Glorified.

---

1. "Will be hidden from Our observation", as stated in the preceding verse.
2. The Quran.

43.　Nothing is said to you that was not said,
　　To messengers before you; but your Lord,
　　Is Most Forgiving and Most Vehement,
　　In Giving Punishment.

44.　If We had made it: a non-Arabic
　　Reading,[1] they would have surely grumbled: "Why
　　Are not its verses clear? It is most cryptic!
　　A foreign message and an Arab guy?!"
　　Say: "It's a Guidance and a Healing,
　　For people who believe; but unbelievers,
　　Who seem to have some trouble with their hearing,
　　Shall be unto it blind; as if a voice,
　　Calls them from a most distant place!

45.　Of old We gave the Book to Moses, yet
　　After a while disputes arose about it,
　　And if it had not then been for a Word,[2]
　　Decreed already by your Lord,
　　Judgment would have surely been passed about
　　People who had many a sickening doubt.

46.　Whoever does what's good and right,
　　Benefits his own soul, and he,
　　Who will do evil, works against it,
　　Because your Lord is certainly
　　Never unjust to His own creatures.

47.　The knowledge of the Hour of Doom,
　　Could be referred to Him alone;

---

1. Or: a Quran.

2. A decree of respite.

No fruit shall come forth from its sheath,
Neither a female bears a burden,
Nor may give birth, without His Ken;
And on that Day when He shall question:
"Now where are My companions?" they shall say:
"We do confess that none of us,
Could be to this a witness!"

48.   And what they used to worship erst,
Leave them now in the lurch,
And they shall know that for escape,
There is no way to search.

49.   Man never ceases to implore
For all good things, but if some evil
Afflicts him, he'll despair and grow
Hopelessly ill!

50.   And when We bless him, after some affliction,
And let him taste Our mercy, he will claim:
"This is my due, and I conjecture that
The Hour is ne'er to come!
And even if I shall be taken back
Unto my Lord, I have been storing some
Good deeds with Him!" But We will certainly
Inform the disbelievers of their actions,
And let them taste some grievous retributions.

51.   When We bestow on Man some favours,
He turns away and goes aside,
But as some evil touches him, he will
Be prayerful, long and loud!

52.   Say: "Think! If this indeed be from
      Allah Himself, and you reject it?
      Who shall be then in greater error
      Than he who has been in explicit,
      Opposition concerning it?"

53.   Soon shall We to them show Our Signs,
      In farthest regions and horizons,
      As well as in their souls, until
      It will become, unto them all
      Most plain that it's the Very Truth;
      Why, is it not sufficient that your Lord,
      Is Witness of all things in sooth.

54.   Behold! They harbour doubts about the Meeting
      With their own Lord. Lo! He's incorporating
      All things indeed.

SURA 42
THE COUNSEL
(AL-SHURAA)

In the Name of God, the Beneficent, the Merciful

1. Haa Meem;[1]

2. 'Ain Seen Qaaf.[2]

3. Thus does Allah, the Mighty, the All-Wise
   Reveal to you, and he has done likewise,
   To those in former times.

4. All that is in the heavens,
   And all that is on earth is His,
   And He's Most High, Most Great,

5. The High heavens almost disintegrate,
   As angels hymn their own Lord's praise,
   And ask forgiveness for the dwellers
   Upon the earth; for God's in truth,
   The Most Forgiving, Full of Ruth.

6. God watches over those who've taken,
   Others beside Him as protectors,
   But you are not in charge of their affairs.

7. Thus have We sent to you a Reading
   In Arabic, that you may warn
   The Mother-Town and people dwelling,
   In her vicinity, and that you warn

---

1. H.M.   2. A.S.Q.

Them of the Day of Gathering-
There is no doubt about it-when
A party shall be in the Garden,
Another party in the Flames.

8.   Had God so willed, He would have made
All of them one *umma*[1] indeed,
But He admits unto His favour,
Whome'er He pleases; and the evil-doers
Shall have no patrons and no helpers.

9.   Have they beside Him taken
Some other patron?
Surely God is the only Guardian:
It's he Who brings
The dead to life again,
And He alone does reign
Over all things.

10.   No matter what it is concerning which
You disagree, with God is its decision;
Such is Allah, my Lord: in Him I trust,
And to Him do I turn on each occasion.

11.   Originator of the heavens,
And of the earth: He it is, Who,
Did give you spouses from among
Your species, and of cattle, too,
Mates of them, that you thereby
Will multiply; in likeness there is nothing
Like Him: the All-Hearing, All-Seeing.

---

1. People, community, nation.

12.   Of the heavens and of the earth,
        Has He alone the treasured Keys,
        He gives abundantly or sparingly,
        Of sustenance to whom He please;
        For cognizant is He of everything.

13.   To you has He prescribed the same,
        Religion He enjoined on Noah,[1]
        And what We now reveal to you
        And what We have commanded ever
        To Abraham, to Moses and to Jesus,
        Is this: Keep up this faith and never,
        Be into sects therein divided.
        On those who worship idols jointly
        With God, what you invite them to,
        Is hard; God chooses for it whom
        He please, and guides to it the people who,
        Turn unto Him time after time.

14.   Yet men, through jealousy and rancour,
        Divided into sects just after,
        The knowledge was unto them preached,
        And had it not been for a Word,
        Concerning an appointed time,
        Already issued from your Lord,
        Judgment would have at once been reached,
        Between them; therefore, those who had been let
        Be heirs unto the Scripture after them,
        Were in perplexity of doubt about it.

---

1. God's Religion is the same in essence, whether given to Noah, Abraham, Moses, Jesus or Mohammad, peace of God be upon them all.

15.   And for this, keep on calling to the Faith
   And steadfastly be walking on the Path,
   As you have been commanded, and do not
   Follow their whims, and say: "In all the truth
   Of the Book, sent by God, do I believe,
   And I have been commanded to decide,
   Justly among you: God is both our Lord,
   And your own Lord; what we do is indeed
   For us, and for you shall be your own deeds;
   Let there be no contentious matter,
   Between us and yourselves; for Allah will
   Be bringing all of us together,
   And to Him is our final goal.

16.   And these who do dispute concerning God,
   After accepting His obedience,
   Futile shall be their argument,
   In the sight of their Lord, and hence,
   On them is Wrath, and theirs will be
   A grievous chastisement.

17.   God is the One Who has sent down
   The Book with truth and a true Balance,[1]
   But how could it be to you known,
   That the Hour, is at no distance?

18.   Those who do not believe in it,
   Would like to hasten it,
   But those who do believe in it,
   Hold it in awe, for they're aware,

---

1. This according to commentators means, "the law contained in the Quran",
"revelations by which we can weigh all questions of right and wrong", or "the
scales for Truth".

That it's the Truth; lo! Have they not,
Those who doggedly doubt the Hour,
Gone farthest into error?

19. Allah is Loving-Kind unto His servants,
To whom He Will, He grants in plenty,
And He's the Strong, the Mighty.

20. Whoever hankers after
The harvest of the other world,
For him We shall increase
The harvest manifold,
And He who hungers for
The harvest of this world,
Of it We give him here,
But He shall have no share,
In the Hereafter.

21. Perhaps they have some partner-gods,
Who, in the matter of religion,
Have for them sanctioned certain things,
Without Allah's permission!
But had it not been for a Word
Of respite, judgment had been given
Ere now among them; surely the impious,[1]
Shall undergo a torment grievous;

22. Aghast at their own vile performance,
Shall you see the unjust,
This will happen, it is a must;
But those who do believe,

---

1. Or: "The unjust, the evil-doers, the oppressors".

And do what's right, will rest
In the Meadows of Paradise,
There, by their Lord, shall they receive
Whatever they desire, and this
Shall be the greatest Grace.

23.   This is a part of the good news
That God unto His servants gives,
To those who do believe and do
What's right. Say: "I demand of you
No wage for this but love for relatives[1] ;"
And anyone who earns a righteous deed,
We give him more of good therein indeed;
For God's the Oft-Forgiver,
And the Most-Grateful Giver.

24.   What! Do they say that "he has forged
Falsehoods concerning Allah? But,
If Allah willed, He could seal up
Your very heart! Nay, God blots out
The falsehood and confirms the truth,
Through His own Words; He's the Awarest
Of what's in every breast.

25.   He it is Who accepts repentance,
From his servants, and pardons,
Their wrong-doings and sins,

---

1. According to most commentators this means "love for my relatives", some,
however, translate this as "love for your relatives", yet, as the Holy Prophet is
a member of the Quraish of Mecca, the meaning would be the same, that is,
he at least has the right to ask that his kith and kin should not persecute him
and his family; and, of course, the general sense of "loving one another" may
also be taken into account.

And knows your whole performance.

26. To those who do believe and do what's right,
Will He listen and unto them augment
His graceful bounties, but the disbelievers
Shall have a grievous chastisement.

27. If God were to bestow abundance on
His servants, they would surely be insurgents,
Throughout the land, but He sends down by measure,
As He pleases, for of His servants,
Is He the Most-Informed Observer.

28. And He's the One who sends down rain,
When they have given up all hope,
And spreads abroad His grace amain;
He is indeed the Praised Protector.

29. And of His Signs is the creation,
Of the heavens and of the earth,
And of the living creatures that He has
Scattered over them both;
And when He Wills, He has the Power
To gather them together.

30. No misfortune unto you happens,
But you have wrought it by your hands,
Yet there are many things He pardons.

31. Be sure you can't escape Him on the earth,
Neither beside God shall you find,
A patron or a helping hand.

32. And ships are also of His Signs,
    That sail upon the oceans,
    Looking like mountains.

33. But if it be his will,
    He is able to lull and still
    The winds, and they'll be static
    Upon its back;
    Truly herein are Signs,
    To all the patient, grateful persons;

34. Or He could let them sink,
    Down to the bottoms,
    For what they've done;
    But many things He pardons.

35. And thus the people who gainsay,
    Our revelations will find out,
    That they shall never get away.

36. Whatever you are given is indeed,
    A passing joy in the life of this world,
    But better and more lasting is a portion,
    With God for the faithful, who in their Lord,
    Will put their trust;

37. Those who avoid all major sins,
    And shun indecencies,
    And even in their anger grave,
    Are ready to forgive,

38. Who to their Lord respond,
    Attend unto their prayers,

Conduct all their affairs,
Through mutual counsel, and expend,
Of that with which We have enriched them,
In charitable alms.

39.　And those who when some wrong is done them,
Are ready to defend themselves.

40.　And let the retribution of
An evil,[1] be to it accorded;
Yet those who pardon and make peace,
Shall be by God Himself rewarded;
For God certainly has no love,
For those who will transgress.

41.　But those who, after being wronged,
Avenge themselves and do the same,
Upon them, there shall be no blame;

42.　The blame shall only rest on those
Who do their fellowmen oppress,
And insolently through the land transgress,
In disregard of justice;
For these there is a torment grievous.

43.　But it would be an act of
Great resolution when a person,
Bears wrongs with patience and will pardon.

44.　Those whom Allah will leave to err,
Shall have, thereafter, no protector,

---

1. Or: "an injury".

And you shall then the evil-doers' comment,
After they see the Torment, hear:
"Is there not some way back from here?"

45.   And you shall see them brought before it,
Shamefully in abasement,
But they shall look at it with furtive looks,
And the believers shall thus comment:
"Truly the losers are the folks
Who lose themselves and their own kin,[1]
Upon the Day of Resurrection;
Shall not the perpetrators of oppression,
Be in eternal Torment?"

46.   And no protector could they have but God
To help them out; there is no way, however,
For those whom God has left to err.

47.   Do hearken to your Lord before the Day,
Shall come, which when ordained by God, none may
Avert at all; no place is there to fly
To on that Day, and nought could you deny!

48.   Now if they turn away and pay no heed,
Remember We have not sent you to be
A watcher over them; yours it is only
To carry on the Message; and indeed,
When We give man a taste of Our own Mercy,
He does in it rejoice, but when some ill,
Befalls him, due to his own former deed,
Lo! Truly man will be ungrateful!

---

1. Or: "followers".

49.   The Kingdom of the heavens
      And of the earth, to God belongs;
      He is ever creating what He will,
      Daughters He gives to whom he please,
      And sons He gives to whom He will;

50.   Or He will give them children,
      Of both kinds, male and female,
      And whom He will, He shall make barren,
      For He's the Wise, the Powerful.

51.   It is not fitting for a mortal
      That God should speak with Him but by:
      Revelation, or from behind a veil,
      Or by the sending of a messenger,
      Who will, by His permission, then reveal
      Whatsoever he pleases,
      For he is the Most High, the Wise.

52.   Thus have We sent to you a spirit,[1]
      By Our command, with revelation:
      You did not know, before this, of the Book,
      Nor of the Faith; yet an illumination
      Did We ordain it, guiding by it,
      Whome'er We please among Our servants,
      And you will surely guide
      Into the Direct Road,

53.   Which is the Way of God:
      To Whom belongs,
      All that is in the heavens,

---

1. Or: "Gabriel".

And what the earth contains;
Behold! Most surely everything,
In the long run, to God returns!

SURA 43
GOLDEN ORNAMENTS
(AL-ZUKHRUF)

In the Name of God, the Beneficent, the Merciful

1. Haa Meem.[1]

2. By the Book in explicitness supreme!

3. We have indeed made it an Arabic,
   Reading,[2] that you perhaps will think;

4. And it's a transcript from the Mother-Book,
   With Us, Sublime and Full of Wisdom.

5. What! Since you are a reckless folk,
   Shall We from you then this Reminder,
   Turn away altogether?

6. Lo! Many prophets have We sent,
   Unto the peoples ancient;

7. Yet never came to them a prophet,
   Whom they would not be scoffing at!

8. Thus We destroyed them, though they were
   Far mightier than these[3] in power;
   But the example of the men of old,
   Who went before them, will still hold.

---

1. H.M.
2. Or "Quran".
3. The Meccans.

9.   Yet if you ask them who created
    The heavens and the earth,
    They will certainly say: It was the Wise,
    The All-Mighty Who did create them both;

10.   Yes, it was He Who for you placed,
    The earth as a cradle, and traced
    Out routes upon it that you may
    Find your own way;

11.   And He's the One Who sends down from the Heaven,
    Water in due degree; by which We quicken
    Every dead land: you will likewise
    Be made to rise,

12.   Who has created mating pairs,
    Of all species, and made the vessel,
    For you, as well as beasts,
    On which you travel,

13.   And on their backs you keep your balance;
    And once you have thus firmly mounted
    Or boarded them, you may remember
    The favour of your Lord, and utter:
    "Glory be unto Him Who has subjected
    These unto us, as we ourselves could never
    Bring them under our dominance;

14.   "But, back unto our Lord, we'll be directed."

15.   Yet: some of His own servants,
    They take as His components!
    Most certainly is man,

A clearly thankless specimen!

16.   Has He, out of His own creation,
      Unto Himself some daughters taken,
      But sons for you He's chosen[1] .

17.   Yet when the tidings of the birth of that
      Which they do set up as a likeness!
      To Al-Rahmaan,[2] is brought to one of them,
      His face will settle into darkness,
      And he'll be filled with pressing sadness!

18.   Females brought up to only look attractive,
      Who are in disputations most defective?![3]

19.   They also make the angels,
      Who are servants of God the One,
      Daughters and females!
      Now, did they witness their creation?
      Surely their witness shall be taken down,
      And questioned shall they be for certain.

20.   They also say: "We would have never
      Worshipped them,[4] if it had not been the will
      Of the Most Merciful!"[5]
      No knowledge have they in this whatsoever,
      Lies only do they tell!

1. Daughters, goddesses: The Arab pagans believed that their female "deities"
   and angels were daughters of Allah (God the One, the Supreme God).
2. The God of Mercy, the Most Beneficent.
3. Could females with such qualities, in the pagans' minds, be partners with
   God?
4. The idols   5. Al-Rahmaan.

21. Or did We e're give them a Holy Writ,[1]
     And they are holding fast to it?

22. But nay! They say: "we found our fathers,
     Upon a course,[2] and we are travellers,
     In their footsteps on the same avenue."

23. In the same way, we never sent, before you,
     A warner to a town[3] whose well-to-do
     Did not cry out: "Surely we found our fathers,
     Upon a course, and we are followers;
     Of their footsteps indeed!"

24. They[4] said: "Even if we do bring you,
     A better guidance and religion,
     Than what you found your fathers on?"
     They said: "We don't even acknowledge
     Your apostolic message!"

25. Thus We exacted from them retribution:
     Behold the fate of those who did engage
     In Truth-rejection!

26. Recall the time when Abraham thus spoke,
     Unto his father and his folk:
     "I totally myself absolve,
     Of everything you serve,

---

1. "Authorizing angel-worship".

2. Also: "Religion, persuasion".

3. Also: "Habitation, nation, country".

4. "All warners, every warner".

27.　　"Except the One Who made me,
　　　　He it is Who will guide me."

28.　　And thus he left this Word[1] behind,
　　　　To last for his posterity,
　　　　That unto Him they should be turned.

29.　　Yea, to these men[2] and to their fathers,
　　　　I have indeed been generous,
　　　　Until the Truth should come to them,
　　　　And an Apostle luminous.

30.　　Now that the Truth has to them come, they state:
　　　　"This is magic and we reject it!"

31.　　They also say: "why was not this Quran,
　　　　Sent down to an important man,
　　　　In the towns twain[3] ?"

32.　　Are they in charge of allocating,
　　　　The Mercy of your Lord?
　　　　We it is Who deal out their livelihood,
　　　　To them, in the life of this world,
　　　　And We have raised some of them higher
　　　　In rank than others, so that they could hire
　　　　Each other's service; better is your Lord's
　　　　Mercy than all their hoards.

---

1. Or "doctrine, message, precept"; the Gospel of Unity: "I worship only Him
　　Who created me."
2. The idolatrous Arabs.
3. Mecca and Taa'if.

33. But were it not that all mankind,
    Would have become a single nation,[1]
    We would have certainly assigned,
    To those with no belief in Al-Rahmaan,[2]
    Houses with silver roofs, and stairways silvern,
    That they by which ascend,

34. And gates of silver to their houses,
    And silver couches to recline upon,

35. Together with: ornaments golden;
    Yet naught is all this but provision,
    Of this world's life; and the enjoying
    Of the Hereafter with your Lord,
    Shall only be for the god-fearing.

36. And he who fails to heed the warning
    Of Al-Rahmaan:
    To him shall We assign a satan,
    And he will be his close companion!

37. And these[3] divert them from the direct Road,
    While they still think that they are rightly guided!

38. At length, when such a person comes before Us,
    He says:[4] "would that 'tween me and you had been,
    The distance of the East and West!"
    What an evil companion!

---

1. "Of disbelievers".

2. The Beneficent One, the God of Mercy

3. The satans, the devils.

4. "To his devil-companion".

39.　　But since you were an evil-doer,
　　　　This Day it will not profit you at all,
　　　　That you, in Torment, have a partner!

40.　　Could you[1] then make the deaf to hear,
　　　　Or to the blind show the direction,
　　　　Or guide the person sunk
　　　　In flagrant deviation?

41.　　We will surely take vengeance on them,
　　　　Whether We take you hence,

42.　　Or let you see what We have promised them;
　　　　For over them We have full Dominance.

43.　　Therefore hold fast to what
　　　　Has been to you revealed;
　　　　Upon the Direct Road,
　　　　Are you indeed!

44.　　Surely to you and to your people
　　　　It is an Admonition, and you all
　　　　Shall be about it questioned.

45.　　Question[2] any of Our apostles,
　　　　We did before you send:
　　　　"Did We ever set up a deity,[3]
　　　　To be worshipped beside
　　　　The God of Mercy?"

---

1. The Holy Prophet.

2. "Examine the Messages of".

3. Or "other gods".

46.   Of old did We sent Moses with Our Signs,
       To Pharaoh and his nobles;
       He said: "Truly I am a messenger,
       Of the Lord of the Worlds."

47.   But after he did show,
       Our Signs unto them, lo!
       They only laughed at them;

48.   Every Sign that We showed them though,
       Was greater than the one preceding,
       And We afflicted them with torments,
       That they might be conceding.[1]

49.   They said: "O you magician,
       Call on your Lord on our behalf,
       To do as He has promised you;
       We will be guided, sure enough!"[2]

50.   But when We did relieve them from the scourge,
       Lo! They did break the pledge!

51.   And Pharaoh made a proclamation,
       Among his nation:
       "O People mine!
       Is not the sovereignty of Egypt mine?
       And aren't these rivers mine,

---

1. That is: "accept the Truth and turn to God".

2. Such statements, half a mockery, half a ruse, were spoken to Moses on different occasions, to stop the plagues that came one after another: each time they promised to obey Allah!

Which flow beneath my feet?[1]
Surely your sight could be no cheat!

52.   "Am I not better than this abject wretch,
Who could hardly express himself in speech!

53.   "Why has he not been given
Some bracelets golden,
Or have no angels come along with
Him in procession?"

54.   Thus he incited his own folk,
To levity, and they obeyed him,
Because they were a people sunk,
In unbridled transgression.

55.   And when at length they had,
Provoked Our anger,
We took vengeance upon them,
And drowned them all together;

56.   And thus We turned them into
An ancient lesson,
And an example unto
Each coming generation.

57.   And when the Son of Mary is held up
As an example,[2] lo! your people,
Raise a clamour in ridicule,

---

1. The abundant streams from the Nile flowing beneath his palace, were evidence of his power, prosperity and sovereignty: he boasted of water and he perished in water!

2. That is: "as a shining example of Divine Power."

58.   And cry: "Is he better than these our gods?"[1]
        This they only set forth in disputation;
        They are indeed a most contentious nation!

59.   Nay! He was just a servant whom We did
        Bless with favours, and made him an example,
        For the Children of Israel.

60.   Were it Our will, We could bring forth
        Angels out of yourselves to be
        Succeeding you upon the earth.

61.   In fact he[2] is a sign of Resurrection;
        Harbour no doubt about it then,
        And follow me: this is the right Direction.

62.   And never be misled by Satan,
        For he's your foe, most open.

63.   When Jesus came with clearest Signs,
        He said: "Unto you have I brought
        Wisdom, and I will clarify,
        To you parts of the things about
        Which you're at variance; thus be
        God-fearing and obey me;

64.   "Certainly my Lord and your Lord,
        Is God the One;

---

1. The Arab pagans' logic was this: 'As Jesus, is worshipped by some Christians
   as a deity, why could they not worship their own gods and idols? They are
   surely preferable to gods of such foreign cults as Christianity!'

2. Jesus.

Thus worship Him alone,
This is indeed the direct Road."

65.   Then different factions[1] fell into disputes,
        Among themselves; but woe to those who thus
        Transgressed, from the chastisement of a Day
        Painfully grievous.

66.   Do they wait only for the Hour of Doom:
        That it should overtake them,
        All of a sudden, least expected,

67.   Intimate friends upon that Day become
        Adversaries to one another;
        Those who feared God, however,
        Shall be excepted:

68.   O My devoted servants,
        No fear shall be on you this Day,
        Nor will you be in any way,
        Sad and dejected;

69.   You are the ones who did believe,
        And unto God truly submitted;[2]

70.   You enter into Paradise,
        With your near ones,[3] delighted;

71.   Golden platters and drinking-cups,

---

1. Jewish and Christian sects.

2. Original: "have been true Muslims".

3. Or: spouses, consorts, companions.

Shall be to them passed round,
And therein will they find,
What every soul yearns after
Whatever eyes delight in;
And there you shall abide for ever.

72.   This is the Paradise,
That you receive as recompense,
For what you wrought;

73.   And for your sustenance,
You'll have abundant fruit.

74.   But the wrong-doing sinners shall,
For ever in Hell's Torment dwell,

75.   Nowise will it[1] be to them calmed,
So there they will be overwhelmed
With absolute despair.

76.   It was not We who were to them unfair,
But they themselves have been,
To their own souls tyrannic!

77.   And they shall supplicate: "O Maalik,[2]
Would that your Lord would ever make
A final end of us!" And he shall say:
"Nay! You are here to stay!"

78.   Surely to you We brought the Truth,
Although most of you hate the Truth!

1. The Torment.

2. A keeper of Hell, in charge of the torments of the damned.

79. What! Have they settled some contrivings?
But it is We Who settle things!

80. Do they reckon We do not hearken their
Secrets and what's said in an undertone?
Aye! And Our angels at their sides,
Do write them down.

81. Say: "If Al-Rahmaan had a son,
I would, in worship, be the first one;

82. But far Exalted is the Lord of
The Heavens and the Earth, Lord of the Throne,
Above those accusations that they have
Against Him thrown.

83. Therefore leave them to babble,
And let them vainly play,
Until they face their promised Day.

84. It's He Who is God in the Heaven,
And God on Earth, and He alone
Is the All-Wise, the Lord of Ken.

85. And blessed is He to Whom belongs
The Kingdom of the heavens,
And of the Earth and all that
Between them lies;
The knowledge of the Hour is,
With Him alone,
And unto Him you will return.

86. Those others whom they call upon beside Him,

Have no authority to intercede,
Save anyone who testifies unto
The Truth, and knows indeed.

87.　　If you ask them who has created them,
They surely answer: "God the One!"
Whence are they then turned from
The right opinion!

88.　　And to his[1] calling: "O My Lord, these men,
Will not the Faith embrace",

89.　　Is said: "Bear with them and say 'peace',
For soon they'll come to notice!"

---

1. The Holy Prophet's.

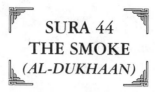

SURA 44
THE SMOKE
(AL-DUKHAAN)

In the Name of God, the Beneficent, the Merciful

1.   Haa Meem.[1]

2.   By the Book in explicitness supreme.

3.   We sent it down upon a blessed night;
     Givers are We of warnings right,

4.   And in it[2] every precept wise was made,
     Most plain indeed,

5.   As a commandment from Ourself;
     We have always revealed,

6.   Blessing of revelation from your Lord,
     Who's Hearing all and Knows of everything;

7.   Lord of the heavens and the earth,
     And what between them lies; in Whom your faith,
     Should be unshaking.

8.   There is no God but He, and it is He,
     Who life and death ordains;
     Your Lord is He, and the Lord of your fathers,
     Of bygone days.

---

1. H.M.

2. During that night.

9. But nay! With doubts they're playing games!

10. Therefore keep waiting and do mark
    Them on the Day wherein the heaven,
    Will bring about a smoke,
    Misty and yet unhidden,

11. Which will enshroud mankind:
    This is a torment grievous.

12. "Our Lord, remove the Torment from us,
    For we are true believers![1] "

13. How do they from the Warning profit
    Now that to them has come a prophet,
    Who all things clears?

14. They turn their backs on him and say:
    "A madman taught by others!"

15. We will remove the plague from you a little,
    Yet certainly you will return to evil.[2]

16. Then on the day when We will strike
    Our most horrendous stroke,
    We'll certainly Our vengeance,
    Upon them take!

17. Before their time, we put to test the people
    Of Pharaoh, after an apostle noble,

---

1. "They shall say".
2. Or: "unbelief"; original: "to it".

Himself to them presented.

18.   "Do send away with me", cried he,
    "Allah's own servants, for most surely,
    I'm an apostle to be trusted;

19.   "And do not ever hold yourselves,
    Above Allah; indeed I bring you
    Some veritable proofs,

20.   "And I take refuge with the One, Who is
    My Lord and your own Lord in truth,
    Against your stoning me to death;

21.   "And if in me you have no faith,
    Do let it not incur your wrath!"

22.   Later he cried unto his Lord:
    "Wicked people are these in sooth!"

23.   "If that's the case, then do march forth
    Together with My servants in,
    The dead of night, for you will be
    Pursued for certain[1] ;

24.   "Then go across the parted sea,
    For they shall be a legion,
    Bound to be drowned!"

25.   How many were the gardens and the fountains,
    They left behind!

---

1. The speaker is God.

26.   And fields of corn, and noble dwellings!

27.   And all the other pleasant things,
       They took delight in!

28.   So was their end!
       And what was theirs, We gave to other men.

29.   Neither the Heaven nor the Earth,
       Over them wept,
       Nay! And no longer were they kept!

30.   Most certainly We saved the Children
       Of Israel from an affliction,
       Wholly malignant,

31.   From Pharaoh; for he was the tyrant,
       Among the most extravagant.

32.   And them[1] did We, in Our cognition,
       Chose above every nation;

33.   And We did show them miracles,
       Which also served as their clear trials.

34.   Yet these people[2] are saying:

35.   "Except for our first death, there shall be nothing,
       And We will ne'er again be rising!

---

1. The Children of Israel.

2. The pagans of Mecca.

36.   "Bring our forefathers back,
        If it's the truth you speak!"

37.   What! Do they think that they are better
        Than the people of Tubba[1] ,
        And others who before them flourished?
        All of them We extinguished,
        For they were sunk in sin for ever.

38.   And We did not create the heavens,
        The earth, and what between them lies, as games!

39.   We did create them for a serious end,[2]
        But most of them do not this comprehend.

40.   Surely the Day of Separation,
        Shall be, for all of them,
        The pre-appointed congregation,

41.   The Day when friends,
        Shall not attend to friends,
        When none any assistance finds;

42.   Save the people on whom:
        God may have Mercy, for He is
        In Might Exalted, Merciful.

43.   Indeed the tree of Al-Zaq-qoom,[3]

---

1. The prosperous, ancient people (and kings) of Hamyar in Yemen, whose
   hegemony once extended over all Arabia to the East African Coast.
2. Original: in truth.
3. The dreadful, bitter tree growing at the bottom of Hell.

44. Shall be the diet of the sinful,

45. It is like molten copper,
And it shall boil inside their womb,

46. Like the boiling of scalding water.

47. "Seize him and drag him down,
Into the midst of Fire,

48. "Then pour upon his head
Of the tormenting, boiling water,

49. "Now taste it! For you are forsooth,
The man of might and honour!

50. "This is certainly what you had
Been puzzling over!"

51. But the righteous who did restrain
Themselves, shall be on safest terrain:

52. Amid gardens and fountains,

53. Dressed in some garments made
Of finest silk and rich brocade,
Beholding one another,

54. Such are to be their stations;
And We shall wed them unto Houri belles,
With eyes after gazelles;

55. Therein they may in peace and comfort,

Have every kind of fruit;

56.   As their first death is passed, they will therein,
        Taste no more death; and He will save them
        From the chastisement of *Jaheem*:[1]

57.   It is the gracious bounty of your Lord,
        It is success supreme!

58.   We have made it[2] easy indeed,
        In your own tongue, perhaps
        They will take heed;

59.   Thus: waiting is what you shall do,
        For they are waiting too!

---

1. The Blazing Hell.
2. The Quran.

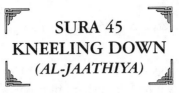

SURA 45
KNEELING DOWN
(AL-JAATHIYA)

In the Name of God, the Beneficent, the Merciful

1. Haa Meem.[1]

2. The revelation of this Book is from
   Allah: in Might Exalted, Full of Wisdom.

3. Most surely in the heavens and the earth,
   Are Signs for those who do have faith,

4. And in your own creation, and that of
   The beasts He spreads abroad, are also Signs
   For people certain of the Truth,

5. And in the alternation,
   Of Night and Day, and in provision
   That God sends down from heaven,
   Whereby he gives life to the earth,
   After its death,
   And in the circulation of the winds,
   Are Signs for those who use their minds!

6. Such are the Signs of God the One,
   That We recite to you with truth;
   So then, in what *hadeeth*,[2]
   Will they have faith, if they,
   God and His Signs deny?

---

1. H.M.

2. Announcement, discussion, report and tradition.

7.   Woe unto every sinful, falsehood-monger,

8.   Who hears God's verses unto him rehearsed,
        And then, as if he heard them not, persists
        In proud disdain! Inform him thus,
        Of a torment most grievous!

9.   When something of Our revelations,
        Comes to the knowledge of such folk,
        They take it as a joke!
        There shall be, for these people,
        A chastisement most shameful;

10.   Hell's in their hot pursuit,
        And all their worldly gains,
        Avails them not a hoot!
        Nor those they took for patrons,
        Instead of God! They shall only receive,
        A torment truly grave.

11.   This is true Guidance:
        Thus those who disbelieve the revelations
        Of their own Lord, shall suffer
        A grievous torment of abominations.

12.   It's God the One Who has subjected
        To you the oceans and the seas,
        That ships traverse it at His bidding,
        And that you may seek of His bounties,
        And that you may be grateful.

13.   He has also subjected to you all
        That's in the heavens and upon the earth,

All of it is from Him; surely in this,
Are Signs for those who ponder on the truth.

14.   Tell the believers that they should excuse
Those who do not expect the Days of God,[1]
For He Himself shall recompense,
Every people according to its deed

15.   Whoever does a righteous deed,
It is to his own benefit,
And whoever does evil, it shall be
To his own hurt,
But then all of you, in the end,
Shall be unto your Lord returned.

16.   To the Children of Israel,
We gave of old the Book and Wisdom,
And the prophetic missions,
And with good things of life, We blessed them,
And favoured them above all nations;

17.   We granted them manifest sanctions
In the Affair;[2] but it was after,
Knowledge was granted them that they,
Fell into schisms with each other,
Through mutual envy,[3] but your Lord,
Will certainly judge any matter,
In which they did between them differ,
Upon the Day of Resurrection.

---

1. Days of victory for God and His prophets, and evil for the disbelievers.

2. The affair of prophethood and the question of religion.

3. Or "through evil motives".

18.   Then We put you[1] upon the Highroad[2]
        Of the Affair;[3] thus follow it, and follow
        Not the low lusts of people,
        Who do not know.

19.   For certainly they shall, against
        Allah, not help you in the least;
        In sooth the evil-doers, the unjust
        Are one another's patrons,
        But the Protector of the ones,
        Who do fear Him, is God the One.

20.   This[4] gives insights to humankind,
        Guidance and Grace it is in truth,
        For people certain of their faith.

21.   Do people who do evil, really deem
        That We shall deal with them as with the folk,
        Who did believe and led a righteous life,
        Or that their lives and deaths shall be alike?
        Awfully ill is what they think!

22.   The heavens and the earth
        Did God create to show the truth,
        And that each soul could be paid back,
        According to its deed,
        That they shall not be wronged indeed.

---

1. The Holy Prophet.
2. Original: *sharia'* meaning "a highway", "a straight course", thus "the way of religion" or "the divine law".
3. Of the issue of faith, religion and divine commandments.
4. "This Book" or "these revelations".

23. Think! Who, but God, may guide a person,
    Whose god is his own lust and passion,
    Whom God has wisely left in error,
    Setting a seal upon his ears and mind,
    And impeding his eye-sight with a cover?
    Will you then not be warned?

24. "Except for this our present life,
    There is nothing, "they claim,
    "And we live and we die, and nought
    Would destroy us but Time!"
    Indeed they have no knowledge of this,
    Unwittingly they only guess!

25. And when our revelations plain,
    Are unto them rehearsed, their logic
    In argument will make them say:
    "Bring our forefathers back,
    If it's the truth you speak!"

26. Say: "It is God Who gives you life,
    And causes you to die, and then,
    He will assemble you upon
    The Day of Resurrection, in
    Whose coming is no doubt; most men,
    However, have of this no ken.

27. The Kingdom of the heavens,
    And of the earth, to God belongs,
    And the day when the Hour is come,
    Yea, on that day, the falsehood-mongers,
    Shall meet their final doom.

28.   You shall see every nation kneeling down,
    And every nation shall be summoned
    Before its book:[1] "You'll be rewarded,
    This Day for all you earned;

29.   "This book of Ours will speak of you,
    With truth, for We have been recording,
    Everything you were doing."

30.   And those who did embrace the faith,
    And did what was righteous and proper,
    Into His Mercy shall their Lord,
    Cause them to enter:
    That shall be the undoubted Bliss.

31.   But the infidels He shall thus address:
    "Were not My revelations ever
    Recited unto you?! Indeed you were
    Puffed up with pride, and then
    Became a sinful, guilty nation;

32.   "And when you were reminded that the Promise
    Of God was true, and that, about the Hour
    There was no doubt, you did profess:
    'Of what the Hour is, we have no ken!
    We really think it's just a guess,
    But We are certainly uncertain!'"

33.   And then the evils of their deeds become,
    Unto them manifest,
    And they, by that at which they used to mock,

---

1. Or: "Record".

Shall be encompassed.

34.   They will be also told: "This Day We will,
        Forget you, as you had forgotten
        Your Meeting with Us, on this day of yours,
        The Fire shall be your eternal den,
        Wherein you will be helped by none!

35.   "That is your fate, for you did take
        God's revelations for a joke!
        And this world's life upon you
        Did play a trick."
        Therefore nothing today unbends
        Them from it, nor given a break,
        Are they to make amends!

36.   Therefore all praise is God's
        Lord of the heavens,
        Lord of the earth, and Lord,
        Of all the worlds!

37.   To Him belongs
        The Grandeur in the heavens,
        And on the earth, and He's:
        The Mighty, the All-Wise.

SURA 46

THE SANDY PLAINS

(AL-AHQAAF)

In the Name of God, the Beneficent, the Merciful

1. Haa Meem.[1]

2. The revelation of the Book is from
    Allah: in Might Exalted, Full of Wisdom.

3. Nay, We did not create the heavens,
    The earth and what between them lies,
    But for just ends[2] and for a settled term;
    Yet those who disbelieve pay no attention
    Unto Our admonition.

4. Say: "If you happen to be truthful men,
    Do think of what you call upon
    Along with God the One!
    Show me what they created on the earth?
    Do they of heavens share a portion?
    Bring me a Book they sent before this,[3]
    Or some vestige of revelation?[4]

5. And who is more in error than the man,
    Who does, instead of Allah, call upon
    Idols that will not answer them until,
    The Day of Resurrection!
    They are certainly unaware of

---

1. H.M.   2. Original: "with truth, in all truth".   3. The Holy Quran.

4. Original: "traces of knowledge": some divine commandment authorizing the
   worship of "other gods" than God the One.

850

Their invocation!

6. And when mankind is brought together,
They'll be hostile to them, and they will counter,
Their own deification.

7. And when Our lucid revelations are
To them recited, those who have no faith,
Say, of the truth which has been brought to them:
"Plain sorcery is this in sooth!"

8. Or do they say: "It[1] is his fabrication!"
Say: "If I have invented it, then nothing
Do you control to save me from God's wrath!
But He well knows what you're about it saying!
Witness enough is He indeed,
Between me and you all,
And He's the Pardoning, the Merciful.

9. Say: "I am not a prodigy among
Apostles, nor do I already know,
What will be done with me and you;
Only what's unto me revealed, I follow,
Giving plain warning is my only mission."

10. Say: "Do think if it[2] be from God,
And you reject it?! When an Israelite,[3]
Vouches for its conformity,[4] and does
Believe it, while you vainly arrogate?!

---

1. The Quran.   2. The Quran, the Message.

3. One of the learned Jews who embraced Islam in its early days.

4. With the divine Law.

Ah! Surely Allah does not guide,
Those given to transgression.

11. The Infidels[1] say of the faithful:
    "If it had been a good thing, then they[2] would,
    Not have believed in it before us!"
    Lo! Since they cannot see in it some good
    Guidance, they charge: "This is an ancient falsehood!"

12. But then before this,[3] came
    The Book of Moses,[4] and this is
    A Book verifying the same
    In the Arabic tongue,
    To warn the people who do wrong,
    And to be giving tidings glad
    To the doers of right and good.

13. Certainly they who say: "Our Lord is Allah,"
    And firmly stay on the road of belief,
    Neither shall they have any fear,
    Nor shall they ever come to grief.

14. They'll be the Guests of Paradise,
    Timelessly there in residence:
    Of their own deeds, the recompense.

15. We have indeed on man enjoined,
    To be, unto his parents kind,
    His mother bears him with much pain

---

1. The rich and the powerful of Mecca.

2. The faithful, mostly from among the poor and the oppressed.

3. The Quran.   4. The Torah, the Pentateuch.

And she gives birth to him in pain;
His carrying until he's weaned,
Is thirty months; and when, at length,
He'll reach the age of fullest strength,
And will to forty years attain,
He says: "Grant me, my Lord, that I may be,
Grateful for favours You bestowed on me
And upon both my parents,
And that I may do righteous works that will
Please You; and pray, in my descendants,
Be to me Gracious; to You I have turned,
And I am to Your will resigned.[1] "

16. These are indeed the folks
From whom We shall accept
Their noblest works, and whose ill works,
Will We pass by; they shall be grouped
Among the heirs of Paradise:
What they were promised proved
To be a truthful promise!

17. But he who says unto his parents:
"Fie on you! Are you warning me
That I'll be taken out,[2] when many
Generations have passed already
Before my time[3] ?" But still the parents,
Implore the help of God and pray:
"Woe to you! Do have faith,
Surely God's promise is the truth";

---

1. Or: "I am a Muslim".

2. "Taken forth from the grave alive on the Resurrection Day."

3. That is: "They are dead and gone away for ever".

And yet he'll say:
"Oh, stories of the ancients!"

18.   Such men justly deserve the Sentence
Passed on the bygone generations
Of Jinns and humans,
Loser indeed shall they be hence!

19.   And for them all, there shall be ranks,
According to their works,
So that God may repay them duly
For their own deeds; but they will surely
Not be dealt with unfairly.

20.   For those who disbelieve, there is a Day,
When they shall be before the Fire placed:
"You squandered your good things and precious gifts,
During your earthly life, and you did taste
Pleasures in them a while; therefore this Day,
You shall be sternly punished and disgraced,
As your reward for being arrogant,
On the earth, and because you have transgressed.

21.   And mention one of Aad's[1] own brethren,[2]
Who warned his people in the Sandy Plains,[3]
-Surely before his time and after,
Did come many a warner-
"Serve none but God: for you, I feel the terror,
Of a Day full of dreadful pains!"

---

1. The people of Aad.   2. The Prophet Hood.

3. Sand hills or sandy dunes: characteristic of the country of the Aad, adjoining
Yemen and Hadramaut in Southern Arabia.

22. They said: "You really come to us to turn us,
    Away from our own gods?!
    Then bring your threatened scourge upon us,
    If you're a man of truthful words!"

23. He answered: "Only Allah has that knowledge;
    And I proclaim to you the message,
    With which I have been sent;
    Nevertheless I do envisage
    That you're a folk most ignorant!"

24. So when they saw a passing cloud,
    Coming straight for their valleys, they cheered loud:
    "This is a cloud that for us carries rain!"
    "But nay! It is that which you wanted hastened:
    It's nothing but a blast of wind,
    Only pregnant with plagues of pain!

25. "Which will demolish everything
    At its own Lord's Command!"
    And that was how the morning found,
    Nothing of them but many a dwelling ruined!
    Thus do We pay back people who have sinned.

26. And We let them have such prosperity,
    Not to you[1] granted, and We gave them,
    Hearing, eyesight and minds, but neither
    Their ears, nor eyes, nor minds could save them,
    A thing of benefit, for they denied
    God's Signs,[2] and what[3] they did deride,
    Encompassed them on every side!

---

1. The Meccans.   2. Or "revelations".   3. The scourge of God.

855

27.   We did, of old, destroy many a town,
    Round about you;[1] yet to them We had shown
    Our Signs already, that they may return.

28.   Now, why was there no help to them,
    Forthcoming from those whom they took
    For gods beside God, as some kindred
    Deities unto Him? Nay! They forsook
    Them utterly: such was their falsehood,
    And what they did wrongfully fake!

29.   Let them know how We to you sent
    A band of Jinns to hearken
    To the Quran:
    No sooner were they in its presence,
    Than they remarked: "Listen in silence,
    And after it was ended, they betook
    Themselves, as warners, unto their own folk.

30.   They said: "Our people! We have heard a Book,
    After Moses sent down, that verifies
    What came before it, and, unto the Truth,
    It guides, and to a Direct Path;

31.   "O People, hearken to the one Who calls,
    You unto God, and do embrace His faith,
    That He may many of your sins forgive,
    And shield you from a torment grave;

32.   "Those who do not respond to Allah's caller,

---

1. The prosperous cities of Sheba, Aad and Thamood lay on the borders of
   Arabia; thus the people of Mecca are told how those living around them were

Shall not escape Him on this earth,
Nor shall they have a patron ever,
Instead of Him; these are in open error!"

33.   Do they not see that God Who did
        Create the heavens and the earth,
        And never was with their creation wearied,
        Is Able to give life unto the dead?!
        Yea, he possesses power,
        Over all things indeed.

34.   The Day is coming when the unbelievers
        Shall be presented to the Fire:
        "Is this not true?!" And they will answer:
        "Yea, by our Lord!" and He shall cry:
        "Then taste the Torment for
        What you used to deny!"

35.   Therefore endure with patience and be steadfast,
        As did the messengers endued with firmness,
        And for them,¹ do not be in any haste,
        For on the Day when they shall witness
        That which they had been Promised,
        They feel as if they had not tarried but
        An hour of a single day! Well-versed,
        Is the Message: Shall any perish save,
        The people who transgressed?

---

aforetime destroyed.

1. "For their doom."

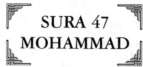

SURA 47
MOHAMMAD

In the Name of God, the Beneficent, the Merciful

1. To nought shall Allah bring,
   The deeds of those who have no faith,
   And try to block His Path.

2. But He will cancel every wrong,
   And rectify the state of whosoever,
   Believes and does what's good and proper,
   And in what has been to Mohammad,
   Sent down, has faith: The very Truth
   From their own Lord.

3. That is because: deniers of the faith,
   Do follow falsehood, while the faithful
   Follow the truth from their own Lord;
   Thus does Allah set forth for people
   Descriptions that with them accord.

4. Thus, when you face the disbelievers,[1]
   Strike off their heads, and once you overcome,
   Their force, do tie them up as prisoners;
   And afterwards grant them their freedom,
   Or also ask for ransom,
   After the battle cries have ended:
   Thus have you been commanded.
   Yet if God had so wished,
   He could Himself have punished
   Them by some scourge, but He would rather

---

1. "Armed disbelievers committing aggression against the Muslim Umma."

Test you by means of one another;
And those who, in the cause of God, were slain,
Will find their deeds were not in vain;

5.   He'll guide them and ennoble their condition,

6.   And will admit them to the Garden,
Of which He gave them information.

7.   O You believers, if you are
Helping the cause of Allah,
He'll help you, and He'll not allow
Your knees to tremble ever!

8.   As for the disbelievers:
Let them be in perdition,
For He has, their endeavours,
Rendered of no fruition;

9.   That is because they hate
What God sends down by revelation!
Thus does He all their actions frustrate!

10.   Have they not ever journeyed through the land,
To see what was their predecessors' end?
Allah destroyed them, and a kindred fate,
Awaits every rejecting pagan.

11.   That is because: God is the Patron
Of those who do have faith,
And those who have no faith,
Will never have a patron.

12.   Certainly Allah will admit the ones,
    Who do believe and do what's right, to Gardens,
    Watered by running streams;
    While the pagans enjoy some worldly feasts,
    And eat, as eat the beasts,
    And their abode shall be the Flames.

13.   How many were the cities,
    Greater in might and clout,
    Than the Town which has cast you[1] out?
    We wiped them off the land,
    Did anyone give them a hand!

14.   Could one who holds on to his Lord's
    Clear teachings, be compared with him whose foul
    Doings seem fair to him, who only follows
    The whims and lusts of his own soul?

15.   Here is a picture of the Paradise,
    Which to the righteous is Our promise:
    Therein run rivers of unstaling water,
    And brooks of milk whose taste will never alter,
    And rivulets of wine, for drinkers' joyful pleasure,
    And burns of honey, of the purest flavour,
    They will therein have fruits of every kind,
    With the Forgiveness of their Lord for ever!
    Does this look like the lot of those who find
    Themselves dwelling for ever in the Fire,
    And, of a scalding water, having sips,
    Which their bowels asunder rips?

---

1. The Holy Prophet.

16.   Indeed there are among them men
Who hearken unto you, but when,
They leave you, they will say to those
Who've been the knowledge given:
"What was it that he said just then?!"
Such are people whose wits God dims,
And who then follow their own whims.

17.   For the guided, He shall further augment,
Their Guidance,[1] and grant them their own Restraint.[2]

18.   Are they then waiting for the Hour of Doom,
That it suddenly come upon them?
Its portents have already come;
But how shall they have their Reminder,
When it's already there?!

19.   Know, therefore, that there is no deity
But God the One: ask pardon for your sin,
And for believers, men and women;
For God has perfect ken
Of your outdoor activity,
And what you do when you are in!

20.   The faithful say: "Would that a *sura*
Were now sent down,[3] but when a forthright
Sura has been revealed, whose burden
Is war, you see the people, in whose heart
Is malice, stare at you, as if they were
Fainting for fear of death! It would, however,

---

1. Spiritual advancement is progressive.

2. The spiritual power to restrain oneself.

3. "Allowing Muslims to fight against the unbelievers."

Have been for them more proper,

21.   If they obeyed and uttered what was fair;
And when the matter[1] was resolved on,
If they were true to God, it would be far
Better for them for certain.

22.   Were you[2] not ready, if you held command,
Surely to spread corruption in the land,
And cut your ties of kith and kin?

23.   Such are the men whom God has cursed, and then
Has made them deaf, and made them blind!

24.   Do they not meditate on the Quran,
Or have they locks upon their heart and mind?!

25.   Those who go back and leave their faith behind,
After the Guidance has been made,
Manifest unto them, have been beguiled
By Satan, and they have been buoyed
Up by him with false hopes indeed.

26.   That is because they say to those
Who hate what Allah has sent down:
"We do comply with you in some affairs!"
But God well knows their undertone!

27.   What will they do then when the angels make
Them to give up their ghosts, while they shall strike
Them on the face and back?!

---

1. "Of fighting the infidels".   2. The hypocrites.

28. That is because they follow whatsoever
Displeases God and do dislike His pleasure,
Therefore, He brings their works to naught.

29. Do the men of malicious mind and heart,
Reckon that God will never bring to light
Their evil thoughts and spite?

30. Had We so willed, We could have pointed them
Out to you, and you would then recognize
Them promptly by their looks, but certainly
You should still know them by the tone and guise
Of their expressions;
And Allah knows your actions.

31. And most certainly We shall let
You go through trials, so that We test,[1]
The faithful strivers[2] and the steadfast
Among you all, thus We shall make
Your mettle manifest.

32. The disbelievers who debar the others,
From Allah's Path, and counter and resist
The Messenger when Guidance has already
Been clearly shown them, shall not in the least,
Injure Allah! He will in fact,
Render their deeds of no effect.

33. O You believers, do obey
God, and obey the Messenger,
And let not your own labours ever

1. "To make known by tests".

2. Those who strive and fight in the cause of God.

Go uselessly astray!

34. The disbelievers who debar the others,
From Allah's Path, and die as disbelievers,
Shall never be by Allah pardoned.

35. Thus do not, out of weariness,
And faint-heartedly, cry for peace;
Surely you'll gain the upper hand,
For God the One is on your side:
He'll never let your labours slide.

36. This earthly life is nothing but
Some idle games and plays,
But if you do believe and guard
Against the evil, He then pays
Your wage and due reward;
But still He does not sanction,
That you give up every possession;

37. If He demanded that, and pressed you,
You would covetously withhold,
And all your hidden malice would unfold!

38. Lo! There you are! The people called
To give unto the cause of God!
And some of you are miserly indeed,
But the miserly is only a niggard,
To his own soul:
God's truly Needles but you are in need,
And if you turn away, He will indeed
Replace you with some other folk,
Who will not be at all your like!

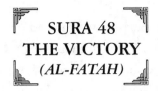

SURA 48
THE VICTORY
(AL-FATAH)

In the Name of God, the Beneficent, the Merciful

1. A glorious victory have We indeed
    Unto you given,

2. That God may cause your faults of past and future,
    To be forgiven,
    And make complete on you His Favour,
    And guide you on a Highway Even,

3. And aid you with His Mighty Aid.

4. He it was Who sent down *sakeenah*[1]
    Upon believers' hearts so that they grow,
    In faith much keener;
    For God has legions in the Skies,
    And on the Earth, and God's
    The Ever-Knowing, the All-Wise;

5. That He may bring believing men and women
    Up into Gardens through which rivers glide,
    Therein for ever to abide;
    And that He may remove from them their vice,
    For this is, in God's sight,
    The grand success.

6. And that He may chastise the men and women,

---

1. Divine calm, tranquillity, serenity; *shekheenah* in Hebrew means "The Holy
   Presence".

Among the hypocrites and faithless pagans,
Who always nourish evil thoughts on God;
On them there shall be evil turns,
Allah is wroth with them, and He has laid,
His curse upon them, and for them prepared,
The Fire of Hell, an evil, final turn.

7.   And legions in the Skies,
And on the earth, are God's
And God is the All-Mighty, the All-Wise.

8.   Indeed We sent you as a witness,
A bearer of good tidings,
And harbinger of warnings,

9.   In order that you all believe in God,
And His apostle, and you may then aid,
And honour Him, and sing His praise,
Mornings and evenings.

10.   The people who unto you swear allegiance,
Indeed they swear allegiance unto Allah,
For God's Hand was[1] above their hands, and hence,
Whoever breaks his oath, will only injure
His very soul, but those who truly guard,
Their pledge with Allah, they shall soon,
Receive from Him a rich reward.

11.   The laggards of the Arabs of the plain,[2]

---

1. Or: "is".

2. The desert Arabs who did not accompany the Holy Prophet on the
Pilgrimage to Mecca in the 6th year after Hijra.

Shall soon to you complain:
"It was our flocks and families
That kept us busy, therefore, please
Implore for our forgiveness!"
Out of their mouths departs,
What is not in their hearts!
Say: "Who could then command a thing
For you from Allah: Whether He intend,
Some loss on you to bring,
Or whether He will give you an advantage?"
Surely it's God Who has full knowledge
Of all that you are doing.

12.   In fact you thought that the Apostle
And the believers would not ever
Come back to their own people;
And this was, in your hearts, so nicely groomed,
That you were thinking nought but evil,
And turned into a people doomed.

13.   And We already have prepared the Fire,
For those who have no faith at all,
In God and in His Messenger.

14.   To God belongs the Kingdom of the Heavens,
And of the Earth; whome'er He Wills, He pardons,
And He does punish whom He will,
For God is Oft-Forgiving, Merciful.

15.   When you set out to gather spoils of war,
The laggards shall be saying:
"Do let us follow you"; do they desire
To change the Word of God?! Say: "Never

Will you follow us, for already thus
Has Allah spoken." Then they will maintain:
"Not so! You're only of us jealous!"
Indeed they hardly understand a thing.

16.   Say to the laggards 'mongst the Arabs of the plain:
You shall be summoned soon to face a nation,
Given to tougher confrontation,
Then you shall have to fight them,
Or they profess submission;[1]
Then if you prove obedient,
You will receive from God
A good repayment;
But if you turn back as you did before,
He shall inflict on you a painful torment.

17.   Upon the blind there is no blame,
Nor any blame upon the lame,
Also unblamed are the unwell;[2]
And whosoever does obey,
Allah and His apostle,
He shall admit him into Gardens
Watered by running streams,
While those who turn away, He shall chastise
With dreadful pains.

18.   Well pleased was God with the believers,
After they plighted fealty
To you under the tree;[3]

---

1. "Submission to the will of the Almighty, becoming a Muslim.

2. "If they do not go to the fight".

3. The ceremony of the covenant of Fealty took place while the holy Prophet
   sat under a tree in the plain of Hudaibiya.

He was Aware of what was in their hearts,
Thus He sent down to them Tranquillity,
And granted them a nearby victory,[1]

19.   And rich booties they gathered as their prize,
For God's the Mighty, the All-Wise.

20.   God has promised you many gains
That you'll acquire, but He has hastened,
These for you beforehand, and has restrained,
From you the hands of men,
That it unto believers be a Sign,
And that He may guide you along,
A Direct Lane.

21.   And other prizes you have not yet gained,
But which God is encompassing,
For God is Potent over everything.

22.   And even if the disbelievers,
Should give you battle, they'd be bound
To turn their backs; then no protectors,
Nor any helpers, shall they find.

23.   Such were the ways of God in foregone days,
And you shall find in God's tradition,
No alteration.

24.   He it was Who their hands from you restrained,
And your hands from them, in the Meccan vale,

---

1. The near victory was obtained at *Khaibar*, soon after the return from Hudaibiya.

After he let you over them prevail,
For God was Watchful of your every action.

25.   It's they who disbelieved and thwarted you,
From visiting the Holy Shrine, and blocked
The offerings to reach their destined venue!
Lo! There were faithful men and women,[1]
Unknown to you, whom you could trample down,
And would, unwittingly, have brought upon
Yourselves some shameful guilt on their account.
But God ordained it thus that He,
Brings whom He will into His Mercy.
If they had been apart, we would then have
Punished the unfaithful among them,
With a chastisement grave!

26.   And, while the disbelievers' hearts were tense,
With rage of prejudice and bigotry
The bigotry of Ignorance,[2]
God sent down His Tranquillity
On His Apostle and the faithful,
And the Word of restraining piety
Did He make on them binding.
For they were of it worthy and deserving,
And God is Cognizant of everything.

27.   God has indeed fulfilled
The vision unto His Apostle shown:
You'll certainly enter the Holy Shrine,
If Allah will, in full security,
With shaven heads or tresses shorn,

---

1. In Mecca.   2. "the ignorance of heathen days."

While fearing nothing.
For He does know what you know not, and thus
He granted you a speedy win before this.

28. He is the One Who has sent forth,
His Messenger with Guidance and the Truth
Of religion,[1] to make it dominant upon,
All of religious faith,
Surely Witness enough in truth,
Is God the One.

29. Mohammad is the Messenger of God,
And his followers should be solid
Of heart, against the disbelievers, but,
Amongst each other, most compassionate;
You see them bowing down, prostrating,
Imploring Grace from Allah and entreating,
His Good Pleasure; their marks are on their faces,
These are, of their prostration, traces;
This is their picture in the Torah,
And in the Gospel, the same aura:
They're as the seedling that puts out its shoot,
Then strengthens it, and it takes root,
And stoutly stands upon its stem,
Making the sowers to rejoice in them;
This fills the disbelievers with disgust,
Yet Allah has already made a Promise,
To the faithful, who do what's right and just,
Forgiveness and a noble recompense.

---

1. Religion of Truth or the true Religion.

SURA 49
THE CHAMBERS
(AL-HUJURAAT)

In the Name of God, the Beneficent, the Merciful

1. Believers! Do not take precedence,[1]
   In God's and His Apostle's presence,
   And be virtuous and god-fearing:
   For God is the All-Hearing,
   Who, of all things, has Cognizance.

2. Believers! Do not raise your voices,
   Above the Prophet's voice, nor speak
   With him at the tops of your voices,
   As you with one another speak!
   Lest your labours should come to nought:
   A loss of which you never thought!

3. They who lower their voices when they talk,
   Unto Allah's Apostle, are the folk,
   Whose hearts has God inclined to piety:
   They'll have Forgiveness and a bonus mighty.

4. Most of the people who call out,
   Unto you while you are within,
   Your private chambers are no doubt
   Ignorant men.

5. If only they were patient and would wait,
   Till you came out to them, it would be better

---

1. Or "Do not enter upon any affair before God and His Apostle, or without their permission.

For them! But God's the Oft-Forgiver,
And He's the Mercy-Giver.

6.   Believers! Should an evil-doer come,
Up to you with some piece of news, be sure
To ascertain the truth at once, lest you,
Harm people, out of ignorance, and be
Remorseful then for doing wrong.

7.   Remember! God's Apostle is among,
You at present: If he were to give way,
To you in many matters, certainly
You would have come to grief,
But God has made you love Belief,
And in your hearts did He it beautify;
And He made you haters of Disbelief,
Wickedness and rebellion; such are they
Who walk in the right way,

8.   Through Grace and Favour which is God's,
And God's the Ever-Knower, the All-Wise.

9.   If two parties among the faithful are
At war, the one against the other,
Make peace between them, but if either
Of them transgress against the other,
Then you must combat the transgressor,
Till it submit to Allah's order,
And when it does so, then make peace,
'Tween them in fairness and with justice,
For Allah surely loves the people,
Who're truly equitable!

10.   Surely the faithful are but brethren,
    Thus 'mongst your brethren do make peace,
    And for God's sake be pious,
    That Mercy may be to you given.

11.   O You believers! Do not let some men
    Be mocking other folks, perhaps the latter
    Are better than the former;
    Nor let the womenfolk make fun
    Of other women, for the latter may,
    Be far better than they;
    And do not try each other to defame,
    Nor call each other by a nickname,
    It's bad to call a person by the same
    Sobriquet when he has indeed professed,
    The Faith, and people who do not desist,
    Are certainly unjust.

12.   You who believe! Avoid being suspicious
    Extremely all the time:
    Suspicion in some cases is a crime,[1]
    And spy not on each other, nor backbite:
    Will there be one among you who would eat,
    The flesh of his dead brother?[2] Do you not
    Find it disgusting! Thus:
    Be god-fearing and pious,
    For God is Lenient and Compassionate.

13.   We have created you, O men,
    From a single man and a woman,

---

1. Sin, vice.

2. Such an abomination it is to speak ill behind people's backs.

And made you into tribes and nations,
For your own mutual recognitions,
Yet, in the sight of God, the noblest
Of you, is he who fears Him most,
And God is the All-Knowing, the Awarest!

14.   The desert Arabs say: "We do believe".
Say: "You do not believe! You better say:
'We do profess Islam', for the true faith,
Into your hearts has not yet found its way;
But if you follow God and His Apostle,
None of your deeds will He belittle,
For God's the Oft-Forgiving Merciful."

15.   Those only are the true believers who
Have faith in God and His Apostle,
Then never do they doubt, but struggle
With all their wealth and lives in Allah's cause;
They are in faith most truthful.

16.   Say: "Do you fancy to apprise
Allah of your religion? When,
God knows all that is in the heavens,
And on the earth; the fullest ken
Has God about all things!

17.   They think that their professing Islam, was
To you a favour;
Say: "By embracing Islam, you did not
Do me a favour:
God rather granted you a favour
By guiding you unto the Faith,
If you are men of truth."

18.   Of the heavens and of the earth,
        Does Allah know all the Unseen,
        And of whatever you are doing,
        God is surely the Seer Keen!

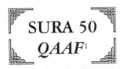

SURA 50
QAAF[1]

In the Name of God, the Beneficent, the Merciful

1. Qaaf;
    By Al-Quran, the Glorified Enough.

2. And yet they wonder that a warner from
    Amongst themselves has to them come!
    Thus are the disbelievers saying:
    "This is indeed a curious thing;

3. "After we're dead and turned to dust...?
    Such a return is too far-off,
    One cannot in it trust!"

4. But We already know how much,
    Of them the earth is to corrupt,[2]
    And with Us is a Book in which
    Every account is kept.

5. Yet they denied the Truth that was
    Unto them sent,
    Therefore they are now in a state
    Of great bewilderment!

6. Do they not ever look up at the heaven,
    Above their heads, to question,
    How We established it,

---

1. The Arabic letter qaaf.

2. That is: The earth only corrupts the body; it has no power over the soul; the
   full account of the soul's doings is in God's Record.

And how with ornaments,
We furnished it,
Without a thing uneven?

7.   The earth have We spread out, and thereupon
Have We set up many a mountain,
And We have caused the growth therein
Of various kinds of beauteous plants,

8.   For the insight and admonition,
Of all imploring servants.

9.   And from the heaven We send down
Abundant, blissful rains,
By which We then bring forth
Gardens and harvest grains,

10.   And stately trees of palms,
With generous, fruitful arms;

11.   For all creatures, their own provision;
And We thereby revive,
Lands that were not alive;
Such is to be the Resurrection.[1]

12.   Others before them[2] treated
Their messengers as false:
The clan of Noah, and the peoples
Of the Thamood and of Al-Rass,[3]

---

1. Original: coming out, rising again.   2. The Meccan pagans.

3. Most probably the people of Prophet Shu'aib; they may have lived in Yamamah.

13.   The Aad and Pharaoh's men,
       And Lot's own brethren,

14.   The Aikah[1] and the Tubba'[2] peoples:
       They all rejected their apostles,
       Justly then did My promise,[3]
       Upon them come to pass.

15.   Were We at all worn out
       By the pristine creation,
       That they should be in doubt
       About a fresh creation?!

16.   We have created man,
       And We are Most-Aware of all
       The promptings of his soul,
       And We are nearer to him than
       His own jugular vein!

17.   Behold! Seated are on his left and right,
       The Noters Twain,[4] minutely taking note.

18.   No word he utters but is taken down
       By an observer, missing naught!

19.   And then the trance of death,[5]

---

1. The Sylvans or the Dwellers of the Forest who lived in Midian.

2. The people of Hamyar.

3. Threat, Warning.

4. Two angels.

5. The stupor or unconsciousness to this worldly life, and the opening of the eyes to the next world.

Shall come with all the Truth:
"This is the very thing you sought,
To do without!"

20.   And on the Trumpet there shall be a blast:
      And it's the Day that has been promised![1]

21.   And every soul shall come together,
      With his evil-impeller,[2]
      And truthful counsellor.[3]

22.   "You surely did neglect,
      This very fact,
      But now We have removed your screen,
      Today then, is your sight most keen."

23.   And his companion[4] says: "with me,
      Has It[5] been ready!"

24.   "Do cast[6] into Gehenna,
      Every ungrateful unbeliever,

25.   "Every forbidder of good deeds,
      Every transgressor, every doubter,

---

1. Or : threatened.

2. Original: The driver, the one who prompts to evil.

3. Original: The witness, the one who calls to truth and righteousness.

4. The accompanying devil at whose suggestions man commits evil deeds.

5. His Record.

6. The verb is in dual form: Presumably every sinner is dragged and thrown into the Flames by two Hell-Guards; the order in this verse and the two following verses comes from God or one of His archangels.

26. "Who set up other gods with God the One;
    Cast them down into torment,
    Most vehement."

27. And His Companion shall then say:
    "Our Lord, it was not I at all,
    Who made him disobey,
    But he himself was far astray!"

28. He'll say: "You twain, wrangle not in My presence,
    For I had sent you warnings in advance!

29. "Altered shall never be My Sentence,
    Nor am I in the least
    To my creatures unjust."

30. On that Day We will ask Gehenna:
    "Are you full to the brim?"
    And she shall say: "Am I to make more room?"

31. And Paradise,
    No longer at a distance,
    Is forward brought unto the righteous.

32. "This is what had been promised,
    To every watchful man of penitence,

33. "Who feared the All-Beneficent,
    Although unseen, and brings along
    A heart repentant;

34. "Do enter it in peace,

This is the Day of Permanence.[1] "

35.   There shall they have all that they can desire,
    And We may still augment their bliss,
    And give them more.

36.   We have indeed destroyed before
    Them[2] many generations, far
    Greater than them in prowess;
    Lo! They did search the land entire;
    Was there for them a shelter?!

37.   There is in this indeed a Lesson,
    For any mindful person,
    Or he who, otherwise,
    Could use his ears and eyes.

38.   The Skies and Earth and what between them lies,
    Did We create within six Days,
    And We were never touched by weariness!

39.   Thus hear with patience all that they express,
    And celebrate your own Lord's praises,
    Before the Sun does set and ere it rises.

40.   And give Him due glorification,
    During the night, and even
    After prostration.[3]

---

1. Or: Day of Eternity.   2. The Meccan pagans.

3. Even after the daily prayers, one should always remember God and continue His glorification; some commentators understand this to mean "extra prayers".

41.   And, for the Day, do listen, when the Crier
       Shall cry out from a place quite near,[1]

42.   The Day when men shall hear,
       That Fateful Shout, will be in truth,
       The Day of Coming Forth.[2]

43.   It's We Who life and death ordain,
       And unto Us shall be the Final Turn,[3]

44.   That is the Day when Earth is rent asunder,
       And all rush out that were thereunder;
       And, this bringing together,
       Is unto Us an easy matter.

45.   Aware are We indeed of what they utter,
       And you shall not at all compel them; then
       admonish every man, who dreads My warning,
       By means of this Quran!

---

1. "Near to everyone alike".

2. "Out of the graves": the Resurrection.

3. "The ultimate turning" or "return".

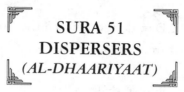

SURA 51
DISPERSERS
(AL-DHAARIYAAT)

In the Name of God, the Beneficent, the Merciful

1. By Winnowing Dispersers,

2. And Heavy-Burden Bearers,

3. And Gliding Floaters,

4. And the Dispensers of Affairs:[1]

5. That which is Promised unto you,
   Is absolutely true,

6. And verily the Judgment
   Shall be a sure event.

7. By heavens full of highways!

8. You are indeed with one another,
   At odds in what you say;

9. Away from it,[2] will be the man,
   Who has already turned away.

10. Perish the falsifiers!

---

1. The elements mentioned in verses 1 to 4 may be winds, angels or other agencies that carry out God's commands and bear His blessings.
2. "From the Truth".

11.   Who wander in the heedless byways,
      Of utter ignorance:

12.   "When will the Day of Judgment be?",
      Do they enquire!

13.   The Day they shall be put to proof upon
      The flaming Fire!

14.   "Now taste the mischief which you sought to hasten".

15.   But pious, self-restrainers shall abide in,
      The midst of Gardens and by Fountains,

16.   Enjoying what their Lord to them has given,
      Because, aforetime, they had been,
      Doers of good and right,

17.   They used to sleep but little in the night,

18.   And at the dawns, they prayed for Pardon,

19.   And in their property, there was a portion,
      For those who begged, and for the men,
      In silent, needful plight.

20.   And many are the Signs upon the Earth,
      For people firm in Faith,

21.   Also in your own selves: will you not be
      Able to see?

22.   And the Heaven is holding both,

Your sustenance and what you're Promised.

23.   Thus, by the Lord of Heavens and the Earth,
      This is the very Truth,
      As true a thing,
      As you're now speaking!

24.   Has the report unto you come,
      About the honoured guests of Abraham?

25.   Behold! They entered unto him and said:
      "All health". "All health", he answered, and he thought:
      "Some people weird!"

26.   Then he betook himself unto his folk,
      And came back with a fatted calf,

27.   And it before them laid;
      "Why don't you eat?" he said.

28.   But then, of them, he grew afraid!
      "Be not afraid", they said,
      And gave him tidings glad,
      Of an-endowed-with-Wisdom lad.

29.   Then came his wife bewailing loud,
      And while her face she struck,
      She thus deplored:
      "Will I?¹ A barren woman old!"

30.   They said: "But thus your Lord has spoken,
      And He is Full of Wisdom, Full of Ken.

---

1. "Give birth to a child?"

31. He asked them: O You messengers,
    Have you a greater errand then?

32. They said: We had been sent,
    Unto a nation sunk in sin,

33. To bring upon them rains,
    Of clayey stones,

34. Marked by your Lord for the extravagant!

35. And we delivered those, therein,
    Who were believers,

36. But there we only found one household
    Of true believers,[1]

37. And left it as a warning sign,
    For those who fear the painful retribution;

38. Behold, this was the case of Moses also,
    After We sent him unto Pharaoh,
    With manifest authorization,

39. But he, relying on his hosts,
    Turned back in condescension,
    And said: "He's a magician, or a madman!"

40. Therefore We seized him and his fighting army,
    And catapulted them into the sea,
    And truly blamable was he!

---

1. Muslims: "submitters to the will of the Almighty".

41.   And Aad, another case to mind!
    We sent on them a blighting wind,

42.   All that it blew upon,
    And, what it left behind,
    Looked like some dust of sand!

43.   So were Thamood, Behold!
    'Enjoy yourselves a little', they were told,

44.   Yet they were in revolt,
    Against the order of their Lord,
    Thus they were stricken by the Thunderbolt,
    As it they did behold,

45.   And yet they had no strength to stand,
    Neither could they themselves defend;

46.   So were, before them, Noah's people,
    They, also, were an evil-doing band!

47.   We built the Firmament with Our Own Hand,
    And it, We shall continue to expand,

48.   And We have made the Earth a wide expanse,
    We're Good at Spreading excellence!

49.   And We created pairs of everything,
    That you may think upon.

50.   Thus flee to God! I am to you indeed,
    From Him, a warner plain,

51.　　And set up not another god with God:
　　　　I am from Him to you,
　　　　A warner plain indeed.

52.　　It's been the same:
　　　　Never before unto them came,
　　　　A messenger but they did claim
　　　　"Magician or a madman!"

53.　　Has there been some transmission,
　　　　By every generation?[1] !
　　　　Nay! They are all transgressors,
　　　　Beyond remission.

54.　　Thus turn your back upon them,
　　　　You shall not be to blame.

55.　　But do keep on Reminding,
　　　　For true believers are,
　　　　To profit from Reminding;

56.　　And Jinns and men have I created only
　　　　That they should worship Me.

57.　　No livelihood do I demand of them!
　　　　Nor do I need them feed Me!

58.　　It's God who is the All-Provider,
　　　　The Very Lord of Power,
　　　　Solid for ever!

---

1. "Have they made this scoff a legacy to one another?"

59.   Indeed the evil-doers are to meet,
       A share of torment that was meted out
       Unto their former mates, so let them not,
       Ask Me a thing to expedite!

60.   Thus woe betide the disbelievers,
       Facing the promised Day of theirs!

SURA 52
THE MOUNTAIN
(AL-TOOR)

In the Name of God, the Beneficent, the Merciful

1.   By the Mountain,[1]

2.   And by the Book already written,

3.   Upon a scroll well spread,

4.   And by the much-visited Fane,[2]

5.   And by the Roof, highly erected,

6.   And by the Ocean, swollen yet restricted:

7.   Certainly your Lord's chastisement,
      Is imminent,

8.   By no means shall it be averted,

9.   That's on the Day when Welkin,[3]
      Will side to side be shaken,

10.   And mountains shall be in fantastic motion;

11.   Thus, woe this Day to those,
      Who did the Truth oppose,

---

1. The Mount is the symbol of Revelation: Mount Sinai, Mount of Olives and
   the Mount of Light (in the case of the Holy Prophet).

2. The Ka'ba.   3. The sky, the vault of heaven.

891

12. Who now engage in vain oration,
    Only for recreation!

13. Upon that Day shall they be ruthlessly,
    Into Gehenna's fires driven:

14. "This is the very Fire, which you treated
    As a big lie;

15. "Is this now sorcery,
    Or do you not see properly?!

16. "Enter the Fire! Whether you bear it,
    Or cannot bear it, it will be
    The same to you, for you shall be rewarded,
    For what you did!"

17. Surely the self-restrainers pious,
    Shall be in Gardens and in Bliss,

18. Rejoicing in what their own Lord,
    Upon them has bestowed,
    Their Lord who did deliver
    Them from the plague of Fire;

19. "Do eat and drink with relish,
    For what you did accomplish."

20. On thrones set in many an ordered line,
    They shall recline,
    And We will wed them unto *houri* belles,
    With eyes after gazelles;

21.   And to the faithful whose descendants,
Followed them in the Faith, We'll join
Their own descendants,[1]
And aught of their own deeds, shall We decline;
Yet every person is in pledge for deeds his own.

22.   And We shall give them fruits and meats,
After the longing of their hearts;

23.   Therein a Cup shall they be passing on,
From had to hand, wherein,
Is nothing vain, nor any sin,

24.   And lads will wait on them, as their own pals,
Lovely as virgin pearls;

25.   And some of them approach the others,
To comment on their own affairs,

26.   They say: "The time when we were living near,
Our kith and kin, we suffered many a fear,

27.   "Then God was to us mercifully Kind,
And He did save us from the Scourge of,
The Scorching Wind;[2]

28.   "For, heretofore, upon Him we did call;
For He is the Benign, the Merciful."

---

1. This is another divine bliss for the faithful: their near and dear ones shall be
joined to them, provided, of course, that the latter were not faithless people,
even though their ranks and individual merits might be less than the former.

2. The flames of Hell.

29.   You just remind and warn then,
       For, by the Favour of your Lord,
       You are no *kohin*,[1]
       Neither a madman!

30.   Or do they say: "he is a versifier,
       Let us await some adverse
       Turn of fortune, him to devour!"

31.   Say: "go on waiting for some evil fate,
       And I, along with you, shall wait!"

32.   Do their illusion-ridden minds
       Them unto this command,
       Or are they rebels gone beyond,
       Whatever binds?!

33.   Or do they say: "It[2] has been by him faked!"
       Nay, they have no belief, in fact.

34.   Let them then bring a like *hadeeth*,[3]
       If they be men of truth!

35.   Were they created by, or out of, nought?
       Or have they brought themselves about?

36.   Did they create the heavens and the earth?!
       Nay, rather, they maintain no faith,
       In any truth!

---

1. Arabic Kaahin: a soothsayer, fortune-teller, diviner.

2. The Quran.

3. Discourse, narration, saying, report, announcement.

37. Do they possess the Treasures of your Lord?
    Are these by them controlled?

38. Have they a special Overhearing Ladder,
    For hearing what goes on up there?!
    Let anyone who's heard enough,
    Bring us his lofty proof!

39. Or, has He daughters only, and you sons?!

40. Are you demanding of them wages,
    That them in heavy debts engages?

41. Have they some knowledge of the Hidden,
    And they can write them down?

42. Have they against you plotted?
    But those who disbelieve shall be
    Themselves outplotted!

43. Or do they have a deity,
    Other than the Almighty?[1]
    Exalted God is far above, what they
    Join with Him as a sharing entity!

44. These people, if they see a portion,
    Of heavens falling down, they'd say:
    "A mass of clouds in motion!"

45. So leave them be, until they face that Day
    Of theirs, when they shall swoon away;

---

1. Allah, God the One.

46.   The Day when their designs avail them naught,
    And none shall help them out.

47.   And there shall be a further woe,
    For the unjust, down in this world;
    But many of them do not know!

48.   And so, wait for the order of your Lord,
    Because you are before Our very Eyes,
    And celebrate your own Lord's praise,
    Whene'er you rise,

49.   And glorify Him in the night,
    And, after stars fade out of sight.

SURA 53
PLEIADES[1]
(AL-NAJM)

In the Name of God, the Beneficent, the Merciful

1. By Pleiades fading away!

2. Your fellow-townsman,[2]
   Is not astray,
   Nor was he led awry,

3. Nor does he ever say,
   Aught of his own imagination;

4. It's naught but Revelation,
   Sent down by inspiration.

5. Instruction was unto him given,
   By one,[3] of mighty sway,

6. Endued with Wisdom; and he was a perfect vision,

7. And he was on the highest point,
   Of the horizon;

8. And nearer did he come while in descent,

9. And was then two bow-lengths away,
   Or closer even;

---

1. Or "The Star".　　　　2. The Holy Prophet.

3. The Arch-angel Gabriel, through whom the inspiration came, according to most commentators.

10.   Then He[1] revealed unto His servant,
The Revelation.

11.   The heart could not deny the vision;

12.   How could you question then,
What he has seen?

13.   And at another such descent,
He saw him once again,

14.   Close to the Sidra[2] of the farthest point,

15.   Adjacent to the Garden,
Of ever-lasting station,

16.   Lo! Sidra was encircled,
Closely encircled;[3]

17.   There could be no delusion,
Nor an insurgent notion,

18.   For he, some of the greatest
Signs of his own Lord witnessed.

19.   Has any of you ever been a muser,
On Laat and Uzza,

---

1. God.

2. Or "the Lote-tree of the extremity" is symbolic of heavenly Bliss; it is said to
grow at the loftiest spot in Paradise, near the Throne of God.

3. "By hosts of adoring angels making the Tree seem enshrouded."

20.   And, thirdly, on Manaat?![1]

21.   Is He to have such maidens,[2]
    And for you will be sons?!

22.   This certainly is an unfair division!

23.   Nothing are these but names,
    That you and your forefathers coined:
    Upon them no authorization,
    Has God enjoined;
    They follow nothing but conjectures vain,
    And their own selfish whims;
    Though certainly the Guidance from
    Their Lord has to them come.

24.   Is man supposed to gain,
    Whate'er he fancies?!

25.   Nay, it is Allah who ordains,
    Both the Hereafter and the Present.

26.   And many are the angels in the heavens,
    Yet nothing shall their intercessions,
    Avail, save after God's permission,
    Is given unto whom He will,
    And is to Him acceptable.

27.   Only deniers of the life to come,
    Give angels female designations;

---

1. The three principal goddesses of Pagan Arab Idolatry; they, as well as angels were called "the Daughters of Allah".

2. Or "daughters, females".

28.   Of this they have no sure cognition;[1]
        They follow nothing but conjecture,
        And never is conjecture,
        For truth, a substitution.

29.   Thus, turn aside from him who turns his back,
        On Our Message, and who will only seek,
        This present world.

30.   And that's of knowledge, all they could afford;
        Surely it is your Lord,
        Who best knows him who is astray,
        And it is He Who's Well Aware,
        Of those upon the guided Road.

31.   Whatever is there in the heavens,
        And everything on earth, to God belongs,
        So He shall recompense the evil-doers,
        According to their doings,
        And He'll reward the ones,
        Who have done good with best of means:

32.   People who do avoid the greatest sins,
        As well as gross indecencies,
        Save small, short-lived offences;
        Surely your Lord's forgiveness is immense,
        He's known you ever since,
        He brought you forth,
        Out of the earth,
        Since you were all some embryos,
        Inside your mothers' wombs;

---

1. Or "certain knowledge".

Therefore, on purity of your own selves,
Do not be feigners,
It's He Who better knows,
The pure restrainers!

33. Do you see him who turns his back?

34. He gave in alms a little first,
But even that, he later ceased!

35. Is he a knower of the Hidden,
And the Unseen he sees?

36. Or has he never been informed of what,
Is in the Scrolls of Moses taught,

37. As well as those of loyal Abraham:

38. No soul shall bear the burden of another,

39. That for a man there shall be nothing,
But the results of his own labour,

40. And that the fruit of his own effort,
Will soon come into sight;

41. Then he shall be rewarded for it,
With a reward complete;

42. And that, unto your Lord, shall be
The final destination,

43.   That He it is Who moves to laughter,
       Or, to weeping in lamentation,

44.   That it is He Who life and death ordains;

45.   That it is He Who has created,
       The male and female twains,

46.   Out of a semen-droplet, when ejected,

47.   And that with Him alone,
       Is the second creation.[1]

48.   That it is He Who could afford,
       To make you rich, and give to hold,

49.   That over Sirius,[2] is He the Overlord,

50.   That He destroyed the Aad of old,

51.   Thamood as well, and of them left no more,

52.   And Noah's people long before:
       Surely they were transgressors bold,

53.   And He did overturn the Ruined Towns,[3]

54.   And covered them with dust in countless tons!

---

1. "The raising of the dead", as a new life in the Hereafter.

2. The brilliant Dog-star; many Pagan Arabs worshipped it as a divinity.

3. The overthrown cities to which Lot was sent for a warning. (Sodom and Gomorrah).

55. Now which, amongst the bounties of your Lord,
     Do you decline?

56. He[1] also is a Warner in the line,
     Of warners old;

57. The E'er-Approacher is already nigher,

58. And yet, but God, none knows its Hour.

59. Are you amazed at this Narration,

60. And laugh, instead of shedding tears,

61. And waste your time in vanities?!

62. Rather fall down then in prostration,
     To God, and offer supplication!

---

1. Original: This (The Prophet).

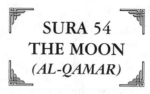

SURA 54
THE MOON
(AL-QAMAR)

In the Name of God, the Beneficent, the Merciful

1. The Hour of Doom is nigher, and the Moon,
    Will rend asunder,

2. But though they see a Sign, they turn aside,
    And cry: "what a magical wonder!

3. Thus they deny, and follow their own lusts,
    But all affairs have a fixed calendar!

4. A Message[1] has unto them come already,
    To warn and serve as their defender,

5. For it's profound in Wisdom; but the warnings
    Did them no profit render.

6. So let them be! The Day the Crier summons
    All to a serious business to surrender,

7. With downcast eyes, shall they come forth from graves,
    Like locusts scattering in disorder,

8. And race towards the Crier. "This Day surely",
    Will say the disbelievers, "is a grinder!"

9. In former times it was the Noah's band,
    Who did reject the Truth amain,

---

1. Or: tidings, Narratives.

And they defied Our servant with the brand:
"He is insane!"
And thus they had him banned.

10.　Then cried he to his Lord and prayed:
"I have been overcome; I need Your aid."

11.　Thus We opened the gates of heavens,
To unrelenting rains,

12.　And made the Earth to burst with gushing fountains,
And water onto water joined,
To the extent ordained;

13.　But him We bore upon the board,
Of something bound with log and cord,

14.　Under Our Eyes did she serenely glide:
A recompense to him who was denied!

15.　And We have left it as a Sign indeed,
But is there anyone who will take heed?!

16.　Thus came My Punishment,
After admonishment!

17.　Indeed We rendered Al-Quran,
Easy for recollection;
But are there any recollectors?!

18.　The Aad also the Truth denied;
How was My punishment,
After admonishment:

19.   Upon a day of unremitting woe,
        We loosed on them a wild tornado,

20.   People were plucked and flung around,
        As hollowed trunks of palms,
        Uprooted from the ground;

21.   That was My retribution,
        After the admonition;

22.   Indeed We rendered Al-Quran
        Easy for recollection,
        But are there any recollectors?!

23.   Thamood were, of Our admonitions,
        Also rejecters;

24.   They argued: "What! Are we to follow
        A man, a solitary fellow,
        Who is among us?!
        Surely in such a case, we will be
        In error, nay, in madness!

25.   "How is it that among us all the office
        Of warning fell on him alone? Nay, rather
        He is a flagrant liar!"

26.   Ah! Surely they shall know,
        Who is the flagrant liar,

27.   Only tomorrow!
        For We will send a she-camel,
        To put them to a trial;

Therefore keep cool and be a watcher;

28. Only inform them that the water will,
    Be shared between them and the camel,
    And they, by turns, will have their proper share.

29. But lo! They called to their own leader,
    And he then took in hand a dagger,
    And did hamstring her!

30. And how was then My retribution,
    After this admonition:

31. Against them did We send a single Cry,[1]
    And they were like some branches dry
    Used by the sheep-fold builders!

32. Indeed We rendered Al-Quran
    Easy for recollection,
    But are there any recollectors!

33. The clan of Lot were of Our admonition,
    Also rejecters,

34. Upon them We sent down,
    A savage stone-charged storm,
    On all except Lot's household, whom
    Delivered We before the dawn:

35. That was Our special favour; for We thus,
    Reward the grateful with a Bonus.

---

1. Or "a Mighty Blast".

36. Indeed he had already cautioned them,
    Of Our severest Seizure,
    But they did not his warnings treasure!

37. They had even his guests from him demanded!
    Their eyes, therefore, We blinded:
    Thus taste My retribution,
    After the admonition!

38. And at the day-break, they were pounded,
    By a constant Affliction:

39. Thus taste My retribution,
    After the admonition!

40. Indeed We rendered Al-Quran
    Easy for recollection;
    But are there any recollectors!

41. And certainly to Pharaoh's people,
    Had come My warnings,

42. But they rejected all Our Signs;[1]
    We smote them thus, after the manner
    Of One Who's Mighty, Full of Power.

43. Now are your[2] disbelievers,
    Better than those, or is there an exemption,
    For you in any Scriptures?!

---

1. Or "miracles".

2. "The disbelievers among the Meccans".

44. Or do they say: "We are an allied host,
    Who will themselves assist!"

45. Soon shall the allied hosts be put to rout,
    And show their backs in flight!

46. But, it's indeed the Hour of Doom,
    That is their promised time,
    And that Hour, shall be by far
    More grievous and more bitter.

47. The guilty are indeed in error,
    And will certainly end up in the Fire;

48. Upon that Day they will, upon their faces,
    Be dragged into the Flames:
    "Now you shall feel the touch
    Of the Thing that will scorch!"[1]

49. All things have We created
    In measures stated;

50. Our Will is executed right away,
    Swift as the twinkling of an eye;

51. And many people of your kind,
    Did We, of old, destroy;
    Are there now any who will mind?

52. And everything that they have ever done,
    Has been kept in the Books,

---

1. Original: saqar.   2. Prepared by the Guardian Angels.

53. Wherein all matters, small or great, are written down.

54. Surely the righteous will be dwelling,
    Amid Gardens and Brooks;[1]

55. And seats of honour will be for their taking,
    In the presence of an All-Mighty King!

---

1. "Of Paradise".

SURA 55
THE BENEFICENT
(AL-RAHMAAN)

In the Name of God, the Beneficent, the Merciful

1. It's Al-Rahmaan,[1]

2. Who has been teaching the Quran,[2]

3. He has created man,

4. And it was He Who granted him,
    Power of expression.

5. The sun and moon both run
    By strictest computation,

6. The stars and trees bow down,
    In adoration;

7. On high did He raise up the heaven
    And He set up the Balance;[3]

8. Behold! Do not upset the balance,

9. And weigh all things with fairness,
    And do not scant the balance.

---

1. The Beneficent, God of Mercy.
2. The Reading, the Revelation.
3. The original Arabic al-mizaan means "the balance of justice", "the scales", and
   the constellation Libra (The Balance).

10. And the Earth, He has laid out for,
     The living creatures,

11. Wherein are fruits and palms,
     With hanging clusters,

12. And grains in husks and herbs of fragrance.

13. Could you[1] indeed afford
     To spurn a bounty of your Lord!

14. He has created humans
     Out of some muddy clay,
     Like that handled by potters!

15. And He created Jinns,[2]
     From smokeless flames of fire.

16. Could you indeed afford
     To spurn a bounty of your Lord!

17. He is the Lord of the two Easts,
     And Lord of both the Wests.[3]

18. Could you indeed afford
     To spurn a bounty of your Lord!

1. The Arabic verb is in the dual form; many commentators believe that here
   the two groups of intelligent creatures, humans and Jinns are being
   addressed. The dual form, however, is sometimes used by the Arabs to give
   force to the meaning.
2. Or "the sprites".
3. Different points of the horizon at which the sun rises and sets at the winter
   and summer solstice.

19. Two seas has He let loose,
    Adjacent, face to face,

20. Between them lies an isthmus,
    That they do not transgress!

21. Could you indeed afford
    To spurn a bounty of your Lord!

22. And pearls and corals have come forth,
    Out of them both!

23. Could you indeed afford
    To spurn a bounty of your Lord!

24. And His are lofty vessels
    Afloat on seas like castles.

25. Could you indeed afford
    To spurn a bounty of your Lord!

26. All that exist upon her,[1]
    Will undoubtedly wither;[2]

27. Only the Image of your Lord,
    In all its majesty and honour
    Abides for ever.

28. Could you indeed afford
    To spurn a bounty of your Lord!

---

1. On the earth.

2. Or "shall pass away".

29.   All that is in the heavens and on earth,
His help implores,
And everyday He in some work,
His own power employs!

30.   Could you indeed afford,
To spurn a bounty of your Lord!

31.   O you two weights of burden,[1]
Soon, shall We give you Our attention![2]

32.   Could you indeed afford
To spurn a bounty of your Lord!

33.   O companies of Jinns and men!
If you could ever smooth the path
to penetrate the outer bounds
Of heavens and the earth,
Do overpass the bounds!
But there shall be no penetration,
Without Authorization;

34.   Could you indeed afford
To spurn a bounty of your Lord!

35.   Flung at you shall be flames of smokeless fire,
And densest fumes: then you shall have no helper;

---

1. Or "two worlds", "two treasures", "two bodies of men and things": The two weights, according to commentators, are men and Jinns who are burdened with responsibility or, as some hold, with sin.

2. Or "settle your affairs", "judge you".

914

36.   Could you indeed afford,
        To spurn a bounty of your Lord!

37.   The Sky is to be rent asunder,
        And look the red of bloodied leather!

38.   Could you indeed afford,
        To spurn a bounty of your Lord!

39.   Yea, on that Day shall neither man nor Jinn
        Be questioned of his sin!

40.   Could you indeed afford,
        To spurn a bounty of your Lord!

41.   The guilty shall be known
        By their own looks,
        And they'll be taken in
        By their legs and their forelocks!

42.   Could you indeed afford,
        To spurn a bounty of your Lord!

43.   This is Gehenna which the guilty,
        Did call a falsity,

44.   Between it[1] and some water boiling,
        To and fro, they'll be strolling!

45.   could you indeed afford,
        To spurn a bounty of your Lord!

---

1. Hell.

46.   But for the people who did dread
    To stand before their Lord,
    There is to be two Gardens[1] ;

47.   Could you indeed afford,
    To spurn a bounty of your Lord!

48.   Full of provisions;

49.   Could you indeed afford,
    To spurn a bounty of your Lord!

50.   There are in them two flowing fountains;

51.   Could you indeed afford,
    To spurn the bounty of your Lord!

52.   In them you'll find of every kind
    Of fruitage twains.

53.   Could you indeed afford,
    To spurn a bounty of your Lord!

54.   On couches they recline, with linings made,
    Of rich brocade,
    And within easy reach are laid,
    The fruits from the two Gardens.

55.   Could you indeed afford
    To spurn a bounty of your Lord!

---

1. The whole scheme of this sura runs in twos, for those addressed are the two
  types of intelligent, responsible creatures God created: Men and Jinns.

56. Therein shall be the bashful virgins,
    Not ever touched by men or Jinns;

57. Could you indeed afford
    To spurn a bounty of your Lord!

58. As if life had been breathed
    Into ruby and coral gems!

59. Could you indeed afford
    To spurn a bounty of your Lord!

60. Shall the reward of goodness
    Be aught but goodness?!

61. Could you indeed afford,
    To spurn a bounty of your Lord!

62. Besides these, there shall be
    Two other Gardens,

63. Could you indeed afford,
    To spurn a bounty of your Lord!

64. Deep-green in colour from
    Watering often;

65. Could you indeed afford,
    To spurn a bounty of your Lord!

66. Each one with its own gushing fountain,

67. Could you indeed afford,

To spurn a bounty of your Lord!

68. Both bring forth fruits and palms of dates
     And blood-red pomegranates.

69. Could you indeed afford,
     To spurn a bounty of your Lord!

70. In each you'll find the fairest maidens:

71. Could you indeed afford,
     To spurn a bounty of your Lord!

72. Heavenly houris purdahed in pavilions,

73. Could you indeed afford,
     To spurn a bounty of your Lord!

74. Not ever touched by men or Jinns

75. Could you indeed afford
     To spurn a bounty of your Lord!

76. On soft, green cushions,
     Set on carpets most fine,
     Shall they recline.

77. Could you indeed afford
     To spurn a bounty of your Lord?

78. Exalted be the Name of
     Your Lord, the Lord of Majesty,
     Glory and Bounty!

SURA 56
THE OCCURRENCE
(AL-WAAQIA)

In the Name of God, the Beneficent, the Merciful

1. When the Occurrence[1] shall occur,
   Forcefully all at once,

2. Then will no soul renounce,
   Its sure occurrence!

3. It[2] will abase,
   It will exalt.[3]

4. When the Earth shall be shaken from its base,

5. And crumbling down shall come the mountains,

6. To turn into some dust of scattered atoms,

7. Then will you be a threesome band:

8. The people of the right hand;
   Who are the people of the right hand?

9. The people of the left hand;
   Who are the people of the left hand?

10. And the first ones, the foremost,
    Ever the first and foremost:

---

1. Or "The Inevitable Event": the Day of Resurrection, the Hour of Judgment.

2. The Day of Judgment.

3. Many people will be brought low and many will be exalted.

11.   These are the Nearest;

12.   They'll be in blissful Gardens;

13.   A multitude from older times,

14.   But fewer from amongst,
       The later generations,

15.   High on luxurious thrones,

16.   Shall they recline,
       Each other facing,

17.   And youths of ever-lasting prime,
       At their service, about them racing,

18.   With goblets, ewers, and a special bowl
       Of Ma'een Wassail[1] ;

19.   No after-ache have they therefrom, nor will,
       Thereby their sense and reason fail.

20.   They'll have whate'er they choose of fruits,

21.   And what they fancy of the flesh of fowls,

22.   And there are *houri* damsels,
       With eyes after gazelles,

23.   Pearls are they hidden in their shells:

---

1. A most pure wine from a special fountain in Paradise.

24. Some prizes for their previous trials!

25. No idle talk therein is ever heard,
    Nor any charge of sin,

26. *All hail, all hail*[1] is gaily offered,
    Again, again and often.

27. And the people of the right hand,
    What of the people in this band?

28. They'll be amidst the thornless spina christi,[2]

29. And palm-trees of a peerless kind,
    That bring forth fruits in plenty,

30. And in the shades that long extend,

31. By waters ever-fluent,

32. And fruits abundant,

33. Never to end, nor ever to be banned,

34. And spouses of exalted kind,

35. Whom We created as special beings,

36. And We have made them ever virgins,

---

1. Original Arabic "salaam" (Hebrew shalom)

2. Original "Sidra": a special kind of lote-tree.

37.   Lovers of their own spouses, and,
        In age, to them as twins:

38.   For the people of the right hand,

39.   They are a multitude from older times,

40.   A multitude as well, from later times.

41.   But the people of the left hand;
        What of the people in this band?

42.   They'll be amidst some pestilential winds,
        And waters flaming,

43.   And in the shadows of
        A black smoke fuming,

44.   Neither cool nor refreshing!

45.   For they were, ere this, truly blessed
        With ease and luxury,

46.   But they indeed used to persist
        In the great blasphemy.[1]

47.   And they were wont to argue: "what!
        Once we are dead and turned to dust
        And rotten bones, shall we be raised?

48.   "And our fathers, those men of past?!"

---

1. Or "wickedness supreme": their associating others with God in His divinity.

49. Say: "Yes, indeed, those of the former times,
    And the succeeding ones,

50. "Shall all be summoned to a meeting,
    Upon a Day of chosen timing;

51. "Then you, O you, the erring ones,
    The Truth-rejecting pagans,

52. "Shall certainly be eating,
    Of the tree of zaq-qoom,[1]

53. "And with it fill your womb,

54. "And over it some boiling water,
    You will imbibe,

55. "Nay, you will lap it like,
    A thirsty camel tribe!"

56. This shall be what, upon the Day of Doom
    For a repast, they shall consume!

57. It's We Who did create,
    You all, why do you not admit[2] ?

58. Only behold the semen you emit!

59. Did you yourselves create it?
    Or was it We Who did it?

1. The bitter and pungent Cursed Tree described as growing at the bottom of
   Hell.
2. "The Truth of Creation and Resurrection".

60. It's We Who have decreed that death,
    Should be your common lot;
    We're not, however, hindered from:

61. Changing your state and form,
    And make you grow into a thing,
    About which you know nothing!

62. Yet you have known the first creation,
    Why do you take no admonition?!

63. Do you not even see the seeds you sow?

64. Do you yourselves cause them to grow?
    Aren't We the very Growers?

65. Were it Our Will, We would have made them,
    Dry chaff, and you'd become some sorrowers:

66. "Certainly have we been at cost,

67. Yet we have been forbidden harvest!"

68. And do you ever think,
    Of the water you drink?

69. Do you then send it from the welkin,
    Or it's a drop of what We work in?

70. Were it Our Will We'd turn it into brine!
    But do you not decline,
    E'er to give thanks?!

71.   And do you ever give a thought
To the fire that you ignite?

72.   Has it been you who reared its timber,
Or is it We Who are the Rearer?

73.   It's We Who made it a Reminder[1],
And an advantage for the traveller.

74.   Thus glorify the name
Of your own Lord,
The Most Supreme.

75.   It need not that I swear,
By the Positions of the stars-

76.   Though it is, if you were aware,
One of the greatest oaths indeed-

77.   That this is the most noble Reading[2],

78.   Out of a Book, well-guarded, most secure,

79.   None touches it except the cleanly pure,

80.   A revelation from the Lord
Of all the Worlds.

81.   Could you at all afford
Such Message to despise!

---

1. The ordinary fire in this world is a reminder of the Great Fire of the next.
2. The Quran.

82.   And make a daily business
Out of your crying lies?

83.   Why, at the moment when it[1] comes
Up to the throat,

84.   When you could only gaze and gloat,

85.   When We are closer to him than you all,
Although you see Us not,

86.   Yes, why is it that you, if nought
Holds you under control,

87.   Do not make it[2] go back?
Answer if it's the truth you speak[3] !

88.   Now then, if he be of the Nearest,[4]

89.   For him there shall be happy rest,
And bounty[5] and the Paradise,
Of godly Bliss.

90.   And if he be amongst,
The people of the right hand,

91.   Then it shall be "all hail to you",
The people of the right hand,

---

1. The soul of the dying man.   2. The soul.

3. "Concerning the claim of independence".

4. The most virtuous in the sight of God.

5. Or figuratively "Satisfaction and Delight".

92.   But if he be a truth-rejecter,
        An erring strayer,

93.   His entertainment is to be
        With scalding water,

94.   And burning in the blazing Fire!

95.   This is indeed the verity,
        Of surest certainty!

96.   Thus glorify the Name,
        Of your own Lord,
        The Most Supreme.

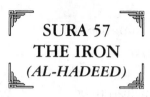

SURA 57
THE IRON
(AL-HADEED)

In the Name of God, the Beneficent, the Merciful

1. All that is in the skies,
   And everything on earth declares,
   The praise of God the One, Who is
   In Might Exalted, the Most-Wise.

2. His is the Kingdom of the heavens,
   And of the earth, and He ordains
   The facts of life and death, and reigns
   Over all things.

3. He is the First, the Last, the Manifest
   And the Hidden Inmost,
   It's He Who is of everything
   The Knower Best.

4. It's He Who, in Six Days, created
   The heavens and the earth,
   And then He mounted,
   His Glorious Throne,
   He knows what goes into the earth,
   And what from it goes forth,
   And what from Heaven may come down,
   And what goes up to it, and He's with you,
   Wherever you may be,
   And He does clearly see,
   All that you do.

5. To Him belongs,

The Kingdom of the heavens
And of the earth, and unto God
Every affair returns.

6.   The night He merges into day
And day He merges unto night,
And He does know the secrets,
In depths of every heart.

7.   Believe in God and His Apostle,
And out of that which God has made
You heirs of, give in alms, for those,
Among you who believe and give in alms,
Are to be paid a great reward.

8.   What has come unto you that you do not,
Truly believe in God? While the Apostle
Invites you to believe in your own Lord,
And he already took your pledge as well,
Provided you are truly faithful.

9.   He it is Who has sent
Clear Signs[1] upon His Servant,
That He may bring you out
Of Darkness into Light;
For God is unto you, in truth,
Most kind and Full of Ruth.

10.   So what has come to you that you,
Do not expend in God's Path, since
The wealth of heavens and the earth,

---

1. Or "revelations".

Is only God's inheritance?!
Equal are not, amongst you, those
Who spent and fought before the Triumph[1] :
They do attain a higher rank than those,
Who spent and entered fighting afterwards;
Yet God has promised good rewards,
To all, for God is Most Informed
Of what you have performed!

11. Who is he that will lend,
To God a handsome loan?
So He will multiply it,
For him, and let him own,
A noble meed beside it.

12. For on that Day, you will behold,
Believers, men and women,
With their own light running before them,
And on their right[2] ; and then[3] :
"Some good tidings for you this Day:
Gardens beneath which rivers stream,
To dwell therein for aye;
That's the success supreme."

13. Upon that Day the hypocrites,
The men and women, will implore
The faithful: "Wait for us, that we
May borrow from your lights!"
And the reply shall be:

---

1. This is usually understood to refer to the conquest of Mecca by Muslims.

2. These lights guide them on their route to Paradise.

3. "Thus shall they be addressed by the angels".

"Go back into the past, seek your own lights!"
Then Separation shall be brought about
Between them with a Wall that has a Door,
Within which there shall be Compassion,
And on the other side, unto the fore,
There will be Retribution!

14.   "Were We not with you?" They to them call out;
"Yes, but you led yourselves into temptation,
You surely wavered and you were in doubt
And your own lusts were your deception,
Until the Doom of Allah came about,
Indeed the Arch-Deceiver did,
Deceive you in regard to God;

15.   "Today, therefore, from you no ransom
Is to be taken, neither from
Any rejecting pagan;
Your home shall be the Fire,
It is from now to be your Patron;
And what a wretched journey thither!"

16.   Has not the time yet come for those
Who truly have believed, to yield
Humbly to God's Remembrance
And to the Truth He has revealed?
And that they never should be like
The people who received the Book[1] ,
Before them, whose lifetime was lengthened,
But whose hearts were then hardened,
And multitudes of them became

---

1. Or "The Scripture".

Doers of evil unrestrained.

17.   Know that it's Allah Who revives,
The earth after it dies;
Already have We made the portents[1] plain,
Perchance you realize.

18.   The men and women who give alms,
And lend to Allah handsome loans,
Will have them back doubled indeed,
Together with a noble meed.

19.   And those who did have faith in God and His
Messengers are the faithful most upright,
As well as witnesses in their Lord's sight:
They'll have their own reward and their own light;
And unbelievers who denied Our Signs,
Shall be the blazing Hell's Companions!

20.   Know that this worldly life is nothing but,
A sport, a pastime and an exhibition,
Mutual boasting and a combat
For more of wealth and children;
It's like the vegetation,
Which spring up after rain,
Whose growth delights the tillers,
But then, away it withers,
And you shall see it turning yellow,
And then becoming stubbles hollow!
And in the life to come there shall be
Either a Torment full of woe,

---

1. Also: signs, revelations.

Or God's Forgiveness and His Mercy,
And pleased Reception:
Surely this temporal life is nothing but
A means of self-deception!

21.   Thus rival one another in the race,
Unto your Lord's Pardon, and tread
After a Paradise, whose breadth,
Shall be the breadth of heavens and the earth,
Prepared for those who do have faith in God,
And His apostles: That's God's Grace,
That unto whom He pleases, He'll dispense,
And God's Graciousness is immense!

22.   Not an affliction e'er befalls
On earth or in your souls[1] ,
But ere We brought it into being,
It was already in Our Scrolls[2],
For that's, for God, an easy thing:

23.   Lest you, over what you may lose,
Shall be disheartened,
Nor over what He's given you
Be vainly heightened;
For Allah does not love the haughty boasters,

24.   Who are misers themselves and do enjoin
Men to miserliness as well, yet men
Who turn away in heedlessness,[3]
Should know that God's the Praised, the Needless.

---

1. "In your own persons", "spiritual crises".

2. Original "in a book".   3. "From almsgiving.

25.   We have already sent Our messengers,
With clearest Signs, and We have sent the Scriptures
And the Balance down with them, that mankind
Might be observing justice;
And We have sent down[1] iron,
Laden with warlike violence
As well as benefits for men,
That God may see who gives assistance
To Him and His apostles when,
Not in public observance;
And God is certainly
The Powerful Almighty.

26.   Noah and Abraham We sent indeed
And We conferred upon their line and seed
Prophethood and the Scriptures[2] ;
And some of them had been the rightly guided,
But many had been men of evil deed.

27.   Then, in their wake, We kept on sending
Our many an apostle,
We then sent Jesus, son of Mary,
And granted him the Gospel,[3]
And placed kindness and mercy,
In the hearts of the people,
Who truly followed him; and monkery

1. "Provided you with".

2. Original "The Book": Revelations from God.

3. Original: Injeel (The Evangel "Good News"): By this is meant revelation made to Jesus by God the One, whether committed to writing or not; regrettably many things have been attributed, sometimes blasphemously, to this most pure, penultimate prophet of God, that may never be believed by those who truly fear God.

Had been their own invention,
What We decreed was the prescription:
To seek God's Pleasure only,
But they did not observe this diction,
As it should have been fostered properly;
We do, however, offer compensation
To those of them who did believe; yet many,
Among them are immoral.

28. O You who have believed!
Fear God and do believe in His Apostle,
And you'll receive from Him a double portion
Of his Compassion,
And He'll provide you with a Light,
Whereby you'll walk aright,
And He will grant you absolution,
For God is All-Forgiving, Full of Mercy;

29. So that the people of the Scriptures,
May know that they have no command
Over aught of God's favours,
And that all Grace is in God's Hand,
That unto whom He pleases, He'll dispense,
And God's Graciousness is immense!

SURA 58
THE DISPUTING WOMAN
(AL-MUJAADILA)

In the Name of God, the Beneficent, the Merciful

1.   Indeed God heard the words of her, who was,
   Disputing with you 'gainst her spouse,
   And was to God complaining;
   And God your dialogue was hearing,
   For God's All-Hearing, Ever-Seeing.

2.   Amongst you those who put away their wives,
   By the assertion "Thee I *ziharize*"[1] ,
   Know that they never shall become their mothers!
   Their mothers are no others,
   But those who gave them birth!
   They surely issue from the mouth,
   A word obscene and lacking truth;
   Yet God is Pardoning, Forgiving.

3.   So those who *ziharize* their wives,
   And then retract what they did utter,
   They have to free one neck amongst the slaves,
   Before they touch each other;
   You are advised to do it,
   And God's Aware of what you're doing.

4.   But whosoever has not got the means,
   Then let him fast for two successive months,
   Before they touch each other,

---

1. A form of divorce among Pre-Islam Arabs; the man would say to his wife:
   From now you shall be to me as (the back of) my mother!

And if he finds himself unable,
he should be feeding sixty, needy people,
This way you show your faith,
In God and in His messenger;
And these shall be the bounds of God,
And those rejecting faith shall suffer,
A dreadful torture.

5.   Those who engage in acts of opposition
To God and His apostle,
Shall be destroyed in degradation,
As those before them rendered humble;
Indeed We have revealed,
Explicit revelations,
So there awaits the faithless heathen
Abasing retributions.

6.   Upon the Day when Allah brings,
Them all to life again,
He shall inform them of the things
They did; God has, for certain,
Recorded all their doings,
And these they have forgotten,
But God does witness everything.

7.   Aren't you aware that Allah kens,
Everything in the heavens,
And all that earth contains?
There is no secret counsel 'tween three persons,
But He's of them the fourth,
Neither among five persons,
But He's of them the sixth,
Nor less or more than that, but He

Shall be with them where're they be.
Therefore upon the Day of Resurrection,
He shall inform them of,
Their every action:
Of everything is God All-Knowing.

8.   Have you not noted those who were forbidden,
To enter into secret conversation,
Yet they return to what has been forbidden.
Unto them, and converse together
Of sin, of enmity and contravention
Against the Messenger;
And when they come to you, their greeting
Is never like as God has greeted you,
And they say to themselves:
"Why doesn't God chastise us for our words?!"
Oh, Hell shall be enough for them,
They shall inside it dwell and burn,
What evil, final turn!

9.   O You believers,
When holding secret counsels 'mongst yourselves,
Then do not counsel one another,
On sin and enmity or disobedience,
Unto the Messenger,
But speak of virtuous goodness
As well as righteousness,
And have a righteous fear of God,
To Whom you shall be gathered.

10.   The secret counsels are indeed,
A deed of Satan,
By which he seeks to grieve,

The people who believe,
Yet he is not to hurt them in the least,
Except by God's permission;
Thus let believers put their trust
In God alone.

11.   O You believers! In a congregation,
Make room when you shall be so bidden,
And God will make you ample room!
And when you shall be told to rise, then rise,
And God will from among you raise,
Those who have faith and those to whom,
Knowledge is granted, unto higher grades;
For God is Cognizant of all your deeds.

12.   O You believers, when you do, in private,
Consult the prophet,
You should, before such conference,
Give something in benevolence;
That's best and purest for you all,
But if you do not find the wherewithal,
Then God's Forgiving, Merciful.

13.   Are you afraid of lacking means,
To give to charity and alms,
Before your private consultation?
Well, if you don't do so, and Allah pardons
You, then keep up the praying recitation,
And pay *zakaat*, and be obedient,
To God and His apostle,
For God, of all you do, is Cognizant.

14. Have you not noted those who have befriended,
     A people[1] under Wrath of God?
     They're neither of you, nor of them,
     And knowingly they swear to falsehood.

15. God has for them prepared a torment grievous,
     For it was evil what they had been doing.

16. Their oaths they only use as covers,
     Only to hinder others,
     From Allah's Path, and thus it is
     That for them shall await,
     A torment that abases.

17. Neither their riches, nor their children could
     Help them protect themselves from God,
     They are the inmates of the fire of Hell,
     Wherein they shall for ever dwell.

18. The Day when God shall raise them all,
     Then will they be unto Him swearing,
     As they now swear unto you, thinking,
     That they do stand on something!
     Beware, they're only liars.

19. Satan has of them gained possession,
     Thus making them forget God's Mention;
     They are the Party of the Devil,[2]
     Indeed the Party of the Devil,
     Shall be the losers.

---

1. The Jews of Medina, according to some interpreters.
2. Original: Satan.

20. Certainly those who act in opposition
    To God and His apostle,
    Are 'mongst the most abased of people.

21. God has decreed: "I surely shall prevail,
    Myself and My apostles;" surely God,
    Is Powerful, the Mightiest of all.

22. You shall not ever find believers,
    In God and in the Final Day,
    To be on friendly terms with those
    Who Allah and His Messenger oppose,
    Not though they be their fathers,
    Their children or their brothers,
    Or those unto them tribed;
    These are the people in whose hearts
    He has the Faith inscribed,
    And with a Spirit of His own, He has
    Confirmed them; and He'll take them into Gardens,
    Watered by running streams,
    Therein abiding, God with them well-pleased,
    And they with Him well-pleased;
    These are indeed God's Party,
    Now certainly God's Party,
    Shall be the prosperous party!

SURA 59
THE GATHERING[1]
(AL-HASHR)

In the Name of God, the Beneficent, the Merciful

1. Whatever is there in the Skies,
    And everything on Earth declares,
    The praise of Allah, for He is
    The Overpowering, the Wise.

2. It's He who drove the unbelievers,
    Among the people of the Scriptures,
    Out of their land of dwelling,
    Upon the early gathering;
    You did not think they would go forth,
    And they were certain that their forts,
    'Gainst God, would serve them as defense;
    But Allah came upon them whence,
    They never guessed, while in their hearts
    He cast such terror that, their homes
    Were broken down by their own hands,
    As well as by the faithful's hands;
    Be thus advised,
    You that have eyes!

3. Had it not been that God already willed,
    That they were to be exiled,
    He would have certainly
    Tortured them in this world,
    But, in the world to come they are to suffer,
    The punishment of Fire.

---

1. This sura is also called "the Banishment".

4.   That is because they were to God,
        And to His messenger, in opposition,
        And he who sets himself 'gainst God, should guard,
        For God is Stern in retribution.

5.   Whatever you cut down of trees of dates,
        Or left them standing on their roots,
        All was by God's permission,
        So that He brings upon the evil-doers,
        A shameful degradation.

6.   And of the spoils of theirs, what God bestowed,
        Upon His Messenger, for them you did,
        No horses gallop, neither camels rode,
        But it is God that His apostles grants,
        Dominion over whom He wants;
        God has power over all things.

7.   What God has taken from the people of the towns,
        And given unto His apostle, now belongs,
        To Allah, His Apostle, and the kith and kin,[1]
        To orphans and the wandering aliens;
        So that it shall not be possessed in turns,
        Among you by your wealthy men!
        So take what the Apostle to you grants,
        And do refrain from what he may prevent
        You from it, and observe the fear of God,
        For God is surely Strict in punishment.

8.   It's also for the poorer emigrants,
        Who from their homes, and their possessions,

---

1. The Apostle's kindred.

Were driven into exile,
For they were seeking God's compassion,
And favour and good pleasure, while
Assisting God and His Apostle;
Indeed they are the truthful.

9. And those who had already set up homes,
And had believed before them, love the ones,
Who fled to them for refuge, who do not
Find in their hearts a need for what,
Was granted them, and them they prize,
Above and over their own selves,
Though poorness be their lot;
And he who overcomes his own soul's greed,
Salvaged is he indeed.

10. And those who after them arrived, announce:
"Our Lord, forgive us and forgive our brethren,
Who in the Faith had over us precedence,
And in our hearts, let there be no aversion
To those who did believe already,
Our Lord, You're Gracious, Full of Mercy."

11. Have you not seen the hypocrites who tell
Unto their fellow-unbelievers,
Among the people of the Scriptures:
"If you are driven out, we also will,
Be going out with you, and at no time,
Shall we obey the men who do you harm,
And if you are attacked, we will be flying
To your defense;" but God is Witness
That surely they are lying!

12.   Indeed if they are driven out,
They won't go out with them,
And if they shall be fought against,
They won't be backing them,
And even if they come forth to assist,
Then they would surely turn their backs:
Helped shall they not be in the least!

13.   The horror of you in their hearts,
Is more outstanding,
Than that of God,
That is because they are a crowd,
Devoid of understanding!

14.   They shall not fight against you all together,
Except in towns well-fortified, or from
Behind high walls. Among themselves their valour
Is great; you think of them united, wholesome,
But they have hearts divided, torn asunder;
Because they are a crowd devoid of wisdom.

15.   Like those of recent times before them,
Who met the evil sequel of their action;
And there shall be a grievous torture for them.

16.   They are like Satan when he urges men
"To disbelieve"!
And when they disbelieve, he, there and then:
"Of you do I myself absolve,
For I have dread of God, the Lord
Of all the worlds!"

17.   Therefore they both shall end in Hell,
Therein for long to dwell;
And that's the wrong-doers' reward!

18.   Have fear of God, believers!
And let each soul consider
What it for its Tomorrow offers;
Have fear of God, since God well knows
Of your affairs.

19.   And do not be like those who did forget
Allah, and so He caused them to forget
Their souls, their selves;
They are indeed the evil-doers.

20.   Equal are not the heirs of Hell,
And those who shall in Garden dwell,
Triumphant are the Garden-dwellers.

21.   Had We sent down this same Quran,
Upon a mountain,
You would indeed have seen it humbly fallen,
For fear of God, and rent asunder;
Lo! for the sake of men, We mention
Such parables, perhaps they ponder!

22.   He's God the One, and there is no
Godhead but He,
The Knower of the Hidden and the Open,
Who is Benefic, Full of Mercy.

23.   He is the One God and, but He,
There is no other deity
The Sovereign Lord, the Ever-Holy,
The Source of Peace, the Fount of Safety,
The Guardian over all, the Mighty,
The All-Compelling, Ever-Dignified;
Far from what they set up with Him,
Allah be glorified!

24.   He's Allah, the Creator,
The out-of-nothing Starter,
The beings' Super-Potter;[1]
The beautifulest Names are His;
Whatever is there in the Skies,
And everything on Earth declares
His glory, and He is
The Mighty, the All-Wise.

---

1. The Designer and shaper of all.

SURA 60
THE EXAMINER
(AL-MUMTAHINA)[1]

In the Name of God, the Beneficent, the Merciful

1. O You believers! Do not take for friends,
   The enemies of Mine and foes of yours;
   You show them friendship while they are the ones,
   Who disbelieved the Truth to you revealed,
   And drove out the Apostle and yourselves,
   Because you did believe in God, your Lord!
   If you come out to struggle in My cause,
   Seeking to please Me, do you then extend
   Secret affection to them as a friend?!
   And I do know full well what you conceal,
   And all that you reveal;
   And whosoever of you may,
   Do this, will surely stray,
   From the right way.

2. If over you they gain the upper hand,
   You find that they are foemen, and,
   They shall unleash their hands and tongues,
   To do you evil wrongs,
   And they will keenly crave
   That you may disbelieve.

3. Neither your kinsmen, nor your children
   Would be to you of any profit
   Upon the Day of Resurrection;
   Betwixt you brings He separation,

---

1. "The Sura that examines" or "The woman who is examined", according to
different pronunciations and interpretations.

948

For Allah Sees your every action.

4.   Indeed you have a fine example,
       In Abraham and his companions,
       When they said unto their own people:
       "Lo! Clear of you are we, and what you pray to,
       Instead of God; we do reject you,
       And enmity and hatred shall for eons,
       Between us run, until you are believing,
       In God alone."
       -Excluding Abraham when saying,
       Unto his father:
       'I plead for your forgiveness in my praying;
       Though getting for you something further,
       From Allah, have I not the power'-,
       "Our Lord, in You alone we trust,
       And to you only do we turn,
       And unto you we come at last;

5.   "Our lord, do not expose us to the wiles
       Of disbelieving, truth-deniers;
       Our Lord, you are indeed,
       The Mighty, the All-wise."

6.   Surely in them you have a good
       Example of the people,
       Who have their hopes in God,
       And in the Final Day;
       As for the ones who turn away:
       God is in need of nothing,
       He is the Ever-Praised.

7.   God shall perhaps establish amity,

Between you and the others,
With whom you are at odds,
For Allah has Ability,
And Allah is Forgiving, Full of Pity.

8.   Respecting those:
Who neither fought you in religion's cause,
Nor did they drive you from your homes,
Allah does not forbid,
That you should do them good,
And be, in treating them, most just,
Indeed God likes the justice-doers best.

9.   But God forbids you to be kind to those,
Who fought you in religion's cause,
And drove you from your homes,
And aided your eviction from behind;
And those who may be to them kind,
Are certainly transgressors.

10.   O you believers, when believing women,
Unto you fly as refugees, examine
Them-but it's God who knows the truth
About their faith-
Now when you find that they are true believers,
Do not return them unto disbelievers:
The former are not lawful to the latter,
Nor are the latter lawful to the former;
But do give back the dowries they've been given,
And if you marry them, there is no sin,
Upon you, once their dowries have been given.
Neither hold on to marriage ties,
With unbelieving wives:

Demand the dowries to them given,
And let the unbelieving men
Demand what they have given;
Such shall be God's injunction,
He is to judge between you all,
And God is the All-Knowing, the All-Wise.

11. And if some portions of your spouses' dowers,
Over to disbelievers goes,
And then you overcome and get them back,
Then pay, of what they gave, the like,
To those whose spouses them forsook;
And have the pious fear of God,
In Whom you are believers.

12. O Prophet, when to you believing women,
Come, giving you their oath of loyalty:
"Never to worship, in association
With God, another deity,
Nor commit theft or fornication,
Nor murder their own children,
Nor speak a slanderous falsity
Of their own fabrication,
Nor disobey your goodly commendation",
Then, do accept their oath of fealty,
And pray to God for them to be forgiven,
For God is Oft-Forgiving, Full of Pity.

13. O You believers, do not take for friends,
A People who the wrath of God incurred,
They have indeed of life to come despaired:
Even as the disbelieving pagans,
Despair of those in tombs!

SURA 61
RANKS
(AL-SAFF)

In the Name of God, the Beneficent, the Merciful

1. Whatever is there in the skies,
    And all upon the earth, declares
    God's Glory and His Praise,
    For He is the Almighty, the All-Wise.

2. O You believers!
    Wherefore do you profess,
    That which you never practice?

3. It is disgusting in the sight of God,
    When you say what you do not practice!

4. God truly loves the ones in ordered ranks,
    Who combat in His Cause as if they were,
    Impervious, solid flanks.

5. Recall when Moses said unto his people,
    "O People mine! Why vex me and make trouble,
    When you have known that I am God's apostle,
    To you?" yet, after they had turned aside,
    Their hearts were turned aside by God, since God,
    The evil-doing people, does not guide.

6. As when said Jesus, son of Mary,
    "Sons of Israel! I am truly,
    God's own Apostle sent to you, confirming,
    The Torah that we've got; and giving,
    The tidings glad:

Of an Apostle after me arriving,
Whose name is AHMAD;"
Yet, when he did come to them with,
Many a lucid Sign,
Said they: "Ah, this is magic plain!"

7. And who shall be more wicked than the one,
    Who forges lies concerning God, while he
    Unto Islam[1] is being called upon;
    And surely God does not direct the people,
    Involved in wrong and evil.

8. Using their mouths, they fancy putting out,
    The Light of God, but God, of His own Light,
    Is the Perfector,
    Despite the dislike of the disbelievers!

9. He is the One who sent His Messenger,
    With Guidance and the faith of Truth,
    So that He may exalt it over,
    Entire, religious faith.

10. O You believers!
    Let Me inform you of a good transaction,
    That saves you from a woeful retribution:

11. Have faith in God and His apostle,
    And in the Cause of God devoutly struggle,
    With your belongings and your beings!
    That is the best for you,
    If you but knew!

---

1. Submission to the will of the Almighty.

12.   We will forgive your sins,
        And let you enter Gardens
        With many a running stream,
        And pleasant mansions,
        Inside the paradise of Eden;
        This is the gain supreme.

13.   And other blessings to you dearest:
        The Help of God and Triumph nearest;
        Therefore, proclaim unto the faithful
        This tidings best.

14.   O You believers!
        Be God's supporters,
        As in the case of Jesus, Mary's son,
        When he to his disciples put the question:
        "Who unto God are my supporters?"
        Said the disciples: "We are God's supporters."
        Thenceforth a party of the Israelites,
        Embraced the faith, whereas the other party,
        Defied it; then We gave a hand
        Unto the faithful 'gainst their foes,
        And they above them rose.

SURA 62
FRIDAY
(AL-JUMU'A)

In the Name of God, the Beneficent, the Merciful

1.   Whatever is there in the Skies,
And everything on Earth declares
God's glory and His praise,
The Sovereign Lord, the Holiest,
In Might Exalted, the Most-Wise.

2.   It's He who raised among the gentiles[1] ,
A messenger from their own midst,
To read to them His Revelations,
To purify them and to teach them,
The Book and Wisdom;
-Whereas before this they were lost,
In error manifest-

3.   And others of them[2] who have not yet joined them,
And He's the Overpowering, the All-Wise.

4.   This is God's Grace,
He grants it unto whom He please,
He is the Owner of the highest bounties.

5.   Those unto whom the Torah was consigned,
And yet they bore it not, resemble,
A donkey laden with some books,

---

1. The word *ummi* carries different meanings in the Holy Quran: illiterate, Arab
polytheist, and non-Jewish or gentile, in different contexts.

2. Meaning other *ummi* nations as well as the generations to come.

Yet worse is the example of the people,
Who Allah's revelations have denied;
For Allah does not guide,
The oft-transgressing folks.

6. Say: "O You of the Jewish faith,
   If you suppose that of all men,
   God's friends are you alone,
   And you do speak the truth,
   Then gladly wish for death!"

7. But never will they for it long,
   Because of what they've done, and Allah
   Knows the people who oft do wrong.

8. Say: "Lo! The death from which you shrink,
   Shall certainly you overtake,
   Then you will be sent back,
   Unto the Knower of the Hidden,
   And of the Open, and He then,
   Enlightens you of what you've done!"

9. O You believers, when the call is made,
   For Friday Prayings, do make haste,
   To God's remembrance, and leave off all trade;
   Would that you knew: that would be for you best!

10. And when the Prayer is ended, then disperse,
    Throughout the land, and go in quest,
    Of Allah's Grace, and oft remember
    Allah, that you may prosper.

11. Yet when they get a sight of merchandise,
Or games, they after them disperse and leave
You standing there alone!
Declare: "What Allah has got in reserve
Is better than some goods or games, for Allah
Is certainly the Best Provider.

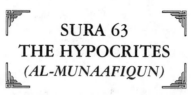

SURA 63
THE HYPOCRITES
(AL-MUNAAFIQUN)

In the Name of God, the Beneficent, the Merciful

1.   When hypocrites come to you, they declare,
"We do bear witness that indeed you are,
God's messenger;"
Yea, God does know you are His messenger,
And God does witness that the hypocrites
Are utter liars!

2.   Their oaths in faith, they use as screens,
So they obstruct the Path of God;
Evil indeed is all their doings.

3.   This is because they first embraced
The Faith, and then denied it, hence
A seal upon their hearts was placed,
And they became devoid of conscience.

4.   Yet when you see them, you will be impressed,
By their fine looks, and when they lecture,
You keenly hear the words expressed;
In fact they are as blocks of timber,
Propped up against a wall,
They think that every, blaring call,
Is meant to be against them;
They are the enemy; beware of them!
God will condemn such folks
Are they not really false?

5.   And when they're told: "Now come,
That God's Apostle may
For your forgiveness pray,
They turn their heads aside,
And you shall see them turn away,
While looking big with pride.

6.   It is the same for these,
Whether you beg forgiveness for them,
Or never beg forgiveness for them;
For Allah has no Guidance for the person
Wickedly sunk in sin.

7.   It's they who recommend:
"Do not a thing expend,
On those who follow God's Apostle
Until they separate and crumble!"
But all the Treasures of the Heavens
And of the Earth are Allah's,
Yet hypocrites do not this realize.

8.   They say: "When we return to Al-Madeena,
The mighty shall, from there, expel the meaner!"
But might belongs to God and His Apostle,
And to the faithful, though
The hypocrites may not know!

9.   O You believers!
Let not your worldly riches or your children,
Divert you from repeating Allah's Mention,
Surely this kind of choosers,[1]

---

1. "Choosing worldly riches".

Will be the losers.

10.　　And from what We for you provided spend,
　　　　Ere death shall one of you attend,
　　　　As then he shall be saying:
　　　　"My Lord, why did you not awhile reprieve me,
　　　　I could have given then in charity,
　　　　And now would have the righteous joined?!

11.　　But God respites the souls of none,
　　　　When their appointed times run out,
　　　　And God is Best-Informed about
　　　　What you have done!

SURA 64
COMMON LOSS-AND-GAIN
(AL-TAGHAABUN)

In the Name of God, the Beneficent, the Merciful

1. All that is in the heavens,
    And everything on Earth declares
    God's glory, and to Him belongs,
    The Kingdom, and to Him is due all praise,
    And over everything He reigns.

2. It's He who has created you:
    Yet, some of you conceal the Truth,[1]
    And some of you have Faith,
    While God is Seeing what you do.

3. The heavens and the Earth,
    Did He create in truth,
    And He fashioned you all, and gave
    You figures brave[2] ;
    And back to Him shall you go forth.

4. Whatever is there in the Skies,
    And everything on Earth, He knows;
    And knows He all that you disguise,
    And what you may disclose;
    Even what lies in depths of hearts,
    God always knows.

5. Has there not come to you the tidings,

---

1. Or "are disbelievers."

2. Fine, excellent.

Of those who disbelieved, in former times,
And had to taste the evil consequence,
Of their own doing,
Who yet shall have to face,
The painful Scourge ensuing?

6. The reason is that unto them,
Their own apostles came,
With clearest Signs,
But they said: "Shall our guides be humans?!"
Thus they did not believe, and gave no heed,
And God was of them in no need,
For God is absolutely Needless,
And He's the Praised, the Glorious.

7. The disbelievers claim that they,
Shall ne'er be resurrected! Say:
Yes, surely, by my Lord, you shall be raised,
And surely will you be advised,
Of what you did;
Easy is that to God.

8. Therefore in God and His Apostle,
Have faith, and in the Light,
That We sent down as well,
And know that God is Best-Informed
Of what you have performed.

9. The day He gathers you, and does
The Day of Gathering ordain,
That is indeed going to be,
The Day of Common Loss and Gain:
As those who did believe in God,

And did whate'er was right and good,
From them shall He their evil cleanse,
And let them enter Gardens,
Watered by running streams,
To dwell therein for times on end;
That is the Triumph grand!

10.   And, disbelievers who denied Our signs,
Are to be Hell's companions,
And there shall they remain for eons;
How wretched are such home-comings!

11.   Afflictions never come about,
Except by God's permission,
And one who does believe in God,
He guides his very heart,
For Allah is the Knower of all things.

12.   Thus obey God, and do obey,
The Messenger;
But if you turn away,
Then it shall be upon Our messenger,
Only the Message plainly to deliver.

13.   There is but God the One, no deity,
So let the men of faith rely
On Allah only.

14.   O You believers, in your wives,
And children, you may have an enemy,
Therefore, of them beware;
But if you pardon and forbear,
And do forgive, then God's as ever,

The Most-Forgiving, Mercy-Giver.

15. And know that your possessions and your children,
    Are only tests,
    And it is merely God with Whom a great
    Repayment rests.

16. Thus keep your godly duties as you could,
    And listen and obey, and spend,
    In charity; it is for your own good;
    For whoever from his own greed,
    Could save himself, prospers indeed.

17. Should you lend God a handsome loan,
    He'll pay you back as much again,
    And sins of yours He shall condone,
    For God is Most-Rewarding, All-Benign,
    All the Unseen and Seen He knows,
    And He is the All-Mighty, the All-Wise.

SURA 65
DIVORCE
(AL-TALAAQ)

In the Name of God, the Beneficent, the Merciful

1.   O Prophet! If you are divorcing women:
You may divorce them only when,
Their periods have their courses run,
Therefore of the appointed period,
Make a record unflawed,
While fearing God, your Lord.
And don't expel them from their homes, nor they,
Themselves should go away,
Unless they have been proven guilty,
Of something lewdly dirty.
And these are bounds by God set down,
And he who goes beyond the bounds of God,
Certainly his own soul he wrongs;
You never know! Perhaps God brings,
To pass, thereafter, novel things.

2.   And when they reach their waiting times,
Either retain them with deserving kindness,
Or part with them on even-handed terms,
And from amongst you, call to witness,
Two men endued with justice,
And only for the sake of God,
Let them establish evidence;
Those who believe in God,
And in the Latter Day,
Shall be exhorted by it,
And whosoever has a fear of God,
For him shall God prepare an exit;

3.   And shall provide for him from whence,
        He could not comprehend,
        And he who puts his confidence
        In God, enough for him is He alone,
        For God His purpose certainly attains:
        For everything a measured providence,
        Is set as God ordains.

4.   If you're in doubt about your women:
        For those who have despaired of menstruation,
        As well as those without a menstruation,
        The waiting course shall be three months,
        And the appointed time for pregnant women,
        Is when they lay their burden down,
        And He shall by His own injunction,
        To him who cares about his duties unto God,
        Provide relief and ease.

5.   That is from God an ordinance,
        To you revealed, and he who has
        The fear of God in him, He shall efface
        His evils from him, and enhance,
        For him the recompense.

6.   You shall provide them lodgings in your homes,
        According to your means,
        And harm them not in order that you harden
        Their situations,
        And if they are expecting children,
        Maintain them till their burden,
        They do lay down;
        And if they for you nurse and suckle,
        Their recompense you have to settle,

And do enjoin each other unto goodness,
And deal in fairness;
But if you clash and quarrel,
Then let for him another woman suckle.

7.   The man of plenty, out of his abundance,
Shall spend, and he who has a mean subsistence,
According to what God has to him given;
God never puts a burden on a person,
Beyond what He to him has given;
God brings about facility,
After adversity.

8.   And many nations have rebelled,
'Gainst the commandment of their Lord
And His apostles! Thus We called
The matter to severe account,
And painful was Our punishment.

9.   Therefore the evil fruit of their own doing,
They tasted, and their final end was ruin!

10.   God has for them prepared a biting torment,
Therefore, fear God, O you who ponder,
And do believe! Now God has to you sent
Down a Reminder:

11.   A Messenger who does to you recite
God's most explicit revelations,
To lead, from darkness into light,
Those who believe and do good actions;
And whoso does believe in God,
And renders righteous deeds,

He shall admit him unto Gardens,
Watered by running streams,
To dwell therein for good;
A goodly sustenance indeed,
Is given him by God.

12.   God is He who created seven heavens,
And earths, in corresponding fashions,
The Order down amongst them runs,
In order that you know that God's
Omnipotent, and that His Knowledge does
Encompass all there is!

SURA 66
THE PROHIBITION
(AL-TAHREEM)

In the Name of God, the Beneficent, the Merciful

1.   O Prophet, why do you prohibit,
What God for you did sanction,[1]
In seeking to solicit
Your spouses' satisfaction?
Yet God's Forgiving, Full of Ruth.

2.   God has indeed for you ordained,
The expiation of an oath,
For God's your Patron, and He is
The Ever-Knower, the All-Wise.

3.   Now when the Prophet something secret,
Unto a wife of his confided,
And then when she disclosed it,
And Allah let him know of what she said,
He part of it to her reported,
And other part avoided;
And when he told her of it,
She said: "who let you on to this affair?"
He answered: "I was made aware,
By the All-Knower, All-Aware!"

4.   Would that you two[2] to Allah turned,[3]
Your hearts are surely so inclined,
But if against him both of you combined,

1. Made lawful.

2. Reportedly two wives of the Holy prophet, Ayesha and Hafsa.

3. "In penitence".

Know that God is his very Guardian,
And Gabriel and virtuous believers,
And angels shall be his relievers.

5.   Were he to give you all divorce,
Perhaps his Lord would, in your place,
Give to him better consorts: Muslim women,
Full of belief, devout, repentant,
Servers of Allah, whether emigrant,
Widowed or virgin.

6.   O You believers,
Do guard yourselves and kindred of your own,
'Gainst a Fire, whose fuel
Is made of man and stone,
With keeper-angels, strong and stern,
Who never disobey what God enjoins,
And promptly carry His commands.

7.   You disbelievers,
Make no excuses on this Day:
Only for what you have been doing,
You're being made to pay!

8.   O You believers,
Repent to God a pure repentance,
Your Lord, perchance will cleanse
Your sins, and let you enter Gardens,
Watered by running streams;
Upon the Day when God shall not discredit
The Prophet, neither his in-faith companions,
Their light shall be resplendent,
In front of them and on their right,

And they shall say: "O Lord, enhance our light,
And unto us forgiveness grant,
You are indeed Omnipotent."

9.   O Prophet, with the disbelievers,
And 'gainst the hypocrites, contend,
Be toughest with them, never bend;
Gehenna shall be their abode,
And it's an evil end!

10.   For disbelievers Allah gives
Examples, in the case of wives,
Of Noah and of Lot: they were
Under the sponsorship of two
Of our sincerest servants true,
But both betrayed them; so they could,
Protect them not from God;
And they were told: "Do enter
The Fire, with those who enter!"

11.   And God has set unto the faithful,
The wife of Pharaoh an example,
She said: "My Lord, build me a house,
Near you in Paradise,
And salvage me from Pharaoh and his vice,
And save me from a wicked race."

12.   And Mary, Imran's daughter: she
Preserved her chastity, so We,
Into her of Our Spirit blew;
And she did testify unto the Words
And Scriptures of her Lord's;
She was a heedful woman true.

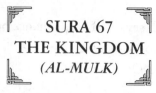

SURA 67
THE KINGDOM
(AL-MULK)

In the Name of God, the Beneficent, the Merciful

1.   Most hallowed is He in Whose hand,
The Kingdom lies,
And He is ably in command
Of all there is!

2.   He who created Death and Life,
That He may put you to a test:
Which one of you shall be,
In doing good, the best;
And Mighty is He, Oft-Forgiving;

3.   He Who created seven heavens,
In elevated constitution,
You shall not see an imperfection
In Al-Rahman's[1] creation.
Now then, turn up your vision,
Could you see any failing?

4.   Then look once more, and yet again,
The vision, stunned and spurned,
Comes back, exhaustion showing.

5.   And this the lowest of the heavens,
Did We with lustrous Lamps adorn,
And We obliged them to perform,
As missiles that assail the satans;

---

1. The Most Merciful God.

And We prepared for them the Pains
Of the All-Blazing.

6. And for the disbelievers in their Lord,
There is the torment of Gehenna,
And it's a bad abode!

7. When they therein are flung,
They from it hear the loudest braying,
While it is wildly boiling,

8. Well-nigh with rage exploding;
Whene're another group is in there thrown,
Its keepers throw at them this question:
"Did ne'er a warner come to you to warn?"

9. They answer: "Yes, indeed,
To us a warner came,
But we denied him, saying:
"No! God has not revealed a thing,
You're just in an illusion grand!"

10. They further say: "Had we but listened,
Or had we used our mind,
We would not be amongst the inmates
Of the Undying Flame."

11. They thus confess their sins, and, just the same,
Avaunt! Will it be to the Inmates
Of the Undying Flame.

12. For the people who fear their Lord,
Although unseen, there is indeed,

Forgiveness and a great reward.

13.   Whether you manifest your word,
Or speak under your breath,
He surely knows the inmost,
Recess of every breast.

14.   Should He not Know? He that created all?
The Subtle-Knower, the All-Knowing?

15.   He is the One who made the earth,
For you level and smooth;
Therefore, traverse its regions,
And eat from His provisions;
And unto Him shall be the Resurrecting.

16.   Are you securely confident that He,
Who is in Heaven, shall not let you be,
Swallowed up by the earth when she
Is like a sandy whirlwind swaying?

17.   Or, are you confident again,
That He, who is in Heaven,
Shall not against you send
A horrid hurricane?
Then you shall comprehend
How is My warning!

18.   Indeed, before them, there were those,
Who to the Truth were crying lies,
And grave was My repaying!

19.   Do they not watch how birds above them,

Their wings expand and fold?
None, save Al-Rahmaan,
Could them uphold;
He does See into everything.

20. And who is He that, like an armoured host,
Helps you, apart from Al-Rahmaan?
Indeed the unbelievers suffer most,
From fancy and delusion.

21. Or who is it that might for you apportion,
If He were to withhold His Own provision?
Yet, they persist in boldness and aversion.

22. Who is more rightly guided: he that goes
Bent down upon his nose,
Or he that upright marches forth
Upon the straightest Path?

23. Say: "He it is who brought you into being,
And ears and eyes and hearts unto you granted,
Yet little is the thank that you are giving!"

24. Say: "He it is who placed you on the earth
And multiplied, and you shall be,
Before Him gathered forth."

25. They ask: "When shall this Promise come to pass,
If it's the truth that you express?"

26. Say: "Such cognition does with Allah rest,
And I am but a warner manifest."

27. But then when they shall see it drawing nigh,
    The faces of the unbelievers will
    Be full of grief, awry;
    And then it shall be mentioned:
    "Here is that for which you petitioned!

28. Say: "Think in depth,
    Whether Allah put me to death,
    And those who are with me, or whether
    He blesses us with His Compassion,
    Yet who will save the unbelievers,
    From a most painful retribution?!"

29. Say: "He is Al-Rahmaan,
    In Him do we believe,
    And Him do we rely upon;
    And soon you shall be knowing,
    Who is in error wallowing!"

30. Say: "Only think, if you awoke to find
    Your waters sunk into the ground,
    Who will it be that for you brings
    Water that springs?!"

SURA 68
THE PEN
(AL-QALAM)

In the Name of God, the Beneficent, the Merciful

1. N, by the Pen, and that which they record,

2. You aren't possessed,
    Thanks to the blessing of your Lord.

3. And you shall be immensely recompensed,

4. For you're endowed with morals unsurpassed.

5. Then you, and they, shall both behold,

6. Which party is possessed!

7. Surely it is your Lord who Knows them best,
    Those walking off His Road;
    And it is He again who does Know best
    The ones on Guided Road.

8. Obey not, therefore, the rejecters-

9. They wish that you should be retreating,
    So that they too could be retreaters!-

10. Neither obey the common swearers,

11. Defamers, slander spreaders,

12. Forbidders of good works and alms,

Transgressing sinners,

13.   Oppressors coming of unsure begetters,

14.   Though with more wealth and sons than others.

15.   When unto them Our revelations
Are being read, they counter:
"Oh, legends of the ancients!"

16.   Shortly we shall be branding
Their nostrils for distinction!

17.   Indeed we have been giving them[1] a probing,
As we did probe the owners of the garden,
Who swore that they would, in the morning,
Pluck their produce for certain,

18.   So certain that they made no reservation[2] !

19.   But while they were asleep, upon them came,
Caused by your Lord, a visitation;

20.   And by the time the Sun had risen,
It was defruited, barren!

21.   And in the morn, they called each other:

22.   "Let us make haste unto our cultivation,
If we should pluck and gather."

---

1. The Meccans

2. Such as: "If God will".

23.   So they departed, whispering together:

24.   "Today you shall let no one enter,
      No needy man, no beggar!"

25.   Thus they betimes went out in haste,
      Fixed in their resolution.

26.   And after seeing it, they cried:
      "We must be in the wrong location"!

27.   "But nay! we have been made deprived."

28.   The modest one among them grieved:
      "Ah, did I not advise
      You to give Praise?!"

29.   "Glory and praise unto our Lord,
      Surely we trespassed", they deplored.

30.   Then they began to blame each other,

31.   Saying: "O woe to us, we were indeed,
      In mutinous error".

32.   "Perhaps our Lord shall to us grant,
      Instead of it, one better;
      We humbly unto Him petition."

33.   Such is the punishment, although
      The Chastisement of the Hereafter,
      Shall be far greater;
      Did they but know!

34.   Surely for self-restraining righteous,
      There shall be, with their Lord,
      The Gardens of Delight and Bliss.

35.   Are we to order parity
      For Muslims[1] and the guilty?!

36.   What's wrong with you? How do you make
      A ruling or a judgment?

37.   Or have you got a certain Book
      That you peruse,

38.   In which for you there is,
      All that you choose?!

39.   Or have We sworn with you a covenant,
      Binding until the Day of Judgment,
      That you must e'er have what you please?!

40.   Ask them, which one of them, this guarantees?

41.   Or have they some associate-gods?
      Then, it's upon them to bring forth,
      Their gods along with God,
      If they are men of truth.

42.   The Day of Dread when knees shall tremble,
      And they are called upon to kneel,
      Lo, they shall not be able:

---

1. Submitters to the will of the Almighty God.

43.   Their eyes dejected, lowered,
Themselves by dust of scandal covered;
Because when they were safe and well,
They had been called upon to offer
Their humble prayer![1]

44.   Therefore, leave Me alone with those,
Who think of this Report[2] as lies,
Soon shall We pull them down
From their high horses,
From whence they cannot recognize;

45.   Yet I shall put up with them for a while,
Powerful and certain is My guile.

46.   Or, do you ask them for some wages
That them in heavy debts engages?!

47.   Or in their hands is the Unseen,
And they, therefrom, just write it down?!

48.   So wait with Patience for the order of your Lord,
And do not be like the Companion of the Whale[3] ,
Who cried out when he was by desperation floored.

49.   Had not a blessing from his Lord been of avail,
He would have been abandoned,
Unto the Wilderness, condemned.

---

1. "But they did not obey."

2. Announcement, revelation.

3. Jonah.

50.   His Lord, then, chose and blessed him
      And 'mongst the righteous placed him.

51.   The disbelievers were about to cast,
      The evil eye upon you,[1] when they heard
      The Message, yet they say: "he's sure possessed!"

52.   But It[2] is nothing less than
      A Message to all men.

---

1. Mohammad (pbuh).

2. The Quran.

SURA 69
THE SURE OCCURRENCE
(AL-HAAQQA)

In the Name of God, the Beneficent, the Merciful

1. The Sure Occurrence,[1]

2. What is the Sure Occurrence?

3. Nay, you do not know what,
   The Sure Occurrence is!

4. Thamood and Aad,[2]
   The Thundering Bang[3] belied,

5. As for Thamood,
   They were annihilated by,
   A crushing, quaking Blast;[4]

6. And as to Aad,
   They were annihilated by,
   A furious, icy gust,

7. That He for seven, ceaseless nights,
   On them unleashed,
   That eight, long days
   Against them lashed;
   So that, one might have seen,

---

1. An inevitable event, the Last Day.
2. Names of ancient peoples in Arabia.
3. Or "the clatterer", "the shocker"; another word for the Last Day.
4. A violent blast, scourge or catastrophe.

The people lying thrashed,
Prostrate as trunks of palms,
Decayed and crashed.

8.   See now if any trace of them remains!

9.   Then there was Pharaoh, and the ones,
Before his times,
And wicked sinners of the Ruined Towns[1] ;

10. For they their Lord's apostle disobeyed,
Thus He upon them sent,
A scourge of punishment;

11. And when the waters overflowed, We made
You, in a Floater, to be carried,

12. That it should serve you as a warning,
-And that attentive ears would it retain.

13. But when the Horn is but once blown,

14. And Earth and mountains shall be borne
Away, and shattered at a stroke,

15. Yea, on that Day, the Great Event shall strike,

16. And heavens, loose today and frail, shall crack
And cleave asunder;

17. And angels there shall stand on every border,

---

1. Settlements of the people of the Prophet Lot (Sodom and Gomorrha).

And eight of them, this Day, will shoulder,
Your Lord's High Throne of Power.

18.   On that Day, you shall be exposed;
No secrets that you had disguised,
Shall be unpublished, undisclosed!

19.   Then he who shall receive his book,
With his right hand, he thus shall speak:
"My record! Oh, come take a look!

20.   "The thought of meeting my Account,
I ne'er forsook."

21.   So he shall lead a life of eden,[1]

22.   In an exalted Garden,

23.   With clusters hanging low of fruitage burden.

24.   "Do eat and drink unto your heart's content,
For what you forward sent,
In days, that went."

25.   But he who shall receive his book,
With his left hand, he thus shall speak:
"Would that my book was never to me given,

26.   "So I knew not what my Account had been!

27.   "O Would that death had made of me an end,

_____

1. Delight, happiness.

28.   "My wealth is useless, nothing it could bend,

29.   My sovereignty? Gone with the wind!"

30.   "Seize him and bind him well,

31.   "Then cast him into blazing Hell,

32.   "Thereafter, in a chain,
Of seventy cubits' length,
Let him remain!

33.   "For he did not believe in God Almighty,

34.   "And never did he advocate
The feeding of the needy.

35.   "So here Today he has no faithful friends,

36.   "Nor any food but filth of wounds,

37.   "Which none shall eat but those who sinned!"

38.   Thus swear I not by what you see,

39.   Neither by what you do not see,

40.   That this is certainly the Word,
Of an Apostle honoured,

41.   And that it's not a poet's diction;
How little you believe!

42.   Neither a Kohin's[1] divination;
         How little warning you receive!

43.   It is indeed a revelation,
         By Lord of all Creation.

44.   Had he[2] some sayings, in our name,
         Pronounced, untruthful an iota,

45.   We would have surely seized him firm,

46.   Then, cut off his aorta,

47.   And of you none could him assist!

48.   Surely it is a warrant unto those
         Who do evil resist,

49.   And We do know that there are some
         Deniers in your midst,

50.   And that it makes the disbelievers,
         Despondently distressed.

51.   For it's indeed the Truth of Certainty;

52.   Thus, glorify the Name of
         Your Lord, the Mighty.

---

1. A Soothsayer.
2. The Holy Prophet.

SURA 70
ELEVATIONS
(AL-MA'AARIJ)

In the Name of God, the Beneficent, the Merciful

1. A sceptic questioned once about the Doom,
   That's bound to come?

2. There is against it no protection
   For the unfaithful pagan,

3. It comes from God, the Lord of Elevations;

4. The angels and the Spirit shall ascend,
   Unto Him in a Day that will extend,
   In terms of years, some fifty thousand.

5. Therefore keep up with graceful patience;

6. Surely they think it's[1] in the farthest distance,

7. But We do see it near at hand!

8. The Day when heavens look like copper molten,

9. And mountains shall be coloured tufts of cotton,

10. And bosom friends shall not each other question,

11. Although they will be in each other's vision;
    The sinners shall be ready to redeem

---

1. The Last Day, the Chastisement.

Themselves from torments of that Day of Doom,
Even by sacrificing children,

12.   Their wives and brethren,

13.   Their Kindest kith and kin,

14.   And all the people on this earthly haven,
If *that* assured for them salvation!

15.   But nay! It[1] fiercely burns,

16.   The fleecer of the skins,

17.   Calling upon the ones,
Who turned and fled from Faith,

18.   And just amassed and hoarded wealth!

19.   Man is indeed by temperament
Hasty, impatient:

20.   When touched by evil, he is deeply grievous,

21.   And when by fortune blessed, ungenerous!

22.   Not so the worshippers,

23.   Who are consistent with their prayers,

24.   Who, of their wealth, assign a portion just,

---

1. Fire of Hell.

25.   Unto the beggars and the dispossessed,

26.   Who do confirm the Day of Judgment,

27.   Who dread the torment,
        Delivered by their Lord,

28.   -"The torment coming from their Lord,
        None could indeed avoid.-

29.   Who always guard their chastities,

30.   -Save from their spouses or their mates of bond;
        Thus they shall not be blamed,

31.   But if they seek to go beyond
        The limits, then they shall transgress.-

32.   Who keep their trusts and treaties,

33.   Who in their witness-giving,
        Are firm and righteous,

34.   Who are attentive to their prayers;

35.   Those are the ones who will in Gardens,
        Reside, with honours.

36.   But what's the matter with the unbelieving,
        Who are, with necks outstretched, around you moving?!

37.   In sundry batches from the left and right?!

38.   Does every man among them long to go,
        Into the Garden of Delight?

39.   It won't be so!
        We have created them of what they know!

40.   Thus by the Lord of East and West shall I not swear,
        That We possess the Power,

41.   To substitute them with some better people
        Than them, and from it nothing could Us cripple!

42.   So let them plunge in follies, let them play,
        Until they face the Day,
        Unto them Promised,

43.   The Day when they shall rise from graves,
        In sudden haste as racing towards some goals,

44.   With downcast eyes, aghast,
        Themselves ashamed, abased;
        That is the Day unto them Promised!

SURA 71
NOAH
(NOOH)

In the Name of God, the Beneficent, the Merciful

1.   Noah We sent unto his clan,
Saying: "Do warn your people ere
A painful scourge them overran."

2.   He said: "My folk, I am to be
To you an open warner:

3.   "Serve God, and fear Him and obey me,

4.   "Your sins by Him shall be forgiven,
And given respite for a season;
As, when the Term by God appointed
Does come, it won't be backward driven;
If only you were men of reason!"

5.   He said: "My Lord, I have been calling
My people night and day,

6.   "Yet all my pleas were only making
Them farther run away;

7.   "So oft as I did call upon them,
That You may pardon them,
They put their fingers in their ears,
And hid themselves inside their garments,
Persisted in their mien,
And prided in their arrogance,
Oh, what an arrogance!

8.   "And then I made to them
My loudest invitation,

9.   "And then I made to them
My open proclamation,
And did in private cautioned them,
A special caution.

10.   "And then I said: 'Do ask your Lord for pardon,
For He's the One, Forgiving Often.

11.   "It's He who sends upon you from the heavens
Abundant rains,

12.   "And strengthens you with wealth and children,
And makes you gardens,
And brings you running streams.

13.   "What ails you that you do not care
For God's commanding grandeur?!

14.   "And it was He who brought you forth
In various forms;

15.   "Do you not see how God the heavens seven
Created, one above the other,

16.   "And made the Moon among them shine,
And set the Sun a lustrous lantern,

17.   "And God it was who brought you forth
Out of the earth, just like a growth;

18. "And then He shall you all to it¹ return,
    And bring you out again,
    A bringing out indeed!

19. "And God has made a vast expanse,
    For you out of the earth,

20. "So that you may therein traverse
    Along extensive paths.'"

21. Then Noah added: "O My Lord,
    They disobeyed me, and they followed
    The man whose wealth and children
    Increases his perdition!

22. "And many horrid plots,
    They did against me plan;"

23. They also said: "Do not forsake your gods,
    And leave not Wadd, nor Suwa', nor Yaghooth,
    Neither Ya'oogh, nor Nasr in sooth!

24. "Indeed they have misled a lot of people,
    So grant the ones engaged in evil,
    Nothing but more perversion!"

25. Thus they were drowned,
    For their own sinful doings,
    And made to enter Fire, where they found,
    That none but God, unto them could extend
    A helping hand.

---

1. The earth.

26. Then Noah said: "My Lord, of disbelievers,
    Leave not a single one upon the land!

27. "For if you let them be, they shall mislead
    Your faithful servers,
    And they shall only breed,
    Unbridled, thankless sinners.

28. "My Lord, forgive me and forgive my parents,
    And him who comes into my quarters,
    In faith, and all believing men and women,
    And don't increase transgressors
    In aught except perdition!"

SURA 72
THE JINN
(AL-JINN)

In the Name of God, the Beneficent, the Merciful

1. Say: it's revealed to me that of the Jinn a horde,
   Gave ear, and then they said: We have indeed a Reading
   heard,
   Truly amazing:

2. It does direct unto the right direction, thus we did,
   Embrace the Faith, and shall henceforward none besides
   our Lord,
   Be ever serving,

3. That He, our Lord-be gloriously exalted-has not taken,
   A female consort, nor has He a son begotten,

4. And that the Fool amongst us used to speak outrageous
   things,
   To God relating,

5. And that we thought that neither men nor Jinn,
   concerning God,
   Could e'er be lying,

6. And that there were some men who used to seek the help
   of Jinn,
   But they misled them into more defying,

7. And that they thought, as you have thought, that God
   would never,

A man be sending,[1]

8.　　　And that we did attempt to make our way to heights of
　　　　　　　　　　　　　　　　　　　　　　　heavens,
　　　　But then we found it full of fearsome wardens,
　　　　And comets flaming,

9.　　　And that we used to sit at certain posts to steal a hearing,
　　　　But now whoever tries to listen, finds a meteor flaming,
　　　　For him in ambush lying,

10.　　　And that we do not know if evil, for the men on Earth,
　　　　Has been intended, or their Lord intends to guide them
　　　　　　　　　　　　　　　　　　　　　　　forth,

11.　　　And that amongst us some are righteous, and of us, some
　　　　　　　　　　　　　　　　　　　　　　　others,
　　　　Are otherwise; we follow many a different path,

12.　　　And that we knew that never could we frustrate God on
　　　　　　　　　　　　　　　　　　　　　　　earth,
　　　　Neither escape from Him by flying,

13.　　　And after we the Guidance heard, then we the Faith
　　　　　　　　　　　　　　　　　　　　　　　embraced,
　　　　And he who in his Lord has faith, he shall not fear when
　　　　　　　　　　　　　　　　　　　　　　　faced
　　　　With loss or suffering,

14.　　　And some of us have now surrendered, but amongst us
　　　　　　　　　　　　　　　　　　　　　　　some,

―――――――――――――――
1. Or "...would not raise any from the dead".

Are deviating, yet whoever does embrace Islam,
He shall be at the right direction aiming,

15. As to the deviators doing evil,
They shall become of Hell the fuel.

16. Now if they firmly keep to the right Way, abundant rains,
We will be to them giving,

17. And thereby put them to a trial;
Yet whosoever from his Lord's Remembrance turns away,
He makes him taste a torment, ever-growing,

18. And that the mosques belong to God, so you shall never,
Invoke in them along with God another,

19. And that when Allah's servant rose upon Him calling,
They crowded him, well-nigh assaulting;

20. Say: "I do call upon my Lord, and never any other,
With Him shall be associating,"

21. Say: "It is not within my power to cause you harm, or any
Virtue unto you bring,

22. Say: "No one could from God protect me, neither shall I
ever,
Besides Him find a shelter,

23. "Unless what I receive from God and His communications,
I do deliver.
And whoso God and His Apostle disobeys, for him,
There is the fire of Hell therein to dwell for ever,

24.   "Till when they see what they were Promised, then they
                                                know,
      Who's weaker in his helpers, and the less in number!"

25.   Say: "I know not if what you're threatened with is nigh, or
                                              whether
      My Lord shall set for it a longer timing:"

26.   The Knower of Unseen is He, and He His secrets never,
      To any is divulging,

27.   Except to some apostles whom He chooses, then a watcher,
      He'll make, before him and behind him, to be marching,

28.   For making sure that they indeed their Lord's
                                  communications,
      Shall have delivered; yet He is surrounding whatsoever,
      Is with them, and He does record the number,
      Of all affairs and actions.

SURA 73
WRAPPED IN MANTLE
(AL-MUZZAMMIL)

In the Name of God, the Beneficent, the Merciful

1. You who have wrapped yourself inside a mantle!

2. Keep vigil in the night, except a little,

3. A half thereof, or make it less,

4. Or add to it, and Al-Quran recite,
   In measured note;

5. For soon shall We to you address,
   Some Word of weight.

6. Indeed at vigils in the night,
   Impression is intense,
   And speech is strong and straight,

7. And in the course of daylight,
   You are in daily work immersed.

8. Thus your Lord's Name commemorate.
   And unto Him yourself,
   Devoutly dedicate,

9. He's the Lord of the East and of the West,
   There is, but He, no other God,
   Thus make Him your protector best,

10.   And all they say, do bear with steadfast Patience,
    And do avoid them, yet a nice avoidance.

11.   And leave Me with the Truth-rejecters,
    The ones enjoying comfort and abundance;
    And for a while, give them a chance!

12.   Surely with Us are hefty chains,
    And Fire that chars!

13.   And food that chokes,
    And grievous pains:

14.   The Day that shakes the Earth with all its mountains,
    The mountains crumbling into heaps of sand,
    Sand in the wind!

15.   We have indeed unto you sent,
    A Messenger, a witness 'gainst you all,
    As We to Pharaoh an apostle sent.

16.   But Pharaoh the apostle disobeyed,
    Thus We on him the hand of seizure laid.

17.   Now if you do persist in Unbelief,
    Then, how will you escape the dreadful Day,
    That turns the heads of children gray!

18.   When heaven is thereby asunder rent,
    His Promise shall be carried out.

19.   And yet, this is an Admonition,
        Thus, one who wills, will take the Road,
        Unto his Lord.

20.   Your Lord does know that you keep vigil,
        For nearly two-thirds of the night,
        Half of it, or thereof a third,
        A group of people with you do as well.
        But it is God who nights and days ordains,
        He knows that you[1] could never keep this up,
        He, therefore, in His Mercy, does relieve you,
        Of these refrains,
        Recite then, what you can of the Quran;
        He knows that some of you shall not
        Be in good-health,
        And others travel through the earth,
        In quest of God-provided good,
        And others fighting in the cause of God;
        So read as many verses as you could.
        And do attend unto your prayer,
        And give *zakaat*[2] unto the poor,
        And lend a generous loan to God,
        Indeed whatever good you send before,
        You shall re-find with God in store,
        And that's repayment, good and grand;
        And, God's Forgiveness, do implore,
        For He is Oft-Forgiving, Loving-Kind.

---

1. The believers

2. Alms-tax, Poor-rate, obligatory charity.

SURA 74
ENWRAPPED
(AL-MUD-DATH-THIR)

In the Name of God, the Beneficent, the Merciful

1.   O You that have yourself enwrapped!

2.   Arise and Caution.

3.   And voice your Lord's magnification,

4.   And give your garments an ablution,

5.   And keep away form all pollution,

6.   And favours do not grant, to hold
      Men under obligation,

7.   And for your Lord be patient
      With resignation;

8.   For when the Trumpet shall be blown,

9.   That is to be a Day of Tribulation,

10.   For disbelievers, not an easy station,

11.   Leave him[1] to me whom I alone created,

12.   And ample wealth for him appointed,

---

1. A pagan chieftain (Walid bin al-Mughirah), according to some commentators.

13. And sons, before him in attendance,

14. And furnished him with great convenience,

15. Yet, he is greedy for My augmentation!

16. No, never! For he is a grudging foe,
    Unto our Revelation.

17. Soon I shall make him take
    A troublesome ascension!

18. For he reflected and he plotted!

19. Confound him, how he plotted!

20. O Perish! How he plotted!

21. And then, he glanced around,

22. And then, he scoffed and frowned,

23. And then, in haughty pride, his back he turned,

24. And said that this[1] was nothing but some charm,
    From others handed down!

25. That this was nothing but the word
    Of humankind!

26. Soon shall I have him into Saqqar[2] thrown,

---

1. The Quranic revelation.   2. Hell-fire.

27. What Saqqar is? You shall not understand:

28. It does not leave a thing behind,
     And nothing does it leave alone!

29. It singes and deforms the human skin;

30. It's guarded by NINETEEN.[1]

31. And we appointed only angels
     To guard the Fire,
     And made their number,
     A subject for dispute,
     Among the disbelievers;
     That those with Scriptures,
     May be convinced,
     And the believers' faith,
     Shall be increased;
     That those with Scriptures, and believers,
     Shall have no doubts,
     And those, with sickness in their hearts,
     As well as disbelievers, grumble:
     "Oh, what could God intend
     By such a parable?"
     Thus whom He Will, He shall mislead,
     And whom He please, He guides indeed;
     And none, except He, is informed,
     About the forces of your Lord,
     And it[2] is nothing other than
     A warning unto man.

---

1. Nineteen keepers, according to most commentators.

2. The Holy Quran.

32.   No, not at all! Now by the Moon,

33.   And by Departing Night,

34.   And by the Dawn that bares the face of Morn,

35.   It[1] is a thing of greatest fright,

36.   Surely a Warning to mankind,

37.   To those of you who would go forward,
        And those who would remain behind;

38.   Each soul is hostage unto what he's earned,

39.   Except the People on the Right,

40.   In their own Gardens, they shall question,

41.   The sinners proven:

42.   "What brought you into Saqqar?"

43.   They shall reply: "We never did a prayer,

44.   "Nor did we ever feed the poor;

45.   "And we engaged in false and idle bickering,

46.   "And we denied the Day of Reckoning,

---

1. This matter of Hell.

47. "Until there came to us the Certain."

48. And now no intercessor's plea shall save them.

49. What is then wrong with them? Why do they turn,
    Away from Admonition,

50. Like frightened asses,

51. That flee from roaring of a lion?!

52. In truth, each one of them wants to be given,
    Some Scrolls unrolled!

53. But no! In fact they do not fear,
    The other world,

54. And yet, this is an Admonition.

55. So let whoever will, to it attend,

56. But no one will it mind,
    Save by the Will of God;
    He is the Source of Righteousness,
    And the Fount of Forgiveness.

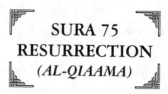

SURA 75
RESURRECTION
(AL-QIAAMA)

In the Name of God, the Beneficent, the Merciful

1. By Resurrection Day I need not swear,

2. Nor need I swear by the Innate Reproacher,[1]

3. Does man suppose that We his bones,
    Shall never bring together?

4. Indeed We can remould his tips of finger,
    In perfect order.

5. Yet man would like indulging further;

6. He questions: "When will be this Day,
    When people shall be Raised?!"

7. But when the sight is dazed,

8. And when the Moon does not emit a glimmer,

9. When the Sun and the Moon shall join together,

10. Man says that Day: "I must escape, but whither?!"

11. Surely there is no shelter whatsoever!

---

1. The reproaching, human self-conscience.

12.   All, on that Day, shall come to rest,
        Before your Lord,

13.   Man, on that Day, will be informed,
        Of deeds sent forth, and of the unperformed;

14.   Man is surely of his own self aware,[1]

15.   Although he some excuses proffer!

16.   -You[2] need not move your tongue in expedition,

17.   It is on Us to see to its collection,
        As to its recitation;

18.   Thus after We have read it,
        Follow the reading with attention,

19.   Again, on Us shall be its explanation.[3] -

20.   But no! You love this fleeting world,

21.   And, to the life to come, pay no attention!

22.   That Day some faces shine with jubilation,

23.   With eyes towards their Lord;

24.   And on that Day some faces show dejection,

---

1. Or "an eye-witness against himself.

2. Mohammad (pbuh).

3. The verses in parentheses are only for the attention of the Holy Prophet.

25. Expecting some immense affliction.

26. Oh, yes! When It[1] shall be about to leave him,

27. With those around him craving:
    "Is there a sorcerer to save him?!"[2]

28. And he is sure that he is Leaving,

29. With pangs of death him overwhelming,

30. Unto your Lord that Day shall be the Driving.

31. For he did not accept the Truth,
    Nor did he pray,

32. But he denied the Truth and turned away,

33. Then he did go back to his household,
    Conceited, bold!

34. It[3] serves you right, you do deserve it,

35. A thousand times you do deserve it!

36. Does man suppose that he is left alone,
    To roam around?

37. A drop of semen issued, was he not?!

---

1. Man's soul.

2. Or: "any charm to restore him?"

3. "This doom" or "the Hour".

38. Which then became a bloody clot,
    That He created, and perfected,

39. And then made into male or female kind?

40. Is He not Able then to raise the dead!

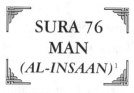

SURA 76
MAN
(AL-INSAAN) [1]

In the Name of God, the Beneficent, the Merciful

1.   Has not Man passed a space of endless time,
   When he was nothing yet to mention?!

2.   The human being We created from
   A sperm of mingled constitution;
   That We may put him to a probing,
   Therefore, We made him Hearing, Seeing,

3.   We have indeed shown him the highway straight
   Whether he be indebted or ingrate.

4.   For disbelievers chains and fetters,
   Have We provided, and a blazing Fire.

5.   As for the righteous, they shall drink from cups
   Tempered at Camphor,

6.   The Spring from which God's servants drink,
   Which runs wherever they prefer.

7.   They who fulfilled their vows and they did fear;
   The Day whose evil flies afar;

8.   And to the poor, the orphan and the captive,
   They, out of love for Him, did victuals offer:

---

1. This sura is also called: *Al-Dahr*.

9.   "We feed you only for the sake of God;
         Rewards or thanks from you, we do not look for,

10.   "The dreadful Day of Anguish of our Lord,
         Is what we fear."

11.   So God did guard them from the evil of that Day,
         And made their faces shine with blissful joy.

12.   And for their being resolutely Patient,
         He did reward them with delights of Garden
         And garments silken,

13.   Reclining there upon luxuriant thrones,
         They shall not find the heat of Sol severe,
         Nor suffer from the cold of Zamharere,[1]

14.   And shadows of the Garden shall embrace them,
         And fruits in clusters, hanging low, shall face them;

15.   And silver vessels shall around them pass,
         And cups translucent, made of glass,

16.   Translucent cups of silver,
         Which they themselves shall measure;

17.   And there they shall be served a drink
         That's mixed and spiced with Zanjabeel;[2]

18.   Poured from a Fountain known as Salsabeel;

---

1. Probably a word of Persian origin: an extremely cold place.

2. Ginger.

19. And youngsters graced with everlasting youth,
    Who in your eyes would look like pearls in motion,
    Shall give them due attention.

20. And when one looks around, then one shall find
    Abundant blessings and a Kingdom Grand.

21. They shall be wearing robes and garments.
    Of fine, green silk and rich brocade,
    And ornaments, silver inlaid;
    And then their Lord shall offer them to swill,
    The purest Wassail:

22. This way you will be prized,
    And your endeavours praised.

23. It is by Us that this Quran
    Is unto you revealed,
    Revealed in portions.

24. Therefore, the orders of your Lord
    Await with Patience;
    And to the sinner or the disbeliever,
    Amongst them, do not pay obeisance;

25. And your Lord's Name, commemorate,
    At dawn and at the evening twilight.

26. And in the night-time, fall before Him prostrate,
    And glorify Him through a lengthy night.

27.   These men,[1] however, love this life in transit,
       And disregard the grievous Day beyond.

28.   We did create them and their fabric strengthened,
       And, if We will, We shall replace them,
       With others of their kind.

29.   This is indeed an Admonition;
       So let whomever pleases take the Road
       Unto his Lord.

30.   Yet, you will not, unless it shall be,
       By God's volition;
       For God is All-Aware, All-Wise.

31.   He will admit to His Compassion
       Whome'er He please,
       But for the culprits of transgression,
       He has prepared a Scourge that plagues!

---

1. The immediate reference is to the Meccan pagans, the general reference is to
   the unbelievers of all ages.

SURA 77
THE EMISSARIES
(AL-MURSALAAT)

In the Name of God, the Beneficent, the Merciful

1.   By Emissaries in succession sent,

2.   Then by the Speeders swift and vehement,

3.   And Those that keenly Dissipate,

4.   Then, Those that sharply Separate,

5.   Then, Those that revelations Intimate,

6.   Either by plea or by admonishment:[1]

7.   That which has been unto you Promised
     Shall come to pass.

8.   That's when the stars are darkened,

9.   When heavens shall be opened,

10. When mountains will, as powder in the wind,
     Be blown away.

11. And when Apostles shall be summoned
     At the appointed time;

---

1. For a better understanding of these oaths, one must consult authentic,
   Quranic commentaries.

12. On what Day is it fixed to happen?

13. Upon the Day of Separation!

14. Would that you were enlightened
About the Day of Separation!

15. Woe on that Day unto Rejecters!

16. Did We not devastate the men of past,

17. Then, them with others, We replaced?

18. Thus do We deal with guilty sinners.

19. Woe on that Day unto Rejecters!

20. Did We not make you from a lowly liquid,

21. And then We lodged it in a place protected,

22. For an appointed period?

23. And fashioned it to flawless measures,
Aren't We Supreme Designers!

24. Woe on that Day unto Rejecters!

25. Have We not made the Earth a bed,

26. To hold the living and the dead,

27. And in there lofty mountains raised,
    And given you to drink sweet waters?

28. Woe on that Day unto Rejecters!

29. "Begone unto That[1] which you cried was lies:

30. "Depart you unto triple-columned Fumes,

31. "Which have no cooling shadows,
    Neither avail against the Blaze,

32. "But send up sparks as huge as castles,

33. "As bright as black-and-yellow camels."

34. Woe on that Day unto Rejecters!

35. This is the Day when they shall not converse,

36. Neither allowed to offer some excuse;

37. Woe on that Day unto Rejecters!

38. This is the Day of Separation:
    "We have you now together gathered,
    And those of bygone generations,

39. "Now if you have some machinations
    Against Me, be attempters!"

---

1. Hell.

40. Woe on that Day unto Rejecters!

41. Indeed the Righteous will be found,
     Amidst the cool of shades and founts,

42. And, as they wish, they take of fruits:

43. "Oh, eat and drink unto your heart's content,
     This is the guerdon of your deeds."

44. Thus We reward the righteous doers.

45. Woe on that Day unto Rejecters!

46. "Eat and enjoy yourselves a little while,
     Since you are guilty sinners."

47. Woe on that Day unto Rejecters!

48. And when it's said to them: "Prostrate yourselves,"
     They do refuse!

49. Woe on that Day unto Rejecters!

50. Thus, after this,[1] in what *hadeeth*[2]
     Will they have faith?!

---

1. This Final Testament, the Holy Quran.

2. Message, revelation, announcement, etc.

SURA 78
THE IMPORTANT NEWS
(AL-NABA'A)

In the Name of God, the Beneficent, the Merciful

1. What are they calling into question?

2. The most Important News,[1]

3. On which they have diverging views?!

4. Not so! They soon shall come to recognition,

5. For sure, they'll come to recognition!

6. Have We not made the Earth a cradle vast?

7. And set the mountains up like pillars?

8. And have We not created you in pairs?

9. And did We not assign your sleep as rest?

10. And brought about the Night that covers?

11. Then Daylight We ordained for seeking rations?

12. And built above you seven, solid Heavens?

13. And made a Lamp that burns and brightens?

---

1. The Day of Judgment.

14. And water we sent down from pregnant clouds,
    That in abundance flows.

15. Whereby all grains come out and herbage grows,

16. And dense, delightful gardens.

17. Beware, the Day of Separation,
    Already is decided,

18. The Day the Trumpet shall be sounded,
    Then you, in groups, attend a Congregation!

19. And, as if it had gates, the Sky shall open,

20. And, mountains shall be set in motion,
    As in an optical illusion.

21. Gehenna lies in wait, behold!

22. For the transgressors, an abode,

23. Wherein, for long, long years they shall be based,

24. Wherein, no coolness shall they taste,
    Neither have any cheering drinks,

25. But boiling water and a food that stinks;

26. Some recompense befitting!

27. For they had not expected an Accounting,

28.   And roundly had denied Our Revelation;

29.   Whereas We counted everything and kept it,
        In writing fashion.

30.   'Now taste it! For We never shall increase
        For you a thing but retribution?'

31.   As for the truly righteous,
        The people always on their guards,
        There is salvation and success,

32.   Gardens and vineyards,

33.   And buxom maidens for companions,

34.   And brimfuls of the purest wines,

35.   Therein they shan't be hearing words
        Of falsity, nor lies,

36.   This is your Lord's reward, the worthy prize,

37.   The Lord of heavens and the earth,
        And what between them lies,
        He's Al-Rahmaan, the All-Beneficent,
        Before Him no one is to raise,
        An argument.

38.   The Day on which the Spirit and the angels,
        Shall stand in ranks; their mouths they shall not open,
        Save him who does from Al-Rahmaan,
        Receive permission, and who tells,

What's right and proper.

39.   That Day is sure to come, so let whoever,
       So wills, go back unto his Lord.

40.   We do forewarn you of a chastisement,
       By no means distant:
       The Day when man shall see what he sent forth,
       And cries he, who denied the Truth:
       "If only I were dust of earth!"

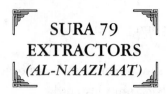

SURA 79
EXTRACTORS
(AL-NAAZI'AAT)

In the Name of God, the Beneficent, the Merciful

1.   By Stern Extractors,

2.   By Soft Releasers,

3.   By Sailing Spacers,

4.   And hence by Pressing Racers,

5.   And thence by Regulators of Affairs:[1]

6.   The Day when comes the thundering Blast,

7.   Which shall be followed by a next,

8.   On this Day hearts are beating fast,

9.   And eyes are humbly downcast.

10. Exclaim they: "What! Are we indeed returned
     Unto our prime condition,

11. "After we into rotten bones were turned?!"

---

1. For a discussion of these oaths, one must consult authentic, Quranic commentaries; it is impossible to carry over such interpretations into our unassuming, literal rendering.

12. They used to say: "Such Repetition
    Would be a losing proposition!"

13. But no! A single Cry it takes,

14. And lo! Each one of them awakes.

15. Have you the tale of Moses e'er been told?

16. When, in the sacred vale of Tuwa,
    His Lord unto him called:

17. "Go you to Pharaoh for he has become
    A rebel bold,

18. "And say: 'Have you the inclination
    To be in soul reformed?

19. 'Then I shall guide you to your Lord,
    So that you may become a man
    Who fears the Lord.'"

20. He did, and then let him behold,
    The Token manifest.

21. Yet, he cried lies of insubordination,

22. And then, he turned away in haste,

23. And, gathering all his men,
    He made a proclamation,

24. And said: "I am your Lord, the highest!"

25. And thus God smote him with the Retribution
Of the next world, and of the first.

26. This surely is preventive admonition,
To those who fear the Lord.

27. Were you the harder to create than Heaven,
Which He has made?

28. Its canopy He did lift up and fashion,

29. And let there be the nights that darken,
While bringing up the dawns that brighten,

30. The Earth unrolling into one extension,

31. Its water drawing out, and bringing forth,
Its vegetation,

32. He also, firmly set the mountains.

33. All this for you, and for your beasts,
As life's provisions!

34. Yet when the Great Disaster shall befall,

35. The Day which brings back recollection,
Of things for which a man has striven,

36. And Hell is brought to exposition,

37. Now, as for him who had rebelled,

38.   And had preferred the life of earthly world,

39.   Certainly Hell shall be the Habitation;

40.   And, as for him who feared to stand
Before his Lord, and thus refrained
Himself from lust and passion,

41.   His Home shall be the Garden.

42.   They question you about the Hour of Doom:
"When shall it come?"

43.   Wherefore are you to have the information?!

44.   Up to your Lord shall be its Termination.

45.   Indeed you are a Warner unto men,
Who are, about it, filled with apprehension.

46.   The day they face It, they perceive,
It was no longer than the previous eve,
Or, of a day, its early portion!

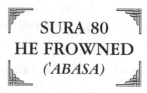

SURA 80
HE FROWNED
('ABASA)

In the Name of God, the Beneficent, the Merciful

1.   He frowned, and he did mind,

2.   That to him came the blind?!

3.   But then, how was it to you[1] known
    That he is not to be refined?

4.   Or that he might be warned,
    And would from Warning something gain?

5.   And yet, the wealthy-looking man,

6.   To him you did attend;

7.   But you would not be blamed,
    If he uncleansed remained.

8.   Yet, he who comes to you with passion,

9.   And feels the fear of God,

10.   Then, you to him pay no attention!

11.   No, no! This is indeed an Admonition,

---

1. Mohammad (pbuh). Although the addressee is the holy Prophet, the first
   verse is subtly styled in the third person.

12.   So let whoever will, take heed and mind it:

13.   In Pages of distinction,

14.   Exalted, purified,

15.   Penned by the hands of Scribes,

16.   Ennobled, dignified.

17.   O Perish man! He has been so ingrate;

18.   Of what thing did He him create?

19.   He did create him from a tiny semen,
      he then, decided his dimension.

20.   And then, his path of growth he softened,

21.   And then, He let him die and be entombed,

22.   And then, He'll raise him up, when He intend.

23.   Alas, what He has bidden,
      Has man declined!

24.   Yet, let man think on what he eats, but once:

25.   Water and rain We pour down in abundance,

26.   And then the soil We split in fragments,

27.   And We therein the grains produce,

28.   And grapes and varied fodder,

29.   And olive-trees and palms of dates,

30.   And gardens dense,

31.   And fruits and plants;

32.   Provisions for you and your beasts.

33.   And then, when comes the Stunning Blast,

34.   The Day when man forsakes his brethren,

35.   His mother and his father,

36.   His wife and his own children,

37.   For, every one of them upon that Day,
       Shall have enough for his preoccupation!

38.   That Day some faces shall be bright and gay,

39.   All smiles expressing jubilation,

40.   And on that very Day,
       There shall be faces grimed with dust and dirt,

41.   Clouded with darkness of contrition,

42.   These are the faces of the disbelievers,
       The brazenly unbridled sinners.

SURA 81
CESSATION
(AL-TAKWEER)

In the Name of God, the Beneficent, the Merciful

1.   When Sol[1] shall cease further to shine,

2.   When stars shall darken,

3.   When mountains shall be set in motion,

4.   When she-camels shall be forsaken,

5.   When beasts are come in their collection,

6.   When seas are set alight,

7.   When souls and bodies reunite,

8.   And when they ask the infant maid,
      The child, alive-begraved:

9.   'What was her crime, why was she killed?'

10.   And when the Scrolls shall be unrolled,

11.   And when the wrapping of the Sky is torn,

12.   And when the Fire shall fiercely burn,

13.   When Paradise is closer drawn:

---

1. The sun.

14. THEN, what each soul with him has borne,
    To him is to be known!

15. And thus I do not call to witness,
    The planets on their orbits,

16. The stars that surface and eclipse,

17. The Night that unto Dawn submits,

18. The Dawn that into Morning bursts:

19. That this is certainly the Word
    Of an apostle honoured,[1]

20. With strength endowed, and highly placed
    By the Possessor of the Throne,

21. There he's obeyed, and held in trust;

22. And your companion: he is not possessed,

23. He did espy him on the clear horizon,

24. And he in truth does not withhold,
    Aught of Unseen unto him told;

25. Neither is it the say of the cursed Satan.

26. So whither are you going?!

---

1. Gabriel.

27. It's but an Admonition
     To all the being,

28. For those of you, who have the will,
     Upon the direct path to travel;

29. And yet, your willing, is of no avail,
     Except that God, the Lord of all the worlds,
     Thus Wills.

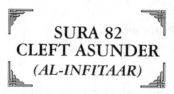

SURA 82
CLEFT ASUNDER
(AL-INFITAAR)

In the Name of God, the Beneficent, the Merciful

1.   When cleft asunder are the heavens,

2.   And when the stars are strewn,

3.   When torn apart shall be the oceans,

4.   And when the tombs are overthrown:

5.   To every soul it shall be known,
     All that he did send forward,
     And what he did postpone!

6.   O Man! What did beguile you from,
     Your Lord, the Gracious One,

7.   He Who created you and fashioned,
     And then proportioned,

8.   In any shape He wilt, he gave you form.

9.   Heedlessly, you deny the Day of Doom,

10. Though over you some Guardians loom,

11. The Scribes of commendation,

12. Who know your every action.

13.   The righteous in the faith shall dwell in Bliss,

14.   And hardened sinners burn inside the Furnace,

15.   Which they shall enter on the Judgment-Day.

16.   And none could from it keep away.

17.   The Judgment-Day? To you it is not known!

18.   The Judgment-Day? You do not comprehend!

19.   It is the Day when every soul shall stand,
Unhelped, alone,
The Day when God shall reign supreme!

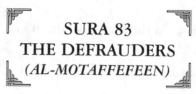

SURA 83
THE DEFRAUDERS
(AL-MOTAFFEFEEN)

In the Name of God, the Beneficent, the Merciful

1. Woe to defrauders!

2. Who, when receiving from the people,
    Exact full measures;

3. But, when they measure or weigh out to others,
    Give less than proper!

4. Do they not think that they shall be awakened

5. Upon the Fateful Day?

6. The Day on which all humankind,
    Before the Lord of all the Worlds,
    Shall have to stand?

7. Indeed the record of the wicked sinners
    Is in Sij-jeen;

8. And what Sij-jeen would mean, one wonders!

9. It is a Register with marks and numbers.

10. Woe on that Day unto Rejecters!

11. Who disbelieve the Day of Judgment;

12. And none deny it but unbridled sinners,

13.   Who, when Our revelations are recited
     To them, cry out: 'Oh, legends of the ancients!'

14.   It is not so! Indeed it is the rust
     Of their own actions in the past
     That has their hearts eclipsed!

15.   Nay, nay, they shall be on that Day debarred
     From their own Lord.

16.   And then, inside the blazing Fire
     They have to tread,

17.   And then, they shall be told:
     "This is that which you had denied!"

18.   In fact the record of the righteous lies
     In Illiyoun.

19.   And what is meant by Illiyoun, one wonders!

20.   It is a Register with marks and numbers,

21.   Which those the Nearest unto Him
     Shall witness.

22.   No doubt the righteous are in boundless Bliss,

23.   On canopied, high couches, they recline,
     Gazing around,

24.   While in their faces you discern,
     The joy and happiness of Bliss;

25. Their thirst is slaked by drinking from a wine
    That's sealed and pure,

26. Whose dregs are musk-and those who for this pine
    Let them aspire;

27. And blended with the waters of Tasneem,

28. The Spring sublime from which imbibe
    The Nearest unto Him.

29. The guilty sinners always jeered and mocked
    The men who did believe,

30. And when they passed them by, they winked
    At one another!

31. And when they went back to their folk,
    They did so, full of pride and pleasure!

32. And when they caught a sight of them, they said:
    "Surely these people are misguided!"

33. But they had never been commanded
    To be their overseers!

34. Therefore today the disbelievers,
    Are being laughed at by the faithful,

35. Reclining on luxuriant thrones,
    Gazing around.

36.   Should not the disbelievers be rewarded,
Also, for what they did?!

SURA 84
BURSTING ASUNDER
(AL-INSHIQAAQ)

In the Name of God, the Beneficent, the Merciful

1. When heavens shall asunder burst,

2. Their Lord obeying as they must,

3. And when the Earth is flattened out,

4. Ejecting all within and clearing out,

5. Its Lord obeying as it must;

6. O Man, you surely then are moving
   Towards your Lord,
   And you shall have with Him a Meeting!

7. Now as to him whose record is
   Into his right hand given,

8. Soon by an easy counting,
   Shall his Account be taken,

9. And to his people he shall be returning,
   By joy and pleasure driven;

10. But as to him, whose record from
    Behind his back, is given,

11. He shall be loudly wailing,

12.   Yet, he shall have to hasten
        To enter Hades blazing;

13.   For he was with his kith and kin
        Joyful in careless living,

14.   In fact, he never even
        Suspected his Returning!

15.   But, there he is! As o'er his every action,
        His Lord was ever Watching.

16.   Thus by the Sunset's Glow I need not swear,

17.   Nor by the Night and what it brings together,

18.   Nor by the Moon when she's in fullest order:

19.   That you shall certainly go further
        In stages, one upon another.

20.   Why, then, believe they not, what is the matter?

21.   And why, when Al-Quran is read to them,
        Do they kneel not in prayer?

22.   Nay, far from it! Those who conceal the Truth,
        Are always crying lies!

23.   And God best knows what they disguise!

24.   Thus, of the painful Scourge,
        Give them the news!

25.   But for believers who do good, there is
A recompense that never fails.

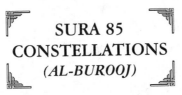

SURA 85
CONSTELLATIONS
(AL-BUROOJ)

In the Name of God, the Beneficent, the Merciful

1. By heavens holding constellations,

2. And by the Day that has been promised,

3. And by the witness and the witnessed,

4. The diggers of the Trenches of Consumptions
   -May they be cursed!

5. Who had the fire well-fed with fuel,

6. Who sat about on seats uprisen,

7. And witnessed what they did unto the faithful.

8. They did not torture them for any reason,
   Except that they had faith in God the One,
   In the All-Mighty, the All-Praised,

9. To Whom the Kingdom of the heavens
   And of the earth belongs,
   And God is Witness to all things.

10. And those who persecute and hunt,
    The faithful men and women,
    And afterwards do not repent,
    For them, there is the torments of Gehenna,
    Together with the Burning Chastisement.

11.   For the believers doing good,
      There will be gardens glad,
      Beneath which rivers glide,
      That is the Triumph grand!

12.   The vengeance of your Lord is unrelenting,

13.   He is the One Who does create from nothing,
      And never stops creating.

14.   And He's the Oft-Forgiving, the All-Loving,

15.   Possessor of the Glorious Throne,

16.   Who Executes intentions of His Own.

17.   Have you not heard,
      The story of the armoured multitude

18.   Of Pharaoh and Thamood?!

19.   And yet, the disbelievers,
      Have constantly the faith denied,

20.   Although they are, from every side,
      By God surrounded;

21.   And yet, this is the Reading Glorified,

22.   Within a Tablet Guarded.

SURA 86
THE PIERCING STAR
(AL-TAARIQ)

In the Name of God, the Beneficent, the Merciful

1. By heavens and by Taariq,[1]

2. On Taariq you do wonder?

3. One of the stars of piercing luster!

4. There is no soul with no observant watcher;

5. Thus, over what he is created of,
   Do let man ponder?

6. He was created of some spurting water,

7. That runs from parts between the loins and ribs.

8. Returning him does rest within His power,

9. Upon the Day, when secrets are laid bare,

10. When one is helpless, nor has he a helper!

11. Now by the heavens of recurring rains,

12. And by the earth, the splitter into greens,

13. It[2] is indeed the last conclusive Sermon,

---

1. The word means: 'the visitant by night'.　　2. The Holy Quran.

14. Not for frivolity and fun!

15. But still they[1] plot and plan,

16. So do I plot and plan!

17. Thus to the disbelievers
     Let's grant a respite,
     A fleeting respite!

---

1. The pagans, polytheists and faith-deniers of Mecca.

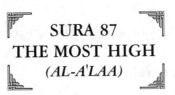

SURA 87
THE MOST HIGH
(AL-A'LAA)

In the Name of God, the Beneficent, the Merciful

1. Exalt and glorify
   The Name, that of your Lord,
   The One Most High,

2. Who did create and did proportion,

3. Who did design and showed the Way,

4. Who brought about the vegetation,

5. Then made them fade into decay.

6. We shall to you recite,
   A gentle recitation,
   So nothing from you slips away,

7. Unless Allah will otherwise;
   All that is manifest, He Knows,
   And all that's in disguise.

8. And We shall guide you to the Smoother Way,

9. Thus Warn them, if the Warning could,
   Be unto them of any good.

10. The ones who Fear, they will take heed,

11. And wretched ones will it avoid,

12.   They shall be cast into the Fire Extensive,

13.   Wherein they neither die nor live!

14.   Successful is the man who purifies,

15.   And magnifies the Name, that of his Lord,
      And to Him prays.

16.   Yet, you prefer the life,
      In the world of the Present,

17.   Although the life to come is better
      And far more constant!

18.   Indeed the same is found in pristine Pages,

19.   The Scrolls of Abraham and Moses.

SURA 88
THE OVERWHELMING
(AL-GHAASHIA)

In the Name of God, the Beneficent, the Merciful

1. You ever heard the news concerning
    The Overwhelming?!

2. That is the Day when certain faces
    Are downcast, shaming,

3. Burdened, exhausted, broken-down,

4. About to enter Hades flaming;

5. They are permitted to be drinking
    Out of a fountain boiling,

6. Their only food is something thorny,
    Acrid and stinking.

7. Hardly nutritious, hunger unappeasing!

8. Yet, other faces that Day are rejoicing,

9. Well pleased with their own striving;

10. Inside an elevated Garden,

11. Wherein you shall no idle talk be hearing,

12. Wherein there shall be many a flowing fountain,

13. Wherein there shall be thrones exalting,

14. And goblets ready to be taken,

15. And ordered cushions silken,

16. And carpets rich outspreading.

17. Do they not even on the camel ponder,
    How it's created?

18. And, on the heavens,
    How they have been constructed?

19. And, on the mountains,
    How firmly they are hoisted?

20. And, on the Earth,
    How vastly it has been expanded?

21. Therefore, keep on reminding,
    You're there to give them warning,

22. You are not to coerce them as a keeper;

23. And as to those who turn back disbelieving,

24. God shall subject them to the Great Tormenting;

25. Surely to Us is their returning,

26. And then, on Us is their Accounting.

SURA 89
THE DAWN
(AL-FAJR)

In the Name of God, the Beneficent, the Merciful

1. By Dawn,

2. By Nights of Ten,

3. By Odd and Even,

4. By Night submitting unto Morn,

5. Is there in this an oath for thinking men?

6. Have you not noted what your Lord
    Did unto Aad,

7. Of Iram, with their buildings proud,

8. The likes of which were never raised
    Throughout the world?

9. And to Thamood,
    Who rocky mountains hewed?

10. And unto Pharaoh, Lord of Multitude?

11. They all transgressed throughout the land,

12. And spread corruption far and wide,

13. And so your Lord upon them poured,
    A scourge of chastisement;

14. Your Lord is ever Watching
    From His own vantage-point.

15. This is the case of man:
    When he is being tested by his Lord,
    Through privilege and bliss, on him bestowed,
    Says he: "My Lord respects me!"

16. But when He, for a different, trying lesson,
    Shall his provisions lessen,
    Says he: "My Lord disgraces me!"

17. No! Not at all!
    It's you who do not ever
    The orphans honour,

18. Who never urge each other
    To feed the needy and the poor,

19. Who greedily devour
    The legacies of others,

20. And wealth you love with all your hearts!

21. But no! When Earth is pounded into powder,

22. And comes your Lord,
    And angels rank on rank will gather,

23.   And Hell, on that Day, flares up nearer,

24.   That Day does man his deeds remember;
What a delayed Reminder!

25.   Says he: "Oh, if I had sent forth whatever,
For this true life of mine!"

26.   But that Day no imagined torture shall
Vie with His Torment,
And no enchainment be,
Like His Confinement.

27.   "O Soul serene, delighting,

28.   "Come to your Lord again,
Enchanted and enchanting,

29.   "And then,
My servants join,

30.   "And step inside My Garden!"

SURA 90
THE TOWN
(AL-BALAD)

In the Name of God, the Beneficent, the Merciful

1.   I swear not by this Town,

2.   Though you live in this Town,

3.   Neither by the Begetter,
     And his begotten children,

4.   That We indeed created Man
     Into exertion and affliction.

5.   Does he suppose that no one,
     Has over him dominion?!

6.   "I have already squandered vast
     Volumes of wealth", he boasts!

7.   Does he suppose he is by no one noticed?

8.   Have We not granted him two eyes,

9.   A tongue and pair of lips?

10. And shown him both the Paths?

11. Yet, he has made no haste
     Upon the Steeper Path,

12. And don't you know the Steeper Path,

13.   That is, the freeing of a bondman,

14.   The feeding in a day of famine,

15.   Of a familial orphan,

16.   Or an impoverished person;

17.   And then one should be of the faithful, hence
Enjoining one another unto patience,
And recommending merciful benevolence.

18.   These are 'the people of the right',

19.   But those who do reject Our Signs,
They are 'the people of the left',

20.   The Fire upon them rains!

SURA 91
SOL
(AL-SHAMS)

In the Name of God, the Beneficent, the Merciful

1. By Sol[1] and by His radiant glows,

2. And by the Moon as Him she follows,

3. And by the Day that His resplendence shows,

4. And by the Night that over Him a curtain draws,

5. And by the Sky and how it was established,

6. And by the Earth and its extension,

7. And by the Soul and how it was accomplished,

8. To which He gave the inspiration,

9. Certainly he who purifies it,
   He shall succeed,

10. And he who does corrupt it,
    He fails indeed.

11. Out of revolt and pride,
    The people of Thamood,
    The Truth denied,

---

1. The sun.

12. When from their midst, the wickedest,
Rose up in rage and haste;

13. But God's apostle to them thus addressed:
"The camel is God's beast,
Do let her quench her thirst",

14. Yet, they did cry him false,
Then put her to the sword,
And for this sin of theirs, their Lord,
His Scourge on them unloosed,
And them He levelled!

15. And He had of its aftermath no dread!!

SURA 92
THE NIGHT
(AL-LAIL)

In the Name of God, the Beneficent, the Merciful

1. By Night that veils,

2. By Day that brightly shines,

3. And by the coming to existence,
   Of males and females:

4. Indeed you strive for divers aims!

5. Yet, he who gives in generous alms,
   And his own self from evil guards,

6. And does affirm the truth of faith,

7. Him We shall grace with Easy Path.

8. But for the niggardly who greeds,
   And thinks that he is free of needs,

9. And truth of faith denies,

10. For him We shall prepare,
    The Way to Toils,

11. And then his wealth shall have no use,
    After he falls.

12. Surely it is for Us to show the Paths,

13. And surely unto Us is tied the First,
    The Last, the Future and the Past!

14. Thus I do warn you of the Fire that blazes,

15. That for none but the wickedest it rises,

16. The ones who did reject the Faith as false,
    And turned their backs.

17. But it shall not approach the ones
    Who do abstain from sins,

18. Who give away their goods and means,
    Themselves to cleanse,

19. And not as recompense for any service,
    That someone has already rendered,

20. But only for the Pleasure of their Lord,
    The Highest,

21. And they shall soon be pleased.

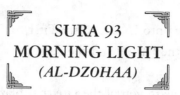

SURA 93
MORNING LIGHT
(AL-DZOHAA)

In the Name of God, the Beneficent, the Merciful

1. By morning light,

2. And falling night,

3. You[1] are not by your Lord abandoned,
   Nor is he with you unconcerned,

4. And that which for you lies in store,
   Excels all that has gone before,

5. And soon you shall be granted
   Such plenty by your Lord,
   That you shall feel delighted.

6. Did He not find you orphaned,
   And He provided you with shelter?

7. Did He not find you drifting,
   And He directed you thereafter?

8. Did He not find you needful,
   And then He made you prosper?

9. Therefore the orphan,
   Do not abandon!

---

1. Mohammad (pbuh).

10.   And then, the needful beggar,
        Do never censure!

11.   But the favours of your own Lord:
        Tell them abroad!

SURA 94
BROADENED BREAST
(INSHIRAAH)

In the Name of God, the Beneficent, the Merciful

1. Did We your breast for you[1] not broaden?

2. Did We not from your back take off the burden,

3. That was about to weigh you down?

4. And have We not exalted your renown?

5. Yea, after hardship there is ease,

6. Indeed with hardship there is ease;

7. Therefore, when comes release,
    Then, do your best,

8. And make the Lord, your only Quest.

---

1. Mohammad (pbuh).

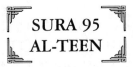

SURA 95
AL-TEEN

In the Name of God, the Beneficent, the Merciful

1.　By Teen[1] and by Zaitoun[2]

2.　And by the Mountain of Seneen[3]

3.　And this protected Town:[4]

4.　We moulded Man into the best design,

5.　And, later, We shall render him,
　　The meanest of the mean;

6.　Those who believe, and proper deeds perform
　　Shall be excepted, and for whom
　　The recompense shall be unending.

7.　What then will cause you to deny the Doom?

8.　Is Allah[5] not the Judge Supreme!

1, 2, 3. Teen means 'fig' and Zaitun 'olive', yet they, together with Seneen, also
　　stand respectively for the Mount of Fig, Mount of Olive and Mount of Sinai,
　　which have obvious divine associations with three prophets of God; therefore,
　　I preferred to keep the original words.

4. Mecca

5. God, the One

SURA 96
BLOOD-CLOT
(AL-ALAQ)

In the Name of God, the Beneficent, the Merciful

1. Read!
    In the name of your Lord,
    Who all created,

2. Created Man from blood, coagulated,

3. Read:
    And your Lord is the Most Exalted,

4. He tutored by the pen;

5. What Man knew not, He helped him ken.

6. Yet, Man is surely insolent,

7. In thinking he is self-sufficient,

8. Certainly everything
    Is to your Lord returning,

9. You see the one who hampers,

10. Our servant in his prayers?

11. Do you think he behaves on guidance?

12. Or whether he directs to godliness?

13. What do you think if he is lying,
    Turning his back not minding?

14. Does he not know that God is Seeing?

15. Beware! If he is not to cease,

16. His forelock We shall seize,
    The forelock of a lying, sinful, person,

17. And then We let him call his right-hand men,

18. And We, in turn, the Guards of Hell shall summon!

19. Nay, nay! Him shall you not obey,
    But bow yourself,
    And unto Us draw nigh!

SURA 97
THE GLORY
(AL-QADR)

In the Name of God, the Beneficent, the Merciful

1. Indeed We sent it[1] down
    Within the Night of Glory.

2. And what could make you comprehend
    The Night of Glory!

3. The Night of Glory, does transcend
    Of months a thousand.

4. The angels and the Spirit,[2] by their Lord's permission
    Concerning every mission,
    Therein come down;

5. Salaam[3] shall reign,
    Till break of dawn.

---

1. The Holy Quran.

2. The Arch-angel Gabriel.

3. Salaam in Arabic and 'shalom' in Hebrew mean: 'submission to the Will of
   the Almighty and, therefore, the untroubled, serene state of mind accruing
   from it.

SURA 98
THE EVIDENCE
(AL-BAYYINA)

In the Name of God, the Beneficent, the Merciful

1.   Nay, never do the disbelievers,
Among the People of the Scriptures,
And those who-but Him-worship others,
Abandon being unbelievers,
Unless they shall be furnished,
With Evidence unblemished:

2.   A messenger from God who would
Be reading Pages pure,

3.   Containing writings right and proper.

4.   Yet it was not till after,
The evidence was to them granted
That People of the Scripture,
Diverged and disunited!

5.   Whereas they only were instructed
To worship God, and to sincerely take
To their religion for His sake,
Hence true believers;
And to attend to prayers,
And give away *zakaat*;[1]
This is religion right and straight.

---

1. Regular charity, legal alms, tithe.

6.   Undoubtedly the disbelievers
    Among the People of the Scriptures,
    And those who-but Him-worship others,
    Shall into the Gehenna fire be cast,
    To be there long abiders,
    They are, of all the men, the worst.

7.   But those who shall the Faith embrace,
    And do good works,
    Surely they are, of men, the best.

8.   The recompense, their Lords' reward,
    Shall be the lasting Gardens
    Of Eden, with their running streams,
    Abiding there for time untold,
    God being pleased with them,
    And they too with Him pleased;
    This is for him who fears his Lord.

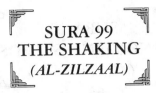

SURA 99
THE SHAKING
(AL-ZILZAAL)

In the Name of God, the Beneficent, the Merciful

1. When Earth is shaken with the last convulsion,

2. When Earth ejects her every load and burden,

3. And Man will cry: "what shall unto her happen?!"

4. That Day she brings her tidings to the open,

5. According to the inspiration,
   That has your Lord unto her given.

6. That Day shall men proceed in groups divided,
   And will be shown all that they did.

7. And then he who an atom's weight of good,
   Has done, shall see it,

8. And he who did an atom's weight of evil,
   Shall also see it.

SURA 100
SNORTING STEEDS
(AL-'AADIAAT)

In the Name of God, the Beneficent, the Merciful

1. By snorting steeds,

2. When striking fiery sparks,

3. That race to morning raids,

4. That blaze a trail of dust,

5. And split the center of a host[1],

6. That Man is to his Lord ingrate!

7. And he himself shall witness unto this;

8. Indeed his love for worldly gains is great,

9. But is he not aware that when
    The graves shall open,
    And Occupants are overthrown,

10. And all the secrets shall be known,

11. Surely is, on that Day, their Lord,
    About them Best-Informed?!

---

1. For detailed interpretations of these oaths, one may consult with authentic,
   Quranic commentaries.

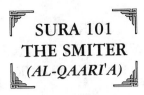

SURA 101
THE SMITER
(AL-QAARI'A)

In the Name of God, the Beneficent, the Merciful

1.   The Smiter!

2.   What is the Smiter?

3.   Would that you recognized the Smiter!

4.   A Day it is when men shall be as moths,
Dispersed by wind,

5.   And mountains shall be coloured tufts
Of carded wool;

6.   Then he whose scales are heavy

7.   Shall dwell in Bliss,

8.   And he whose scales are light,

9.   His home is the Abyss.

10.   And you know not its nature;

11.   It's of the blazing Fire!

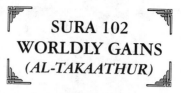

SURA 102
WORLDLY GAINS
(AL-TAKAATHUR)

In the Name of God, the Beneficent, the Merciful

1. The craze for more and more of worldly gains
   Has made you fall into a swoon,

2. Until you come unto the tombs;

3. Indeed you shall know soon!

4. Undoubtedly you shall know soon!

5. In fact, if you with certainty had known,

6. The fire of Hell you would have seen;

7. But then, you shall be surely seeing it,
   With eyes of certainty,

8. And then, that Day, you shall be questioned
   About the blessed Bounty.[1]

---

1. All the blessings and comforts of life granted by God.

SURA 103
TIME
(AL-'ASR)

In the Name of God, the Beneficent, the Merciful

1.   By Time!

2.   Man is in loss forsooth,

3.   Except such as have Faith,
     And carry out benevolence,
     Enjoining others unto Truth,
     And recommending Patience.

SURA 104
THE SLANDERER
(AL-HUMAZA)

In the Name of God, the Beneficent, the Merciful

1. Woe unto every blaming, smearing, slanderer,

2. Who heaps up wealth and hoard it for the future,

3. Thinking his wealth ensures his life for ever!

4. By no means, no! He shall be handed over
    Unto the Hutama;

5. And what is Hutama, you wonder?

6. The Fire of God, the kindled blazer,

7. That leaps up unto hearts,

8. That shall be on them closing over,

9. In columns waxing further.

SURA 105
ELEPHANT
(AL-PHEEL)

In the Name of God, the Beneficent, the Merciful

1. Did you not note the doing of your Lord,
   Upon the Army of the Pheel![1]

2. Did He their cunning plot not foil,

3. By sending swarms of Ababeel?[2]

4. That showered upon them stones of hardened clay,

5. Which left them just as chewed up hay?!

---

1. Or al-Fil means 'elephant'; these were the troops of Abraha, the ruler of
   Abyssinia, who invaded Mecca with a large army, in which were some
   elephants.

2. The miracle consisted in the birds (ababeel) coming in large flights and fling-
   ing stones which destroyed the whole of the Abraha's army.

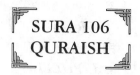

SURA 106
QURAISH

In the Name of God, the Beneficent, the Merciful

1. For the Quraish[1] protection,

2. Protection of their mission,
   In winter, and of summer season,

3. Indeed they ought to worship
   The Master of this Mansion,[2]

4. Who fed them in the face of draught,
   And made them free from fright.

---

1. The chief, Mecca tribe to which the holy Prophet belonged.

2. The House of Ka'ba at Mecca.

SURA 107
CHARITY
(AL-MAA'OUN)

In the Name of God, the Beneficent, the Merciful

1. Do you know him who disavows the Judging,[1]

2. He is the one who drives away the orphans,

3. And urges not unto the poor a feeding;

4. Then, woe unto the praying persons,

5. Who do not heed their Praying,

6. Who make a show of piety,

7. But nought give they to charity.

---

1. The Judgment-Day.

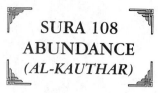

SURA 108
ABUNDANCE
(AL-KAUTHAR)

In the Name of God, the Beneficent, the Merciful

1. Indeed We granted you[1] Abundance,[2]

2. Thus pray unto your Lord,
   And for Him sacrifice,

3. It is your foe indeed,
   Who'll go without a trace!

---

1. Mohammad (pbuh).

2. The pagans and disbelievers of Mecca taunted the Holy Prophet as 'abtar' ('having no male child, being unproductive, hopeless in progress'). Here God Almighty assures him of 'kauthar' ('the abundant bounties and blessings bestowed on him here and in the hereafter'). Even in the strict sense of the word, 'kauthar' is realized in the person of his daughter, Fatima (AS), whose marriage with Ali (AS), has issued numberless descendants, known as 'sadaat', who are found in every part of the world today, and, nothing remains of the enemies of the Prophet (pbuh).

SURA 109
THE DISBELIEVERS
(AL-KAAFIROON)

In the Name of God, the Beneficent, the Merciful

1. Say: O You disbelievers!

2. I do not serve that which you worship,

3. And you serve not what worship I,

4. And never have I worshipped
   The things that you have worshipped,

5. And you serve not what worship I,

6. To you be your religion,
   And my religion, mine!

SURA 110
HELP
(AL-NASR)

In the Name of God, the Beneficent, the Merciful

1.   When comes the Help of God, and Victory,

2.   And you see men embracing God's religion
In many a legion,

3.   Then praise your Lord, and seek His Mercy,
Since He's Most Prone to Pardon.

SURA 111
FIBRE
(AL-MASAD)

In the Name of God, the Beneficent, the Merciful

1. The arms[1] of Abu Lahab[2] shall be broken,
    Himself he shall expire,

2. By his own wealth and all his gains forsaken,

3. Soon shall he burn inside a flaming Fire,

4. With him his wife,[3] the one with fire-wood laden,

5. Around her neck, a rope of palm-leaf fibre!

---

1. Or 'hands', signifying power, might, authority.

2. The holy Prophet's paternal uncle, a wealthy, ruthless arch-enemy, the nick-name means 'father of flames'.

3. An unbelieving, spiteful woman, often wearing a highly priced necklace.

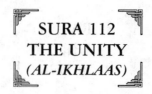

SURA 112
THE UNITY
(AL-IKHLAAS)

In the Name of God, the Beneficent, the Merciful

1. Say: He is Allah, God the One,

2. God is the Absolute, Eternal One.

3. He fathered none,
   Nor was He born,

4. And equal unto Him is none.

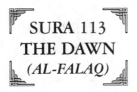

SURA 113
THE DAWN
(AL-FALAQ)

1. Say: I seek refuge in the Lord of Dawn,

2. From evils of the creatures of His Own,

3. And from the evil of the Dusk descending,
    To darkness tending,

4. And from the evil of enchanting women,
    On knotted cords a-breathing,

5. And from the evil of the envious, when
    Their envy will be blazing!

SURA 114
THE MEN
(AL-NAAS)

In the Name of God, the Beneficent, the Merciful

1. Say: I seek refuge in the Lord of men,

2. The King of men,

3. The God of men,

4. From Evil of the Tempter urging often,[1]

5. Who whispers in the hearts of men,

6. Be they of Jinn or men.

---

1. Tempters and whisperers (satans) who approach man over and over again until they win him over to their evil side.